The Architecture of Rome
An architectural history
in 402 individual presentations

edited by Stefan Grundmann

with contributions by
Ulrich Fürst
Antje Günther
Dorothee Heinzelmann
Esther Janowitz
Steffen Krämer
Ilse von zur Mühlen
Antje Scherner
Philipp Zitzlsperger

Edition Axel Menges

© 2007 Edition Axel Menges, Stuttgart/London
2nd, revised edition
ISBN 978-3-936681-16-1

Reproductions: Bild und Text GmbH Baun, Fellbach
Printing and binding: Everbest Printing Co., Ltd.,
China

Translation into English: Bruce Almberg, Charles Earle,
Michael Robinson and Katja Steiner
Design: Axel Menges
Layout: Helga Danz
Cover photo: James Morris

Contents

UF Ulrich Fürst
SG Stefan Grundmann
AG Antje Günther
DH Dorothee Heinzelmann
E J Esther Janowitz
SK Steffen Krämer
I M Ilse von zur Mühlen
AS Antje Scherner
PZ Philipp Zitzlsperger

Foreword

No other city featured in travel guides as early as Rome. Pilgrims were able to refer to the famous mirabilia and form an impression of the holy city for themselves as early as 1144. No city took up as much space in the most famous German-language guide on Italy as Rome. Jacob Burckhardt's *Cicerone* of 1855 is one long love letter to the eternal city. And no city is better suited than Rome to provide a true guide through the history of art, a guide that does not just give information about each item in isolation, but uses them as a basis for a history of art and arranges them to form a complete picture. Burckhardt did this in his day, and the present guide is going to try to work like this as well, as this approach seems to have been neglected for some time.

To this end, architecture was selected, as undoubtedly the most important genre in Rome (although the most significant paintings and sculptures in the buildings are always mentioned). The city of Rome made such an impact on architecture at almost all periods that the buildings of Rome form the scaffolding of architecture in general. Rome was the only ancient metropolis that did not go down with its empire, but played a leading role in Europe in post-ancient occidental history at most times. It is thus possible to assemble an unbroken chain of buildings in which certain developments took place. At every point it is possible to identify preceding or subsequent buildings, and also the origins or later history of the works (which has been done in detail). And at every point readers can form a clear impression of these other buildings from the copious illustrations in the guide, and if their curiosity is aroused they can go and look at them, as they are seldom very far away. Rough lines of development are traced for every epoch in an introductory text leading to the works, and also a few circular walks, moving readers on a few decades from one building to the next, meaning that they constantly move forward historically, without making unduly large detours in terms of space.

For the eternal quality of Rome can be experienced only by someone who sees how the main buildings in the city came into being, and who understands how architectural history came to be written here: naturally in the ancient Roman period, in which architecture as the art of enclosed space, of walls and interiors with different structures, first emerged; then with the early-Christian basilica, which developed in Rome in the 4th century, looking backwards to ancient Roman types, and which spread throughout Europe from there, becoming the basis of the Romanesque and Gothic movements; later with Bramante and Michelangelo, who created the flower of Western architecture in the High Renaissance, and whose architectural work is to be found almost exclusively in Rome; and lastly again with Bernini and Borromini, whose influence can be clearly seen in a very concrete way in almost every Baroque building, right down to the late 18th century. Rome also led the way in the field of fascist architecture, and its buildings have been much more interesting than many people imagine in the last fifty years. This sequence will be demonstrated by a new concept in this architectural guide: the 400 buildings are arranged chronologically (by the date of the design and the date when building started, sometimes according to the date of the most important section) and not – as is usually and rather randomly the case – alphabetically or topographically. And so we follow history, stage by stage, almost always illustrated – right down to the most recent times. The eternal city lives on. SG

The development of the city

Today the characteristic features of the terrain are not as striking for the visitor as they were in ancient times, or even 120 years ago. The eternal city's seven hills have been worn down by thousands of years of development, and they are no longer as steep and pointed as they were. In fact the point at which urban settlement started, the Palatine hill, did no longer have a pointed top even in imperial times, but formed a broad plateau, as considerable substructures were required for the palaces that were built here (see A27). Thus steep ridges like the one between the Capitol and the Quirinal hill were removed, in this case to make room for the imperial forum of Trajan (see A29), and Domenico Fontana, Sixtus V's architect and engineer, thought it particularly worth mentioning that hills were removed and valleys filled in the course of his extensive urban operations.

In the same way the Tiber is much less present in the urban picture than it was in the 19th century, at the end of which the high embankment walls were built to prevent the annual flooding (see K10). This meant not only the destruction of many buildings by the river, but above all direct access to the river from developments on the Tiber bend was cut off, as the older buildings were about 5 metres below the level of the roads along the banks.

If we also include the draining of the Forum marshes, which was brought about early in the ancient period by the creation of the Cloaca Maxima (see A1), then we have mentioned the three natural components that particularly affected urban development. These are first of all the river, which separates Trastevere and the Vatican from the rest of the city. Then come the seven hills, the Palatine and Capitol hills, which are central both in terms of space and their significance, and then (arranged to the east of the two, in a semi-circle round them, from south to north), Aventine, Caelian, Esquiline, Viminal, Quirinal (and later still in the north the Pincian hill and the Janiculan Ridge in Trastevere). And finally come the lower areas extending between the hills, especially those that run down to the river on the Tiber bend (west or north-west of the Corso, the ancient Via Lata, of the Capitol and the Palatine).

Antiquity

The beginnings

The settlement of Rome started on the Palatine hill. It was here that the walled original cell that the Romans called »Roma Quadrata« was built – according to Varro in 753 BC. In fact Iron Age huts have been found, including the so-called House of Romulus, that can be dated to the 9th century BC by their funerary urns. There were unhealthy marshes in the Forum hollow at the foot of the Palatine at that time. The city border seems to have run along the later Via Sacra, as their are also buildings from that period on this side, for example the Shrine of Vesta (A40), but only tombs on the other side. In about 600 BC the forum was paved for the first time, which shows that it had previously been drained (by the New Cloaca Maxima). This was the work of the Etruscan kings, who had taken Rome over (according to tradition in 616 BC). And so if the valley was occupied from that time, then it is to be assumed that the other two adjacent hills, the Quirinal and the Capitol, were also settled about then as well. In fact the largest Etruscan temple came into being on the Capitol (for Jupiter Optimus Maximus), although this was not consecrated until 509 BC. The foreign kings were driven out in the same year, and the Republic founded.

The Republican period

The Forum became the first centre of monumental architecture in the Republican period. Numerous temples were built (see A1 for detail), and probably also the most important political centre, with the Comitium and the Curia (see A16), and additionally in the early 2nd century BC the basilicas as a specific form of forum building with stock exchanges and court functions (see A11 for detail). And in the 1st century BC, under Sulla, the Forum also acquired a magnificent show façade on the Capitol side, in the form of the Tabularium (A9). The Capitol had long been the cultic centre, and the state archives were housed behind the show façade. Thus at the beginning of the imperial period the Forum started to be a coherent area of Roman monumental architecture. At this time the Palatine hill was the preferred residential area of the Roman upper classes, as is shown by the so-called House of Livia. Augustus was also born here. Later he bought up more houses and linked them together. The – probably authentic – »House of Augustus« was built.

The second main development in the Republican period – alongside the further development of the nucleus of Palatine, Forum and Capitol – was that the city expanded and an appropriate infrastructure was created. At first, even before the middle of the 4th century, the Rebublican city wall was built, which fixed the so-called Pomerium. This created not only a defensive complex, but an area that was sacrosanct in many respects. Military authority was not valid in the Pomerium, no burials could take place (but see A29), and no temple to foreign gods could be built. An important part of the run of the wall is that it excluded the whole of the Tiber bend (called the »Campus Martius« in ancient times), and also the whole of the far bank of the Tiber, and the Pincian hill as well. Only the seven hills were enclosed. In 312 BC Appius Claudius Caecus, with the Aqua Appia and the Via

Appia, laid the basis both for the network of aqueducts that gave Rome a unique position among European metropolises in terms of water supply (for the entire system see A22), and also for the system of main roads radiating out of the city. One of these, the ancient Via Flaminia, then later, when the city spread out in this direction, the ancient Via Lata, is still clearly visible today, the dead straight Via del Corso, which links the Piazza del Popolo and the Piazza Venezia.

Only two complexes have survived on any significant scale, both between the Capitol or the Palatine and the Tiber, of the development in the pre-Imperial period (outside the Palatine, Forum and Capitol): the (foundations of the) group of temples on the Largo Argentina (A3) and the group of temples on the Forum Holitorium and above all on the Forum Boarium (see A4, A6, A7), linked by the Velabrum, the hollow between the Capitol and the Palatine, through which the Cloaca Maxima also runs, to the Forum Romanum. Thus the Velabrum and the Forum Boarium permitted access from the Forum to the Tiber. However, the Forum Boarium was also in the middle of another important thoroughfare, thus at the intersection of the central axes of early Rome: near to the Forum Boarium the Pons Sublicius led over the Tiber and with it the trade road that continued to the south through the later area of the Circus Maximus (leading into the Via Appia at the end of it) and to which Rome owed its creation. First of all, Rome stood at a point where the Tiber could be crossed. Here too, according to legend, Romulus and Remus were stranded in their little basket. And the Forum Boarium, the ancient cattle market (now: Piazza Bocca della Verità) was the trading place at this crossing. The crossing of axes with the Forum Boarium, the trading square (and its extension to the south-east), with the Forum Romanum, the monumental zone with the political centre, with the Palatine as the most refined residential area and the Capitol as the cultic centre was thus fixed at the beginning of the imperial period.

The Imperial period

In the Imperial period the focus of urban and architectural development fell in the period of almost two centuries from Julius Caesar (in Rome: 48–44 BC) to Hadrian (AD 117–138), in other words under the Julian and Claudian dynasty (Caesar to Nero, murdered AD 68), the Flavians and the early adoptive emperors (Trajan, AD 98–117 and Hadrian). This is true first for the centre, the forum and the adjacent hills. Development was particularly intensive under Caesar and Augustus. The Forum, in terms of the remains visible today, goes back almost entirely to these two rulers, above all Caesar, and the measures they took to redesign it, both in terms of the complex as a whole and almost all the individual buildings. The Forum Romanum is the Forum of Caesar and Augustus (see A1 for detail).

Both also opened up the series of imperial forums (A13, A20), that begins to the east of the Forum Romanum and took up the remaining space in the lowlands on this side of the Esquiline and Viminal hills. A series of imperial forums were added on, the latest and largest being that of Trajan (A29). The monumental area at the heart of Rome was thus almost doubled in its extent under Caesar and Augustus. It also increased in quality. In his res gestae, or report on his life, Augustus not unjustly wrote that he had inherited a city of clay and left behind a city of marble. The adjacent Palatine hill was also subjected to fundamental change. Here, first of all under Tiberius, but on a much larger and more permanent scale under Domitian towards the end of the 1st century AD, the palace area of the Roman emperors (see A27) came into being, which was to be the model for palace building throughout the Western world.

Between Tiberius and Domitian the focus of building shifted to the southern end of the Forum for a time – the monumental centre began to thrust forward in this direction. The reason for this was Nero's efforts to express his claim to power by building an enormous villa – very diverse, but not yet monumental and block-like, as Domitian's palace was to be. This so-called domus aurea (A24) extended from the slopes of the Esquiline over the hollow containing the Colosseum, to the south of the Forum, down to the slopes of the Palatine. Nero was deposed, Vespasian, as the father of the Flavians, was less patrician in attitude. He had most of the villa pulled down and had a building for the amusement of the people built on the site of the great lake in the garden, the Colosseum (A25). Later the Flavians also placed the most important triumphal arch in this area (A26). The functional buildings – like the Colosseum, and later the baths – were increasingly to leave the temples behind from then on, and parallel with this, though not directly linked, building with cement and brick was increasingly to force out domestic stone. For after the fire of Rome under Nero the so-called urbs nova was built in this new material, largely with a number of storeys, as can be seen above all in the palace on the Palatine hill, and in Ostia, which developed considerably at this time. Rome also became a commercial city in building terms, and a large city, with a big population. Among the three great urban developers from the ranks of the dictators or emperors, who set out to redesign Rome fundamentally, the measures taken by Sulla left their mark in at least one striking place (on the Capitoline show wall), those of Caesar (and Augustus) clearly more (in the whole of the Forum, the imperial forums and the Campus Martius), those of Nero the least, because most was built over.

Of the areas of Rome outside the original centre the principal ones to be developed were the Campus Martius (Tiber bend) and the area that was later to become the Vatican. The low Campus Martius, which was outside the Republican city wall, was not built on

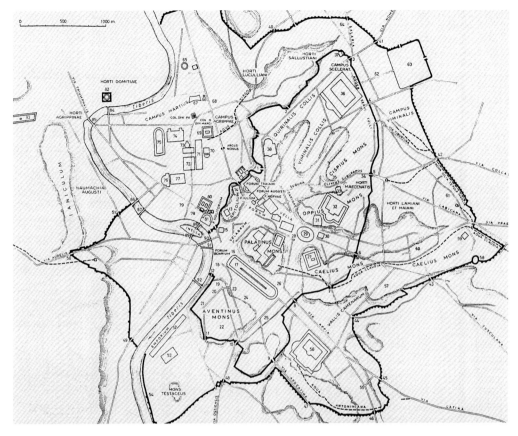

Rome at the time of the late Imperial period

until the reign of Augustus. It became a second monumental zone (alongside the one in the Forum), particularly through the work of Augustus, and later extensively of Hadrian, over a century after. Augustus established the mausoleum for almost all the emperors of the 1st century AD here (A15), the Ara Pacis (A18), and a forerunner of the Pantheon (by Agrippa). Hadrian had the Pantheon (A31) built, and a whole group of temples in this context, extending from the Corso to the Pantheon (see A36), and also a second mausoleum on the other side of the river, to which access was provided by a bridge, the present Castel Santangelo (A33). The network of streets in the Tiber bend was immediately related to this bridge, or linked up with it. As well as the stadium of Domitian (AD 81 to 96), whose form has survived in the Piazza Navona (B61), two major axes from all this can still be seen today. One of these is the ancient Via Triumphalis (parallel with the Tiber), which Julius II was to revivify along with the ancient street linking the Vatican and Trastevere, on the other side of the river, in the form of his Via Giulia and Via della Lungara, creating such

large axes again for the first time at the beginning of the modern age. The other ancient road axis, the so-called Via Recta, which ran from the Tiber right across the Tiber bend almost to the column of Marcus Aurelius (now the Piazza Colonna) by the Via Lata (the present Via del Corso), still cuts through the urban fabric today, but was never widened, and so tends to go unnoticed. Hadrian's mausoleum is the first of the changes realised in the Vatican area. The area was occupied by imperial gardens and the largest tomb city after the one on the Via Appia. Thus the majority of the ancient tombs and catacombs are to be found in these two areas. Even Piranesi's famous engraving of St Peter's Square is captioned: »Caesar's and Nero's gardens and circus«. In fact there was considerable building activity under Nero in the Vatican area. Nero did not just build a circus here, from which the obelisk in St Peter's Square comes; the Borgo, the core development in the Vatican area for the common population also dates from Nero's times, and it was here that homeless people who had not received any substitute accommodation settled after the fire in AD 64. Most of these came from Central Europe, where settlements were given the name of a »Burg« (castle) or »Bourg«, hence »Borgo« here.

After Hadrian, in other words from the second half of the 2nd century AD, the development of the city slowed down, with some exceptions. These include Septimius Severus in particular and his son Caracalla, and the soldier emperor Aurelian. At the time of the Severans, about 200 AD, and from then on, the major buildings of the late-ancient period were erected, increasingly far from the city centre, above all the Baths of Caracalla (A43) and of Diocletian (A46). Of the Forum buildings the basilica of Maxentius (A50) belongs here, which was already part of the considerable upsurge in architecture in the early 4th century AD, at the time of Constantine, although the basic urban co-ordinates were little affected. The so-called marble urban plan, perhaps the most important source of our knowledge about the urban picture in ancient Rome, also came into being under Septimius Severus. Under Aurelian (270 to 275 AD), because Rome's military might was no longer sufficient to keep enemies far away from Rome, the Aurelian Wall was built; this shows the approximate extent of late-ancient Rome, and remained Rome's outermost border until after the First World War. It included the Tiber bend, the Pincian hill and also parts of Trastevere (cf. A33, A44).

Medieval Rome lay mainly to the south of the old city centre, and Renaissance and Baroque Rome north of it.

Christian late antiquity and Middle Ages

In ancient Rome a very simple distribution of the most important building types and residential areas crystallized out: the monumental centres were the Forum (down to the Colosseum) and (less densely built up) the Campus Martius (Tiber bend); the Capitol was first and foremost the cultic centre; the other hills were the smart residential areas, whose former smartest place became the site of the imperial palace; the simple population lived in the remaining, unhealthy lower areas. As well as this, the city area extended to the Aurelian Wall. Both these things changed fundamentally in the Christian Middle Ages. For one thing, the city shrank. One of the most important reasons for this was the shift of the capital city to Constantinople (330 AD). The building of the main basilicas had started earlier (the Lateran basilica in 313 AD, the Old St Peter's in 324 AD). There are no reliable figures, but even in the 5th century, Rome seems to have had only 250 000 to 500 000 inhabitants (as opposed to 600 000 to 2 000 000 in the imperial period), and from the 6th century scarcely more than 30 000 inhabitants. For in 537/38 AD, when the (then Byzantine) city of Rome was under siege by the Ostrogoths, the aqueducts had been destroyed, which also meant that the hill sites were without water from then on. The figure in the Trecento, in other words that of the papal exile in Avignon, can be relatively reliably estimated at 15 000 to 17 000 inhabitants, which is tiny in comparison with London, Paris or even Venice. Only just under a third of the area enclosed by the Aurelian Wall was even approaching being fully settled. The second important change is also addressed by the definition of the settled area: relatively soon after 537/38 AD the hills became deserted, and ultimately they were avoided altogether. Only mercenaries lived there, the French on the Esquiline, for example. The settled areas were now on the lower land, the Tiber has become the city's lifeblood. The medieval settlement area can be easily discerned on an engraving by Brambilla dating from 1590, by mentally removing the building inside the area starting with the Piazza del Popolo to about the level of Castel Sant'Angelo and Piazza Colonna. So the settled area was roughly in the shape of an oval with vertices in Castel Sant'Angelo and the Capitol, with one short side following the whole loop of the Tiber, the north eastern broad side running through the Piazza Colonna and the south western from the Sant'Angelo bridge along the Tiber to the Ponte Sisto and on in a curve to the Capitol. The Pincian, Quirinal, Capitoline and Palatine hills thus formed (still in 1590) a border for the settled area and were not included in it. It is significant that the Capitoline hill had now become known as the goat hill (monte caprino) and the Forum Romanum behind it was called the cow meadow (campe vaccino). The principal ancient sites were now grazing land.

The development of church building confirms this development impressively, both the shrinking of Rome and the withdrawal from the hills. If one considers the important church buildings in late-ancient Rome in the period of Constantine, of the so-called Sistine Renaissance (C7–C10) and to a limited extent from the time of Byzantine rule (C12–C14), then it is clear for all of them that they are either far away from the city centre, regularly even outside the Aurelian Wall, or on the top of hills. This shows: the city was still large, and people were living on the hills. But the latter is no longer true of the Byzantine period. If one excepts buildings that were erected on ancient houses belonging formerly to martyrs (C3, C4) or built into the ancient Roman Forum buildings (C11, C12), then this is true without exception. Such an assumption recommends itself because martyrs typically came from the poorer strata of the population, whose houses were in the lower-lying areas, and using them as starting points for cult sites suggested itself. The spatial distribution of the churches changed during the two dark centuries after the collapse of the Byzantine empire in Italy and before the Carolingian group of buildings came into being (C15–C21), in which the High Middle Ages proclaimed themselves stylistically as well, and which were very different from the late-ancient period (see C20, for example). The built-up area of Rome decreased dramatically, new church buildings appeared only rarely near or outside the Aurelian Wall (C24, for example). And when in the 11th century the northern Italian cities started to be renewed, Rome was asleep. No cathedral was built in the Middle Ages that could have borne comparison with those in the cities north of the Alps or in northern Italy. S. Maria in Trastevere (C28), the largest Roman church of the period, seems small in comparison with those. And most of the churches were not built on the hills any more, but on the plains (even since the Byzantine period). Admittedly the sites were often dictated by older centres (see C18, C22, C23, C25, C30, C36), monasteries could have different sites (C34); to the extent that the site could still be chosen, there was almost no new building on the hills (see for example C19, C20, C24, C27, C29; exception: C17). Once this had become the case, then it was frequently considered necessary to emphasize this exception with an addition like »ai monti« (for example C21). All the great churches built in the High Middle Ages were sited on the plains near the Tiber, S. Maria in Trastevere (C28), S. Maria in Cosmedin (C26, based on a Byzantine diaconate), S. Cecilia (C16) and S. Maria sopra Minerva (C37). The church sites are almost a dating criterion, so significant is the break between late-ancient times and the Byzantine or Carolingian period.

Besides the churches it is above all the bridges, two streets and the Papal residence that are important for the basic structure of the medieval city of Rome. Three bridges (one divided into two) survive in the Middle Ages, the Ponte Sant'Angelo in the north, the Pons Fabricius (A10) and the Pons Cestius in the south, both of which lead to the island in the Tiber and thus together form a Tiber crossing, and also, even further south, the Pons Maior, which collapsed for the first time in 1557 and finally in 1598, and was known from then as Ponte Rotto. If the Ponte Sant' Angelo was important for access to the Vatican, then the sites of the other bridges show that the southern section of the Tiber had become the heart of medieval life in Rome. With S. Cecilia, S. Maria in Trastevere and S. Maria in Cosmedin, most of the major new church buildings since the Carolingian period were in this (physically very limited) zone. To this extent it is not surprising that new church buildings on hills are to be found on the southern ones, the Aventine and the Caelian.

On the other hand, the Ponte Sant'Angelo (B96) provided access to the Vatican. And from it the two most important roads started, which entirely served pilgrimages and processions, and linked the Vatican with the important centres. Both ran in a longitudinal direction through the oval settlement area: the Via Papalis, somewhat further to the north, from the Ponte Sant' Angelo to the present Piazza S. Pantaleo with the Palazzo della Farnesina ai Baullari (H21), from there to Il Gesù (B1), running in the same way as the

present Corso Vittorio Emanuele (K11), then branches off to the Capitol from the square outside Il Gesù; and the Via Peregrinorum, which led from the Ponte Sant' Angelo along the present Via dei Banchi Vecchi to the later Palazzo Farnese (H25) and the Theatre of Marcellus (A17), and on from there to the Lateran.

The latter was the actual papal residence, and had been a palace even in the Carolingian period (C15). This was entirely committed to the idea of renewing the greatness of ancient Rome, more particularly the palaces of the Roman emperors, and was to have a lasting influence on the palaces of the West. But it is important for the cityscape of medieval Rome that it was if anything further from the centre than the Vatican, where the only buildings on a monumental scale were Old St Peter's (and the Castel Sant'Angelo), and there was no large residence. The papal residence was thus a long way outside the settled area. Nicholas III, by building the Pasetto walls, which linked the core of the Vatican with Castel Sant'Angelo, in 1277, prepared for a shift of residence to the Vatican, but this did not happen until precisely a hundred years later, after the popes had spent the greatest part of the intervening period in exile in Avignon.

For as long as the pope was resident in the Lateran, the people of Rome were less exposed to his political and military power than they were from the moment that the Castel Sant'Angelo was at his disposal (from the Vatican). When another large church, S. Maria in Aracoeli (C36), was built (exceptionally) on the top of a hill, then it (and above all the open steps leading to it) was also a symbol of the city's bourgeoisie. The Commune of Rome has been founded in 1143/44. For this reason numerous family towers were built in the inner city (as in other Italian cities); these included the Torre delle Milizie (C35), and those of the Frangipani (in the Colosseum and on the Arch of Janus Quadrifons, A51), of the Colonna in the Mausoleum of Augustus (A15) and of the Orsini on the Theatre of Marcellus (A17). The formation of a strong Commune (and appropriate urban structures) had been prevented by the popes since their return from Avignon. Rome developed differently from other Italian cities.

Late Middle Ages and early Renaissance

In 1377 the papal residence was moved back to Rome from Avignon, but not to the medieval residence in the Lateran but (predominantly) into the Vatican. In fact it was not the medieval centre of Rome that was the starting-point for the new development, but the Vatican. Because of the Pasetto walls connecting it with Castel Sant'Angelo, the Vatican Palace was considerably more secure than the Lateran or the city, which some later popes, particularly Clement VII, 1527, came to be very pleased to know. Additionally the city could be completely dominated from the Castel Sant'Angelo. This new direction for planning in general shifted the Ponte Sant'Angelo to the centre of town-planning considerations, it was the papal city's actual access to the city of Rome. The first to hit on the plan of making the Vatican and Rome of a similar size to ancient Rome was Nicholas V (1447–55). In his day there were again about 40 000 people living in Rome. He had summoned Alberti, the most important architect of the early Renaissance (with Brunelleschi) to Rome. Alberti wrote his architectural treatise here, and planned a Vatican city with all the facilities, with gardens, theatres and a large chapel. He also went about some enlargements of Old St Peter's, though did not yet project rebuilding it (see H7). He also planned to renovate all the usable public buildings, and especially the forty most important churches. Nicholas V died too early. Even so, the nucleus of the later Vatican palace wings had been built in the form of the Cortile dei Papagalli (F1), and one of Nicholas's successors, Sixtus IV, realized the plan for a large chapel in the Vatican (F13; now named after him). Under this pope, who acquired the title Restaurator urbis, the great early-Renaissance churches also came into being (F7, F14, F16), the first streets cut through, and also, in the form of the Ponte Sisto, a first bridge between the Ponte Sant'Angelo (B96) and those on the lower reaches of the Tiber (in the south). Also the first monumental palaces since the ancient and Carolingian periods in Rome were built after the time of Nicholas V, in the form of the Palazzo Venezia (F5) and the Palazzo della Cencellaria (F19), probably built to plans by Alberti.

High Renaissance and Mannerism

But Alberti's ideas did not really bear fruit on a larger scale until the papacy of Julius II (1503–13). His architect Bramante now actually created – on the scale of an ancient imperial garden or stadium – the gardens of the Belvedere courtyard, which created and opened up an entire landscape (H6). He also created a palace façade for the Vatican, visible over a distance, open and »extrovert« (H11). However, he was above all concerned with rebuilding St Peter's, whose effect on the cityscape as a whole was not very great for as long as Old St Peter's survived, with its rectangular forecourt. And at that time the most important access road, the Borgo Alessandrino, named after Alexander VI (1492–1503), approached the palace and not the church. The straight Borgo Alessandrino was not only a model for later street axes of this kind, but also the starting point for the first ambitious further development: Julius II had the idea of making the Tiber the centre of a first system of streets and axes. To this end he laid out the Via Giulia (based on the ancient Via Triumphalis) and the Via della Lungara, on both sides of the river and largely parallel to it. These

streets were cut almost at right angles from the Via Alessandrina in the north and correspondingly in the south from the Via dei Pettinari, which leads from the Ponte Sisto to Trastevere. This produced an extended rectangle of streets running north–south, with the two new streets on the long sides. The Via Giulia was planned as a magnificent prospect, framed by Renaissance palaces, though some important ones remained incomplete, like Bramante's Palazzo dei Tribunali.

Julius's successor Leo X (1513–21) commissioned the Via Leonina (now della Ripetta), a similarly straight axis from the Via Recta (and thus indirectly from the Ponte Sant'Angelo) to the Piazza del Popolo. Seen from the Piazza, this was the furthest to the right of the three great street axes that start here. The central one is the ancient Via Lata, now the Via del Corso. The Via del Babuino on the left followed under Paul III (1534–49). Northern Rome, in the triangle between the Castel Sant'Angelo (A33), the Piazza del Popolo and the Piazza Colonna, indeed even SS. Trinità dei Monti (H44), could now be reached with ease. And in fact the increasing amount of settled area in the 16th century, compared with that of the Middle Ages, was in that area in particular. This can be seen in Brambilla's engraving of 1590 (the year in which Sixtus V, the great urban developer, died). Paul III additionally completed the square at the end of the Ponte Sant'Angelo on the city side, the so-called Platea Pontis, by pushing the Via Trinitatis through to the Via Giulia, thus linking this early-Renaissance street to the Castel Sant'Angelo and at the same time completing the system of streets radiating from it. These were the first two stelliform complexes actually to be realized in the High Renaissance. The immediately surrounding area had acquired considerable significance because the banking area had grown up here opposite the Castel Sant'Angelo, which was the papal treasury, particularly the Zecca, the mint (H23), on the Via dei Banchi Vecchi, which acquired its name in this way. It was under Paul III that the first Renaissance squares elsewhere in Rome were created, outside the Palazzo Farnese (H25) and on the Capitol, where the epitome of a monumental and uniform square design for the early-modern period immediately came into being (H27). Pius IV continued to build long street axes, but now much more clearly to the south-east, the second area into which the city was to extend beyond the medieval settlement area. He built the Via Pia (the present Via XX Settembre), now starting at the Quirinal, i.e. another papal palace, whose square also had a particular aura of ancient Rome (as the Dioscuri had been discovered there). And additionally Michelangelo – and this is new – gave the square a definite focal point by designing the Porta Pia, in which the idea of (intersecting) routes and urban structures was to acquire intense pictorial expression (see H43).

Baroque and Rococo

The work of Sixtus V

So when Sixtus V (1585–90) embarked upon his great urban development projects, a great deal had already been devised: the concept of long, straight streets, as well as putting them together into systems radiating from a particular point, streets directed at a monument to catch the eye at the end, but also the formation of uniform, monumental squares. And yet Sixtus V was much more consistent in his efforts than his predecessors, and is thus considered the greatest urban developer of the 16th century. Before him most of the axes that had been created had been short and isolated. It is true that a start had been made on a coherent system, but it was not until Sixtus V that the whole city was analysed in terms of urban development, and this meant above all a network of streets for access to the south and east. Sixtus V wanted these areas to experience a population upsurge similar to that seen by the north in the early 16th century. Almost two thirds of the area inside the Aurelian Wall was in fact still unsettled, and in addition these were the healthier areas on the hills. And so

Rome in an etching by A. Brambilla, 1590

Sixtus V had the axes put further through into the more rural areas beyond the Capitol. Giedion has provided us with a masterly description of Sixtus V's urban development work, and has also presented it graphically. Sixtus V started immediately with the first axis, which ran right through the city from the extreme north to the extreme south-east, from the Piazza del Popolo to S. Croce in Gerusalemme (B134), 4 kilometres long, through very hilly territory, and dead straight. This was the so-called Strada Felice (now the Via Sistina etc.), never completed in its northern section. The Palazzo Barberini (B45), one of the main palaces on this road, shows in its diagonal placing how consistently (and uncompromisingly) this street thrust through urban areas. Sixtus V and his architect Domenico Fontana were also particularly proud of this masterpiece of town planning, and Fontana emphasized that it had been Sixtus V who had removed the hills and filled the valleys, and thus made Rome into a city of more gentle waves. But Sixtus V's magnificent achievement was not just this single street, with which he began, but the simultaneity of his projects, the fact that he started in many places at once. For a long time, during his »exile« in a vineyard near S. Maria Maggiore, in the reign of his rival Gregory XIII (1572–83), he had been able to reflect about his planning of linking the parts together to form a coherent

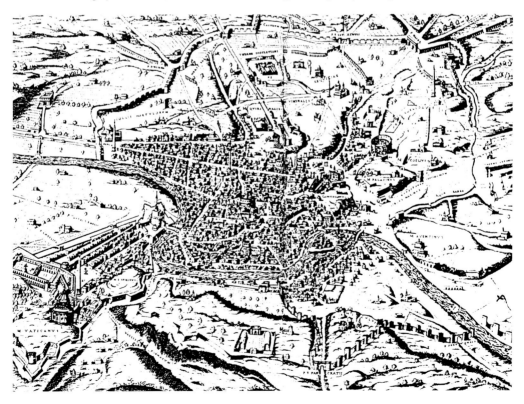

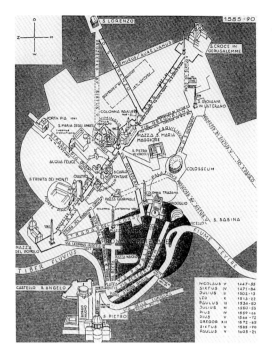

The planning of Rome by Sixtus V

network. There were probably iconographic considerations behind this overall concept as well. Sixtus wanted to make Rome into a »single shrine« (Pastor), and to make it easy to reach the most important churches. But this is only one aspect. His plans were no longer like those of Nicholas V and Julius II, who had built on to systems that already related to one of the main churches, like St Peter's, for example. And so it was no longer the old idea of similitude, according to which the earthly city was supposed to be built as a copy of the kingdom of God, that formed the basis of his concept. He was also no longer thinking of the humanistically inspired ideal city concepts of the High Renaissance with their stellar complexes. It would be to misunderstand the arrangement of streets (also stellar) around S. Maria Maggiore (C7) to try to explain it with concepts of this kind. Sixtus V in fact came close to smashing the concept of the stel-liform, walled ideal city of the High Renaissance. He was concerned, even though his concept was church-related, primarily to relate his overall concept of urban access to function. And thus he was the first to lay the foundations of the modern city plan.

This general plan was flanked by a series of special measures. Sixtus V took up the newly developed tradition of squares in front of the principal buildings and made »space« in front of the Quirinal Palace and the Lateran Palace, for example, and started to do so in the Piazza Colonna as well (all admittedly less inter-

esting designs artistically). Then he had obelisks built to catch the eye at the ends of axes or in exposed places – and this then also affected the third papal palace, the Vatican. He had four of these obelisks built: in both the Vatican and the Lateran, at S. Maria Maggiore and in the Piazza del Popolo (and also the columns of Marcus Aurelius and Trajan). The Vatican obelisk was the first and biggest. With this Sixtus also inaugurated a new axis for the Vatican, which seemed to have been shifted so far to the side in terms of his thinking as a whole. For this new obelisk related to St Peter's itself, and not to the Palace. And under Sixtus V the building itself was also completed for the time being by the vaulting of the dome (in a mere 22 months). It also fitted in with the new definition of the axis that Sixtus V again formed the plan of puling down the central row of houses in the Borgo, which led to St Peter's, the so-called Spina del Borgo – like Nicholas V before him, with Alberti, and Julius II, and later Carlo Fontana (1694), Morelli (1776), Napoleon (1811), Pius IX (1850) and the general development plan in 1881, until ultimately under Fascism and later it was realized (1936–50) with the Via della Conciliazione. As another flanking measure Sixtus V also restored the water supply, which had simply laid damaged and completely useless since the time of Alexander Severus (AD 222–35), not only to the valleys, but also to the hills. And the show façade of the Acqua Felice (B18), as contemporaries were already aware, may have been in bad taste, but made an uncommonly proud impression in the figure of Moses, with an almost Biblical sense of mission. And the Fontana di Trevi also got the Acqua Vergine back again (the ancient Aqua Virgo), although at the time this was only for the washing of wool.

The structure of the city of Rome, as fixed by Sixtus V, was already practically identical with that at the time of the Second World War, and in terms of population size with that in the early days of the kingdom (1870/71). It was not until the 1950s that the city started to extend over the whole area outside the Aurelian Wall. If we look at the population increase, then the time when the axes were cut through in the last two thirds of the 16th century represented an enormous upsurge. After the number of inhabitants had gone down again after the Sack of Rome (1527) to about 30 000, in 1599, not even ten years after the death of Sixtus V, it was 110 000, in other words four times as large. After that growth was steady until 1870, and clearly slower with about 147 000 inhabitants in 1799 and about 200 000 in 1870.

The further development in High Baroque and Rococo

The possibilities for urban development that remained for the great era of the Baroque and Roman Rococo therefore seem modest at first sight, but affects the artistic side more, the side of life, while for Sixtus V function remained in the foreground. It was he who created the great axes, the traffic routes or the infrastructure, but his successors created pleasant spaces for lingering within the structure of the city. The greatest of these creations, the framing of St Peter's square by Bernini's Colonnades, is the most eloquent example of conveying the gigantic size of the church and the palace precinct to the more human scale of the surrounding buildings, and using perspective and an abundance of visual axes to fuse an enormous ensemble (consisting of the church and parts of the palace, but also the adjacent streets and the Borgo development) together visually and make it open to experience. Until the pontificate of Alexander VII (1655–67), in which St Peter's Square was built, it is true that Rome had hardly any centrally sited proud squares, but then they came into being in rapid succession over a period of fifty years. Alexander's predecessor Innocent X (1644–55) had made a start by designing the Piazza Navona (B61), and under Alexander VII there came the square in front of S. Maria della Pace (B79) and the Piazza del Popolo with its twin churches (B87/88) and – in the Rococo period now – the Spanish Steps (B115) and the Fontana di Trevi, together with the area around it (B126). And this omits a number of smaller squares altogether (see only B72, B85, B93, B95, B118). The characteristic feature of these squares built in the 1660s and 70s is the dense building around them, and not so much a sense of opening up into axes leading into the distance. And they were also not (or if so, only peripherally) related to a monument in the middle, like an obelisk, for example, but to all the surrounding monumental buildings. These typically showed, frequently within themselves, but certainly from one square to another, a considerable range of design forms. Hans Rose spoke of a »lack of symmetry tantamount to genius« in this context. What happened here was that Maderno, in S. Susanna (B30) was the first to include the adjacent buildings in the façade design of the main building, and this idea was developed from then onwards. But what this produced was not, as in the cities of Upper Italy or north of the Alps, rectangular squares with largely linear limits, the phenomenon that Lotz called the »piazza salone«, but lively space with an uncommonly individual style to it.

It was not until the late 17th century that Carlo Fontana once more took up the idea of routes and axes (although only in isolation), which Domenico Fontana had launched so impressively a century earlier, under Sixtus V. He wanted to repeat the trapezoid piazzetta in front of St Peter's on the other side of the oval piazza where the Via della Conciliazione starts today, thus giving St Peter's Square a long-drawn-out effect. Of course the complex would not have been anything like as cramped and squashed as it was in the late 16th century. The project was not carried out. But just under fifty years later, the high

Baroque tradition of creating squares as a space for lingering was brought into the most felicitous harmony with the idea of creating axes in the Spanish Steps (B115). The steps give access to the Pincian hill, but at the same time de Sanctis wanted to create a space that seems majestic but comfortable, and thus attracts people to linger. Another route that already earlier became a place in which to linger was the Ponte Sant'Angelo, in the design by Bernini (who, with his own project, also had a considerable influence on the realization of the Spanish Steps). Bernini designed the bridge, which was an important part of the processional route, to be a place of leisure as well, by providing the angels as objects of contemplation, and all this already using the gracious overall forms of incipient late Baroque and Rococo (B96). This perfect balance between movement and repose finally showed even in the design of the Ripetta Harbour, in which the river was given a flowing façade that was entirely appropriate to it, making a vivid impression (ill. p. 171).

Classicism and Historicism

Classicism's great town-planning project was the Piazza del Popolo. Here Valadier used existing features very skilfully, especially the twin idea, which had already been realized with the pair of Baroque churches and which expressed the vestibule or gateway character of this square so well, but he also developed some uncommonly modern ideas: by interlinking green and built-up areas and also by fitting together various planes (see p. 277 and K1). Thus the first large public park in Rome emerged on the Pincian hill in this context.

But two other 19th-century measures are even more important for the Roman cityscape. First of all there were excavations and exposure of features of the Forum Romanum, the Forum of Trajan and the Colosseum in particular. But a piece of town planning in the more restricted sense was a second bundle of measures. Their principal characteristic is above all that they shifted the gateway to the city of Rome: the early railway age did not lead only to building up a considerable area on the Viminal, but also to the fact that the most important town-planning measure started near the station: the first years of the kingdom produced a large east–west axis to complement the great north–south axis of the Corso (see plan with K11). It started at the Piazza Esedra (now Piazza della Repubblica), which was also designed in a monumental fashion towards the end of the building works (K16). From here the Via Nazionale (K9) leads to the Piazza Venezia, which was subsequently greatly enlarged, and the monument for King Vittorio Emanuele II (K15), visible for a considerable distance, was added. Starting from the Piazza Venezia, what had been started in the Via Nazionale was continued

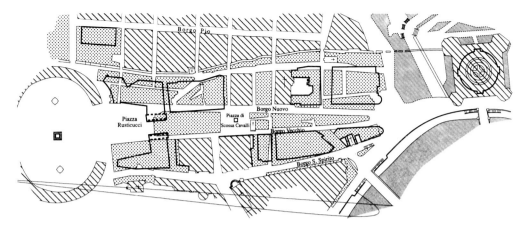

in the Corso Vittorio Emanuele (K11), which since then has cut through the Tiber bend in an east–west direction. Thus the Piazza Venezia became the point of intersection between the ancient Via Lata (the Via del Corso) and the 19th century Via Nazionale and Corso Vittorio Emanuele. Other new streets were created to do justice to the newly emerging traffic requirements, especially from the station via the Via Barberini and Via del Tritone to the Piazza Colonna. A great deal of attention was paid to monument protection in the course of this work. The town-planning measures are effectively the core of architectural development in the second half of the 19th century and are thus described more specifically in the appropriate chapter (see pp. 278, 279).

Modernism

Rome expanded enormously in the period after the First World War. After it became capital in 1870/71 the population doubled within 30 years to a good 400 000 inhabitants. Coherent settlement beyond the Aurelian Wall was established for the first time in the early 20th century, though at a measured pace. Workers' quarters came into being in the south-west, the Quartiere Testaccio (K22) and the Quartiere Garbetalla (M2, M3) from the 20s onwards. A more refined residential area formed by the Via Nomentana, near to the Porta Pia (H43), including many of the most interesting villas and small palaces (very early: K19, Ximénes). The expansion of Rome became a positive programme under Fascism: partly because of a conscious policy of reducing the population in the cities (see p. 297), and partly (and particularly visibly) with the aim of linking Rome to the sea. The E'42/EUR centre (M24) was planned at the halfway mark,

and access to it provided by fast roads with many carriageways. Of the other large and prestigious projects the Foro Mussolini (now Foro Italico, M5) and the university (M9) were built outside the Aurelian Wall, but close to it. Very dense expansion of the city did nor start until after the Second World War, largely in stages and rings: in the late 40s and 50s still quite close to the old town (for instance M40, M41), otherwise (largely workers' estates) on main roads out of the city like the Via Tiburtina (for example M37, M38), because that is where industry was sited; this phase of settlement was dominated by the Neo-Realistic design mode (»rustically attractive«). Before the start of the second phase, because of the Olympic Games in 1960, the area around the Via Flaminia and the EUR became a focal point for building (see M45, M46, M48, M49). In the second phase, starting in the mid-sixties, settlement started near to the Grande Raccordo Annulare, the motorway ring that was being built; this was mainly in the form of large, block-like complexes with comprehensive infrastructure, very much in the spirit of the International Style (for example M53, M55, M64, M67, M68). The area beyond the motorway ring was settled almost at the same time, frequently (especially in the north) on the popular hill sites, but usually not in the form of large complexes, but as more fragmented development (for example M62, M65, M66). It is precisely these areas, which seem to have no particular order, that show that the almost revolutionary set of town-planning guidelines and instruments formulated in the law of 1942 in Italy were never followed consistently.

Building activity slowed down considerably from 1973 (because of the oil price shock and the world economic crisis), leading to a phase (as at the time of early-Mannerism, see for instance H31) in which a large number of projects originated that had no chance of being realized (often on the basis of Giambattista Noli's famous town plan of 1748). The inner city in particular again became the site of many very carefully adapted building measures (see M63). There

well as the axis leading to the principal site of Catholicism, two more were created on the key sites of imperial antiquity. The first, and the more famous, the Via dei Fori Imperiali, leads from the Piazza Venezia past the left of the Capitol to the Colosseum (A25), through the middle of the Fori Imperiali, and the other, the Via del Teatro di Marcello, curves past the right of the Capitol, then passes the Theatre of Marcellus (A17) and on to the Forum Holitiorum, the commercial centre of ancient Rome. Thus these two axes opened up the entire core of the ancient city. The reference to the ancient Roman imperial period, and especially to the Augustan era, showed in many of the measures taken, from the uncovering of ancient buildings (excavation of the Forum Romanum was concluded in the Fascist period) to the choice of the so-called Stile Littorio (for detail see pp. 297–299). The new show boulevard of the Via dei Fori Imperiali is characteristic of the development of Fascism in Italy to the extent that this link with ancient times was very decidedly built into a fundamentally Modernist mood, a mood of new beginnings. The idea of taking traffic past the monuments of antiquity on a multi-laned dead straight fast road was rightly seen as part of the intellectual property of Futurism, as its ideal of technology and rapid movement was obviously a key feature. In fact, unlike German Fascism, the Italian version was by no means scornful of Modernism (see pp. 297/298). Comparable expressways were built to provide access to Mussolini's own large buildings, for example the E'42/EUR (M24). The present had found its way into the oldest centre of the Eternal City. SG

Two Fascist axes east and west of the Monumento Vittorio Emanuele II cutting through the ancient Imperial city (1936–38)

was even a plan at this time to break up the Via dei Fori Imperiali again.

This addresses the very heart of the city, which in fact was redesigned at two significant points in the three quarters of a century after the First World War, although the urban design given to it by Sixtus V and continued in the 19th century was largely retained. Mussolini's Fascist regime was responsible for both redesign operations, and both were very typical of it. In 1932 the principal architect of the Fascist era, Piacenti, carried out a measure that was in fact based on centuries-old ideas, the opening up of the Via della Concilazione, a visible expression of the normalized relations between Italy and the Vatican State, introduced at the latest with the concordat of 1929. As

Antiquity (753 BC to AD 313)

It does not do justice to ancient Roman architecture to view it primarily in terms of the history of style. It is much more important that it was highly original in developing building types and forms, and the techniques necessary for this. It is this, and not the development of style that provides the key points in a chronological arrangement. The independence of Roman architecture, particularly in terms of Greek architecture, cannot be emphasized to energetically. A whole series of characteristic and fully independent features emerged, which was not the case in sculpture. Roman town planning, which is addressed only peripherally here, is discussed at some length in the entries on the Forum (A1) and on Ostia (A30).

Building types, forms and techniques

Numerous building types developed in Roman architecture, partly based on Hellenistic forerunners: from aqueducts via baths and amphitheatres (and freestanding theatres, see A17) to the triumphal arches. And the standard type of Roman square with its framing porticoes, with the principal building added on one side should also be mentioned here (see A13). One building type is particularly outstanding, the basilica. It represents Roman architecture's most important contribution to Western building history. This was where the form emerged of a structured and directed interior with a higher central section and adjacent side sections or aisles (see A11 for detail). This building type was used for non-religious purposes in the Roman world. There are three principal points that should be emphasized. Firstly, the basilica became the dominant type of church building, i. e. for the building task that was the most important until the Renaissance, which was then joined by (only) a second that was similarly important, the building of palaces. Thus the significance of its development was considerable. If one looks here at further elements like the apse, the ceremonial and the mosaics, then the effect Rome had on the Western Christian world becomes all too clear. In Rome the apse (which can already be found in Hellenistic predecessors) became increasingly significant as the place of greatest distinction (for the emperor's throne or the cult statue). Ceremonial, as continued in the West, went back to Domitian (A27), and mosaics were omnipresent in the Roman world. Secondly, the fact that a secular building type was adopted for ecclesiastical architecture shows how functional Roman architecture was, in that its types could be used for a number of purposes. Constantine may have taken over this building type for Christian church architecture for a number of reasons (see p. 67). But the very fact that it was taken over shows that building types in Rome were perceived to be able to fulfil various functions.

The basilica, the court building or market hall, became a church. The design of the imperial chamber in Domitian's palace on the Palatine was interestingly very similar to that of the halls in baths, but in the 2nd century AD also influenced the architecture of temple interiors, an entirely different problem (see A36). Forum, especially the imperial forum, and temple precinct had fundamentally the same structure, and they both comprised a temple. This flexibility of building types has been convincingly interpreted as being the expression of the very close link between religious and public life in Rome. But the most important point, thirdly, is that it was with the basilica that the idea of the designed interior made its breakthrough. When the Roman basilica was developing as a building type in the early 2nd century BC, the interior became the central design theme. Designed interiors had previously been found at most in Hellenistic antiquity, but they were far more modest. Anyway it was Roman interiors that radically changed the history of architecture. The entire later Western development would be unthinkable without it. In Rome itself the first important objects for interior design were the baths, then, as a related building form, palaces (A27), later, in the mid-2nd century AD, the cult room as well. In religious history this can be seen as the transition from the blood sacrifice, which was celebrated in the open air, to the rite of consecration.

The most important innovations in the realm of building forms are also associated with the increased importance of the interior. The column was adequate as the central expressive form in an architecture in which only the exterior was designed throughout. But if the interior was to be designed as well, then new building forms were needed for the walls. Ultimately the principal innovations in Roman architecture in terms of building forms always affected either the interior or the exterior wall, or its link with the column order. This applies first to the way in which the wall runs. In this respect the most interesting forms were those that went beyond a simple box shape. The first of these is the rotunda, the vaulted, cylindrical building form. In Roman architecture it was usually surrounded by a circle of niches. For the interior lighting was the principal problem here, and for the exterior the revelation of the rotunda form (and beyond this the form of the circle of niches). Lighting was achieved at first through the apex of the dome (in early examples in Rome from the Augustan period onwards; see also A31), later through windows in the drum or clerestory (in examples from the time of Hadrian onwards, but above all in the 3rd and 4th century AD); the openings became larger and larger. In the first rotundas, in the 1st century AD, the exterior was not yet fully revealed (see A24). Development in this respect was not concluded until late antiquity (see A31, A53). A second central building form for interiors was that of the groin vault, the vault created when two barrel vaults intersect at right angles. In Roman architecture they were made of cast masonry – developing beyond previous Hellenistic buildings. In Republican examples the bays were further separated by transverse arches (A9). These had to be omitted when the groin vaults were intended for use as a system that could be extended at will in two directions; this step fol lowed in the 2nd century AD (A29, A50). Because in Roman architecture circular lines so often occur in combination with straight ones, the concept of »architecture with mixed lines« was coined for this. Before Roman times, correspondingly curved building forms are found, even in Hellenistic architecture, only in transient small buildings, never on a large scale. It is obvious that architecture since the Renaissance, especially the »mixed-line architecture« of the Baroque period, owed everything to these developments in ancient Rome. Mixed lines in ancient Roman architecture can be seen even more clearly if one considers the second-mentioned element, the order of columns. Two developments are central to this: their connection with the wall and above all their connection with the round-arched form, both contradicting the Greek system of column order with horizontal entablature and not recorded in Hellenism until 100 BC. The Greek column order was connected with the wall by applying the orthogonal order of column and entablature to the wall, into which an arch was cut, the pier arcade; this continued in the Republican period (A9). Under Domitian a column order placed in front of the wall came to be taken for granted, it became a column »curtain« in front of the wall. The column came into even more intensive interplay with the wall as soon as it clearly replaced parts of it. In places it now replaced the piers in the pier arcade, and the wall arch was placed directly on top of it, and in places it replaced the corner pier of a groin vault and this vault was placed directly on top of it, thus creating the form of a baldacchino. Completely formed examples of both phenomena are not to be found until late antiquity (see A30 and A50).

The most important of these building forms were made possible only by the invention of new building techniques, above all of Roman concrete (opus caementicium). First mortar was taken from the Greek cities in southern Italy, a mixture of sand and burnt lime that reacts when water is added, creating artificial limestone. This technique was known in Rome in the 3rd century BC. Roman concrete was then derived from the chance discovery that the combination became waterproof and pressure resistant to an enormously high degree if the sand was replaced with (volcanic) Pozzolan earth. Even the greatest technical achievements of Republican Roman architecture could scarcely have been realized without this invention, for example the shrine in Palestrina (A8) or the aqueducts. Vitruvius describes this technique in detail in the early 1st century AD. Usually, but not always, the opus caementicium is clad, at first with opus incertum (polygon), then with opus quasi reticu-

latum and opus reticulatum. In the 2nd century AD brick cladding made a general breakthrough. This building technique was essential for many building forms, because it was easy (and cheap) to model walls and construct oblique surfaces and vaults. All that was needed for the shuttering was a good carpenter. After the fire of Rome in AD 64 the city was rebuilt using this technique. It appears very extensively in Ostia (A30), which experienced its heyday in the 2nd century AD. Lavish spatial forms like those used in the Domus Aurea (A24) and the palace on the Palatine (A27) would not have been possible without this technique, nor would it have been possible to build the Pantheon (A31) or the basilica of Maxentius (A50). But it was some time before the (brick-clad) »concrete« wall appeared on the outside without order or decoration, and the building derived its effect from the frugal aesthetics of light and dark, of wall and hollow. The functional buildings (A29, A37) were the first here.

Chronological survey

The Republican period (A2–A12)

Hardly any independent developments took place in Rome during the first three centuries of the Republic. Etruscan influence can be seen in the broad, flat, short proportions of the temples (for example in the Temple of Jupiter on the Capitol, see A1, or in temple C in the Largo Argentina, A3). This changed from about 200 BC, when Greek models replaced the Etruscan ones. Most significant is the change in proportions, which now became considerably more slender and tall (see first A7). An intensive process of Hellenization started in Rome. But this was only one trend in the last two centuries before Christ, which was not even the more consequential one for Western architecture, as it was in this period that the principal characteristics of Roman architecture were established. It has already been pointed out that the basilica developed as a type in the early 2nd century, and also the triumphal arch, and in the 1st century BC the amphitheatre and probably bath architecture as well. Central design forms developed, especially for the temples. This happened firstly under Sulla, or shortly before, when high, dominant terraces were developed for them – in Tivoli, Terracina and Palestrina (A8) – and when the column order was first connected with the wall (A9). Secondly this happened in a rather more general way in the two centuries when the Roman temple (under Etruscan influence) gained a clear orientation. Thus the round temple (tholos) was given a porch in almost all cases (see A3, A6, A31, A40), and the peripteros, i. e. the rectangular temple with columns running round all four sides, was modified to become a podium temple in the form of a pseudoperipteros, i. e. a temple whose rear section (the cella) was clearly distinct from the front section (the columned hall); in this case the stylobate, the base with steps on all sides, was replaced by the podium, a base whose sides have no steps, but have a flight of steps to provide access at the front. A similar spirit can be detected even in ensembles of several buildings: all the temples in the largo argentina face in the same direction (A3). This continued in the Julio-Claudian period: when squares were designed (the fori imperiali, for example), the temple did not stand freely in the middle, but was linked with the framing buildings at one end of the square (A13, A20).

Early Julio-Claudian period (A13–A23)

The fori imperiali address two fundamental characteristics of the Julio-Claudian period. For Rome this was the beginning of a period of urban development intended to impose order and at the same time the period of imperial forms. In Rome this regularization (unlike Miletus, in the Greek classical period, or Roman provincial cities) never affected the whole of the city, but always just selected public centres. Thus Augustus and Caesar redesigned the Forum Romanum to impose order (A1) and at the same time devalued it as a political centre. It was enough for imperial pride that Augustus was turning Rome into a city of marble. He had 82 temples restored and built 10 new ones. The marble quarries needed to do this (in Carrara) were opened in 36 BC. If one also adds in the necessary preparation time, then it was probably Caesar who took the initiative. As well as the fori imperiali, the great monuments that in the Republican period had flourished as a building exercise for the whole of the upper class were now used to serve only the rulers, and at the same time monumentalized. This was particularly true of tomb building (see A15, A12). The triumphal arch found what was later to be its customary form in this period, in that here too column order with column and entablature was applied to building with mass and walls (piers, arch and attica), for the first time under Augustus in the Forum Romanum (see A1, A26). The high plinth on which the single temple was raised also gave an impression of grandeur. And at the time of Augustus the Corinthian order made a breakthrough in Rome, and from then onwards it was used exclusively. Here the Ara Pacis (A18) led the way, and the Temple of Mars-Ultor (A20). The model predominantly used by Augustan architecture, in the frieze of figures on the Ara Pacis, for example, was Periclean classicism (see A18, A20, also A31). The Hellenistic garland frieze was another frequent feature.

At the same time, the Augustan period was predominantly conservative, and so opportunities for innovation were ignored. It is well known that Augustus always emphasized old Roman values, and presented himself merely as primus inter pares. The content expressed by Augustan art and architecture can be reduced to a common denominator: Roman spirit in Graeco-Periclean clothing. They were also conservative in matters of building. There was scarcely an architect who would trust in the effectiveness of the wall alone (without column order). Column order was probably used extensively as well to maintain a sense of »decorum« (A17) in precisely those buildings and building types that had previously been considered a threat to Roman morality and, like stone theatres, had been realized only in isolation. Vitruvius, the great architectural theoretician of antiquity, embodied this conservatism. The opportunity of using opus caementicium, which was now completely mastered technically, to find a new aesthetic language was not taken. The impression of heavy walls, already conveyed by architecture under Sulla and even before that, did not come about. What was known as gravitas romana was frequently lacking. This did not change until the reigns of the last emperors in the family. Under Claudius, rusticated stone, left in its roughly hewn condition, became the most important expressive feature (A22, A23). Even more radical was the new start under Nero.

The 2nd half of the 1st century (A24–A27)

Two tendencies dominated the period from Nero to Domitian. Firstly, brick-clad concrete and thus the wall became dominant. Rome was rebuilt after the fire in AD 64 using this economical technique. The second tendency seemed to contradict this, but in fact did not: the first magnificent spatial complexes tailored especially to the person of the emperor came into being, the Domus Aurea (A24) and the palace on the Palatine (A27). Their builders, Nero and Domitian, who lived according to the image of the divine emperor, were assassinated for precisely this reason, and became victims of damnatio memoriae. But their buildings were masterpieces of a spirit that was to win through later. Nero and Domitian, unlike Augustus, no longer wanted to relate the unfolding of imperial magnificence to tradition and the community, but to the person of the emperor alone. Each built a residence, in the first case a villa that had been moved into the city and blown up to gigantic proportions, and in the second the prototype of the Western palace. Both ensembles showed a quite new complexity in terms of spatial sequences and the shape of individual rooms, varied, oblique-angled, and frequently lavishly articulated with niches. This was particularly true of the rooms that surrounded the central octagon of the Domus Aurea like »leftovers«. A lavish sequence of spaces also developed in the building of baths under Nero (see A28). Pleasure taken in complex spatial sequences, and partly also in playing with illusion, is paralleled in contemporary painting in Style IV in Pompeii. The fact that we know the names of the architects, Severus and Celerius or Rabirius, speaks for the high quality of both building complexes. Imperial splendour was demonstrated even more vividly (for detail see A27) in the palace on the Palatine, in which Domitian lived out the Hellenistic idea of the divine Emperor and created the court ceremonial that was later to become customary in the West. The walls were lavishly articulated with niches, thus the fact that concrete can be shaped was used to the full, and the wall could be perceived as a mass; this was the beginning of Roman mass building (see also A25). In addition, an extravagantly rich play of columns was placed in front of the wall – like a curtain. This form of wall with a sense of movement (with niches and free-standing columns in front of the wall) remained dominant until late antiquity. Coloured stone was used for decoration. Rooms were immensely high and awe-inspiring. The column developed comparably under the Flavians, with each one being placed on its own high plinth (A25, A26). Spatial height and layered construction are also typical of the second masterpiece from the period of Domitian, the Arch of Titus with its high attica, and also of its relief style (A26). Both works are the epitome of what was called »Flavian Baroque«. The great political break, the fall of Nero, thus had no lasting effect on the history of architecture. Domitian took up the building style of the age of Nero. The only change was an interim one, under Vespasian, who was a Flavian, and thus the first person who was not a member of a noble family to come to power. Vespasian built modestly (in the case of his temple in the Forum Romanum, A1), but also ostentatiously, when erected for the people the largest building in Rome, the Colosseum (A25), over Nero's villa.

The adoptive emperors (A28–A38)

The largest imperial forum was built under Trajan, together with market buildings (A29), baths (A28) and a harbour, which led to the rise of Ostia (A30). These buildings represent considerable change. In the imperial forum and the markets Trajan was clearly turning more to the community as a whole again, and also to tradition. The Basilica Ulpa in the Forum of Trajan was the last and largest of these basilicas committed to the classical model, and also the last large secular building in Rome with a Greek row of columns and epistyle. But Trajan's period was also marked (in a different way from the Augustan period) by further advances in concrete and brick building. It saw the first group of buildings in Rome that relied solely on the frugal aesthetics of this material. In the mean time, designing large, complex spaces in concrete had become commonplace (A29). Ostia (A30) embodies this age better than Rome. Ostia is to the era of Trajan as Herculaneum and Pompeii were to the pre-Flavian era.

Commentators like to see Trajan's successor, Hadrian, as a phil-Hellene. But his love of Greece was substantially different from that displayed under Augustus, the moralizing element in particular being absent. Architecture under Hadrian can no longer be reduced to the common denominator of expressing the Roman spirit in Greek clothing. Numerous developments in the field of architecture fell into the age of Hadrian that do not show even the slightest Greek influence: Hadrian built the first temple that was dominated by its interior, and this was a concrete and brick building (A31). Three-dimensional forms in concrete and brick were developed in an almost virtuoso fashion under him (A32). Circular form dominated ground plan and elevation (rotunda), especially in the predominant type of arch, the Syrian arch. And even the Villa Hadriana, which seems eclectic in many ways, was specifically of its time in its shifted axes and highly innovative forms in terms of space, elevation and vaults. In the Pantheon, this period produced one of the most impressive »classical« spaces in Rome, but at the same time the Villa Hadriana was built, an ensemble of buildings with which Post-Modern architects have always felt a sense of empathy because of its complexity.

An era of great buildings came to an end with Hadrian. Domitian had established the palace as a type, Trajan left behind the great imperial forum, and in the Pantheon Hadrian found the quintessence of the Roman rotunda. His successor Antoninus Pius was an architectural classicist (A35); only two buildings have survived from his period in Rome. For the first time building activity outside Rome, in Baalbek, for example, put building in the capital clearly in the shade. Clearly the provinces were getting stronger – in fact they had been providing the emperors since Trajan.

The Severans, Maxentius and Constantine (A39 to A54)

Only the Severans built on a large scale in the period of just under a hundred years between the adoptive emperors and the Tetrarchs. The only exception here was the Aurelian Wall (A44). Under the Severans, the first non-European emperors, architects returned to tried-and-tested building types, but the nature of design did change. A tendency to megalomania, (in the building of baths) became stronger (A43), and a completely new atectonic approach can be sensed in the buildings of this period. The design of the arches in particular seems ornamentally atectonic: their articulation seems to be overrun by »carpets« of reliefs, thus losing the impression of lucid articulation (A41, A42). Also eastern cults were promoted for the first time at the highest levels of state, a (lost) temple of Serapis was built. All this was to bear rich fruit in late antiquity; its relief style was already starting to show through (A42). The Severans were responsible for a whole range of buildings – baths (A43), sections of palaces on the Palatine (A27) and a triumphal arch (A41) – and thus the last large dynastic building programme before Maxentius and Constantine. Even before their day the Baths of Diocletian were built, the last large baths to be built in Rome (A46).

The Arch of Constantine is probably the best-known building dating from the first three decades of the 4th century, and it could convey the impression that architecture under Maxentius and Constantine was conservative. The arch is traditional in type and its reliefs were largely taken from other buildings and adopted (A52). But this impression is deceptive. Vaulting technique and mass building found their most expressive forms in the Basilica of Maxentius (A50). Here these forms were now transferred to the basilica itself. Articulated building, which was combined with mass building in this basilica, found forms that were bolder and lighter than ever before (A53). Openings had never consumed so much of the wall. The niches were now as close together as possible. Even the dome was no longer a simple hemisphere, but was articulated by ridges, first of all by mere reinforcements (see A47, A53), and not until later by ribs. Two central developments came to fruition in these decades: now the centrally arranged structure stood freely within the outer building, its lavish articulation recognizable down to the last concha. Now the form of the interior could be clearly recognized in the exterior (A53). And the »final fusion of the Hellenistic column apparatus into the structure of the wall« now took place »in the form of the columned arcade« (Rakob). The arcade was now placed directly on the column, not on the pier (see A30). And from then on the column, in combination with the groin vault could replace the (wall)pier, producing a baldacchino shape (A50). The highest stage of spatial differentiation and vaulting technique had been achieved. All this was to live on in Byzantium. But in Rome the simple, box-shaped space of the basilica, that had been developed under the Republic, was adopted once more for the new large churches. The reasons for this are unclear: did inventive powers decline when the residence was moved? Were the complex spatial forms considered to be too »coloured«, i. e. much too tailored to imperial and ancient and pagan building requirements? In any case a large proportion of medieval Western architecture was based on the rediscovery of the art of vaulting and handling space in ancient Rome. The old capital in the West was thrown back into a state that had already been achieved in Republican architecture, which had a strongly Hellenistic tinge. But Byzantium inherited Roman vaulted construction, the least Grecian building form that ancient Rome produced.

The independence of ancient Roman architecture

Richness of invention in terms of building types and forms was probably the most important characteristic of Roman architecture. The independence of this art, which contrary to a current prejudice did not get stuck in imitative dependence on Greek architecture, can also be seen in many other characteristics. Roman architects often thought in systems. This was particularly clear in town planning and the design of squares. It is probable that they saw enclosed precincts, the templum, for example, as sections detached from cosmic order. Orientation had qualities of the sacrosanct. Even in the Republican period this essentially Etruscan concept was already combined with an element of Greek origin, in that porticoes were introduced as framing sections of the building. Among the first surviving examples are Tivoli and the Julian imperial forums in Rome (A13, A20). The temple – as such already oriented – was once again specially bound into these squares and acquired further orientation, as it was placed on one of the narrow sides and connected with the framing porticoes, while in Hellenistic building complexes it stood freely in the middle (see A34). The significance of orientation can also be seen, particularly clearly, in isolated buildings. Circular buildings – the tholos or rotunda – were given a porch; this is different only in exceptional cases (A6) and sometimes also in tomb architecture (but see also A47). The oriented podium replaced the stylobate, which had steps on all sides. Ultimately entire landscapes were subjected to this orientation system, for example under Sulla in Palestrina (A8). The desire to impose order on the Forum Romanum also reveals a similar spirit (A9 and A1). The landscape became part of the architectural system in a large number of ways. These include gigantic terraces with substructures (A8 and A32), and also new designs for whole chains of hills (A29) and the fact that theatres were no longer built in natural troughs, even though there were plenty of these available in the city of seven hills (A17). Gardens (A32) and tumuli were increasingly brought into architectonic form (see A12, A47).

But there were also obvious breaks in this systematic thinking. Under Hadrian, discontinuity, along with richness of imagination, seems to have been almost a programme in its own right for a few years (A31, A32). At least in the Republican period one can detect a profound break between popular and high art (see A14). And with column architecture and wall architecture two strands ran alongside each other for a long time. It is precisely in this last point, so central to Roman architecture, that its power to bind things together and to create systems is shown. The wall could be combined with the order, and the column with the round arch. A similar synthesis of different details within one system can be seen in the fact that elements of movement developed in Roman architecture and appropriate ideas were perfected. Spaces and buildings were designed in a great variety of ways and drawn together as a sequence within a complex. Changing spatial impressions, squares and interiors followed each other in complexes of this kind (A8, A29, A11). Many of these design forms had Hellenistic roots, though most of them were considerably more modest.

In Roman architecture the concept of the façade became a central theme. It was used to hide walls or rooms. Façades used in this way are found for the first time in Palestrina (A8). A design form used in Domitian's palace on the Palatine also fulfilled the function of a façade (A27, see also A51). Here dense colonnades, true curtains of columns, were placed in front of the wall, changing its character considerably. It was only in the later period that the interior or exterior wall was increasingly allowed to make an impact in its own right, for instance as a curved wall with openings (see A29, A49, A53).

Roman architecture aimed at functionality in many respects. When Frontinus praised the aqueducts (see A22), this was by no means an isolated case. The key building technique of Roman architecture, opus caementicium, was able to meet functional needs. Functional buildings – aqueducts, but also baths and amphitheatres, for example – were valued more highly than they had been in Greece, where many functional types – the theatre, or even the stadium – served cultic purposes, and were not there just for pleasure.

It is a fundamental misunderstanding of Roman architecture to suggest that its principal characteristic is an imitative dependence on its Greek precursor. The phase in which ideas were taken over directly was very brief, and affected mainly the 2nd century BC, of which scarcely anything remains in Rome. Even in the 1st century BC a process of romanization was taking place, under which Greek and Hellenistic roots increasingly diminished in significance. Roman art was independent above all in the phases from which the great monuments derive. Buildings travel only seldom, the craft relates to places. Thus a completely independent architecture came into being in Rome, on the basis of its own needs and an indigenous building technique. Wall (mass) and interior are genuinely Roman themes, and so are vaulted building forms with mixed lines (which are thus linked with mass and interior). Greek column building, which is conceived to be looked at from the outside, could achieve none of this. »Roman art stands at the beginning of Western art« (Kraus) is particularly true of architecture. SG

A1 Foro Romano
Via dei Fori Imperiali (plan V 1/B)

Many of the chief buildings of Roman-antique architecture stood in the Forum Romanum. They bear witness to different architectural ideas, structural tasks, and commissioners. This is how they will be described in their individuality and in their chronological context (A9, A11, A16, A26, A34, A35, A40, A41, A49, A50). However, the Forum Romanum is also the centre of ancient Rome, which was the dominating power in ancient Europe. The consistent and magnificent design of that ancient centre will, by way of introduction, be described here: an invitation to take a walk around it.

The first settlement in Rome was on the Palatine hill. At that time there were unwholesome marshes in the hollow where the Forum is located. The boundary of the town seems to have followed the course of the later Via Sacra, because buildings from that period – the Vesta shrine (A40) and the Regia (12) – are found within that limit, while beyond it there are only tombs. The Forum was first paved around 600 BC, in connection with two further events: the Cloaca Maxima, the main drainage channel which also drained the Forum, was built at that time, and the Etruscan kings took power over Rome (tradition has it that this was in 616 BC). Thus if use was now being made of the valley, it may be supposed that the other two adjoining hills, the Quirinal and the Capitol, were included in the settlement no later than at this time. The largest Etruscan temple, to Jupiter Optimus Maximus, was built at that time. It was though not consecrated until 509 BC, the year when the foreign kings were expelled and the republic was founded.

The temples of Saturn (5) and the Dioscuri (6), two important shrines, were erected at the very beginning of the republic. The Temple of Concord of C. Flavius (3) followed in 367 BC after his victory over the Gauls. When Rome took over the hegemony of the western Mediterranean following the Punic Wars, the building density increased. It was though still disordered, owing to the plurality of powerful Maecenases. Nonetheless, the basilica, the type of building necessary to Rome as a centre of power, was developed in the early 2C BC. Two of these basilicas also predetermined the later arrangement of the square (A11). But only one republican building survived into the imperial period. This was the Tabularium (A9), which also introduced a new development: its tall show wall gave the Forum a point at which to aim, and thus began to make it more orderly.

The work which Sulla, the leader of the Optimates' party, had begun by building the Tabularium was completed not much later by Caesar, who was the leader of the opposing Popular party, and by Augustus, Caesar's adopted son and successor. All the buildings in the Forum proper go back to their period of rule, apart from individual monuments (columns, etc., 9–11), the Temple of Vespasian (4), and the Arch of Septimius

Severus (A41). The Forum proper is the area between the Capitol and the Temple of Caesar (7).

When Caesar was setting out this area, he was helped by the fact that significant lines for the formation of a city square had already been laid down in the two flanking basilicas. These lines were more clearly emphasized under Caesar's supervision (A11). But Caesar made the decisive intervention when he moved the Curia (A16) away from the Comitium. The Comitium (1) was a circular open place where the people's assembly was held, with surrounding terraces for listeners and a speaker's platform, the Rostra, which formed a segment of the terraces. The Curia, the place where the Senate met, adjoined this exactly to the north, as points of the compass were regarded as magic in Rome (cf. also A30). Caesar now

built his own Forum (A13) here and relocated the Curia. The consequences were radical: by means of this relocation, he was expressing the fact that he was going to erect his own new Curia Iulia (A16) and thus take the Senate's own building away from them. The Curia was even attached to the corner of his own Forum like a vestibule. At the same time the Comitium was partly built over by the new Curia, and its chief feature, the speaker's platform, was removed: the platform was relocated and placed in front of the large backdrop of the Tabularium (2). This rearrangement was a direct attack against the two highest instruments of state. Their disempowerment was, by architectural means, made very apparent to the onlooker. Compared with such radical changes, the fact that Caesar was closing an open section by moving the Curia towards the

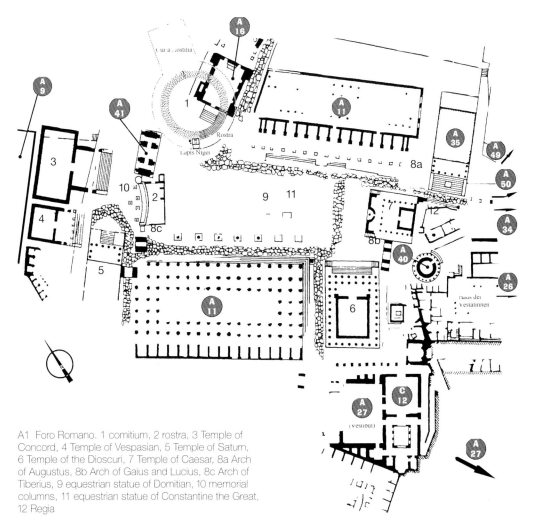

A1 Foro Romano. 1 comitium, 2 rostra, 3 Temple of Concord, 4 Temple of Vespasian, 5 Temple of Saturn, 6 Temple of the Dioscuri, 7 Temple of Caesar, 8a Arch of Augustus, 8b Arch of Gaius and Lucius, 8c Arch of Tiberius, 9 equestrian statue of Domitian, 10 memorial columns, 11 equestrian statue of Constantine the Great, 12 Regia

A1 Foro Romano

nascent square appears of only secondary importance.

After Caesar was murdered at a session of the Senate, Augustus continued what had been begun, but more cautiously. The first commission which he ever awarded for building work in Rome is also his own really independent contribution to the design of the square. In the place where the people had, in a spontaneous ceremony, honoured and cremated Caesar's body as it lay in state, Augustus built a temple, a six-columned prostyle (consecrated 27 BC) (7). Caesar's statue was set up in the low cella where it could be seen from the outside, and an image of the comet which had appeared on the day of his death was placed above its head. The front of the tall temple podium was in the form of a rostra: that is, it was without the conventional central staircase, and only had narrow stairs at the side. In this way a new rostra was placed opposite the one which Caesar had moved to a new location in front of the Tabularium. Ships' beaks (rostra) which had been captured at the battles of Antium, 338 BC, and Actium, 31 BC, were attached to both structures. The temple was dedicated to the god Caesar, and is thus the first temple in Rome by which a dead person was deified. The duplication of the speaker's platform expresses the intertwinement of the state and the ruler's own dynasty, a notion which from now on was to be a central theme in Augustus' architectural propaganda (cf. also A20). The square became bipolar, with the Temple of Caesar dominating. The most significant factor from the point of view of city planning is that Augustus, by building

the temple, closed the Forum and formed it into a square. Such a square was also to be found in Caesar's Forum, and later also in that of Augustus. All that remained to be done under Augustus was to close certain gaps: some older structures which burned down in 12 BC were, over the following twenty years, either rebuilt (Basilica Iulia) or replaced by larger, marble structures (the temples of the Dioscuri and Concordia, both by Augustus' stepson Tiberius). The Temple of Saturn had already been erected by Munatius Plancus in 30 BC. A third element of Augustus' design of the square was the arches occupying three of the four corners of the square that had taken shape (8a–c): to the right and left of the Temple of Caesar the three-gate Arch of Augustus and the arch for his grandchildren and designated successors Gaius and Lucius; and the Arch of Tiberius on the Capitol, opposite his own arch and likewise spanning the Via Sacra. It was long before a comparable monument to an emperor was placed in the fourth corner, in front of the Senate's Curia (A41).

The temples all had those upright proportions, with majestic podia, which are typical of the Augustan period. The two which are still prominent today, to the left and right of the Basilica Iulia, had a particularly old and venerable origin. Although the Temple of Saturn (5), a prostyle, was consecrated for the first time only in 498 BC, it had also served an Etruscan deity who was greatly revered. The Saturnalia were among the main religious festivals in Rome. The state treasury was housed in the temple. The Temple of the Dioscuri (6), a peripteros, owes its creation to the legend which relates that two horsemen miraculously appeared at the battle of Lacus Regillus (499 BC) in order to help the Romans achieve victory. The fact that Greek heroes were so prominently revered, and that this was done by using a purely Greek type of temple (cf. A34), probably goes back to the influence of the aristocracy, whose especial tutelary deities the Greek heroes were.

The platform which was created for the Forum is entirely independent. It differs from the standard Roman (and Hellenistic) form embodied by the imperial fora which were given a uniform (and monotonous) shape by the porticoes that framed them. In the Forum Romanum, by contrast, the square is formed by buildings which do not merely provide a frame, but have a very independent function of their own, and do not surround the Forum in a uniform way, but are of differing shapes, heights and widths. On the other hand, another distinction of the city-square shape taken by the Forum is that – in contrast, for example, to what normally happened in the Middle Ages – the square is framed not by normal buildings made up of small sections, but by specific Forum buildings, particularly basilicas. Both these factors taken together give the square its very individual character, which is though at the same time also lordly and regularized, and one feature brings both factors out very clearly: the square is almost rectangular, but narrows slightly towards the Temple of Caesar. The tension that lies in this trapezium shape given to the square was later to be utilized by Michelangelo on the Capitol (H27) on the other side of the Tabularium (and the Senators' palace).

The square and its buildings came into being under Caesar and Augustus. Although many of them had to be rebuilt in AD 283 after a major fire (cf. for example A16), the old forms were evidently preserved. The only temple to have been fitted in at a later date is also a subordinate feature, and it only filled a gap in the structure (4). Thus the appearance which the principate had given to the square for the benefit of the community being governed remained largely preserved. The only special features added by later emperors were monuments. The first to do this was Domitian, who ventured to set up his equestrian statue (9) in the square in AD 91. He was the emperor who built the palace on the Palatine, developed court etiquette and, for the first time ever, postulated the deification of the ruler while the ruler was still alive (A27). This emperor also gave the main square an entirely new character by placing the statue in it; he emphasized the centre and weakened the bipolarity. The ancestors and the community were no longer the centre of attention. Domitian was murdered and his statue removed. The second monument, the Septimius Severus arch (A41), did not follow until a century and a half later. Although this emperor's arch comes obtrusively close to the Curia, it is only a continuation of the idea already conceived in the three arches which date from the period of the principate and stand in the other three corners (8a–c). Diocletian, who was also responsible for the reconstruction in AD 283, ordered

five memorial columns – one to each emperor and one to Jupiter (10) – to be erected in an elevated position above the Rostra to celebrate twenty years of the system of tetrarchy. Now that the dominate was replacing the principate from the point of view of public law too, there were imperial insignia above the (republican) speaker's platform. The square was once again more strongly oriented towards the Capitol, as it had been in the period before Caesar ever since the Tabularium was built. The last monument, once again an equestrian statue, was built for Constantine the Great (11) in AD 334, when he was already residing in Byzantium.

The upper part of the hollow which extends upwards from behind the Temple of Caesar as far as the so-called Velia with the Arch of Titus (A26) is located outside the ancient Forum. Despite this, it houses the religious centre which includes the Vesta shrine (A40) and the Regia (12). The latter is the house of the pontifex maximus and, ever since early times, has repeatedly been rebuilt with the same oblique angles. Here there are also some splendid individual monuments commissioned by those emperors who evidently respected the Forum's orderliness once it had been created: the very modest monument by Antoninus Pius (A35) is diagonally behind the Temple of Caesar, and particular mention should also be made of the buildings by Hadrian (A34) and Maxentius (A49, A50), as well as of the Titus arch (A26) which is the distant, elevated lookout point for viewing the Forum. SG

Bibliography: M. Grant, *The Forum Romanum*, 1970; Ch. Hülsen, *Das Forum Romanum*, 2nd edn., Rome, 1905; P. Zanker, *Forum Romanum. Die Neugestaltung durch Augustus*, Tübingen, 1972.

A2 Mura Repubblicane
(plan VI 1/A)
mid 4C BC

The Etruscan kings of Rome evidently also provided the impetus for the city fortifications: Servius Tullius is said to have built the first wall in the 6C BC. Its ashlar stones made from the local Cappellaccio tufa are preserved in parts of the wall's foundations, and show that much of it followed the same course as the later republican wall. But the visible sections – in the Piazza del Cinquecento and Viale Aventino – of the so-called Servian Wall are from a later period, namely the mid-4C BC, when the republic, unsettled by the Gallic invasion of 387 BC, rebuilt the fortifications in a large-scale endeavour which was technically well organized throughout.

The ring of walls was 11 km long and encompassed over 400 ha, although the entire field of Mars was not yet included within it. Rome was at that time already by far the largest town in Italy. The wall itself was built of the solid, bright tufa from the quarries, known as Grotta Oscura, of Veji who had just been conquered. The blocks, which were about 60 cm high (2 Roman feet), became a typically Roman form of ashlar masonry known as opus quadratum: layers of stretchers (stones laid lengthwise along the wall) alternated with layers of headers (stones leading into the inside of the wall) up to a height of 10 m, with the wall attaining a possible thickness of over 4 m. There were evidently not yet any towers at this time. A ditch 17 m deep and 36 m wide was additionally built on the plateau, particularly exposed to danger, between the Quirinal and Esquiline hills. The earth excavated for this ditch was piled up on the city side of the wall to form an immense rampart, the so-called Agger.

The wall was no longer kept in good repair after the end of the civil wars, as by then no one was able to threaten the capital of the empire. UF

A3 Area Sacra dell'Argentina
Largo di Torre Argentina (plan IV 2/B)
from 300 BC

The Area Sacra on the Largo di Torre Argentina provides a view of the architecture of the republican period. It shows its architectural types and shapes in the form of a whole group of temples which are a consequence of the densely populated Roman world of gods and grew up over a period of centuries in repeated new campaigns of building work.

The temple of the Italic deity Feronia (C) was the first to be built in c. 300 BC. It is a typical podium temple (cf. A7) from the early period, being built of tufa stone and having three-dimensional terracotta decorations. Its cella was surrounded by rows of columns on three sides (a so-called pseudoperipteros). The Temple of Juturna the naiad (A) followed a little later. Its relatively good state is the result of later rebuilding work (columns from the imperial period, and the apses were only added when the structure was converted into a Christian church). The largest temple, which is that of the seafarers, called Lares Permarini, and is built of travertine (D), was begun in the early 2C BC and documents the later republican period. The parallel alignment of the temples indicates that city planning was taken into account from the very beginning. After 111 BC, the entire area was re-paved and surrounded with colonnaded halls which combined it into a self-contained group, the former portico of Minucia Velus. In

A3 Area Sacra dell'Argentina

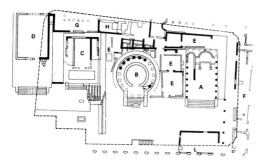

A4 Tempii del Foro Olitorio (today S. Nicola in Carcere)

the early 1C BC, the existing gap was filled by a round temple to an unknown goddess (B): it stood on a round podium, had a portico, a temple frontage and a flight of outdoor steps, and it fitted into the straight line formed by the temple façades.

All this was exposed from 1926 onwards in the course of demolition work in preparation for the construction of a large square, and in 1933 it was made the centre of that square, so that today's traffic now travels around this monument to the historic past. UF

A4 Tempii del Foro Olitorio (today S. Nicola in Carcere)
Via del Foro Olitorio (plan IV 2/B)
c. 200 BC, AD 1128 and 1599

Another characteristic group of temples from the republican period (cf. A3) was built on the Forum Holitorium, the Roman vegetable market near the Tiber. The three buildings standing close to one another can be identified as temples to Janus and Spes and, in the middle, a temple to Juno Sospita. The construction of the latter, in 197–93 BC, was ordered by C. Cornelius Carthagus.

The use to which this group was later put is of particular interest. It was probably in the early 12C (date of consecration: 1128) that the complex was, in a very rational way, converted into a basilica with a nave and two aisles, with the nave being of about the same width as the cella of the middle temple, whereas the aisles were extended beyond the middle temple as far as the adjoining rows of columns of the two neighbouring temples. The Ionic row of columns to the right, and the Doric row to the left, have been exposed again ever since restoration work was performed in 1932. The columns of the false arcades inside the complex are also spoils from other ancient buildings. In spite of later interventions (coffer-work ceiling under Pius IX, 1865), the medieval basilica is still the dominant feature.

In 1599, Giacomo della Porta was awarded the commission to convert the plain façade wall. Two surviving Ionic columns in the frontage served as an inducement for him to design the entire façade using a single motif: a large aedicule with two columns and a temple gable. He was though not concerned with archaeological reconstruction. The ponderous attic, and the motif of the façade panel between the columns, generate hard contrasts: their bulkiness and angularity opposes the roundness of the columns. The mannerism of the façade is shown in this and in the classical-style ornamentation consisting of small sections. UF

A5 Ponte Milvio
Piazzale di Ponte Milvio / Viale Tiziano (plan I 2/A)
109 BC

The Pons Milvius was one of the main means of access to ancient Rome. Coming from the north, people entered the city by proceeding along the Via Flaminia and through the Porta Flaminia, today's Porta del Popolo. The Via Flaminia was built as early as 220 BC, so that the bridge must have been usable no later than then. A piece of literary evidence in Livy (XXVII, 51, 2) confirms that it already existed in the 3C BC. The bridge was completely rebuilt in 109 BC by the censor Marcus Aemilius Scaurus. It became a historic milestone in AD 312, when Constantine the Great defeated his fellow-emperor Maxentius in the famous battle at the Milvian Bridge. After this, the emperors of Christian Europe, from Charlemagne onwards, traditionally marched into Rome across this bridge. In 1805, as part of a restoration of the bridge being conducted under Pope Pius VII, the bridge tower added at the northern end was rebuilt to a design by Giuseppe Valadier. The four middle arches of the bridge are all that survives today of the original ancient Pons Milvius. This bridge of stone, with its semicircular arches, is one of the trailblazing inventions of Roman architectural engineering. Its massive arched construction is a masterly technical achievement. Its prominent

A5 Ponte Milvio

A6 Tempio di Vesta

arches have become an architectural feature which shapes the landscape. Strong, statically solid piers in the river support the round arches, whose thrusting forces, operating diagonally outwards, are absorbed by massive abutments on the shore, which are on-land bulwarks. The asymmetrically shaped piers in the river are a characteristic feature. Breakwaters which taper to a point are to be found on that side of the piers which faces the current. Above the breakwater of every pier there is an opening, the aim of which is to prevent the bridge from being flooded by large masses of backed-up water surging against it. AG

A6 Tempio di Vesta
Piazza Bocca della Verità (plan VII 2/A)
late 2C BC

This round temple by the Tiber embodies, like no other temple in a Roman town, the type of the Hellenistic tholos, transplanted to Italic soil. Not only the building material, which was Pentelic marble from Attica, but also the builders, came from Greece. Hermodoros of Salamis, a Greek, may have been the designing architect. M. Octavius Herrenus, who had become rich thanks to the oil trade, ordered the temple to be built in the late 2C BC, probably in honour of Hercules Victor, also known as Hercules Olivarius. A Greek stylobate, low in height and with steps, supports the circular hall (peristasis) consisting of 20 unusually slender, fluted, Corinthian columns. They are placed so close together that the intercolumniations are equal to the lower diameter of the column shafts – a value lower than the measurements which Vitruvius gave for the pycnostyle, the temple with close-set columns. This means that the overall impression is shaped by the circular hall. The cella retreats almost entirely into the background behind the dense ring of columns. The purely Greek character of the temple is revealed in the fact that there is no portico aligning the structure; Roman tholoi and rotundae are usually distinguished by a portico. This elegant structure was one of the first pieces of marble architecture in the city. It was only from the time of Caesar onwards that larger quantities of brightly shimmering marble were used in Rome. In addition to bronze, marble was the quintessential material of the Greek art which was so greatly admired. Before Caesar's time, it could not be expected that there would be any competent »marmorarii« living locally. The comprehensive restoration of the temple after the great flooding of the Tiber in AD 15 proves that, 100 years after the Hellenistic temple was built, Rome had developed its own tradition where marble was concerned. EJ

A7 Tempio della Fortuna Virile
Piazza Bocca della Verità (plan VII 2/A)
c. 100 BC
It was not until the 20C that an area of temples, the Area Sacra di S. Omobono, was excavated to the north and south of the Cloaca Maxima on the Forum Boarium. The latter was the cattle market of ancient Rome and was located immediately by the river port outside the city wall, in the valley between the Capitol, Palatine and Aventine hills and the Tiber. One of the temples in this area may have been dedicated to Portunus, the god of river- and seaports. This temple was probably the Templum Fortuna Virilis. The reason for its excellent state of preservation is that it was converted into a church in 872 (S. Maria de Gradellis, known since the 15C as S. Maria Egiziaca). This temple was built in the 1C BC from tufa and travertine blocks, and stood on the foundation walls of an older building. It was originally coated with a fine layer of stucco, which was replaced by an altered and rougher outer covering. The temple is an outstanding example of Roman urban architecture in the republican period, an architecture marked by the merging of Graeco-Hellenistic elements with Etruscan and Italic ones. The elements of a Greek peripteros with a surrounding ring of columns, an entablature, a gable and a cella were adopted, but they were converted into a pseudoperipteros, a structure oriented in a particular direction. Because the cella wall has been moved towards the outside

A7 Tempio della Fortuna Virile

and merges with the slender Ionic columns, the round structure, which would otherwise lack orientation, becomes a building with a front and rear façade. This lends much greater weight to the wall, and thus to the space surrounded. The shrine, which stands on a high podium, can only be entered via the frontal flight of outdoor steps. A vestibule known as the pronaos, which is four columns (a tetrastyle) wide and two intercolumniations deep, is situated immediately in front of the cella. It is in the distinction between the show façade and the rear side that the pseudoperipteros, in which the axes of the columns measure 9.20 x 17.76 m, shows the form of the Italic temple. AG

A8 Santuario della Fortuna Primigenia, Palestrina
Palestrina, Piazza della Cortina (plan G2 4/A)
c. 80 BC
In 82 BC, Sulla, the leader of the Optimates' party (the patricians), conquered the ancient Praeneste, the last bastion of the followers of Marius, the social reformer. He ordered the male members of the old families to be executed. The place became a colony for his veterans. Two structures were erected. They both lie along the same axis, but are not linked to one another by, for example, any staircases. The lower structure is secondary. It did not house a shrine as some authors think, but a Forum. This is because in the centre there is a basilica, that is to say a building with a large interior (A11), and temples did not have a large interior until the time of the Pantheon onwards (A31). Before then the cult was celebrated outdoors.

The upper complex of seven terraces is well preserved in its load-bearing structure. It was dedicated to Fortuna Primigenia. Primigenia means (Jupiter's) »firstborn daughter«, but here it is more of an honorary title, as the first statue of Fortuna depicted her with Jupiter and Juno on her lap like a mother, whereas the statue from the Sullan period shows her in a suspended position (some remains are in the museum). The substructure of the complex is formed by three of the terraces, all of which are of conventional material. The two lower ones are of polygonal masonry (opus incertum), and the third is of tufa ashlar blocks. The ramps in the wings of the terraces give access to the shrine. Walls on the ramps block the view on to the plain, except in the middle. The upper terraces were already built in concrete (opus caementicium). For this purpose, limestone was mixed with sand (and later with pozzolana, which was still better suited). This material withstands great pressures and can be filled up with rubblestones. This technique made possible two basic structural forms of Roman architecture: substruction (particularly in the cryptoporticoes with their barrel-type and groined vaults), and vaulting. Via these terraces, a central staircase leads up to the orchestra and the shrine. The last two semicircular terraces are still part of today's surmounting Palazzo Colonna Barberini (11C, with alterations dating from 1493 and 1640; today museum with architectural fragments).

A8 Santuario della Fortuna Primigenia, Palestrina

The cradle of Roman architecture lies in Sulla's epoch. Shrines were now built on high terraces (this was also done in Tivoli and Terracina). They create a commanding and patrician impression (cf. also A9). They were also a great step forwards in the architectural design of entire stretches of land. The Greek classical age gave preference to autonomous individual structures, out of which the Hellenistic period then formed complexes and long axes. Only later did Roman-Italic architecture intensify the axiality and make it unshakeably symmetrical, thus more strongly constraining humans to come within the architecture, the intention being that they should walk across it (cf. also A29). All this can be felt in the ramps. The view of the valley is obstructed until the balcony in the middle is reached; the only view revealed is one of symmetry. For much of the way, people walked through penumbral, unified, colonnaded halls and did not come out into the light until the end. The shrine is revealed only gradually. A second pair of ramps flanks the first and is located diagonally behind it. This emphasizes the symmetry, and makes the architecture still broader and thus still weightier. The weightiness always so typical of Rome, the gravitas romana, thus begins here. The landscape is dominated.

The design of the individual structural members is also new. This applied initially to the idea of developing façades. In contrast to Greek column structures, Roman concrete walls had to be given a facing. It is true that for two centuries Greek forms, consisting

of columns, columned halls, and entablature, were used for this. But it was not only walls, but also parts of the inner area, that were faced over. On level IV, for example, the attic of the (surviving) eastern exedra masks the barrel vault which runs straight across behind it; this attic, with its row of pilasters, also feigns the presence of a second storey, which does not exist, inside the building. Thus this was a deceptive wall placed out in front for show – a »facciata«. At the same time the structure is marked by various combinations of column and round shape. Columns support the above-mentioned barrel vault on level IV. In addition, on level V, and in a similar way on level VI, columns stand in front of a row of arches and thus form what is known as the tabularium motif (A9). All that is still missing is arches which are built directly on to the column and are thus called arcades (cf. A30).

The two-aisled hall of columns at the top is in the form of an exedra and was surmounted by a tholos with a Fortuna Nike. Thus the building was a victory monument for Sulla, who defeated his last opponents here and called himself »Felix Sulla« after the goddess Fortuna. There was one feature of this magnificent terraced shrine which was not imitated for a long time: exedrae with a monumental appearance were not built again until the time of Trajan (A28, A29) and, later, in the court and villa architecture of the High Renaissance (H6, H16). SG

Bibliography: H. Kähler, *Das Fortuna-Heiligtum von Palestrina Praeneste*, Saarbrücken, 1958; F. Fasolo and G. Gullini, *Il santuario della Fortuna Primigenia a Palestrina*, Rome, 1953; see also at A9.

A9 Tabularium
Foro Romano (plan V 1/B)
78 BC

Sulla, the leader of the Optimates' party (A8), gave instructions to erect this structure, which is the best-preserved republican building in Rome and has an inscription giving its date. Consul Lutatius Catulus, Sulla's successor, ordered its actual construction. The building, intended as a state archive, stands in an elevated location in the Asylum, which is the small hollow between the two rounded tops of the Capitol hill. The

A9 Tabularium

Asylum was sacrosanct and provided protection from persecution. Proudly patrician like other Sullan buildings (A8), the building was meant to dominate the Forum. Sulla was thus the first person to attempt to give the Forum an orderly shape (cf. also A1, A11). This trapezium-shaped structure (73 x 45 m) built of regular tufa ashlar blocks is only well preserved in the part facing the Forum.

The façade had three storeys. The second storey, a row of open arches (arcades), which formerly numbered eleven, rises above a gigantic base course with small square windows which illuminated a lower corridor. Three of the arches on the second storey are today open again. It is here that the so-called tabularium motif, which is the pathbreaking innovation in this structure, is to be found. This motif consists of an arcade of pillars (square pillars with a wall arch built directly above them) and the order of columns, here Doric, placed in front of it. The order of columns is used in an ennobling way which subdivides the wall. The order of columns is Greek in origin and was created for the open colonnaded hall which, like a sculpture, produces its effect only towards the outside. The arcade of pillars, on the other hand, is a chief element of Roman architecture: substructions are formed from it, and it cuts into the wall. Massive structures, and interior architecture, could not have come into being in Rome had it not been for substructions and walls. The release from Greek ideas began with the tabularium motif, basic solutions used in later Western architecture were developed here. This motif must not be confused with its Hellenistic precursors in which, if the distances between the columns (the intercolumniations) became too large for the horizontal architrave, pillars were placed behind the columns and projected laterally further into the intercolumniation and thus narrowed it. The order of columns in the tabularium can no longer be understood as being load-bearing, but only as having a subdividing function. The tabularium motif was subsequently applied to various buildings: basilicas (A11), theatres (A17, A25), triumphal

A9 Tabularium

A10 Pons Fabricius

arches (A26), city gates (Porta Nigra in Trier), and all façades having openings for arches. Initially the main aim was to make the building more impressive. The wall and the order of columns which subdivides it were from then on the basic elements of Western architecture. The third storey has been lost. There was probably a portico here, consisting of a colonnaded hall with the entablature as horizontal conclusion.

The passage behind the façade is divided into eleven individual vaults, each of which rests on four arches, so that eleven bays are created. The first groined vaults known in Roman architecture are found here. They are formed by two barrels intersecting at right angles: one of them consists of several individual transverse barrels opening towards the Forum, and the other is the lengthwise barrel. This invention did not develop its full spatial effect until there were no longer any wall arches dividing up the vaulted area (A29, A50). A second vault shape, the pure and unsegmented barrel, is found in the imposing passageway leading down from the Asylum to the Forum. SG

Bibliography: R. Delbrueck, *Hellenistische Bauten in Latium*, Straßburg, 1907.

A10 Pons Fabricius
Isola Tiberina (plan IV 2/B)
62 BC

The Pons Aemilius was the oldest link with the island in the Tiber, and the first bridge in Rome to be built of stone (179 and 142 BC). All that survives of it is a single arch, known as »Ponte Rotto«. The Pons Fabricius leads to the island in the Tiber from the left bank, while the Pons Cestius does so from the right. Both bridges connected the field of Mars with Trastevere. The Pons Fabricius, 62 m long and 5.50 m wide, was built in 62 BC by L. Fabricius, the curator viarum (inspector of roads). The constructor's name is known to posterity from the inscriptions above the bridge's large arches. Slightly smaller dedications to M. Lollius and Q. Lepidus, who were the two consuls in the year 23 BC and ordered the bridge to be restored, are to be found on the left arch of the bridge. Only some remnants still survive of the formerly elegant travertine facing. The core part of the bridge is of tufa and pepe-rino blocks. In 1679, Pope Innocent XI (inscription) ordered the construction of the brick facing which is still there today. The link between the two shores is provided by only two slightly surbased arches, each with a wide span of 24.50 m. The deeply carved-out overflow above the breakwater alters the optical impression given by the massive, wide pier of the bridge and converts it into two elegantly curving supports. Ponte dei Quattro Capi, the bridge's new name which originated in the Middle Ages, refers to the ancient bronze parapet, now destroyed. The name derives from the four-headed hermae which served as the pillars of the ancient railing.

The Pons Cestius was also built in the 1C BC, this time to the instructions of Cestius, another inspector of roads (62–27 BC). The bridge was torn down in 1889 and rebuilt in 1892, with the old material being used in the central arch of the bridge. AG

A11 Basilica Aemilia and Basilica Iulia
Foro Romano (plan V 1/B)
179 BC (main alterations in 78, 54 and 34 BC), 54 to 46 BC

There is no type of building that was created so specifically for the Forum as was the basilica, neither is there any other type that shaped the Forum to such an extent. It was for a long time a multi-purpose structure, a roofed-over area for all matters being dealt with in the Forum. The first basilicas were built in Rome: the Basilica Porcia (189 BC), the Basilica Aemilia (179 BC) and the Basilica Sempronia (170 BC). The two last-named flanked that upper part of the Forum which Sulla provided with a regularizing conclusion in the shape of the Tabularium (A9). Caesar made use of this when working on that new arrangement of the Forum which he initiated and Augustus completed (cf. also A1). After fires had destroyed all three basilicas, Caesar ordered only the two flanking basilicas to be rebuilt. He subsidized the reconstruction of the Basilica Aemilia, and himself ordered a larger version of the Basilica Iulia to be erected on the spot on which the Basilica Sempronia had formerly stood.

The name »basilica« is Greek (from »basilieus« = king) and refers to royal halls. However, the type of building known to us is Italic. The fact that the Romans did not come up with a name of their own for the first key type of building which they invented is evidence of their lack of interest in theory. Although Hellenistic vocabulary – such as porticoes, columns, architraves – was often used for parts of the basilica, the uniformly self-contained, subdivided and oriented area is Italic. A particular type of structure, resulting from the fact that the parts making up a basilica were becoming more exactly fixed, only became more strongly defined in the 1st century AC. The following basic elements are of decisive significance: this is a box-type structure, and its central section projects further upwards, with lower sections either only flanking

it or surrounding it on all sides. In the first type, there is a nave and two aisles, lower in height, on both sides. The second type is more common in ancient Roman architecture. The higher and lower sections, such as the aisles, are separated from one another by rows of columns, two storeys high in some cases. The differing heights of the nave and aisles, or of other sections, enable storeys to be formed; hierarchies arise between the different components of the building. The central section is lit from above by the clerestory, which is the wall projecting above the separating rows of columns. This is a centralizing feature. However, in the oldest known basilica (in Pompeii), this central section was still probably open, thus resembling a Hellenistic peristyle courtyard. If the central section was surrounded by columns on all sides, the building – as in other examples of Roman architecture (cf. A8, A29) – became revealed only a little at a time: in order to arrive at the other and usually more important end, the walker passed through various inner sections: first a low section, then a higher one, and then a low one again, with rows of columns in between. Porticoes were often attached to the outside of ancient basilicas, and in the case of the two basilicas being described here the porticoes were added no later than the Julian period. Thus the basilica was oriented towards both the inside and the outside. The discovery that the interior was also an architectural task was a central contribution made by Rome to the development of Western architecture. It even surpassed the achievements of Greece.

A basilica could have its façade along its long side, as in the case of the Basilica Aemilia (about 70 m x 29 m) with its three gates leading on to the Forum. It was mainly used as a market hall, this being one of the two main functions which were increasingly developing. With its two aisles in the north and one in the south, it was irregular in structure but divided the area up in a functional way. Space for shops (tabernae) was found behind a double portico in the exterior, facing the Forum in the south. The design of cor-

A11 Basilica Aemilia and Basilica Iulia

ners for which this basilica is known can still be discerned today: pillar and column were combined, thus creating an impression of solidity.

A basilica could also have its façade along its short side, and this applies to the Basilica Iulia (about 101 m x 49 m), which served as a judgement hall, the second possible main function. It had a nave and four aisles, and as there are two storeys in the side aisles, there were probably three in the central nave section. Greek forms, without any arches, were used for many basilicas, including the Basilica Aemilia. In contrast to this, it is mostly Roman forms that are to be found in the largest basilica in the Forum: along the walls there are weighty arcades with columns standing in front of them as in the case of the Tabularium (A9), and the side aisles had barrel vaults instead of a flat ceiling. SG

Bibliography: V. Müller, »The Roman Basilica«, *American Journal of Archeology*, 1937, p. 250.

A12 Tomba di Cecilia Metella
Via Appia Antica (plan G2 3/B and plan VIII 2/C)
c. 50 BC

22 tomb structures along the consular roads, mainly the Via Appia, were built since the Sullan period. 30 years later, the Metella tomb was constructed, a structure which influenced later buildings, was later adopted in a monumentalized form in the emperors' mausoleums (A15, A33), and, in terms of size, was surpassed only by them. Cecilia Metella was the daughter-in-law of Crassus, who formed the first triumvirate together with Pompey and Caesar. Her husband served under Caesar as a general in Gaul.

A cylinder 29 m in diameter, built of travertine, rises dominatingly above a square substructure. The upper conclusion is decorated by a frieze of garlands and bulls' heads – typical motifs in tomb architecture (cf. A33) – as well as of Gallic shields alluding to Metella's husband. The structure was completed at the top by a round mound of earth. Cypresses stood on this mound. The cylindrical interior structure harbours two rooms: the burial chamber proper is underneath, and above it is a high vaulted rotunda.

A12 Tomba di Cecilia Metella

A13 Foro di Cesare

The tumulus is the second main type found in Roman tomb architecture, the burial tower being the first. In all the pre-Roman examples, the tumulus consisted only of a mound of earth with cypresses. In the Roman period, the mound was the rounded top section, but in other respects the design went beyond the natural form (cf. also A8). The scene is characterized by the architecture, which here consists of a cylinder as a large, dignified shape which iself takes in the tumulus and raises it. In Rome, the interior was important too. Thus the cylinder became a domed, cultic area in which it was possible to walk about. The division, typical of Roman tomb architecture, into a burial chamber below and a shrine above is here found for the first time (cf. A29). Around 1300 the tomb became part of some fortifications, and the upper crenellation was built. SG

A13 Foro di Cesare
Via dei Fori Imperiali (plan V 1/B)
46 BC

In spite of later restorations, the remains on the eastern slope of the Capitol, which make up about a third of the former structure, go back, where their core structure and their design are concerned, to the Forum which Caesar consecrated in 46 BC and Augustus completed. The new Corinthian marble columns, and the rich architectural ornaments of the temple that occupies the northern side, came into being under Trajan in AD 113. The double row of granite columns, which is a U-shaped double portico measuring 150 x 75 m and frames the area and the temple, was rebuilt by Diocletian in AD 283.

The new and provocative feature of this group of buildings is to be found neither in its elements, nor in its strict regularization which accords with Vitruvius' theory of architecture. In a temple standing on a podium – here it is a peripteros with eight columns at the front and no hall at the rear –, the only important innovation lies in the vaulting, and the apse, of the cella. Patterns which influenced the porticoes were to be found on the southern field of Mars: the portico of the theatre of Pompey (55 BC), and the Metellus portico

(146 BC), whose constructor had made it into a private victory monument by erecting a temple to his personal tutelary deity. But what was unprecedented was the fact that such a structure was built not outside the walls, but immediately next to the city centre, and also that, being a Forum, it was made into a place of public and economic life (see the row of shops along the columned halls in the west). What is more, it was only Caesar's ambitions that enabled the new Forum to be turned into a place of self-portrayal. An image of Venus Genetrix, the tutelary goddess of the Julians, stood in the temple apse, while in the square Caesar was depicted on an equestrian monument as a triumphant victor. Caesar himself, enthroned on the podium, received the Roman Senate. UF

A14 Tomba di Marco Virgilio Eurysaces
Piazzale Labicano (plan IX 2/D)
c. 40 BC

Eurysaces the baker, who was also a magistrate working in the field of bread distribution, built this trapezium-shaped travertine tomb for himself and his wife. It was later part of the Aurelian Wall for many centuries (A44). The substructure is formed by vertically located cylindrical shapes which depict measures of cereal or (as in the frieze) containers for kneading dough. It is followed by the inscription which calls the building a »panarium« (bread basket), and by a massive block in which the same cylindrical shapes, placed horizontally, form the decoration. The depiction of the married couple on the main side of the building (in the east) has been moved to the Capitoline Museums. Today the building concludes with the frieze depicting the details of the dead man's trade: washing the cereal, baking the dough, delivering the bread.

The tension between the individual and the masses, the patrician and the plebeians, typified the later republican period. Civil war was always smouldering. The tendency towards self-portrayal was greater than at any later date (A12). This tomb is the proudest existing monument to popular art. Its date is close to that of the Ara Pacis (A18), and it is evidence that stylistic differences in Rome were a matter rather of social class than of period. There was no homogenous development as there had been in Greece. In Rome, everyday life was transformed into art, especially on tombs. SG

Bibliography: P. Ciancio Rosetto, Il sepolcro del fornaio Marco Virgilio Eurisace a Porta Maggiore, 1973.

A15 Mausoleo di Augusto
Piazza Augusto Imperatore (plan IV 1/A)
32–28 BC

This mausoleum to the young Octavian was completed in the field of Mars in 28 BC, immediately after the victory over Mark Antony, the last rival in the civil war. The princes Gaius and Lucius, and the emperors from Tiberius to Nerva, were, along with Augustus and

A15 Mausoleo di Augusto

others, interred in this family tomb, the »Tumulus Juliorum«.

But even today's ruins still indicate that the tomb was chiefly intended to express the power and greatness of the person who ordered the building work. The sheer mass of this round structure, 87 m in diameter, is overwhelming; it even surpasses the archetype of all tomb monuments, which is the edifice of the Carian dynast Mausolos in Halicarnassus. But its structural principle is simple: within the external walled ring (about 9 m high) there is a massive cylindrical wall some 35 m in height, and this in turn harbours the round cella containing the actual burial chamber. A mound of earth, ascending towards the centre and with trees planted on it, was heaped up between the tufa walls which are faced with marble and travertine; a walled passageway leads to the centre. Thus the mausoleum arouses various associations: it is the size of a Hellenistic ruler's tomb; it has a hill shape as in the tumuli of heroes from early times; and finally the cylindrical wall can be interpreted as being an enormous pedestal for the colossal statue of Octavian which originally stood on the peak high above Rome. Octavian, the autocrat, self-assuredly erected a symbol of victory before he restored the res publica in 27 BC and demonstrated some other virtues: the piety and modesty of Augustus. After his death, bronze tablets giving the »res gestae«, the biography of Augustus, were put up at the entrance. They also report that he left behind him a »city of marble«. UF

A16 Curia Iulia
Foro Romano (plan V 1/B)
29 BC, AD 283

The Senate, which was the assembly of aristocrats and consular officials, had been meeting in the Curia, directly beside the Comitium, ever since the legendary early period. After the fire in 52 BC, Caesar rebuilt it, moving it to its present location, so that this Curia Julia became an annexe of his new Forum. Augustus also left his mark on the building: at the consecration in 29 BC, he erected a Hellenistic statue of Victoria, his personal goddess of victory. After another fire in

A16 Curia Iulia

AD 283, Diocletian ordered the Curia to be rebuilt in close imitation of its old forms. It was used as a church from the 7C on and remained very well preserved, so that in 1930–36 success was achieved in recreating the state of the building as it was in the late classical period.

The simple brick panel of the façade has a triangular gable, three large windows, and a portal (whose surviving bronze doors are to be found in the middle portal of San Giovanni in Laterano). Today's onlooker must imagine to himself that this panel was formerly complemented by a marble facing and a vestibule. However, the interior – a magnificent, lapidary, box-shaped space, which rises steeply to a height of 21 m, is 18 m wide and 27 m long and has a (reconstructed) flat ceiling – shows that a respectable severity was always maintained in this building. It must ultimately remain an open question whether these grand proportions go back to the time of Caesar or to that of Diocletian. Apart from some niches for figures, all that is to be found on the long sides is the steps for the senators' seats; the presiders' place was on the podium by the rear wall, at the feet of the statue of Victoria. Thus the character of this tall building lay mainly in the noble spatial proportions, and not so much in the original marble fittings, of which the floor, which is largely original, has survived. UF

A17 Teatro Marcello
Via del Teatro Marcello (plan IV 2/B)
13 BC
The Marcellus theatre on the Forum Holitorium is a torso. The section where the stage was has not survived, and neither have the two flanking halls which

may have replaced two old shrines on this site. In the Middle Ages, the auditorium, which could accommodate some 15 000 people, was transformed into a fortress which Penuzzi then converted into a Renaissance palace, today's Palazzo Orsini. In the excavation works of 1926–32, a segment of the old exterior structure came to light again. It is the most important relic of a sudden upsurge in theatrical architecture, in the course of which theatres having space for 40 000 visitors were built on the field of Mars within the space of 50 years. The first and largest theatre of stone, whose architectural forms probably also influenced later buildings, was erected by Pompey in 61–55 BC (some remains of the hemicycle still survive in the Via di Grottapinta on the Campo dei Flori). Caesar ordered the construction work to be begun by the Tiber, but it was not until 13 or 11 BC that Augustus dedicated the building to Marcellus, his nephew and designated successor as emperor. A third theatre was financed by Balbus in 13 BC.

During the republic, the Senate had not permitted such buildings in Rome, as the organizing and financing of plays by ambitious donors was an undesired political event which provoked demonstrations. All that was done was that temporary theatrical structures made of wood were built in connection with the cult attached to the festivals of the gods. Augustus eagerly seized upon the example of the triumvim and sought publicity in the theatre, where the agreement between people and ruler found expression in the welcomes and the applause, and in exceptional cases also in the protests. In addition, the example of the Greek dramas was intended to have an educational function in Augustus' programme of cultural renewal. Augustus' interest in the theatre was reflected even in the law: the Lex Iulia Theatralis arranged the order of

A17 Teatro Marcello

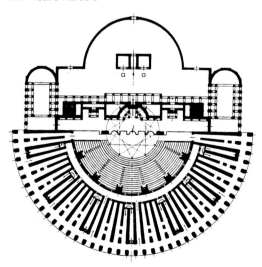

seating and precedence in such a way as to reflect human society. Senators, priests and the municipal authorities sat in the orchestra, the knights were in the terraces, then came the free citizens, and sections for women and foreigners were reserved at the top.

The type of structure was still determined by classical Greek theatre, with an orchestra (it was still a complete circle in that theatre) and an ascending semicircle – the cavea – for the spectators. But there was now no longer a view of the landscape, as a multi-storeyed decorative wall rose up behind the stage, and the terraces were now not built into a concave slope as before, but were placed on substructions. What this means for architecture is shown by the surviving section of the Marcellus theatre. The fact that the tabularium motif (cf. A9) was repeated 41 times over several storeys, thus shaping the exterior structure, by no means points to a lack of imagination; instead, it emphasizes the majestic size (a diameter of about 130 m), and its theme is to show, in the exterior, the roundness of the cavea in the interior, so that the purpose of the building could be seen even without the decorative sculptured theatrical masks on the arches. What is more, the regular arcatures also indicate the constructive principle: it lies in the ascending stretches of wall which radiate out from the centre and are linked by barrels and arches. And finally, the orders of columns placed in superposition out in front provided a festive splendour, emphasized by a new kind of intensification of the orders – Doric, Ionic and Corinthian – in the attic storey which have been altered today. The approach employed in the Marcellus theatre meant that the constructive and practical requirements, the architectural design of a theatre, and the claims to impressiveness, were all convincingly united and were lent shape in such an unconstrained way that the empire's theatres and amphitheatres (cf. A25) adhered to this pattern for generations. UF

A18 Ara Pacis di Augusto
Via Ara Pacis (plan IV 1/A)
13–9 BC

In 9 BC, this altar was dedicated to Pax Augusta, the peace which the Senate had promised in 13 BC on the occasion of Augustus' return from his campaigns in Gaul and Spain. Thanks to chance finds, this shrine has been known since the 16C, but only in the 20C was it systematically excavated, reconstructed and housed in a modern exhibition building next to the Augustus mausoleum. It originally stood at the edge of today's Corso.

The monument consists of a rectangle of walls (11.7 x 10.6 m); the visitor passes through two entrances in the long sides and, via a few steps, reaches the small altar in the centre. The architecture is witness to Augustus' demonstrative modesty in his later years. This small structure avoids the pomp of large Hellenistic altars; the delicate order of pilasters on the outside is restrainedly decorative in character.

A18 Ara Pacis di Augusto

It is the cycle of reliefs, which includes almost all the programmatic themes in the Augustan world of images and depicts them with utter perfection, that makes the altar into the main work of official state-sponsored art in the early imperial period. Even the ornaments are expressive. Their dominant theme is the famous climbing plants which adorn the outer walls of the lower half of the Ara Pacis; they became the symbol of the new era of peace, because they combined luxuriant fertility and a full life on the one hand with well thought-out, regular orderliness on the other. In the statuary reliefs above them, a reference to early Roman history is to be found on both sides of one of the entrances: Aeneas sacrificing to the Penates, and Romulus and Remus outside the she-wolf's cave. The other entrance is flanked by a much-damaged relief of Roma and by a depiction of a maternal goddess, a typical example of the Augustan language of images. Although this depiction is rich in natural forms and sensual features, it does not relate a myth, neither is it a depiction of the landscape. The scantily clad female figure embodies the general idea of fertility and prosperity. Every object becomes an attribute of the state of happiness achieved in the Pax Augusta: the twins signify having a large number of children, the cattle and the ears of corn stand for rural prosperity, and the female figures on the swan and dragon (aurae) are reminders of the climatic advantages of winds coming from sea and land.

On the narrow sides of the altar, the onlooker learns how the state was organized under Augustus. The ceremonial procession in which the Roman leaders went to the altar is to be seen here. Augustus has joined the procession of priests with his head enshrouded; he is in this way showing his piety and his constant concern for religious cults. His family, including his two grandchildren who were his designated successors, also follows the procession; this expresses Augustus' dynastic intentions. But the status of all of them falls within the procession of dignitaries, and individual special features only play a subordinate rôle, with even Augustus merely being a primus inter pares. When it is a matter of piously making sacrifices,

A19 Piramide Cestia

bricks, and is thus one of the oldest dateable buildings in Rome to use this technique.

Egyptian examples had been the fashion in Rome since the time when Egypt was conquered and incorporated within the Roman Empire in 30 BC. For the first time ever, Augustus ordered an obelisk, specially imported, to be set up in Rome (in the Circus Maximus). Several temples to Isis were built under Domitian and Caracalla, including one on the site of today's Jesuit church of S. Ignazio (B46). The pyramid as an architectural type, being a tomb in its quintessential, venerable, sacred form, was frequently adapted in Rome. A monument comparable to the tomb of Cestius stood near the Angels' Fort until the 16C.

The only Protestant graveyard in Rome, in which those buried were mostly artists, came into being beside the pyramid in the early 19C in the face of tough resistance from the Popes. This is probably one reason why this impressive site is today a popular destination for all those travelling to Rome.

The Cestius pyramid presents itself today as a curiosity resulting from a comparatively brief trend in the fashion of ancient Rome and, together with the surrounding graveyard, is one of the city's most atmospheric sites. EJ

the order of priority within the community is determined as if of its own accord, and herein lies the real meaning of this portrayal.

The depictions on the interior walls concentrate on the cultic ritual: its symbols are bucrania (skulls of sacrificed cattle), sacrificial dishes, and garlands with ribbons. The stylized beams and boards underneath suggest the wooden barriers delimiting an altar area. UF

Bibliography: E. Simon, *Ara Pacis Augustae*, Tübingen, 1967; P. Zanker, *Augustus und die Macht der Bilder*, Munich, 1987.

A19 Piramide Cestia
Piazzale Ostiense (plan VII 2/B)
11 BC

The fashion for Egyptian things in the Rome of the 1C BC is very clearly expressed in the structure of the Cestius pyramid on the Via Ostiense near the Porta S. Paolo. Gaius Cestius was a people's tribune, a praetor and a member of a priests' council which organized and financed cultic banquets. He ordered this pyramid, 37 m high, to be built for himself outside the city as a tomb structure which was later included in the Aurelian city wall (A44).

The pyramid is faced with tufa stone at its base and with marble slabs elsewhere. Originally it had columns at its sides and was decorated with several bronze statues of the deceased. The entire structure is of opus caementicium. The barrel-vaulted burial chamber measuring 4 x 6 m formed a recess within the massive rubble-work structure and was faced with

A20 Foro di Augusto
Via Alessandrina – Via dei Fori Imperiali (plan V 1/B)
consecrated in 2 BC

In 42 BC, on the occasion of the victory over Caesar's murderers, Octavian promised to build a temple to the avenging god of war. The Temple of Mars Ultor was erected as the core structure of the new Forum, which was directly attached at right angles to Caesar's previous Forum (A13). Augustus ordered the entire building to be constructed at his own expense and on his own plot of land. He consecrated the temple in 2 BC. Apart from the usual functions of a Forum , it primarily became a venue for political ceremonies on the topic of warlike foreign policy. The Senate made decisions on war and peace here, and it was here that victorious campaigners laid down their triumphal insignia. Foreign rulers swore the oath of allegiance before the image of Mars Ultor.

This main work of Augustan state-sponsored architecture is unfortunately largely in ruins. Today the Via dei Fori Imperiali runs unconcernedly across the front section of the Forum. The only well-preserved part is the magnificent wall at the rear side, 30 m high, built of solid, dark peperino. The wall is an eloquent work of architecture: on the one hand, the many-cornered course which it pursued respected the old residential areas of the densely populated Subura, while on the other it clearly separated the splendid Forum from those areas.

Following the example of Caesar's Forum (A13), the structure was conceived as a rectangle with open colonnaded halls on the long sides; but two semicircular exedrae were attached at the sides of the porticoes, and the particular feature is that the temple comes far forward on to the surface of the inner courtyard. It dominates the courtyard and presents itself as the quintessential paragon of Augustan temples. It continues the Roman tradition by following the type of the podium temple, having at its front a deep vestibule and an outdoor staircase (cf. A7). But the novel features are the elaborateness of the work, and also the outward appearance: the material, which is radiantly bright Carrara marble, and the high-standing columns with their splendid Corinthian capitals, are intended to compete with the pomp of Hellenistic temples. But another example was followed for the detail: some capital shapes, column bases and coffer work in the ceilings are clearly taken from Greek art in the high-classical period. The caryatids in the attic storey of the colonnaded halls (to be found today in the antiquarium of the Augustus Forum) even copy the caryatids in the Erechteion on the Acropolis in Athens. These imitations and references can be read as a political programme: ancient Roman virtue, Greek culture, and Hellenistic columnar splendour, all combined, are intended to impart an idea of the new greatness of the empire in the Augustan era.

The original programme of sculptures was equally expressive. Mars, who according to legend was the father of Romulus and Remus, and Venus, the mythical ancestress of the Julian family, to which Augustus belonged since being adopted by Caesar, stood side by side in the cella of the temple. The combination of myths relating to the state and to leading families was repeated in the exedrae in the statues of Aeneas who was Venus' grandson, and of Romulus. These were followed in the niches of the outer walls (surviving in the left-hand exedra) by meritorious men from the family of the Julians and by great names from Roman history. In this idealized depiction, that history looks as

A20 Foro di Augusto

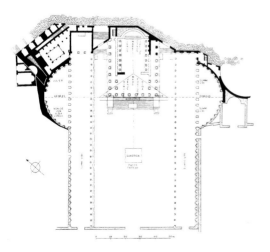

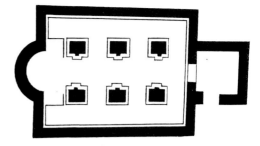

A21 Basilica Sotteranea

though it is being interpreted by stressing the saving acts of the gods: the happy combination of family and state began with the two ancestors Mars and Venus, continued with the constant rise of Rome, and found its heyday under the rule of Augustus. UF

Bibliography: P. Zanker, *Forum Augustum*, Tübingen, 1968.

A21 Basilica Sotteranea
Porta Maggiore (plan IX 2/D)
1st half of 1C AD

The well-preserved underground structure of the so-called Basilica Sotteranea was discovered in 1917 in the course of building work outside the Porta Maggiore, and is frequently interpreted as being a significant heathen forerunner of the Christian basilica. The reason for this is the sequence of the rooms: a square anteroom reminiscent of an atrium; a room measuring 9 x 12 m, subdivided into three barrel-vaulted aisles by two rows of pillars; and an apse on the central nave. But the parallels are rather the result of chance. It is not a basilica, as the aisles are of approximately equal height and there is no clerestory. Neither should reference be made to the architectural type known as a hall church; the tall, narrow rooms are derived from a plain, ancient form of enclosed room, namely the vaulted cryptoporticoes. Such subterranean passages in basements are also – for example in villa architecture – found in an arrangement with more than one aisle and a separating row of pillars. This is basically a type of concealed basement architecture, which was made to serve cultic or sepulchral purposes by providing an anteroom and an apse. A basilica, on the other hand, is a specifically Christian transformation of the market and judgement halls of Rome.

What is more significant is the luxurious decoration with white stucco reliefs. The framework for them in the vaults is the flat surface upon which figures can be depicted. The exact intention of the building cannot be deduced from the varied topics of these depictions, taken from Greek and Roman mythology. But the scenes prove that the unknown people who ordered the work attached great importance to decorative qualities. The reliefs are a leading work of Roman sculpture at the end of the republican period. UF

A22 Aqua Claudia

A22 Aqua Claudia
(plan G2 4/B)
AD 38–53
The treatise by Frontinus, who from AD 97 on was a
»curator aquarum« (inspector of aqueducts), gives us
very good information on the water supply of Rome.
He lists the 24 aqueducts, including some secondary
runs, in chronological order: Aqua Appia, Anio Vetus,
Aqua Marcia, Tepula, Iulia, Virgo, Alsietina (Augusta);
then Aqua Claudia and, built at the same time, Anio
Novus, the largest aqueduct; there followed Aqua
Traiana and Alexandriana. The system adopted was
devised for the construction of Aqua Appia under the
censor Appius Claudius Caecus in the 4C BC: following the example of the drainage channels which were
so important, the open gutter was used, and it was
decided not to employ the pressure water piping
found in Alexandria. The aqueducts were developed in
order to bridge valleys and, near the towns, to prevent
contamination and the unauthorized removal of water.
Since the time of the Aqua Marcia (early 2C BC), they
were so high that they were also able to supply the
hilly areas in Rome. Very advanced measuring techniques made it possible to build them over a distance
of almost 100 km with a constant and very slight gra-
dient. Almost all the channels entered the city in the
south-east at the Spes Vetus, except for firstly those
which supplied Trastevere, and secondly the famous
Aqua Virgo, which came from the north and today still
feeds the Fontana di Trevi (B126). The latter is a de-
scendant of the aqueducts' concluding sections,
which were of splendid architectural design and were
called naumachiae (fountains) and castelli (distribution
structures). Under Trajan, more than twice as much
water was available to every Roman than in 1968.
   Aqua Claudia is neither the largest channel nor the
oldest. It is nonetheless unique and, to Pliny, was the
finest thing on earth. Domus Aurea (A24) and the
buildings on the Palatine (A27), which are the two
large emperors' palaces after the time of Claudius,
were supplied from it. Frontinus, formerly a senator, a
proconsul in Asia Minor and a governor in Britain, by
no means thought of his new office as inferior to the
others. He wrote: »Compared with the many and necessary aqueducts, what are the completely useless
Pyramids or the universally known creations of the
Greeks?« What prestige aqueducts possessed! It was
this way of understanding them that promoted, under
Claudius, the creation of a specific aesthetic, which
had been foreign to the Greeks, in the field of structural engineering. The weighty row of arches in the Aqua
Claudia, and its headstone in Rome (A23), are early
examples of their kind. SG

A23 Porta Maggiore
Via Praenestina (plan IX 2/D)
AD 52
Aqua Claudia (A22) and Anio Novus, the Claudian
aqueducts, are here, in pipes lying one above the
other in the high attic, routed on two arches over the
Via Praenestina and Labicana. The complex became
a city gate only after AD 271, when it was incorporated
into the Aurelian Wall (A43) and reinforced by adding
towers and an additional gate (torn down today). The
fact that there are two passageways, something inconceivable for a triumphal arch (A26, A41), shows
that it is only a functional building.
   Augustan classicism was forsaken under Claudius.
Functional architecture came to the fore, and aesthetics changed. Just as functional building work in the
19C was the ferment for modern architecture, post-
Augustan functionalism was evidently the stimulus for
the peak period of Roman architecture, from the time
of Nero to that of Hadrian. It was now not only the
type, but also the language of spaces and forms, that
became completely disassociated from Greek models:
it was now only the wall that dominated, and no
longer the Greek order of columns. In the spatially

A23 Porta Maggiore

A24 Domus Aurea of Nero

oriented art works created under Nero and Domitian, that order was reduced to being merely the wall's decoration. During the rule of Claudius, the new feature of the language of walls lay in the dressing of the stones: they remained rough-hewn. In the Roman antiquity, this is hardly found except in the middle of the 1C (the late-Roman Porta Nigra in Trier is incomplete). This technique, so fundamental to the Renaissance, lends the wall a rich, three-dimensional appearance, in which there is an alternation between round and angular shapes, between rough and detailed work; here, the latter refers to the gables and cornices. At the same time the decorative, non-load-bearing use made of the order of columns is a pathbreaking feature: the aedicule, which is a framing motif consisting firstly of a pair of columns or pilasters and secondly of a gable, had not previously been such a dominant feature, neither had it been so much disassociated from the rhythm of the wall. Whole »carpets« of aedicules were increasingly employed from now on, thus creating very animated surfaces and walls (cf. A27). SG

A24 Domus Aurea of Nero
Via del Monte Oppio (plan V 2/B)
Severus, Celer
begun AD 64

Only the human imagination can measure the value, in terms of city planning, of Nero's Domus Aurea, built after the great city fire. It is the first genuine emperor's residence after Augustus' small habitation and Tiberius' disputed edifice on the Palatine. This structure follows the type of a rich private individual's villa suburbana, but transforms it to a gigantic size, provocatively taking up a large part of the city area: beginning at the Colle Oppio, it bordered on the Forum, included the Palatine hill and, in the south, only ended when it reached the Circus Maximus and the city wall. This artificial landscape included not only larger sections of buildings, but also small pleasure buildings, fountains, nymphaea and an artificial lake, as well as game preserves, small woods, and even vines and fields which were rural idylls.

After Nero's death, public buildings (A25, A28, A34) were ostentatiously erected on this area. The only part to have survived is that underneath Trajan's thermal springs (A28). This almost endless succession of spaces measures 300 x 100 m and is ordered by courtyards and symmetrical and axial relationships. The curious main hall, an octagon adjoined by other rooms and having a vault which passes into an open circle, is architecturally significant. It was probably a dining hall mentioned by Suetonius, with a rotating vault of heaven: one of the many mechanical wonders.

But it was the decorative wall paintings that had the greatest subsequent effect. These underground »grottoes« were known since the late 15C and were studied by, among others, Raphael's fellow-worker Giovanni da Udine. They influenced ornamental Renaissance art, with the name »ornamental grotesquery« being given to the genre. UF

A25 Colosseo
Piazza del Colosseo (plan V 2/B)
AD 72–80

After the Pyramids, the Colosseum is the largest building in the ancient world: the quintessential monument to massive Roman building work. The unbelievably short time of as little as just under ten years taken to build it was a supreme achievement of Roman engineering and organization. It was begun by Vespasian after the Jewish War as a three-storeyed amphitheatre and elevated by the addition of another storey under Titus. It proved possible to consecrate the building as early as AD 80, with accompanying games that lasted 100 days. Such games, which could always be visited free of charge, had since the republican period increasingly been employed as a means of political propaganda. Vespasian, the first emperor not to be of aristocratic stock, used it as a major political demonstration for the Flavian imperial family. Even the choice of site was a political matter. An artificial lake built by Nero as the centre of his Domus Aurea (A24) was formerly located in the hollow between the Palatine, Esquiline and Caelian hills. When the Colosseum, the first large monumental structure of the Flavians, was built on top of it, the area of the gigantic private villa once again became part of the city's public space. The name Colosseum has been customary since the early Middle Ages. However, it does not derive from the theatre's enormous size (its long side measures 188 m), but goes back instead to a colossal bronze statue of Nero, 35 m high, which formerly stood beside the amphitheatre. The type of the free-standing, oval-shaped amphitheatre, enclosed on all sides, takes shape in exemplary fashion here for the first time ever. From then on it continued to be a model for

A25 Colosseo

both classical times and the modern era. This purely Italic architectural type was already developed in the 5C BC, but initially only in the form of temporary wooden stands. A freely-rising stone structure was built in Pompeii in 80 BC. It is the oldest surviving example of this type, which found its definitive architectural formulation in the Colosseum.

The exterior subdividing work, with a three-storeyed, regular wall of arches and a complete order of columns standing in front, is a direct continuation of the Tabularium (A9), the Basilica Iulia (A11) and the Marcellus theatre (A17). In no other building in Roman urban architecture is it possible to gain a better grasp of the fact that the nature and function of an order of columns is to subdivide the wall and give it a structural framework. Two supports in each case, the concluding entablature, and the interval in between – these are the three basic elements of the order – form the bays, each of which frames an arcade of pillars. The order of the half columns presents itself in superposition, that is to say in a perpendicular arrangement one above the other through several storeys. The load-resistant Tuscan order stands suitably enough at the very bottom, followed by the light Ionic order, with the dignified Corinthian order forming the conclusion. The fact that the columns are placed on high separate pedestals is a specifically Flavian feature. The fourth storey, with its subdivision consisting of composite pilasters, of the alternation of windows and bronze plates (now lost), and of the encircling corbels (a device for holding the wooden poles of the immense awning), was added at a later stage by Titus, who thus decisively altered the previously compact appearance of the building. The uniform succession of the large arches in three storeys one above the other is made more varied only by some rather more elaborate portals on the four main axes, but, despite the endless rows, does not look monotonous. It is only the uniformly surrounding arcatures of the arches, combined with the order of columns, that is able not only to compel the immense building to take on a certain shape, but also to lend proportion to this gigantic monument whose mass becomes visible in the intradoi of the arcades of pillars.

The interior of the amphitheatre, an oval cavea which ascends all round, today gives an insight into the complicated substructions and exposed skeleton of this giant edifice which formerly shimmered in its marble splendour. The basic principle of the design is still discernible. Seven concentrically arranged ring walls, and the retaining walls radiating out from the centre of the building, form the supporting framework of the spectators' terraces, which in many cases rested on groined vaults and diagonally ascending barrel vaults. A complicated, multipartite system of staircases was housed in the wedge-shaped sections (cunei) which were subdivided by the radial walls, and it functioned as a distributor leading to the spectators' terraces. The concentrically surrounding passages have circular barrel vaults, whose beginnings on the exterior structure are marked by cornices. Apart from the four main terraces (maeniana), there were also the honorary lodges and the imperial lodge (pulvinar) on the main axes. At the very top, an open colonnaded gallery with standing room for spectators encircled the enormous round shape that was the cavea. As in the case of the Marcellus theatre (A17), the strict hierarchy of Roman class society was reflected in the precisely regulated and legally determined arrangement of the places for spectators. The arena originally had a wooden floor covered with fine sea sand (arena). Today the onlooker sees a confusing labyrinth of underground service passages with many spaces for stage machinery and scenery.

From here a passage led directly into the adjoining Ludus Magnus, the chief Roman school for gladiators. Its foundations were only discovered in 1937. This structure, whose architectural type is related to that of a barracks, is the only one of its kind to have survived. In the courtyard there was a small amphitheatre which served as a training ground. The gladiators were made to maintain most strict discipline, and here underwent severe training to prepare them for their

A25 Colosseo

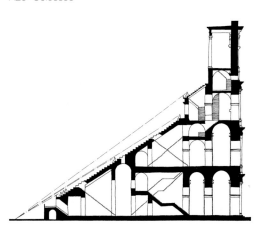

deaths. The gladiators' fights, which had developed from Etruscan burial rites held at funeral ceremonies, remained customary into the 5C.

In its size and unity, in its rational design tailored to meet practical and technical requirements, and in the severity and clarity of its structuring which takes in the vast mass of the building, the Colosseum is a very impressive document to the nature of ancient Roman architecture. To the architects of the Renaissance, the Colosseum was the very quintessence of all Roman architectural achievements, a living textbook of classical orderliness. EJ

Bibliography: G. Cozzo, *Il Colosseo*, Rome, 1971; F. Colagrossi, *L'anfiteatro Flavio*, Florence, 1913.

A26 Arco di Tito
Foro Romano (plan V 1/B)
AD 81

The triumphal arch is a genuinely Roman invention and remains one of the great architectural motifs up to the present day. Built in honour of historic personages on the occasion of a victory or a conquest, its main function was »to elevate above the ordinary world« (Pliny) the image of the honoured person, usually in the form of a statue with a quadriga. None of these groups of figures has survived, so that all triumphal arches are basically torsi. It is still unclear today whether the arch was more important as a supporter of other structures, or as a place under which to pass; in the latter, modern interpreters claim to see a ritual ceremony in which the campaigner who had returned home washed himself clean of the blood of war. The Titus arch, the oldest surviving arch in Rome, was built by Domitian in honour of the deified emperor Titus in »summa sacra via«, where its western frontage is oriented towards the Forum Romanum. The Frangipani incorporated the mighty edifice within their fortifications in the Middle Ages. Giuseppe Valadier excavated the arch in 1822.

Two large reliefs in the archway remind us of Titus' victorious campaign and of the destruction of Jerusalem in AD 71. The emperor's triumphal entry is depicted on the north side, and on the south side is the procession with the spoils from the devastated temple of the Jews, including the menorah. Both panels are exemplary of the pictorial relief style of the late-Flavian period, a style which displays parallels with the architecture of that period, two instances being the tall spaces for the depictions, and the principle of having many graduations in the layering. Built ten years after the military victory, the Titus arch is part of a major propaganda campaign conducted by the Flavian imperial family with the aim of improving the reputation of the »gens flavia« and thus consolidating the position of the dynasty, which did not have a long tradition behind it. That relief in the apex which is to be found in the archway and depicts the apotheosis of Titus shows that it was less a matter of honouring earthly triumphs than of deifying the Flavian emperor. This de-

A26 Arco di Tito

ification is much more strongly expressed here than at the time of Augustus. The emperor originally appeared as an honoured »divus« on a quadriga which had four elephants and stood atop the monument.

The Titus arch employs the older and simpler type of the single-gate triumphal arch which, in contrast to the more elaborate three-arched type, is to some extent the »normal« Roman arch. A single, large, barrel-vaulted archway is bordered by two mighty pylons. The high attic above it formerly bore the lost group of statues. Each face of the arch forms a show façade subdivided into three bays by an order of columns standing on high pedestals. The bays are of differing widths, and together they form one combined rhythmic bay. It is only this order of columns placed out in front for show that tightens up the building, gives it clear proportions, and, what is more, ennobles it thanks to the fluted column shafts and the rich splendour of the composite order of columns (the earliest such surviving in Rome). The entablature is bent at right angles above the columns in such a way that the central bay comes forward and thus expressively frames the archway. The rhythmic subdividing of the substructure then continues into the attic. Here, the panel of inscriptions in the very clear-cut frame takes up the width of the emphasized central bay, so that a vertical course is created which formerly came to an end in the statue, now lost, of the emperor. Three-dimensional decorations are largely absent from the façade of the arch, with the result that the proud inscription consisting of monumental roman letters cast in bronze is elevated into becoming the real decoration of the triumphal arch.

The particular quality of the Titus arch lies firstly in the noble restraint shown in the three-dimensional decorations, which remain strictly limited to the marked-out pictorial areas, secondly in the clear structure of the building, thirdly in the energetic articulation which stands on high pedestals and for the first time, in contrast to older triumphal arches, firmly incorporates the archway into the overall structure, and fourthly and most importantly in the well-balanced proportions. EJ

Bibliography: M. Pfanner, *Titusbogen*, Mainz, 1983.

A27 Palazzo dei Flavi (Domus Flavia and Augustana)
Monte Palatino (plan V 1/B–1/C)
AD 81–92
Rabirius

Human settlement in Rome began on the Palatine hill. It was here, in 754 BC according to Varro, that the hypothetical original cell, which was surrounded by a wall and was called »Roma Quadrata« by the Romans, came into being. Iron Age huts, including the so-called House of Romulus which was revered and repeatedly rebuilt, were in fact found here. The cinerary urns which were found permitted the house to be

A27 Palazzo dei Flavi (Domus Flavia and Augustana)

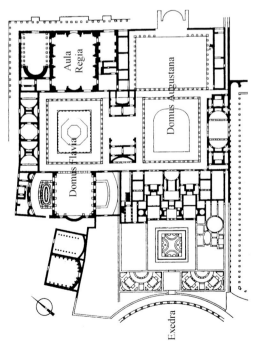

dated in the 9C BC. The surroundings of this building are that section of the Palatine upon which no palaces were later erected. Identifiable buildings from the republican period survive on both sides. They are: the remains of the substructure of a Cybele temple (2C BC); the House of Augustus; and the so-called House of Livia. The point is that during the republican period the Palatine became the preferred residential area of the Roman upper classes. Augustus, too, was born here. Velleius Paterculus and Suetonius report that Augustus later bought up several houses one by one and linked them together. The »House of Augustus« is thought to be authentic, because it agrees with tradition by adjoining the House of Romulus and the Temple of Apollo (36 BC). And in contrast to all the other republican houses, nothing was built on top of it. The domicile of the man who founded the principate was evidently held in high esteem. The succession of spaces is architecturally insignificant. These are plain private houses, not palaces. In contrast to this, the paintings are among the best in the so-called style II of Pompeii (c. 30 BC).

Due to the very strong example set by Augustus, the Palatine became the emperors' residence from the time of Tiberius onwards. The term »palace« derives from the name of the hill. The palace on the Palatine really did become a structure which had an influence upon the work of building palaces. It was not yet the palace of Tiberius, of which only a peristyle and cryptoporticoes underneath the Farnese Gardens survive, which created a type, and neither did the (built-over) end portions of the Domus Aurea (A24). But the palace of Domitian did become typological. The very fact that the complex was left untouched throughout the entire imperial period is evidence of how convincingly the building task was performed here. The area now built over was stately in size, as was the Domus Aurea: the vestibule of the complex was several hundred metres away and laterally adjoined S. Maria Antiqua (C12). This reception area was of gigantic dimensions (33.10 x 24.50 m) and had a barrel vault. For the palace itself, Rabirius, who was Domitian's court architect, built an artificial terrace placed on substructures and above an earlier (Neronic and republican) structure. The palace was in three parts, all of them integrated into an almost square block of outer walls: they were the Domus Flavia which with its large rooms served the functions of state, the Domus Augustana with its private rooms, and the so-called stadion. The three parts were erected in the order given, and building work was still being done on the stadion after the complexes of rooms had been inaugurated (AD 92).

The Domus Flavia is in three sections, with a peristyle courtyard in the middle, a triclinium in the south, and a wing in the north. The middle of that wing is formed by the Aula Regia, flanked by a basilica (formerly with a barrel vault and a nave and two aisles) and the lararium, which was probably a room for the guard. The Aulia Regia, the audience room, was entirely new in both design and architectural type. This almost square room is characterized by a succession of round and rectangular niches. The wall was hollowed out by them, and its mass thus became perceptible. At the same time it makes an animated impression. The columns formerly placed in front of it for show also contributed to this. Whether the room had a barrel vault is disputed. There was enough knowledge of the use of concrete in construction work to make it possible to create, for the first time ever, such large vaults. The above-mentioned vestibule, which was even larger, is evidence of this. It is not likely that the aula would have had a more modest design than the vestibule. The barrel vault would also have contributed enormously to the impression of size and weightiness. The peculiarity of the »Flavian Baroque«, observable in similar fashion in the relief-work art of the period (cf. A26), is shown in the immense height of the room and the animatedness of the wall. Domitian ordered this new type of structure to be built because his image as emperor had changed. Here he presented himself as »deus et dominus«: the idea of divine emperorship was born. The emperor was »put on display« in the apse of the room (the basilica, and the triclinium which is the banqueting hall, also have apses). He sat in it like the statues of gods in the room's other niches. There were also mosaics, and the brightly-coloured stone which from Domitian's time onwards was preferred to white marble. Today it is known that Domitian also developed the ceremonial which later became the Papal and, via the Byzantine Empire, the Western ceremonial. The picture is completed by the balconies by which the three rooms were opened up towards the Forum. Domitian was able to step out on to these balconies as on to a benediction loggia. The high terraces from the Sullan period (cf. A8) were here utilized for a new purpose. The triclinium opposite was of a known type, but what is new, here too, is the size and the openings at the sides. The view through these openings, albeit impeded by a row of pillars, fell upon two nymphaea. This design type also remained influential from then on (cf. A32, A30, and also A53).

The structure of the Domus Flavia differs from the earlier Domus Aurea in that it emphasizes the axes. This is the root of the enfilade, which is the suite of rooms found in later castles. An axis of this sort, extending from one peristyle courtyard to another, also links the Domus Flavia with the Domus Augustana. The latter is laterally adjacent, but clearly separate. This gives the structure an exemplary bipolar and well-ordered appearance.

The above-mentioned peristyle courtyard stood in the rear section of the Domus Augustana. Thus this section is oriented in the reverse direction: the main façade, a large exedra, points southwards towards the Circus Maximus. This is another balcony giving a distant view. The south-western section of the Domus

A28 Terme di Traiano

Augustana is better preserved, is grouped around a second courtyard, and has two storeys. The upper storey is on the same level as the Domus Flavia, while the lower storey is further down. Buildings with more than one storey had become customary at the time when Rome was rebuilt in Roman concrete after the fire of AD 64. In this part of the Domus Augustana, the typically Flavian abundance of curving shapes, assembled in a complex manner, is still more strongly evident than in the Domus Flavia.

The so-called stadion was not roofed. It was surrounded on all sides by two-storeyed porticoes: arcades of pillars on the first storey, and above them were colonnaded halls with a horizontal entablature. The northern corner, now rebuilt, gives an impression of this. The stadion was probably used as a garden, and also as the hippodrome as which it is described in that section of the history of martyrs which deals with St. Sebastian. From then on there had to be a hippodrome in every Roman imperial residence (cf. A48).

Septimius Severus expanded the complex in the south-east. Part of it, the septicodium, is among the most splendid show walls in ancient Rome. It is typically Severan in its abundance of columns (cf. A41), and here, on the Via di S. Gregorio, it survived until the 16C. SG

Bibliography: G. Cantino Wataghin, *La Domus Augustana – personalità e problemi dell'architecttura flavia*, Turin, 1966; H. Finsen, *La Résidence de Domitien sur le Palatin*, Copenhagen, 1969; B. Tamm, *Auditorium and Palatium*, Stockholm, 1963

A28 Terme di Traiano
Viale del Monte Oppio (plan V 2/B)
AD 104–09
Apollodorus of Damascus

The thermal baths which Trajan opened in AD 109 were built in an elevated location at the southern end of the Esquiline, next to the Colle Oppio. The palace of Nero (A24) was partly built over in this process. Thanks to the inexhaustible imperial resources, the design was completed in the space of only five years.

This complex occupies a key position in the development of Roman architecture in the field of thermal baths. The first public baths in Rome had been built on the field of Mars by Agrippa, Augustus' son-in-law. Another milestone was Nero's ruined thermal baths near the Pantheon; a ground-plan drawing by Palladio shows that a central axis with a succession of bathing rooms was, for the first time, flanked here by ancillary rooms, arranged symmetrically in pairs, and by sports halls. Trajan's architect followed this model, but he surrounded the large, self-contained block structure of the baths with encompassing wings on three sides (outer length of the sides of those wings: 337 x 296 m), so that an enormous U-shaped inner courtyard came into being. This created the type of Roman imperial thermal baths that was retained until the late-classical period (cf. A43 and A46). Exemplary use was made of the heat of the sun in the afternoons by orienting the hottest bathrooms towards the south-west.

Relatively little has survived of Trajan's thermal baths. But some large exedrae still produce an impression of their liberal dimensions and magnificent spatial effect. UF

A29 Foro di Traiano
Via dei Fori Imperiali (plan V 1/B)
AD 107–13, from AD 100
Apollodoros of Damascus

Trajan ordered the construction of the last and largest imperial Forum. It made Apollodoros into Rome's most famous architect. He had previously built bridges across the Danube on Trajan's campaigns. Between the Capitol and the Quirinal there ran a narrow ridge, which according to an inscription was at the same height as today's column of Trajan. The ridge was completely cleared away. Thus the landscape was radically reshaped, as occurred elsewhere in Roman architecture (A8). On the Quirinal hill, a slope came into being which was supported by the market buildings, and this was why these were the first to be

A29 Foro di Traiano. TF1 basilica, TF2 library, TF3 Column of Trajan, TF4 Temple of Trajan, TM1 markets, TM2 Via Biberatica, TM3 market hall

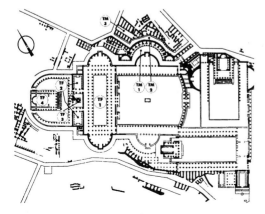

erected. Nero and Domitian had built palaces, but Trajan, reverting to Augustus, once again chose to order a Forum to be constructed. The new wall architecture of Nero and Domitian continued in the 2C, and so too did more traditional forms. The contrast between Trajan's Forum and his Market shows this quite clearly.

The Forum of Trajan was entered from that of Augustus by passing through an arch in the convexly shaped entrance wall. The complex as a whole ascended towards the rear up a few steps. The first square, rectangular and surrounded by colonnaded halls, was dominated by an equestrian statue of Trajan and concluded by an immense, transversely located basilica (TF1). The Greek and Latin libraries (TF2), arranged symmetrically to the left and right, adjoined the basilica in the rear. The column of Trajan (TF3) stood between them, framed by their porticoes and some surrounding columns. The last courtyard was dominated by the Temple of Trajan (TF4). The Forum combined two matters: it took over the severe orderliness, and the framing portico, from the imperial Fora, while at the same time adopting from the Forum Romanum the complexity and – for the first time ever in an imperial Forum – the basilica as being the quintessential structure in a Forum. The symmetry of this Forum is of an ideal type and, in typically Roman manner (cf. A8, A11), was revealed only when passing through it. Constantly changing spatial impressions – squares and interior areas – followed one after another.

The Basilica Ulpia, so called after the name of Trajan's family, was the last and largest in heathen Rome. The architectural type is traditional, but the shape it takes is very splendid: a nave and four aisles, with large exedrae at both ends (hidden today underneath the Via dei Fori Imperiali and the Scalinata di Magnanapoli), as well as the colourfulness so typical of the period of the adopted emperors, when materials from all the provinces were replacing the marble. The building had a far-reaching effect. From that time on every imperial Forum in the provinces had a basilica. And it was probably the prestige of this basilica that induced Constantine to build Christian assembly rooms in the form of basilicas. The old St Peter building (p. 67) was then of almost exactly the same size.

The column of Trajan (AD 110–13) is a revolutionary invention. There had in the republican period been columns devoted to fame. But what was new is the fact that it was covered with a strip of reliefs: the idea that a chief architectural element could become merely a surface for carrying images is quite in accord with Roman thinking (cf. A42, A51). The shaft and capital measure 100 feet (29.78 m), and with the base and the statue pedestal the figure rises to 39.86 m. Some 2,500 figures (casts of them are to be found in the Museo di Città Romana) on a strip 200 m long, with 23 bends (ranging from a height of 3.65 m below to 3.83 m above), give depictions of the Dacian wars. They were still oriented on the Hellenistic ideal of imitating nature (though less so than under Augustus),

A29 Foro di Traiano

and there are no late-classical graphic elements. Trajan does not dominate, and the enemy is portrayed as having human features. This shows that stoical, philosophical ideal of rulership upon which the system of adopted emperors was based even before the time of Marcus Aurelius. The column is not merely a monument to victory, but also primarily a tomb. Eutropius stresses that only Trajan was given a tomb in the pomerium, the core area of the city. The design was based on the structure of burial towers, with the burial chamber below and a temple, which contained an element of apotheosis, above. Here the temple is a statue of the deified emperor (since 1588 the statue has been of Petrus). The idea of purification was depicted in the zone in between, by means either of gates (as in the burial towers) or of the strip of reliefs which displays the achievements of Trajan's life. Thus the column was not built for human eyes, which were unable to follow the ascending spirals, but for the open sky into which it thrust upwards out of its surrounding structure.

The Temple of Trajan completes the Forum, which was designed to include it. As custom demanded (cf. A35, A36), it was not built until after Trajan's (and Plotina's) death and deification (AD 121). Nevertheless, the imperial cult was now so strong that, for the first time ever, a Forum was dedicated entirely to the emperor and a temple was built to him.

The customary high wall of peperino surrounded Trajan's imperial Forum. The façade of the markets was not then freely exposed as it is today. It stood behind the exedra of the first courtyard on the right, and was itself formed as an exedra (TM1). The lowest street giving access to the markets was in the intermediate space, a second such street, the Via Biberatica (TM2), followed a W-shaped course behind the first row of market buildings, and there was a third street at the very top. There were some 150 shops along the streets, and a few larger buildings, chiefly

the market hall (TM3). The further the visitor walks away from the symmetrical Forum and upwards towards the hill, the stronger the functional asymmetry becomes. The basic unit is formed by the barrel-vaulted taberna (shop). The exedra contains eleven tabernae in a radial arrangement. They support the hill in the same way as the barrel vaults support the Colosseum (A25). There are two characterizing contrasts: that between the wall surface and the hollow space of the barrels, and that between the wall colour and the bright frame of the openings. These frugal aesthetics, which are determined solely by the prescribed design, had never previously been seen in such pure form in Rome. Tentatively commencing after the fire in AD 64, they shaped the 2C (cf. A30). One remnant of the subdividing work here is the gable, only to be found on the upper row of arches in the exedra. The supporting framework used in the construction of the large market hall shows how good a knowledge of concrete building there was by that time. What a ponderous impression the republican forerunners in Tibur and Ferentino make by comparison! There are six pairs of shops on every level. Those below open directly on to the hall, and those above on to a gallery. Isolated supports of travertine stand on the parapet of the gallery, well inside the area and not on the outer wall of the hall. They bear the groined vault, which is formed by the main barrel and by the transverse barrels of the individual shops. The era of large vaults commences here (A31, A36, A43, A50). SG

Bibliography: F. Florescu, *Die Trajanssäule*, Bonn, 1969; Ch. Leon, *Die Bauornamentik des Trajansforums und ihre Stellung in der früh- und mittelkaiserlichen Architekturdekoration Roms*, Vienna, 1971.

A30 Ostia Antica
Ostia (plan G2 1/C)
Ostia, located on the mouth (Latin: ostia) of the Tiber, served to supply Rome. Founded as a castrum in 338 BC, it experienced an upswing after the harbours of Claudius and in particular Trajan (hectagonal, and today restored) had been built. The interesting functional buildings which make up the main part of the town largely date from the first two thirds of the 2C AD. They are still to be seen in Ostia, whereas in Rome they are lost. Ostia became deserted when Constantine conferred the status of a town upon Portus Traiani in 314.

The layout of Ostia is similar to that of most Roman towns. The determinant feature is the design of the castrum, with a rectangular rampart and two main streets crossing one another at right angles: these were the Cardo running from south to north, and the Decumanus. As Rome itself was older in origin, it remained full of nooks and crannies and was an exception here. The Forum in such towns – in Ostia this was done under Tiberius – was built at the intersection of the two main streets by expanding one of them into a square. Although the castrum was no more than the nucleus, the network of other streets was also oriented on it. Only the Decumanus, which ran parallel to the ancient bed of the Tiber, forked at the western gate of the castrum. The expanded town walls and gates (1) were built by Sulla (c. 80 BC). They remained determinant later too. If there was not enough space, more than one storey was built. In similar fashion to the flight of birds, which was used for making prophecies, the right-angled layout of a town seems to have been regarded in Italy as, among other things, an image of the cosmic order.

Few buildings were erected in Ostia in the Julio-Claudian period, when Rome was becoming a city of marble: a Temple of Roma Augustus (2) under Tiberius, and under Augustus himself a theatre with a colonnaded hall (5). The history of this theatre is typical of Ostia. Its colonnaded hall became the »place of the corporations«. Projecting walls were inserted between the columns, thus creating tabernae (shops) (cf. A29). Mercantile agencies (corporations) from all countries came and depicted their activities and coats of arms on the mosaics. The basilica constructed under Domitian (4) only had to perform judicial functions.

A30 Ostia Antica. 1 town walls, 2 Temple of Roma-Augustus, 3 temple on the Capitol, 4 basilica, 5 theatre, 6 Horrea Epagathiana, 7 house with the mosaic niche, 8 Casa a Giardino, 9 Casa di Diana, 10 House of the Triclinia, 11 House of the Muses, 12 House of Amor and Psyche

The horrea, storage halls with sales premises, were one of the central architectural types in this seaport. In classical times, economic affairs were otherwise conducted in the countryside, in Latifundia, but this was not the case in Ostia. Almost all the horrea (and cereal mills) were on the side of the Decumanus towards the Tiber. These new functional buildings were favoured by the harbour and by the new building method, which was a core of cement mortar faced with bricks. This was how Rome had been rebuilt after the fire of AD 64. The markets of Trajan are the chief work to employ this method (A29). Ostia experienced its peak period from the time of Trajan onwards. The façades had previously been painted colourfully, whereas the aesthetic attraction of the brick structure lies in the contrast firstly between the walls and the cavities and secondly between the bricks and the (differently coloured) ashlars. The best example is to be seen in the Horrea Epagathiana (6). This three-storeyed ashlar structure with its six window axes has a chief motif, namely the portal with its aedicule frame. Contrary to what is customary in Roman architecture, the portal is not symmetrically placed. Its function determines its appearance (cf. A29). It is adjoined by shops whose storehouses were lit by small (mezzanine) windows. Dwelling rooms were located above. The structure of the Horrea Epagathiana accords with that of large apartment blocks. That is to say, the rooms are grouped around an arcaded courtyard. This type was later used when developing the Renaissance palace.

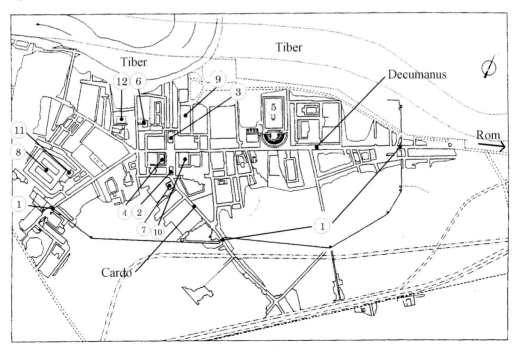

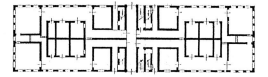

A30 Ostia Antica. Casa a Giardino

The residential houses accord with those in Rome. Evidence of this is provided by the ruins of the apartment block (insula) on the Capitol in Rome, and by the so-called marble plan (p. 11). The single-storey domus was – in Pompeii, for example – predominant in the pre-Flavian period. This changed after the time of Nero. The regional catalogues stated that there were 1790 domus structures in Rome in the early 4C, but 46 000 insulae. Almost all the pre-Flavian domus in Ostia have been built over (one exception is the house with the niche containing mosaics (7)); any later domus are only to be found south of the Decumanus. The insulae were planned to have more than one storey. Thus the upper storeys possess an identical or similar ground plan, and usually have their own staircase leading to the street. The insulae were evidently built very high, having up to five floors. It would otherwise not have been necessary, under Trajan, to prescribe a maximum height of 60 feet or to provide such a high podium for the temple on the Capitol in the Forum (3). In contrast to the domus, which was a house with an atrium, the insulae opened towards the outside. The doors and windows ensured that light came in from the street. In an initial stage of development, a succession of dwelling rooms was placed above the shops. They were reached by some stairs inside the shop (examples are to be found in the part of the Cardo towards the river). The size of an insula unit was then doubled by placing two of them back to back, with independent staircases located at the corner or in a passageway. This was the minimum standard for the 2C. The Casa a Giardino from the period of Hadrian (8) is a model example of this type: it has identically carved dwellings, two in each of the two blocks. This insula also demonstrates that in Ostia a surrounding garden compensated for anything very narrow and high. The six fountains served primarily to supply the upper storeys, which had no water. The best-developed type is found in the Casa di Diana (mid-2C) (9): when the buildings were longer and broader (23.3 x 39.3 m in this case), courtyards, which again had fountains, had to be included, especially if, as here, older building work cut off the light on two sides. Courtyards fulfilled the high-class demands imposed if they were made into broad peristyle courtyards, examples being the House of the Triclinia (10) and, in particular, the House of the Muses (11). Brickwork was used in all these types, as it was in the horrea. A separate subdividing element created for the insula was a row of balconies, especially splendid in the

Casa di Diana (9). The balcony was indeed a mere subdividing element, because it was too narrow to be used and does not follow the level of the floors.

Ostia became deserted after the 2C. One gem from the later period may though be mentioned: it is the House of Amor and Psyche (c. 300) (12). The structure has become freer here, and asymmetry is built into it. The house has underfloor heating and a nymphaeum. One of the earliest examples of a columned arcade, that is to say a combination of column and arch, is to be found in the courtyard. Shortly before, an arcade such as this had been first evolved in Diocletian's palace in Split. SG

Bibliography: R. Meiggs, *Roman Ostia*, Oxford, 1973; G. Calza and G. Becatti, *Ostia*, Rome, 1984.

A31 Pantheon
Piazza della Rotonda (plan IV 1/A–2/A)
AD 118/19, AD 125–28

The Pantheon is the unsurpassed ideal model of a rotunda. An inscription on today's structure still names Agrippa as the constructor. However, brick stamps are evidence that it was erected in the time of Hadrian. The building which Agrippa erected for Augustus in 27 BC had looked different: it had a transversely rectangular cella and caryatids, like the Erechteion from the Periclean period. Today's structure was created in barely ten years. This was possible because standard structural elements, namely columns measuring exactly 40 feet, were employed and there was an excellent knowledge of concrete building methods (cf. also A29). A ring of foundations 7.3 m wide and 4.5 m deep supports the whole. The dome, with its diameter of 43.3 m, is today still the largest in Rome. The reason why the building is so well preserved is that Boniface IV reconsecrated it as S. Maria ad Martyres in 609. Only the bronze facing was lost: Constantius II »looted« the inside of the dome in 663, and Urban VIII (Barberini) did the same to the vestibule when he was building the Baldacchino (B42).

The Pantheon was part of a larger group of buildings from Hadrian's period. Thus no more imperial Fora were built after Trajan's time (A29), but Hadrian, who was for a long time the last to do so, continued the tradition of rather large imperial complexes of buildings. Within this group of buildings, the walker passed from the Corso to the square in front of the Pantheon by going through two temple areas (A36). In this square, which was at that time a lengthwise rectangle framed by colonnaded halls, he turned left and saw to the south the front section – massive, and filling up the square – of the Pantheon. Thus the latter was the final point in the chain.

All that was formerly to be seen of the outer structure in the oblong square was the portico. Five steps also led from it to the square, so that the building resembled a podium temple (A7). This achieved two things: tradition was preserved in the outward appearance, and the rotunda, which adjoins at the rear and was, in itself, a structure without orientation, was given an orientation: a process typical of Roman architecture (p. 23). The vestibule, 33.1 m wide and 15.5 m deep, consists of a gable and 16 Corinthian columns. What might be called a nave and two aisles comes into formation between them. The outer aisles end in a round niche (which at the time probably contained statues of Hadrian and Augustus, upon whose work Hadrian drew, cf. also A33). The nave and aisles were flat-roofed. The central nave leads to the entrance and was barrel-vaulted.

A31 Pantheon

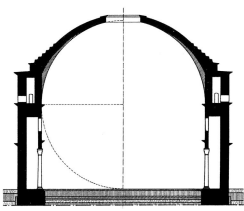

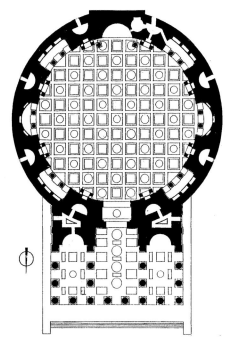

Thus the cross-section of the roof was in the form of the Syrian arch popular under Hadrian. A second and different type of building adjoins the temple façade.

The rotunda, and particularly its interior, is the showpiece of the Pantheon. Interior architecture developed much more strongly in Rome than in Greece, and this applies both to the structural types (A11) and to the shapes (A9). In the Pantheon, a temple was for the first time built in such a way that it was mostly the interior that was to be used. The cult had previously been celebrated outside the temple. The archetypal rotunda, consisting of a cylinder and a hemisphere, was also created here. The structure is shaped by the simplest possible dimensions: the overall height is exactly equal to the diameter, and the dome, a perfect hemisphere, is of exactly the same height as the cylinder. This gives the structure its monumental tranquility and simplicity, which are chiefly derived from its agreeably broad proportions. The structure is indeed determined by aesthetic considerations. The point is that its actual appearance differs from what might be imagined from its design: it can be seen from the outer structure that a flatter dome, which is the so-called testudo (tortoiseshell) of cast cement and is an artificial monolith, rests on the walls; the material still required to round off the hemisphere was filled in. It is an impressive engineering achievement: the largest dome made of a natural monolith is in the tomb of Theodoric in Ravenna and is 9 m in diameter.

It is not merely the overall shape that is imposing. The appointments, the subdividing work and the individual shapes are spectacular too. In no other building from the classical period are the appointments similarly well preserved. The rich colourfulness created by pavonazetto, porphyry, giallo antico and grey granite is a real experience in the Pantheon. It was first seen under Domitian (A27), but did not appear continuously until the time of the adopted emperors. The subdividing work contributes greatly to the spatial feeling of an agreeable broadness, as it is the horizontal level that dominates in the cylindrical section. The building is divided into two storeys: they are wide, low, round shapes. Something similar applies to the dome which dominates the whole: although its lines point towards the sky, its immense span contributes further to the impression of weightiness. Quiet, uniform light flows into the area through the opaion above, which is the only source of light. One peculiarity of the subdividing work has always been surprising: the second storey, whose ancient state has only been preserved in one section to the right of the main niche, is subdivided by delicate, closely placed pilasters and windows (their aim is to light up the niches, which come up to this level). The pilasters are not in superposition, that is to say they are not perpendicularly above those in the first storey. Bandinelli said that there was a »rhythm of hours« below and a »rhythm of minutes« above. Such a feature is an exception in Roman architecture, but sudden interruptions, and angular displacements, were highly regarded in the period of Hadrian (cf. A32). This peculiarity in the subdivision gave the second storey its lightness and a certain rotating effect. The pattern on the floor contributed to this. Among the individual shapes, particular mention should be made of the seven niches, entirely accommodated within the thickness of the wall. They make the thickness referred to (6.2 m) very evident. The gravitas romana, which is a continuous characteristic, is seen here too. It is also clear that the shape of the interior was – as opposed to what then happened in the late-classical period – not intended to become discernible in all its parts (including the niches) in the exterior structure. The niches are rectangular on the diagonals, and round on the main axes. They are marked out by columns. This lends nobility to the edifice. At the same time, the combination of cylindrical wall and row of columns is an invention which, where the development of architecture in the early Middle Ages is concerned, can hardly be overestimated. Another individual form is still more celebrated. The main niche is framed by columns standing in front of it. Along with the arch which penetrates the entablature, the columns form the so-called Pantheon motif, of which there was much emulation, from the Pazzi chapel in Florence to the AT&T building in New York.

There is speculation about the purpose to which the Pantheon, the »temple for all the gods«, was dedicated. It should be stressed that the rotunda as an architectural type was previously found in palaces and thermal baths, that is to say in building complexes which had a strong imperial stamp, but never in cultic edifices. The Pantheon may have been intended to house the cult of the emperor, which was now becoming established. The adopted emperors now declared their belief in stoa, the philosophical tendency which had developed the pantheistic idea that there was a divine permeation running through the entire universe. Cassius Dio, Hadrian's biographer, actually regarded the Pantheon as a likeness of the vault of heaven. According to him, the opaion is the sun, and many matters could be associated with the planets: Mars and Venus who were the ancestors of Rome, or the surroundings of the emperor.

Only the dispute between Bramante and Michelangelo will now be picked out from the truly never-ending history of the influence produced by the Pantheon (cf. e. g. A47, A49, H4, H31). Bramante loved the delicate encircling roundness of the second storey. He intended, in imitation of it, to place a ring of close-standing columns on the inside of the drum of St Peter's. He was followed in this by domes in England, the USA and Paris. Michelangelo felt that the delicate second storey of the Pantheon, where there is no superposition, was too weak, and he mocked it. The result of his words was that Vanvitelli redesigned it with stucco in 1747. SG

Bibliography: K. Fine Licht, *The Rotunda in Rome*, Copenhagen, 1968; R. Vighi, *The Pantheon*, 1955.

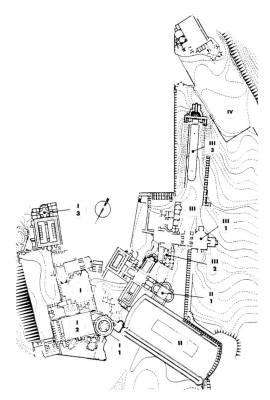

A32 Villa Adriana, Tivoli. I villa, I/1 villa standing on an island, I/2 villa with peristyl, I/3 Piazza d'Oro, II poikile, II/1 triclinium, III canopus complex, III/1 vestibule, III/2 baths, III/3 canopus, IV academy

A32 Villa Adriana, Tivoli
Tivoli (plan G1 3/B)
AD 118–34
Hadrian built his villa on some 300 hectares of hilly ground at the edge of the Sabine hills. It comprises four complexes with four differing axes. The two outer complexes are fairly parallel with one another. They follow the course of the adjoining chains of hills, and the difference in height, amounting to 53 m, is noticeable here. The so-called academy (with the tower of Timon) is in the south (IV), and to the north are the palace with its peristyle (I/2) and, at a slight angle to this, the Piazza d'Oro (I/3). A horseshoe-shaped chain of hills runs diagonally in between. The canopus (III/3) is bedded in its valley and, together with the entrance vestibule (III/1) and the thermal baths (III/2), forms a third complex. The fourth complex stands diagonally to the third, and the so-called poikile is its central feature (II). This complex stands next to the palace complex and is linked to it by the villa (I/1) which stands on an island and is round like a hinge. The chief work of the first phase of construction (118–25) was the island

villa, and that of the second (125–33) was the Piazza d'Oro; the canopus was built after 130. The whole villa is based rather on a loose succession of ideas by the emperor than on a uniform overall design. Spartian, Hadrian's biographer, named the prototypes, which stood in various eastern provinces: the Stoa Poikile, the Lykeion and Prytaneion, the academy in Athens (with the tower of Timon), and the canopus, which is the only prototype identifiable with certainty.

It was mainly the Post-Modern critics who were fascinated by the interruptions between the axes and by the lack of continuity. Some authors regarded this as a borrowing from Greek art. It is true that angular displacements are known from the Periclean classical period, but only between independent individual structures (the Acropolis). They will be sought for in vain in interconnected building complexes, especially those of the Hellenistic period. But they are only rarely found even in Roman architecture. This is different though in Roman painting, which only developed what is known as aggregate space, and did not evolve a uniform perspective.

The palace (I), the main section, stood at the edge. Contrary to what is the case on the Palatine (A27), the state and private rooms were no longer clearly separated, and were not located at opposite ends of the palace. The imperial chambers were housed in tiny spaces which were located not centrally, but in the island villa (Teatro Marittimo) and – adjoining the latter, and reached by a hidden staircase – in the two-storey tower with its belvedere. The perfectly circular Teatro was surrounded by a ring-shaped canal with an external wall. Only swivelling wooden bridges led across the canal. The entire range of items found in a villa was integrated on the island, an area barely 40 m in diameter. The villa's ground plan is based on circle segments in multifariously varied shapes. The triclinium in the south, a room for resting, was the main room; thermal baths and a library adjoined it. The only open visual axis led across from the triclinium to the garden in the north. The visual axis was though at the same time interrupted by a waterworks which trickled down from on top. Contrary to the 1C structures (A27), a free view as from a belvedere was no longer sought after here. The design of the Teatro renders clearly discernible two further principal features of the villa as a whole: they are the dominance of the circular line (in ground plan and vertical projection), and the return to privacy and intimacy. The moat and wall are the ideal types for a retreat (in Latin: privare). But in the interior the shapes are free and flowing.

The other end of the complex is taken up by the second spatial work of art to justify the villa's fame: this is the Piazza d'Oro (I/3). The variety of shapes is once again to be seen in the entrance vestibule, has its roots in some spaces on the Palatine (A27), and displays as its prime feature the alternating succession of round and rectangular niches. But what is new is that the richly subdivided form of the interior is now

A32 Villa Adriana, Tivoli. Canopus

visible all around the exterior structure too. This did not become a standard practice until the late-classical period (A53). There is an audience room at the rear end. The concave-convex shaping of the wall, without any insertions, is a celebrated feature here. In the chief axes, the wall was replaced by rows of columns, and was thus transparent. This enabled the route to be continued into a nymphaeum at the rear, and at the sides into light-wells around each of which five rooms were grouped. Here, as is also the case in the other complexes, the orientation was thus once again turned through a right angle within the complex.

The Teatro Marittimo is adjoined by the poikile (II), whose name makes reference to the famous square in Athens, framed by porticoes. This was a square which had a belvedere and, standing on large substructions, projected into the Campagna. However, here too, no importance was attached to obtaining a distant view, because it was mainly the triclinium (II/1) that invited the visitor to linger a while. This was another room full of curving shapes: a room with three conchae. And the onlooker's gaze, which here went back to a tholos in the poikile, was once again interrupted – this time by rows of columns.

The other buildings in this complex are at right angles to the poikile. They provide the transition to the vestibule, and then on to the canopus (III/3). The blueprint for the latter was the channel which led to the celebrated shrine of Serapis in the Nile delta near Alexandria. But the orientation was now reversed: the grotto, a triclinium, is not the point at which the onlooker's gaze is aimed, but the point from which it starts. The onlooker sees the semicircular colonnade which stands opposite and – although not in itself an uncommon feature in villa architecture – had a specific design that was original and full of new ideas: the Syrian arch, which was an uninterrupted piece of entablature bending upwards into a circle in the middle, was known in the time of Augustus (the triumphal arch in Orange), but then it only occurred sporadically and in less important locations. But here the arch became a row of arches. For the first time the sequence appears as an arcaded row, a series of arches borne on columns such as was only put into effect in the late-classical period (cf. A30, last paragraph). The arch penetrated the solid system of column and horizontal architrave.

This villa's architecture is not eclectic at all, but full of ideas and rich in ambivalences, especially because of the interruptions between the axes and the visual axes. Villas were a ferment for further development even in the 1C, especially Nero's villas in Anzio and Subiacum, which were a model for the Domus Aurea (A24). It was now, in the Villa Adriana, that virtuosity reached its culmination, before a more conservative basic approach once again found acceptance under Antoninus. The abundance of vault shapes (in the Piazza d'Oro, on the Temple of Serapis, in the thermal baths) was one feature. Another is the lost gardens. They expressed the Roman interpretation of art (cf. A8): they were architecturally designed with walls and substructions, and the views obtainable were routed into channels. These gardens stand at the very outset of Western garden architecture, which then blossomed anew first of all in Italy, one example being in the Villa d'Este nearby. From there it radiated out to other countries. In Tivoli, one has the impression of seeing the emperor, this almost modern romanticist, who climbed up to the top of the Aetna to see the sunrise, from close by. SG

Bibliography: H. Kähler, *Hadrian und seine Villa bei Tivoli*, Berlin, 1950; M. Üblacker, *Das Teatro Marittimo in der Villa Hadriana*, Mainz, 1985.

A33 Mausoleo di Adriano, today Castel S. Angelo
Lungotevere di Castello (plan IV 1/A)
AD 135–39, later additions
Demetrianus

After the burial of Nerva, the mausoleum of Augustus (A15) did not have the space for another emperor. Burial in the emperor's own forum, as in the case of Trajan (A29), had to remain an isolated instance. Hadrian therefore ordered the construction of a mausoleum for his family and future emperors. It was once again directly by the Tiber, opposite the field of Mars, which was also built on in Hadrian's period (A36). Free imperial gardens and what, apart from the Via Appia, is the most significant tomb area (around St Peter's) were located here. In order to give access to the mausoleum, the Pons Aelius was built (AD 134), so called after the name of Hadrian's family and the tutelary deity Helios. The mausoleum was not completed and consecrated until AD 139, under Antoninus Pius.

Most of the building survives. A cylinder 21 m high and 64 m in diameter rises above a square substructure with a height of 15 m and sides measuring 89 m. The cement mortar core, encased by ashlars of tufa, peperino and travertine, can still be seen today. It extends as far as the projecting ring above the battlements which were added under Benedict IX (1033–44). However, the building lost much of its marble facing,

A33 Mausoleo di Adriano, today Castel S. Angelo

which had surrounding columns or projecting pilasters, when the citizens of Rome were planning to raze this (papal) fortress in 1379. Some remains of the frieze, where there are garlands and bulls' skulls, display stylistic features from Asia Minor, but are of local marble. This demonstrates that since the time of Hadrian, workshops whose style was derived from Asia Minor but which were evidently located in Italy led the field in architectural decoration. Cypresses were planted on the cylinder, and a cubical base course with sculptures on top stood in the middle of it. They were probably a quadriga, with Hadrian as Helios. The core of the inner structure also survives: below is the vestibule with a niche for Hadrian's statue (today in the Vatican), above the square, barrel-vaulted burial chamber, and, linking the two, there is a barrel-vaulted passage which describes a complete circle and ascends by 12 m.

The form of the building shows that Hadrian, despite his love of Hellenistic architecture, did not intend to construct a mausoleum inspired by it, but instead was planning another architectural tumulus like that built by Augustus before him: the exterior dimensions of the substructure are almost identical. The form was simplified. The five circles were replaced by a single circle on a square substructure. Thus a republican model stood sponsor here (A12). At the same time the principate was also drawn upon. But the form was enriched as against that of the Augustus mausoleum. The Roman square-shaped crematorium was included in the substructure and given a monumental size.

This mausoleum is the second largest classical building in Rome after the Colosseum. It excels all the other witnesses to the city's development in the postclassical period. It lost its peaceful function a century later. This was because Aurelian's plan for protecting Rome rested on three supports: the walls (A44) which surrounded the area on the right side of the Tiber (and also surrounded the south of Trastevere, where the vitally important mills were); the river; and – in the middle of the unfortified section of the river – the fortress of Hadrian. The fortress was reconsecrated as Castel Sant'Angelo when, in 590, Pope Gregory the Great, during a procession aimed at banishing the plague, saw St Michael descending above the building. At that time the fortress was already serving a new protective purpose: since the time of Totila (547) it opposed the city and the Roman people; it was therefore planned, even at that time, to place walls around the Borgo and the Vatican. Nicholas III put the plan into effect in 1277 when he built the so-called Pasetto walls because he was planning to move into the Vatican (cf. p. 12). The building itself was also increasingly fortified: Boniface (1389–1404) substituted a central tower for the classical quadriga plinth. After the people of Rome had expelled Eugene IV, the predecessor of Nicholas V, from Rome for ten years, Nicholas (1447–55) added four square-shaped corner towers, each of them dedicated to an Evangelist. The present corner towers (Sangallos the Elder) were built under Alexander VI (1492–1503), and the outer pentagon of bastions was finally erected under Pius IV (from 1561 onwards). A second sequence of extensions and conversions served to make the building into a comfortable papal residence: it was particularly under Nicholas V, but also in the 16C under Julius II and Paul III, that the central tower was, by degrees, turned into a longitudinal section. It was only Urban VIII who abandoned his predecessors' age-old fears and ordered that the walls linking the fortress to the bridge be razed (cf. B96). SG

Bibliography: C. d'Onofrio, *Castel S. Angelo*, Rome, 1984; S. Rowland Pierce, »The Mausoleum of Hadrian and the Pons Aelius«, *Journal of Roman Studies*, 1925, p. 75.

A34 Tempio di Venere e Roma
Foro Romano, Piazza del Colosseo (plan V 1/B)
AD 135

The design for the Temple of Venus and Roma (begun 121, consecrated 135) is said to derive from Hadrian himself. An enormous platform (145 x 100 m) was erected on the site of an atrium belonging to the Domus Aurea (A24). Its long sides supported large porticoes – many of their granite columns have been set up again – which marked out a kind of Forum of Hadrian, entirely dominated by the largest temple in Rome. The monastery of San Francesca Romana (B36) has been built over part of the temple. Remains of the cella are still visible. Bushes mark the place where the columns stood (10 columns at the front, 20 on the long sides).

The core of the building, with the double cella, makes a very Roman impression, but its form derives from the time of reconstruction under Maxentius after a fire in AD 307. In contrast to what occurred in Greece, the two cultic images stood in apses whose backs here abut upon another. The columns inside the building do not divide the area into aisles; they elaborately subdivide the side walls with their niches. The flattened cupola of the apse – with its interesting lozenge-shaped coffers –, and the barrel vaults in the halls, are leading works of Roman vault architecture.

This temple was nonetheless an extraneous element in Rome, a homage to the Greek temple, because it stands above a stylobate, which is a substructure with steps on all sides, and its surrounding ring of columns make it into a genuine peripteros. When the emperor, with the power of Rome at its zenith, built a joint shrine to the goddess of the city and the tutelary deity of its Caesars, he followed his cultural preferences by doing this in the forms of the Greek temple. It may be that this incongruity provoked Apollodoros the architect into uttering his sharp and apposite criticism, which is said to have cost him his life. UF

A35 Tempio di Antonino Pio e Faustina
Foro Romano (plan V 1/B)
AD 141

Larger complexes of buildings were for a long time hardly erected any more after the time of Hadrian. Antoninus ordered, in particular, two temples to be built, one for his predecessor Hadrian (A36) and, before that, one for his wife who died in AD 141. Thus Antoninus allowed the system of adoptive emperors, which emphasized family ties, to shape his architectural programme too. When he himself died in AD 161, he was included in the dedication (in the frieze).

This temple is a podium temple in the form of a prostyle. This type had previously been used for the Temple of Caesar (A1) which was located diagonally in front and in which all that was missing was the colourfulness, a feature that was not added until the time of Domitian (A27) and Trajan (A29). Antoninus was known for acting in a traditional way. This applied in particular to the Roman cult and gave him the epithet of Pius. A time of innovations, such as that in the period from Nero to Hadrian, was not to begin again until a century and a half later. Hadrian's temples either had no prototype (A31) or, being peripteroi, were strongly oriented on extraneous designs, namely Greek models (A34). Antoninus did though adopt the last-mentioned type in the temple he built for Hadrian.

The history of this structure in the post-classical period is exemplary of tendencies in the development of Rome. In the 11C it was integrated into the church, a new building, of S. Lorenzo in Miranda. The first major excavation works on the Forum were performed in the early 16C. The spirit of these years was still having an effect in 1536 when the temple, in preparation for the visit of Charles V, was stripped of all its post-classical additions. Torriani surrounded it with building work again in 1602, as the Christian cult was now again held in higher regard in the Counter-Reformation after the Council of Trent. The new façade followed the type coined in Il Gesù (B1), the main building of the Counter-Reformation. SG

A35 Tempio di Antonino Pio e Faustina

A36 Tempio di Adriano
Piazza di Pietra 91 (plan IV 2/A)
AD 145

This building was part of the larger group of buildings from Hadrian's period on the field of Mars. Two temples standing one behind the other, which both had an eastern staircase and were flanked on both sides by basilicas or porticoes, extended from east to west, from the Corso to the east side of the square in front of the Pantheon. The way led from east to west. A third temple, the Pantheon, stood on the southern side of the square just referred to (cf. A31). The more westerly of the first two temples mentioned above was built by Hadrian for his mother-in-law Matidia. The other temple, which is the most recent in date, opens towards the Corso and was built for Hadrian by his successor Antoninus Pius. This was what custom required. The building was a peripteros which probably had 8 x 13 columns and stood on a high podium. The following features can still be seen today in the wall of the stock exchange: eleven columns from the northern flank; the pedestal built of peperino, 4 m high and located below street level; and the cella wall, formerly with a marble facing. Thus the exterior structure follows a traditional type.

Things are different in the interior of the cella (remains of it can be seen in the stock exchange). A rectangular fringe of columns on high pedestals supported a coffer-work barrel vault which spanned 17 m. Thus, as under Hadrian, the temple interior is intended to be monumental and weighty (cf. A31). The pedestals of the columns had on them depictions of the provinces (today most of them are in the Palazzo dei Conservatori), and this indicates that the provinces were becoming stronger. This was the first time the emperors had come from the provinces: Trajan and Hadrian were both from Spain. Hadrian's administrative reform made the provinces into centres of decision-making. Here the provinces symbolically support the empire.

This building is an eloquent example of the juxtaposition, typical in the period of the adopted emperors, of traditional and progressive structural components (cf. also A29, A32). It is particularly the exterior of temples that follows tradition here (cf. also A31, A34). SG

A37 Tomba di Annia Regilla
Via della Caffarella (plan G2 3/A)
AD 161

This building was formerly thought to be a Temple of Deus Rediculus, the god who had forced Hannibal to retreat. Today it is regarded as the tomb of Annia Regilla, who died in 161. It is part of an entire villa complex which her husband, the rhetorician Herodes Atticus, ordered to be built in memory of her.

Marcus Aurelius ascended the throne the same year. The building is witness to important and radical changes which occurred while he was emperor. This »philosopher on the emperor's throne« had to spend 20 years on his campaigns. It was only the Severans, a later family of emperors, who again built monumental structures. Tomb architecture gained in importance. The only building (A38) erected by this emperor also comes under this category. Regilla's tomb belongs to the type – which was then coming into fashion – of tombs in the form of a house. Many of them are to be found on the Via Appia and in the area around St Peter's. The structural form selected is evidence that people were switching over to burying the dead in sarcophagi. Only the emperors adhered to the

A36 Tempio di Adriano

A37 Tomba di Annia Regilla

method of burial in urns, a method which strikingly explains the small size of the container that held Trajan's tomb (A29). As in some earlier examples (A12, A29), it was intended to portray the ascent of the soul, so that the structure selected was one with a burial chamber below and a temple – here, a podium temple – above. Two octagonal columns in round niches tower above the centrally located door of the burial chamber.

Brick-built structures – a core of cement mortar, faced with bricks – had their heyday under Trajan and Hadrian, when their design principles were fathomed (A29) and they were employed for lofty functions, such as those of the cult (A31). Now, in the conservative second half of the century, this revolutionary technique was also transferred to old architectural types (such as the podium temple), and had thus definitely become respectable. The method of work also became more refined. The clinker was no longer baked after it had been divided up. Instead, a large piece of it was baked and then sawn into pieces, so that deformations occurring during baking were avoided. Borromini (B74) and Portoghesi (M72) later remembered this technique. SG

A38 Colonna di Marco Aurelio
Piazza Colonna (plan IV 2/A)
AD 180–93

Although Marcus Aurelius is buried in Hadrian's mausoleum (A33), his colossal column in the field of Mars is also related to the memory of the dead man: the temple of the deified emperor, and his ustrinum, which is the rectangular crematorium, were located close by. The emperor's column is the third in Rome after those of Trajan and Antoninus Pius, and also accords with the first of these two (A29); its shaft measures some 100 Roman feet (29.6 m), is made up of marble blocks, and, on its spirally arranged relief strips, portrays campaigns, this time against the Germanic tribes and the Sarmatians. However, the composition is much simplified and abandons the naturalism of Trajan's period: the scenery of the regions is reduced to a few abbreviated set pieces; the criterion for the human figures lies in how significant they were; and the narrative tone displays a drastic and ferocious mood.

Ever since the Corso – which runs past the column and was in classical times the Via Lata or Flaminia – was regularized under Paul II, this standing remnant of the classical period has once again played an urbanist rôle. Sixtus V gave the column a new pedestal, an inscription and a statue of Paul the apostle. When some smaller houses outside the façade of the Palazzo Aldobrandini-Chigi (B23) were torn down in around 1660, this gave the area around the column a rectangular shape: it was the Piazza Colonna. Thus this column in Rome was not only the paragon of the imperial column – this was adopted by Fischer von Erfach in the façade of the Karlskirche church in Vienna, because it was a unique and stately form –, but it was also the imperial column in its rôle as the monument dominating a city square. This model was also employed by the emperors of the early 19C: witness Napoleon's Colonne de la Grande Armée in the Place Vendôme (1810), and the column of Alexander (1814) in the palace square in St Petersburg. UF

A39 Catacomba di S. Calisto
Via Appia Antica 102 (plan G2 3/B)
since c. AD 200

The early-Christian catacombs, which in accordance with Roman burial customs are located outside the city walls, are Christian community graveyards in their early form. They often originate from private pagan hypogea (underground burial chambers) which only later, under Christian management, were linked to one another and expanded into long passage systems. The prescribed area was not allowed to be exceeded, but the burial of bodies, which was the only permitted burial-form for Christians, required ever-increasing amounts of space. The passages were therefore embedded into the ground in several storeys. The catacombs had their peak period in the 3C and 4C, but bodies were still being placed in them in the 5C.

The oldest of the Roman catacombs is the Calixtus catacomb which is located on the Via Appia and is named after its earliest administrator, who later became Pope Calixtus I. It dates from c. 200 and was for long used as a burial site for the Roman bishops. The passages laid out in four storeys take up an area of some 300 x 400 m and extend for nearly 20 km. The most frequent form of burial consists of simple niches which were embedded into the walls of the passages and closed in the front with slabs of brick or marble. There are also wall tombs, which have a

A38 Colonna di Marco Aurelio

A40 Tempio di Vesta

round arch, usually with coloured decorations, above the burial site. A more elaborate architectural design, with the niches and columns positioned symmetrically and usually also carved from the unworked stone, is found only in some tomb chapels which branch off from the passages, are imitative of pagan burial chambers in their design, and were able to accommodate united family organizations or colleges. DH

A39 Catacomba di S. Calisto

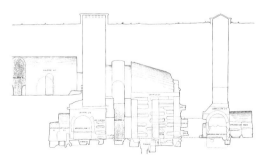

A40 Tempio di Vesta
Foro Romano (plan V 1/B)
c. AD 200

This temple is among the most significant shrines in Rome, and its tradition dates back to the period of the city's foundation. Its cella harboured the holy fire – which had been burning since time immemorial – of Vesta, who was the goddess of the domestic hearth and was among the most important deities in the cult of the Roman state. The round temple is an unusual form for Rome and is explained by the fact that the tholos as an architectural type was intended for chtonic deities, of whom Vesta was one. But it is also reminiscent of the archetypal Italic round hut, which was the focal point of the Roman state. The preceding building, which is alleged to have been founded by Numa Pompilius, the second king of Rome, also adhered to this type. The Temple of Vesta is thus the oldest Italic round temple. The present structure is a modern reconstruction of the building which Julia Domna, the wife of Septimius Severus, ordered to be built. A podium, which was very high by Roman architectural standards, supports the circular hall of Corin-

A41 Arco di Settimo Severo

thian columns, and there are corresponding half columns on the cella wall. Each column stands on its own high pedestal, as in the case of the Arch of Septimius Severus (A41), and also in the Flavian period previously (A25/A26). The rich marble facing, and the vigorous and thorough articulation with its impressive projections and recesses which generate a rich play of light and shade, are typical of Severan and Flavian architecture.

The temple directly adjoins the vestals' house, the courses of whose walls are still discernible. The priestesses lived here in strict seclusion. Their chief task was to maintain the holy state fire, which was never allowed to go out. EJ

A41 Arco di Settimio Severo
Foro Romano (plan V 1/B)
AD 203

By comparison with the Titus arch (A26) which is over 100 years older, the triumphal Arch of Septimius Severus is distinguished by the richness of its architectural subdividing work and of its three-dimensional decorations. It was built at the time of the first Soldier Emperor, under whom the pictorial aspects of Roman architecture gained in significance and the architectural structure was positively flooded with extravagant decorations. The senate and people of Rome built the arch on the west side of the Forum Romanum in AD 203 in honour of the emperor and his sons Caracalla and Geta. The occasion for this was the tenth anniversary of the emperor's rule, and at the same time his victories over the anti-emperors Niger and Clodius Albinus were also commemorated. As in the case of the Titus arch, the onlooker must here imagine the arch as having been surmounted by a quadriga with the statues of the emperor and his sons.

The Septimius Severus arch has a large archway in the middle, flanked by two small ones, and thus follows the type of the tripartite triumphal arch, which is an elaborate variation on the arch of honour that was first developed in the Tiberius arch in Orange and was introduced to Rome in the shape of the Augustus arch (29 and 19 BC, at the eastern end of the Forum Rom-

anum, not preserved). There the side arches were formed as aedicules loosely oriented on the main arch. In the Septimius Severus arch, all three arches are in a single massive block of masonry reaching its conclusion in the weighty attic which is broad throughout. Both façades of this massive block structure have, by way of orchestration, a composite order of columns which, as in the Titus arch, forms a rhythmic bay in each individual case, and thus creates an impressive show wall. The columns, on their plinths and tall pedestals, stand freely in front of the rear wall of the arch and are only attached to that wall by the moulded entablature: this is a particularly graphic example of the type of column that stands out in front. Here the columns also have pilasters behind them. Behind the columns placed loosely out in front, the reliefs exhibit an agitated surface which covers the whole show wall of the arch, and only leaves free the edges of the building. The history of Septimius Severus' victorious campaigns against the Parthians and the Arabs is – in several registers, and with the customary range of triumphal items being employed – related in the four large relief panels above the small arches, beginning on the side towards the Forum and continuing from left to right on the other side. The depiction of the army's departure commences the sequence, which then proceeds with the liberation of the town of Nisibis, the siege of Edessa and the subjugation of the Osroans and King Abgar, and continues to the conquest of the towns of Seleukia and Ktesiphon. The captives of the ancient Romans appear on the tall column pedestals at the feet of the triumphal arch, so that they appear to be carrying the entire weight of the monument. The relief style marks the beginning of relief-work art in the late-classical period, and is related to that found on the column of Marcus Aurelius (A38). The scheme of column reliefs with a surrounding frieze of images was probably taken over from there and here adapted to a horizontal arrangement. Apart from the reliefs, it is mainly the large number of arches that constitutes the particular richness of this triumphal monument.

Apart from the three gates in the façade, there are two smaller arches which are at right angles to them and link the lateral gateways with the central one. The result of this, when the structure is looked at obliquely, is an impression of diversity and abundance, with the light and shade on the intradoi and curvatures of the arches making the massiveness of the building visible. Elaborate in its architectural type, extravagant in its three-dimensional decorations, and ennobled by the free-standing, completely round columns, the Arch of Septimius Severus is among the most splendid triumphal arches in Rome. It seems that one intention in erecting this arch was to surpass the richness and variety found in any comparable triumphal monuments. But this is only achieved at the expense of the proportion and classical balance displayed, for example, by the Titus arch. The Septimius Severus arch is the very model of the architectural type which consists of a three-gate triumphal arch with a rhythmic bay in front of it. This type was to attain great significance in the architecture of more recent times. Since 1470 at the latest, when Alberti adapted the three-gate triumphal arch into a large show façade at the entrance of S. Andrea in Mantua, the triumphal arch was among the great motifs in architecture from the end of the Middle Ages onwards (cf. H7 and elsewhere). EJ

Bibliography: R. Brilliant, »The Arch of Septimius Severus«, *Memoirs of the American Academy in Rome*, 1967, p. 29.

A42 Arco degli Argentari
Via del Velabro, Via Teatro di Marcello (plan VII 2/A)
AD 204

The money changers (argentari) and cattle traders in the Forum Boarium built this arch in honour of the royal family. With its height of 2.90 m, the structure looks too low today in this terrain which has been filled up with earth. Caracalla ordered the name of his wife Plautilla to be removed from the inscription in 211, and that of his brother Geta in 212, on each occasion after they had been murdered. He did the same when deposing his father-in-law Plautianus in 205.

The structure looks small when compared with the imperial buildings which started being built again in the early period of the Soldier Emperors, because peace again prevailed (A41, A43). What is more, the architecture is unpretentious and is reduced to the pilaster pillars and a simple architrave or door lintel. Thus interest is concentrated on the order of pilasters and the reliefs. Late-antique design principles are

A42 Arco degli Argentari

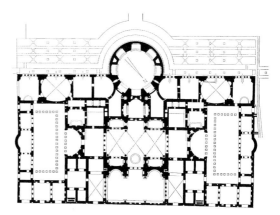

A43 Terme di Caracalla

discernible for the first time: the decorations cover the architecture, including the order of pilasters, like a carpet. The Greek heritage of clarity and tectonics is thus abandoned (cf. A51, of later date). The same applies accordingly to the relief-work sculptures which depict, in the right-hand intrados of the arch, Septimius Severus and his wife Julia Domna making a sacrifice and, in the left, their sons Caracalla and Geta (now removed): the artist did not chisel all round the figures, but used a drill. This is why there is something of drawing or woodcut about them. The content of the reliefs also shows late-antique features: the beards and locks of hair seem to have been taken over from the adopted emperors, but in reality the fact that the locks come in threes points to the cult of Serapis. The same applies to the posture adopted by Julia Domna when praying. The first non-European emperor was here, for the first time, celebrating Eastern cults at the highest level of state. SG

A43 Terme di Caracalla
Viale delle Terme di Caracalla (plan VIII 2/B)
AD 216

The thermal baths on the southern fringe of the city were built during the Severan emperors' dynasty. Opened by Caracalla in 216, they were in operation for over three centuries. They are an ideal embodiment of the type of structure known as imperial thermal baths (cf. A28); it can still be seen today that their purpose extended far beyond mere cleaning requirements. They were among the most important places in public life: the inhabitants of Rome were able, when enjoying a bath, to experience directly the greatness of the imperial founder, and the magnificence of the empire, by admiring the enormous dimensions, the technical perfection, and the luxurious appointments. The standard of those times was never attained again.

The extensive rectangle formed by the surrounding sections of the building is today marked by its ruins and by rows of trees. This was the site of the services that were part of the bathing activity: halls for lectures, libraries and inns, and also cisterns, platforms for spectators, and dwellings for the staff, were located here. The rectangle was adjoined on the inside by parks and areas for sports.

The bathing activity itself took place in the enormous block structure (220 x 114 m) in the centre. Two advantages of the compact concrete of which it is built take effect here: it is resistant to damp, and it is an ideal heat accumulator. Visitors could not see the engineering work, which consisted of the system of water pipes, fires and maintenance passages underneath the bathing rooms. The bathing water was heated in large copper boilers. Hollow areas (hypocausts) below the floors were used to heat the rooms. The hot flue gases coming from the heating, which was done with wood, passed through the hypocausts and, via vertical chimney flues, even heated the walls.

The basis principle of the arrangement lies in placing the bathing rooms in rows along a central axis, with the room temperature increasing continuously. The alignment of the rooms begins in the north, where the large swimming pool, the natatio, is located. The cold bath (frigidarium), the largest room (58 x 24 m), follows next. It is a hall structure, to whose monumental spatial character the surviving side aisles and incipient vaults bear witness. The visitor passes via the tepidarium, which was smaller in size and was a restrained transitional zone, into the large rotunda of the caldarium with its hot-water baths (the ruins are today used as a stand for musicians). Rooms with accompanying functions grow out of this central axis like symmetrical wings. The succession of rooms along the southern frontage probably included some more hot baths, such as the hot-air bath known as the laconicum. The sports halls with their flat ceilings and U-shaped covered walks take up the most space. The entrance areas and changing rooms (apodyterium) are to the north. Staircases led to the sun terraces on top of the complex.

The onlooker must always imagine the sumptuous appointments as having been on a larger scale than what remains today. Enormous monoliths were used for the bathing pools (now on the Piazza Farnese) and the colossal columns. The massive, weighty structures were faced with marble slabs and stucco decorations, the floors were covered with mosaics (the gladiator mosaic is today in the Vatican Museums), and the openings in the walls were closed by large glass windows. There was a very extensive programme of sculptures, as in all thermal baths. The famous classical works of art in the Farnese collection were found here: the bull, the Hercules and the Flora. UF

Bibliography: E. Brödner, *Untersuchungen an den Caracallathermen*, Berlin, 1951; id., *Die Römischen Thermen und das antike Badewesen. Eine kulturhistorische Betrachtung*, Darmstadt, 1982.

A44 Mura Aureliane
(plan II 2/D and plan VIII 2/B)
begun AD 271

After the general decline of the empire in the anarchic circumstances of the 1st half of the 3C, success was, from the time of Gallienus onwards, achieved in recovering its military striking power. This included the building of a new city wall under Aurelian, the Soldier Emperor (AD 270–75); after the fall of the Limes, barbarian invasions had to be expected in Rome.

The wall was 19 km long, extended far beyond the earlier course of the wall, and incorporated large areas in the south and east, as well as Trastevere, which was a part of the city on the other side of the Tiber, and the field of Mars. Existing structures such as the Praetorian camp, the Amphiteatro Castrense, the Cestius pyramid (A19), and the Porta Maggiore (A23), were integrated into the line of defence. It was fortified by nearly 400 rectangular towers which stood 30 m (100 Roman feet) apart and projected beyond the line of the wall. The gates were flanked by round towers. But Aurelian only began the structure. His brick-faced wall (opus latericium) was 6 m high and 3.5 m across,

A44 Mura Aureliane

A45 Porta Appia or Porta S. Sebastiano

and had a concrete core. It was first reinforced by Maxentius (306–12), who used a different masonry in which layers of brick alternate with layers of tufa stone (opus vittatum, cf. A45). In 401/02, under Emperor Honorius and his military campaigner Stilicho, the walls and towers were doubled in height, a second set of battlements was installed, and some gates were, by building additional gates opposite them, expanded into self-contained fortresses (Porta Ostiense). One of the most immense fortifications of the late-classical period thus came into being. It has also been used since the Middle Ages and has repeatedly been restored. This explains its good state of preservation. UF

A45 Porta Appia or Porta S. Sebastiano
Via Ardeatina (plan VIII 2/C)
late 3C AD, converted 5C AD

The Porta Appia, known in the Middle Ages as Porta S. Sebastiano, is the largest and best-preserved city gate in the Aurelian Wall (A44). The present structure replaces an older and much lower edifice with half-round towers and two gates (the Porta Ostiense gives an approximate idea of it). When Honorius, in the early 5C, ordered the city wall to be increased in height, the Portia Appia also had two storeys added to it and was enlarged by adding rectangular flanking towers. The battlemented towers now rise from massive, angular substructures, which a gallery-like upper storey combines into a kind of fortress. The gate was protected on the side towards the field by a portcullis, and on the city side it could be closed by the wings attached to it. Today the Museo delle Mura is inside the gate.

The gate took its name from the Via Appia, which ended here, in the south of the city. Tradition has it that it is the oldest Roman road. What is unusual is that its name is not derived, as was otherwise customary, from its point of destination (Via Ostiense) or from its function (Via Salaria), but from the name of its builder, the censor Appius Claudius Caecus, who completed the road in 312 BC at the same time as the first Roman water channel, the Aqua Appia (A22). The significance of the Via Appia was initially mainly military. It ran along the coast through the Pontine Marshes as far as Capua, and was later continued to the seaport of Brindisi. The road surface, built above a supporting structure of lime mortar, was a paving made up of hard basalt stones and has survived to the present day. EJ

A46 Terme di Diocleziano
Piazza della Repubblica (plan VI 1/A)
AD 298–306

The most important new building constructed in Rome in the period of the tetrarchs was the thermal baths which Maximian erected in AD 298–306 and dedicated to the second Augustus Diocletian. Imperial thermal baths were a proven architectural type (cf. A28 and A43) which, here, was altered only in the de-

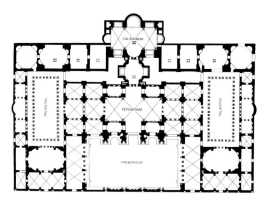

A46 Terme di Diocleziano

tails. Space was created for the record figure of 3 000 bathers.

The appearance of these baths today differs from that of the ruins of Caracalla's thermal baths, as the large main rooms never fell down. This was why the Renaissance architects took particular interest in them (there are valuable drawings of the structure mady by Palladio and Anonymus Destailleur) and from the 16C on they were included in the new building work. Such parts as the caldarium and the surrounding sections were largely destroyed in this process, while others are outstandingly well preserved because they were put to a new use. The frigidarium and a domed room in the southern corner were converted into churches (H42 and B32), the tepidarium serves as an entrance area, and a smaller room with hot baths became a planetarium. The large exedra suggested the idea of providing a strong urbanist emphasis (K16). In 1889, the Museo Nazionale Romano was set up in the eastern sections, which are not only an ideal framework for the celebrated sculptures in this museum in the thermal baths, but also show the effect produced by, and the vistas to be found in, the ancient successions of rooms. The remains of the show wall, nearly 100 m wide, of the natatio can be seen in the courtyard, and they are the best-preserved example in Rome of this type of façade, which probably derives from theatre architecture. It consisted of column orders, aedicules and niches for statues in a luxurious arrangement. UF

A47 Tor De' Schiavi
Parco dei Gordiani (plan G1 3/C and plan IX 4/D)
c. AD 300

This round structure built in c. 300 stands on the site of the Gordian villa on the Via Praenestina and is a tomb temple. It is called Tor De' Schiavi after a later owner. What with the segment of wall that has been broken out of it, the temple resembles an architectural model in that it displays the wall-building engineering, the thickness of wall, and the architectural design, that were found in the late-classical period.

A47 Tor De' Schiavi

This concrete rotunda is a successor to the Pantheon (A31), having similar niches in the interior. They are alternately semicircular and rectangular in shape. The diameter is reduced (about 14 m), and the structure is simplified. But the lighting by means of oculi at the onset of the dish of the dome is an important innovation. The exterior is also faithful to the prototype in that it is a bare cylinder structure with a few cornices; there was also a vestibule, here with four columns at the front and an open-air staircase.

However, the different structural idea should not be overlooked. It is reminiscent of older cylindrical mausoleums (A12, A33). The rotunda, which is here completely exposed like a monument, harbours within its tall, round podium an entire basement: this is a circular hall with a barrel vault and a sturdy central column. The niches in the outer wall here were intended to contain sarcophagi which were accessible via an entrance at the rear of the building. The free-standing mausoleum in the form of a two-storeyed round temple with a separate burial chamber is a particular late-classical type which, after having its beginnings in Diocletian's temple in Split, reached its peak in Rome.

This picturesque ruin in the Campagna met with much attention on the part of the architects of the Renaissance and the Baroque, both as a mausoleum and certainly also because of the idea of the oculi, which was capable of further development. UF

A48 Villa di Massenzio
Via Appia Antica 153 (plan G2 3/B and plan VIII 2/C)
AD 306–12
Maxentius ordered a spacious complex to be built on the site of a 2C villa on the Via Appia. Some monumental rooms intended for display, of which the con-

cha of the throne room has survived, were built within the previous structure. The real core of the complex is a centrally planned structure surrounded by a vaulted portico measuring 100 x 85 m, and stands directly on the Via Appia. The surviving basement of the large rotunda is a burial chamber which is reached by some elaborate staircases, so that the rotunda is regarded as the mausoleum of Romulus, Maxentius' son who died young. But the mausoleum was probably, in imitation of other imperial tombs (cf. A15 and A33), intended as the mausoleum of a future dynasty of Maxentius. This would have meant that the upper storey was the Temple of Hercules, his personal tutelary god.

Games in honour of the deceased were held in the adjoining circus, which is among the best-preserved racecourses for horses to survive from classical times. The racecourse, 520 m long, is divided in the middle by a tall barrier (spina) with a water pond and round half-way marks. Numerous fittings are today scattered across Rome. The entire western side is taken up by the starting arrangements (oppidum), with its tall towers and, between them, the masonry-work starting boxes (carceres). The western side is rotated away from the axis in such a way that all the teams had equal chances at the start. The stands for some 10 000 spectators, and the remains of the imperial lodge upon which the organizer allowed the crowd to honour him, can also be seen. In the late-classical period generally, the circus had become the site of the ruler's cult, and this was why no imperial residence was without one (cf. also A27). UF

A49 Tempio di Divo Romolo
Foro Romano (plan V 1/B)
AD 307
This small domed building on the Via Sacra is in outstandingly good condition, and stands outside the southern part of today's church of S. Cosma e Damiano (C11). Erected in the early 4C, is was restored in the 17C and given a lantern. Even the building's original bronze portal, a typically Roman one with a frame and panels, has been preserved.

The purpose of the building is disputed. The rotunda is usually described as a Temple of Divus Romolus, as the building work was probably begun by Maxentius, the father of Prince Romulus who died young,

A48 Villa di Massenzio

A49 Tempio di Divo Romolo

and can be related to images of memorial round edifices to be found on coins minted in honour of Romulus. But perhaps it was a matter, here too, of portraying Maxentius' dynastic intentions (cf. A48). Interpretations alleging that it is a Temple of Jupiter Stator are based on classical descriptions of the buildings in the Forum. Others see the rotunda as a monumental entrance area leading to the Forum Pacis.

In terms of its architectural layout, the temple is a group of three structures consisting of a rotunda flanked by two rectangular halls with their long sides facing forwards. There are apses in the halls. The combination of a round building with a façade which, being concave, curves away from the building behind it is of interest from the point of view of architectural history: this curving show wall, with its niches for statues, contrasts excitingly with the rotunda. The flanking rectangular structures are less well preserved. Along with the columns standing in front of them, they combine with the façade and the rotunda to form a richly subdivided architectural group. It cannot be denied that Baroque architects were inspired by it (cf. e.g. B71). UF

A50 Basilica di Massenzio
Foro Romano (plan V 1/B)
begun AD 308

The building work actively pursued under Maxentius reached its peak in this basilica on the Via Sacra. It was precisely here that he proved to be the »conservator urbis suae«. Following the tradition of the great emperors, he gave the Forum a new basilica which had a larger volume (the main room alone measures about 80 x 25 x 35 m) than any other enclosed area there. As a type it is based on the thermal bathing

halls, and it is among the very highest achievements of Roman vaulted architecture.

Confusion reigns as regards the assessment of the architectural forms, as the word »basilica« refers not only to the practical purpose but also to an architectural type (A11), and today has the third sense of an honorary papal title for churches regardless of their form. Only the first of these applies here: it was a market and judgement hall. But there is only one aisle; the only possibly basilican feature is the cross-section. The surviving northern series of three partial rooms shows that the rooms were not aligned; each room is an extension or an attached room that relates to the dominant central hall. The attached rooms are divided up by the large projecting walls which also had the technical function of abutments supporting the main vault. The passageways through the walls are of no importance to the spatial impression created. The barrel vaults are at right angles to the main room. The architect was not concerned with adding any aisles, but with providing a subdivided but coherent spatial volume, and with creating a spatial impression which was oriented on the central axis, was of monumental effect, and included the idea of the enormous attached rooms subordinating themselves to the larger main room like satellites.

Only the beginnings of the vault of the central room are still discernible. It was a typically Roman groined vault with coffer work, and had a large, simple but dignified form without subdividing wall arches. The continuous barrel was intersected by lunettes which resembled transverse barrels and led to the large windows of the clerestory. As the barrel and lunettes approach their lowest point, they converge into narrow bases located at the feet of the vaults, above the colossal columns of the main room. One of the columns remained in situ until 1614 (today it stands outside S. Maria Maggiore). It therefore looked as though eight columns were supporting the bold vault with its wide span. But at the same time the solidity of the structural design above the walls of the attached rooms also remained perceptible to the onlooker. In this architectural type, the building as a whole, and the subdivisions in the form of massive walls on the one hand

A50 Basilica di Massenzio

and colossal, well-structured columns on the other, combine to create a full and powerfully emotive spatial impression.

The basilica of Maxentius perfects the type of structure found in thermal bathing halls, but this fact only encompasses part of the architectural idea. Those bathing halls were always transversely located, whereas the large apse in the west here provides a new kind of orientation in the longitudinal axis. Under Maxentius, it was here that the body of judges sat. But the apse was not a real point of aim, because it was separated from the hall by barriers. It was only later that Constantine the Great, to whom the Senate dedicated the building in AD 313 after his victory at the Milvian Bridge, discerned the tendencies to be found in the succession of transverse vestibule, hall and apse: this is the type, widespread in the late-classical period, of the imperial throne room, which is also found in the basilica in Trier, said to have been built by Constantine. He therefore placed his own image, a colossal seated statue, in the apse (today its remains are in the Palazzo dei Conservatori). A new apse on the north side, and another entrance towards the Via Sacra, were added for the tribunal. Building work in the Forum reached its truly imperial conclusion in this combination of the hall structure from the imperial thermal baths on the one hand and the imperial throne room on the other. UF

Bibliography: H. Kähler: »Konstantin 313«, in: *Jahrbuch des Deutschen Archäologischen Institutes*, 1952, p. 130.

A51 Arco di Giano

A51 Arco di Giano
Via del Velabro (plan VII 2/A)
early 4C AD

Today this building is identified as the Arcus Constantini, which Constantine's regional catalogues mention for Regio XI. It is a tetrapylon with four arches, and two passages which intersect in the form of a cross. This type of structure was known since the time of Augustus (Cavaillon), but equal importance was not given to all four sides until the Arch of Galerius was built in Thessaloniki in the period of the tetrarchs. It was in that period that Constantine then assumed the dictatorship. Like the earlier examples, Janus Quadrifrons was probably topped by a superstructure, but this was removed in 1830 along with the medieval tower which the Frangipane family had placed on top.

Janus is the Roman designation for this structural type, and is at the same time the name of the god of routes and beginnings. His shrine in the Forum Romanum consists of two passages which were opened in wartime and closed in peacetime. Constantine chose the point where two old routes intersected as the site for this structure. One of them ran from the venerable Forum Boarium (cf. A7) to the Velabrum depression and thus to the political Forum Romanum. The Cloaca Maxima also followed this route. The second route, proceeding from north to south, was the trade route to which Rome owes its origin (p. 9).

There are two characteristic design principles, both of them in the Roman late-classical spirit: the building is subdivided by niches with shell-shaped vaults and, between the niches, by small columns (now lost) supported on corbels. These elements are placed so regularly and so close together that the impression of a glittering carpet is aroused, very much at variance with the weighty, cube-shaped mass of the building. A feature of similarly atectonic, late-classical design is the horizontal strips which line Janus Quadrifons on all sides, even in the passages, thus degrading him to a mere bearer of linear decoration. SG

A52 Arco di Costantino
Via di S. Gregorio (plan V 1/B–1/C)
AD 312–15

This, the largest and best-known triumphal arch in Rome, is a repetition of the type found in the magnificent triumphal Arch of Septimius Severus (A41). As with that arch, the reason for building it was the emperor's tenth anniversary, but the prime intention was to set up a monument to Constantine the Great's victory over Maxentius at the Milvian Bridge in 312. For the first time, it was not Rome's triumph over a foreign people that was now being celebrated, but instead the elimination of a Roman rival. Thus the arch is witness to the inner disintegration of the Roman Empire, which was soon to collapse. In 1536 Charles V, who regarded himself as a successor to the first Christian emperor, marched into Rome through Constantine's triumphal arch.

A52 Arco di Costantino

The Constantine arch follows the type of the three-gate triumphal arch, with an order of columns on high pedestals standing in front of it, and with the characteristic graduation of the heights of the three arches. Once again, a rhythmic bay is created. It forms the large gateway in the middle and the two lower arches into an impressive show façade. A tall attic, adopting the rhythmic subdivision of the structure beneath it, forms the upper conclusion of the monument. The Constantine arch does not, in terms of structure, contain any new inventions when compared with the Septimius Severus arch (A41) which is about 100 years older. But its subdivisions are better proportioned and it is more well-balanced in the distribution of the surfaces and in the arrangement of the relief-work panels. This weighty monument is broad and solid, and the three gates fit harmoniously into the massive structure. The broad arrangement of the structure, and its secure firmness, distinguish this arch from the Septimius Severus arch with its tall proportions, the narrow design of its gates, and the attic above which weighs down too heavily upon it. The significance of the Constantine arch is primarily due to its abundant reliefs. Like the architectural subdividing elements, nearly all the reliefs derive from older buildings which stem from the time of Trajan, Hadrian and Commodus and were veritably cannibalized in order to decorate this arch. The development of relief-work art over a good two centuries can here be followed as in a museum collection. As in the Septimius Severus arch, captive barbarians, and goddesses of victory, are depicted on the column pedestals. On each of the façades there are four tondi from the period of Hadrian, which are the most striking decorations here. They depict hunting scenes whose subject matter belongs in another context. All that was done was to re-work the heads of Hadrian and turn them into portraits of Constantine. Statues of Dacian warriors stand above the columns. The attic itself is faced with large relief panels from the time of Commodus (scenes from the war against Quadi and Marcomanni). The reliefs from the Constantine period are a narrow frieze of figures which runs around the arch above the narrow archways and continues beyond the flanks. They illustrate the historic event which marked a turning point in world history and was the reason for building the arch. Beginning on the narrow western side and continuing via the southern side to the northern, the reliefs portray the army's departure from Milano, the siege of Verona (above the left southern arch), the battle at the Pons Milvius (above the right southern arch), the triumphal procession in Rome, the speech made by Constantine from the Rostra (above the left northern arch; a rare depiction of the Forum Romanum with the triumphal arches of Severus and Tiberius and the Basilica Iulia) and, finally, the »congiarium«, the distribution of money in Caesar's Forum on 1 January 313. The rough, ungraceful working and the severe, hierarchical style of the figures mark a fundamental reorientation in Roman relief-work art and directly foreshadow the art of the Middle Ages. The use of spoils taken from older Roman buildings, and the lack of innovation, express the diminishing greatness of Rome and the heralding of the end of the Roman Empire.

The well-balanced, broad proportions and impressive size of the monument, the quality of the reliefs assembled here, and not least its historical value as the last Roman honorary memorial to have been erected, all rightly go to make the Constantine arch the most famous of all the Roman triumphal arches. EJ

Bibliography: A. Giuliano, *Arco di Costantino*, Milan, 1955.

A53 Ninfeo degli Horti Liciniani
Via G. Giolitti (plan VI 2/B)
AD 320

This ten-sided room, 33 m high and just under 25 m in diameter, is, by reason of stamps on the bricks, dated in the late-Constantine period, and no longer in that of Galerius (c. 300). The incorrect notion that this nymphaeum was dedicated to Minerva Medica de-

A53 Ninfeo degli Horti Liciniani

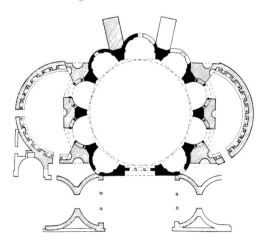

rives from a Minerva statue which was discovered. This building, as its size suggests, served to impress the onlooker. Its original structure was not massive enough and too audacious. When the work was finished, some rooms attached for support, and the transversely oval vestibule, therefore had to be added. Despite this, the dome fell down in 1828.

The ten-sided room is surrounded by a ring of conchae which is interrupted on the entrance side; until the first renovation, the two pairs of conchae at the sides were translucent. The wall was replaced by open, curving rows of columns. Here, the architecture of Hadrian's period, particularly the Piazza d'Oro in Tivoli, clearly served as a model (A31, A32). But the alternation of round and rectangular niches is now dispensed with, and the conchae stand directly next to one another in a row. Neither are the conchae now concealed from the exterior view, but instead they shape the building. The drum above the row of conchae also has ten sides, and is breached by large windows. In the time of Nero and Hadrian, the light was allowed to enter only through the apex of the dome (A24, A31), whereas later, under Caracalla, it could come in laterally through the clerestories or the wall of the drum (A43), but the openings had never been as large as they are here. The round dome is reinforced by brick nervations, which do not though conduct away any of the pressures. No dome in Rome had ever previously made such a free outward impression as did this one. The circle of niches, the centrally planned type of building, and the nervations, mean that the building is probably the most important forerunner for such Byzantine structures as S. Sergios and Bakchos (Byzantium) and S. Vitale (Ravenna). This nymphaeum later aroused the enthusiasm of Renaissance architects. Even the very first genuine centrally planned building, Brunelleschi's S. Maria degli Angeli, followed its model. SG

A54 Mausoleo di S. Elena
Via Casilina 643 (plan G1 3/C)
before AD 330

The reason for this building's present name, Pignattara Gate, is that amphoras (pignatte) were built into the vault in order to reduce the weights to a minimum. This was just as important to Roman concrete building as was the stable chemical compound of lime and pozzolana earth. But this is a detail. This round structure was originally planned as a mausoleum for Constantine. When he moved the seat of government to Byzantium in 330, his mother, St Helena, was buried here.

At first glance, this is an ordinary late-classical tomb rotunda, as it again has windows at the onset of the dome, and niches which are alternately semicircular and rectangular (cf. A47). The porphyry sarcophagus of the deceased stood in the eastern niche. However, this rotunda goes far beyond its predecessors in terms of shape and architectural idea. The sarcopha-

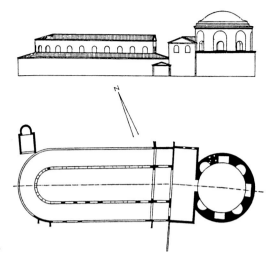

A54 Mausoleo di S. Elena

gus is now no longer placed in a burial chamber in the basement. The rotunda itself becomes the burial chapel. And it is no longer isolated, but is linked by a narthex to the basilica in the west, which has today been excavated, to form a bipolar group. That combination of burial chapel and cemeterial basilica which remained characteristic of 4C basilicas (except for the Lateran basilica) is here found for the first time: all these structures are tomb churches which are dedicated to martyrs or saints, in the present case the martyrs Marcellinus and Petrus. Thus it is typical for a memorial building for saints or martyrs, in the form of a basilica with an ambulatory, to be combined with another structure, frequently a mausoleum in the form of a rotunda. It was commonly the mausoleum of the founder, in this case St Helena (cf. similar examples in C1, C14). The exterior of the rotunda is marked by a low surrounding circle which partly anticipates the ambulatories found in the tomb rotundas of slightly later date (C1), and also by the window openings which are covered by trough-shaped intradoi. It is here (and contemporaneously, and still more clearly, in Trier) that the Romanesque arcature begins to take shape. Many of the tendencies in medieval church architecture are already to be found in this rotunda. SG

1 day: A1, A9, A11, A16, H36, A27, A26, A40, A35, A49, A50, (A34), A52 (Forum Romanum and Palatin).
1 day: A15, A18, A31, (A36), (A38), A13, A20, A29, (A24), A25, (A43), A6, A7, A42, A51, A17 (early Imperial period and Forum Holitorium).

Christian late antiquity and Middle Ages (313 to 1377)

Constantine and the beginnings of Christian church building (A54, C1)

In the early 4th century Rome's late-antique cityscape was dominated by the building activities of the pagan emperors. The Christian community, which at first included only a small proportion of the population, led a subordinate, inconspicuous existence, dependent on the favour of the emperor of the day. Their places of assembly were private houses, which were called »tituli« according to the names of their owners (e.g. »titulus Clementis«), of which there were about 25 in Rome in the 4th century. Christian burial places, the extensive catacombs, remained concealed under the ground. The crucial turning-point came in the year 312 with Constantine's victory over his co-emperor Maxentius at the Milvian Bridge, which he ascribed to support from the Christian God. It was not until he entered the city and subsequently issued the Edict of Milan (313), which permitted unlimited religious freedom, that the way was cleared for Christian architecture.

As well as some important public buildings, which derive at least in part from Constantine's initiative (see Introduction to the ancient period A50, A52), he and his family had a decisive influence on subsequent Christian architecture with the earliest official buildings for Christian worship that they founded. Constantinian church building has a number of characteristic building types and functions.

The first building he commissioned, shortly after 313, is the Lateran basilica (S. Giovanni in Laterano), which was built on imperial land on the edge of the city, and was presented to the bishop of Rome as his cathedral. The original structure, which still survives amidst the Baroque rebuilding (B66), was a basilica with nave and four aisles; there was a clerestory above the nave, and the aisles became successively lower. Nave and aisles had an open roof structure. A characteristic feature are the colonnades edging the sides of the nave, while the aisles were separated by columned arcades. At the west end – Constantinian basilicas did not yet face east – a semicircular apse concluded the nave. Before this apse side rooms emerged from the ground plan, but these did not develop into actual transepts until later buildings. The form of the Lateran church is a direct continuation of the building type of the pagan basilica with several aisles that was widespread in Roman antiquity (A11). Its fundamental characteristic was to serve as a poly-functional spacious assembly hall. In contrast to these pagan basilicas which are rarely be found unambiguously oriented by an apse, the early-Christian basilica is now submitted to a strictly hierarchical orientation to an apse constituting its liturgical centre. However, it is typical of ecclesiastical building under Constantine, and points the way for all medieval architecture in Rome, that the building is not vaulted, which clearly distinguishes Christian architecture from monumental (pagan) structures like for example the basilica of Maxentius (A50), which was completed just before the Lateran church.

The exterior of the Lateran basilica was strikingly plain, in brick, while the interior was lavishly decorated with mosaics, marble and spoils (reused parts of ancient buildings, especially columns and architectural ornament) – an important feature of early-Christian architecture. Constantine built a free-standing baptistery west of the basilica (C8), and an accommodation for the bishop nearby, which formed a complete cathedral complex.

The first church of St Peter, initiallly constructed in the second quarter of the 4th century, on the site of the apostle's traditional grave, was also a basilica with nave and four aisles, and again on imperial land (Old St Peter's). Constantine had large areas of an ancient (pagan) necropoly filled in so that the choir of the church, in the west, could be situated directly above the apostle's grave. While the basilican form of Old St Peter's, which survived until the church was re-built under Julius II (H7), and has been well preserved in drawings, is close to that of the Lateran church, a crucial innovation are the transepts inserted between the main building and the apse. Lower than the main building, they were separated from the nave by an arch, the so-called triumphal arch, and from the aisles by inserted columns. This meant that the transepts were part of the apse in liturgical terms. A baldacchino at the point of transition between transept and apse indicated the apostle's tomb below, while the altar was placed in the semicircle of the apse. To the east of the building was a preceding courtyard, the atrium. Thus here the basilica with nave and four aisles, in contrast to the Lateran cathedral, functioned as a tomb church above the grave of the apostle prince, thereby acquiring particular distinction.

S. Giovanni in Laterano

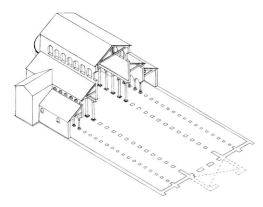

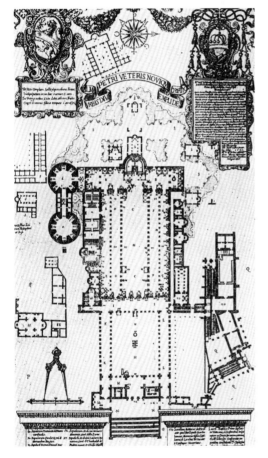

Old St Peter's

ambulatory around the apse in the west. They are known as ambulatory basilicas because of their form, or cemetery basilicas because of their situation and function.

The earliest example of this type was the basilica consecrated to the martyrs Marcellinus and Petrus, buried in a catacomb on the Via Labicana, again on imperial land (A54); other examples are S. Lorenzo fuori le Mura (C13), S.Agnese fuori le Mura (C14) and S. Sebastiano (B37). It is typical of these memorial buildings that they were not built directly above the martyrs' graves, but at places close by, while the grave itself was marked quite simply (or in later times, as in the case of S. Lorenzo and S. Agnese, with fairly modest church buildings). These basilicas, whose interiors were themselves burial places, were usually surrounded by mausoleums, of which two of the imperial ones are significant: that of the emperor's mother Helena (A54), which is assumed to have been originally intended for Constantine himself and was added to the east of the basilica of SS. Marcellino e Pietro, and that of his daughter Constantina, which was situated at the side of the basilica of St Agnes (C1, C14) founded by her.

The third group of Constantinian buildings includes centrally-planned buildings with various forms and functions: one is the Constantinian Lateran baptistery (C8), which presumably took the form of a timber-clad octagon. It was the first free-standing baptistery, and inaugurated a building type that was particularly effective in Italy until the High Middle Ages. As well as this he had built the imperial mausoleums of Helena and Constantina (A54, C1), also centrally-planned buildings, which as vaulted rotundas with niches used familiar forms of Roman architecture (A53).

Thus Constantinian architecture shows close connections with that of ancient (pagan) Rome, adapted very slightly to the needs of Christian worship. The basilica type was established as the dominant form of Christian ecclesiastical building in Constantinian architecture, which was varied for use as a cathedral, tomb or memorial church. However, the most distinctive feature of Constantine's building policy was that Christian churches were built mainly on imperial land, which meant that they were clearly private foundations by the emperor, alongside his public urban building activities. With the exception of S. Giovanni in Laterano, which is just inside the city walls, and the nearby palace church of S. Croce in Gerusalemme (B134), his foundations – appropriately to their status in relation to tombs, which were never inside the city precincts – were all on roads leading out of Rome and thus outside the city proper. No churches were built in the Roman old town, where the Christian community continued to use the earlier house churches (tituli) for their assemblies.

The second building type established by Constantine includes memorial basilicas, which were built at venerated martyrs' graves or memorials, and were in the form of a piered basilica with nave and two aisles; the aisles were arranged as a semicircle as an

The architecture of the post-Constantinian period (C2–C14)

After the foundation of Constantinople in 330 and the emperors' move from Rome their building activities in Rome declined considerably. The great reduction in population and economic losses at the time of the migration of peoples – the Visigoths under Alaric took Rome in 410, destroying a great deal – meant that only very few secular buildings were erected in subsequent centuries. People settled increasingly in a cramped central area and used the surviving buildings from the imperial period, so that new buildings from the medieval period are almost exclusively ecclesiastical. It was only at this time that churches started to acquire increasing political significance, especially as under the emperor Theodosius in 391 all pagan worship was forbidden and Christianity became the state religion.

After an interruption following the death of Constantine, new church buildings did not start to appear until the late 4th century. The building commissioned by the three reigning emperors Valentinian, Arcadius and Theodosius in 386 over the tomb of the apostle Paul (S. Paolo fuori le Mura, C2), where Constantine had built only a small sanctuary, takes over the Constantinian basilica with nave and four aisles. The building, which is considerably larger than Constantine's basilicas, is directly modelled on Old St Peter's, but introduced crucial changes by using columned arcades instead of colonnades in the nave as well, and by the fact that the church faced east, the first example in which this can be proved. It also deviates in the form of the transept, which runs through unbroken (e. g. by a crossing) as in Old St Peter's, but is the same height as the nave. The position of the altar has also changed. It is now placed directly above the apostle's tomb, which establishes a concrete connection between the altar and the reliquary for the first time. S. Paolo fuori le Mura is the last of the Roman basilicas with nave and four aisles, and also the last imperial foundation; from now on all the churches in Rome were to have ecclesiastical funding (by bishops, popes, congregations).

The next century (late 4th century to c. 500) saw a particularly large number of new churches. There were isolated new foundations, and many existing tituli were replaced by churches, now starting to appear in the inner city as well. All buildings in this period follow a modest deviation from the Constantinian basilica in the form of a basilica with nave and two aisles, usually with columned arcades and immediately adjacent apse, with no transepts. S. Sabina (422–40, C6) is a particularly good example of the high point of this period. Here too the plain exterior in brick stands in marked contrast to the decorative interior, which was lavishly provided with mosaics in the apse and on the walls, costly marble incrustation and ancient spoils (some renovation). Large windows corresponding with the intercolumniation below make the building very light. This form was now to become »standard« for Christian basilicas in Rome, and with slight variations (piers instead of columned arcades in S. Lorenzo in Lucina, for example, C29; insertion of a transept in S. Pietro in Vincoli, C9) remained the principal type in Rome until the High Middle Ages.

Two important papal foundations differ from this: S. Maria Maggiore (C7) and S. Stefano Rotondo (C10), and also the alterations to the Lateran baptistery (C8), all of which go back to Sixtus III (432–40) or his immediate successors. In S. Maria Maggiore we see the basilica with nave and two aisles in especially lavish, classical form. The usual arches are replaced by colonnades with an austere entablature reminiscent of Constantinian buildings leading directly to the apse, which was originally immediately adjacent. The building, which is also larger than other basilicas of this type, is also closer to the Constantinian foundations in this respect. A completely new and singular spatial form was found for S. Stefano Rotondo, a circular, centrally-planned building whose basilican raised central space was originally separated from two ambulatories by an inner colonnade and an outer columned arcade. Thus the scheme of the Constantinian basilica seems to be transferred to a centrally-planned building, with the outer ambulatory additionally divided into various spatial compartments. Also the alterations to the Lateran baptistery put in train by Sixtus III show more strongly classical features with an austere inserted colonnade, so that it is possible to speak of a first (Sistine) renaissance within early-Christian architecture.

There was practically no new building in Rome in the 6th century, probably because of political unrest and clashes with the Ostrogoths and Lombards. Characteristically this period saw the first examples of ancient buildings, at first only secular ones, being converted into churches (which was probably why they did not succumb to dilapidation or destruction). Examples include the incorporation of the church of SS. Cosma e Damiano (C11) into a Roman building in the Forum Romanum or the erection of S. Maria Antiqua (C12) in ancient buildings at the foot of the Palatine, and also the conversion of the Curia (A16) into S. Adriano. It was not until 609, under Boniface IV, however, that the first pagan temple, the Pantheon (A31) was consecrated to Mary, which represents a crucial step.

There was very little new building at the turn to the 7th century, but the few examples include the basilicas of S. Lorenzo and S. Agnese fuori le Mura (C13, C14), now both built directly over the tombs of the saints. They both represent the type of the basilica with galleries, which is unusual in Rome, though common in the Eastern Roman empire. The architectural ornament in both churches also shows clear borrowings from Byzantine models, which seems to be a characteristic trait of this epoch and shows the increasing influence of Constantinople, as the Byzantine empire had spread over large sections of Italy after the Ostrogoths were driven out after about 550. The desire to place the altar over the martyr's tomb and for better access for the increasing number of pilgrims, which is presumably expressed in the galleries of these buildings, which were directly accessible from the outside, was a characteristic of the policy of Gregory the Great (590–604), who had numerous diaconates built to accommodate pilgrims. The original building of S. Maria in Cosmedin (C26) is an important example of this. In accordance with the increasing veneration of relics he had a circular crypt built around the apostle's tomb in Old St Peter's, which made it possible for the pilgrims to circulate with ease, and that here too it was possible for the altar to be placed immediately over the tomb.

The idea of Renovatio Imperii Romani under the Carolingians (C15–C22)

After the influence of the Byzantine East had had a decisive influence on Roman architecture in the 7th and 8th centuries, in 800, under the Carolingians, there was a clear tendency to think back to the tradition of early Christian late antiquity. Charlemagne's coronation as emperor in Rome marked the beginning of an ambition to continue Roman world domination. Charlemagne was not just Caesar and Augustus, he explicitly proclaimed that his intention was a »Renovatio Imperii Romani«, a revival of the Roman past, as it had been before Byzantine dominance. This concept of renewal was all the more heterogeneous as knowledge of ancient Rome was at best vague; among other things the »Golden Age« was to be conjured up again, during which Rome was the city of the emperors, above all of Constantine the Great, and the capital of the Christian world. Above all there was a desire to be independent of the Byzantine supremacy of the immediately preceding centuries.

Building measures under Pope Leo III (795–816) marked the turning point between a fundamentally Eastern building tradition and the new tendency to think back to early-Christian architecture. The rebuilding programme for the church of S. Anastasia, which has Baroque cladding today, was influenced by early-Christian models, and so was the partially destroyed new building of S. Stefano degli Abessini behind St Peter's. In S. Anastasia the borrowings from early-Christian buildings in the 4th century can be seen above all in the monumental proportions, which include larger, axis-related windows, and the addition of an atrium. It is even possible to identify definite models for similar features in S. Stefano degli Abessini. The entrance to the church was through an atrium, colonnades divided the nave from the aisles, the transept was linked with the aisles by double openings, the triumphal arch between the main building and the transept was supported by piers, and a semi-circular apse with a circular crypt and confessio beneath it concluded the continuous transept. All these elements are clear reminiscences of 4th century early-Christian architecture in Old St Peter's and the early 5th century in S. Paolo fuori le Mura (C2). Subsequently Eastern building forms with their complicated spatial arrangements (galleries, pastophories) were completely abandoned in favour of the more lucid spatial divisions of the early-Christian basilicas. Under Pope Paschal I (817–824) a series of church buildings bearing the mark of early-Christian architecture came into being (C17, C18). In S. Prassede (C18), a well-preserved example, the scheme of the colonnaded basilica with nave and two aisles with continuous transept opening into the aisles with double passages, and a semicircular apse with circular crypt below has been applied. The spatial proportions in the nave are light and open, borrowing from those in the models, Old St Peter's and S. Paolo fuori le mura, the window openings are double and oriented strictly axially to the colonnades. Despite the reduction in building forms in comparison with the great basilicas there was no lack of splendour. The interiors of the Carolingian buildings are resplendent in magnificent, extravagant decoration with marble, ancient spoils and mosaic. Even the technique of regular brick masonry, which can be seen in the window arches, which are constructed of three rows of brick, a technique that had disappeared since the 6th century, was used again, even though the technical quality of early-Christian architecture was never achieved again. Even the additional chapel of S. Zeno records a return to »forgotten« tradition. In the 4th century S. Peter, S. Paolo fuori le Mura and S. Sebastiano were surrounded by mausoleums with centralized ground plans. The S. Zeno chapel combines this function with that of a memorial chapel. S. Maria in Domnica (C17) and S. Pressede (C18) pick up building types developed in the 4th century, and are thus perfect examples of the renaissance of the early-Christian basilica, which characterized Roman architecture in the decades between 800 and 820.

For the next generation of churches, built between 820 and 850, other models clearly became influential. A debt was still owed to early-Christian basilicas, but now more notice was taken of the large 5th-century basilicas (C16, C20). The hallmark of this phase is greater plainness and simplicity. In S. Cecilia (C16), a building conceived very similarly to S. Prassede, there was no transept and the walls are supported by columned arcades. S. Marco (C19) is also similar to the great 5th-century basilicas without transept like for example S. Sabina (C6). A variant on this is S. Martino ai Monti (C21), whose colonnades are more reminiscent of S. Maria Maggiore (C7).

In the mid-9th century new influences start to show. In the pontificate of Leo IV (847–855) the two churches of S. Maria Nova (S. Francesca Romana, B36) and SS. Quattro Coronati (C22) were built. Archaeological traces suggest that S. Maria Nova was a smaller version of S. Martino ai Monti, with the fundamental difference that the classical atrium was again replaced by the roofed porch (narthex), which was usual until the 8th century. Even more obvious are the changes in the church of SS. Quattro Coronati. The rows of column in the nave are here interrupted for the first time by a central pier. A pilaster on the front of it and reaching to the roof-truss divides the main section into two bays, which interrupted the flow of accumulating columns and made the space rhythmical. The massive gatehouse tower, probably also an influence from north of the Alps, brought an unusual accent to the fixed ensemble of atrium and church building. The great variety of building forms that characterized Carolingian building north of the Alps admittedly has no parallels in the tradition-conscious building style in Rome. When the Carolingians lost power (from 860) the short but vigorous building spurt in Rome came almost to a standstill.

The early-Christian architectural tradition in the Romanesque period (C23–C37)

Before Roman architecture was able to be reborn in the early 12th century the city sank almost into insignificance for almost two centuries. Power struggles among the Roman aristocracy, who controlled the fate of Rome and the papacy, caused a situation that was often like that of a civil war. The papacy had reached its nadir in terms of morals, finance and political power. Pope and emperor fought bitterly to defend their power bases, and were not afraid to go to war over this. Sacking by the Normans under Henry IV in 1084 had a devastating effect on the architecture of Rome.

It was from the reforming orders, first and foremost Cluny, from whose ranks constructive opposition grew in the 11th century. The Cluniac Benedictine monk Pope Gregory VII (1073–85) emerged as the leading mind in the second half of the 11th century. He vehemently defended the Papal guidelines in the investiture dispute, and his policies were a turning-point for Rome.

In the early 12th century significant building activity once more started, hesitantly and modestly, after only small, unimportant chapels or Christian churches had been built in ancient temples since the last flowering of architecture in the Carolingian period (A4). A number of variations on the basilica, which were to determine the image of medieval churches, developed as new, large-scale building projects were initiated. The great Roman building tradition started again with the new building for S. Clemente (C25). Between 1110 and 1130 the 4th century early-Christian structure was replaced by a new building richly decorated with

mosaics and liturgical equipment. The plan of the church is simple, with its nave and two aisles divided by columned arcades, the small, closely-placed clerestory buildings that are typical of this period and the large main apse. The building's exquisite quality lies in the use of ancient spoils from its predecessor and above all its magnificent furnishings. Striking spatial proportions, which have survived in their purest form in S. Giovanni a Porta Latina (C24) and S. Maria in Cosmedin (C26), are also a feature of the architecture of this period. The naves are steep, but never cramped, as the foundations of previous, early-Christian buildings were often used, the windows are small and do not relate to the arches below, or to the colonnade zone. The early-Christian basilica with nave and two aisles and a main apse is retained as a scheme, but now appears in a completely new guise. The simplest possible architecture is used as a frame for the most lavish furnishings, principally based on Cosmati work (often inscribed Cosma), by the group of craftsmen, who operated in Rome from the 12th to the 14th century and specialized in decoration using the finest marble inlay work (incrustation). New parts of the building like the cloister, the campanile with its typically Romanesque blind galleries and the colonnaded porch, placed in front of a simple basilican cross-section façade are the hallmarks of medieval architecture in Rome. A particularly well-preserved example of this type is S. Maria in Cosmedin, where the rich exterior ensemble of church, porch and campanile has survived, and the interior reflects medieval furnishing with schola cantorum and Cosmati floor.

All medieval churches in Rome completely eschewed features of Romanesque architecture north of the Alps like articulation of the wall by placing things in front of it, monumental vaulting or »tower landscapes« that are visible and effective over long distances. In this they remained obliged to the late-antique tradition. The church of S. Maria in Trastevere (C28) shows how harmoniously the early-Christian building tradition mixes with elements that are entirely ancient. The size alone, which is about the same as S. Sabina (C6), is impressive, and underlines the great prestige of the new building. While in the interior the period of Christian antiquity seems to have been resurrected, the exterior of the church and the characteristic composition of its elements – the basilican cross-section façade has a narthex in front of it and a campanile on the right aisle – reveals that it was built in the 12th century. But late-ancient components in the interior are the two magnificent rows of columns composed of ancient spoils that fringe the nave and direct the eye to the triumphal arch, which is also supported by massive columns. The short transept inserted before the apse shows links with Old St Peter's and S. Paolo fuori le muri. The small clerestory windows, however, are anything but ancient. The three apses that conclude the nave and both aisles and the transept, which scarcely rises above the side aisle, certainly show that the 12th-century building type is rooted in the great early-Christian basilicas, but the immediate model is to be found in the important abbey of Monte Cassino (started 1071).

A version of the 6th-century galleried basilica also found its way into medieval architecture. Galleries, opening to the nave in triple arches, were introduced into the smaller new building for SS. Quattro Coronati (C22) after destruction by the Normans in 1084. During the next hundred years the image of the medieval church changed very little. The building form and decoration of S. Maria in Trastevere were used again for S. Lorenzo fuori le Mura (C13) about a century later. Only individual elements vary the standard type, as for example in the tri-apsidal eastern conclusion of S. Saba (C30). Existing older buildings were often given colonnaded porches or gabled porticoes as motifs for their entrances, and the popular campanile, in wich all the delight on decoration of the Romanesque period could be developed, was often simply added later – because it was free-standing. The blind galleries that appeared so much in the north remained alien to Rome. It occurs only in the apse of SS. Giovanni e Paolo (C5). Not least of the features

to establish itself in Roman architecture was the continuous, high transept, as presented as a model in S. Paolo fuori le Mura (C2). Even Old St Peter's was given a »proper« transept in 1154, and so were S. Croce in Gerusalemme (B134), S. Maria Maggiore (C7) and the Lateran basilica (B66) as late as 1291.

Finally, the church of S. Maria in Aracoeli (C36) shows the consistency of the Roman building tradition. Gothic with its characteristic steep spaces had already spread throughout Europe when Rome was still clinging on to brightness and breadth, columned arcades and the flat roof of buildings shaped by early Christianity. It is at most in detail that the Gothic formal repertoire has made its mark. The only exception is the Dominican church of S. Maria sopra Minerva (C37), to which the Gothic church of S. Maria Novella in Florence served as a model, despite the continued effect of the Roman building tradition.

The Middle Ages came to an end in Rome with a final phase of deep recession. When the popes left Rome to live in Avignon in the great schism of 1309 to 1377, this lead to profound political and financial collapses. Nothing large or significant was built in this period. It was only when the popes returned that architecture began to flourish again. AG/DH

The »Sette Chiese« in 1575. Etching by A. Lafréri

C1 S. Costanza

C1 S. Costanza
Via Nomentana 349 (plan G1 2/B and plan II 3/D)
c. 326/29

In the early 4C, Constantina, the daughter of Constantine the Great, ordered the mausoleum to be built for herself as an annexe to the large basilica (C14) founded in honour of S Agnese.

The simple rotunda on the model of Roman tombs was given considerable variation and expansion in S. Costanza. The structure of the building – an elevated circular edifice with a concentric double ambulatory – can be seen from its exterior. The outer ambulatory, which has not survived, was formerly an open, circular, colonnaded hall which, following the tradition of the classical circular temple, lent the building a distinctly ancient Roman character. However, the step-like graduation of the heights and rear sides of the various buildings transcends Roman models and here, for the first time, shows the basilican scheme being transferred to a rotunda (but also cf. A54). The mausoleum could be entered from the southern aisle of the basilica via a vestibule which has not survived, but was transversely arranged and had apses at the sides.

The core of the complex is a tall, perfectly round, domed room. Inside, twelve arcades on double columns support the drum-like cylindrical wall which opens far above into a bright fringe of large round-arched windows. A dome, formerly open at the apex, completes the room. The twelve arches are arranged above a circular ground and make for a circular continuum of twelve arcades. However, the emphasis is less on the arcades that are cut evenly into the wall than on the splendid pairs of columns which are lent special significance by the massive entablature sections which, what with the swelling frieze, make a very three-dimensional impression. It is only this entablature, resting weightily on the rich composite capitals, that orients the double columns radially towards the centre. The columns are the delimitation between the core structure and the low ambulatory, which surrounds the bright domed area like a dark background

shade. The weighty circular barrel vault which only has small slits for lighting, and the massive circular wall whose thickness is only made all the more apparent by the fringe of wall niches, render the ambulatory narrow and dark. Thus the emphasis is on the greatest possible contrasts, in which bright breadth is opposed by dark narrowness, the lightness of the arcades differs from the heaviness of the wall which harbours the fringe of niches, and the circular structure of the column stands against the hollowness of the niche. Another finesse is the manner in which the two visual axes crossing one another are subtly emphasized within the central structure: firstly by means of the arcades of the main axes which, here, are broader and higher and whose columns are oriented almost orthogonally and not radially, and secondly by the niches which are on the main axes and are continued down to the floor. The main axis from the entrance to the altar is also accentuated by the differently coloured column shafts of red granite. Those shafts also lend distinction to Constantina's splendid porphyry sarcophagus (today the original is in the Vatican) which is placed in front of the main niche. Originally, the princess's mausoleum gleamed in shimmering splendour. All the walls were, on the model of large Roman staterooms, incrusted with marble, and the vaults and floors were covered with delicate mosaics. The furnishings were lost when the building was made Baroque in 1620, but have been very exactly handed down to posterity in Antonio da Sangallo's drawings and elsewhere. They show that some chief elements of the architectural subdividing work have been lost along with the system of decorations. Thus the domed area originally had a two-storey order of pilasters which axially combined the arcature and the fenestration in vertical paths. These paths were continued across the mosaics of the drum and into the apex of the dome. In this way the central area was linked into a wider architectural context. The only surviving mosaics are in the ambulatory. In each case there are two mosaic panels located opposite one another and agreeing with one another in the ornamentation, which extends from severely geometrical patterning (probably an adaptation of ancient vault patterns) through scattered patterns against a bright background to arrive at depictions of Cupids harvesting and pressing grapes. The only distinctly Christian portrayals are in the mosaics of the niches, showing the law and the keys being handed over to St. Peter.

The furnishings and architecture mark S. Costanza out as a typical building from the transitional period. A new kind of spatial interpretation announces itself in the differentiated lighting arrangement, in the decided distinction between main room and side room, and in the abandonment of clear surveyability and of regular half-light. EJ

Bibliography: F. W. Deichmann, *Frühchristliche Kirchen in Rom*, Basle, 1948; A. Schmarsow, *Der Kuppelraum von S. Costanza*, Leipzig, 1904.

C2 S. Paolo fuori le Mura
Via Ostiense (plan G2 3/A and plan VII 1/C–2/C)
384–410, 1823–54

The tomb of St Paul lay on the road to Ostia, far out-side the Aurelian city wall (A44). The foundation stone for what, until St Peter was rebuilt, was the largest church building in Rome was laid in 384 under the emperors Valentinian II, Theodosius and Arcadius above a small sheltering hut which had served as a memorial site. S. Paolo is one of the seven pilgrimage and cardinal churches, and counts among the five pa-triarchal churches, the basilicae maiores. Although lo-cated outside the territory, the church and monastery are part of the Vatican State. This immense basilica with a nave and four aisles was completed after the very short construction period of less than ten years. But the furnishings were only finished between 400 and 410 under Emperor Honorius. In 441, a fire or earthquake caused great damage to this building which the poet Prudentius (384–405) extolled as the »Golden Cathedral«. Rich mosaic decorations, of which some much-restored remains survive on the triumphal arch, were donated by Pope Leo I (440–61) and Empress Galla Placidia as part of the repair work. Only a few structural alterations to S. Paolo were made over the centuries. A Benedictine abbey (cf. the cloister in C32) was built on the southern side in 936. Alessandro Galilei placed a portico in front of the façade in 1750, during the rule of Pope Benedict XIII. If a devastating fire on 15 July 1823 had not almost completely destroyed the outstandingly well-preserved early-Christian building work, then the most pristine of the significant early-Christian churches would have come down to posterity in the shape of S. Paolo. But as it turned out, although the historicizing reconstruc-tion by L. Poletti (completed in 1854) attempted to re-produce the old structure largely in accordance with the original, hardly even any remains still survive of the old substance of the building. All that was spared by the fire is the mosaics on the apse and on the trium-

C2 S. Paolo fuori le Mura

phal arch. Numerous engravings and drawings pro-duced before or shortly after the fire give an authentic idea of what the overall original structure looked like.

The early-Christian succession of rooms, with the atrium placed in front of the church façade, has been rebuilt in S. Paolo. The historicism of the reconstruc-tion falsifies the original in a slightly sugary way, but this is negligible in view of the significance of the over-all ensemble. This elongated church building is plain and undecorated on the outside. The idea of an early-Christian imperial basilica can still be sensed in the interior. Like Old St Peter's, this basilica with a nave and four aisles has a continuous transept which has apses but, in contrast to the older structure, was of the same height as the nave. Despite the greater sig-nificance of Old St Peter's, this type of transept pre-vailed in the Christian churches built in the following centuries. S. Paolo is the first large basilica whose nave and aisles are separated by columned arcades. The nave is characterized by lucid breadth and mod-erate brightness. Its proportions date back to the orig-inal structure and show the characteristic well-bal-anced weighting of the individual architectural ele-ments. Mural paintings were attached above the ar-cades in the nave. The round-arched windows above them, with their transoms, bathed the interior in a uni-form light. The formerly open roof frame was, after the reconstruction, replaced by a closed coffer-work ceil-ing. The windows in the clerestory, above the arcades of the inner aisles, were walled up, and as a result the aisles are now much darker than previously. Here, it is now only the proud abundance of columns with a Corinthian order that is effective. Seen in combina-tion with the columns leading to the nave, they form a positive forest of columns. This richness of individu-al elements comes to a resounding conclusion in the immense triumphal arch which is supported by two colossal granite columns with an Ionic order. The point upon which the main longitudinal section of the church is oriented is the semicircular main apse and the apostle's tomb in the transept. The splendid trium-phal arch gives the apse and the tomb an ennobling framework, while at the same time the area behind them is marked off from the congregation area and stands out separately. AG

C3 S. Balbina
Piazza di S. Balbina (plan VIII 1/B)
2nd half of 4C

A new structure, whose earliest mention as a church dates from 595, was erected in the 4C above a Ro-man residential house from the 2C. Apart from some later alterations, mention should be made of a thor-ough restoration in 1929–39, which attempted, in rad-ical fashion, to recreate the original state by rebuilding the parclose and the transom windows.

The interior is a broad area to each side of which six chapel niches, low in height, are attached; they have alternately rectangular and semicircular conclu-

C4 S. Pudenziana

sions. The clerestory lit by large windows, and an open roof framework, both rise above this. The room is oriented on the apse which opens out in tall and broad fashion. A niche with a bishop's throne placed in it stands in the middle of the apse. The altar placed beneath the triumphal arch, and the restored schola cantorum, impart the typical impression of an early-Christian church. What marks out this 4C structure, apart from its unusual breadth, is firstly the rare occurrence of a hall type (replacing the basilican form) with lateral chapel niches, which was not unusual in heathen buildings, and secondly the separate niche located in the apse (cf. the so-called basilica of Junius Bassus, c. 350). The question arises of whether the S. Balbina edifice was very strongly influenced by contemporaneous heathen structures or was perhaps itself built as one such, especially as its mention as a church dates from as late as 595. Examples like S. Balbina may have been a model for early-Renaissance churches, whose architectural type is frequently that of a hall area with lateral niches (cf. F17). DH

C4 S. Pudenziana
Via Urbana (plan V 2/B)
c. 390
The façade of S. Pudenziana – a modest historicizing conversion by A. Manno, 1870 – does not look very promising, but the great age of the façade can be inferred from its location well below today's street level. Legend has it that Pudenziana, whose father gave shelter to St Peter, founded the building. But in reality this is the only instance in which a secular ancient basilica was converted into an early-Christian church (between 390 and 400). The basilican thermal bathing hall with columned arcades along each side dated from AD c. 150, and was turned into a church by converting one of the short sides – they curved in segmental arches – into an apse. This was done by walling up the clerestory window and attaching the famous, but much-restored, mosaic showing Christ teaching. In addition, the entrance had to be moved from the long side to the other short side.

However, this basilican construction, with its delicate marble columns, often had to be rebuilt. The main longitudinal section of the basilica was lengthened in the 6C with the use of some original columns that were still available. In the high-medieval period, a campanile typical of those times was built, the aisle walls were repaired, and the arcades in the nave were reinforced. To this end the columns were encased with pillars and the arches were strengthened with cross girders. The building reached final degeneration in the late 16C when F. de Volterra gave it a barrel vault with lunettes and, in the choir, built an intersection with a dome over it. The aisles were partly converted into chapels. It is therefore a great advantage that the restoration performed in 1927 uncovered the ancient substance of the walls with their arches and columns, with the aim of directing the onlooker's interest towards the building's venerable age and architectural history. UF

C5 SS. Giovanni e Paolo
Piazza dei SS. Giovanni e Paolo (plan VIII 1/A)
c. 400, 12/13C
This basilica is on the western slope of the Caelian hill, directly on the Clivus Scauri, an ancient stretch of road whose old paving is still discernible. The original structure of today's building was erected above a complex of ancient residential houses in which the Roman palace officials Johannes and Paulus suffered martyrdom in AD 362. Pammachius, a student friend of Hieronymus – the latter was a Father of the Church – abandoned the first oratory and, in c. AD 400, built above the ancient residential structures a columned basilica (one nave, two aisles), the core

C5 SS. Giovanni e Paolo

structure of which still survives today. Conversion works were performed in the mid-12C, when the vestibule and campanile were added. Further alterations made in the early 13C give this early-Christian basilica the appearance of a Romanesque structure today. The old interior fell victim to being extensively redesigned in the Baroque style in 1715–19. The building's original state, at least in its exterior structure, was restored after 1948.

The church façade by Pammachius is obstructed today by the Romanesque columned portico, but was originally a magnificent show wall which opened towards the east as a double-storeyed columned arcature. The five large arches in the end wall of the nave had their counterpart in the substructure, where the arches of the columns led directly into the church interior. This church, which was in this way entirely opened up to the light, was aptly described as a »basilica aperta«. The clerestory had a double row of windows, with round arches and circular windows whose traces can still be clearly seen in the masonry. The large apse, whose massive roundness rises high above the slope of the Caelian hill and is visible from afar, is also part of the basilica by Pammachius. Since the 13C, it has had a dwarf gallery of the Lombardic type, consisting of radially oriented transverse barrels above small free-standing columns. The image of the apse seen from the old Clivus Scauri road which is spanned by weighty relieving arches has since time immemorial been one of the best-known and most beautiful sights in Rome. The richly articulated campanile above the remains of the temple of Claudius (AD 54) completes the group of Romanesque additions.

Despite being redesigned in the Baroque style, the interior has retained the proportions of the early-Christian basilica. It follows the type of columned basilica which has a nave, two aisles, no transept, some arcades in the nave, and a main apse in the east. This broad and formerly still taller space (the coffer-work ceiling was not inserted until 1598) was majestically tranquil and well-balanced. It was not until the 13C that the broad nave was subdivided and rhythmized by the addition of flying buttresses.

Today the visitor walks from the right aisle into the ancient substructures. The confusing complex of buildings includes three residential and kitchen buildings, which are separated by a narrow courtyard and form an insula on the angular plot of land between the Clivus Scauri and the temple of Claudius. These are rare examples of urban apartment blocks whose two-storeyed façades can still be discerned on the outer wall of the northern aisle. The refined domestic culture of Roman classical times is documented by the furnishings, some remains of which survive. There are a wine cellar, a hypocaust bath and an elegant nymphaeum. In the 3C, the two houses on the Clivus were converted into a private house which also contains the first oratory, the germ cell of today's church. A confessio, from whose windows there is a view of the martyrs' tombs, was later installed above the ancient stairs of the house. For the reason that it is pervaded by ancient and early-Christian structures, SS. Giovanni e Paolo is a significant historical building in which the creation of early-Christian architecture can be followed very graphically. EJ

C6 S. Sabina

Piazza Pietro d'Illiria (plan VII 2/A)
422–40

The construction of the church during the pontificate of Coelestin I (422–32) is described in large mosaic letters in a dedicatory inscription in the interior, on the entrance wall of the basilica. This states that it was built to the order of a presbyter known as Petrus who came from Illyria. From an entry made in the Liber Pontificalis under Pope Sixtus III (432–40), it may be deduced that the church was probably not consecrated until that Pope's period of rule. But most of the construction work was almost certainly performed during Coelestin's pontificate. A Roman private house was excavated underneath part of the church, and this lends probability to the old tradition which relates that the new structure was built above a titular church in the private house of Sabina, a Roman matron. The former overall complex, which included a basilica, a quadriportico and a baptistery, extended between the two ancient routes of the Aventine hill, namely the Vicus Altus in the north-west and the Vicus Armilustrii in the south-east. In 1219, Pope Honorius III handed the church over to the Dominican order. The latter ordered the building of a Romanesque cloister which is a model of the Romanesque joy of ornamentation. The conversions carried out on the church in the 16C and 17C were eliminated when it was restored from 1914 to 1919, so that although this basilica with a nave, two aisles and a central apse is largely undecorated today, its architectural shape has been entirely preserved. S. Sabina is a particularly good example of the normal type of a 5C basilica.

The exterior of this simple and severe brick building is best looked at from the Parco dell'Aventino (Parco Savello). The only decorations in the energetically rounded apse and in the walls of the main section of the building are the large round-arched windows which surround the entire upper part of the building. The colonnades of the portico on the west wall were closed with masonry in the 10C in order to protect the valuable doors of the main entrance. The famous wooden doors date from the 5C. Scenes from the Old and New Testaments are depicted in the reliefs, the technique for which was learned from late-classical sculptural art.

The interior of the columned basilica (one nave, two aisles) displays the following features which characterize this architectural style stemming from the late-classical period: a harmonious ratio of height to breadth, of bright expansiveness, and of well-balanced elegance in the proportions. The architectural means are

C6 S. Sabina

employed sparingly but effectively. The round-arched arcades of the aisle run towards the massive central apse without being interrupted by a transept. The apse is the point on which the church is oriented. The arcades are borne by twenty exquisitely chiselled, fluted columns with Corinthian capitals dating from the 2C AD (spoils). The comparatively widely set columns are typical of the 5C in which the basilica was built (contrast the forest of columns in S. Paolo fuori le Mura, C2). The fact that there is neither a transept nor any additional aisles amounts to a reduction in the architectural means employed, accompanied by a concentration on the basic shapes. The marble incrustations in the arcaded zone are a small surviving remnant of the originally rich wall decorations. The wall zone above the arcades was, like the apse and the triumphal arch, decorated with mosaics. The characteristic lighting conditions are a factor in the overall impression created. The large round-arched windows, which almost entirely break up the clerestory and continuously surround the entire building, light up the nave with uniform brightness. The openings are closed by transoms which in this case consist of extremely thin alabaster segments. This, despite the numerous large openings, means that the light is by no means harsh, but only pleasantly bright. The slightly shaded aisles complete the splendid main room. AG

C7 S. Maria Maggiore
Piazza di S. Maria Maggiore (plan VI 1/B)
432–40
S. Maria Maggiore is the first monumental church dedicated to the Mother of God, and this makes it the »mother« of, and the model for, numerous subsequent churches. It is one of the seven pilgrimage or cardinal churches of Rome, and also one of the five patriarchal papal churches, the basilicae maiores. It was of central significance to the propagation of the cult of the Virgin Mary from early-Christian times onwards. Despite numerous alterations, the spatial impression produced by the splendid 5C papal basilica, with its nave and two aisles separated by colonnades and the large

semicircular apse framed by a triumphal arch, has been excellently preserved.

It is recorded that a church was founded on the peak of the Esquiline hill in the period of Pope Liberius (352–66). But the furnishings and structural forms of the church that survives today, and the entries in the Liber Pontificalis, suggest that this first church foundation was largely destroyed when the Vandals invaded. It is a proven fact that Pope Sixtus III (432–40) issued the order to erect a new building. Once the Visigoths were expelled in 410, heathendom was finally defeated. Christianity gained a position of power which grew ever stronger and had to be demonstrated to the outside world by means of splendid church buildings. The new architecture harked back to the splendid architecture of the Roman Empire's classical peak period, the aim being to manifest the significance of the new Rome, which was not to be inferior in any way to the now-extinct Roman Empire. S. Maria Maggiore is the chief building of this so-called Sistine renaissance, which is rich in variations, and in which the basilican scheme was re-interpreted, while new formulations (C8, C10) of the centrally planned structure so popular in the classical period were also put into effect.

It was not until the late 13C, under Pope Nicholas IV (1288–92), that the narrow transept with its two apses was inserted between the church's main longitudinal section and the original apse. It is not clear whether that old apse, with its late-classical mosaics, was completely destroyed in that process or whether parts of it were re-used.

The church was given its new, splendid campanile in 1377, with the old Romanesque parts being employed. With its 75 m, this campanile is the highest in Rome, and also has the most decorative subdivisions found in that city. They differ from storey to storey. In contrast to the earlier campaniles (cf. e. g. C21, C26, C28), that of S. Maria Maggiore is a self-contained structure. The onlooker's gaze is captured by the rich

C7 S. Maria Maggiore

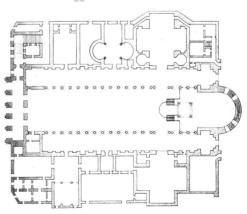

decorative forms placed upon this building. It may be assumed that, here too, the size and exuberance of the decorations amount to public expressions of will, because it was particularly in the 14C that, owing to the papal schism, little building work was being done in Rome, and it is very probable that the campanile, visible far afield, can be interpreted as a symbol of the Roman papacy's dogged resistance.

In the mid-16C, building work was begun which radically changed the church both outside and inside. In the interior, the clerestory of the nave was redesigned in 1593. The old stucco framework was taken down, and every second window was walled up. In the 16C to 18C, chapels were attached and the façade and apse were redesigned (cf. B20, B97, B132), with the result that hardly any of the early-Christian church is still discernible in the exterior structure.

Despite the conversion work inside the basilica, the outstanding grandeur of the congregation area (one nave, two aisles) from the early-Christian period is still preserved. A classically formed entablature is supported by two rows, each of twenty columns, which are admittedly spoils, but nonetheless harmonize excellently in terms of both size and material. The architrave which runs horizontally right across, and the well-oriented Ionic capitals, intensify that optical impression of depth which comes to its magnificent conclusion in the semicircle of the apse. Each of the majestic columns with their precisely worked capitals is a dignified form in itself. Placed in succession close together in the typical early-Christian way, they look almost never-ending, and create a processional route possessing a festive majesty that can scarcely be excelled. The nobility of the impression produced is characterized by a workmanlike and artistic precision. The entablature – which is sculpted in masterly fashion and consists of architrave, fascias, cyma (egg-and-dart moulding) and a frieze depicting creeping plants – is concluded by a moulded corbel. The large order of pilasters in the clerestory wall continues the rhythm of the columns. This means that, despite the dominant gap created by the entablature, the upper section is linked to the lower.

The delicately-worked former stucco decorations no longer survive today. The windows, which are now walled up, also render the original structural idea unclear. In similar fashion to S. Sabina (C6), the onlooker must imagine to himself that there was formerly an uninterrupted row of transom windows. These were framed by small columns placed within, which themselves stood on some other short, small columns surrounding the mosaic panels. The mosaics were in a layer which stood further back, and they were framed by aedicules that had alternately segmental and triangular gables. The light which entered in uniform fashion, along with the late-classical mosaics that still survive today, gave the wall structure a shimmering and uncommonly splendid appearance. The perfection of the former decorations can best be reconstructed by examining the mosaics that still survive. The composition, the gravity of the figures, their gestures and poses, the colours, and the impressionist technique employed, all stem from the artistically outstanding frescoes and book illuminations of antiquity.

The flat coffer-work ceiling from the late 15C accords with a similarly designed early-Christian conclusion to a spatial area. This building was a kind of public declaration of policy: the ancient classical period and imperial splendour were here reborn in the Christian spirit. AG

C8 Battistero S. Giovanni in Fonte
Piazza di S. Giovanni in Laterano (plan VIII 2/A)
after 313, 432–40

There was a Roman villa which belonged to the Laterani family and had existed since the 1C AD. In connection with the Lateran basilica, Emperor Constantine ordered a baptism church to be built above a circular hall which was part of the villa's thermal baths. This baptistery is among the earliest surviving, and numerous later baptisteries were influenced by its shape. It has not yet proved possible to clarify its architectural history, as the building erected by Constantine was subjected to considerable changes under Sixtus III (432 to 440), and also in the 16C and 17C, and there are differing views regarding which of these periods

C8 Battistero S. Giovanni in Fonte

the individual changes belonged to. The baptistery is to the north-west of the basilica. The present structure is a plain octagonal brickwork building in front of which, to the south, there stands a vestibule which has two porphyry columns placed within it and ends in two apses. The octagon and vestibule form a visual unit and are typical for late-classical architecture.

Compared with the clearly structured exterior, the interior has a more complicated shape. The octagon surrounds an area which is divided into a central section and an ambulatory by the insertion of a two-storey architecture of columns which is itself octagonal. The entire width of the central section, which is higher than the ambulatory, surrounds the late-16C round piscina which serves as a font and is the functional centre of the baptistery. The lower colonnade consists of monumental porphyry columns supporting a massive architrave which bears an inscription concerning Sixtus III, and above this there follows an upper order of columns, which is lighter because the columns are smaller. The chapels on the sides of the octagon were added from the 5C to the 7C. The decorations of the entire main inner area date from the 16C and 17C.

It has not yet been possible to clarify which sections of the baptistery go back to the Constantine structure and which others are part of the later alterations. The octagonal columned insertion is, due to Sixtus III's inscription on the inner architrave, usually said to be part of the conversion work performed under Sixtus III, but the shape of the original Constantine structure is unclear. It is true that the octagonal shape, and the vestibule which ends in two apses, are both features which are typical of late-classical and early-Christian architecture and were also employed in Constantine architecture (the octagon in the Church of the Nativity in Bethlehem, the vestibule in S. Costanza, C1). Nonetheless, the fact that the forms of the entablature in the inserted Sistine colonnade and in the outer vestibule are homogeneous might support the theory that the octagon was completely rebuilt under Sixtus III. Round-shaped foundation walls might even prompt the assumption that the original structure was round, thus adopting the round shape of the previous thermal bathing hall. But it is to be noted that the centrally planned architectural form, suitable for a baptistery, characterizes this early-Christian building. Although that form was often employed in the classical period for other structures such as thermal baths and mausoleums, it is linked here with the vestibule in a manner typical of early-Christian architecture. It is probably the earliest baptistery to have the form of a detached centrally planned structure, and is thus likely to have inaugurated this architectural type which, particularly in Italy, remained effective until the end of the high-medieval period. DH

Bibliography: G. B. Giovenale, *Il Battistero Lateranense*, Rome, 1929; G. Pelliccioni, *Le nuove scoperte sulle origini del Battistero Lateranense*, Vatican City, 1973.

C9 S. Pietro in Vincoli

C9 S. Pietro in Vincoli
Piazza di S. Pietro in Vincoli (plan V 2/B)
before 439

Eudoxia, the wife of Emperor Constantine III, ordered the construction, above a Roman domus, of a basilica to house the chains of St Peter which had been transferred to Rome. It was consecrated by Sixtus III in 439. The building was altered, mostly under Giuliano della Rovere, who was the titular cardinal of the church and later became Pope Julius II. He attached the cloister and portico to the exterior and extensively restored the interior, with the groined vaults in transept and aisles coming into being in this process (his tomb, designed by Michelangelo, is in the southern transept). The interior was decisively altered in 1705 when Francesco Fontana inserted a flat-vaulted ceiling in the nave, thus impairing the original lighting conditions.

This early-Christian structure, of which much survived, consists of the main basilican area (one nave, two aisles), an apse, and a transept which does not extend beyond the outside lines of the aisles. Close-standing rows, each consisting of ten classical Doric columns, support round-arched arcades which probably originally continued in the transept, thus producing a tripartite transept. This arrangement is unique because it differs from the continuous »Roman« transepts of Old St Peter's and S. Paolo fuori le Mura (C2) in employing a new method which is an extraneous element in Rome, with models presumed to derive from the Greek East. The proportions of the basilica, with a very broad nave and narrow aisles, are a feature which lends the continuous rows of columned arcades the impression of a broad street of columns. Although S. Pietro in Vincoli is, in this respect, a typical example of early-Christian architecture in Rome, it did not initiate a trend: the other form of transept had no successor. DH

C10 S. Stefano Rotondo

C10 S. Stefano Rotondo
Via S. Stefano Rotondo (plan VIII 2/A)
468–83

This building erected under Pope Simplicius (468–83) came at the end of the first post-classical renaissance which Pope Sixtus III began with his buildings (C7, C8) and in which the complexity of late-classical interior design was, for one last time, revived over a period of nearly 50 years. The structure consisted of a central rotunda, surrounded by two concentric circles (overall diameter 65.80 m). Thus the design of the large basilicas with a nave and four aisles is here – a unique feature for Rome – transferred to the rotunda. Four chapels also cut into these circles and projected above them, although in the ground plan they were flush with the outer circle. Thus a Greek cross graphically pervaded the rotunda. The central rotunda (23 m high, 22.30 m in diameter) is formed by a circle of 22 Ionic granite columns which have a horizontal architrave and support a cylindrical wall that formerly had 22 round-arched windows. The first circle, an ambulatory, still survives, while the second was divided into eight parts, four of which contained chapels, while in those in between there were probably gardens. Each of the gardens was entered through two doors in the circular wall. The visitor passed from the gardens through arcades into the ambulatory, or else laterally into the chapels. Thus the second circle was not a mere decoration, and was separated from the first by arcades.

The building still makes a light and diaphanous impression today, but it is much reduced. The Romanesque masonry suggests that it was Innocent II (1130 to 1143) who made the main alterations, probably as a result of the devastation of Rome by the Normans (1084). The building had to be consolidated. To this end a three-part arcade was built transversely across the rotunda. Of the four chapels, only the eastern one was retained, and of the gardens, only the one adjoining to the north: it was to this garden that the entrance was moved. The 36 arcades which stood between the ambulatories and were borne by columns were walled up. This was how today's outer wall came into being. It can still be seen in that wall that

the arcades for the chapel entrances (in each case there were four columns flanked by two pillars) extended further upwards than those that led to the gardens (here there were five columns and six arcades in each case). The spatial impression suffered again under Nicholas V (1452–54): 14 windows in the central rotunda were walled up, and the others reduced in size. The chapel in the east had a further chapel added to it in the 18C.

The building's function is unclear. It has the round shape of early-Christian martyria and is dedicated to the arch-martyr Stephanus, whose cult began to prosper when his tomb was found near Jerusalem in 415. However, the building never housed a relic of the saint. Neither is it mentioned as a diaconicon or titular church before 1118. For these reasons, where the architectural idea is concerned, reference is made today to the (ruined) Anastasis, the church of Jesus' resurrection, in Jerusalem. That church probably had a lightweight, conically shaped dome (cf. Calot's engraving, 1609), and it can be supposed that S. Stefano also had one such, because although the narrow surrounding cornice in the rotunda makes it possible to infer that there was a vault, it would only have been a lightweight vault made of earthenware tubes. Thus it would for the first time no longer have been the late-classical tomb rotunda that served as model, but instead a church of the Resurrection such as then became usual in the Middle Ages. Martyrdom and resurrection are quite lively expressed in the central rotunda which, amidst dark ambulatories, is flooded with light. The Acts of the Apostles relate that Stephen saw the open sky when martyred. Thus, at the end of the series of classical round buildings, there comes another with an altered structural idea. The building also stands on the threshold of the Middle Ages. The rotunda loses its late-ancient character through combination with the cross form. Roman spoils were used for the arcades between the first and the second ring, but the medieval impost appears for the first time. And these arcades are no longer tight and firm as in S. Costanza, but loose, and different in height. SG

C11 SS. Cosma e Damiano
Via dei Fori Imperiali (plan V 1/B)
c. 530, 1632

When looking from the former Via Sacra on the Forum Pacis of Vespasian (Forum Romanum), it can still be seen that the church of the two saints and medical doctors Cosmas and Damian, who were from the Orient, was originally part of an ancient complex of buildings. During the pontificate of Pope Felix IV (526 to 530), the splendid hall on the Via Sacra – which up to then had been either an audience hall for the city prefects or possibly also part of a library –, and its vestibule, a centrally planned domed structure, were consecrated as a church. The rotunda is a simple brick structure which, step by step, tapers off towards the top and is crowned by a lantern. The entrance gate

C11 SS. Cosma e Damiano

C12 S. Maria Antiqua

to the church on the opposite side derives from the Baroque period. This very high archway looks like an extraneous element, squeezed in as it is between the plain monastery buildings of the Franciscan order. The visitor goes through a long passage into a small arcaded courtyard articulated by simple fascias. The interior of the church is a simple hall area, with a late-classical apse attached in the rotunda. The apse and triumphal arch are decorated with early-Christian mosaics depicting Christ handing over the scroll to Peter and Paul (traditio legis divinae), along with the patrons of the church, St Theodor and the founder. The classical interior decoration, consisting of opus sectile and coloured marble, in the rest of the church survived until Luigi Arrigucci's Baroque conversion in 1632. AG

C12 S. Maria Antiqua
Foro Romano (plan V 1/B)
6C
The origins of this church date back to the 6C, when Rome was under Byzantine supremacy. Located below the Palatine on the southern side of the Forum Romanum, the church was incorporated into the complex of imperial palaces in which, by then, the Byzantine viceroys were residing. The function of the adapted buildings is not known. Probably there was a praetorium here, a guardroom for soldiers, located next to the monumental vestibule by which the imperial residence on the Palatine was opened up towards the Forum (A27). A community of monks established here, at an early stage, a diaconicon which took over the Roman sanatorium at the nearby Juturna spring. Johannes VII particularly promoted this church. In 705–08, he attached a bishop's palace which was later repeatedly used as a papal residence. Endangered by an earthquake in 847, the church was moved elsewhere during the rule of Leo IV (B36), and was entirely abandoned no later than the 12C. The new Baroque building by Onorio Longhi was torn down in 1900 in order to uncover the old church. The structure of the previous building is still shown by the succession of rooms in the church: an atrium lined with niches, a main area with an inserted quadriportico

of pillars and granite columns, and three small rooms used as a presbytery. The ancient quadriportico was converted into an area with a nave, two aisles, and a barrel-vaulted narthex which was moved to the inside of the church. The choir on the opposite side balanced the narthex. The presbytery with its shallow apse was flanked by two adjoining rooms. The latter, known as pastophoria, are Byzantine in origin and suggest that the church was founded by one of the Byzantine viceroys, either Narses or Belisar. EJ

C13 S. Lorenzo fuori le Mura
Piazzale di S. Lorenzo (plan IX 2/C)
4C, 6C, 13C.
This structure originated in the tomb of St Laurentius, who was buried in a catacomb on the Via Tiburtina in the 3C. In c. 330, Constantine ordered a basilica over 80 m in length, the »basilica maior«, to be built to the south of his tomb. Known only from excavations, it can be mentally reconstructed as having been a basilica with a nave, two aisles, colonnades, and a western apse around which the aisles were routed in the form of an ambulatory. It belonged to the structural type known as cemeterial or ambulatory basilicas. These were memorial structures which, in the Constantine period, were erected in the area of martyrs' burial sites (cf. A54 and C14). The tomb itself was only given a small sanctuary.

It was only later that Pope Pelagius II (579–90) ordered a church to be built directly above the martyr's tomb. The church was considerably enlarged under Honorius III (1216–27) by the addition of a new basilica to the west. This involved abandoning the western apse of Pelagius' structure, which now took over the function of a choir, while the new structure approximately surrounded the area of the today's nave.

The exterior is a massive structure whose masonry makes it possible to discern the two different phases of construction: the 13C nave and today's choir from the 6C. The medieval ensemble is completed by the 12C campanile, and by a vestibule and cloister from the period of the Honorius basilica (with works by the Vassalletti). But it becomes particularly clear in the

C13 S. Lorenzo fuori le Mura

interior that the basilicas were of two different types. The earlier Pelagius structure, which was formerly oriented towards the west, is a basilica with a broad nave and two very narrow aisles which surround the area on three sides. A gallery storey, which has lightweight columned arcades opening on the central area, rises above a massive colonnade of which only about half has been visible ever since the choir was heightened in connection with the addition of the nave. Above the gallery there follows the clerestory with its large window openings (transoms added later). All the structural elements consist of ancient spoils, as becomes particularly clear from the composite entablature of the colonnade. If the building is imagined in its state without the heightened choir, the result is a structure of very high proportions which is surrounded on all sides by a shell-type space with an horizontal level strongly emphasized by the weightiness of the lower colonnade. This is the first certain example in Rome of a galleried basilica, and S. Agnese fuori le Mura (7C, C14) is the only surviving building to parallel it. This structural type was particularly widespread in the Byzantine area, and demonstrates the strong Eastern influence in Rome in the period around 600. That influence is also seen in the employment, unusual in Roman architecture, of impost blocks to contain the arcades in the gallery, and also in the mosaic decoration of the former triumphal arch (today they are on the western rear wall of the choir).

A feature clearly differing from the Pelagius building is the nave, also basilican, which adjoins in the west and is characteristic of 13C Roman architecture. The lower colonnades accompany its nave like a street of columns, and lead to the choir area in almost monotonous rows. The clerestory without a gallery, and an open roof frame, rise above the severe continuous entablature. The floor, and the furnishings, complete the 13C appearance. Having comparatively tall proportions, the nave follows the type of a regular colon-

naded basilica which, since the rebuilding of S. Crisogono (C27), became a model for the architecture of the period around 1200 (cf. S. Maria in Trastevere, C28). DH

C14 S. Agnese fuori le Mura
Via Nomentana 349 (plan G1 2/B and plan II 3/C)
4C, 625–38

S. Agnese fuori le Mura is one of the best-preserved churches in Rome to derive from the early-Christian period. The whole complex is closely related to that of S. Lorenzo fuori le Mura (C13). Constantina, the daughter of Constantine, ordered a memorial basilica to be built near the burial site of St Agnes so as to form a direct link with her own mausoleum (S. Costanza, C1). Like the basilica maior of S. Lorenzo, this basilica was also located in the area of a necropolis and had a nave, and two aisles which, in the form of an ambulatory, were routed around the apse in the west. Some remains of this building can be clearly discerned north of the mausoleum. It was only later that Honorius I (625–38) ordered a basilica to be built directly above the martyr's tomb in the catacombs. Despite later alterations, that basilica has preserved its character as an early-Christian edifice.

The basilica has a characteristic location. It is oriented towards the east, and is built into the hill of the catacomb so that the altar can be placed directly above the saint's tomb. Thus although the brickwork exterior makes the basilican graduation discernible, it does not make it possible to recognize the building's height, which is only visible in the western façade.

C14 S. Agnese fuori le Mura

The interior has, by Roman standards, an unusually high nave, framed on three sides by columned arcades which stand above one another in two storeys. The apse, which takes up almost the entire width of the nave, follows immediately in the east, without a transept. A very low clerestory, with small windows corresponding with the intercolumniations, provides for subdued lighting in the interior. The galleries are at the level of the street in the east and are accessible at ground level from there. The comparatively narrow proportions of the aisles make them into a background spatial layer lining the nave, and they lend a dignified appearance to the double columned arcades which, taken together, occupy the height of the apse arch.

The columns in their close rows are ancient spoils, whereas typical (and rare) examples from the 7C are to be found among the capitals (the stylized Ionic capitals in the narthex gallery are one example). As in S. Lorenzo, impost blocks in the delicate gallery arcades form the link between columns and arches, and they are a Byzantine element which is an extraneous feature in Rome; its only surviving parallel is in S. Lorenzo. On the other hand, galleried basilicas of similarly tall proportions were widespread in the Byzantine area, even though this applies mostly before the 6C. The mosaic in the apse is an important example of 7C Roman mosaic art, and indicates as well the influence – very strong at that time – of the Byzantine East. The facing of the lower zone of the apse is of porphyry and grey marble, still survives in the original, and is the only example of its kind to have been preserved in Rome.

The proportions here are markedly steeper than in S. Lorenzo, and the choice of arcades alone, instead of the severe lower colonnade found in S. Lorenzo, lends the area greater lightness and elegance, especially as the storeys are more subtly coordinated with the design of the apse. Taken as a whole, the S. Agnese building, in its present shape which is still largely that of the original, is an outstanding example of an early-Christian basilica in Rome and, along with S. Lorenzo, it demonstrates the very strong Eastern influence in the period around 600. DH

C15 Triclinio Leoniano (former Lateran Palace)

Piazza di Porta S. Giovanni (plan IX 1/E)
c. 800

The Carolingian triclinium, which no longer survives today, was the papal palace that was named after its main room and was located by the Lateran church. It was one of the largest palaces of its period. Begun under Pope Zacharias (741–52) as a new building above some preceding Constantine structures, it took over a hundred years to construct, and created a conglomeration consisting of various spatial groups. In the late-16C, the entire complex had to give way to Sixtus V's new building (B21), and here all that survived of

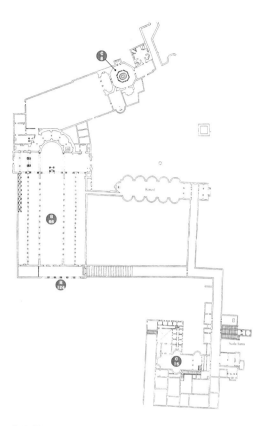

C15 Triclinio Leoniano (former Lateran Palace)

the medieval structures was the Sancta Sanctorum, the popes' private chapel that dated back to the 13C. The complex, which had been developed around various inner courtyards, adjoined the Lateran basilica and stood to the north-east of it. The most important sections were two triclinia (banqueting halls) built under Leo III (795 to 816), one of which was in the form of a trikonchos (a room with three apses; a reconstruction by F. Fuga, 1743, of one of the apses is in the square outside the basilica). The more famous triclinium, which gives the building its name, consisted of an elongated room with an apse at the front and five apses on each of the side walls. Another trikonchos was added to the palace under Gregory IV (827–44). It is not only the trikonchoi that point to late-antique models. The large triclinium with its eleven apses has a single parallel in the imperial palace in Constantinople, and permits the conclusion that this architectural form, as well as some of the ceremonies, were directly adopted from there. But this building dates from the very time when the Roman papacy was becoming detached from Byzantium and there was a stronger leaning towards the Frankish Empire (the Pepin Donation), so that the papacy's claim to the primacy of the Roman church is shown by the adoption of these imposing late-antique and Byzantine spatial shapes. DH

C16 S. Cecilia in Trastevere
Piazza di S. Cecilia (plan VII 1/A)
817–24 (and later)

An early-Christian titulus was, no later than the 5C, established in a Roman house in whose caldarium St Caecilia is said to have been martyred in the 2C. Today's basilica was built under Pope Paschalis I (817 to 824) and was later much altered. It must be regarded as a significant example of early-9C architecture in Rome, although its spatial appearance today is shaped by 13C furnishings (ciborium by Arnolfo di Cambio, fresco by Pietro Cavallini) and in particular by structural changes made in later centuries. There was rebuilding work in the 15C and 16C, and Cardinal Aquaviva ordered considerable further renovations between 1721 and 1742. Later alterations date from the early 19C.

The former atrium situated in the east is today occupied by a forecourt. The design of its portal and of the upper church façade dates back to the work performed by Ferdinando Fuga under Aquaviva in 1741. A vestibule standing in front of the basilica, the campanile, and a cloister which adjoins in the south, were all built in the 12C.

Inside, the first surprising feature is the spaciousness of the nave, which is almost all that remains of the original structure built under Paschalis. Narrow, unlit aisles (groined vault from c. 1500) are today sep-

C16 S. Cecilia in Trastevere

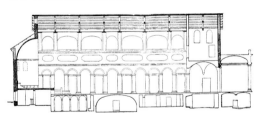

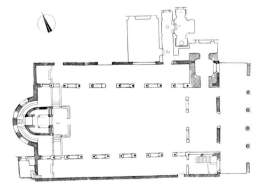

arated from the nave by pillars, the basilica's original columns were encased and every second arch in the arcade was closed (1822). The mezzanine with coretti which follows above this derives entirely from the renovations performed under Aquaviva (1724). The clerc story is formed by rhythmized round-arched windows which have lunettes cutting into a barrel vault with a three-centred arch. In the 16C, the nave of the church was slightly shortened by the insertion, in front of the inner façade wall, of a nuns' gallery concealing the fresco by Cavallini which is located here.

The original elevation of the Paschalis structure can be reconstructed on the basis of the existing substance of the building: a broad wall area stood above two rows each consisting of 13 columned arcades, and above this again there were round-arched windows which were oriented axially on the arcades and stood below an open roof frame. The point upon which the nave is oriented is still today the apse which, in the calotte, has retained the mosaic as a valuable witness to the period of the church's construction (cf. also S. Prassede, C18), whereas the marble incrustation beneath this has been renovated, albeit on the basis of early-Christian models such as S. Agnese fuori le Mura (C14). A circular crypt (confessio) stands below the apse, following the latter's roundness, and originally opened the way into a memorial room which was replaced in c. 1900 by a historicizing hall crypt. In the east there follow some accessible, excavated rooms of the Roman residential house. Above its caldarium, a memorial chapel which was attached to the northern aisle dates back in its core structure to the 9C and, in terms of design, is closely related to the Zeno chapel – likewise erected by Paschalis I – in S. Prassede (C18).

After the 6C and 7C buildings (S. Lorenzo fuori le Mura, C13; S. Agnese fuori le Mura, C14), Carolingian architecture in Rome once again followed more closely the methods employed by early-Christian church architecture in Rome. With its original properties as a columned basilica, S. Cecilia is a typical example of that Carolingian architecture: it has a broad nave, narrow and unlit aisles, an apse in the west, is without a transept, and possesses a circular crypt. DH

C17 S. Maria in Domnica
Via della Navicella 10 (plan VIII 2/A)
c. 817–24

This church, one of the three whose construction was ordered by Paschalis I (817–24), displays the spatial appearance deriving from the Carolingian period as purely as does any structure except S. Giorgio (C20). Major alterations were made only by Giovanni de' Medici, who later became Pope Leo X. From 1489 on, he ordered the ceiling and clerestory to be redesigned; the windows had previously been higher and narrower, and – as was usual in Rome in the Middle Ages – ended in round arches at their tops. He also caused the façade to be erected, with its dominating

C17 S. Maria in Domnica

vestibule. The latter, a very good High-Renaissance work, was for long attributed to Raphael, but now to Sansovino (1513/14). Conciseness, combined with swelling strength, typifies the architecture of that period. Thus pillars in the vestibule, with slender Ionic pilasters projecting in front of them, support three-dimensionally moulded archivolts.

Since the time of Paschalis I, church architecture more strongly pursued the idea of a revival (renovatio). The large early-Christian basilicas were emulated. In the present building, these were the basilicas of the period around 400, in which rows of arcades separated the nave and aisles from one another (C2, C6). This building makes an early-Christian impression by reason of its broad proportions, which are still broader than in its prototypes, and also because the apse (with splendid contemporaneous mosaics) takes up almost the entire wall, which thus resembles a triumphal arch. At the same time, though, the prototypes are reproduced in a very simplified way: the aisles are reduced to passages (3.80 m), there is no transept, and neither is there even the circular crypt usual for Carolingian churches in Rome. Thus the very first building, which embodies in its pure form the idea of a Carolingian revival, shows a basic tendency: in the North (Aachen, Lombardy), new architectural types and vaults of the late-classical period were used again when putting the idea of renovatio into effect, whereas in Rome only the Constantine basilica, and even that in a reduced language of forms, was employed. SG

C18 S. Prassede
Via di S. Prassede (plan VI 1/B)
c. 822
This church dedicated to St Praxedis, the sister of St Pudentiana, is an outstanding example of the idea of renovatio in the Carolingian church architecture in Rome. There had been an assembly room on this site since the 5C. In c. 822, Pope Paschalis I ordered the church to be built and decorated. It was intended to accommodate those numerous remains of martyrs which had been buried in ruinous graves and rescued and assembled by Paschalis. The church passed into

the possession of the Benedictines in 1198. The first redesigning works were carried out in the 13C, the second in the 16C, but both of them only partially altered the structure that dated from Carolingian times.

The architectural model for the Carolingian building is evidently the early-Christian St Peter's, but the dimensions are much smaller and the structure is much simplified. Paschalis built a small copy of Old St Peter's above a circular crypt which can today be entered from the nave. The atrium which formerly stood in front of the church is ruined today. The low western façade is plain and almost undecorated. Its Renaissance portal was inserted later. The unplastered brickwork in approximately even layers visibly expresses the fact that the architect had also reverted to the 4C and 5C where building techniques were concerned. On the outside of the clerestory, the ten small round-arched windows are also to be seen which, as in S. Paolo fuori le Mura (C2), have a double covering. They were walled up and replaced by four large windows.

Following the example of Old St Peter's, the type chosen was a colonnaded basilica with a narrow transept which did not project beyond the aisles and did not have a separate crossing. The interior has none of the tallness of later medieval buildings. Instead, a lucid breadth dominates, as in the early-Christian prototypes. The semicircular central apse is framed by a splendid triumphal arch. There are numerous details which make the reduction, and the similarity with the prototype, both equally evident. Only a nave and two aisles were built in S. Prassede instead of a nave and four, the architrave is borne by only 11 columns instead of 22, and the aisles have only a double arcade opening on the transept, and not a threefold arcade as in Old St Peter's. But the spoils for the columns

C18 S. Prassede

and architrave were chosen just as carefully as in early Christianity. The spatial impression originally produced by the Carolingian structure is much impaired by the flying buttresses in the nave, which dominate the area and are supported by massive pillars reinforcing the columns. The buttresses were inserted in the high-medieval period for structural reasons. Nevertheless, the architecture and decorations – the overall impression is well completed by the splendid 9C mosaics – mean that an outstanding Carolingian church building has been preserved in Rome.

The S. Zeno chapel by the right aisle was built under Pope Paschalis I between 817 and 824, and is the most important example of Byzantine influence in Rome during the Carolingian renovatio. A small centrally planned area, whose groined vault is supported by four columns inserted in the corners, rises above a cruciform ground plan. The function of the small chapel is not clear. It is natural to suppose that it was used as a memorial structure for Theodora Episcopa, the Pope's mother. The great precision and unusual beauty of the individual architectural elements are remarkable here, as in the rest of the church. Roman spoils form the frame around the entrance to the chapel. The architrave, borne by two sumptuous porphyry columns, dates from the 1C AD. The depictions in the mosaics can be traced back to Byzantine models and were not customary in Rome until this period. AG

C19 S. Marco

C19 S. Marco
Piazza di S. Marco (plan V 1/B)
833, converted 1465

The basilica founded in 336 by Pope Marcus, who was later canonized, is today surrounded on almost all sides by the complex of the Palazzo Venezia (F5 and F6). But the basilica's spatial appearance today still bears witness to Gregory IV's new structure dating from 833. This was a columned basilica (one nave, two aisles, open roof frame) which had a crypt but no transept, and ended in simple apses.

The venerability of the building legitimized the fact that the papal residence was moved into it under Paul II, but he converted it again in 1465–70. In order to make space for the divine services held by the papal clergy, the presbytery was expanded by means of two high arcades leading into the transverse sections of the aisles. The nave was given one of the earliest Renaissance coffer-work ceilings in Rome, whereas the aisles have groined vaults above wall arches and projecting pilasters. The design of the exterior wall in the aisle is important to this new type of classical-period appearance: it has a succession of dark conchae with shell-shaped flattened cupolas, but today its effect is reduced by architectural insertions. The vaulting also made it necessary to reinforce the columned arcades by means of pillars and cross girders. The combination of pillared arcade and half-column was reminiscent of the massiveness of ancient Roman buildings, but this fact is no longer apparent, because the columns were finally made to stand free again in the Baroque period.

Although these alterations were caused by dilapidation and liturgical necessities, they show that Paul II and his architect Francesco del Borgo selected the classical language of shapes in this renovation too. But they did not proceed dogmatically: the clerestory windows display the embellishment of Gothic tracery windows. UF

C20 S. Giorgio in Velabro
Via del Velabro (plan VII 2/A)
c. 827–44

In erecting this church, Pope Gregory IV (827–44) was building over a diaconicon which since 752 had harboured the relics of the head of St George. Ever since some later insertions were removed in 1924/25, there has probably been no other late-Carolingian interior in Rome to have survived in such a pure form. The exterior was built later: the portico and campanile are from the 13C, and the upper section of the façade from the late 18C (Valladier).

As in the case, for example, of S. Maria in Domnica (C17), S. Giorgio is a columned basilica with a nave, two aisles, and a row of arcades (there is no transept). Thus as in the example given, the structure was based on the large basilicas of the period around 400 (cf. also C2, C6). Again as in the example, the much-simplified design is a striking feature, but in this case so too is the altered proportion: the overall proportions are taller, thus anticipating the tendency of the high-medieval period. And the distances between the columns are large. Thus the arcades almost become three-centred arches, and the energetic rhythm which, in early-Christian structures, is produced by the closely-placed row of columns and by the narrow, high arches following one another in rapid succession is lost here. The aisles contribute more strongly to the effect created. This building's second main characteristic, its inclination to be irregular, is seen in the arcatures and in the path they follow: the building tapers from a width of 19.60 m at the entrance to 14.70 m at the apse wall, this tapering being very marked in the right aisle, in which there is also a bend. What is more, the door and the apse are not in the main axis. Irregular foundation walls from the diaconicon were evidently used again. The rectangular windows are also known in diaconica, but not in medieval Roman churches. Their small size anticipates high-medieval taste. SG

C21 S. Martino ai Monti
Viale del Monte Oppio (plan VI 1/B)
4C, 6C, from 847
Along with SS. Quattro Coronati (C22), S. Martino ai Monti completes that series of churches from the late 8C and the 9C in which the idea of the Carolingian renovatio took shape (cf. C17, C18, C19, C20). Here too,

C20 S. Giorgio in Velabro

C21 S. Martino ai Monti

the early-Christian type of an architrave basilica was emphatically reverted to. The core of the structure is a Christian assembly room situated in a 3C private house whose remains were located in the spacious crypt. In the 4C, Pope Sylvester I ordered a new church to be built above these walls. The conversion work performed under Pope Symmachius in the 6C was replaced by what was largely a new structure, begun under Pope Sergius II in 847. The atrium and circular crypt from that period no longer survive. The church was given its present shape in 1650 under the guidance of Pietro da Cortona, but the original Carolingian structure remained partly intact.

In the exterior, the onlooker's eye is caught by the massive round shape of the red-brick Carolingian apse. The façade dating from 1676 displays a simple, self-contained wall surface subdivided by pilasters and cornices.

In the interior, the fact that the early-Christian basilicas served as models is to be seen from the broad, settled proportions in the nave, with the narrow aisles and the wide apse. The columns with their Corinthian capitals are ancient in origin and support an architrave. The more modest dimensions and the reduced shape are typically Carolingian. The articulation of the high wall, with its alternately painted round-arched niches, its foreshortened architectural forms, and the sculptured coretti placed in front for show, dates from the Baroque period. Three large 16C frescoes in the left aisle show interior views, important as documents, of ruined early-Christian churches. AG

C22 SS. Quattro Coronati
Via dei Santi Quattro (plan VIII 2/A)
847–55, 1091-1116
Devastation, conversion and reduction characterize this originally impressive building of the Carolingian renovatio. Under Pope Leo IV (847–55), a magnificent columned basilica with a nave and two aisles was built on the Caelian hill above the foundation walls of a late-classical assembly room which was dedicated to four martyrs. After being devastated by the Normans in 1084, it was rebuilt in 1091 and 1116 under Pope

C22 SS. Quattro Coronati

Paschalis II. Remnants of the Carolingian church, which was over 50 m long, can still be seen. An enormous gate tower, rare for Rome, rises above the entrance to the atrium. Along with the massive round shape of the apse which stands in the west, with its undecorated exterior dominating the way up to the monastery like a bulwark, this brick-built church today still demonstrates its proud Carolingian claims. The surviving circular crypt with its confessio also displays the typical reversion to the early-Christian architectural tradition. The remains of the columned basilica, which formerly had a nave and two aisles, are located in the second forecourt and in the interior of the church, but are covered over by other building work. The much smaller early-12C church was, with its nave and two aisles, fitted into the western section of the nave of the Carolingian structure. The old walls of the nave retained their original height, and are now the outer walls. The spatial impression produced in the interior is shaped today by the contrast between the narrow, dark, nave of the church and the broad and bright Carolingian apse. The narrow and tall basilican nave, with its galleries, stands adjacent, and the cross-shaped pillar in the middle of it lends it a rhythmizing turning point. Such a switchover in the supporting structures is an original feature for Rome, and points to influences from north of the Alps. The individual architectural members, such as the columns and capitals assembled from spoils, are heterogeneous but nonetheless of high quality. AG

C23 S. Prisca
Via di S. Prisca (plan VII 2/A)
3C, 11C, 1660

This extremely plain and simple building is one of the oldest titular churches in Rome. The chief feature of importance for this church is its location above Roman building work, some of which has been excavated, from the republican period. In the late 5C, a church was built above the Roman houses, which according to the legend were thought to include the house of Aquila and Prisca, the first Christian married couple in Rome. However, today's proportions are not those of the early-Christian church, but mostly derive from an 11C conversion. The originally simple arcaded basilica, which was tall in the high-medieval style and had small windows at a high location, appears today in a Baroque form, due to conversion work in c. 1660.

The exterior hardly has any peculiarities. The Baroque façade was erected by Carlo Lambardi and follows the widespread architectural type of the aedicule façade. Like the exterior, the interior, in its Baroque covering, shows little inventive power. However, the ancient columns which, as spoils, improved this plain medieval room are still visible.

A museum has been set up in the labyrinthine building work below the church, and this area is of greater significance. From here, access can also be gained to the crypt, a barrel-vaulted hall which was inserted into the existing Roman masonry. Next to the crypt is a 3C mithraeum which joins that in S. Clemente (C25) in being one of the two best-preserved examples of such a heathen cultic room. It is also a barrel-vaulted room, with benches for reclining set into its long sides. There is a round niche to the left of the entrance, and another to the right. Another round niche with a high relief depicting the god fighting the bull is to be found on the front side of the room. AG

C24 S. Giovanni a Porta Latina
Via S. Giovanni a Porta Latina (plan VIII 2/B)
6C, c. 1100

This church which stood on the Aurelian city wall, far outside the city centre, was founded during the 60 years of the Byzantine occupation of Rome in the 6C. One relic of this phase of Eastern influence is the three-sided main apse which is broken up polygonally on the outside and was incorporated into the later new building, being given two additional flanking apses at that time. The church was rebuilt in c. 1100. It was only in 1191, almost 100 years later, that the church was consecrated under Pope Coelestin III. The 11C and 12C were not a brilliant period for Rome, and only a few churches were founded at that time. The financial resources, scanty in any event, went to support the costly crusades. S. Giovanni a Porta Latina is a very well-preserved example of the few churches which date from the period around 1100 and, due to the lack of funds, were very modest in design.

Five plain round-arched arcades form the entrance to the vestibule. The columns of marble and granite, with their Ionic order, are spoils. The campanile, also from the 12C, is a model example of Romanesque architectural subdividing work. In order to express graphically how the campanile develops as it ascends, the subdivision becomes successively more rich and filigreed as the tower grows higher. The simple niches placed in front for show are, above them, developed into round-arched openings, and the openings in the upper three storeys are formed by acoustic arcades standing on delicate little columns.

After a restoration, the interior of the church appears in its 12C state. The arcades of this basilica (one nave, two aisles) each have only five columns with shafts of differing lengths, and are made of various materials. The base courses, the plinths and some of the Ionic capitals are also spoils. The modest character of the building is underlined both by its low height and by the small windows. The inserted apse has a semicircular conclusion on the inside. AG

C25 S. Clemente
Piazza di S. Clemente (plan VIII 2/A)
4C, from 1108

Despite the 18C alterations, S. Clemente is an outstanding example of a 12C Roman church, with an architectural and cultic tradition that has continued since ancient Roman times. Today's basilica was, from 1108 onwards, erected under Pope Paschalis II (1099–1118) as a new structure, with a previous early-Christian edifice (probably 4C), which had itself been constructed above Roman buildings, serving as the foundation. Carlo Fontana redesigned it in Baroque style under Clemens XI (1700–21).

The origin of the structure is located some 20 m below today's street level and consists of two Roman buildings: they are an early-1C tufa stone structure in the east, and a 2C brickwork residential apartment block in the west. In the 3C, the central area of the apartment block was converted into a sanctuary of Mithras, which with its two lateral benches, its niche for the statue and its flat barrel vault is a well-preserved example of this type of building in Rome (cf. C23).

In the later 3C, a large hall was built above the adjoining eastern building. The function of the hall is uncertain, but it may have been the Titulus Clementis, which is known from sources and is one of the 18 Roman titular churches documented from before the year 385. According to this theory, the direct coexistence of the Christian and Mithraic religions might have been very graphically evident here until heathen cults were finally banned in 391. In the 4C, this hall was converted into a basilica (the lower church), with columned arcades and an apse in the west above the sanctuary of Mithras which had by then been abandoned. This early-Christian structure is typified by its proportioning, with a strikingly broad nave which is more than twice the width of the aisles, while the

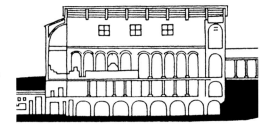

C25 S. Clemente

overall length is relatively short. But the spatial impression is considerably disturbed by wall sections inserted for the purpose of building the upper church.

When the upper church was built in the 12C, the lower basilica was pulled down as far as the level of the capitals, filled in and used as a foundation, but the proportions were characteristically altered: only the southern aisle accords with that underneath it, whereas today's nave and northern aisle take up, between them, the dimensions of the lower nave. The reduced width thus achieved is in accord with the narrower and taller proportions aimed at in the 12C. The nave and aisles are separated from one another by columned arcades above ancient columns which consist of spoils and have Ionic capitals. In the middle of the nave the two rows of columns are interrupted by a longitudinally arranged pillar marking the end of the liturgical area of the choir, which is itself limited by a schola cantorum with relief- and mosaic-work barriers, two ambos and an Easter candlestick. The floor with its Cosmati work, the altar ciborium, and the unique apse decorations with fresco work and mosaic on a gold background are also all part of the original furnishings. Thus the architectural type of this 12C building follows that of the columned basilica which has a nave, two aisles and an apse, but no transept. That type is typical of early-12C Roman architecture (cf. S. Maria in Cosmedin, C26).

The well-preserved atrium, which has colonnades at the sides and an original protyron, follows in the east, in front of the façade designed by Fontana. Although it was made Baroque in the 18C, the overall ensemble of basilica and atrium is thus still an exemplary and largely intact building from 12C Rome. DH

C26 S. Maria in Cosmedin
Piazza Bocca della Verità (plan VII 2/A)
c. 780, 1120–23

This building stands in the ancient Forum Boarium (cattle market). Thus remains of several ancient buildings are to be found in it. The area of the church (with its tower) was divided into two at that time. The dividing line was at the level of the fifth column inside the church and ran at right angles to the nave and aisles. Until 780, a Flavian temple podium, made of tufa ash-

C26 S. Maria in Cosmedin

lars, occupied the rear section. From the 4C on, the front section was taken up by a transversely rectangular hall whose rear wall ran along the above-mentioned dividing line and on whose other three sides magnificent Corinthian columns stood (seven at the front, three on each side). Some of them are still to be seen today in the tower walls and church walls in the front half. It was into this hall that a diaconicon was inserted in the mid-6C. This was a building serving the interests of pilgrimage, which was becoming popular. In the diaconicon, to the left and right of a hall (the latter was identical to the front half of the nave), there were groups of rooms, and on the second storey groups of open arcades (galleries). Hadrian I (772–95) ordered the first church to be built in the area of the diaconicon (at the front) and of the temple podium (at the rear). The interior was redesigned under Calixtus II (c. 1120–23). The sections which lend shape to the exterior, namely the vestibule and the campanile, were entirely new features added at this time.

Ever since Sardi's splendid rococo façade dating from 1718 was, along with some other baroque inclusions, removed in 1892–98, the vestibule and campanile have once again shaped the appearance of the façade. The seven-storey campanile, one of the finest in Rome, is subdivided by clearly defined cornices and by arches which, in the lower section, have arcatures. The latter, passing through two intermediate stages,

are varied until, at the top, the treble windows with arcades supported by columns are reached. The campanile is counterbalanced by the two-storey vestibule with its continuous row of pillared arcades and its portico projecting in the middle. Here, the pillared arcade replaces what is otherwise usually found in the narthex in Rome, namely a row of columns with a horizontal architrave. The projecting portico accommodates the gabled shape of the nave. Thus arcades and the gabled shape, in several variations, are the uniting elements of vestibule, nave and campanile. There is also the forceful contrast between the horizontal and the vertical. In the left of the narthex is the »Bocca della Verità«, an ancient river-god mask which, in the Middle Ages, was believed to possess magical powers: anyone placing his hand into its mouth and telling an untruth was to remain caught there.

In the interior, only the crypt retains its Carolingian appearance. Circular crypts consisting only of a semicircular passage had existed since the time of Constantine (S. Lorenzo in Milano). They were particularly widespread in the Carolingian period (cf. C16, C18, C19, C22, C27). But in S. Maria in Cosmedin a further step was taken. The first hall crypt in Rome, and probably in the whole of Western Europe, was created: the passage is adjoined by a hall with a nave, two aisles, a transept and a separate crossing. This accords with the basic structure of a Constantine basilica. Thus this crypt is an early, restrained example of the idea of Carolingian revival (C17, C18). From now on, the hall crypt as a structural form was a standard component of Romanesque churches (but only outside Rome). Round niches, two of them located one above the other in each case, are set into the walls. They were intended to accommodate the relics which were very eagerly assembled under Hadrian I. They are reminiscent of early-Christian catacombs (cf. A39), and so too is the technique of »negative« architecture: the room was not built, but was hewn into the tufa of the Flavian temple podium.

C26 S. Maria in Cosmedin

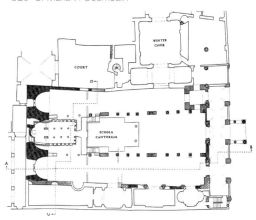

Only parts of the Carolingian core built under Hadrian I (772–95) are still discernible in the interior. The church was built as a basilica with a nave, two aisles and three apses, but no transept. The diaconicon hall (with galleries) was used as front half of the church. The structure was expanded and completed by a newly built rear half, but here the galleries were replaced by mere arcatures. In this half, the temple podium had to be taken down. Parts of it were used as foundations, as a casing for the crypt, and as a support for the back of the presbytery. Thus the entire nave wall had the same structure: the row of columns (spoils) with a horizontal architrave (parts of which are visible to the side of the apse) was underneath, and above this were the arcades of the galleries. This is how one of the few galleried basilicas in Rome (cf. C13, C14) came into being. There was also an upwards expansion: a third storey was added to the wall all along its length. This is the wall section in which the clerestory windows can still be seen today; the galleries were vertically underneath them. The building also deserves attention by reason of its three-apse conclusion. The latter was frequently regarded as the second great invention of the structure from Hadrian's period (the first being the hall crypt). That is only partially true. This form was invented in Syria and Palestine, being transmitted via the Adriatic towns of Salona and Parenzo. But it probably really was from S. Maria in Cosmedin that it started spreading over the whole of Western Europe (but again without having much effect in Rome itself). The three-apse conclusion can be explained from liturgical necessities in the Eastern Church, and the building from Hadrian's period, located in the Greek part of Rome, was intended for a Greek congregation.

The interior was given its present appearance under Calixtus II (c. 1120–23). The galleries were walled up. Under Hadrian I, the tall proportions resulted from the existing gallery storey, but now they accorded with the taste of the high-medieval period. And without the galleries, the area makes a narrow, shaft-like impression. The pillars, and the arches resting on them, are of the same Romanesque brickwork. Thus the wall above was retained, but the row of columns and the horizontal architrave below were replaced successively by arches and by a row of pillars and columns, thus creating the typically high-medieval alternation in the supporting structures. The intercolumniations were also altered in this process, and their vertical correspondence with the windows was lost. The furnishings are also from the early 12C, and are more splendid than any others in Rome except those in S. Clemente (C25). The floor is of opus alexandrinum, the style of stone inlay work developed by the Cosmati family. Opus sectile, the small-sectioned mosaic work dating from the 8C, is to be seen at the high altar. The presbyter's throne with its nimbus and ancient lions was added in the apse. The parclose and the schola cantorum which contains lecterns and pro-

jects into the nave also date from the 12C. Only the ciborium, another Cosmati work, is Gothic (1294). The furnishings dating from 1123 were donated by Alfanus, who is buried in the narthex. SG

C27 S. Crisogono
Viale di Trastevere (plan VII 1/A)
731–41, 1123–30

After Constantine the Great issued his tolerance edict in 312, public meetings of Christians were permitted for the first time. The titular church of S. Crisogono is the first known building which was used solely for Christian divine service. The initially simple, barn-like structure had a baptistery added to it in the 5C.

The church was enlarged and converted in 731–41. At the same time it was given a circular crypt. In this way an architectural type which was no longer customary – it had been inserted into Old St Peter's in c. 600 – was adopted anew. It came back into fashion in the following hundred years. Some walls in the existing church, and in the lower church some fragments of mural paintings from the 8C–11C and the horseshoe-shaped confessio, all survive from this structure.

The next great phase of construction, which is regarded as the highest in quality and shaped the building's present appearance, followed under Pope Calixtus II in 1123–30. The structure created at that time is, in its scheme and in the richness of its furnishings and decorations, comparable with that of S. Maria in Trastevere (C28). In the exterior, the quality of this building can be well seen in the rich articulation of the Romanesque campanile. Although the interior was made baroque in 1626, the monumental spatial impression which was aimed at can still be sensed. This basilica (one nave, two aisles) derives its noble character from the two rows, each of eleven sumptuous, ancient, grey and red granite columns, which lead up to the two immense porphyry columns supporting the triumphal arch. The wide nave ends in a broad semicircular apse. The transept between them gives an impression of having been inserted. Like S. Maria in Trastevere, S. Crisogono, with its colonnades, narrow transept and characteristic proportions, is a vivid example of the renewed reversion, in the 12C, to the early-Christian architectural tradition. AG

C28 S. Maria in Trastevere
Piazza di S. Maria in Trastevere (plan VII 1/A)
1140–48

S. Maria in Trastevere is probably the most significant and elaborate 12C church building in Rome. It was the first church of St Mary in Rome, having been founded by Pope Julius I (before 352) on the site where a source of oil was, in 38 BC, interpreted as a portent of the coming of the Messiah (northern parclose). Innocent II ordered a new building to be erected in 1140–48, but it was not until 1215 that it was consecrated by Innocent III. Despite later alterations,

C28 S. Maria in Trastevere

this building has preserved its medieval spatial appearance outstandingly well.

Following the tradition of the preceding structure, the church is oriented towards the west. A vestibule by Carlo Fontana (1701/02) stands in front of the surviving Romanesque structure. The upper part of the façade derives largely from 19C modifications, but it preserves a mosaic from the late 12C or 13C below the gable panel. The campanile, which stands further back in the north, also dates from the 12C.

The interior follows the type of the colonnaded basilica with a nave, two aisles, a transept and a semicircular apse. The nave and aisles are separated from one another by colonnades, and ancient granite columns, with mostly Ionic capitals, support the massive continuous entablature (spoils from the thermal baths of Caracalla, A43). Above this are the clerestory, redesigned in baroque style, and a coffer-work ceiling designed by Domenichino. The nave, despite the broad areas opening towards the aisles, has tall proportions which are counteracted by the rows of the colonnades. The transept does not project beyond the line of the aisles, and is a continuous structure without a separate crossing; this is the characteristic form found in the early-Christian basilicas of Old St Peter's and S. Paolo fuori le Mura (C2). The transept is immediately adjoined by the semicircular apse which, when opening towards the nave, is almost as wide as the nave (famous 12C mosaics on the apse arch and in the calotte, late-13C mosaics by P. Cavallini in the lower round part of the apse). The 12C spatial appearance is completed by some original furnishings (bishop's throne, Easter candlestick, Cosmati-style floor). Adjoining chapels from the 16C and 17C (including the Avila chapel, B101) expand the nave and aisles without impairing the predominant medieval spatial impression.

S. Maria in Trastevere is a very typical example of church architecture from further on in the 12C in Rome. That architecture once again harks back more strongly to the beginnings of early-Christian architecture, although it is the taller dimensions characterizing the high-medieval period that predominate. After the buildings by Paschalis II and his immediate successors (cf. S. Clemente, C25), S. Crisogono (1123–30, C27) is the first to display two new elements: the continuous transept which does not though project beyond the lines of the aisles, and – in the nave – colonnades instead of the round-arched arcades which had predominated until then. S. Maria in Trastevere follows S. Crisogono directly in both ground plan and elevation, and even adopts the motif of the columns supporting the triumphal arch. However, this architectural type is here presented in larger dimensions and greater pretensions, and this means that it may be regarded as specific for the 12C, especially in view of the further buildings that followed the same type (e. g. S. Croce in Gerusalemme, B134, S. Francesca Romana, B36, extension of S. Lorenzo fuori le Mura, C13). DH

C29 S. Lorenzo in Lucina
Piazza di S. Lorenzo in Lucina (plan IV 2/A)
432–40, 1130, 1196

The complex architectural history of S. Lorenzo dates back to ancient times. A residential apartment block, whose rooms were, from no later than the 4C onwards, used by a Christian community as an assembly place (»Titulus Lucinae«; the excavations are accessible), was built in the 3C in the northern part of the Campus Martius, near to the Ara Pacis (A18) and above the paving of Augustus' sundial. Above this, Pope Sixtus III (432–40) ordered a church to be built. Although only a few remains survive of it in the foundations and above-ground structure, this church fundamentally shaped the form and structure of the present building. The church was a basilica with a nave, two aisles and an apse, but no transept. It is very

C29 S. Lorenzo in Lucina

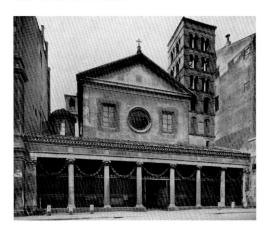

probable that the nave and aisles of this early-Christian building were separated from one another by pillared arcades at that time, and this means that S. Lorenzo is a rare example when compared with those basilicas with columned arcades which were otherwise customary in the 5C.

After severe devastations, probably by the Normans, a largely new structure of identical dimensions was erected in the early 12C (1099–1118, consecrated in 1130 and 1196) under Pope Paschalis II. Its characteristic columned portico and campanile (late 12C) shape the building's external appearance today. But the impression produced by the interior was fundamentally altered in the 17C when the floor was raised in height and a flat ceiling was inserted. The main change here was that the former aisles were, by means of internal walls, transformed into side chapels, thus producing the hall structure existing today (Cosimo Fanzago, c. 1650). DH

C30 S. Saba
Via di S. Saba (plan VII 2/B)
590–604, 12C, 15C.
In the 6C, a church was built above the house lived in by St Silvia, the mother of Gregory the Great (590 to 604), who was the first monk to become Pope and was one of the four Roman Fathers of the Church. The building was dedicated to St Sabas, who founded an order of the Eastern Church, lived in the first half of the 6C, and died in 532 in the Mar Saba monastery near Bethlehem. This early-Christian church was replaced by a new structure in the 12C.

In the mid-15C, the exterior, with its striking façade, was given a new appearance. A palace-like panelled façade was erected at the western end in the quattrocentro period, with the basilican design of the medieval church being entirely negated. The vertical structure is in three zones, alternating between open pillars and arcades on the one hand and the closed masonry wall on the other. On the ground floor, massive pillars support an architrave. The self-contained wall area above is broken up only by small window openings and, like a broad strip, separates the vestibule below from the loggia above. The latter is the elegant conclusion of the transom-like façade. The low campanile is almost completely concealed by the façade.

Inside, the modest 12C basilican standard prevails, with the typical tall proportions in the nave, and the small windows at a high location (cf. S. Maria in Cosmedin, C26). The two apses flanking the main apse enrich this architectural type which lacks a transept. This makes the ground plan very similar to the basilicas in the Alpine region which were built at about the same time. This basilica (one nave, two aisles), whose arcades are supported by spoils, was expanded in the 13C by the addition of another short aisle beside the left aisle. The oratory of St Silvia, which was excavated in the early 20C and is a small room with an apse, dates from the 4C or 5C. AG

C31 SS. Quattro Coronati: cloister

C31 SS. Quattro Coronati: cloister
Via dei Santi Quattro (plan VIII 2/A)
late 12C
The cloister is an important part of a medieval monastery. Together with the church, it forms the core of the monastery. All the areas important to monastery life are accessible from here. The roofed passage, separated from the outside world, gave the monks and nuns peace in which to contemplate. The special feature of the medieval Roman cloisters is their splendid furnishings which were produced by specialist craftsmen, the so-called Cosmati, who were active in Rome and the episcopal seats of Latium from 1150 to c. 1320. Their decorative wall, column and floor mosaics were developed from Arab-Sicilian wall decorations.

The cloister of SS. Quattro Coronati is the first cloister in Rome to have been built by Cosmati artists. Begun in the late 12C, it is markedly simpler than, and not so sumptuous as, the later examples in S. Paolo fuori le Mura (C32) and S. Giovanni in Laterano (C33). But the structural scheme, in which pillars and columned arcades constitute the turning points, is already completely developed here. The succession of narrow columned arcades is rhythmized by narrow pillars with pilasters placed in front of them for show. The arcades rest on domed double columns. The impression of delicacy is formed by the double sawtooth

C32 S. Paolo fuori le Mura: cloister

frieze and by the rich decorative strip of inlay work typical of the Cosmati. The »Roman« way of building cloisters was developed here. The individual components were not manufactured on site. Instead, entire cloisters, taken to pieces, were transported over considerable distances. A rare feature for Rome is the masonry-work barrel vault which, instead of an open roof frame, covers the passage, and is the more significant in that vaulting never gained acceptance in medieval Rome. The fountain in the middle of the cloister dates from the time of Paschalis II (1099–1118). AG

C32 S. Paolo fuori le Mura: cloister
Via Ostiense (plan G2 3/A and plan VII 1/C–2/C)
1205–41

The cloister of S. Paolo fuori le Mura fortunately escaped being destroyed in the devastating fire of 1823. It adjoins the southern transept, and was built in 1205 to 1241 under the abbots Petrus of Capua and Johannes of Ardea. It was built at the same time as the very similar cloister of S. Giovanni in Laterano (C33), so that it can be presumed that the Cosmati artists of the Vassalletto family worked on S. Paolo too. Although the structural scheme is comparable with that of the cloister of SS. Quattro (C31), the impression of multifarious variety, and the abundance of individual shapes, are much more strongly prevalent in. To take only one example, the splendid and differently shaped double columns, which are either flat or fluted, with the columns of each pair either turned in towards one another or woven together out of two strands, were here executed with very great mastery. This cloister is the most successful of the three that have survived, because its proportions are also very well balanced: the openings are bright and wide, corresponding with the size. The eastern and western wings are each divided into five compartments by pilasters which are bent at right angles in the entablature. Each of the compartments contains four round-arched arcades, and a fifth, slightly elevated arch, flanked by splendid projecting half-columns, is inserted in the middle compartment. This arch marks

the passageway. The northern and southern wings are somewhat narrower. Four compartments, each with four round-arched arcades, are accentuated at their centres by an inserted columned arcade which frames the opening leading on to the garden. The marble reliefs in the spandrels between the arches display the entire repertoire of medieval symbolic depictions of plants, masks and animals. To make the overall appearance more splendid still, a richly articulated entablature was inserted between the roof and arcades. AG

C33 S. Giovanni in Laterano: cloister
Piazza di Porta S. Giovanni in Laterano (plan VIII 2/A)
c. 1220–40

Although the cloister of S. Giovanni in Laterano was begun some 20 years later than that of S. Paolo fuori le Mura (C32), it was completed at about the same time. The order to carry out this leading work of Cosmati-work art was placed during the pontificate of Honorius III. The work was completed in c. 1240, during Pope Innocent IV's pontificate. A striking feature is that the proportions are somewhat more compact than in the S. Paolo cloister, while on the other hand the detailed shapes are more finely elaborated. Here too, the little columns are alternately either plain or fluted, and either turned in towards one another or woven together out of two strands. This interplay, and the shimmering mosaic inlays, disguise the supporting function of the little columns and make them into a decorative element in their own right. The compartments, again articulated by pilasters, each consist of five arcaded arches. The arches which stand all around are scarcely interrupted by the passageways. The relatively uniform overall shape directs the onlooker's gaze to the abundance of imaginative details. The quality of the craftsmanship is seen not only in the delicate shaping of the arches, but also in the marble reliefs in the spandrels, depicting animal figures, leafwork and masks. Further examples demonstrating that the Vassalletti were superb sculptors are the sphinxes by the exit in the southern wing, the capitals with their figures in the northern wing, and the splen-

C33 S. Giovanni in Laterano: cloister

C34 Abbazia alle Tre Fontane

didly decorated leaf-work capitals. Below the mosaic frieze of the richly adorned entablature, there is a geometrical pattern accompanied by the proud inscription of Vassalletto father and son, the two artists. The entablature is concluded above the frieze by a cornice decorated with leaves, masks, lions' heads and palmettes. Among the fragments exhibited in the cloister, mention should be made of the remains of Cardinal Annibaldi's tomb (1276) by Arnolfo di Cambio. AG

C34 Abbazia alle Tre Fontane
Via delle Tre Fontane (plan G2 3/B, plan VII 2/C and plan VIII 2/C)
begun 1221

This monastery was built on the site on which, according to tradition, Paul the Apostle was executed. The monastery was given its name by the three springs which, so the legend relates, started from the ground here after Paul's head had struck it three times. No remains survive of Pope Honorius I's original building dating from 625. The earliest surviving component in the monastery section is built into the gatehouse. The barrel-vaulted brickwork passageway, with a columned gallery above, is interpreted as being part of the oratory from the S. Giovanni Battista baptistery dating from 780.

After the Cistercians took over the monastery in 1140, they began in 1221 to erect the new structure of the monastery church of SS. Vincenzo e Anastasio, which still survives today. Although it was built as a basilica in the Roman tradition, it is shaped by the frugal, severe architectural philosophy of the Cistercians. This plain brick structure is, in the interior, made somewhat rigid by the massive, angular pillars dividing the tall nave from the very low aisles which make a squat impression, and also by the uniform wall area above the arcades with their long spans. Some typical features of Cistercian architecture are the choir with its flat conclusion, and the transept which projects only a little way and is also lower than the central part of the nave of church. This order's preference for vaulted church structures did not gain acceptance in Rome. An open roof frame was inserted instead of

the planned barrel vault whose beginnings are still visible in the clerestory.

The monastery complex is supplemented by two simple centrally planned buildings, S. Paolo alle Tre Fontane and S. Maria Scala Coeli (B13), erected by Giacomo della Porta in the late 16C. AG

C35 Torre delle Milizie
Via Quattro Novembre (plan V 1/B)
13C

This tower between Trajan's markets (A29) and the church of S. Caterina a Magnanapoli (B47) is among the most significant secular architectural monuments of medieval Rome. It was one of the few family towers surviving in Rome, and was used as a fortification by the most influential Roman aristocratic families, including Annibaldi, Caetani, Conti and Colonna. It took its name from a barracks which formerly adjoined it and was used by Byzantine militias. There was a previous 12C structure, and the tower surviving today was probably built in the early 13C as part of a fortification, although no exact chronological information is available. The building frequently changed hands, with the result that there were repeated alterations and restorations.

The tower, projecting far above the surrounding buildings, is made of a tall upright structure which is not subdivided except for a few small window openings, and of a smaller cube rising above this. Both sections are of pure brickwork, but the upper part contrasts with the lower because its external wall stands some way back and its edges are rounded, and chiefly because it is articulated by projecting pilaster strips. Originally there was another storey above this, but it fell victim to an earthquake in 1348; today the tower ends in a crenellation at the top.

At a height of over 51 m, the Torre delle Milizie is the most massive of the medieval family towers still surviving in Rome, and is thus an important example of this architectural type which shapes the characteristic medieval townscape of some other Italian towns such as San Gimignano, but hardly finds any parallel in Rome itself. DH

C36 S. Maria in Aracoeli
Piazza Venezia (plan V 1/B)
1250

Its excellent location alone makes the church of S. Maria in Aracoeli very significant. It stands on the site where a temple of Juno, the shrine of Virgo Caelestis, and the Auguraculum, all stood in classical times. A monastery is recorded as having been founded on this site in the 8C. It passed into the possession of the Benedictines in the 10C. When the Roman senate was reinstated in 1143, there began to be a close link between the city's government and the monastery. The nearby Capitol hill had since classical times fulfilled important functions as a symbol of civic power in Rome. This tradition was now continued by the church and monastery. It was here that the city parliament met and courts of justice were sometimes held.

In 1249, Pope Innocent IV donated the monastery to the mendicant order of the Franciscans. The following year the Franciscans began a new church building, whose design corresponded to that of today's structure. Probably in order to lend further distinction to the site, a legend has been in circulation since that time. It concerns an altar which Emperor Augustus is said to have founded here when the Tiburtine Sibyl foretold to him that the time was near when a divine child would be born who would defeat the old gods and found a new era. In 1348, the Roman people, as a token of gratitude for being saved from the plague, presented to Madonna of Aracoeli the staircase of 124 steps leading upwards. The cross-section façade, which is still undecorated and unfriendly today and has a cavetto-work conclusion (cf. S. Maria sopra Minerva, C37), was given its true character at that time. Along with the ramp on the right, which leads to the Capitol in terraces consisting of broad steps (H27), the stairs present an architectural sight unprecedented up until then. The broad steps of the ramp are a relatively comfortable way of reaching the Capitol, the public square. On the other hand, some effort is required in

C36 S. Maria in Aracoeli

order to climb the steep and narrow steps up to the church. The Romans were rightly proud of this unique structure and immortalized its architect, Lorenzo di Simone Andreozzi, in an inscription beside the main portal.

The mid-13C period when the church was built, and the fact that its appearance was only slightly altered in the baroque period, show that the High Gothic, which was flourishing in Northern Europe, scarcely found an echo in Rome (cf. S. Maria sopra Minerva, C37). This large columned basilica has a nave, two aisles, and a short continuous transept which does not extend beyond the alignment of the aisles. The shape and proportions of the nave follow early-Christian models. The round-arched arcades are borne by varying columns, and the spoils derive from the Palatine and the various buildings in the Forums. The rather settled broadness of the nave contrasts with the low and narrow aisles. The slightly inserted, almost square, box-shaped choir, with a short bay in front of it, is improved by the doubling of the two splendid triumphal arches which mark off the transept. The splendour is heightened not only by the spoils, by also by the floor, a work by the Cosmati artists. The Gothic style prevails only in a few details, such as the slight pointedness of the arcaded arches; the design as a whole is based on the tradition of early-Christian Roman basilicas. The wooden ceiling with the symbol of navigation was donated in 1571 in memory of the naval victory at Lepanto. The first family chapels were attached next to the choir in the late 13C. They are the earliest demonstrable examples of this architectural type in Rome. They were followed by numerous others, which soon surrounded the entire church. In this way the church structure visibly expanded into a basilica with a nave and four aisles. The most famous of these chapels is by the right aisle. It was decorated in 1485 with frescoes by Pinturicchio. AG

C37 S. Maria sopra Minerva
Piazza della Minerva (plan IV 2/B)
begun 1280, 1450 to late 15C

A political power struggle between the two great mendicant orders of the Franciscans and the Dominicans led to the construction of the only church in Rome to have been built in the Gothic style. In order to disassociate themselves, in terms of architecture too, from the competition of the Franciscans who, shortly before, had built a church (C36) in the tradition of early-Christian Roman basilicas, the Dominicans chose for S. Maria sopra Minerva, the church of their order, the modern Gothic architectural style, which had been almost unknown in Rome until then.

It has been demonstrated that, in the 8C, a church was founded to the east of the Pantheon, where a monumental square stood in ancient Roman times. The epithet »sopra Minerva« is based on an error, because there was not a temple of Minerva beneath the church, but instead a shrine of Isis. But it has been

C37 S. Maria sopra Minerva

proved that a small round temple of Minerva Chalcid-
ica, above which the small church of S. Marta was
built, stood a little further to the east, on the Piazza del
Collegio Romano. The mendicant order of the Dominicans obtained the area in c. 1280, and work on constructing the new church was begun immediately. The
Gothic vaults were only inserted after 1450, and the
entire building was finally completed in the late 15C.
In 1453 the church was given a Renaissance façade,
which until the 18C was similar in form to that of S.
Maria in Aracoeli (C36). Restoration work performed
in 1848–55 slightly altered the vault and the original
system of projections.

In 1725, the undecorated, plastered Renaissance
façade was subdivided by flat pilaster strips, with the
upper gable-shaped conclusion (cavetto work) being
removed in this process. The three marble portals
date from the 15C, but have been altered in parts. The
eye-catching feature of the façade is the elephant on
the square outside the church (B95). It bears an obelisk which had been excavated in this area. In 1667,
Ercole Ferrata, following a model by Lorenzo Bernini,
created this lovable elephant which bears its heavy
load not without humour.

The church interior is indebted in many respects to
the Dominican church of S. Maria Novella in Florence,
begun some 40 years earlier. The ground plan and elevation system, and also the spatial proportions, are
foreign to the Roman architectural tradition, and are
clearly derived from the older church of the Dominican
order. But the Dominican church in Rome is not a
copy of the Florentine model, but combines the Roman architectural tradition with the new Gothic language of forms. The ground plan (one nave, two
aisles) of the main part of the building is adjoined in
the east by a projecting transept with five choir chapels on its long eastern wall. These choir chapels are
of differing, graduated depths, and are accentuated
by the main apse which is located in the middle and is
broken up polygonally. The richly graduated choir section with its apses had been widespread in the architecture of monastery churches since the Ottonian pe-

riod. The system is simplified in S. Maria sopra Minerva, and the secondary chapels have a flat conclusion. Unlike their prototypes, they do not present,
from the outside, a rich architectural sight consisting
of graduated three-dimensional round structures.

A feature shared by the Roman church and by
S. Maria Novella, its model in Florence, is that they
both follow the architectural type of the basilica with
a nave, two aisles, a groined vault and a projecting
transept. The spatial proportions are already set forth
in the six approximately square-shaped bays of the
nave which are flanked in the aisles by narrow bays
having a lengthwise rectangular shape. The spatial impression produced by the nave of the church is determined by the broadness of the way in which the
arcades open towards the aisles; the latter are themselves scarcely lit and are therefore seen in a single
unit with the nave. In this respect, this Gothic church
differs from the previous Roman architectural tradition
and, in its hall-like breadth, displays a great affinity
with the Gothic buildings in Central Italy. But in contrast to S. Maria Novella, where this hall-like width of
the spatial character is more predominant, S. Maria
sopra Minerva remains indebted to the Roman buildings where the greater emphasis placed on the nave
is concerned. In the older church, the rows of arcades
are lent rhythm by the alternation of pointed and
round arches, whereas its Roman successor, with
its uniform rows of pointed-arched arcades, more
strongly emphasizes the nave. The nave is also more
clearly delimited from the aisles by the shape of the
pillars which, in spite of the four half-columns placed
in front of them in each case, present themselves
much more decisively as a united mass. Finally, the
design of the transept – which was originally planned
to be lower, and was given its tall ribbed vault in the
15C – can be compared with that of Roman transepts in its tendency to be set off from the nave of
the church. The sculptures in the capitals are also the
work of Roman stonemasons because, by comparison with related Northern works, they display the classical repertoire of shapes inspired by the ancient Roman period.

The decision in favour of a stone vault instead of an
open roof built of wood was something of a sensation
for Roman medieval architecture. Large buildings had
not been given vaults since the classical period. However, the impetus for this was provided not by classical times, but by the systematic architecture of the
Gothic period. It is possible to discern a close relationship with S. Maria Novella in Florence, but Roman
building traditions have also left their mark in Rome's
only Gothic church. AG

1 1/2 days: C4, C7, C8, (C15), C10, (C17), C5, C6,
C20, C26, C16, C28 and – as a transiton to the Renaissance – H4.

Christian late antiquity and Middle Ages

Late Middle Ages and early Renaissance (1377–1500)

Martin V (1417–31) moved to Rome in 1420, after 100 years of absence by the popes, and made the city the centre of the Christian world once more. By restoring papal power and authority he proved to be the man who actually re-established the Roman papacy. From this point the popes were the most influential building clients, who stamped a new image on the city with their major projects. During the Avignon exile (1309–77) and the subsequent schism (1378 to 1417) Rome had sunk into complete insignificance and building activity had come to an almost complete halt. Martin V came back to a desolate, lifeless city; cows grazed in the Forum and the Capitol had declined into Monte Caprino, the goats' meadow. The building tradition had been interrupted for a full century. In Florence Filippo Brunelleschi was producing the first masterpieces of Renaissance architecture, but in Rome the worst of the damage had to be made good first of all. Rebuilding the city walls and roads, bridges and water supplies – renovation of the infrastructure – and the restoration of the 40 main churches delayed the development of the new style of architecture for about half a century. Martin V proved his farsightedness as a large-scale town planner by reviving the office of magistri viarum, the master builders for roads, whose tradition went back to the imperial period. By making it part of the papal administration the popes had got their hands on the most important instrument of urban building policy, which was to have an effect during the High-Renaissance and and Baroque period.

Eugenius IV (1431–47) continued the restoration work, concentrating on Rome's three most important centres: the Capitol, the Lateran and the Vatican. The idea of renovatio and the aim of restoring Rome's former splendour and lost greatness was also propagated by the humanists who had started to collect at the papal court. A first step towards the renovation of the ancient buildings was the uncovering of the Pantheon porch. Despite this, rebuilding the city inevitably went hand in hand with the destruction of ancient Rome, whose monuments were exploited as quarries until well into the 16th century.

Nicholas V (1447–55) was the first manifestation of the huanistically educated Renaissance pope, who wanted to display the papacy's new prestige in architecture above all, and to by associating it directly with Roman antiquity. Despite fragmentary realization, his wide-reaching plans set the scale for all future planning and anticipated the ideas of the High Renaissance in their splendour. The creator of these ambitious projects was L. B. Alberti, a humanist and architectural theorists who had been with the Curia since 1431 and dedicated his architectural treatise De re aedificatoria, in which he had formulated the theoretical basis of the new style, to the pope in 1451.

Even if there is not a single building in Rome that can be directly linked with the name of Alberti, he was a major influence in the development of Roman Renaissance architecture. He brought unity and antique form to Nicholas V's bold plans for redesigning the Vatican and rebuilding St Peter's – the first far-reaching urban development concept since ancient times. The densely built-up area between Castel Sant'Angelo and and St Peter's, the so-called Borgo, was to be organized by three radially spreading streets lined with porticoes, focused at a newly arranged St Peter's Square, which already anticipated Bernini's dimensions (B80). The square was to become the forum of quintessential Christendom – consciously borrowing from imperial models. Such an all-embracing adoption of key ancient structures had awakened memories of Roman rulers even for contemporaries. Only a few fragments remain of the planned, massice fortress complex that would have secured the Borgo as a separate district, as the city of the Curia and the papal residence. The extension of the Vatican, which had replaced the Lateran as the official papal residence since the return of Martin V, remained incomplete, with the exception of the Cortile dei Papagalli (F1).

The focal point of the whole complex was the rebuilding of St Peter's (H7). A massive vaulted structure was to be added to Constantine the Great's nave and aisles. It would have put all previous Renaissance buildings in the shade and articulated the »grand style« inspired by Roman antiquity. Choir and transept were to be spanned with mighty groined vaults on columns, centred by an enormous crossing dome. The foundations of the so-called Rosselino choir, the only fragment of this gigantic project, were still used by Bramante to give scale to his plans (H7). The plans for St Peter's, which founded the new, specifically Roman style of Renaissance architecture, filled with the spirit of antiquity, in contrast with Florence are reflected by project like for example the ancient-Roman style vault of S. Maria sopra Minerva (C37), S. Maria del Popolo (F7), S. Agostino (F14) and even for the building of S. Giacomo degli Spagnuoli (F2), which is generally unusual for Rome. The epoch-making building of the Roman Renaissance and its spiritual father can scarcely be grasped in Rome itself and were not to develop the full range of their significance until almost the end of the century.

Pius II's (1458–64) first commitment was to making his home town of Pienza into the first ideal city of the Renaissance. But he did continue Nicholas V's building projects by building a benediction loggia in front of St Peter's; its appearance is preserved in a drawing by Heemskerck: a three-storey, backcloth-like show façade with columns in front of it made a magnificent setting for the papal blessing. The splendidly staged tabularium motif (A9) was used here for the first time in Renaissance architecture, and the direct

Old St Peter's: loggia of benediction

adoption of the articulation of the Colosseum (A25) was to turn out to be one of the most important and momentous innovations in modern architecture, which was immediately followed in Rome itself (F5, F6). Placed in front of St Peter's in the ancient garb of the Colosseum, the benediction loggia demonstrates the Roman pontifex's lofty claim to be the direct successor of ancient power. The architect of the loggia, Francesco del Borgo – presumably a pupil of Alberti – distinguished himself particularly through the direct proximity to antiquity, which also illustrated the high rank of papal architecture in other buildings (F5, F6). He was one of the few tangible architect personalities of the Roman quattrocento, which unlike Florence tended to remain anonymous, and produced few noteworthy masters.

Paul II (1464–71), a Venetian lover of pageantry, who adopted a prestigious lifestyle, was late to recognize and use the talent of Francesco del Borgo. But finally he handed him the biggest building project of his pontificate, the extension to the Palazzo Venezia (F5), which set new standards for Roman palace building in the quattrocento. Palaces built before this one (F1, F3) still showed their origin in medieval-feudal fortress building, despite a few Renaissance elements like the cross window, for example. The Palazzo Venezia's status as a pioneering building in modern palace architecture is justified above all by its truly monumental dimensions, the regularization of the whole complex with the first enfilade of modern times, the balanced proportions and the urban function of the building. Size and seriousness, a block-like quality and weight were to remain, in contrast with the Florentine tradition, the characteristic features of Roman palace building (H25).

The reign of Sixtus IV (1471–84) is seen as one of the »darkest« episodes in the Renaissance papacy, because ecclesiastical matters came well behind his worldly and political interests. Nepotism, providing his relatives with livings and key position in the ecclesiastical hierarchy (including Pietro Riario and Giuliano della Rovere, later to be Julius II), and external political ambition led to financial ruin, war and general unrest in the church state.

But art and building flourished under these circumstances; the Papal Bull of 7 December 1473 makes the following programmatic demand for Rome: »Because for her above all, who is the head of the earth as seat of the Apostle-Priest asserts its primacy over every other city, it is seemly that externally as well she should be the cleanest and the most beautiful city.« Here Sixtus is following his predecessors, but the scope of his activity was unique and earned him the honorary name of restaurator urbis suae.

The authority of the magistri viarum was increased. Whole streets were completely renewed, e. g. the Via Recta, now dei Coronari, or the Via Sistina, now di Monte Brianzo – regular, straight axes in the heavily populated Tiber bend. Many of the measures were of great use in terms of civilization: street straightening and street paving, the building of the Ponte Sisto (F11), the first new bridge since ancient times, and of the Ospedale di S. Spirito in Sassia (F8).

According to the life by Giorgio Vasari, Baccio Pontelli, who came from Tuscany and was trained at the ducal court in Urbino, is said to have played a leading role as an artistic advisor for Sixtus's building enterprises. But his actual involvement in individual buildings is questionable, as Pontelli, a trained artist in intarsia and carver, can be shown to have worked in Rome only late in the pontificate of Sixtus, and then mainly as a fortress architect (citadel in Ostia).

While hitherto palace building had predominated (F1, F3, F4, F5), church buildings now acquired particular status , as the Pope or his cardinals wished to immortalize themselves as builders (F7, F9, F13, F14, F16). In fact it was not until the reign of Sixtus that the long series of Roman Renaissance and Baroque churches started, and the buildings show clear signs of being pioneering work. Quality varies considerably, for example the clumsy formal language of S. Agostino (F14) can only be called provincial. More successful formal language, like that of S. Maria del Popolo (F7) or the perfect spatial proportions of the Sistine Chapel (F13) did not have an impact on the shaping of style. But the diversity of building types and ideas is astonishing. In the exterior of buildings the older loggia type is used (F9), and also the forward-looking cross-section façade type (F7. F14). Interiors include: the great hall space of the Sistine Chapel (F13), variations on the vaulted basilica like S. Maria del Popolo (F7) and S. Agostino (F14), the highly modern combination of hall and central space in S. Maria della Pace (F16) and an interesting variation of the church with crossing dome in S. Maria della Pietà on the Campo Santo Teutonico (F12). As a contribution to future development this wealth of ideas was as important as the constant adoption of individual ancient motifs.

Church buildings after 1484 (F17, F18, F20) once more extend the diverse image of the early Renaissance in ecclesiastical building. Overall the pontificates of Innocent VIII (1484–92) and Alexander VI (1492–1503) started no significant trends. One exception here was the ambitious Cardinal Raffaele Riario, whose palace, the later Cancelleria (F19), of enormous dimensions and the highest architectural quality and featuring momentous innovations in the art of the façade like mezzanine floor, ressaut and rhythmical bay in pilaster order formed the climax of the epoch. In palace-building the early Roman Renaissance achieved significance throughout Europe. UF/EJ

F1 Vaticano: Cortile dei Pappagalli
Città del Vaticano (Plan III 1/A)
c. 1450

The complex of buildings which is the Vatican Palace makes a confusing impression on most visitors, but its present shape is the product of a simple succession of events in the history of architecture. The four-winged building which surrounds the Cortile dei Pappagalli was the nucleus and starting point. In the period that followed, that building remained visible towards the south, where the forecourt of the basilica adjoins it.

Sixtus IV ordered the first extension, the Sistine Chapel (F13), to be built in the west of that building, towering above it and standing at an oblique angle to it. The buildings by Bramante followed from 1503 onwards. These were the belvedere courtyard to the north (H6) – extensions to it were built at its far northern end in the 20C (cf. M7) – and the eastern façade of the original four-winged building. That façade was later repeated on two further sides, thus developing the structure into the U-shaped Damasus courtyard which is open towards the south (H11). Finally, Fontana's four-winged structure followed. It adjoins the eastern arm of that courtyard, and is today the section projecting further than any other towards St. Peter's Square (B19).

This entire complex of buildings came into being in its present form from 1450 onwards. Until the time of exile in Avignon, the residence of the Bishop of Rome was the Lateran (cf. C15), and it was not until 1378 that the first conclave was held in the Vatican and Gregory XI moved his residence there. The dimensions and appearance of the early-medieval buildings, the first of which were commissioned by Pope Symmachus in c. 500, are largely unknown. It is more likely to have been a fortress-like structure, consisting of towers and barracks, than a palace; all that there is

Γ1 Città del Vaticano with Cortile dei Pappagalli

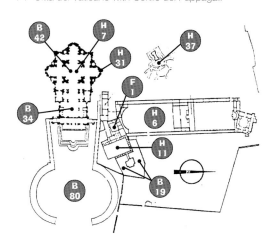

F2 S. Giacomo degli Spagnuoli (Nostra Signora del Sacro Cuore)

much of to see today is the course of the walls built by Pope Leo IV (846–55), which made the area of St. Peter's into a fortified city (»Città«). From that time onwards, an initial conglomerate of buildings was erected over the centuries, but it fell into ruin during the exile in Avignon. It was only later that Pope Nicholas V (1447–55), in building the Cortile dei Pappagalli, created the nucleus of today's complex of buildings. Under this first great rebuilder of Rome, the Vatican thus became the heart of papal architectural policy and of the »renovatio imperii«.

Nicholas V had planned a four-winged building, of which the section that is still the most significant today, namely the three-storeyed northern wing with its basement, was erected in c. 1450. Each of its upper storeys (today the Appartamento Borgia and the Stanze of Raphael) was given three rooms. A little later, the complex was finished with the western wing and the irregular, sombre, inner courtyard, the Cortile dei Pappagalli, came into being. From the windows of the narrow corridor behind Raphael's Stanze, the visitor can look at this courtyard with its forms typical of the 15C: these are the corbelled entablature, and the flat façades with irregularly distributed windows and no division into storeys. The name of the courtyard refers to the frescos which formerly decorated the façades and depicted parrots and other animals, alluding to a former aviary in the eastern arm. SG

F2 S. Giacomo degli Spagnuoli (Nostra Signora del Sacro Cuore)
Corso del Rinascimento (Plan IV 1/A–1/B)
1450 to late 15C
S. Giacomo degli Spagnuoli was, by order of Alfonso Paradinas, the Spanish prelate, built from 1450 on wards as the national church of the Spaniards. It is

the earliest of the few hall churches in Rome (cf. F20). Various later alterations greatly transformed the building. It was not originally made to relate to the Piazza Navona, and its façade was oriented on the eastern Via della Sapienza. It initially consisted of three aisles of equal height, each with three bays which had groined vaults. Only later, in preparation for the jubilee year of 1500, did Alexander VI order it to be lengthened as far as the Piazza Navona (B61) and given a façade there. However, this was only a show façade because, inside the building, the high altar was placed in front of the walled-up main portal. In contrast to the articulation in the interior, this façade was of a basilican cross-section design (today's façade was altered in the 19C). The original (eastern) façade, and the entire first bay, were pulled down in the course of building the Corso del Rinascimento in the 19C.

The interior is shaped by the forms of the quattrocentro. Two striking features are the wide way in which the bays open towards one another, and the uniform spatial character which results from the equal height of the aisles and from the absence of a clerestory. This is a hall room which is shaped not by clear emphasis in one particular direction, but by a free view of all the aisles – a form atypical for Rome and used only in buildings for foreigners. DH

F3 Palazzo Capranica
Piazza Capranica 98–101 (Plan IV 2/A)
begun 1451
The Palazzo Capranica is one of the first large cardinals' palaces which were built in Rome after the popes returned from Avignon and which demonstrate the increase in self-assurance among leading circles in Rome. Cardinal Domenico Capranica began building the palace in the 1450's, including within it some

F3 Palazzo Capranica

F4 Casa dei Cavalieri di Rodi

older residential structures. He set up the Collegio Capranica here, which in 1478 was moved to a separate
section that was attached to the palace at right angles
(and was converted in 1955). If contemporaneous
Florentine palace buildings, which already embody in
perfect form the prototype of the Italian Renaissance
palace, are considered, the Roman tradition of palace
architecture seems to be not very well developed. The
façade of the palazzo is not yet designed to a uniform
plan, and shows that Roman palace architecture in
the early Renaissance was greatly indebted to older
traditions. The building was later altered by adding another storey, walling up the windows and installing
shutters. Despite this, it clearly shows some specifically Roman features: the unsubdivided and smoothly plastered surface of the brickwork, the block-like
nature of the massive structure, the absence of decorations in the façade which is marked only by two
large cross-shaped windows in the piano nobile, the
tall and formerly self-contained ground floor, the
asymmetrically placed entrance portal (the western
portal followed in 1478), and the massive, compact
tower with its belvedere placed on top (the earliest
known belvedere in Rome). Even here it can be seen
that simple but effective large size, and unadorned
dignity, were the features aimed at in Rome, and this
contrasted with the richly subdivided Florentine palaces. Simplicity and monumentality, instead of abundance and variety in subdivision and surface relief,
were the factors that counted. EJ

F4 Casa dei Cavalieri di Rodi
Piazza del Grillo 1 (Plan V 1/B)
begun 1466
The palace of the Knights of St. John of Jerusalem,
known since the 16C as the Knights of Malta, was
built from 1466 onwards for Marco Barbo, who was
a cardinal, a pope's favoured nephew, and the prior of
the Knights of St. John in Rome. The building is one
of the urbanist plans of Paul II – the latter wanted to
revive the ancient centre (cf. F5) –, and is attributed
to his architect Francesco del Borgo. The extensive

complex would highly merit investigation in more detail.
The staircases and halls, whose detailed shapes
are reminiscent of the Palazzo Venezia, have been
skilfully integrated into the ancient masonry of the annexes in the Forum of Augustus (A20). The window
openings in the exterior wall of the Forum make the
defiant, embossed masonry work of the ancient dividing wall into a palace façade of grandiose pretensions.
The windows themselves are if anything antiquated
in form: they are biforia with projections and pointed
arches above. Such delicate Gothic formations were
at the time also found in Florentine palace architecture. The topmost point in this multi-storeyed building
is occupied by a loggia which is opened up on two
sides by columned arcades. Ancient spoils were used
for their shafts and Ionic capitals. Thus an airy belvedere was created. It invited the visitor not only to look
at the large-scale ruins of the Forum of Trajan (A29)
and the Maxentius basilica (A50), but also to pursue
humanistic reflections on Rome's ancient greatness,
the recreation of which was the purpose of the Renaissance popes' programme. UF
Bibliography: C. Ricci, »Il Foro d'Augusto e la Casa
dei Cavalieri di Rodi«, in *Capitolium*, 1930, 157.

F5 Palazzo Venezia
Piazza Venezia / Piazza S. Marco (Plan V 1/B)
begun 1466
Francesco del Borgo
The complex of the Palazzo Venezia is among the
most significant early-Renaissance buildings in Rome.
A building that was determinant in palace architecture
from the end of the Middle Ages onwards was erected
in a new attempt to use the resources of architecture
to present the magnificent grandiosity of the papacy
and the splendour of its power. After being elected
Pope Paul II, Pietro Barbo, who was a Venetian and a

F5 Palazzo Venezia

favoured nephew of Pope Eugene IV, took the spectacular decision to expand the existing cardinals' palace near his titular church of S. Marco (C19) and turn it into a papal residence in the centre of the city, far away from the Vatican and near the great ancient monuments. His architect was Francesco del Borgo, a humanist and papal official who, at the papal court, was probably influenced by the architecture of Alberti, and also by the latter's scientific study of the classical period. He certainly also knew the architectural projects of the Curia from the time of Nicholas V onwards (cf. introduction).

The palace consists of three parts whose very arrangement set a trend in the urban development of Rome. The palace (A) and the large courtyard (B) are a compact block around the old colonnaded basilica (C; cf. C19), whereas the rectangle of the so-called Palazzetto Venezia (D) was originally attached at its tip to the south-eastern edge of the palace. That is the edge which today projects freely into the Piazza Venezia. Thus two city squares came into being in this formerly densely built-up area: one was outside the palace façade (E), and the other outside the new benediction loggia (cf. F6). They were rectangles about twice as long as they were wide, and thus reflected the recommendation which Alberti, in his treatise on architecture, made for city squares. Since the late 19C it has no longer been possible to gain a mental picture of this, as the older building work in the section nearer the Capitol has been removed and the entire Palazzetto has been moved to the west in order to create some empty space outside the monument to Vittorio Emanuele (K15). Thus it was that today's much larger Piazza Venezia came into being.

The starting point for the new palace (A) was the preceding structure that stood on the eastern side of S. Marco, was a typical cardinals' palace dating from c. 1455 (cf. F3), and is still discernible from the fact that the windows in today's eastern façade stand closer together. The new sections adjoined it in an L-shape around the church choir. Special attention was paid in the planning to the orderly succession of impressive papal rooms. In accordance with established court etiquette, there is on the first floor, called the piano nobile, a succession of rooms which grow continuously smaller: the Sala Regia, the two rooms of the Sala Ducale, the anteroom known as Sala dei Paramenti, and finally the audience room which was called Sala del Pappagallo and was adjoined by the existing private apartments in the older sections of the building. A decisive factor here is that the door openings are kept in a straight line in such a way that there is a continuous axis, both visually and where walking through the rooms is concerned. Thus this was an enfilade which, as a principle was used in a succession of palace architecture. This internal arrangement was so important that the irregular distances between the façade windows were thought to be quite acceptable, and the exterior view is in any case very re-

F5 Palazzo Venezia

strained. The building is concluded by the crenellation, which adds a fortifying and at the same time crowning touch. The smooth cubic structure is traversed only by cornices which indicate the division into three storeys and lend the windows an expressive stability. The windows display a geometrical regularity of simply shaped round arches and rectangles. But it is precisely this undecorated austerity that guaranteed the building's powerful effect, its gravitas, which was now to characterize palace architecture in Rome for a long time.

The exterior of the Palazzetto Venezia (D), being a somewhat smaller crenellated cube shape, is closely related, even though it has two rows of round-arched windows in its two storeys. However, apart from a small apartment, it does not contain any dwelling rooms, but firstly a hidden private garden measuring 36 m x 36 m with its soil elevated above ground level, and secondly that garden's architectural surroundings: a two-storeyed, rectangular, surrounding loggia used by the pope for strolling and as a place for private audiences. Neither secret gardens nor inner courtyards were anything new in Renaissance architecture, but a particular architectural quality is seen in the detailed formation of the arcatures. The lower arcades have typical early-Renaissance octagonal pillars, perfectly formed. It was particularly the capitals that became exemplary in Rome: they consist of beautifully curved, chalice-like shapes on all four sides, filled up with the papal coat of arms or the palmette ornament, while their ends coil up into scrolls on the chamfered edges of the pillars. But the fact that ancient Rome and its classical canon of shapes had been studied is noticeable in the entablature above this, and particularly in the sturdy Ionic columns of the upper arcature. The design of the upper entablature can be rated as a genuine piece of humanist architecture, because success was here achieved in using, for the entablature, a clearly ancient form which was borrowed from the Colosseum and was based on an ancient writer who was an authority. In his well-known treatise on architecture, Vitruvius, a Roman, stated that the entablature of an order of columns was derived from the wooden buildings of earlier times and from the designs of their beams. This is why here, in the Palazzetto, the entablature covers the beams of the roof frame.

A separate inner courtyard (B) attached to the western flank of the basilica is the third part of the palace. Visitors entered this courtyard through the main entrance in the north before proceeding to the stairs leading to the audience rooms. Although the courtyard was only begun after the architect's death, it nevertheless displays his style. Compared with the courtyards of the Florentine Renaissance, this inner courtyard, which has the dimensions of a city square, was a tremendous innovation. The same applies to the two-storeyed loggia, whose structure was no longer a light and airy columned arcature, but instead displayed the tabularium motif (cf. A9): this was a much more closely linked combination consisting of pillared arcades and an order of half-columns placed out in front. This lent the courtyard an ancient character. But here too, a detailed study of ancient Rome goes hand in hand with the architect's own ideas: the arcades, as compared with the Colosseum, are elongated and more slender. The horizontal level is dominant in the far-projecting entablature of the Colosseum, whereas the returned entablatures of the courtyard more strongly emphasize the verticality of the columns. In addition, this emphasizes the superposition of the columns. The overall tone is lighter and applies rather to the individual members than to the massiveness of the architecture.

The fact that only a small part of the enormous courtyard was built was probably not due to the death (1468) of the architect or to that (1471) of the orderer of the work. Paul II, while still alive, seems to have been assailed by doubts regarding his project for a private papal residence. After a murder conspiracy had been uncovered outside the palace, the security problems in the closely-built old core area of the city became apparent, and for this reason the fortified tower in the south-eastern corner of the Palazzo was built in 1470. From then on, building activities concentrated more intensely on the Vatican, as if Paul II was once again giving preference to the location, so rich in tradition, near St. Peter's. Although later owners, and also some popes, carried out further work on the furnishings, the palace became the residence of the Venetian embassy in 1564. Since 1916 it has been State-owned and houses a well-known art collection. Mussolini who was head of State, and his State council, resided in the large staterooms between 1929 and 1943. UF

Bibliography: Ch. L. Frommel: »Francesco del Borgo: Architekt Pius II und Pauls II. Zweiter Teil: Palazzo Venezia, Palazzetto Venezia und San Marco«, in *Römisches Jahrbuch*, 1984, p. 711.

F6 S. Marco: Benediction Loggia
Piazza S. Marco (plan V 1/B)
begun 1466
Francesco del Borgo

The fact that the Palazzo Venezia was intended as the residence of Pope Paul II is also shown by the façade which was placed for show in front of the associated basilica of S. Marco (C19). Reduced to two storeys and three bays, it is a repetition of a main work of the early Renaissance: this was the benediction loggia which belonged to St. Peter's, was never completed, was later torn down, and had been begun under Pius II by the same architect in c. 1460.

The upper storey was built in altered shapes after the death of Paul II, but the lower storey ostentatiously imitates the imperial classical period. The tabularium motif (cf. A9) taken from Roman theatrical architecture forms the façade, and here the parallels with the nearby Colosseum (A25) – from which travertine, the building material, was also taken – extend as far as the precisely observed detail of the profiles, cornices and capitals. What is more surprising still is that even the massiveness and weighty appearance of the prototype have been captured. But at the same time the architect also permitted himself to make alterations: he used the composita, the most distinguished order of columns, on the ground floor. He was more interested in verticality, and therefore formed the horizontal entablature less strongly, interspersing it with corbellings above the columns.

In expressing the new grandiosity of the papacy by combining the gravitas of the Roman classical period with ideas and architectural functions of a new kind, Francesco del Borgo was really already laying down the programme for the High Renaissance. UF

Bibliography: see F5.

F6 S. Marco: Benediction Loggia

F7 S. Maria del Popolo

F7 S. Maria del Popolo
Piazza del Popolo 12 (plan I 3/D)
1472–77
Andrea Bregno (?)

S. Maria del Popolo, the church of the Lombard congregation of the Augustinian hermits, is among the
most significant early-Renaissance church buildings in
Rome and is one of Sixtus IV's numerous projects. It
houses the tombs of several cardinals from the della
Rovere family.

Some alterations made by Bernini must be taken
into account in the façade: there were originally no
gable sections at the sides, and the window openings
must be imagined as having included tracery-work
panels. The reason why this building became typological for Rome (cf. H26, B1) is that the façade is not designed as a projecting loggia (cf. F6, F9), but instead
reflects the interior, and thus ultimately follows on from
Alberti's conversion of S. Maria Novella in Florence.
The two-storeyed cross-section façade gives an indication, on the outside, of how the church is structured: the lateral bays stand in front of the aisles, and
the narrower upper storey in front of the raised nave.
Further similarities with Alberti's architecture are the
staircase which becomes a regular step-shaped base
course, the triangular gable as a dignified religious
form, the incipient curves leading up to the higher
middle section, and finally the oculus, placed in the lower part of its wall panel. The building's marked individual character, on the other hand, derives firstly from
its material, the bright Roman travertine, and secondly
from the large blank areas in the façade. To the architect – it is often thought that he may have been Andrea Bregno –, the order of pilasters was only a thin,
flat feature indicating the storeys and bays. He was
aiming at perfect proportioning – an agreeable equilibrium of height and width –, and also at masterful restraint in the detail. In this way he succeeded in designing the best church façade in early-Renaissance
Rome.

The basic character of the interior is very conservative. Its type is that of a basilica with a nave, two
aisles, a transept and choir above a cross shape, and
accompanying chapels at the sides. Where this architectural type is concerned, the literature tends to
make reference to Lombardic predecessors. The rela-
tive height of the aisles, and the structure of the nave
of the church, accord with medieval buildings in Italy:
round projections are placed around the pillars so that
the result resembles cross-shaped pillars; some of the
projections prepare for the vaults, while others support the arches of the dividing arcades. This corresponds exactly to S. Maria sopra Minerva (C37).

It is only at a second glance that the visitor notices
the Renaissance elements. Early-Renaissance capitals, and entablature blocks above them, cause the
round projections to resemble orders of columns. But
the fact that the half-columns are of differing heights
and are therefore variously proportioned, and also do
not have any entases, does not bear witness to classical training. The vault in the nave has no ribs or
transverse arches; it is designed as a continuous Roman groined vault and corresponds to the thermal
bathing halls of classical times (cf. A46), even though
it does not attain their monumentality. The motif of the
conchae at the conclusions of the transept arms is
also reminiscent of classical buildings (and so too,
originally, was the basic form of the locations of the
secondary altars). In particular, the octagonal drum
dome was an epoch-making invention, rich in consequences. Thus the Renaissance reveals itself in the
details, but not in the style, which makes more of a
Romanesque than a classical Roman impression. UF

F8 Ospedale di S. Spirito in Sassia
Borgo S. Spirito 3 (plan III 2/A)
1473–78, before 1600
Baccio Pontelli (?) or Ottaviano Mascherino

This, the oldest hospital in Rome, was founded by Innocent III in 1198, was entirely rebuilt by Sixtus IV in
1473-78 after a fire, and was enlarged by Mascherino
in the late 16C. It was the prototype for a building
serving this purpose in Rome. Located on the route
from the city to St. Peter's, the building was intended
to show that its founder was attending to both the

F8 Ospedale di S. Spirito in Sassia

physical and the spiritual welfare of the population. The pope ordered the hospital to be immortalized in Botticelli's fresco of the »Temptation of Christ« in the Sistine Chapel (F13), also founded by him.

The wings of the men's and women's sections are two lengthwise rectangles which together form an infinitely long rectangular parallelepiped, the original structure. Only in the middle is the long row interrupted by an octagonal domed area (with a chapel), resembling the crossing of a cathedral. This is one of the first large centrally planned areas of the early Renaissance. Thus church architecture was reverted to in choosing the shape of the hospital. In the exterior, the length of the building's sections is emphasized by the surrounding portico, with its groined vault and its infinite-looking row of arcades (part of it was later walled up). The pilaster strips of the arcades have a Doric order and clearly point to the Renaissance, as the tabularium motif (cf. A9) was employed in them. Otherwise one feels that a Gothic and an early-Renaissance sense of form are seen combined in most of the individual shapes, as well as in the gable of the show frontage (reconstructed in accordance with Botticelli's fresco) facing the Tiber: this applies to the round arches, which at the same time are narrow, tall and made up of endless rows; and also to the Gothic tracery-work windows with their horizontal roofing and the sparse early-Renaissance pilasters framing them. SG

F9 SS. Apostoli: vestibule
Piazza SS. Apostoli 51 (plan V 1/A–1/B)
1473–81
Where its architectural type is concerned, this vestibule, which was built outside the venerable basilica of the Apostles Philip and James under the pontificate of Sixtus IV, has nothing new to offer. Vestibules with an upper storey were not a rarity in medieval churches in Rome (cf. H26).

Nonetheless, this is an illuminating building. The regularity and respectable size of this two-storeyed piece of arcaded architecture indicated to everyone

F9 SS. Apostoli: vestibule

F10 Palazzo del Governo Vecchio

at that time that Rome was to be given a new appearance in the shape of its façades. The building also makes it clear what the model was on which the new early-Renaissance language of shapes was basing itself. If one leaves out of account those window panels in the upper arcades by which Carlo Rainaldi altered the overall character of the façade in 1675, then this structure literally repeats the arcades of the Palazzetto Venezia (F5), but not its benediction loggia. The cardinals' palace, which adjoins this vestibule on the left and was built at the same time as it, copies the façade of the Palazzo Venezia. Finally, the person who ordered the building work is of significance. This was Giuliano della Rovere, who was the nephew of Sixtus IV, later became Pope Julius II and, when he was cardinal, also ordered the portico outside S. Pietro in Vincoli to be built. The reason for building the new structure at SS. Apostoli lay in more than a cardinal's care for his church or in the architectural immortalization of his name, because the basilica was actually the family church of the Colonna, a powerful aristocratic family. Pope Martin V Colonna had previously renovated it, and the enormous family palace of the Colonna (B76) adjoins it to the right. The fact that an oak tree – the coat of arms of the della Rovere, who were constantly feuding with the Colonna family – shines forth resplendently on the church façade must be described as the result of the architectural policy of papal nepotism. UF

F10 Palazzo del Governo Vecchio
Via del Governo Vecchio 39 (plan IV 1/A)
1473–77
Cardinal Stefano Nardini ordered this palace to be built for him as a grand residence standing on the old Via Papalis, which ran from St. Peter's to the Lateran

basilica. In 1624, Urban VIII bought up the property to use it as the residence of the governor of Rome. When the governor moved into the Palazzo Madama in the 18C, the former cardinals' palace was given the name it has today.

The palace was at the time regarded as one of the largest and most impressive complexes. Built on a spacious area, it originally comprised no less than three courtyards and several large residential sections, which were grouped around three massive towers. This palace was thus anything but a uniform structure designed on a regular ground plan and in accordance with a superordinate overall scheme. Such structures had already been developed in the Florentine palaces of the early Renaissance. The heterogeneous collection of different sections, courtyards and towers still accords, ultimately, with medieval practices. Thus the Palazzo is less similar to a »modern« cardinals' palace than it is to a medieval fortress and, thanks to the crenellations and towers which formerly existed here, it had a well-fortified character. A feature worth seeing today is the large cortile which is surrounded on three sides by multi-storeyed loggias and is overtopped by the only surviving tower, surmounted by a belvedere. An inner courtyard surrounded by arcades was a novelty which had only just been imported from Florence to Rome, along with the cortile of the Palazzo Venezia (F5). Alterations made after 1500 mean that it is no longer possible mentally to reconstruct the original design of the main façade on the Via del Governo Vecchio. The old portal, which is surrounded by a frame containing diamond shapes and is decorated with a palmette frieze, is another notable feature, and connoisseurs consider that it is among the best house entrances of the period. EJ

F11 Ponte Sisto
Via di Ponte Sisto (plan IV 1/B)
1473–75
Baccio Pontelli (?)

It was in connection with Sixtus IV's urban projects that the bridge named after him – the only one erected in the area of the city of Rome between the ancient period and the 19C – was built for the holy year of 1475. It was not merely intended to give pilgrims a further link between the old core area of the city and the Vatican (this is what the inscription states), but was also meant, among other things, to provide a more direct road link between Trastevere and the market areas around the Campo dei Fiori.

The new building was erected on the foundations of the Pons Aurelius (3C AD), which had been completely destroyed in 792. Four semicircular arches, the two central ones being higher than the two at the sides, are inserted between three bridge piers, which taper to a point in the upstream direction and end in semicircular shapes downstream. The Occhialone, a perfectly circular opening for the purpose of lessening

the water pressure at high water, is located above the central pier. The front faces of the bridge are built of travertine. They were originally concluded by a railing which was made of brick slabs between travertine pilasters, and was replaced in 1877 by the not very appropriate iron webs. Slender arch framing is the only decoration on the wall surfaces. The form that is suited to the bridge's function is the dominant feature, and gains elegance thanks to its well-balanced proportioning, stylish materials and simple shape. Vasari states that Baccio Pontelli (c. 1450–92) was the artist, but he would have been very young when the bridge was built, and this is why the attribution is uncertain. What is typical of this early-Renaissance work is that it closely imitates the city's ancient bridges in its shape and materials, and even in such determinant factors as the Occhialone and the shape of the cut-waters of the bridge piers (e. g. Pons Fabricius, A10). DH

F12 S. Maria della Pietà
Campo Santo Teutonico (plan III 1/A)
c. 1475 to 1500

The tradition of the Campo Santo Teutonico, the graveyard of the Germans and Flemings in Rome, dates back to the establishment of a Schola Francorum, first mentioned in 799. The Schola received an impetus in the mid-15C when some German members of the Curia founded a poor souls' fraternity and at the same time had the graveyard and the church belonging to it restored. But the construction of a new church was begun a little later, probably in connection with the holy year of 1475, and it was consecrated in 1500.

F12 S. Maria della Pietà

The church stands to the east of the graveyard and rises above an approximately square-shaped ground plan, which is adjoined to the south by the main apse and to the north by another apse (they both have a polygonal facing on the inside, and a semicircular one on the outside). Four massive pillars subdivide the area into nine bays having groined vaults. The corner bays have lower vaults, so that the result is approximately the centrally planned shape of a Greek cross with secondary centres in the corners of the arms of the cross. This shape imitates the Byzantine architectural type of a cruciform domed chuirch. But it also differs from it, because here there is no dome over the crossing, and the two apses emphasize the longitudinal direction. The interior is characterized by a very plain surrounding area, with restrained individual forms and white colouring which contrasts with the red brick of the architectural subdividing framework.

The choice of a centrally planned building at this early point in time is noteworthy in the context of the nearby St. Peter's. DH

F13 Città del Vaticano: Capella Sistina
Città del Vaticano (plan III 1/A)
1477–81
Baccio Pontelli

This building, constructed under Sixtus IV to a plan by Baccio Pontelli, was the second major architectural step which the Renaissance popes took at the Vatican, the first having been the section that surrounds the Cortile dei Pappagalli (F1) and was built under Nicholas V. It was intended as the church of the papal chapel and of the capacious courtly household, and is today still the place where the conclave meets. But this bare brick structure, which rises up like a tower, was at the same time a fortress, as is indicated by the spacious upper storey with its battlements and crenellation. The papal chapel in Avignon had also been a fortress, and the political circumstances still called for a massive fort in the Vatican.

F13 Città del Vaticano: Capella Sistina

F14 S. Agostino

Neither the motifs nor the vaulting of this plain rectangular structure indicate that there was any plan to hark back to ancient Roman times. The flat barrel vault with its lunettes is designed in the manner of a hollow vault and rounds off the box-shaped room unobtrusively. The decorativeness of the room lies entirely in two factors, the first being the high-set row of windows: the tympana surround the round-arched windows concentrically, so that the lunettes tend to surmount the beautiful window motif. The other factor lies in the attention paid by the architect to the proportions (40.5 m x 13.4 m, 20.7 m high), which also have an effect on an onlooker who does not know their symbolism (the ratio of the length to the width follows the dimensions of the Temple of Solomon). The area is tall and upright, but not narrow or steep. It is liberal in length, but does not become lost in its depth. The proud spatial impression is based solely on the proportions, and has its share in the effect produced by the mural paintings: these are the cycle of frescos which are on the walls and date from the time of the building's construction, and the later work of Michelangelo: Sistine Ceiling and Last Judgement. UF

F14 S. Agostino
Piazza S. Agostino (plan IV 1/A)
1479–83
Jacopo di Pietrasanta, Sebastiano Fiorentino

This Augustinian church, a high-ranking building founded by the powerful Cardinal Estouteville, who became Camerlengo under Sixtus IV, shows that early-Renaissance church architecture in Rome was at a provincial level. Although the cross-section façade follows the type found in Alberti's modern architecture (cf. F7), there is an accumulation of deficiencies in the shapes: the overall proportions are too broad and portly, the strange bevelling of the cornice above the lateral bays must be adjudged to be an error, the weighty scrolls seem almost to be sliding off the façade, and the surrounding framework is distributed almost arbitrarily across the façade. When compared with this, the high quality of the façade of S. Maria del Popolo (F7) becomes noticeable.

In the interior of the basilica, which has a nave and two aisles and stands above a Latin cross, the Renaissance elements are again unmistakable: the aisles are expanded outwards by conchae; the crossing formerly had a drum dome; and, in the nave, half-columns and pilasters in superposition form a two-storeyed order upon which there stands a classical Roman groined vault without any wall arches. But the fact that the building is nonetheless rather more medieval in style can be seen from its narrow, tall proportions which are reminiscent of the Gothic manner, and also from the structure of the nave which is typical of vaulted Romanesque churches in Italy and Germany: every compartment of the nave combines two pillared arcades and thus two compartments of the aisle on one side of the church. UF

F15 S. Giovanni dei Genovesi: cloister
Via dei Genovesi (plan VII 1/A–2/A)
begun 1482
The hospice of the Genoese near the Ponte Sisto (F11) in Trastevere was founded by Maliaduce Cicala, a rich Genoese. The hospice was intended to provide maintenance and accommodation for those of his compatriots living in Rome, particularly the sailors from his home town who had come ashore in the nearby harbour of Ripa Grande. The cloister is all that survives of this complex structure, and is among the finest and most typical examples of its kind. The visitor entering the courtyard is surprised by its wide and liberal dimensions. The double-storeyed ambulatory, with its four times nine axes, gives on to the bright, open courtyard which resembles an enclosed square. Large arcades on slender octagonal pillars lend articulation

F15 S. Giovanni dei Genovesi: cloister

to the ambulatory which is at ground level and has a groined vault. In the upper storey, similarly well-developed pillars support an open roof frame. This contrast between the solid arcature and the almost ethereal colonnade placed above it is an idea which Bramante, using different shapes, later adopted in the cloister of S. Maria della Pace (H3). One striking detail is the octagonal pillar. This is a favourite motif in quattrocento architecture under Sixtus IV in Rome where, in contrast to Florence, it was the pillar rather than the column that became the established feature. In the present case, the pillar shape and the overall complex follow on in direct succession to the nearby courtyard, begun in 1475, of S. Cosimato. The correspondences are so clear that it can be presumed that the same stonemasons' lodge produced both courtyards. EJ

F16 S. Maria della Pace
Piazza di S. Maria della Pace (plan IV 1/A)
begun 1482
It was on the occasion of the longed-for peace with Naples and Milano that Sixtus IV founded the church of S. Maria della Pace within the bend, very densely populated at that time, in the Tiber. He granted it important privileges and handed it over to the canons of the Lateran. But this building must also be seen in the context of his overall ambitious architectural programme (cf. F8, F11, F13, etc.) which caused Sixtus' contemporaries to give him the name of »restaurator urbis«. This is also why it is attributed to Baccio Pontelli, his main architect.

S. Maria della Pace is probably the most interesting early-Renaissance church in Rome, as it combines a longitudinally with a centrally planned building. The nave of the church, a hall structure which has relatively small dimensions and is spanned by two groined vaults and flanked by apses, renounces the basilica as an architectural type, and this is significant in view of the congregation areas that were built later (cf. H17). (The elaborate expansion of the Capella Cesi, to a design by Antonio Sangallo the younger, was not carried out until 1530.) The original façade (B79) was of the kind seen today in, for example, S. Pietro in Montorio (F17): it was only a plain panel with a triangular gable and pilasters at the sides. These features made S. Maria della Pace into the standard for church architecture in Rome at that time.

What is more important is the attached centrally planned area, which with its imposing height of almost 28 m dominates the nave of the church. The architect was here presenting a new variation on a theme which had been occupying Italy's leading architects for quite a long time. In the case both of S. Andrea in Mantua (from 1472 onwards) and of the so-called Tempio Malatestiano in Rimini (c. 1450), Alberti had intended a large centrally planned structure at the end of a nave. In neither case was this structure actually built, so that its more precise specifications are unclear. Building work on the large choir rotunda attached to the nave of SS. Annunziata was carried out in Florence from 1444 onwards. The interest taken in ancient Roman centrally planned buildings is reflected in all these projects. In selecting the spatial form, the architects of S. Maria della Pace were going back to Rome's real tradition, to octagonal domed rooms with low apses and an octagonal cloister vault. Such rooms can still be seen today in the Roman imperial thermal baths (cf. A43). The only discernible early-Renaissance feature in this purely ancient type of building is the thin order of pilasters which is not really able to lend powerful articulation to the interior. This order was also limited to the lower half of the building (the order above it dates from Pietro da Cortona's conversion work in c. 1655; cf. B79); the second storey with its large windows must originally have made a stark and simple but effective impression.

The exterior points to a particular type of classical domed structure. The only outside additions to the large cubic shape of this octagon are some very long, bent pilasters at its edges. Above this there follow an attic and a ring of four steps. The attic and steps conceal the semicircular ascent of the outer shell of the dome, and only leave visible a flat segment of that shell. The exterior of the Pantheon (A31) was the mod-el here, except that a large lantern was placed on the opening admitting light in the apex of the dome. UF

Bibliography: *Quaderni dell'Istituto di Storia dell' Architettura*, 1981, fascicle 163–168.

F16 S. Maria della Pace

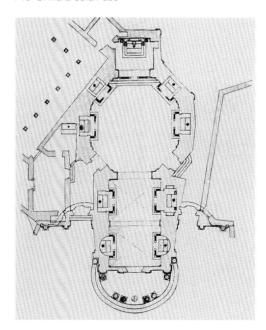

F17 S. Pietro in Montorio

F17 S. Pietro in Montorio
Piazza Pietro in Montorio 2 (plan VII 1/A)
1481–88
Baccio Pontelli

This small monks' church – the structure preceding it was handed over to the Franciscans by Sixtus IV in 1472 – stands on the eastern slope of the Gianicolo hill.

The monastery had been abandoned for a long time prior to this, but was now given a new impetus, the result of which was that masterpieces of all types of art were created for the new building over a period of two centuries. The most important work is probably Bramante's Tempietto in the monastery courtyard (H4). Bernini designed the Cappella Raimondi (B54) in baroque style.

The church structure itself is indebted to the Renaissance. The new building was begun in 1481 with the generous support of the Spanish King Ferdinand IV and his wife Isabella. The plans are probably the work of Baccio Pontelli, who can certainly be described as a good technician, but not as one of the great Renaissance architects. Vasari nonetheless relates that Pope Sixtus IV never ordered a building to be begun without obtaining Pontelli's expert opinion. Vasari also benevolently ascribes to him many buildings in Rome (S. Maria del Popolo (F7), Cappella Sistina (F13), Ponte Sisto (F11), etc.), but it is still sometimes disputed who their architects were.

The façade is of a mute plainness which, when the outside of the building is considered, permits the conclusion that this two-storeyed gable façade, which consists of only one bay and has only one portal at its centre, bears a consistent relationship to the interior. The latter has a nave and no aisles, and accords entirely with the architectural type of a hall church with apses. The apses on the right-hand side still survive in their original dimensions, while on the left the regularity is disturbed by the baroque extensions. Four bays in the wall area are subdivided by the tabularium motif (A9), but each of the groined vaults above spans two bays of the wall area and thus obtains a square shape. This is ultimately still the Romanesque rectangular termination, but understood in a monumental way. The crossing is central in character, what with its flat umbrella dome which is surrounded by two apses in the transept and, in the west, by the choir bay with its polygonal apse. »This little church forms an excellent integral whole, and if it had its original decorations it would produce an outstanding effect.« (J. Burckhardt, *Der Cicerone*). PZ

F18 S. Salvatore in Lauro: cloister
Piazza S. Salvatore in Lauro (plan IV 1/A)
late 15C

The small and little-known cloister of S. Salvatore in Lauro was probably built in the late 1480's and is a very high-quality work of the Roman quattrocento. After the church (B27) was completed, Cardinal Orsini called upon the canons of S. Giorgio in Alga to come here from Venice. The recently restored courtyard is the only original section of the monastery buildings to have survived. This so-called Chiostro Grande surrounds a square-shaped area having four times five axes. The upper storey, a 16C extension, consists of pillared arcades with a Tuscan order of pilasters placed in front of them, and impairs the finely balanced proportions of the lower passageway. The lat-

F18 S. Salvatore in Lauro: cloister

ter is opened up towards the courtyard by means of arcades above marble columns standing on a parapet wall which surrounds the courtyard on all sides. The arcade arches have fine outlines which, in the manner of Brunelleschi, blend together above the capitals and, where they make contact with the capitals, are of the same width as the column shaft. This detail lends the arcades a particular elegance and lightness. The perfect proportions, the exquisite fineness of the Ionic-style capitals, and the clearly traced outlines of the arches, all betray the hand of a master who must have been familiar with the quattrocento architecture of both Urbino and Tuscany. It has recently become more clear that Baccio Pontelli was the architect responsible. The shaping of the arches is unusual for Rome and is also to be seen in the courtyard of the Cancelleria (F19), where Pontelli probably worked. The original method used for the corners, where there is in each case a corner pillar with two half-columns placed in front of it, had already been developed in the courtyard of the Ospedale di S. Spirito (F8), which is probably the work of Baccio Pontelli. EJ

F19 Palazzo della Cancelleria
Corso Vittorio Emanuele II (plan IV 1/B)
c. 1487/88 to 1495
Baccio Pontelli (?)

Roman palace architecture in the quattrocento reached its peak in the immense structure of the Cancelleria. This palace was one of the most splendid since ancient times and at the same time the first to bear comparison with ancient architecture. Rome's ascent to its leading role in architecture began no later than the time of this great urban palace. The palace is today the seat of the pope's office, after which it is also named. This enormous structure was originally a private undertaking by Cardinal Raffaele Riario, who was a nephew of Sixtus IV and financed his ambitious project out of large gambling winnings. Having been appointed titular bishop of S. Lorenzo in Damaso in 1483, Riario decided to tear down not only his predecessor's palace but also the old titular church, a 4C colonnaded basilica. Building work began in c. 1487/88, and the main façade with the founder's proud inscription on it was completed in 1495. The palace is not a homogeneous, uniformly designed block. Instead, its ground plan fits into the square shape between the streets called Corso Vittorio Emanuele and Via del Pellegrino. Further irregularities permit the conclusion that it was built in two stages. The first plan provided for a considerably smaller building next to the old church. Only after the plans were changed in c. 1489 was the complex extended as far as the Via del Pellegrino, thus doubling its size. The broad courtyard of the Cancelleria now stands above Old S. Lorenzo (excavated in 1988). The new church (H1) has entirely disappeared behind the long palace frontage, as if the immense cardinals' residence had "swallowed" it. The fact that Riario caused one of the

F19 Palazzo della Cancelleria

most elegant titular churches in Rome practically to disappear behind the splendid façade of his private palace is evidence of his high-handed awareness of his own power.

The glory of the palace lies in its main façade. This frontage is faced entirely in travertine taken from the Colosseum and the Forum, is of immense dimensions and enormous length, and extends over a total of thirteen axes. Its architectural design is a combination of a flatly laid order of pilasters on the one hand and graceful rustic slabs on the other, and derives from the Palazzo Rucellai in Florence. It was there that Alberti had, for the first time, transferred to a palace façade that classical order of pilasters in superposition (A25) which had been adopted from the Colosseum. The adoption and further development of Alberti's ideas led, in the Cancelleria, to the construction of the first architecturally articulated palace façade in Rome. In contrast to the Florentine prototype, the ground floor is treated as a tall, massive base course which is interrupted only by small round-arched windows and supports the two richly articulated main storeys. The differentiated succession of storeys, consisting of base course, piano nobile, and lower upper storey with mezzanine windows (the latter idea set a future trend), develops the building further as compared with its prototype. The same applies to the subdividing work consisting of delicate, extremely thin pilasters above tall pedestals which are linked into an attic-like cornice. The paratactic arrangement of the rows of pilasters in the Florentine palace has here been abandoned in favour of a harmonious and stimulating rhythmizing approach. The alternation of narrow, self-contained bays on the one hand, and wide bays with windows on the other, forms an interlinked, rhythmic succession. Whenever the end of the façade is reached, one of these bays projects slightly in front of the façade. Thus the basic element of the subdividing work is openly emphasized at the ends of the façade. This part of the façade is known as »risalto« in Italian, from the Italian »risalire« meaning »to project«. In this particular case it is a corner risalto. It is in the Cancel-

leria that the risalto, which was to become a motif in baroque façade design, first occurs in palace architecture. It can be seen here that the risalto is never an independent structure, but always remains a component of the wall. However inconspicuous this projection of the wall may be, it does have the strength firmly and decisively to contain the façade, whose enormous width threatens to make it spread out in different directions. The corner risalto and the rhythmic bay were invented because it was necessary to provide the almost endless frontage, which runs along in tiring monotony, with an architecturally designed »face«, a facciata. Success was undoubtedly achieved in this by an ingenious further development of Alberti's ideas. But there is a strangely tense relationship between the enormous size of the façade on the one hand, and the gracefulness of all the details, which are worked with a precision like a goldsmith's, and the delicate relief which makes an almost linear impression, and in which the pilasters and the cut ashlar stones are combined, on the other.

The adoption of the classical order of pilasters in superposition betrays a desire to vie with classical antiquity. But what this building lacks when compared with ancient Roman architecture is massiveness and monumentality. The graceful subdivision by means of pilasters is a purely ornamental grid based solely on the wall surface. The crystalline severity of the design, and the way in which it been mathematically thought through, are two further factors linking the Cancelleria to the Florentine quattrocento. The wall is still understood as being a neutral surface upon which the tectonic forces are, so to speak, reflected. This fundamental characteristic was later rejected by Bramante.

The unusually large and wide inner courtyard contrasts charmingly with the two-dimensional façade of stone. The architecture of the courtyard opens up in a spacious and broad way, being surrounded on all four sides by a two-storeyed arcaded wall, an airy structure made of delicate granite columns (spoils from Old S. Lorenzo). The strengthening of the corners by pilaster pillars is a typically Roman feature.

F19 Palazzo della Cancelleria

The question of who the architect of the Cancelleria was is today still one of the great puzzles of Italian architectural history. Bramante was long thought to have been the designer of the Cancelleria. But Bramante did not arrive in Rome until 1499, when the palace had already been completed. The most recent research is beginning to point to the theory that Baccio Pontelli, who trained in Urbino and had since 1487 been in the service of Sixtus IV, may have been the architect of the Cancelleria. It is possible that he knew Alberti's plans for the palaces that were to be built all over the Borgo area near St. Peter's, and put those plans into effect here. Following the tradition of Florence and Urbino, he gave further development to Alberti's ideas and formed them into a new system which was superior to all the previous palaces that presumed to imitate classical antiquity. EJ

Bibliography: A. Schiavo, *Il Palazzo della Cancelleria*, Rome, 1965.

F20 S. Maria dell'Anima
Via di S. Maria dell'Anima (plan IV 1/A)
1500–42

In contrast to the basilican church, the hall church as an architectural type (its nave and aisles are all of the same height), although particularly widespread during the late-Gothic period in Germany and Austria, was hardly ever adopted in Roman architecture. Only two hall churches were built in Rome. They both belonged to foreign nations, and were constructed between 1450 and 1540 (cf. also F2).

An oratory of the German-speaking nations, which had existed since the 14C and was linked to a hospice, was first enlarged in 1431–33. In 1499 it was decided to build it anew. The foundation stone was laid in 1500, and the choir was consecrated in 1510 and the whole building in 1542. The architect's name and nationality are unknown. The prescribed area permitted only limited dimensions for the building work, so that today's church, with its associated priests' college, is fitted into a narrow space between the street and houses. The result is a slightly irregular ground plan, and the church is oriented towards the west.
All that can be seen of the exterior is the north-eastern half with its towering façade which, while retaining the same width throughout, is divided into three storeys and concludes with a straight entablature at the top. A façade having this form may suggest that the shape of the church is not basilican, but the third storey is only intended to conceal the roofing. Another unusual feature is the campanile which stands by the choir and has tiles with colourful glazing.
The interior is divided into two areas: the main nave with two aisles, each of four bays; and the deep choir which continues the nave. Pilaster pillars on high pedestals separate the nave and aisles. The counterparts to these arc pilasters on the exterior walls, and between these approximately semicircular chapels are built into the thickness of the walls. There is no gra-

F20 S. Maria dell'Anima

duation as in a basilica, and the nave, aisles and side chapels are all of about the same height. A barrel vault with lunettes rests above the strongly shaped entablature sections of the pillars in the nave, whereas the aisles have groined vaults towards which the calottes of the chapels are opened. Hall churches are usually lit through the side walls, but here the lighting is restricted to the large windows in the façade wall, because the surrounding area is built up. The building is relatively short in length, while its transverse direction is at the same time emphasized by the side chapels, the result being that the spatial appearance is almost square-shaped, with overall proportions that are high and upright. It is instructive to compare this church with the hall church of S. Giacomo degli Spagnuoli (F2), built a little earlier: the proportions of S. Maria dell'Anima are markedly higher, and the hall character is much more strongly brought out.

Besides the general «Gothic» form of the building, the most remarkable elements are the individual shapes of the decoration/articulation: examples being the pedestals, the capitals and in particular the entablature sections, which are clearly indebted to the early Renaissance. The rounded chapel niches, decorated with frescos, are a further typical element of this period (e. g. S. Agostino, F14). The result is a unique combination of northern Gothic ideas and Roman Renaissance elements whose roots ultimately go back to the ancient Roman tradition. DH

F21 Palazzetto Turci
Via del Governo Vecchio 123 (Plan IV 1/B)
c. 1500

This palace, built by an unknown architect in c. 1500, was commissioned by G. B. Turci, the papal scribe. He evidently wanted to go along with the latest achievements in architecture, because the forms found in the Cancelleria (F19) were used for the sub-dividing work on this four-storeyed building, as if the Cancelleria was a book of architectural patterns. This can be clearly seen from the larger shapes right down to the smallest detail.

But it was not the well-thought-out, rich layout of the prototype that was being imitated. Instead, the motifs established there were used to create an individual and plainer succession of features. The rustic slabs are limited to the ground floor, where the round-arched openings leading to the shops indicate the owner's middle-class business interests. The order of pilasters and round-arched window shapes of the Cancelleria are to be found in the upper storeys. The forms of the window openings start with small windows, proceed to large windows having horizontal concluding cornices, and finish with a combination of round and mezzanine windows. The proportions of the bays range from compressed to excessively slender.

This simple but consistent development in an upwards direction is no match for the subtlety and fascinating effect of the Cancelleria. In contrast to, for example, the Palazzo Giraud-Torlonia (F22), the aims here were more modest from the start. It is though still evident that the effect produced by magnificent proto-

F21 Palazzetto Turci

F22 Palazzo Giraud-Torlonia

types was able to raise, at a stroke, the quality of the local architecture. UF

F22 Palazzo Giraud-Torlonia
Via di Conciliazione (plan III 1/A)
begun 1501

This palazzo is on the former Via Alessandrina which Alexander VI ordered to be built across the densely built-up Borgo S. Pietro area as a wide axis linking St. Peter's and Ponte Sant'Angelo. He issued a decree ordering that impressive new buildings be erected on this boulevard which was opened in 1499. It is probable that the pope personally took part in building the Palazzo Torlonia, especially as Adriano Castellesi, the client for whom the Palazzo was built, was an ardent follower of the Borgias' party. The Palazzo, with its order of pilasters in superposition and its cut ashlar stones, is a smaller replica of the Cancelleria (F19), but does not attain the latter's quality. In particular, the scheme of the façade has been misunderstood in several respects. The enclosing corner risalti are absent, and the pilasters have now been moved together in such a way that neither a rhythmic bay nor a genuine double pilaster is formed. This means that the façade has lost its best features, namely the enlivening rhythmizing effect and finely balanced proportions which distinguish its prototype. The square-shaped courtyard begun in 1507 is probably the work of Bramante. The simple but effective plainness of the slender, undecorated pillared arcades, and the delicate wall relief in the ambulatory, are typical of his Roman style. The visitor originally passed from here into the garden, and also into the stables – which may also have been designed by Bramante – in the basement of the main section. With its well-thought-out spatial arrangement, its elaborate travertine façade, and its uniform overall appearance, this Palazzo still reflects something of the splendour of the former boulevard. Like the Cancelleria, the Palazzo may have been a reflex response to Alberti's plans to erect buildings all over the Borgo area near St. Peter's, and to the standardized type of palazzo which was developed for that purpose. EJ

High Renaissance and Mannerism

Bramante, Raphael and the heyday of the High Renaissance (H1–H23)

»Bramante was the first to bring good and beautiful architecture to light again, which had been forgotten from ancient times until his day.« Palladio used these words to justify including Bramante' Tempietto as the only modern building in the fourth book of his treatise, which dealt with the great ancients. The Tempietto (H4) already had everything. Here ancient qualities were not just suggested, as throughout the quattrocento, but actually reborn in their full abundance, for example in the colonnade (the ancient tholos) or in the dome, a perfect hemisphere cast in cement, all completely new in post-ancient architecture (cf. A31). Despite its small dimensions the Tempietto had all the weight and simplicity, the gravitas romana, that Bramante recognized so accurately as the central vivid value of ancient Roman architecture, and which he used again and again, with particular mastery in the monks' choir of S. Maria del Popolo (H5). The programme that ancient building was in the service of Christian architecture and that it should be outdone by it is already present in the Tempietto. And the Tempietto had the advantage over all other great works by Bramante that it was completed by the master himself, and thus his handwriting remained pure. With it Bramante created his own architectural style around 1500, characterized by incomparable, monumental formal beauty and a genuinely Roman approach, a point of culmination that was always considered as the height of Classicism. Here the Roman building style was not following the early northern Italian Renaissance, in which ancient monumentality was never fully assimilated; on the contrary, the genius loci and the style of the times were able to combine most purely in Rome. A personal language was created that everyone was intended to understand and from whose force no one could escape.

The ancient buildings were an astonishingly fertile intellectual breeding-ground for the new style, a re-strengthened papacy and the excellent commissioning situation that this provided formed the material basis. Great foreign artists no longer came to see the antiquities, as they had in the 15th century, but to build in Rome. As Milan had fallen to Louis XIII of France in the previous decade, and as in Florence after the death of Lorenzo the Magnificent a short-lived religious republic had come into being, Rome was able to move into the power vacuum left by the old northern Italian centres. If Rome was to become a European metropolis it was also essential that Rome should become not just one, but the centre in Italy. The guiding theme here in the political sphere as well was the heritage of Roman imperial power. The pontificate of Julius II was the key era of this period. This name was chosen by Cardinal Giuliano della Rovere after his election in 1503 as a reference to Julius Caesar. He proudly had the title pontifex maximus inscribed on one major work, the Belvedere (H6). For ten years he exercised his office with a decisiveness bordering on hybris, which later brought him the name »il pontefice terribile«. He was the quintessence of Renaissance man with his claims to be absolute, which peaked in his decision to build a new and better mother church for Christianity, St Peter's, and to pull the old one down. He was syphilitic, a sodomite, general and despot, of whom Hutten is said to have said that he wanted to storm heaven with force when he was refused entrance up there. Nevertheless he smoothed the way to a level of artistic will that had scarcely been known before, and in the ten years to 1513 he managed to identify the best artists with unusual perception and to make demands on them and promote them to extremes. At this time Rome was able to attract the most famous artists from their former strongholds at will. In 1505 Julius II called Michelangelo to Rome to hand over his gigantic tomb project and commission him to paint the Sistine Chapel ceiling. Michelangelo remained in Rome to the end of his life, and played a substantial part in the architectural design of the city. In 1508 Raphael came to the Vatican to paint the Stanze. Bramante then introduced him to architecture. The number of other important architects is considerable; they all (with the exception of Michelangelo) worked under Bramante and made the basic concepts of his style obligatory for at least the whole of Italy. Even Raphael's work owes almost everything to Bramante's model; the most important other architects were Antonio and Giuliano da Sangallo, Baldassare Peruzzi and – more important for northern Italy – Raphael's pupil Giulio Romano as well as Sansovino and Sanmicheli.

Bramante came to Rome after fleeing from Milan in winter 1499/1500. He was fifty-six at the time, and had already studied the works of late antiquity in Milan, but had always adhered to the Lombard, very intricate, style of decoration. In Rome he had very little reputation at first and had plenty of time to study quite different and more monumental ancient Roman buildings. His style became simple and monumental. The first work which can be attributed to him with certainty in Rome, the cloister of S. Maria della Pace (H3), showed the essence of Roman High-Renaissance architecture in an exemplary fashion: dignity and weight (gravitas) were to be shown vividly, without their clarity being reduced by decorative elements. Harald Keller calls them the absolute dimensions, the absolute measurements that were being mastered artistically for the first time since the ancient world: »Nowhere do these massive dimensions seem like impermissible enlargements of smaller buildings, which are cheated of their best properties by being translated into the large format.« In the cloister the delicate North-Italian column is replaced by the massive pier, above which the arch curves powerfully, and

St Peter's

which seems fully appropriate as support for a full storey. The powerful thickness of the walls is made completely visible in the combination of arch and pier, as these perfectly represent the remains of walls from which the archway is cut. At the same time this considerable weight, the gravitas romana, never seems ponderous or ungainly. Similar values could be sensed earlier in the powerful pillared hall of S. Lorenzo in Damaso (H1), for which reason the work is usually attributed to Bramante, and shortly afterwards in the monks' choir of S. Maria del Popolo (H5). Bramante, as Raphael and Michelangelo were soon to do as well, successfully took the step from architecture dominated by painting, in which the main concern was geometrical and systematic correctness, as in the representation of central perspective, to an sculpturally perceived architecture in which the impression of wall mass and weight became the main factor, from the dominance of the (show) screen to that of the three-dimensional and massive wall. This was the step to a sensual and vivid High Renaissance.

When Bramante built the Tempietto (H4), timelessly beautiful in its design, Julius II appointed him as the first director of the stonemasons' lodge for the new St Peter's (H7). Bramante showed all his successor architects the way in this case as well: he set dimensions for his dome- or crossing-piers that had previously been found on that scale only in ancient baths architecture, the Pantheon and the Basilica of Maxentius (A31 and A50), but were hitherto unknown in Rome's Christian building tradition. He also knew how to make fruitful use of ancient ideas in the most important articulation elements. The gigantic pilaster capitals are nothing other than an enlargement of those of the Pantheon, in a ratio of 5:12. But what is even more important is that Bramante understood how to use the structure of the triumphal arch, and developed from this a sequence of axes of alternating width, the so-called rhythmic bay, for the interior of St Peter's. Bramante had already experimented with a chain of triumphal arches in S. Maria in Abbiategrasso and then above all on Rome in the Belvedere courtyard (H6). It was to Bramante's great credit that he transferred the poised and harmonious power of ancient monumentality to Christian architecture and found a new language in this synthesis. It was for this reason that Castiglione wrote to Leo X in 1519, and Serlio then similarly in his treatise of 1537, that it was Bramante who breathed a new life into architecture.

On the basis of this style and in this ambience of extraordinary and artistic productivity, Bramante and the other architects mentioned devised numerous new architectural forms derived from antiquity. This, unlike the establishment of types in the second half of the century happened in such an immediately complete form that entirely accurate artistic implementation was to be found even in the very first work. Key features are palace architecture, landscape and villa architecture and above all church building. For urban palace architecture Bramante took the first step beyond the Palazzo Venezia (F5) and also the Cancelleria (F19) with the Palazzo Caprini, later acquired by Raphael and therefore also known as Raphael's house. The starting point for the design was the ancient insula, the rented block of the imperial period, with shops at street level and a central courtyard from which steps led to the dwellings in the upper storeys. But the insula was occupied by many families, in contrast with the splendid Roman buildings of the Renaissance. Bramante also placed shops (bottege) on the ground floor, which meant that the palace seemed very fully integrated into the life of the city. This level was in rustic work, thus identified as base and a functional storey, and thus entirely separate from the upper storey, the piano nobile, which seemed formal, as it had an arrangement of columns made up of alternating double columns and aedicule windows, which emphasized the actual dwelling in a solemn and magnificent fashion. The burgeoning power of the High Renaissance is clear from the fact that for the first time the half-column replaced the pilaster, which is found in Florentine palace building, for example the Palazzo Rucellai, and thus the relief quality of the wall was considerably increased. At the same time filling parts, like the wall, and bearing parts, like the order, were also distinguished from each other by the choice of different building materials, and thus structure was emphasized to an extreme extent. In the 16th century the Palazzo Caprini was considered to be the most important palace. The effective force of this invention was to be demonstrated in the work of Giulio Romano, Sanmicheli, Sansovino and Palladio. Nevertheless the palace was pulled down when Bernini's Colonnade was being built. The only surviving building of this type, the Palazzo Vidoni-Caffarelli (H22) seems to be more powerfully articulated horizontally, and despite all its quality lacks secure balance with the other direction, the vertical, through perpendicular relation.

Raphael showed the most original hand with this heritage, particularly in palace architecture. He not only took over direction of the St Peter's stonemasons' lodge after Bramante's death (1514), but also created the most interesting variant on the Palazzo Caprini. His Palazzo Branconio dell'Aquila, which also no longer exists, shows the diversity of his imagination and how he strove for more lavish forms. The classical division into shop level, piano nobile and where appropriate a third storey was retained, but the structural articulation of the walls seems to break out of the frame. The leitmotifs are no longer load and support, but the opposite: now the shop level is given the column order, and its columns support niches in the upper floor, in other words empty spaces, that had previously always been expected between supporting elements (not above them). The bearing element was isolated, robbed of its supporting role in the building. The diversity of decoration made the surface of the façade infinitely rich and soft, while Bramante always repeated the same shorter, clearer sequence of double column and aedicule. »It is as though the hard, brittle material of the Renaissance had become juicy and soft.« (Wölfflin) Raphael himself said of his teacher that his buildings came very close to antiquity, but admittedly without achieving the richness of »ornamenti«. Raphael had become the foremost curator of the ancient buildings and also built into his work, much more than Bramante, their luscious splendour and festivity.

A look at three other buildings shows how rich a range of palace designs emerged in less than two decades. The façade of the Vatican Palace, which later became the Damasus Court (H11) by the addition of more wings designed in the same way, comprised, over a base storey covered by a wall, three storeys, which were completely broken up into open arcades. No palace façade had ever been so extroverted, or has so dominated the view of the city. In the Palazzo Alberini (H14) the articulating elements became particularly shallow, reduced almost to

Palazzo Branconio dell'Aquila

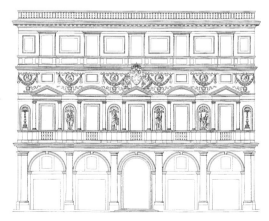

frames and panels, thus anticipating Mannerist design methods. At the same time the weight of the central portal increased, and in the Palazzo Alberini (H14) it was to drive out the bottege completely, which meant that a completely new type had been produced: rustic work on the palace as a whole was missing (of the kind that was often to be seen in Florence, in the Medici Palace, for example), and there was no articulation in the tradition of Bramante and Raphael either. By using horizontal cornices and rows of windows in a plain wall, as well as reinforcing edges by rustic work, Sangallo created a new, much simpler type, whose greatest representative was to be the Palazzo Farnese (H25). The palaces that have been mentioned already embody the whole range of possibilities for future centuries. Until the second half of the 17th century the standard type was derived from the Palazzo Farnese. The Mannerist tendency to see façades as bearers of images would have been unthinkable without the Palazzo Branconio – and without the Vatican façade, now part of the Damasus Court, the first palace of the High Baroque, the Palazzo Barberini (B45) with its open series of arcades would have been unimaginable.

The integration of landscape into architecture also harked back to antiquity. Generally the essence of Roman architecture in the High Renaissance was to allow buildings to appear as an ensemble, in other words as part of a greater effect: thus at this time the first long street appeared, the Via Giulia, with flanking palaces, and also the first complete design for an urban square, the Capitol (H27). Bramante realized an ensemble effect particularly magnificently and at an early stage, by developing a garden landscape with the Belvedere Court (H6) that seems as though it is part of the palace building. He successfully mastered the slope in the long complex by the use of steps, and at the same time created a gigantic garden landscape that was to be visible throughout its length. The complex could be very extensive as it was on the edge of the city. Hitherto the only comparable effect had been in the old imperial palaces, which Julius II wanted to outdo on the Mons Vaticanus: in Nero's Domus Aurea (A24), the Palatine Hippodrome (A27), the Villa Hadriana (A32). Here the way to treat nature and art was established for posterity.

This introduced the development to the suburban villa, first represented by Peruzzi in the Villa Farnesina (H8). The villa became even more significant, and monumental for the first time in the modern age, with Raphael's Villa Madama (H16). Outside the city, this villa took up ancient elements, in that it was provided with courtyards, an atrium and grotteschi (stucco work rediscovered in the Nero's Domus Aurea at this time). Here he created the extensive programme of an ancient imperial villa, and not the much more reduced forms of an Italian early-Renaissance villa. It can again be seen that Raphael lavished even more splendour on the building than Bramante himself, in other words joined monumentality and decoration much more, and brought all three genres together here for the first time. Another characteristic of Raphael's style can be seen in the fact that in the Villa Maderna all the parts were no longer visible at a glance as was the case in Bramante's Belvedere Court. On the contrary, they were sealed off from each other, sometimes placed back to back, like for example the theatre and the villa.

The differences in style that have been mentioned between the two principal masters of this period, Bramante and Raphael, can also be seen in ecclesiastical building, especially in comparing Raphael's Capella Chigi (H12), his third masterpiece, with Bramante's St Peter's: here too Raphael made a much clearer distinction between decoration and structure, the decorative sections seem full and splendid, while at the same time look almost as though they could be taken out, while in Bramante's work the structure and the (sparser) decoration are firmly combined. Two major, striking values were implemented and harmonized with each other in architecture in hitherto unsuspected way in the High Renaissance: lucidity of composition (rationality) and wealth of invention.

Developments in ecclesiastical building took place in the first decade in particular. Apart from the Tempietto (H4), the monks' choir in S. Maria del Popolo (H5) and above all St Peter's (H7) the only outstanding works are Raphael's previously mentioned Cappella Chigi and a small work by Michelangelo, the first in Rome, and the only one for about 25 years: the façade for Leo X's chapel in the Castel Sant'Angelo (H13) was actually a reduced version of Michelangelo's most important unbuilt façade project, for S. Lorenzo in Florence. Here Michelangelo not only invented a façade type of his own, but it could be seen for the first time with that unusual density and energy the master could interlink elements of articulation, even at that time more dynamically than even Bramante and Raphael. The historic outcome of this façade is a paradigm: alongside St Peter's much in ecclesiastical building remained an idea, many great plans were not implemented, particularly in relation to the idea of the centrally-planned building. This is most painful in the series of plans by the most important architects of the High Renaissance for S. Giovanni dei Fiorentini (B16). Important though the idea of the centrally-planned building was for the High Renaissance and its aesthetic of complete equilibrium, only a handful of centrally-planned buildings were realized, most of them on a small scale (cf. H45 and H4, H7, H10, H12, H20, H40).

The years after the death of Raphael (1520) and before the Sack of Rome (1527) saw only a few experiments. Raphael's favourite pupil, Giulio Romano, became court architect in Mantua. The first blossoming of the High Renaissance was over.

From the Sack of Rome (1527) to the Council of Trent (1545) (H24–H29)

The Sack of Rome, the conquering and plundering the city by the Catholic Emperor Charles V, had a shock effect on the architectural scene in Rome as well. The city – after Bramante, Raphael and Giulio Romano – again lost many of its best architects, including Michelangelo for a time. In the 30s and 40s the Eternal City's dominance over Florence and northern Italy was greatly weakened. Church building came to a standstill, almost totally in the case of St Peter's. Only one church of status, S. Spirito in Sassia, was built, apart from small brotherhood churches.

This started to happen even under Paul III. He was a man of great willpower, who followed the weak and vacillating Pope Clement VII, who had caused the catastrophe of 1527. Paul III's achievements included summoning the Council of Trent, thus strengthening Rome and the Catholic Church again, and moving on to the offensive. Paul III was responsible not only for many campaigns for furnishings in the Castel Sant' Angelo and the Vatican (the Last Judgement, the Sala Regia and the Cappela Paolina came into being under him), but also for the most monumental secular buildings of the time, the Palazzo Farnese (H25) and the design of the Capitol (H27), and important urban interventions in Castel Sant'Angelo (cf. B96).

His architect was Antonio da Sangallo the Younger, director of the St Peter's stonemasons' lodge until 1546, thus for longer than anyone before or after him. And yet Raphael's successor was unable to leave any enduring marks on the building. With the exception of the Palazzo Vidoni-Caffarelli (H22) and the Palazzo Massimo alle Colonne (H24) Sangallo acquired every large commission in Rome from the mid-1520s to a few years before his death (cf. H20–H29), when designing the Capitol was transferred to Michelangelo (H27, H30). Sangallo's dominance in this period was due to the fact that even in the 20s he was almost the last direct pupil of Bramante and Raphael in Rome. Giulio Romana had gone to Mantua in 1524, Peruzzi fled in 1527 and came back to Rome in 1535 for only a year before his death (1536). Thus Sangallo was the only architect in the Bramante tradition during the upsurge under Paul III. He was not a painter or sculptor, but came up through the craft of building, and was thus more of an engineer than an artist. Thus he was an exception among the High-Renaissance architects, who were mostly also painters or sculptors – probably because these other genres particularly intensively conveyed the values of light, composition and proportion, which the High Renaissance was especially concerned to represent in a vivid fashion. Of the »artists« in the school of Bramante, above all Giulio Romano and Peruzzi, only the latter left a (single) great work in Rome, the Palazzo Massimo (H24). Even so, the existence of a pupil of Bramante was enough to exclude Michelangelo from public commissions to a large extent. Bramante's renown continued to make an unusual impact. Before the death of Sangallo in 1546 Michelangelo was commissioned only to design the Capitol, and at first this involved nothing but setting up an ancient sculpture.

The quality for which Sangallo was esteemed was the correctness with which he passed on Bramante's classical vocabulary. While Bramante had planned a treatise, but apparently found no time for theory, and his pupil Peruzzi also abandoned plans of this kind, Peruzzi's pupil Serlio published the famous IVth book of his treatise in 1537. Vignola and Palladio published two more treatises, while the High Renaissance, the great age of new beginnings, produced nothing at all. A little earlier Peruzzi had left behind an extensive series of drawings for St Peter's, of which apparently not a single one was intended for execution. All this shows an awakening academic tendency with a preference for theory and experiment for the sake of experiment. This preference was always seen as a key characteristic of Mannerism, which was in fact flourishing in other regions in the 30s and 40s. A cursory glance gives the impression that architecture developed quite differently in Rome. Mannerism seems to have been inhibited in Rome by the predominance of Sangallo. Under Bramante and Raphael lucidity of structure and composition, and richness of invention, were fused into a single entity, but after 1526 striving for simple composition asserted itself under Sangallo. Wealth of invention receded behind this, while conversely outside Rome, following a certain preference by Raphael, who died later, invention was over-emphasized and striving towards simple composition was neglected. Exceptionally complex compositions were produced. How little Sangallo was able to apply his concept to new commissions can be seen in the series of arcades and supports that would have covered the exterior of St Peter's with alarmingly monotonous correctness if his design had been followed (H31). This is an exemplary demonstration of how the vivid impression of external planning came surprisingly near to the actual counter-movement to Sangallo's style: from the 40s, this style was established in buildings whose façades became mere supports for pictures (H28, H32, H27, finally B35), thus in which order and decoration fused into an unbroken carpet, a tendency that Raphael had introduced in his Palazzo Branconio. Both styles, that of Sangallo and that of the counter-movement, are Mannerist in the sense that they isolate one of the values that Bramante and Raphael were concerned to demonstrate vividly as an unbreakable union in the High Renaissance, and that they thus exaggerated this one value and destroyed the equilibrium. This Mannerist development appeared increasingly in the 30s and 40s, but was rooted in the High Renaissance of the second decade of the century, in the Palazzo Branconio, for example, or the Palazzo Alberini-Cicciaporci (H14).

After the Palazzo Farnese (H25) two buildings by Sangallo stand out, and both of them have a feature that constantly characterized Mannerism as an era between High Renaissance and Baroque. Sangallo creates types both in the design for the façade of the Banco di S. Spirito (H23) and also with the design for the interior and façade of S. Spirito in Sassia (H26). The first case is especially characteristic to the extent that Sangallo, by using the triumphal arch as an articulation device remained almost slavishly attached to the design of the uppermost terrace of the Belvedere (H6), but then used the colossal order for this articulation, using it for the first time in palace architecture and thus anticipating the articulation of Baroque façade art, which was more inclined to involve all the storeys together. And S. Spirito in Sassia, taking up designs from late-quattrocento Florence, both for the cross-section façade and the interior (a unified space with low chapels set at right angles), was to have a crucial effect on the type of Il Gesù (B1). Another important feature of the façade was that here, as in the Palazzo Massimo (H24) as well, the façade was increasingly seen in isolation from the body of the building, thus enhancing its urban effect. It was precisely this approach that was to have a considerable effect in the Baroque.

Three large individual buildings were to have and even stronger influence on the period under discussion here than the general dominance of Sangallo. They were all secular: one by Peruzzi, one by Sangallo, though it was later redesigned by Michelangelo, and one by Michelangelo. Peruzzi's Palazzo Massimo is a solitaire, very independent vis-à-vis Raphael's Palazzo Branconio, to which it is closest. It remained without successors. The two large and vivid values that are shown in the building are its complexity – in individual forms, in façade design and also in the linking of façade, vestibule and courtyard – and the immoderate weight with which it bears down. Thus the palace is the main example of a typically Mannerist building in Rome. The two other buildings had an enormous long-term effect, especially in the Baroque. The Palazzo Farnese (H25) established the tradition of large palaces built by the papal family of the day – especially throughout almost all the 17th century. An almost completely new and extended plan was produced for the palace, which was already under construction, in 1534 when Alessandro Farnese became pope Paul III. For the first time in Rome this also had a square in front of it, which was to be a common feature of the Baroque, and neighbouring buildings were removed as appropriate. The palace itself, which corresponded with Sangallo's first palace building, the Palazzo Baldassini (H15) in terms of articulation, was the subject of a competition in 1546. This was looking for the best solution for the top of the building, and only painters and sculptors were in-

vited to participate: they seemed to be trusted more when it was a question of proportions. Michelangelo won with a proud, towering wall and powerful cornice. Despite all the veneration of antiquity Peruzzi was able to say of Vitruvius, the author of the central ancient treatise, at this time: »Vitruvius was neither a painter nor a sculptor; for this reason he had no eye for the element that creates the true beauty of architecture.« The enormous effect that the palace had on its contemporaries because of its proportions can be seen simply in the fact that the type established for its structure and articulation remained obligatory until well into the Baroque period, beyond the middle years of the 17th century. Michelangelo walled up the open arcades in the upper storey in the courtyard, to give it a closed character and a feeling of being lived in. With this same combination of open arcades below and a closed wall above them Michelangelo achieved the first closed square design of the (High) Renaissance, the Capitol (H27, H30), without which none of the great Baroque squares is conceivable. The way in which Michelangelo made the small statue in the centre seem monumental by relating a large oval area to it alone was already wonderful, and so was the way in which he raised the senatorial palace above the flanking buildings by saving the colossal order for the upper storeys, above a rusticated base storey. In these flanking buildings, which are artistically even more significant, he at the same time brilliantly solved one of the basic problems of post-ancient architecture: how could the ancient system of column and horizontal entablature be combined with the wall architecture of the West, especially for palaces? Michelangelo combined large and small order, openness and closure for the wall. No solution that was anything like as conclusive and new had been found for this basic problem since the Tabularium (A9), which is a few metres away. Palladio was to use it most fruitfully for church architecture a little later.

The era of Michelangelo and Vignola (H30–H45)

The Capitol was not conceived until shortly before Sangallo's death (1546), and the solution for the top of the Palazzo Farnese even after it. It was only from this date that Michelangelo started his (late) architectural work in Rome. For this reason the mid-1540s represent a crucial turning-point for architecture in Rome. In comparison with this the beginning of the Council of Trent, 1545, and the Counter-Reformation that it introduced was less significant. Vignola's work is also all dated after 1546. These two great men determined developments for the next twenty years, and Vignola for even longer. There are only two further sets of buildings to be considered alongside the work complexes of these two masters: the group of buildings that are distinguished by a carpet-like surface design (H28, H32, H37, finally B 35), and a very few buildings that were started early in the century and completed from the 60s onwards (H44, H45, also B16). A striking feature of the period under discussion here is the not very long pontificate of Julius III (1550–55), the last humanist on the throne of St Peter.

Michelangelo's work on St Peter's outshone everything else in these two decades – despite the completion of the Palazzo Farnese and even despite the design of the Capitol (H27). At no point is the energy of movement that Michelangelo was able to convey to his buildings as clear as in the oblique sections of the exterior, which seem to have been almost forced out by the truly titanic pressure of the two basic forms, the square and the conchae of the Greek cross. Nowhere else was he able to bring together all sections of the building together in the horizontal and (unlike the work of Bramante, for instance) in the vertical plane and play them through as conclusively as he did in the exterior of St Peter's. Nowhere else was his understanding of buildings as sculptures and his striving for the greatest possible succinctness as striking as they are here. And not least with the dome, which he perceived for the first time as a uniform building unit here, together with the drum, he formulated the crown of ecclesiastical buildings in a completely new way, which was to be obligatory for the next two centuries.

Three centrally-planned buildings, the Cappella Sforza, (H40). S. Giovanni dei Fiorentini (ill. B16) and S. Maria degli Angeli (H42) appeared alongside the works that are also monumental in terms of their scale, Palazzo Farnese, the Capitol and St Peter's. The first of these turned out distinctly smaller (but still monumental), the second was not built and the third is an ancient bath redesigned, and not a centrally-planned building in the stricter sense. They all share an unusually sculptural view of space, which in each case seems to expand and move in an almost titanic fashion: in the Cappella Sforza the Greek cross lost its static quality; one beam of the cross seems to move outside the centre , an enormous tension is thus created H40). The ancient alternate series of rectangular and circular chapels, seen in the Pantheon (A31) in particular, was borrowed in the design for S. Giovanni, but here it seems to surge incomparably more strongly; the chapels thrust over each other and the circular rotunda is even stretched to form an oval rotunda (cf. also even H27). And in S. Maria degli Angeli the old baths were oriented against the Western way of looking at things – the short axis became the main axis and the massive hall the transverse axis – thus building up a tension that Mannerist architects in particular were unable to resist (cf. for example B28, but also B91). All three projects al-so have in common that the column in the core space was revealed like a monument, and towers up proudly and with an enormously sculptural quality.

S. Giovanni and S. Maria degli Angeli also show a characteristic feature of Michelangelo's handling of antiquity. Michelangelo corrected antique solutions very decidedly and worked out his topos that Christian and Western architecture should not simply build on that of antiquity, but should reach out beyond it, with great determination (cf. similarly H27). Even Bramante, whose work most clearly took the same line up to this time (H4, H6) did not go anything like as far. The radical nature of Michelangelo's approach can be seen in the contrast with the almost antiquarian care taken by an architect like Pirro Ligorio (see below) and also in the fact that Michelangelo was not afraid to criticize part of the principal work of ancient Roman architecture, the Pantheon (A31), and to recommend that it should be redesigned. All of the three centrally-planned buildings are very individual in character, the have no real precursors and also did not establish any types. Nevertheless their influence on late Mannerism and above all the Baroque should not be underestimated.

Michelangelo had scarcely any successors. His pupil Giacomo del Duca continued his imaginative approach to design in a very few works (H45, B8), and his second pupil, Giacomo della Porta, completed – with certain changes – the Capitol and St Peter's, but came under the influence of Vignola's style. As a result of Peruzzi's influence Vignola himself was very close to the Bramante tendency, so that this continued to have an effect alongside and after Michelangelo, although this influence was weaker in Vignola's case than it was for Bramante's immediate pupils. The young architect very much went his own way. The most important works in the three decades after Sangallo's death (with the exception of Michelangelo's) are all by him: S. Andrea in Via Flaminia (H34), the Villa Giulia (H35), the palace in Caprarola (H38), the steps in the Farnese Gardens (H36); finally, already marking the start of a new era, Il Gesù (B1) and S. Anna dei Palafrenieri (B5). He became famous for the first oval rotunda actually to be built, although this applied at first only to the dome area (H34), but was then carried out in a more complex fashion at a later stage from the ground plan right through to the dome (B5). Seen from the outside, these buildings look like orthogonal spatial shells, like cuboids, giving no idea of the shape of the interior. This fundamental divergence between interior and exterior can be seen throughout Vignola's oeuvre (cf. also H35, H38) and makes him fundamentally different from the great masters of the High Renaissance, who saw the exterior as a reflection of the interior; this is particularly true of Bramante (H7) and Michelangelo (H31). This break between individual sections is a general characteristic of Vignola's work. Thus in S. Anna it is not just the interior and exterior that are fundamentally different, but the two façades with five axes as well. For this reason Vignola is able to combine various palace types within one façade

(H38). This makes for very complex art and shows a certain inclination towards eclecticism. In terms of individual forms in particular Vignola stands for the tendency that can be generally observed in the third quarter of the century of designing orders strictly according to prescribed patterns (from antiquity or treatises) and without alienation. It is no coincidence that in 1562 he published a treatise on the »Five Orders«, which on the basis of the accuracy of the engravings in particular influenced design of these forms a very great deal and was to lead to a certain uniformity.

The dynamic potential is unusually strong in Vignola's designs, and this made him a major influence on the Baroque. None of his buildings has the titanic energy and movement of Michelangelo's exterior for St Peter's, but both Michelangelo and Vignola introduced a thrust of motion that guided the eye in many of their buildings, something that runs through the architecture. Michelangelo designed parts of the Palazzo Farnese (H25), for instance, in such a way that not only did a single thrust of movement run from the square through the vestibule into the courtyard of the palace, but also from its rear, which faces the Tiber, through loggias and on over a bridge to the Villa Farnesina. And in the case of the Porta Pia (H43) he took up, in the long, intensively articulated, vertical central strip, the Via Pia as a newly designed work by city-builder Pius, as it thrusts through the Aurelian Wall (A44) as the old, earth-covered, transversely placed section of the building. In Vignola's case something like this can be found in almost every work. This applies to the duplicated flights of steps leading up to the Farnese gardens (H36) and also to the round forms multiply encapsulated one behind the other in the ground plan of the Villa Giulia (H35) or to the long axis and open steps leading to the Palazzo Farnese in Caprarola (H38). Even the oval probably emerged for him because he perceived ecclesiastical buildings above all as a way from an entrance, the façade, to the altar. For this reason as well his works acquired a main façade and a distinct space for the altar. This was completely new for centrally-planned buildings. If the route between the two was to be surrounded and shaped by a space-containing shell, then the oval was almost the inevitable solution.

Alongside Vignola and Michelangelo only Pirro Ligorio successfully developed a recognizable formal language. His principal work, the Villa d'Este in Frascati (H33) is linked with Vignola's palace in Caprarola to the extent that both are among those mid-century country houses in which the step was completed from villa in the country to palace in the landscape, typical on the eve of absolutism. The Villa Madama was merely a precursor, the first villa (H16) to be devised monumentally (and imperially). Strong cardinals under weak popes had built palace-villas of this kind, many of them near to the heart of Rome as well. Of these latter the Villa Medici remained (B4), but many

disappeared; they were either destroyed (like the Villa Farnese on the Palatine hill) or incorporated in other buildings (the second Villa Este became part of the Quirinal palace). With their landscape-dominating approach, the geometrically laid out gardens and the fountains the Villa d'Este in Frascati was an incunabula for Baroque country palaces. Comparable designs were previously always very much smaller, now these ideas increased to a monumental scale. In the zig-zag paths and carpet-like arrangement of the parcels the gardens also share the most important characteristic of Ligorio's other work. Ligorio was the most important exponent of the tendency that has already been mentioned that started in the forties in which buildings were seen largely as supports for pictures and were carpeted with ornament, busts and reliefs. The order was not longer intended to express the forces of support and load vividly, the view had become atectonic (cf. especially H32). Ligorio was above all an antiquary; ancient works were now to be copied as faithfully to detail as possible, which of course meant an admittedly free implementation of ancient texts. So in the Casino Pio (H37) Ligorio followed the description of an ancient villa by Pliny the Elder. The circular or oval centrally placed inner courtyard that is to be found in the Villa Giulia, in Caprarola or in the Casino Pio, and that could be seen as early as the Villa Madama (H16) derives above all from this description. In fact this stronger antiquarian tendency goes back to Raphael as the supreme papal curator of antiquities in his day. Dependence on antiquity had become greater, as is proved by all three great treatises (by Serlio, Vignola and finally Palladio). But Bramante and Michelangelo had a more secure grasp on the monumental spirit of Roman antiquity. SG/PZ

H1 Palazzo della Cancelleria: S. Lorenzo in Damaso
Corso Vittorio Emanuele II (plan IV 1/B)
1493–96
Donato Bramante (?)

In 1483, Raffaele Riario, the nephew of Sixtus IV, became the titular cardinal of S. Lorenzo, a basilica which was of the Constantine type and was erected by Pope Damasus I in 380. Riario immediately set about building the Cancelleria, the most sumptuous palace of its period (F19). Contrary to what occurred in the similar case of S. Marco and Palazzo Venezia (C19, F5, F6), the venerable basilica was torn down, and a newly built church disappeared entirely behind the uniform palace façade.

Bramante's career in Rome probably began when he became Riario's adviser in 1493. The church, which was the last part of the palace to be built, may therefore be his first work in Rome and may thus constitute the prelude to the High Renaissance, although its date is earlier than some late buildings of a less definable early-Renaissance character (F19–F21). Even as early as this building, Bramante makes his main objective clear in exemplary fashion (cf. also H4, H7), and in this respect the design of the building differs fundamentally from that of the palace façade (F19): the massive ancient Roman structure was to be recreated in a new look. For this purpose Bramante, despite using a different orientation, was sensitive enough to adopt the basilican shape of the original structure, but replaced the lost columns by pillars. Those bays above columned arcades which had been customary in the early Renaissance now gave way to bays above much weightier pillared arcades.

Thus Bramante adopted the quintessentially Roman form of the cryptoportico with a groined vault (A9, A21). He adhered to this system for the whole building, and also did not separate off the vestibule. This makes the overall space appear much larger, and one section even has a nave and four aisles. It is only on one third of the ground area, in the nave proper, that the church projects into the piano nobile – the latter was important to the client and takes up some space there. The large niche which concludes the nave is also more reminiscent of the Maxentius basilica (A50) than of early-Christian churches.
SG

H2 Palazzo Fieschi-Sora: façade
Via Sora (plan IV 1/B)
begun 1500
pupil of Donato Bramante

The outstanding significance of the palazzo – it was begun in 1480 as an early-Renaissance columned courtyard, and was continued after 1500 with a new design for the façade – is only noticeable to a limited extent today, as work on the piano nobile of the western façade was continued to an altered design from 1523 onwards, and that façade was shortened by two window axes when the Corso Vittorio Emanuele II was built.

The original design for the façade dates from 1500, is still readily discernible on the ground floor, and was a sensation at that time. Thus the approach adopted by the architect in designing the window aedicules and incorporating the basement windows into the structure of those aedicules was exemplary as regards the subsequent High-Renaissance palace architecture (cf. H22). But what is much more important is the way in which the façade is divided up by risalti: an order of pilasters, whose entablature projects beyond the straight line of the cornices, causes the portal, and also the outermost axes of the windows, to move forwards by one layer beyond the surface of the wall. It is true that risalti had already appeared in the Cancelleria (F19), but the full harmony of the order of pilasters now makes the risalti into weighty structures which have firm edges, show additional frames in the intercolumniation, and would originally, like towers, have risen beyond the central section. Where this basic idea is concerned, the Palazzo Fieschi reflects one of Bramante's main projects, although it never went beyond the initial stages and its detailed shapes were quite different: this was the Palazzo dei Tribunali. The unknown architect also proved to be a quick-to-learn pupil of Bramante's when it came to the details of the order of pilasters (cf. H6). UF

H3 S. Maria della Pace: cloister
Vicolo della Pace (plan IV 1/A)
1500–04
Donato Bramante

The cloister is the first work that is certain to have been produced by Bramante in Rome. He fled from Milano to Rome in 1499 and, under Julius II, elevated his new home town into an architectural world power. This small, two-storeyed pillared courtyard reveals the transformation in Bramante's style. The initial impression produced by massive ancient buildings made him abandon his small-sectioned Northern Italian style. Strange rifts and contradictions occurred in this process. Bramante here placed two entirely different systems one above the other. The lower storey consists of a pillared arcature in front of which there is an Ionic order of pilasters standing on high pedestals. In this way a specifically Roman motif, the so-called tabularium motif, was created (A9). Bramante had been able to study it in the Colosseum (A25) and elsewhere, and it already had been adopted in modern times in the courtyard of the Palazzo Venezia, and the benediction loggia of S. Marco (F5, F6). Firstly the emphasis upon the massive wall and the supporting function of the arches, and secondly the severity and sparingness of those elements, contrast greatly with the easy colonnade which is found in the upper storey and consists of an alternation of column and pillar. The design of the corner, with an inserted pillar and projecting pillars on both sides (instead of a »weak« corner column or two pillars placed together), is an elegant solution of this well-known dilemma. The unorthodox use of different types of capital – composite for the pillars, Corinthian for the columns –, and also the position of the columns above the apex of the supporting arches underneath, gave rise to great criticism among Bramante's contemporaries. But Bramante's aim was to employ abundance and »variatio« in order to accentuate the upper storey and create a graceful, easy type of »round dance« there. Its delicate multifariousness follows in the tradition of the quattrocento and characterizes the courtyard as being a connecting link between Bramante's buildings in Lombardy and his later masterpieces in Rome. EJ

H4 Tempietto
Piazza S. Pietro in Montorio (plan VII 1/A)
1503
Donato Bramante

It is impossible to assess too highly the significance which Bramante's Tempietto in the courtyard of the monastery of S. Pietro in Montorio possesses for Roman Renaissance architecture. Not only was it the initial building of the Roman High Renaissance and thus pointed the way for all subsequent architects, but it also constituted a great step forwards in developing the Renaissance idea of the centrally planned building. Attempts were made in the 15C to locate the precise spot at which Peter the Apostle is said to have been martyred in AD 66. The hill called Gianicolo was chosen for this, and was given the name of »mons aureus« (Montorio). But the place where St Peter was actually put to death was probably in the area around St Peter's, as the early-Christian custom was to bury the martyrs not far from where they suffered their martyrdom. The monastery church (F17) was built by 1488, but the really honourable location, the site of the martyrdom, was left largely untouched. In 1503, the Spanish king (it was at the time of Alexander VI, the Spanish pope) commissioned Bramante to build a memorial above the site in question. Bramante had arrived in Rome in 1499 and was now able to absorb classical antiquity and put it into practice in his own architecture (cf. also H3). He planned to construct on the Gianicolo a large round courtyard which was to be surrounded by a loggia and in whose centre the memorial proper was to stand. The memorial was conceived as a »martyrion«, and thus as a centrally planned building. All that was built was the memorial, known as Tempietto. Thus today's rectangular courtyard by no means corresponds to the original plans, and the interplay between the round courtyard with its loggia on the one hand, and the Tempietto in the middle on the other, would have more strongly emphasized the centrally planned character of the building. It is tempting to regard Bramante's overall scheme as an ideal design for a centrally planned building. However, then as now, the Tempietto is all that is granted to the onlooker to admire. Nevertheless, this round temple

H4 Tempietto

with its ring of columns (a round peripteros) succeeded in achieving its effect from the very outset, even though it lacks a corresponding framework in the form of a round courtyard: Raphael immediately adopted the architectural idea in his painting work (*Marriage of the Virgin Mary*, Milano). Palladio also included Bramante's Tempietto in his fourth book on architecture (1570), which was really devoted to the ancient Roman temples. But, to him, the Tempietto was the paragon of beautiful proportions and of a well-decorated style of architecture, and, moreover, was the first example of its kind in the post-classical period.

Thus two phenomena triggered that enthusiasm for this building which continues to the present day. Firstly, the Tempietto was the first example of the consistent adoption of ancient architecture, combined with Bramante's creative powers. Secondly, and independently of the first phenomenon, the stupendous beauty of the Tempietto's forms anticipated matters by already achieving the apogee of absolute proportions.

Many questions arise regarding the first phenomenon: the prototypes for Bramante's Tempietto are being sought by research workers. Many round buildings with a circle of columns are to be found in the remains of ancient Roman architecture; it is certainly probable that Bramante knew the Vesta temple in Tivoli. In the eighth chapter of his fourth book, Vitruvius, an ancient Roman writer on architectural theory, commented on the architecture of a peripteros, stating the exact proportions. But the Tempietto does not fit well with these prototypes: its proportions are taller, and a two-storeyed building is not found in such a context in ancient architecture. The ancient peripteral round temple, exemplified by the Vesta temple and described by Vitruvius, consists only of a round cella, a circle of columns, and the hemispherical dome of the cella. But Bramante placed the dome on a drum, thus creating a second storey. Thus this new type of temple having an ancient appearance was Bramante's invention. It must be added that this invention certainly grew out of innumerable previous ideas and various studies, including some by Bramante's contemporaries (examples include architectural sketches by Leonardo da Vinci). The way in which the drum and dome project beyond the ring of columns indicates that this Christian building lays claim to being an improvement on classical architecture, and one is almost inclined to say that it wishes to portray something of the martyr's soul ascending.

This new type of round temple was combined with the courtyard, which had a loggia, surrounded the temple concentrically, and did not go beyond the planning stage. It is astonishing that this architectural type was not specifically imitated in the form in which it was designed. One reason may be that it could not be used as a place of liturgy: its small dimensions (the cella is about 5.5 m in diameter) make it clear that the Tempietto was mainly conceived as a memorial site lending a dignified setting to the place of crucifixion.

The second phenomenon referred to above, the beauty of the Tempietto's forms, should also be explained in more detail. The way in which Bramante lent to his Tempietto the dignity which it required by reason of its stated function lay in a previously unmatched feeling for forms which requires no improvement and admits of no alteration. This feeling for forms has a certain power resting within itself, and amounts to a perfect creation in which nothing »cramped or inhibited, uneasy or excited« (Wölfflin) can be found. This heavenly peace which the Tempietto radiates was the feature that produced a real influence upon the world of art.

Three concentric steps lead up to the stylobate upon which the circle of columns in placed. Sixteen Doric columns surround the cella at a relatively short distance from the cella wall (the distance was larger in ancient times, cf. Vitruvius and the Vesta temple). The Doric entablature makes a very classical impression, with its architrave, its frieze with a triglyph, and its cornice. The Doric order was deliberately chosen in order to give the building the necessary static tranquility, and was repeated in the form of pilasters on the outer wall of the cella. The imaginative subdivision of the wall, combined with the Doric order, generates an enlivening interplay between the pilasters; in particular, there is a fine chiaroscuro effect. As it approaches the upper storey, the weighty force of the Doric order is lent a more varied appearance by an architectural element which had only recently been introduced. This was the balustrade, which Giuliano da Sangallo, in conspicuous fashion, had adopted in palace architecture in 1479, probably for the first time. In the Tempietto, the balustrade is given a wonderfully harmonious setting. Together with the entablature, it forms a balcony-like conclusion to the circle of columns, from the centre of which the drum of the dome rises up as a continuation of the cella. The subdivision of the wall of the drum resumes that of the cella wall, but with slight variations and somewhat more delicately. The order of columns now consists only of linear outlines, there are no longer any bases or capitals, and the entablature becomes a plain strip. The building is finally completed by a round conclusion consisting of the hemispherical dome which has been gently prepared for by the round-arched niches in the subdivision of the wall. The basic stereometric elements are circle, cylinder and sphere. Taken on their own, they are scarcely able to give the Tempietto its timelessly harmonious overall effect. But the effective force which no one can resist lies firstly in the perfect interplay between the decorative elements and the columns, whose force imperceptibly evaporates in the balustrade, and secondly in the absolute proportions of the substructure, drum and dome. PZ

Bibliography: H. Günther, *Bramantes Tempietto – die Memorialanlage der Kreuzigung Petri in S. Pietro in Montorio*, Rome, 1973.

H5 S. Maria del Popolo: monks' choir
Piazza del Popolo 12 (plan I 2/D)
1503–09
Donato Bramante

In the first few years of his pontificate, Julius II commissioned Bramante to attach a fairly large choir to S. Maria del Popolo (F7). The tombs of the two cardinals Ascanio Sforza and Girolamo Basso della Rovere were placed in this separate section, which is today marked off by a large Baroque high altar. These tombs are masterpieces by Andrea Sansovino. Proceeding on the basis of tripartition and of columns standing in front – these are two features found in Roman triumphal arches –, they established an important type of High-Renaissance tomb.

Bramante tried to divide up this long room in a centralizing way by placing a central rectangular section between two barrel-vaulted sections. The windows in their high locations are a first-rate invention: the arcade and colonnade are combined into a tripartite motif which was put into effect here for the first time and later became famous as the Serliana or Palladian motif. But a more important feature is the conclusion of the choir, where Bramante's unique power of creating shapes turned two banal elements, namely

H5 S. Maria del Popolo: monks' choir

a barrel-vaulted section of the room and an adjoining concha, into a fascinating feature of the High Renaissance. His means for this lay in the wall's replete thickness which he displayed in the window jambs, and in deep, sharply carved ceiling bays, two of which were expanded into genuine window shafts. Thus the concha with its shell-shaped flattened dome is perceived not as the thin shell of a wall, but as the hollowing-out of a powerful and massive wall – an embodiment of ancient-Roman gravity. UF

H6 Città del Vaticano: Cortile del Belvedere
Città del Vaticano (plan III 1/A)
1503–23
Donato Bramante

The significance of the belvedere courtyard to secular architecture was similar to that of St Peter's to church architecture. A founding coin was minted for both of them. Today the impression of the courtyard is spoiled. Innocent VIII (1484–92) had left behind him the belvedere, an irregular building with a loggia, at the higher northern end of the Vatican gardens. Bramante's first chief work for Julius II came into being when Julius intended, on an uneven piece of land, to cause the belvedere to be linked to the nucleus of the Vatican palace, which was himself not very regularly built (F1). Bramante proposed a magnificent regularization consisting of two connecting sections, each about 300 m long and at a distance of some 70 m from one another. The gaps in the ascent which were located between these sections were to be bridged by three terraces, and a backdrop with a large central ex-

edra was to link the heads of the connecting sections. This is the large-scale approach which is characteristic of the High Renaissance and was here seen for the first time. The eastern (and outer) connecting section, the backdrop and the terraces were all built by 1523. It was only from 1560 onwards that Pirro Ligorio erected the section on the garden side, after he had previously added a storey to the backdrop and exedra, thus creating the nicchione (the enormous niche). Domenico Fontana, working for Sixtus V, spoiled the complex in 1587–89 by inserting a transverse arm between the lower and middle terraces. (He also produced the articulation in the lower courtyard which was thus created and is today's belvedere courtyard.) Finally, Raffaele Stern, operating for Pius VII, did the same between the middle and upper terraces in 1817 to 1822.

The complex as a whole was oriented on the papal rooms (Stanze) in the palace. A symmetrical backdrop came into being: below there was a courtyard for games and processions, with a still-surviving semicircular stepped exedra below the Stanze (it was consecrated in 1565 at the time of the marriage of Annibale Altemps, the pope's favoured nephew); at the end of the courtyard there stood a central flight of stairs which led to the second terrace and was flanked on both sides by structures which projected slightly into the courtyard and were a restraining element; at the end of this terrace was a frontage which was designed like an ancient triumphal arch and was flanked on both sides by staircases, each having two flights of stairs (today it is in the inner courtyard, between the transverse sections); and on the third terrace, as in the area below, there was a large central exedra with concentrically rising steps towards which there ran a wall that was subdivided by triumphal-arch motifs. The steps later had to give way to Michelangelo's staircase. The entire complex remained closed towards the outside (except for the arches on the upper storey), and it opened up towards the inside in the form of loggias (facing towards the festival ground and the gardens of the two upper terraces). This feature accorded with the ancient Roman tradition (A27) and continued to be adhered to in Rome (H25, H35). The three parts of the connecting sections are three, two and one storeys high, thus balancing the ascending garden, and coaches could drive on the flat roof.

Bramante was the first to study ramps and the central exedra in Palestrina (A8). Nothing comparable had been seen since classical times. Here we find splendid staircases, and the architectural regularization of entire tracts of land. In brief, this is the monumental spirit to which the later villa and garden architecture owes everything (H33). Julius II wanted to outstrip the ancient villas, and at the same time – this was typical of his period – create an antique feature.

Bramante also had to develop a system for the articulation of tremendously long walls. In doing so, he showed in captivating style that his period was always also endeavouring to outdo the classical period. Firstly, he articulated the lateral walls of the three terraces in different ways, and created a break which was formed by the receding structures at the foot of the second terrace. Secondly, he made each storey one-quarter more flat than the one below it. This greatly increases the foreshortening, especially as the number of storeys decreases towards the rear, and as a result the complex looks longer and more impressive. In both these points, Bramante differed diametrically from the method used in the Colosseum (A25), the most significant ancient Roman endless façade. Thirdly, he gave the wall a much richer articulation than is the case in the Colosseum. A little of this can still best be sensed in today's Cortile della Pigna (pine cone), where there is a row of interlinked triumphal-arch motifs, that is to say alternately narrower and wider bays. Bramante was not the first to use the triumphal-arch motif in modern architecture (it was Alberti who did that), neither was he the first to employ the so-called rhythmic bay (it is found as a mere row of pilasters in the Cancelleria, F19). But he was the first to combine the two into a long, firmly subdivided wall, whose thickness is also rendered perceptible by niches and, in the lateral sections, by open arcades. There is hardly a building in Rome whose recreation one yearns for more strongly than the belvedere courtyard. SG

H6 Città del Vaticano: Cortile del Belvedere. Two stages of construction in Bramante's project

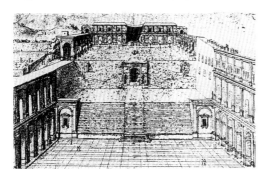

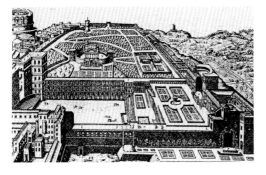

H7 St Peter's: the core area
Città del Vaticano (plan III 1/A)
1506–14
Donato Bramante

A good 150 years were spent in planning, building and altering New St Peter's. Many architects contributed their theoretical and practical creative powers. But, as if guided by a mysterious hand, it was always only the best-perfected ideas that were put into effect. The genius of those responsible was shown precisely in their way of resolving the constantly new problematic situations that arose. The church is the largest in Christendom, being 186.3 m long and 46 m high (the dome is 119 m in height and 42.34 m in diameter), and is today one of the most consummate buildings in the history of architecture.

It was Alberti who, in 1451, first considered the idea of redesigning the basilica which had a nave and four aisles and dated back to the time of Constantine the Great (326–49). He had observed that the walls of the nave of the church were inclined by some 2 m from the perpendicular, but probably exaggerated this somewhat in order to make building work appear indispensable. According to his plans, the arms of the transept were to be enlarged and, like ancient thermal baths, be covered over with groined vaults resting on columns that stood in front. In the nave, weighty pillared arcades were probably intended to replace the ancient columns and the entablature. Rosselino, who was the building supervisor of Alberti, constructed some sections of the transept – and of the longitudinally rectangular choir with its polygonal conclusion (the so-called Rosselino choir) – so that they extended slightly beyond the foundations.

After the death of Pope Nicholas V (1447–55), the building work came to a standstill for fifty years, and then the phase of radical innovatio followed that of mere renovatio.

This was because, on 18 april 1506, Pope Julius II laid the foundation stone for a complete new building of an entirely different nature. A coin issued to mark this building's foundation shows the planned exterior structure. But as it ultimately turned out, Bramante only realized the core area of the interior. His ideas on this subject are reproduced in the first surviving design, which is Bramante's plan (the so-called UA1) for the Uffizi, drawn on parchment. It was produced in six months of intensive planning in the winter of 1505/06, and the later plans that were actually put into effect were based on it. The ground plan is a fragment, but almost all the researchers assume that it is meant to be supplemented and thus formed (by reflection) into a design for a centrally planned building. The result is then a Greek cross which has apses and whose crossing is expanded by bevelling the pillars, thus making room for an enormous dome. There are four indentically formed secondary centres in the corners of the cross.

H7 St Peter's: the core area. Old St Peter's in a drawing by M. van Heemskerck

Characteristic for the design are the enormous dome, the pillars and the richness in forms and articulation. It was the enormous dome that was important to Bramante. He combined two traditions, firstly that of the smaller early-Renaissance domes which stood above a circular ground plan, fitted into the modular system of a bay in the nave of the church, and were consistently hemispherical, and secondly that of medieval cathedrals (Siena, Florence, Pavia) in which the diameter of the dome exceeded that of the nave, but whose domes were made up of individual segments. The dome was no longer meant to rest on the inner corners of the pillars, but on their centres. The pillars were the main feature of the design. They were no longer square- or cross-shaped pillars, but were massive structures that could be individually and sculpturally moulded by bevelling and the formation of niches. The volume, and the weightiness of the wall, became visible. This did not merely amount to the invention of the type of pillar which was employed from then until the end of the Baroque. Over and above this, Bramante was using a sculptural approach to architecture in order to replace the approach which was shaped by painting work and in which the main concern (in the early Renaissance, for example) was the articulation of the flat wall. He made the thickness of the wall visible. Bramante could only have recourse to ancient buildings when looking for this kind of monumentality and thickness of wall, and according to Vasari he actually wanted to place the Pantheon (A31) on top of the temple of peace, which was the Maxentius basilica (A50). But Bramante made alterations to the simple shapes, the rectangle and the circle, of that basilica's ground plan. He planned to surround the central dome with secondary centres. This large number of different sections, this combination of rectangular and round shapes, or, expressed in more general terms, this combination of geometrical shapes, united by true proportions, is what shapes the plan: the circle

of the domes, the square of the overall ground plan, and the Greek cross. The building could have been entered through twelve porticoes, four of them in the apses, and two of them in each of the four secondary centres. The prototypes for this kind of openness, monumentality and richness in form could be found in antiquity (cf. A53, C5, C10 and the Hagia Sophia).

Certain peculiarities of the plan are more clearly revealed by looking at the exterior (which was never built): the coin commemorating the foundation also shows a Greek cross with apses, main and secondary domes and two façade towers, to which two more towers in the rear corners (above the octagonal corner rooms) were intended to correspond. The secondary centres were meant to appear subordinate: the towers were to rise less high than the dome, and the secondary domes were intended to be less high than the transept arms. This view of the exterior makes it clear that the main dome was based on that of the Pantheon: the hemisphere inside the church was intended, in the building's exterior outline, to be replaced by a so-called testudo (tortoise). At the same time it becomes clearer that the aim was to place not merely the Pantheon's dome on top, but rather the entire Pantheon, and that the cylindrical wall found there, was, as was the case in the Tempietto (H4), to be combined with the other ancient type – the tholos – that also stands above a circular ground plan. Thus the magnificent, and technically too daring, feature of the plan was that the main building of the Roman classical period was to be lifted into heaven on four pillars and no longer rest on the well-founded earth.

Despite all the stimuli he received, Bramante's great achievement lies in that he did not merely reproduce ancient architecture, but, while having recourse to the ancient period, monumentalized Christian and Western art in an undreamed-of way, and discovered that a wall was a shapeable mass and thus that space had an entirely new corporeality. But his plan was not put into effect. This is probably because (if Rosselino's foundations had been included) the Apostle's tomb would have lain between the western pillars of the crossing, and not below the dome. The chief part of the church would have been without a function. Bramante proposed that the Apostle's tomb be relocated; even so high-handed a pope as Julius II would not tolerate this idea, and he said that it was written that it was not the tomb that was to be placed inside the temple, but that the temple was to be built around it.

The plan to which the builders set about the construction work is reproduced in a sheet in the Soane museum and in a sketch by Heemskerck – they both record the state of the work at the time of Bramante's death in 1514. At this point, the pillars of the crossing, with the wall arches and end supports, had been constructed. All the other sections visible in the Heemskerck sketch were later torn down or replaced: the nave walls of Old St Peter's in the foreground, the protective structure in the crossing above the Apostle's tomb, but also the western choir which is visible in the background and which Bramante, providing it with a barrel vault and the shell-shaped flattened apse dome that he so loved, had erected above the foundations by Rosselino (cf. also H5). The alterations by which the new building was made feasible result mainly from the ground plan. The spatial programme was made more concise; that is, the centrally planned areas in the first plan, which were located in the diagonals, were omitted. This caused the crossing to be moved westwards to the very beginning of the choir, while the

H7 St Peter's: the core area. Ground plan by Donato Bramante and coin by Caradosso (1506) commemorating the church's foundation.

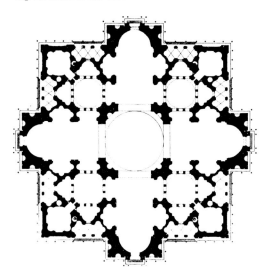

dome came to stand above the Apostle's tomb. The intention evidently now was that the church should also have a nave; from then on, the shape for the ground plan alternated between Greek and Latin crosses in a long series of plans. The pillars of the crossing were massively reinforced, but not sufficiently so for the dome described above which, as Serlio precisely stated in his treatise, was planned to be cast from cement. Michelangelo was obliged to reinforce the pillars once more, although the dome which he was building had two shells and was thus lighter.

The enlarged pillars caused the pilasters of the wall arches to move further apart. Between the pilasters, a separate wall panel was created, and along with it a so-called rhythmic bay consisting of an alternation between narrow wall panels between the pilasters and wide ones between the pillars. This scheme of subdivision is discernible in the ground plan of the detailed drawing, and was repeated in the first pillars in the main longitudinal section. Heemskerck's sketch shows the pilasters extending as far as the beginning of the wall arches, so that they accord entirely with the building as it is today. These colossal pilasters extend beyond an individual storey and are tremendously weighty, but lend human proportions to the pillars and their inhuman dimensions. It is true that Alberti had already employed colossal pilasters and a rhythmic bay in Mantua (cf., in Rome, F19), but the way in which the space was occupied was a new feature and made the design of the crossing in St Peter's appear akin to the triumphal arch (e.g. A26), which is the ancient archetype of these forms of design. The greatest innovation in the articulation lay in its immensely increased solidity. Pilasters when bent no longer had only seven flutes but two times five. It was not until thirty years later that Michelangelo once again entirely understood the value of this crossing's monumental simplicity, and made it into the principle behind the remaining part of the new building, completed by him (H31). SG/PZ

H8 Villa Farnesina
Via della Lungara 230 (plan IV 1/B)
1508–11
Baldassare Peruzzi

The Villa Farnesina marks the turning point between the early and the High Renaissance in the development of the princely country seat. The clear and severe subdivision of the building, and the way in which it is linked into an artistically laid-out park, both point to ancient prototypes found in the villa suburbana, whose combination of imposingness and private utilization became exemplary for 16C villa architecture.

In 1505, Agostino Chigi, the pope's banker, commissioned Baldassare Peruzzi to build the villa, which was constructed between 1508 and 1511. For the design, Peruzzi employed an earlier plan for the Villa Le Volte near Siena, but in the Villa Farnesina he modified and brought to classic consummation the plan of that early work.

The villa was moved some way away from the Via della Lungara. This emphasizes the house's private nature. At the same time the building was given a villa-like character, similar to a free-standing «casino» in a park. This simple structure above a U-shaped ground plan has two wings framing a loggia which is located in the main block, opens towards the north, and is today closed by windows.

The exterior, in its self-contained unity, presents itself as an integrated whole, but does not make a tedious impression. The two storeys, separated by a prominently projecting cornice, are, window axis by window axis, subdivided by delicate Tuscan pilasters. The subdividing work found in the lower storey is, by way of a sensitive and harmonious coordination of the proportions, slightly reduced in the upper. The attic area, decorated with stucco-work putti and garlands, forms a rich conclusion. An essential contribution to the unity of the whole structure lies in the inconspicuous device of placing the mezzanine windows almost underneath the cornice, thus firstly creating a counterweight to the attic windows in the upper area and secondly lending weight to the accents. The cornice which separates the storeys, and the overhanging roof, both emphasize the horizontal levels, thus contributing to the rural character of the villa. A severely classical feature, on the other hand, is the uneven number of axes (nine on the long side and seven on the short sides), with the centre emphasized. Corner pilasters, marked off by their colour, indicate the beginning and end, and guide the onlooker round the building.

The ancient villa suburbana had a tradition of combining imposingness and private use and putting these into effect in architecture. This tradition was also adopted in the Villa Farnesina. In the part facing the road, the building presents itself as having the self-contained façade of an urban palace. But on the more remote side facing the garden, the severe subdividing scheme is rendered more varied, and the private area is elevated into what – owing to its increased splendour – is really the main façade. The five large arches of the loggia open up to mark out the former entrance area, and the centre, once again in classical style, is accentuated by a slightly larger arched opening. But the front sides of the wings are conceived in an entirely unclassical style, as the centre is here in each case formed by a pilaster. The side of the building towards the garden is marked by openness and permeability which produce a relationship with the surrounding park.

The inner structure of the plan for the villa is not entirely symmetrical as it is in the work of Palladio and Giuliano da Sangallo, two later architects. Peruzzi nevertheless distributed the massive structures in a well-balanced way by dividing up the rooms according to their functions. But this arrangement was altered in the 19C when the entrance was moved to the southern side. The fame of the villa derives in particular from its decorative frescos, in which Peruzzi himself, Giulio Romano, Penni, Sodoma and Raphael all had a share. AG

Bibliography: Ch. L. Frommel, *Die Farnesina und Peruzzis architektonisches Frühwerk*, Berlin, 1961.

H9 Oratorio di S. Giovanni in Oleo
Via di Porta Latina (plan VIII 2/B)
1509, 1658
Donato Bramante (?), Francesco Borromini

This oratory near the Porta Latina is a building commemorating John the Evangelist's martyrdom by oil, which legend relates took place here. Since the late-classical period, many mausoleums had stood close together in the area between the Via di Porta Latina and the Via di Porta S. Sebastiano, and the oratory probably itself stands above an ancient preceding building. Today's structure was built in 1509 and was founded by Benoit Adam, a French prelate. Its attribution to Bramante is disputed. In 1658, Alexander VII gave Borromini the task of restoring the building.

The oratory is a centrally planned building, thus following the late-classical custom where memorials were concerned. This small structure, self-contained in the style of a monument, rises above a low travertine base course. The edges of the octagon are occupied by bent pilasters, causing the building to gain in shape and solidity. The polygonal sides made of plastered brickwork are left empty; the only decorations are the two Renaissance portals bearing the founder's coats of arms and Alexander VII's Chigi emblem. The building was formerly concluded by the entablature. Today this is surmounted by the roof designed by Borromini in the shape of a sloping cone made of stone. The circle at the foot is richly decorated with acanthus calyces, palmettes and rosettes. A fanciful ornament, consisting of bent-open acanthus leaves and a knob decorated with rosettes, stands atop the roof. These small but purposeful alterations lend the building the character of a sumptuous decorative casing. The interior is covered by a flat dome and decorated with frescos and stucco work (both 17C) by L. Baldi. EJ

H8 Villa Farnesina

H10 S. Eligio degli Orefici

H10 S. Eligio degli Orefici
Via S. Eligio (plan IV 1/B)
begun 1509
Raphael

This small church of the gold- and silversmiths faithfully reproduces Raphael's design in its original state,
although it is largely a reconstruction by Flaminio Ponzio (1602–04) who, after the building had partially
caved in, raised the height of the dome and drum and
added the façade.

Raphael, possibly working in conjunction with Bramante, built a centrally planned area in the shape of
a Greek cross with short, barrel-vaulted arms. This
was one of the first centrally planned areas in the
High Renaissance, and accorded with the latter's preference for this spatial form. The arms of the cross
formerly projected in the exterior too, but when the
church was rebuilt they were inscribed within a
square, so that the exterior now no longer reflects the
ground plan. Four pillars tapering off slightly towards
the top support the hemispherical dome which stands
on an originally low drum with oculi that have today
been replaced by four open and four blind windows.
Although the building was evidently also a trial speci-
men for St Peter's (H7), the pillars are not bevelled,
but give the impression of having sharp edges. The
tall lantern (it is not original) and the Palladian windows – an invention of Bramante's (cf. H5) – in the attic zone of the front walls of the cross's arms contribute further to the uniform lighting of the interior. The
very restrained, but at the same time immensely firm,
subdividing work in this plain and almost austere
room consists firstly of a framework of flat pilaster
strips and secondly of flat arched panels and flat blind
panels (»windows« and »doors«). On the other hand,
the stucco decorations – also very exactly formed –
on the surrounding architrave and at the feet of the
circles (which follow models from antiquity) of both
drum and dome look almost splendidly rich. The stupendous harmony of the room derives from the fact
that extreme severity and plainness are combined with
purity, splendour and sharpness in all the forms. SG

H11 Città del Vaticano: Cortile di S. Damaso
Città del Vaticano (plan III 1/A)
begun 1512
Donato Bramante

Bramante designed, for Pope Julius II, a multi-storeyed piece of loggia architecture that was placed for
show in front of the eastern wing, which faced the city,
of the old core structure of the palace (F1). In doing
this he widened towards the south an older, multi-storeyed arcaded frontage by including an additional five
bays to reach today's total of thirteen, and at the
same time he added to the frontage a storey with a
loggia. Bramante also adopted the lowest portico of
the preceding structure, but made its arched openings uniform by including round-arched arcatures
(which were later closed up by Antonio da Sangallo
for reasons of statics) and a flat order of pilaster
strips. On this basis, he erected the two galleries, each of
them 65 metres long, consisting of round-arched arcades which have thirteen axes and stand on pillars
with an order of pilasters and half columns which is
placed out in front for show and in the lower storey
has Doric, in the upper storey Ionic capitals. Thus the
building became much greater, not merely in its dimensions, but also in its form. The motif of the pillared
arcade which was linked to the order of columns and
was ennobled by it points to a great ancient heritage
consisting initially of the tabularium (A9), and then –
by reason of the several storeys in which the motif appears in rows – also of the greatest building of Roman
antiquity, the Colosseum (A25). The monumentality
and spiritual greatness of ancient Rome were intended to be aroused again. But at the same time the ancient prototype was not being slavishly imitated but, in
parts, also being »corrected«. The proportions look

H11 Città del Vaticano: Cortile di S. Damaso

less massive, the arched openings appear to be wider and the pillars seem more slender, with the result that supports brimming with energy appear to replace supports that are all too massive. The same applies to the lively-looking balustrades between the pillars, and also to the materials in which there is a distinction between the brick wall and the architectural order that is placed out in front and is made of travertine, whereas in the ancient preceding structure the entire massive block had been of travertine.

After Bramante died in 1514, Raphael completed what Bramante had left behind. Operating on behalf of Pope Leo X (1513–21), he and his fellow-workers decorated the vaults of the loggias in the second storey with scenes from the Old Testament, and the rear wall and pillars with grotesqueries made of painted stucco (known as »Raphael's loggias«). He also completed the loggia façade on the fourth floor to his own plan. Here, the pillar was replaced by a column and the arch by an architrave. Bramante had already put such a combination into effect in the cloister of S. Maria della Pace (H3). But there two columns stood in the place of each pillar, and the upper storey was markedly lower. However, an example of classically correct architecture was being aimed at in the inner courtyards of both these structures; Alberti had earlier emphasized that an arch should be combined only with a pillar, whereas a column should be linked only with a horizontal architrave.

In using this combination of various kinds of classically correct structure for the storeys, the High-Renaissance buildings were meant to outshine the ancient prototypes. The rich show frontage not only looked very open and extroverted to an eye trained on the self-contained walls of the Middle Ages, but also, given its open loggia and the grotesquerie paintings, included some elements of villa and garden architecture. What is more, its splendour also fulfilled the highest claims to impressiveness. After all, at that time the papal benediction loggia, which had been built under Pius II (1458–64) and was also an arcaded architectural structure with three storeys and a tabularium motif, but did not rise up so high (it had four axes), stood to the left of this façade, outside Old St Peter's. Only when Paul V caused the façade for New St Peter's (B34) to be built did the benediction loggia disappear.

Bramante's façade created the basis for expanding the papal palace eastwards. After 1563, a wing was built that had thirteen axes; it pointed eastwards and adjoined at right angles the northern edge of the Bramante façade on which it was modelled. Gregory XIII (1572–85) ordered his dwelling rooms to be fitted out for him in this wing. The Damasus courtyard became a genuine inner courtyard when a third eastern wing, which though only had eight axes, was added opposite the Bramante façade. It was planned and begun by Martino Longhi and Ottaviano Mascherino from 1578 onwards, and Domenico Fontana completed it later, during the rule of Pope Sixtus V. It was now interpreted as being part of the head building of the Vatican Palace, which was being newly erected (B19). The Damasus courtyard was created in this way and was open towards the south. It was named after a spring which the saint is said to have guided towards the font of St Peter's. Innocent X (1644–55) ordered the spring to be surrounded by a fountain, and thus made the Vatican self-sufficient in terms of its water supply. SG

H12 S. Maria del Popolo: Cappella Chigi
Piazza del Popolo (plan I 2/D–3/D)
1513–16
Raphael

In designing this tomb chapel in 1513, Raphael was planning for his friend and patron, Agostino Chigi the banker, a »universal art work«, which was though unfinished when they both died in 1520. Some of the decorations date from the first half of the 16C, but it was not until the time of Fabio Chigi, who later became Pope Alexander VII, that the figured adornments were completed by Bernini. Nevertheless, the chapel in its present shape is the quintessence of a building which walks the narrow ridge, typical of the High-Renaissance epoch, between splendour and purity.

In its overall shape, the chapel is a domed, square-shaped, centrally planned space with a short, barrel-vaulted bay at the entrance and three still shorter cross-arms on the other three sides. The four arms were linked by diagonal sections. By this design, Raphael was alluding to the octagonal shape of the late-classical Heroon, and in this way the building's function as a tomb chapel was also being referred to. But the real prototype for this spatial form is to be found in Bramante's plan for the crossing of St Peter's (H7). Both structures have bevelled pillars in a pendentive domed church above a Greek cross.

The structural framework for this church consists of fluted Corinthian pilasters. It was continued around the entire church, above the diagonal sections and the cross-arms. The intercolumniations had alternating widths and differing designs, so that a rhythmic bay was formed. A surrounding architectural order was intended and therefore bent pilasters were chosen. It is hardly possible to say that the wall is articulated, as it looks like a skin which has been pushed against this framework from the outside. The wall looks detachable, while on the other hand the structure of the fluted order presents itself as firm and solid. Raphael increased the number of flutings to eight as against the six or seven that were usual, thus obtaining a stable-looking pilaster on each side of the bend and, by doubling even these numbers at the entrance, he enhanced once again the solidity which this section possesses – like a door lintel for the whole chapel. Firstly the sharp distinction between structural and filling-up sections, and secondly the enormous solidification of the structural sections, which though at the

H12 S. Maria del Popolo: Cappella Chigi

same time do not look frugal, but splendid and rich (richer than previously in Bramante's works): these are the two features representing the golden balance and the »maniera grande« that are regarded as the quintessence of the High Renaissance. At the same time, by no longer placing the pilasters on high pedestals, Raphael made the area appear more immediately present to the onlooker than did Bramante who, in St Peter's, had used pedestals over 3 m high! As compared with this, Raphael no longer gave the onlooker the impression that he was standing underneath the space and looking up into it.

The manifold and very decided reference to antiquity is another typical feature. The altar with the altarpiece depicting the Birth of the Virgin Mary stands against the wall opposite the entrance, whereas pyramid-shaped tombs imitating classical antiquity (they are for the brothers Agostino and Sigismondo Chigi) are located in the other two arms of the cross. The bevelled corners of the domed pillars contain, in round-arched niches, the statues of the four prophets who foretold the Resurrection: Jonah on the whale (to the left of the altar) and Elijah in the desert (to the right of the entrance), the work of Raphael's pupil Lorenzetto, and Habakkuk (to the right of the altar), with an angel carrying him by one hair to Daniel in the lions' den (to the left of the entrance). The two last-mentioned statues are by Lorenzo Bernini and, being genuinely Baroque sculptures, burst out of the narrow framework of their niches and project far into the room, conceptually traversing it.

As regards the topics dealt with in them, Platonic ideas were combined with elements of Christian belief,

and this is typical of humanism. Between the windows, Genesis is depicted. The cycle of the seasons of the year in the tondi is probably to be understood as a symbol of eternity. The cosmos was formed by the seven spheres for the seven planets, each of which was set in motion by an angel, and also by the eight spheres of the fixed stars. It is through the spheres that the souls return to their creator, who is depicted in the figure of God the Father in the zenith of the dome. Thus Christian ideas – and this is again typical of humanism – were here understood as being the glorious completion of ancient ideas. SG

H13 Castel S. Angelo: Cappella Leone X
Lungotevere di Castello (plan IV 1/A)
1514–16
after Michelangelo Buonarroti

The right-hand side wall of Leo X's chapel – the latter is part of the papal apartments in the Castel Sant' Angelo – points towards the Cortile dell'Angelo. Michelangelo designed a façade for that wall in 1514. It was the first building of his to be put into effect, though it was actually erected by A. da Sangallo the Younger.

The centrepiece is formed by an aedicule consisting of two Doric columns and a triangular gable. These are on a broad basis like temple frontages elsewhere. This centrepiece is subdivided within, so that four panels are created (in the plan, they are all square and equal in size), all of them open (in the plan, the round openings also took up the entire quarter). A self-contained bay with a horizontally concluding entablature adjoins each side of the centrepiece. Here too, the plan left more space (with a flat wall) at the top, above the wall niches, especially as the lion masks alluding to Leo X were absent.

Church façades that were actually built were rare in the early cinquecento, because the centrally planned building which was more popular at that time was understood as being a body which lacked a proper façade (cf. e. g. H31). This small façade thereby gains in significance. It embodies in a nutshell Michelangelo's idea for the large contemporary project, never

H13 Castel S. Angelo: Cappella Leone X

executed, for the façade of S. Lorenzo in Florence. The basic theme of a lateral extension to the temple frontage is common to both works. In this, Michelangelo is deviating from the model found in the most significant early-Renaissance façade, namely that of S. Maria Novella, which is by Alberti and still had its effect in Il Gesù (B1). The taller centre and the lower sides are united in the uniform entablature, and there is no bridging motif, such as a scroll, to link them. In this way Michelangelo was interlinking the vertical with the horizontal in a very compact way that almost resembled a grid (similar, later examples are H30, H31). The centrepiece also projected, so that he was lending depth to the façade and, for the first time, was touching upon the topic that was to be central to the façades of the next three hundred years, namely the two sections that seem to penetrate one another: here they are the transverse bar shape and the aedicule frontage or temple frontage that thrusts forth from it. SG

H14 Palazzo Alberini-Cicciaporci
Via del Banco di S. Spirito 12 (plan IV 1/A)
1515–21
Raphael

The Via dei Banchi (today the Via del Banco di S. Spirito) is a famous Renaissance street by Julius II. It led to the Ponte Sant'Angelo, and was the financial centre of Rome and the site of the major Florentine banks. Giulio Alberini, a merchant and speculator, rented out the shops of his new palace to Verrazzano and Rucellai, two Florentine bankers, in this way financing the costly new building. According to the most recent research, Raphael was the designing architect, and not Giulio Romano as stated by Vasari.

As to its architectural type, this palace reverts to Bramante's famous »Casa di Raffaello« (Palazzo Caprini) (cf. p. 117), a building which no longer survives but in which Bramante created the prototype of the Roman High-Renaissance palace. In that building there was a fully worked-out contrast between the massive base-course storey of raw, »ancient Roman« rustic work and the elegant, subtly elaborated columned architecture of the piano nobile, but here Raphael subdues this contrast in favour of a delicate wall relief. The joints of the rustic work, with their alternation of narrow and broad layers of stone, lie above the base-course storey like a fine piece of drawing. Those low openings for shops which are cut evenly into the wall are covered by an architrave-like block of masonry, each of whose voussoirs forms a straight arch. The semicircular lunettes in the mezzanine supplement the openings, thus creating the overall form of an arcade. Bramante had introduced to palace architecture this motif deriving from classical times, his aim being to illustrate that architecture's ancient Roman basis. The turning point between the lower and upper structures is formed by a broad strip which is decorated with a frieze and above which the

H14 Palazzo Alberini-Cicciaporci

two storeys (they each have seven axes) rise, concluding in a cornice.

Raphael abandoned the classical principles of orderliness when designing the façade. Supporting and resting architectural components are here replaced by wall panelling consisting of framed and recessed sections which divide up the surface of the wall into a multi-layered relief. The supports, which in the piano nobile are still reminiscent of Tuscan pilasters, are in the upper storey dissolved entirely into wall panels. The outlines of the frames of the panels – the latter are recessed into the wall – form here, along with the imaginative window framings, a still richer wall relief. The uncanonical treatment of the details, the introduction of abstract shapes springing from the designer's imagination, and the picturesquely decorative conception of the façade above whose subtly layered wall relief a rich interplay of light and shade unfolds: all this betrays the hand of the painter who also included in his calculations the greatly foreshortened lower view. The dissolution of classical orderliness – and at the peak of Renaissance architecture! – here already proclaims the switch to Mannerism. EJ

H15 Palazzo Baldassini
Via delle Coppelle (plan IV 1/A)
1516–19
Antonio da Sangallo the Younger

This palace, which Melchiorre Baldassini, the protégé of Leo X and intimate friend of Hadrian VI, ordered to be built in 1516–19, was the first palace designed by Sangallo in Rome, but already reflects his plans for the Palazzo Farnese (H25).

In contrast to Bramante's and Raphael's palace architecture (cf. H22), Sangallo once again continued the type of the Palazzo Venezia (F5): a three-storeyed cube which is subdivided only by cornices and rows of windows and concludes in a principal cornice. The fact that this is plainly a High-Renaissance building can be discerned from the detailed shapes which fundamentally alter its appearance: the sturdy colonnaded portal; the massive bosses of the border-tile ribboning which consolidate and intensify the edges of the building; and the characteristic way in which the scroll motif links the windows of basement and ground floor.

The inner courtyard, which was restored and rebuilt in 1956 and is now once again accessible, can also be regarded as an example of the High Renaissance according to Sangallo. Owing to the small size, a loggia could be built only on the entrance side, but it was in a systematic and academically correct way that Sangallo subdivided the structure into three bays in each case, even above the closed window walls: the tabularium motif with a Doric order of pilasters is found below, and above there is only an Ionic order on the three closed sides. The simple bent pilaster was chosen as the method to employ in the corners. The result is an entirely regular square of lucid clarity and the best possible structural proportions. In it, all the detailed shapes, including the window roofings, have been designed with a methodical perfection. UF

H16 Villa Madama
Via di Villa Madama (plan I 1/B)
1516–23
Raphael

In 1516/17, Cardinal Giulio de' Medici, later Pope Clement VII, commissioned Raphael to build a country seat outside the city gates. Such villae suburbanae had, in ancient Roman architecture, a long tradition which Raphael and his fellow-worker Giuliano da Sangallo followed up. However, only a few sections of the ambitious project were completed.

This elongated building was intended to be erected on three terraces, thus taking into account the charming scenery of the location on Monte Mario. A large circular courtyard standing on the middle terrace and linking all the areas of the villa was planned to be the centre of the complex. The splendid rooms intended for dwelling and imposingness were called the Casino. In accordance with Vitruvius's guidelines, they were moved into the northern section. A garden loggia with three axes opened up at the north-western end of the main axis, opposite the entrance area with its atrium. A semicircular theatre was to be built on the topmost terrace on the hillside, and the domestic rooms and baths would have been housed in a cryptoportico on the lowest terrace. This ambitious project was left uncompleted, owing to the death of Raphael in 1520 and that of his client a year later. All that was finished was half the central courtyard, part of the apartments, and the large garden loggia. The existing structure is a fragment, but the intention behind the design is clearly visible. Ancient Roman architecture is reborn in the monumental conchae, in the massive vaults and in the compact, severe way in which the loggia is subdivided by pilasters. The plan of an ancient villa unites a genuinely Roman architectural type with the language of shapes found in ancient monumental structures – and this combination, by which the first villa to be conceived as a monument came into being, was new. Another reference to antiquity is the stucco-work decorations which were carried out by Baldassare Peruzzi and Giulio Romano on the model of Nero's Domus Aurea (A24). AG

H16 Villa Madama

H17 S. Maria di Monserrato
Via Monserrato (plan IV 1/B)
begun 1518
Antonio da Sangallo the Younger

The foundation stone for S. Maria di Monserrato, the national church of the Aragonese and Catalans, was laid in 1518. The plan is by Antonio da Sangallo the Younger, but Antonio da Sangallo the Elder may also have been involved, because the new building was decided upon as early as the pontificate of Alexander VI.

The architectural type of this church is a barrel-vaulted hall area with accompanying chapels and an attached sanctuarium, and is of great significance in the history of building development. It rejects not only the basilica which has a nave and at least one aisle, but also the High-Renaissance ideals of the centrally planned building. This type was developed for the purposes of religious fraternities – this is why it is also known as a congregational church -, and is a room which unites the priests with the laity when it comes to preaching and the Sacrifice of the Mass. With a flat roof, it occurs several times in Rome in the first half of the 16C, examples being S. Marcello al Corso (B103) and S. Spirito in Sassia (H26). But it did not attain outstanding significance until the orders of the Counter-Reformation adopted it in a monumental form (B1).

The structural elements here possess the methodical correctness characteristic of Antonio: a longitudinal barrel with flattened domes, chapels which are clearly subordinate to the hall, and that large order of pilasters, with its continuous entablature, which subdivides the arcaded wall.

The façade with its five axes forms a relief (Francesco da Volterra, 1582-84) which is moulded in an angular way throughout and is typical of the late 16C. Salvatore Rebecchini built the upper storey in a brittle and hard style in 1929. UF

H18 Villa Lante
Passeggiata del Gianicolo (plan III 1/B)
begun 1520
Giulio Romano

Baldassare Turrini da Pescia was until 1521 a high official at the Curia, and he began in about 1519/20 to plan a villa whose construction was begun in c. 1521. Giulio Romano was persuaded to be the architect. It is possible in this work to discern hints suggesting that he was a pupil of Raphael's and was now trying to liberate himself in terms of style.

In particular, the entrance frontage and the garden frontage differ immensely from one another. Double pilasters form the vertical axes on the entrance façade, with a Doric order underneath and an Ionic one on the first floor. In this way three bays are formed, and the middle one, intended for the portal, is wider. The entrance portal is emphasized by half columns and an entablature bent at right angles, thus resembling the

H18 Villa Lante

ruined Palazzo Branconio dell'Aquila by Raphael. The half columns are applied to the façade, as though pretending to ignore the subdivision of the façade.

All four bays on the side facing the garden are of the same width, but the architectural theme is unusual: the motif of the Serliana here has narrow and confined round arches, but possesses not only Doric columns which are of good and tall proportions, but also a well-developed entablature. This motif forms a ground-floor loggia and thrusts the upper storey aside. In fact, its arches which extend beyond a single storey deprive the façade of the overall tectonic solidity which the onlooker's eye is accustomed to seeing and which is to be found in the entrance frontage. The garden façade looks like a slight piece of playfulness, supported by a well-fortified substruction. Giulio Romano is also playing with unconventional proportions: the pilasters at the edges are wider, and thus give a framing impression. The pilasters on the first floor have only four flutings (sometimes only two on the garden side), and look delicate and decorative. That systematic lack of system which was finally to turn Giulio Romano into a master of Mannerist architecture is already hinted at here. PZ

H19 Palazzo Stati-Maccarani
Piazza dei Caprettari (plan IV 1/B)
c. 1520–36
Giulio Romano

This palace designed in c. 1520 is Giulio Romano's last Roman work, and leads up to his Mannerist buildings in Mantua. Although Giulio is still continuing the architectural type of the Roman Renaissance palace, which was a tradition initiated by Bramante and given further development by Raphael, he is starting to depart from classical methods.

The main façade is very closely related to that of the Palazzo Alberini (H14). The tendency, there introduced, to abandon canonical principles of orderliness is continued further here. The rusticated ground floor is brimming with energy. Gigantic voussoirs are joined into massive straight arches above the shop openings. The fact that forces and energies directed against one another are being made visible is particularly noticeable in the main portal which is the focal point of the façade and in which the heavy, wedged-in voussoirs of the door lintel are threatening to burst apart the gable of the portal. The dynamism of the base-course storey is lost in the piano nobile, whose elegant double pilasters, together with the recessed wall panels of the windows, form a delicate wall relief. The emphasis is here entirely upon the aedicule windows, which look like sculptured appliqué work. The loss of substance, three-dimensionality and dynamism is greatest of all in the topmost storey. A flatly layered relief made of pilaster strips and wall panels replaces a full order of pilasters.

The uncanonical use made of the obligatory classical apparatus of shapescharacterizes Giulio Romano's departure from the High Renaissance and the beginning of Mannerism. EJ

H20 S. Maria in Porta Paradisi
Via di Ripetta, Via Antonio Canova (plan I 3/D)
begun 1522
Antonio da Sangallo the Younger
The planning of this small church next to the Ospedale di S. Giacomo was begun in 1519, but it was the plague epidemic of 1522/23 that gave the real impulse for building not only this church but also S. Maria di Loreto (H45). Sangallo was responsible for both churches.

H20 S. Maria in Porta Paradisi

Sangallo's church architecture is easy for the onlooker to survey, and is shaped by the idea of a centrally planned building. An octagon surrounded by a square-shaped wall covering is often found in it. S. Maria in Porta Paradisi is another such domed area with a square surrounding wall.

The façade can be explained as according entirely with the High Renaissance in harking back to ancient times. But this resulted here only in a very sober, almost listless copy of the Titus arch in the Forum Romanum (A26). The massive main entablature, a cross-beam not bent at right angles, is particularly plain. The brick wall, now bare, was originally covered with marbled plastering.

The interior of the centrally planned area takes on the shape of an equilateral octagon. This is also found in ancient Rome: in the palace on the Palatine (A27) and in the late thermal baths (A43, A46). The shape was adopted again here. The spatial design initially leant heavily on that of the Chigi chapel of S. Maria del Popolo (H12), but Raphael's prototype was later largely ousted by that adopted from ancient times.

S. Maria in Porta Paradisi is certainly not a high point in Sangallo's work, but the church nonetheless shows the extent which faithfulness to ancient prototypes could reach in the High Renaissance. PZ

H21 Palazzetto Farnesina dei Baullari
Corso Vittorio Emanuele II / Via dei Baullari
(plan IV 1/B)
1523–30
Antonio da Sangallo the Younger
From 1494 onwards, the prelate Thommas Le Roy was in the service in Rome of the French king Charles VIII. After being raised to the nobility by Francis I, the successor to the French throne, he was allowed to include the French lily in his coat of arms. From 1523–30 he built himself a palace in the Via dei Baullari. The heraldic lily, which is also part of the Farnese coat of arms, still appears today in the frieze of the entablature. This inevitably resulted in cases of mistaken identity, and the palace was soon wrongly named »Farnesina ai Baullari«. On the basis of stylistic comparisons, Antonio da Sangallo the Younger may have been the architect.

The building was extensively altered in the 19C. When the Corso was being built, a third of the substance of the palace was removed in the east. The result is that this building, which today gives an impression of lacking uniformity, provides a free view of the cortile. The façade facing the Corso must be thought of as originally not having included the right-hand section which is opened up by a Serliana. That façade had five axes and a large portal at its centre. The emphasis on the use of rustication in the base-course storey and even in the piano nobile is unusual for Sangallo the Younger in palaces which date from later than 1520 and were commissioned by private persons (cf. H25). On the other hand, the window frames, with

H21 Palazzetto Farnesina dei Baullari

their alternating gable shapes in the piano nobile, point to him. The leitmotiv of the cortile on the ground floor is the Serliana. This architectural form, which is also known as the Palladian motif, was not yet widespread in Rome at this time (cf. H5). PZ

H22 Palazzo Vidoni-Caffarelli
Via del Sudario 10–16 (plan IV 1/B)
begun 1524
successor of Raphael

Today, the palazzo which Bernardino Caffarelli caused to be built from 1524 onwards embodies, in the clearest way, a tendency of a basically different kind from that which, within the Roman High Renaissance, was represented by the Palazzo Farnese (H25). Up until the 19C, its façade was extended several times and had a storey added to it; the seven centrally located window axes of the total of seventeen axes in today's Via del Sudario were part of the original structure, as is easily discernible in the base-course storey, because there are not yet any gabled window frames in it. Thus the effect originally aimed at was solely that produced by the weighty rustic work, whose bosses have smaller sections than in the extended parts of the façade, but possess sturdier and more solid shapes and, taken as a whole, form a compact block which supports the elegant upper storey with its pairs of columns and its window balconies. When the building with its seven axes is reconstructed mentally, its particular qualities become discernible: the upright stance of the palace, its consummate overall propor-

tions, and the well-thought-out rhythm of the wall openings in the base-course storey. In that storey, arcades alternate with openings having a straight arch. The latter is a form in which the voussoirs of the rustic work are joined together as in an arch, but form a horizontal conclusion below; the largest opening is formed by the main portal at the centre.

The palace of Caprini, a cleric of the Curia, was the first building to pursue this tendency. It is ruined today, but has come down to posterity in an engraving by Lafréri (cf. p.117). It was begun by Bramante later than 1501, and in 1517 Raphael purchased it and selected it as his place of residence. Thus the building's decided division into two parts goes back to Bramante: below, two age-old Roman shapes, the pillared arcade and the rustic work with bosses (cf. A9, A23), are combined into a structure of weighty massiveness and compact energy. The shops which open on to these arcades, as they did in the houses of ancient Rome, are only insignificant space-fillers in the arcades. The elemental power of the rocky stone is combined with precisely joined individual forms, particularly in the voussoirs, to form a spellbinding, fascinating sight. Above, however, the surface of the wall is accentuated, with its order of Doric pairs of columns which is placed out in front and is itself not lacking in energy but concentrates it on the beautifully swelling, cultivated shapes of the columns. There are also the slender, delicate outlines of the window aedicules, and the decorativeness of the thin balustrades. The upper storey presents itself as another world which, although repletely abundant, makes it clear in no uncertain

H22 Palazzo Vidoni-Caffarelli

terms what a piano nobile is. The upper and lower storeys, taken together, make Bramante's version of the »gravitas romana«, a version based on subdivided masses and concentrated energy, into the starting point for a number of illustrious successors such as Raphael (H14), Giulio Romano (H19) and Scamozzi. Palladio also drew such a building.

The architect of the Palazzo Vidoni-Caffarelli followed this prototype very closely, limiting himself to slight variations, the chief of which in the upper storey was the attempt, by means of framed panels, to arrange into layers the smooth surfaces of the intercolumniations and firmly to tie those surfaces to the sculptural column motif. The design was formerly ascribed to Raphael, who had though died in 1524; Vasari records that Lorenzetti, one of his pupils, was the architect. UF

H23 Palazzo del Banco di S. Spirito (Zecca)
Via del Banco di S. Spirito 31 (plan IV 1/A)
1525
Antonio da Sangallo the Younger
It is not so much the palace, but rather its façade, that is an astonishing monumental achievement by Antonio da Sangallo the Younger. It already incipiently anticipates the Baroque style.

The mint (Zecca) had already frequently changed its location since ancient times. Not until the pontificate of Julius II did it move into the building on the corner of the Piazza dei Banchi. That side of the house which faced the Piazza was torn down in 1525. The new frontage thus created was built upwards in a slightly concave shape, according with the curvature of the Piazza. The clients who ordered the building work were firstly the Fuggers who were resident as the mintmasters of the Vatican, and secondly Cardinal Armellini.

The façade is designed to produce a long-distance effect, and its monumental appearance makes it into a dominating element in the Piazza, against which it forms a combined front. Here, its monumentality is intensified because it is placed on a base course. The sculptured rustic masonry with the usually low ashlars suggests that the superstructure weighs heavily upon it. A large order of pilasters is now used for that superstructure: the pilasters cover two storeys, whose value thus recedes. The triumphal arch at the centre is an expressive architectural theme, a setting for the papal coat of arms, framed by the narrow articulations of the rhythmic bay. The Baroque could hardly add anything to the fact that the principal cornice is bent to right angles by the projecting pilasters and that the base course is bent in the same way by pedestals. A large order spreading across the piano nobile and the upper storey had never previously been seen in palace architecture. The façadei is no longer a setting for the piano nobile as it is with Bramante and Raphael; instead, the building as a whole is here being presented as a triumphal piece of architecture. PZ

H23 Palazzo del Banco di S. Spirito (Zecca)

H24 Palazzo Massimo alle Colonne
Corso Vittorio Emanuele II 141 (plan IV 1/B)
1532, 1535–38
Baldassare Peruzzi
The brothers Angelo and Pietro Massimo were able to trace their ancestry back to Fabius Maximus Cunctator, who saved Rome from Hannibal. They persuaded Peruzzi, who at that time was, after all, the architect of St Peter's, to rebuild their palace which had been devastated in the Sacco di Roma. The most that was already in existence so that Peruzzi could rebuild it was the round shape of an odeon of Domitian, located underneath the building site. In this late work of his, he surpassed the Villa Farnesina (H8), which had been very delicate, and created the chief work of Roman Mannerism.

The overall shape of the façade is marked by the fact that the three central bays follow a segment of a circle and that the lateral bays go along the tangents, that is to say the straight lines, that start at the ends of the central bays. The curvature of the columns is matched with further curvature, and the flatness of the pilasters is matched with straightness. In this way Peruzzi generated various effects. The street was formerly much narrower, and every item made a stronger separate impression. The curvature of a palace façade is in itself an entirely new feature. Serlio and Cataneo,

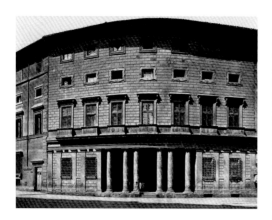

H24 Palazzo Massimo alle Colonne

Peruzzi's two pupils, actually became proponents of the cylindrical palace. The curves followed the configuration of the street, but at the same time distinguished the palace from other palaces. A still more future-oriented feature, central to the Baroque, is the idea, first hinted at here (in a subdued way), of subdividing a palace façade into centrepiece and wings. Contrary to what would be the case if the curvature were continuous, the tension of the façade as a whole looks like that of a bent piece of sheet metal. This effect is enhanced by the way in which the central bay springs up more widely. In addition to this unresolved tension, typical of Mannerism, there was also the fact that – if the onlooker walking along the narrow street was going along the curvature only a little at a time – the centre, upon a close view, was very strongly perceived to be a superelevated frontage.

This palace is indeed thought of as being the chief example of Mannerist palace architecture in Rome, and also a point of reference for Vignola and Pirro Ligorio, the architects of the next generation. »Mannerism« here means complexity, and in particular the absence of hard and fast rules. Here, Peruzzi was influenced not so much by Giulio Romano's Palazzo del Tè, which was the chief work of his generation and of the Mannerism that was exported to Northern Italy, as he was by Raphael's Palazzo Branconio dell'Aquila in Rome (cf. p. 117 and H32). Peruzzi formulated the only congenial answer to that Palazzo. Both Palazzi have a base-course storey with Doric articulation, and three upper storeys which rest with a tremendous weight and do not have a full order of columns. Raphael had in this way already fundamentally modified Bramante's façade scheme which followed the principle that the building was based on the weighty rustic work in the ground floor and was articulated and ennobled in the piano nobile by the order of columns (H22). It is also a Mannerist trait to design the wall so that – and this contrasts with Raphael – it looks as if it was covered by a rigid net.

The order, which is Doric, is unusual. The frontage with its seven axes has the order only on the ground floor, with an order of twin columns in the three central bays replacing the twin pilasters in the side bays. At the transition, the pilaster and column jointly form a pair of supports. Above this a sharp division is created by the projecting entablature, whose weight is optically emphasized by combining the window sills into a single strip. The upper storeys are without an order. The weightiness and preponderance of this section were emphasized more strongly by Peruzzi than by Raphael before him. Peruzzi accentuated its height firstly by means of a doubling – unique in Roman High-Renaissance architecture – of the row of windows in the mezzanine, and secondly by the monotonous design which only has a pattern of cut-stone ashlars and windows. There are no balustrades, niches, friezes, wall panels or columned aedicules. Both these design devices contribute to the structure's second main characteristic: due to the lack of subdivision, the wall looks very flat, and not as if it contained space as it does with Raphael. It was not a building with spatial depth that was here being taken as a theme, but only a façade. Thus, the edges of the façade have not been given separate treatment, and there is therefore no reference to the three-dimensionality of the block. The arrangement of the windows does not accord with that of the storeys behind them. And the very regular cut-stone patterning of the entire wall makes it look like an unfriendly suit of armour. Wurm thought that this was expressive of the ancient Roman virtue of »sodezza« (fitness to fight), but what is perhaps more likely to be reflected here is the gloomy mood of the years following the Sacco di Roma. The subdividing elements are distributed so regularly, and with such little concentration on particular locations, that they look like a net. This applies to the double row of windows, which looks purely geometrical, in the mezzanine. And it also applies to the twin supports below, which adopt Bramante's ideas, but are neither placed close together (as is the case in Bramante's work where they look solidified) nor form a rhythmic bay (cf. H22, H6). Instead, they are like a curtain covering the ground-floor wall. Moreover, the panels of the walls and windows above are of the same size, so that the whole façade looks as though a net-like structure consisting of few firm, flat subdividing elements has been stretched over it.

The columns in the portico are positioned in a way that they are prepare for the courtyard. The columns were not new. They were part of the old palace, and explain the new palace's name. What was new was the horizontal architrave. It was an example of that »correct« faithfulness to antiquity which was being more intensely striven after in the second third of the century. Alberti had deplored the combination of column and arch, and Bramante had therefore replaced it in upper storeys by combining columns and horizontal architrave (H3). What is Mannerist in the present palace is that this portico is located rather unorganically in the façade – it is followed in the interior by a narrow passage that does not have three axes –, and that with this portico (and this differs from what happens with a portal) Peruzzi was knocking a hole into the block-like building which the High Renaissance had created.

The corridor no longer adjoins the courtyard axially, but instead tangentially. The entrance wall and rear wall were opened up into loggias here, while the side walls remained closed. Thus the division into a central section and wings was taken over from the façade. As in the exterior, the ground floor is subdivided all round by a uniform Doric order with a weighty entablature. It is true that a uniform Ionic order again appears in the piano nobile, but the lower right-hand side wall does not have a piano nobile, and on the left-hand wall the Ionic order of the courtyard was here underlaid with the cut-stone patterning taken over from the façade. All this is indicative of two matters: the way in which other sections were visually linked to the courtyard became much more complex and almost more accidental than previously, when there was a liking for showing the corridor and courtyard in a uniform wall system, as in Palazzo Baldassini and Palazzo Farnese (H15 and H25). And Peruzzi loved to have a large number of angles of view, asymmetries, which, as for example in the lower side wall on the right, he could have avoided without much difficulty. SG

Bibliography: H. Wurm, *Der Palazzo Massimo alle Colonne*, Berlin, 1965.

H25 Palazzo Farnese
Piazza Farnese (plan IV 1/B)
begun 1516, plans altered 1534
Antonio da Sangallo the younger, Michelangelo Buonarroti

Alessandro Farnese, who was just as well known as an art collector and humanist as he was as a powerful Curia cardinal from the time of Pope Alexander VI until that of Pope Clement VII, expressed his ambitious

H25 Palazzo Farnese

H25 Palazzo Farnese

pretensions in one of the largest palaces in Rome. The project, begun by Antonio da Sangallo the Younger in 1516/17, was enlarged again in 1534 when the cardinal became Pope Paul III, although it had previously already been perfectly sufficient for papal status. The later involvement of Michelangelo (1546–49) led to major alterations in the upper storeys. Vignola and della Porta completed the building in the second half of the 16C, altering the rear sections with the gallery, whose paintings by the Carracci are a key work of Baroque painting in Rome. The palace passed into the hands of the Bourbons by hereditary succession, and is today the French ambassador's residence.

In the exterior, Sangallo was creating a counterpole to the palaces in the style of Bramante (cf. H22). He was not concerned with the distinction between base course and piano nobile, but with the building as a whole, the large cube-shaped palace. His three-storeyed structure thus, if anything, follows on from palace architecture in Florence, while the effect of the bare wall is continued from the Palazzo Venezia (F5). But these structures were not true prototypes. Sangallo was here creating nothing less that a congenial equivalent to the buildings of the Roman classical period. This equivalent was the quintessence of the »maniera grande« of the Roman High Renaissance. Freestanding on all sides, it towers over the buildings of the city's old core area. The forecourt was planned from the outset, so that the effect produced by this king of Roman palaces would be unrestricted. Sangallo limited the weighty rustic-work bosses to the portal and to the border-tile ribboning, which marks the edges of the cube with great trenchancy and bears witness to its solidity. Neither does the subdivision into storeys curtail the effect of the cube; the energetic cornices are strips which place it in its shape, ensure a clear and incisive orderliness in the façade, and allocate places for the windows. The rectangular windows on consoles below, and the aedicule windows with columns in the upper storeys, lend the building its aspect, but never become an exuberant ornament, even though the individual shapes differ and the gables alternate. Everything is in a mood of monumental tranquility, stability and a self-evident, reliable orderliness throughout.

Michelangelo altered two features of this frontage: the group of windows above the portal was not given any gables, but did receive columns and pilasters in dense concentration, so that the compact massing of the motifs, and the coat of arms, make this honorary loggia very eyecatching. The fact that the third storey was also raised and that a projecting, weighty principal cornice was placed on it means little in terms of material, but much in terms of effect: the building was given a free and tall brow, and another powerfully combining accent in the upper part. In this way it proved possible to increase and outstrip the monumentality of Sangallo's project.

The architecture of the thoroughfare behind the simple voussoir façade of the portal has a status of its own. It seems that it was only designed with three aisles in order to unfurl a replete array of ancient articulatory art: two colonnades with sturdy Doric columns in a close row, and a sculptural wall relief with half columns and niches at the sides: all this was powerfully combined and restrained by the large motif of the coffer-work barrel vault above the thoroughfare.

In this way the architect puts the onlooker in the right mood for the inner courtyard, whose type and subdivision were not really anything new at that time. Sangallo designed it as a large, regular square shape, something which evidently accorded with the High-Renaissance ideal, and he subdivided the two lower storeys of the surrounding loggias by giving them the well-tried tabularium motif (cf. A9, F5). He nevertheless accomplished a work of the High Renaissance. Firstly, he was concerned, as in a textbook, with perfection in the detail, as can be studied in many individual points. Examples are: the jutting entablature which is not bent to right angles and once again emphasizes the horizontal; the splendour of the Ionic order with its garlanded frieze; and the harmonious relationship between the pillared arcades, their imposts and the outline of the arch on the one hand and the columns and entablature on the other. The problem of the corner was also solved in masterly fashion: he subdivided the L-shaped piece of wall in the corner by providing a full half column on each side, and he placed in the corner the edge of a pilaster pillar. This solution links an entirely harmonious structural system to an expressive quality of solidity and concentrated energy. And it is precisely in the weighting of the elements and in their perfectly balanced interrelationship that it turns out that Sangallo was more than an academic only concerned with »correctness«, and this is also confirmed by a comparison with the other Roman examples. By the yardstick of the Palazzo Venezia (F5), what is shown here is not only an improvement in detail, an example being the absence of pedestals

below the columns, but also a superior power and security in the final shaping, which can now really compete with imperial Rome.

Michelangelo altered the courtyard even more than the façade. He closed the arcades of the second storey on two sides, and in the 19C this was also done on the other two sides. And he designed the upper storey as a windowed frontage subdivided by pilasters. These pilasters with their broad recessed layers can be compared with Sangallo's half columns only in terms of their expressive significance, but belong to a quite different mode of design and also generate a new theme: Michelangelo was opposing the uniformity of the storeys by employing a consistent further development: this ranged from Sangallo's tabularium motif below to the self-contained wall of windows subdivided by pilasters above, from the structure of the support components to the wall relief arranged in strong layers, and from the regularity of the round arch openings to the angular, weighty shapes of the window frames. The harmony of the High Renaissance thus developed into what Michelangelo was always striving after: the opposition of compacted three-dimensional forces. UF

H26 S. Spirito in Sassia
Borgo di S. Spirito (plan III 1/A–2/A)
1538–45, 1590
Antonio da Sangallo the Younger

After the oldest hospital in Rome (cf. F8), and also a church tower, had been built as new structures under Sixtus IV, it was not until 1538–45, under Paul III, that the associated church was erected to a design by A da Sangallo the Younger. The façade, which was only built in 1590 under Sixtus V, probably also goes back to Antonio.

The interior is a flat variant, with a coffer-work ceiling, of the aisleless nave with apses (cf. H44, B1), which here accompany the main area as a succession of conchae. The façade is more significant. Although it follows on from a type which had been common in Rome since the late 15C, namely the cross-section façade with scrolls, a triangular gable and a double-storeyed order of pilasters (cf. F7), it lifts that type to a new architectural level.

In S. Spirito, the order of pilasters becomes a dominant factor which really gives the façade its shape and, being a well-ordered continuum, distinguishes the components: below, outside the apses, a lateral bay adjoins each of the three rhythmized bays at the centre. The proportions of the order of pilasters give the structure a severe character, making it a proud and towering façade, and this impression is intensified by an additional vertical element, namely a path consisting of a frame, a wall niche and a frame. The detail, too, is masterly: the cavities of the niches lend the façade a certain substance and take away from it its board-like flatness, and the linking scrolls above the lateral bays look like elastic cross struts. Thus San-

H26 S. Spirito in Sassia

gallo was not only creating the pattern for the most significant Roman façade type since the end of the Middle Ages, but was also setting new standards in the quality of the shaping and of the articulation. UF

H27 Campidoglio (Capitol)
Piazza del Campidoglio (plan V 1/B)
begun 1538
Michelangelo Buonarroti

The Capitol, the smallest hill in Rome, was at the same time the most important, being the religious and political centre of ancient Rome. The present square is in the ancient Asylum, the hollow between the two rounded hilltops upon which there stood the temple of Jupiter and some buildings that were the forerunners of S. Maria in Aracoeli. The ancient triumphal processions ended here, and the state archive was also here (A9). In the 12C, although the city had shrunk and now only filled the bend in the Tiber, the citizens of Rome once again chose for themselves this hill as a site for the conservators (the executive authority) and the senators (the judicative authority).

When Charles V visited Rome in 1536, some buildings (12C and 15C) that were forerunners, some of them very irregular and full of nooks and crannies, stood in this area, as yet unpaved, on the site of today's palace of conservators and senators. To the left, the onlooker's gaze fell upon the church, standing on higher ground, of S. Maria in Aracoeli (C36). Charles V's procession through the city (cf. A35, A52) was meant to end on the Capitol. This plan failed. This was probably why Paul III set about redesigning the place. He started by ordering the only surviving ancient equestrian statue, that of Marcus Aurelius, to be transferred here from the Lateran in 1538. The overall management of the project was given to Michelangelo. This was his first major architectural commission in Rome.

Michelangelo's plan is recorded in Dupérac's famous engraving of 1569. The onlooker's eye is caught by the perfect regularization. An argument in favour of the unusual quality of the project is that it was put into effect mainly after the master's death without any reductions worthy of mention being made. In view of the size of the project, this is a unique occurrence in the history of architecture. The new conservators' palace on the right (H30) was the first structure to be erected, and the last was its counterpart on the left, the Palazzo Nuovo (Museo Capitolino) by Girolamo and Carlo Rainaldi (1644–55). The Palazzo Nuovo had no specific practical function. It served the sole aim of creating symmetry and preventing S. Maria in Aracoeli from being perceived as towering over the square. The senators' palace in the middle was built by Giacomo della Porta and Girolamo Rainaldi (1582–1605). All that was done for this purpose was to encase an older structure which had itself been placed on top of the ancient Tabularium (A9). The towers of that structure are still discernible in the side walls. The façade is subdivided by risalti projecting on the left and right, and also by three storeys, one in rustic work and above it two more which are combined by a large order of pilasters. The building is concluded by a balustraded cornice. The bell tower was added by Martino Longhi the Elder (1578–82) in answer to a portico planned at the top of the stairs.

These stairs are the only part of the design to have been built (1541–54) while Michelangelo was still alive. In the early Renaissance, Alberti and others gave

H27 Campidoglio (Capitol)

scant regard to the architectural task of constructing stairs. It is true that from 1500 onwards stair structures having two flights were found in garden architecture (H6), but not yet in palace architecture, in which they advanced in the Baroque period to become not only the most important place of ceremony but also probably the central architectural task. Michelangelo created the early example of them. In this specific location, the two-flighted stairs combined three advantages: the stairs did not take up much space, they led directly to the main entrance in the piano nobile, and it was possible to preserve the fountain below with its ancient statues (Nile, Roma and Tiber). The portico planned at the apex would have satisfied imperial and papal pretensions.

Such Renaissance architects as Filarete and F. di Giorgio drew ideal cities, but none of them was given the chance comprehensively to redesign a square. The one who came closest to this was Alberti's pupil Rosselino in Pienza. Michelangelo was thus able to create the ideal image of a square for the next few centuries. From then on the cour d'honneur, the entrance area of a palace, was given a U-shape with two lower flanking structures, a taller main structure, and a symmetrical axis. Michelangelo attached great importance to the formation of the cour d'honneur, although he had initially only been commissioned to create, for this irregularly built-over area, an access structure which led to it from the city side and was called the Cordonata. The later castle structure differed in only one point from the method adopted by Michelangelo: in Michelangelo's design, the three sections are still three unconnected buildings. He nevertheless regarded them as belonging together, as being the three walls for a »city-square theatre«. This is why the façades only point towards the square and extend around the corners only to the extent of two axes. Thus Michelangelo found a classical balance between the autonomy of the individual buildings and the synthesis of the whole. Buildings had also preserved their autonomy in the Greek classical period (see the Acropolis), but in the Hellenistic period, the Baroque of ancient times, they coalesced into complexes.

Two shapes in the square deserve particular attention: the trapezium and the oval. The square tapers off towards the access ramp, and is thus trapezium-shaped. The sharp angle between the conservators' palace and the senators' was found in the older buildings which were taken over. But Michelangelo did not balk at tearing down part of a structure if, as in the case of St Peter's, the existing method went against his aesthetic feeling. The trapezium shape is not without its prototypes. Reference is usually made to Rosselino's design of a square in Pienza, where the rectangular patterning of the square is though a disturbing feature. To Michelangelo, who was still »living« the classical period, it was certainly much more important to know that, in the classical period, the same shape for a city square had, beyond the Capitol, existed be-

H27 Campidoglio (Capitol)

low the Tabularium, which was the main building in the square (A1). Thus he was only transferring the ancient shape from one to the other side of the Capitol, the side facing the city – and this reversal of polarity is in any event one of the basic ideas behind the square's design. At the same time, the shape of the square probably satisfied his aesthetic sensitivities. It opposes the foreshortening (and Michelangelo's building work was often contrary to visual habits). The shape therefore makes the main building appear taller, narrower and more impressive. This is why Bernini also adopted this shape the next time a main square was built in Rome (B80). This platform gives the onlooker who climbs up via the ramp and reaches the square a stronger feeling of being accepted and included within a space that closes behind him.

An oval shape with two steps leading to it is recessed into the centre of the square. Apart from some small structures, this oval is the first built since the end of the Middle Ages. Vignola introduced it to church architecture a little later (H34). For both architects, the charm of this shape was that it made it possible to accentuate both the central axis and the middle of the square. In the Capitol, where it is the first such work, this means that it was possible simultaneously to relate the design both to the senators' palace and to the equestrian statue, the latter being emphasized by the patterning of the square.

The interaction between the oval and trapezium shapes says much about Michelangelo's feeling for style. Steps and patterns mark the oval out as a special area. Neither did Michelangelo tolerate any paths cutting into this oval as they do today. In this way an awe of this area was imparted to the onlooker: the area is vaulted, and is therefore convincingly interpreted as meaning that a part of the earth's globe was intended to be expressively uncovered: the Capitol as the navel of the world. Thus the onlooker approaching the senators' palace was brought close to the flanking palaces. The straight paths were displaced, and Michelangelo gave the viewer a sense of almost oppressive constriction. It was precisely to this extent that della Porta modified the design. He selected a pattern of rays which was removed in the early 20C, and ordered paths to be cut into the oval. Thus he decided to give the square a flowing Baroque appearance.

The orderer of the work, and the artist, of course also intended to make specific statements in the design of Rome's most important square. Paul III ordered his coat of arms to be attached to the pedestal of the ancient statue of the emperor. This was meant to express the idea that the citizens' square was conquered and its power broken. Michelangelo, himself an ardent advocate of citizens' rights, did though carry through a considerable enlargement of the design programme. The papal statement was absorbed in a more comprehensive one.

One of the two dedicatory inscriptions praises the revival of ancient Rome and is dated in accordance with the year of Rome's foundation, while the other opposes this by invoking Christ and is dated in accordance with his year of birth. Until the 16C, the Capitol had been reached from the Forum, along routes to the sides of the Tabularium, but Michelangelo built the main access structure on the side towards the city, thus giving the Capitol a new orientation. The senators' palace was in any case already placed on top of the ancient Tabularium. The statement made is clear: the ancient, heathen square was to be honoured anew, but was now to be given a reversed orientation, towards the Christian city. It therefore now appeared both as an ancient temenos (sacred precinct) and as the final point of a pilgrimage route. Its pattern with the number twelve could allude to the ancient cosmos, the signs of the zodiac, but also to the twelve Apostles. Thus the final point of the High Renaissance are to be seen in the square, because the glorification of the ancient classical period as being a forerunner of Christianity is a specifically humanist idea. SG

Bibliography: H. Siebenhüner, *Das Kapitol in Rom – Idee und Gestalt*, Munich, 1954; H. Thies, *Michelangelo – Das Kapitol*, Munich, 1982.

H28 Palazzo dei Pupazzi
Via dei Banchi Vecchi 22 (plan IV 1/B)
um 1540
Giulio Mazzoni (?)
The palace was the residence of Pietro Crivelli, a Milanese goldsmith. This building, very imposing for a mere artisan, was later taken over by Sixtus V as a cardinal's residence. The façade, which is fitted into

the confined row of houses, initially had only three axes, but later had a fourth added to it, with the old angular rustic work remaining preserved.

The architectural subdivision, originally consisting of three storeys above a rusticated base-course storey with shops, is of less interest. The façade lives by its rich stucco decorations which are attributed to Giulio Mazzoni, the creator of the elegant stucco façade of the Palazzo Spada (H32). The adornments consist of festoons, garlands of fruits, masks, putti, satyrs and trophies (from which the name »dei Pupazzi« may derive), and fill the narrow surfaces between the windows. Two relief panels with scenic images are recessed into the third storey. They depict Charles V kissing Paul III's feet, and Paul III reconciling Charles V and Francis I, who had opposed one another. This subject matter is no more suitable for the house of a goldsmith than are the large papal coats of arms in the frieze below the aedicule windows. These decorations, which deal with the dominating position of the papacy, were probably not created until the time when Sixtus V was turning the house into a cardinal's residence. This would also explain why the stucco work on the façade is not better developed in three dimensions. Following in that tradition of the stuccoed palace façade Raphael's Palazzo Branconio, the Palazzo dei Pupazzi is a good example of a significant alternative to the Sangallo style of the 1540's. EJ

H29 Porta S. Spirito
Via de' Penitenzieri (plan III 1/A)
1543–44
Antonio da Sangallo the Younger
In 1543/44, as part of some fortification work being done in the Borgo Leonino, Paul III ordered the southern access – it is the old Porta Saxorum – to be rebuilt. The architect in charge of the fortifications was Antonio da Sangallo the Younger, who had also been commissioned to rebuild the neighbouring church of the hospital of S. Spirito (F8, H26). Although the gate was not completed and was later given a makeshift

H29 Porta S. Spirito

H30 Palazzo dei Conservatori

upper conclusion, the desired monumentality and pretensions of the structure are unmistakable. The gate façade built of travertine rises above a ground-plan line in the shape of a segmental arch. In imitation of ancient truimphal-arch architecture, the façade is subdivided into three bays, the central one of which is occupied by the archway that opens at a high level, while the smaller ones contain round niches standing upon tall pedestals. Strong, unfluted three-quarter columns above projecting pedestals divide the sections from one another and thrust their way through a horizontal cornice which not only supports the archway and the calottes of the niches, but also firmly unites the building; the result is a variant on the tabularium motif (A9). It can be assumed that a uniform entablature and an attic zone above it were intended as the upper conclusion. A characteristic feature is the plastic, space-containing structure of the gate. This produces a particular effect, achieved by the basic form of the segmental arch, by a monumental order of columns, and by the niches with their pedestals that arch forwards convexly. Thus although the Porta S. Spirito, in closely imitating the shapes of ancient triumphal arches, embodies the ideas of the High Renaissance, its three-dimensional language of shapes seems to anticipate essential features of Baroque architecture. DH

H30 Palazzo dei Conservatori
Piazza del Campidoglio (plan V 1/B)
begun 1544, 1563–75
Michelangelo Buonarroti

The conservators' palace was the first new building to be erected on the Capitol (H27). Apart from the central window, Giacomo della Porta adhered strictly to Michelangelo's plans when constructing the building (1563–75).

A colossal Corinthian order of pilasters with a high entablature and a cornice projecting far forwards articulates the building. Seven bays are created. The building is concluded by a balustrade surmounted by statues. The pilasters and entablature both have a re-

cessed layer which surrounds them like a frame. The wall itself, in which the windows are located, is set back by a further layer. On the ground floor, an Ionic order of columns with its own entablature is inserted into the colossal order of pilasters.

The colossal order had already existed before Michelangelo. Alberti used it for the façade of S. Andrea in Mantua (from 1470 onwards), and A. da Sangallo the Younger later also employed it for palace architecture (H23). They were though both still pursuing the aim of developing the shape of the ancient triumphal arch into a type of façade. It was only Michelangelo who made entirely independent use of the colossal order, and only he comprehensively utilized its design opportunities and linked it much more closely to the other parts of the building.

The final shape given to the wall as a surface is immensely dense and consistent. The architrave and cornice of the small order overlap the above-mentioned recessed layers of the colossal order, are bent to right angles at this point and are themselves overlapped by the colossal order. In this way both orders seem to be woven into one another and form a grid. This impression is intensified by the fact that the recessed layers of the pilasters conceal the pillars. From a visual point of view, the building thus became a structure made up purely of articulations: only the pilasters, columns and architraves appear to support anything, and the remaining parts of the wall only fill up space. No previous façade had ever been quite so interlinked in all its individual parts, just as much vertically as horizontally. The basis for this principle was laid down in Michelangelo's early work (H13). He resumed the principle and carried it through into the third dimension in the exterior of St Peter's (H31). Where the subdivision of façades is concerned, that interlinking of a large and small order which is found in the conservators' palace is – apart from the rhythmic bay (cf. H6, H7, F19) – the most significant invention of the High Renaissance. Palladio and Baroque architecture would be inconceivable without it.

The third dimension has also been tremendously solidly worked into the wall as a surface. The depth of the building can be sensed and becomes a key theme. The close interlinking of a large and a small order again has its effect here. This is because whereas the large order dominates the wall, the small inserted order creates depth. For this purpose, Michelangelo gave, to the two columns inserted into the wall, two additional columns on the rear wall of the passage where they serve as counterparts. In each case, he combined these four columns by means of an architrave and a flat vault, so that a succession of baldachins was created on the ground floor. Michelangelo's intention of employing depth as a theme in the small order can be seen from a trendsetting detail: he modified the classical Ionic capital with its flat front, turned the scrolls outwards and placed them diagonally.

The open ground floor is an unusual feature. The early-15C building had already possessed this, and Michelangelo placed a façade in front of that building for show (all he did was to replace the succession of arcatures by a succession of horizontal entablatures, which he preferred because they were flat and looked ancient). However, since the time of Alberti the ground floors of palaces had been solid and self-contained. Even in the 1520's and 1530's, the united block was only penetrated by openings here and there (cf. H24). Michelangelo probably intended something different: the succession of openings is typical of inner court-yards, and the Capitol was intended to present itself as one such.

This succession contributes to the overall effect of the square in other respects too. It more strongly em-phasizes the central axis leading to the senators' pal-ace than would have been possible if the centre of the flanking palaces had been emphasized. The colossal order combines the buildings into large horizontal blocks. The senators' palace is lent prominence in this way too. At the same time, the colossal order forms the strongest counterpoise to the horizontal move-ments which thrust into the square. SG

H31 St Peter's: conchae and exterior
Città del Vaticano (plan III 1/A)
1546–93

The only people who succeeded Bramante as archi-tects of St Peter's after his death were his pupils: Ra-phael, Fra Giocondo, Giuliano da Sangallo, Baldas-sare Peruzzi, Antonio da Sangallo the Younger and, for a few months in 1546, Giulio Romano. Only once the last pupil had died was the way made free for Mi-chelangelo, who completed the work congenially and harmoniously. When the main longitudinal structure by Carlo Maderno (B34), which was added later, is left out of consideration, the building today – apart from the floor at a higher level – is solely the work of Bra-mante (in the core structure, H7) and Michelangelo.

H31 St Peter's: conchae and exterior. Design by
Sangallo

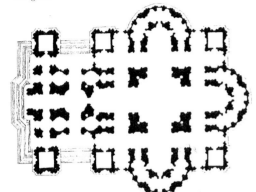

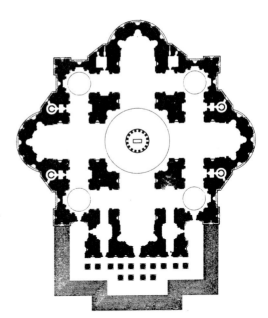

H31 St Peter's: conchae and exterior. Design by
Michelangelo

Others to have left their traces are chiefly Raphael and Sangallo. Under Raphael and after him, the un-certainty caused by Bramante's death was seen in the immense number of drafts, which either did or did not include the Rosselino choir, either did or did not have an ambulatory around each of the conchae, and were sometimes drawings for a centrally planned building and sometimes for one with nave and aisles. Peruzzi developed a new form of drawing which united ground plan and elevation and anticipated isometry. Raphael appointed an executive assistant, because the increased complexity of the plans was placing too much strain on the stonemasons' lodge. In the period from 1529–40, Sangallo achieved little, due to the scanty funding which amounted to only 17 620 duc-ats, but in 1540–46 he used the 162 000 ducats avail-able in those years to raise the floor by 3.2 m and to build a wooden model. This led to the disappearance of the tall pedestals upon which Bramante had placed the pilasters and which gave the visitor the impression of looking from underneath into the building and its or-der of pilasters. Raphael had already departed from such pedestals in the Chigi chapel (H12), and Serlio wrote: »Columns resting on the floor are much more beautiful than columns on a pedestal.« Three main features characterize the wooden model: very monot-onous rows of identical small-sectioned arches and supports in the exterior; a sombre interior (according to Michelangelo it was ideal for raping nuns), because Sangallo provided galleries above the ambulatories around the conchae, but deleted the clerestory win-

H31 St Peter's: conchae and exterior

dows which Bramante had planned to locate in the arms of the cross; and an awkward and, where cost was concerned, entirely utopian combination of a centrally planned building and a building with a main longitudinal section: it was intended that an independent façade section should stand in the east, outside the centrally planned building. And Sangallo opted for a steep dome.

Michelangelo made a clean sweep from 1546 onwards. According to his own words, he intended to recreate Bramante's plan, whom he had hated before his death. For this purpose, with an unshakable consistency, he transferred, in the elevation, the two chief elements of Bramante's design to the entire interior and exterior. These elements were the weightiness of the wall and the colossal order with the entablature employed as a brace (without the small columns, that are found in Raphael and Sangallo). And in the ground plan, he firstly returned decisively to the centrally planned building, and secondly eliminated all the ambulatories, gallerics and adjoining rooms which rendered the structure unclear and had been thought up by Bramante's successors. Michelangelo's plan was even more simple than Bramante's: Michelangelo did not surround the crossing – which had already been built – with secondary centres, but only with a large square space, beyond which only the conchae in the arms of the cross projected. The adjoining rooms were deprived of their autonomy, and the way now always led back to the crossing.

On the basis of the plan approved in 1549, he firstly tore down the ambulatory which had been placed out in front of the southern concha built by Raphael/Sangallo, secondly constructed the concha, with its single shell, in 1551–58, and thirdly during the same period erected the northern concha and – after the domed pillars had been reinforced – also the drum. All these works were almost complete at the time of his death in 1564. The massive attic was not added until work was being carried out on the northern concha, and

that attic was then transferred to the southern concha. From 1585 onwards, della Porta, Michelangelo's successor, also replaced the Rosselino-Bramante choir by a concha following Michelangelo's model, and built the dome in only 22 months in 1588–90 (lantern added in 1593). In the interior, Michelangelo's hand is seen in the drum, the conchae and the lighting (but not in the dome or the arms of the cross – they are by della Porta), and also in the entire exterior (with some alterations in the outline of the dome). There were two main reasons why Michelangelo achieved success after a long standstill in his architectural work: firstly his prestige, especially as he declined any remuneration, and secondly the fact that the project and the surface area were, by his work, made smaller and that the building work thus became much cheaper and also considerably more compelling in its aesthetic formation. According to Vasari, Michelangelo made the building »greater« by reducing its size.

Michelangelo designed the new sections in a very personal style; a real stroke of genius lies in the way in which, by making a few deletions, he lent to the project, which had become complex and immobile, the dynamism typical of him. The reason why a complete change in style did not amount to an incongruity – as it does in Gothic cathedrals and in Renaissance castles in the Loire –, but also did not have to be suppressed – as it was in those churches of the Italian early Renaissance that were structured in a severely modular way –, is that this building, being the paradigm of a High-Renaissance building, did not come into being as a chain of units, but as a circular creation, just like a living organism. In this way it actually became the temple, altogether harmonious within itself, of a complete Catholic church and of the Eternal City of Rome, and not merely the temple of an individual architect. The great extent to which Michelangelo's dynamic interpretation differed from Bramante's static and mathematical understanding of the matter, and also the way in which the gravitas romana and the great architectural order produced a strong uniting effect, are excellently shown by looking from Bramante's core area through the arms of the cross and into Michelangelo's conchae. The architectural order and the wall are here energetically separated, something typical of Michelangelo's skeletal method of construction. The wall makes no more than a space-filling impression, and its decorative elements, such as the aedicules, are so large that they seem to be confiningly compressed within the architectural order. Michelangelo designed the windows to be immense and simple. His chief concern was evidently the light, which blazingly breaks in, is not filtered through an ambulatory located outside, makes the thickness of the wall tangible, and causes that wall to vibrate. This created a most energetic contrast to the long arms of the cross which stand in front and are so dark that they almost resemble tunnels. Taken all in all, the wall looks riven and immensely structured and enlivened, and is not so very flatly layered as it is in Bramante. This is Michelangelo's so-called terribilità in its pure form. The influence of this upon the Baroque style was to be considerable. Only the eastern concha was provided with a means of access to the church. In contrast to Bramante's building which had many articulations and could be entered from all sides, only one access route was designed, so that the impression of movement into the building became to that extent much more energetic.

The showpiece of Michelangelo's design is the exterior, in which it is also possible to see the extent to which dynamism on the one hand, and the ideas of a centrally planned building on the other, could be harmonized with one another. It is precisely here that the immense simplicity is found. The substructure is marked by two shapes, the cross and the square. The diagonal elements are the link between the two, but without giving up their autonomy. But the primary interpretation given to the shapes is not geometric as it is in Bramante, but organic, so that they resemble muscles. Neither are the diagonals arranged at an angle of forty-five degrees, but look as though they have positively been squeezed out by a titanic kinetic energy which consists in the urge of the two basic forms which are thrusting against one another. The building seems to be breathing in and out, a feature later often found in the Baroque (cf. e.g. B52). By adopting the system of articulation, consisting in the rhythmic bay with its colossal Corinthian pilasters and its weighty entablature, Michelangelo succeeded in combining Bramante's interior with the exterior. This combination was more intense than in any previous design, especially as the shape of the interior penetrates through into the exterior and even the diagonal sections are reminiscent of those of the crossing. The three-dimensionality of the inner space also became perceptible in the exterior and was even exceeded there. It could be experienced as an energy which urged its way outwards from inside and gave dynamic tension to the exterior shell. The design is once again not so much static; instead, the rhythmic bay emphasizes the impression of a pulsating organism to which a whole forest of pilasters lends tautness. As in the conchae, Michelangelo gave great depth to the wall here too, and the surface appears almost rugged. Michelangelo's style of planning was also organic: while the structure was being built up, even the weighty entablature seemed too weak to him. He added to it the massive attic, which not only weighs heavily on the pilasters that have no pedestals, but also accentuates the character of the substructure as a free-standing sculpture and base course for the dome. Like a pilgrimage church, the building stands unobstructed. Even Alberti, in the first great Renaissance treatise on architecture, had demanded that the main temple of a city should be a centrally planned building and should stand in an isolated location on a podium.

The substructure does indeed present itself as a base course for the dome. This is because Michelangelo succeeded in combining the articulations very closely with one another not only in the horizontal sequence, but also in the vertical. That net-like linking of all the articulations of a building which is typical of Michelangelo (cf. also H13, H30) was absent in all his predecessors, including Bramante. Their plans were horizontally subdivided, with the elements of subdivision being employed more in rows than combiningly. Michelangelo achieved the vertical link by copying in the entablature, but particularly in the attic, every projection of the order of pilasters in the substructure, by including in the twin Corinthian columns of the drum the vertical lines which were continued in this way, and by causing the energetic ascending impression to take effect right up into the ribs placed on the outside of the dome. At the high level, that is to say in the drum, these articulations are then fully three-dimensional and look more liberated. On the other hand, at every turning point, Michelangelo placed energetically moulded horizontal strips which braced the vertical lines together. In the design of the drum, he removed the regular, static-looking surrounding colonnade planned by Bramante, and replaced it with a rhythmized succession of twin columns energetically projecting out in front.

Two shapes for the outline of the dome replaced one another in the plans. They were the hemisphere and the taller shape which della Porta ultimately built. They both make a beautiful impression of perfect shape. Michelangelo had himself started out from this taller shape, in which the pent-up energy seems to flow out more strongly in the upwards direction. This Florentine patriot evidently proceeded on the basis of the similarly outlined dome of the cathedral in Florence. He had ordered measurements to be taken of that dome. It was tempting to transfer it to the greatest church in Christendom. Indeed, Michelangelo always retained the lantern and the double shell, which was technically easier to build and also permitted the interior contour to be routed differently from the exterior one. But from the very outset he intended to give the double shell a more dynamic appearance by increasing the number of ribs from eight to sixteen and placing columns on the drum. The real onwards development in Michelangelo's plans related to the outline. He increasingly went over to the use of the hemisphere, but on the other hand extended the lantern, and thus did not alter the overall height. A dome of this shape would have given the impression of restraining the upwards energy to a much greater degree and would have introduced a retarding element, before that energy had flowed out heavenwards through the longer lantern. The impression of breathing in and out, of alternating between a titanic urge and an easy relaxation, would have been once again imparted at the top. In any event, Michelangelo understood how to use vivid means of expressing a combination of ancient weightiness and medieval upwards movement, and was the first to interpret the drum and the dome as a united architectural task, something which from then on became generally customary: he shaped the drum above a circular ground plan, and no longer as an octagon and thus as a mere clerestory of the octagon in the crossing. None of this was comparable with Bramante's plan dating from 1505/06, which concealed the hemisphere on the outside.

St Peter's lives by so many great ideas. A unique feature is the linking of Bramante's early High-Renaissance aesthetic – which was more committed to making a static impression and to the centrally planned building – to Michelangelo's late High-Renaissance aesthetic: in the latter, movements, dynamism and a striving for climaxes were more important, and the basic preoccupation of the Baroque was anticipated. To sum up, it can thus be said that Michelangelo proceeded from the basic value which Bramante had succeeded in expressively portraying: the gravitas romana. He adopted Bramante's rather static and resting colossal architecture, but also made it dynamic. In particular, he caused the three-dimensionality of the interior, as being a force urging its way outwards, to appear tremendously vividly in the exterior too. The great extent to which Michelangelo was able to harmonize weightiness and unity on the one hand with dynamism and kinetic energy on the other is shown by his proposal for resolving the question of how a clear orientation for the building could be achieved while still preserving the idea of a centrally planned building. After what has been said, this was a basic problem which ran through the whole architectural history of St Peter's since the time of Bramante. Michelangelo made the subdivision of the exterior surround the building without a break, but nonetheless emphasized the eastern side, where the entrance was, by providing a Corinthian columnar portico which was also colossal. In this way the structure was given orientation, but without the continuum of the centrally planned building being abandoned. However, this method of design was not ultimately put into effect (cf. B34). SG/PZ

Bibliography: D. Gioseffi, *La cupola vaticana*, Trieste, 1960; R. di Stefano, *La cupola di S. Pietro*, Naples, 1963.

H32 Palazzo Capodiferro-Spada
Piazza di Capo di Ferro 13 (plan IV 1/B)
begun 1549 (façade), 1632–35 (vestibule)
Giulio Merigi da Caravaggio with Giulio Mazzoni,
Francesco Borromini

Girolamo Capodiferro held high offices in the Vatican. His election as cardinal in 1544 was probably the decisive factor leading to a new palace being built. But it was not until 1549 that building work began. The richly decorated façade which faces the Via Capo di Ferro, and whose appearance looks unaccustomed when compared with other 16C façades, dates from

H32 Palazzo Capodiferro-Spada

this period. Moreover, Giulio Merigi da Caravaggio, the architect, did not leave any other buildings in Rome to posterity, and may therefore be regarded as more of a marginal figure in Roman palace architecture. However, the façade is not his invention, but instead would have been inconceivable had it not been for Raphael's architectural prototype.

The division of the façade into three storeys is conventional, with a rusticated base-course area, a piano nobile with a mezzanine, and the concluding upper storey. But what is unconventional is the way in which the piano nobile presents itself. The windows are not larger than those in the base course, and are given very little accentuation; they are not placed in the setting of an energetic aedicule, and there is merely an inconspicuous cornice projecting above them like a small sun roof. The accent is between the windows, where deep niches, surmounted by triangular gables, provide space for statues of ancient emperors and heroes. Above the niches there are cartouches. The stucco work by Giulio Mazzoni, which was praised very highly not only by Vasari, plays its part in emphasizing the niche axes: seraphs and putti hold garlands and festoons in such a way that the onlooker's gaze is repeatedly directed towards the niches and coat-of-arms cartouches. The mezzanine windows become quite submerged in this round dance. This shifting of the accents means that there can be no vertical axiality. The interplay between a vertical and a horizontal axis is a thing of the past. There are no pilasters serving as architectural articulations. A restless Mannerist decoration, instead of an appearance of supporting and weighing down, takes power of the façade. Such an unusual kind of façade design had been found in Rome thirty years earlier. Raphael's design for the Palazzo Branconio dell'Aquila, which was torn down in the 17C, did not prevail in architecture, and was well received only in the Palazzo Spada. There too, the vertical axes which were to be expected are interrupted by niches and stucco decoration, but it is all more sculptural, more emphatic, and pondered out with more genius.

The large cortile is of lesser quality. For reasons of space, only three of its sides are opened up into loggias, so that it gives an impression of incompleteness. However, a passageway formerly opened up on the closed side, and it led into a smaller courtyard whose colonnades, built by Borromini and located on the opposite side, are today still meant to give the impression of an extravagantly large palace area. This is because Cardinal Bartolomeo Spada took over the palace in the 17C. He commissioned Borromini to carry out extensive conversion work. The stairwell, formerly more of a makeshift structure, was expanded to an impressive size, and a curiosity of theatrical architecture came into being (1632–35) in this smaller south-eastern palace courtyard. Borromini, a master at making use of cramped building sites, was, here too, able to demonstrate how to create something magnificent and monumental within a limited space. A feignedly long and massive passage (a vestibule) in the form of a Tuscan colonnade with barrel vaulting (like, for example, Sangallo's vestibule in the Palazzo Farnese) leads from the small cortile into another and ostensibly large courtyard in which a big sculpture catches the eye. But in reality it is all different: the colonnade measures just 8.58 m, the courtyard at the end is really a light-shaft, and the sculpture is more of a doll. By means of perfect foreshortening, Borromini succeeded in making something small into something large, an effect which is only revealed when the visitor walks through the structure. »Although the eye is the cleverest of the senses, it has a strange desire to be deceived by the art of perspective.« (Pozzo) PZ

H33 Villa d'Este, Tivoli
Tivoli (plan G1 3/B)
begun 1550
Pirro Ligorio (?)

The villa of Cardinal Ippolito II d'Este, son of Duke Alfonso I and of Lucretia Borgia, is a prime example of Roman villa architecture in the mid-16C. Ippolito II entered upon the office of governor of Tivoli in 1550, and soon began radically to alter the governor's previous residence which was attached to a Franciscan monastery. Only under his successors was the building completed in the early 17C. The name of the architect is unknown, but it is probable that Pirro Ligorio created the design, due firstly to numerous mentions relating to horticultural elements of the villa and secondly to his close connections with the owner of the building. Beside the residential structure, to the villa belongs a large park which, on the slope below the conventual buildings, extends down into the plain, where some architectural remains bear witness to an ancient villa in this location. The gardens are among the earliest of their kind and are the most significant element of the villa.

The broad residential structure dominates the overall complex and is its upper conclusion. In close imitation of the façade articulations of Roman city palaces, three very plain storeys rise above a base course between two slightly projecting corner risalti. A prominent note is formed by the richly subdivided stairs of two flights made of travertine and standing in front of the centre of the building, with its first main storey opening up into a splendid loggia. Michelangelo's staircase of the senators' palace (H27) had been built shortly before and was clearly the model here. This projecting central staircase accentuates the point at which the main axis of the whole garden complex is aimed. That complex is strictly symmetrically composed, with one main axis and various transverse axes.

For the first time, the entire terrain of the villa is here included in a large uniform plan. The access route to the villa from the plain was originally on the line of the main axis, with the result that the park extending up the slope, with the Palazzo as the upper conclusion, immediately presented itself to the approaching visitor in an easily surveyable way. The planted vegetation consisted mainly of hedges and groups of cypresses, but the greatly overgrown state of the park today hardly makes it possible to gain a panoramic view of the entire complex.

In a Mannerist exaggeration, the garden is dominated by the element which was the main attraction of Roman summer villas: the water. The sight and sound of water were longed for in the hot season and, in very imaginative variations, became the leitmotiv of the garden. This required some very great technical achievements, as the demanded masses of water had to be routed to the park from the Aniene river, which was rich in water, along aqueducts, some of them specially built. Diverse fountains with allusive mythological figures and heraldic animals form the points at which paths are aimed, and further transverse axes were created by cascades, other fountains and rows of ba-

H33 Villa d'Este, Tivoli

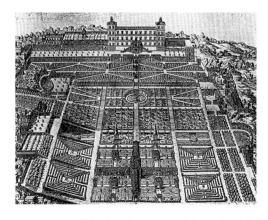

sins. Elements which play with sound effects, such as a hydraulic organ and a fountain that imitates bird-calls, play a considerable part. Surprise and imagination are chief elements of the garden design, but there was no all-embracing programme determining the layouts of the fountains.

The elaboration of the Villa d'Este goes far beyond the model of previous Renaissance villas. In the grandly conceived layout of the garden, with its continuous axes and the planted vegetation which underlines the overall composition, the work anticipates some chief elements of Baroque villas, and it is no mere chance that the arrangement with a palatial residential building and axially oriented gardens having very varied waterworks became the model for numerous Baroque villas. Compare, for example, the Villa Aldobrandini in Frascati (B33). A typical feature is the interest in the ancient Roman period, the tradition of which it was intended to some extent to continue in villa architecture. It is recorded that Ippolito d'Este commissioned Pirro Ligorio to carry out studies in the nearby Villa Hadriana (A32), from which some ancient statues were also taken over as furnishings for the villa, but the severe symmetry of the overall complex was not predetermined by the Villa Hadriana. The demands of the building's owner are here no longer expressed solely by an imposing type of architecture. Instead, the decisive factor is the opportunity, according with the purpose of a summer villa, to enjoy the garden. The owners' liberality and culture are revealed in the variety of the things portrayed, and also in the surprises found. DH

Bibliography: D. R. Coffin, *The Villa d'Este at Tivoli*, Princeton, 1960; C. Lamb, *Die Villa d'Este in Tivoli*, Munich, 1966.

H34 S. Andrea in Via Flaminia

Via Flaminia (plan I 2/C)
1550–54
Giacomo Barozzi da Vignola

Immediately after being elected Pope in 1550, and in connection with the construction of the nearby Villa Giulia (H35), Julius III awarded the commission to build the small church of S. Andrea on the Via Flaminia. In this he was fulfilling a vow, so that this church is to be regarded as a memorial or votive building. The designing architect was Vignola. The first religious building certainly by him is S. Andrea.

The brick-built exterior consists of a massive cube-shaped structure above a slightly elongated rectangular ground plan. A tall cylindrical wall, set off by a bracketed cornice, rises above this. The flat-domed vaulting of this cylinder is almost covered over by another bracketed cornice. On the outside of the part of the building facing the street there is a temple frontage flatly subdivided by pilasters. Its triangular gable, combined with the cube and cylinder, results in a composition of geometrical shapes effectively coordinated with one another. The exterior with its brickwork and

its subdivision as a temple frontage is reminiscent of examples of Roman sepulchral architecture, whereas the combination of the three chief geometrical shapes and of the flat dome above the cylinder clearly indicates that the Pantheon was being imitated (A31).

The interior is a uniform space which has a slight longitudinally rectangular elongation and whose orientation is also emphasized by a small rectangular apse which is the altar space. The four side walls conclude in segmental arches at the top, while in the corners pendentives lead up to a projecting bracketed cornice which serves as the support for a dome which is elongated into an oval as befits the spatial shape. Just as in the Pantheon, the cylinder of the exterior does not correspond to a domed drum in the interior, but already takes up most of the vaulting in the dome. The design of the wall is subdivided in an original style: this is a grid-like system of articulation which is placed in front of the walls, regulating all the walls equally, consisting of pilasters, a surrounding cornice and pilaster strips above, and – set off by its colour – standing out strongly against the wall panels located in between. Different wall layers are subtly distinguished by the graduation of these subdividing elements, and also by flat niches which are recessed into the wall panels. Although this richly differentiated wall articulation gives the building its tectonics, no satisfactory transition has been achieved between the substructure and the domed vault.

H34 S. Andrea in Via Flaminia

A centrally planned building, which is the ideal Renaissance form, particularly for commemorative buildings (cf. the Tempietto (H4)), has here been abandoned in favour of a slight elongation (the ratio of length to width in the substructure is 5:4, and in the dome 8:7). This is accompanied by a clearly emphasized orientation, expressed on the outside by the formation of the façade and on the inside by the altar niche. In the oval dome, Vignola is taking up a theme which had previously occurred in drafts but not in structures that were actually built, and which became a leitmotiv in 16C Roman church architecture: it is the oval space. In S. Andrea, an early work by him, this shape was initially restricted to the dome, but S. Anna dei Palafrenieri (B5), a late work of his, is a further development of this type, with the oval here shaping the entire interior.

The dimensions of the S. Andrea building are only small and the impression of experimentalism is still perceptible; however, not only the elaboration of the exterior with its clearly defined structures and its direct reference to ancient prototypes, but also the differentiated interior design, contain particular qualities which document firstly the very great claims of the client and secondly Vignola's joy of invention. DH

Bibliography: W. Lotz, »Die ovalen Kirchenräume des Cinquecento«, *Römisches Jahrbuch für Kunstgeschichte*, 1955, p. 1, esp. p. 35 ff.

H35 Villa Giulia
Piazzale di Villa Giulia 9 (plan I 3/C)
1550–55, 1561–65

Julius III ordered his belvedere to be built on the northern slope of the Pincio, probably as a counterpart to the Villa Madama (H16) which Clement VII had left incomplete on the other side of the Tiber. Clement was the pope who was responsible for the Sacco di Roma, during which the building's owner was taken prisoner, and while in captivity he promised to construct his second major building, namely S. Andrea in Via Flaminia (H34). The Villa Giulia is the chief work of the brief humanist phase which, under Julius III, once again interrupted the anti-humanist, inquisitorial era of the Counter-Reformation that had begun in c. 1540. The villa is based on an overall plan by Vasari, and is divided into two main complexes: the front complex, the Casino, is Vignola's first work, and the rear structure, the nymphaeum, is by Ammanati. Both had been completed when Vasari left Rome in 1553. There followed the lower connecting walls (1553/54) and the loggia which adjoins the nymphaeum and leads to a garden (1561–65).

The entrance façade of the Casino is unfriendly and severe. The eclecticism in Vignola's style is seen in it (and also in H38 and B3): the system, preferred by A. da Sangallo the Younger, of a blank wall and edges reinforced by bosses (H25) was combined with that of Bramante and his school (it included Peruzzi), who subdivided the wall by an order (H22). Here, Vignola

H35 Villa Giulia

placed the subdivided section, which consisted of two triumphal-arch motifs one above the other, into the façade in an abrupt and not very organic way.

The side towards the courtyard is linked to this entrance façade by the recurrence of the double triumphal-arch motif at the centre. Now the upper arch is a window frontage. But here the shapes are round and soft, and the articulations have been simplified into panels. Thus the central design idea is that the villa presents itself as being closed towards the outside, and only opens towards the rear and inwards. The previous villas in Rome (H8, H16) had been articulated similarly on all their sides, and had been open. But Vignola's idea had its parallels in contemporaneous church architecture (H31) and much later in Modernist villas (this is evident in Le Corbusier's Villa Stein in Garches). The design was also interpreted as meaning that now, in the Counter-Reformation, the cheerful atmosphere of the side facing the courtyard should be veiled by an entrance façade which preserved the decorum, the severe dignity. Vignola combined various sources of inspiration also for the articulation of this courtyard façade. The Villa Giulia, being a counterpart to the Villa Madama, is marked by its round overall shape. Continuously tapering off, that shape also becomes the guiding shape for the rear sections of the villa. Dead areas came into being as a result of the attempt to merge rectangular and round shapes. There is therefore only a small amount of space in the Casino, and it was probably not planned as a residence. The Vatican is really only a short distance away. The system of articulation is very complex, and reads as follows for both storeys:

    a a bbbbb a C a bbbbb a a
    A a bbbbb a A a bbbbb a A

In addition, a large architectural order was, on each storey, combined with a smaller inserted order, whereas Michelangelo had used this system to articulate the entire building as one unit (cf. H30). This complexity, chiefly intended for connoisseurs, was typical of Mannerist architecture since the time of Giulio Romano's

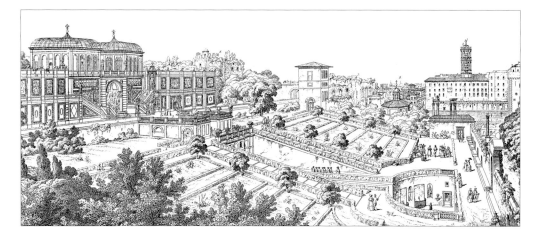

H36 Giardini Farnesini: stairway

Palazzo del Tè in Mantua (1525–35). As against this, the employment of the column which, in faithfulness to antiquity, had only a horizontal architrave was specific to 16C Roman architecture in general (H3, H24).

The visitor reaches the nymphaeum by a staircase and a landing; this intermediate section was self-contained, and was not as today opened up into a Baroque vista. The Mannerist architect wanted to surprise the onlooker, and the villa was intended only to open up as he walked through it. Constantly new impressions were offered: space surrounded by buildings; wall and nature; water and sculpture. The visitor leaves the intermediate section by going a long way down some round stairs, which are located on both sides, and into the nymphaeum. The round shape reappears several times. The waterworks do not yet possess the Baroque exuberance. Instead, the Fontana dell'Acqua Vergine looks hidden, dark and dead. The articulation is of a similar complexity to that of the Casino, but is less subtle. The leitmotiv of the double triumphal arch reappears here too, at the centre, which is a didactic piece of Mannerist architecture: the tectonics of the structure are twice vividly disturbed, firstly by causing the weakest articulating elements, the caryatids, to function as supports below, and secondly by knocking large openings into the block-like shape in the topmost storey. Behind the openings, though not visible through them, lies the garden. SG

Bibliography: M. Bafile, *Villa Giulia. L'architettura, il giardino*, Rome, 1948.

H36 Giardini Farnesini: stairway
Palatino and Via di S. Gregorio (plan V 1/B)
begun 1555
Giacomo Barozzi da Vignola

After the great families of Rome had, in the 16C, set out gardens and villas upon the wildly overgrown an-

cient Palatine, Paul III purchased the entire hill as a rich source of antiques and as a site for a pleasure garden which was to surpass all others. His grandson Alessandro completed the garden and ordered Vignola to build a staircase with which to make it accessible from the Forum. Excavations conducted from 1882 onwards ruined parts of the still-intact complex.

The portal, which measures 11 x 15 m and can today be seen at the place of access to the Palatine in the Via di S. Gregorio, consists firstly of a central section that is rusticated throughout and has a triumphal-arch motif and secondly of a window (lost today) located at each side and having a prominently projecting frame. Above this an arcade opens up, framed by an aedicule made of a segmental gable and herms. The owner could, like a Roman emperor (cf. A27), pass through the arcade and go on to a balcony high above the Forum.

A frontage with five axes, and above it an enormous arch, now in the form of a niche with a fountain, are both found again within the stairs. Vignola combined the exterior with the interior in this way in other works too, several times providing arches above one another and designing the central section as rustic work (H35, H38). But what is fundamentally new here is the large number of flights of stairs (cf. H27, a little earlier). Three parallel ramps lead upwards from the vestibule, which is the narrow, shaft-like »theatre of sculptural busts«. The central ramp proceeds to the level of the grotto and balcony, and the two outer ones – which are steeper and pass through tunnels part of the way – to the next higher level. From there, meandering flights of stairs go up to the fountain niche, around both the niche and some aviaries (added later), and up into the gardens. The Baroque staircases followed this model, except in one point: there was a harking back to the noble simplicity of the High Renaissance, and the many flights of stairs were routed in a much more teleological way. SG

H37 Casino Pio IV.

Giardini Vaticani (plan III 1/A)
1558–62
Pirro Ligorio

The popes' summerhouse (»Casino«) is in a remote location in the Vatican Gardens, which extend to the west of the belvedere courtyard. The building is a work by Pirro Ligorio of Naples. Having been commissioned by Paul IV, the strict reforming pope, he completed the Casino under Paul's successor Pius IV in a much more luxurious design than originally intended. This graceful ensemble of buildings is nimbly and skilfully grouped around the oval courtyard which is decorated with fountains. Two small, vestibule-like gates on the short sides of the oval courtyard give access to the complex which is enclosed like an island. The two main buildings – the open loggia built above a nymphaeum, and the tall Casino – occupy the long sides of the oval, but without following the course it pursues. A stone bench which runs around on all sides and is decorated with vases lends the courtyard an intimate and private character. The structures are lavishly adorned with stucco decorations, mosaics and statues, and are like sumptuous, precious miniatures. The greatest abundance unfolds on the Casino façade, where Ligorio displays a plenitude of ancient decorative shapes. They show the positively scientific interest taken by this learned antiquary, who had been in charge of the excavations at the Villa Adriana and was impressed by the stucco decorations of the early imperial period. But there is also a clear reversion to

H37 Casino Pio IV.

H38 Palazzo Farnese, Caprarola

Peruzzi, who at a very early stage, though only on paper, experimented with an ovally shaped ground plan. Taking up the villa tradition of the cinquecento, Ligorio created a sumptuous, decorative architecture which forms the peak of the tendency which was initiated by Raphael, became more intense in the 1540's (H28, H32), and lay in turning buildings into bearers of images. This architecture therefore contrasts greatly with the weightiness of Michelangelo's contemporaneous structures. EJ

H38 Palazzo Farnese, Caprarola

Caprarola, Piazza Farnese (plan G1 1/A)
1558–73
Giacomo Barozzi da Vignola

Those ideas of city design which made Rome into the mother city of the Baroque were briefly and concisely developed for the Palazzo Farnese in Caprarola. The Farnese acquired the terrain from Julius II in 1504. From 1521 onwards, A. da Sangallo the Younger and Peruzzi, having been commissioned by Pierluigi Farnese, laid the foundations for a pentagonal citadel. It probably already had the corner bastions. In 1534, after Alessandro Farnese had been elected Pope Paul III, the building work began to falter. In 1559–73, Vignola (after a competition with Paciotto) built, on the foundations of the planned citadel, a summer residence for Paul III's grandson, whose name was also Alessandro Farnese.

In any other epoch, such a flagrant alteration of the building's function would have been shied away from, but not so in Mannerism. Contemporaries called the work fascinating. In Mannerism, the forms employed in one building task could be transferred, in any way desired, to another. A citadel became a country house, and by the same stroke what had been planned as corner bastions was turned into terraces. The borderlines became blurred. The shape of the villa was also altered, and it was now block-like in the manner of a city palace (cf. H25). This form of a rural castle which had been heightened in significance was to have abundant successors in the Baroque.

The five sides of the block are articulated almost identically, and all that the main side facing the town possesses in addition is a (formerly open) loggia in the piano nobile and a rusticated entrance gate. Vignola reproduced the latter in his treatise on architecture. Each façade is, in its horizontal and vertical extensions, divided into three. In the exterior, the terraces and above them the risalti project, and the central façade section comprises seven axes and has an order of pilasters in the two upper storeys. The articulation of each façade is a didactic piece of eclecticism in Vignola's style: the blank wall, subdivided only by windows and bossed edges, was preferred by Sangallo (cf. e. g. H25). The central façade sections, on the other hand, are subdivided by an order, thus following the model of Bramante (cf. H22). Here, the pilasters were now almost reduced to pilaster strips, as was the case with Bramante's pupils Raphael and Giulio Romano (H14, H19), and also in Vignola's Villa Giulia (H35). Vignola combined the windows in the topmost section into a tripartite vertical group, a ribbon formation. The arcades look exceptionally long. All this lends the wall a carpet-like Mannerist character, and there is little that is solid about it. Two further Mannerist and anti-classical features are that, in the piano nobile of the lateral façades, Vignola employed rustic work, which had previously been the essential feature of the solid foundation, and that – amidst nature! – he selected unnatural colouring.

The building seems to hover above its surroundings in a tall, unapproachable and unreal way. This impression is reached by introducing several levels, whose system in Mannerism, contrary to what later occurred in the Baroque, was complicated, additive and not discernible from below (cf. also H36). For instance, the onlooker was surprised by the glacis which opens up above the round stairs. The latter, when compared with Baroque designs such as Bernini's colonnades (B80), still look Manneristically narrow and do not reach out in a liberal way. The three-arched frontage amidst this staircase makes the main portal look as though it was small and far removed, and thus contributes to the impressions already described. Contrary to the earlier Villa d'Este (H33), the castle dominates more than just a garden (instead, the garden is behind it and is a masterwork of late-Mannerist garden architecture, being a mixture of sculpture and nature, fragmented by deep cuts). The block now dominates an entire town. The expansive force which was to characterize Baroque castles is here found for the first time. But everything is narrower and more constricted, especially the long axis which leads through the town to the castle and was soon to find its first successor in Rome (cf. H43). Once again, a magnificent building of the Roman cinquecento owes much to the ancient Roman staircase shrine of Palestrina (A8, cf. earlier in H6).

The inner courtyard is round. Sangallo and Peruzzi loved this shape (H23, H29; H24). Vignola here se-

H39 S. Caterina dei Funari

lected a subdividing system which was different again. The combination of a rusticated ground floor and a piano nobile with a subdividing order had been known since the time of Raphael's house (cf. ill. p. 117), and Vignola found a series of triumphal-arch motifs in a row (in the upper storey) in Bramante's belvedere courtyard (H6).

The spiral staircase also resembles that found in the belvedere courtyard, but is again elongated in a Mannerist fashion and is strangely dismembered by subdividing work. It leads up to the rooms which are full of nooks and crannies. The ingenious cycle of frescos (by Zuccaro and Vignola himself) in the rooms made the building into an overall Mannerist work of art. SG

Bibliography: G. Labrot, *Le Palais Farnèse de Caprarola – essay de lecture*, Paris, 1970.

H39 S. Caterina dei Funari
Via dei Funari (plan IV 2/B)
1560–64
Guidetto Guidetti

S. Caterina dei Funari was a small preexisting medieval church built anew, and was erected in the part of the city inhabited by ropemakers (funai). The church was part of an asylum for poor girls which Ignatius de Loyola had founded in 1536 and which he managed together with Cardinal Federico Cesi. As the façade inscription states, the rebuilding work ordered by Cardinal Cesi was finished in 1564. Guidetti based his project on the spatial scheme and façade design of S. Spirito in Sassia (H26).

The two-storeyed façade is graduated like a basilica and divided by pilasters into five and three bays. The storeys are interrelated by scrolls. Slight projections in the entablature accentuate the outermost pilasters and the three central façade bays. Niches and framed panels fill the strips of wall between the pilasters. This subdividing method creates a decorative and surface-filling design for the façade. The niches, pilasters and framed panels are interrelated in a way that lacks tension but is well balanced. A comparison with the façade of Il Gesù (B1), built about ten years later, whose forerunner S. Caterina is thought to be, makes clear that neither the intensification of the articulating elements towards the centre, nor the relationship, rich in tension, between undecorated and decorated wall panels, is the dominating feature in S. Caterina, but that a static and two-dimensional interpretation of the façade still prevails.

The interior (accessible on the feast of St Catherine, 24/25 November) is a hall with three hemispherical chapel niches on each side, and an elevated choir, narrower than the nave. In this, Guidetti was again following the model of S. Spirito in Sassia (H26). AS

H40 S. Maria Maggiore: Cappella Sforza
Piazza S. Maria Maggiore (plan VI 1/B)
c. 1560–73
Michelangelo Buonarroti

The Sforza chapel is among Michelangelo's greatest inventions. It anticipates some essential ideas of Baroque architecture. Michelangelo drew up the plans for the tomb chapel of Cardinal Guido Ascanio Sforza in c. 1560, shortly after the designs for the centrally planned church of S. Giovanni dei Fiorentini (B16). Although the building work was only carried out after Michelangelo's death in 1564, by Tiberio Calcagni and later Giacomo della Porta, the novel shape of the ground plan, the concept of the front elevation, and the choice of travertine, an unusual material for an interior, must be regarded as achievements and decisions by Michelangelo, who was then nearly 90 years old. His successors seem to be responsible for the rather sober and conventional language of shapes found in the architectural elements as built, and also in the altars.

Michelangelo designed a centrally planned space above a cruciform ground plan. The longitudinal and transverse axes of the chapel are of equal length as in a Greek cross, but the transept has been moved towards the chapel entrance. In this way the shallow entrance area is opposed by a deeper altar space. The »crossing« of the chapel is moved away from the centre towards the entrance. The concentration on the geometrical centre of the centrally planned building is thus abandoned, and the longitudinal axis gains in significance. Nevertheless, Michelangelo's chapel does not look like a longitudinal structure. Rather, the lighting and wall articulation accentuate the transverse axis. As old engravings show, the original structure

had three windows in each of the apsidial ends of the cross arms: two at the sides of the tombs and a third in the vault. The altar space, on the other hand, was intended to receive light only from a window above the altar. Thus the greatest brightness prevailed in the lateral apses, whereas the altar remained in semidarkness. This impression has been lost, because in the 18C additional windows were opened up in the altar area and the transept windows were blocked up. Nevertheless, even today, the formal design of the transept apses makes them the most important – and in terms of an understanding of the architectural idea the most informative – parts of the chapel. The apses adjoin the square-shaped core area not as pure semicircles, but as segments of a larger cylinder. They cut in behind the columns and pillars of the square core area, and give the impression of continuing behind them. Similarly, the apex of the vaults of the apses is at a higher level than the apex of the other parts of the chapel, and so the space seems to continue. Seen together with the «crossing«, the transept apses give the impression of being too large and of having been attached from outside. This unusual method adopted also attracts attention to the »crossing« and its structure: it is marked by a pendent dome supported by four columns. This architectural form which looks like a stone baldachin, and is therefore called the baldachin motif, is clearly differentiated from the rest of the area by recesses and graduations. This is underlined by the pedestals of the columns, which are set diagonally to the crossing.The impression created is that the baldachin could exist entirely independently.

H40 S. Maria Maggiore: Cappella Sforza

It contrasts with the rest of the architecture, being an architectonic entity of its own. The baldachin is a dignifying motif which emphasizes the centre of the chapel. In this way, a counterpoise, which ties the chapel together and makes it into a centrally planned structure, stands in opposition firstly to the longitudinal axis preferred in the ground plan and secondly to the transverse axis accentuated by the lighting.

In this building, Michelangelo articulates several ideas significant to Baroque architecture. The fact that purely geometrical figures of the ground plan, namely the circle and the Greek cross, with their balanced proportions, are abandoned in favour of a tension-laden opposition between the axes points beyond the Renaissance conception of space. In the Sforza chapel there also arises the idea, so important to Baroque architects, of combining the centrally and the longitudinally planned building. Another novel feature in the Sforza chapel is the way in which the baldachin is articulated as an independent space within the overall space of the chapel. It was only in the late Baroque that architects again created such independent spatial elements within a larger structure. AS

Bibliography: J. S. Ackerman, *The Architecture of Michelangelo*, Harmondsworth, 1961, new edition 1986.

H41 Palazzina Pio IV.
Via Flaminia (plan I 2/C)
1552, 1561
Bartolomeo Ammanati, Pirro Ligorio

This small palace, in which Pius IV sought refuge during the summer heat, stands outside the Porta del Popolo, where the gardens of the Villa Giulia (H35) formerly extended down to the Tiber. In 1552, Julius III commissioned Ammanati to build a public fountain at the crossroads between the busy Via Flaminia and today's Via di Villa Giulia. The fountain was fed by the restored Acqua Vergine, which also supplied the nymphaeum of the nearby Villa Giulia and flowed into the Fontana di Trevi. When the villa and gardens passed into the possession of Pius IV, he caused the fountain, along with the nymphaeum behind it, to be developed

H41 Palazzina Pio IV.

H42 S. Maria degli Angeli

into a summerhouse for himself. Ligorio skilfully incorporated the existing façade into the new building. On top of the concavely shaped, tripartite show frontage by Ammanati, which is reminiscent of Sangallo's façade for the Banco di S. Spirito (H23) and later became one of the great Baroque themes (B103), he placed a storey adorned with guardian angels and coats of arms. In doing so he adopted the concave course pursued by the façade, whose projecting central motif is a straight aedicule. Architectural theoreticians criticized, at an early stage, the uncanonical arrangement of the Ionic order above the existing Corinthian one. On the ground floor, the façades adjoining the angled frontage present themselves as naked, undecorated walls which surround, in the manner of a hortus conclusus, the garden that is located to the rear and has a nymphaeum and a lobby. The walls protect the garden from the traffic in the busy street. Only on the upper storey does an elegant loggia open up, offering a distant view across the Tiber landscape where there were once no buildings. EJ

H42 S. Maria degli Angeli
Piazza della Repubblica (plan VI 1/A)
begun 1561, 1749
Michelangelo Buonarroti, Luigi Vanvitelli

Work on building the church of S. Maria degli Angeli was, by order of Pius IV, begun in 1561 for the religious order of the Carthusians. This was done in connection with planning the Via Pia (today's Via XX Settembre). The church was, to a design by Michelangelo, to be set up in the ancient ruins of Diocletian's thermal baths (A46). A requirement here was that as much as possible of the surviving ancient building work should be preserved. After some conversion work under Gregory XIII (1572–85), the building was considerably reworked in the 18C and given a new interior design which was by Luigi Vanvitelli (1749) and today determines the spatial appearance.

The large central bathing room (the frigidarium, cf. A43, A46) had been used as a church earlier than this, but with the orientation lying in the transversely located direction running from north-west to south-east. To counter this, Michelangelo turned the main orientation through 90 degrees, thus selecting, as the church's main axis, the symmetrical axis of the ancient thermal baths. The several sections follow one another from the south-west towards the north-east: the main entrance in one of the niches of the ancient caldarium, a domed round room (the tepidarium), the former frigidarium which is transversely located and is now the main hall, and finally a deep choir with an apse today polygonal but formerly semicircular, and extends into the area of the ancient natatio. The associated cloister of the Carthusians was accessible from here.

The main hall can be regarded as an outstandingly well-preserved and almost unique example of the monumentality firstly of ancient architecture and secondly of thermal baths, as the ancient Roman architecture of the space was largely retained. Even the vaults of the frigidarium were preserved in an unruined state. Ancient porphyry columns placed in front of the wall subdivide the broad room into three approximately square-shaped bays, each of them covered with groined vaults in whose lunettes large windows open up. The dark stucco and marble decorations in the lower part of the area date largely from Vanvitelli's redesigning, whereas the nakedness of the vaults give an impression of the rather more sober design work of Michelangelo, who was trying to make the ancient architecture visible by if possible not covering it. The monumental vaulting of the main hall therefore graphically displays the technical peculiarities of ancient Roman vault architecture: firstly, the feet of the groined vaults rest on the free-standing columns placed out in front of the wall, and not on the wall proper; secondly, the shape of each of the groined vaults corresponds to two regular intersecting tunnel vaults (cf. Trajan's markets, A29, and the basilica of Maxentius, A50).

The main area was originally larger on its front sides, because there were two square-shaped adjoining rooms with additional side entrances. The result, in terms of the shape of the church, was an overall complex whose axes were almost equal in length, with the main hall characteristically accentuating the transverse axis in the sequence of rooms. This interplay between the orientations, and the emphasis upon the transverse axis, are features which belonged to Mannerism and pointed the way for ideas in Baroque architecture (cf. also B28, B91).

Despite later alterations (chapels were separated off, the side entrances were closed, and there were decorative elaborations), the structure of S. Maria degli Angeli today still offers a unique opportunity of obtaining an idea of the spatial power of ancient buildings, especially thermal bathing rooms. DH

Bibliography: H. Siebenhüner, »S. Maria degli Angeli in Rom«, *Münchner Jahrbuch der Bildenden Kunst*, 1955, p. 179.

H43 Porta Pia

Piazzale di Porta Pia (plan II 2/D)
1561–64
Michelangelo Buonarroti

The Porta Pia is one of Michelangelo's last architectural works, and is a significant example of Mannerist architecture in Rome. Commissioned by Pius IV, it was built in 1561–64 to designs by Michelangelo, after whose death it was completed by his pupil Giacomo del Duca. The structure is closely connected with extensive urbanist projects by Pius IV, particularly the Via Pia which crosses the Quirinal and was named after him (today it is the Via XX Settembre). The Porta Pia is the end point of the Via Pia and is integrated into the Aurelian city wall (A44). It replaced the previous Porta Nomentana – the latter stood a little to the south -, thus making it possible to continue the Via Pia straight into the Via Nomentana which leads to S. Agnese. The Porta became particularly popular because it was here that the royal troops broke through in 1870.

The gate structure is a square-shaped building around an inner courtyard. Although it was conceived

H43 Porta Pia

as a city gate, the imposing façade was not, as in other cases, built on the far side from the city, but instead on the rear side. It is thus clearly oriented on the Quirinal street. The side of it facing away, on the other hand, was left without a proper design until the 19C, and only in 1861-68 did Virginio Vespignani give it its façade which is reminiscent of ancient triumphal-arch architecture. Vespignani also recreated the upper conclusion of the side facing the city.

The main façade consists of a broad show wall which is built of red brickwork and whose centre has a tall extension towering above it. The central section is taken up by the richly designed gateway built of white travertine, and is therefore clearly set off, both in materials and in richness of adornment, from the plainer lateral bays. The latter are framed at the sides by corner pilasters, also of brick, are surmounted by merlons, and are each articulated only by three items above one another: a window, a rectangular frame reminiscent of mezzanine windows, and a blind tondo in the upper storey which is set off by a travertine ribbon shape. With this arrangement which, unlike the design of approximately contemporaneous gate structures, does not imitate the shapes of ancient triumphal arches (cf. H29, B8), the Porta Pia is more reminiscent of palace façades than of gate buildings.

A still more eccentric feature, indicative of Michelangelo's Mannerist style, is the elaboration which employs a large number of original and in some cases functionless individual shapes that always aim to contrast with, and to alienate, the accustomed architectural methods. One example of this is the design of the portal which is built up of several layers, the front one of which, what with its fluted pilasters, its entablature, and its broken, segmentally arched gable, stands out against the bossed, flat rear layers which conclude in a triangular gable. A new feature here is the interlacing of triangular with segmentally arched gable. These gables, combined with additional decorations employing scrolls and garlands, result in an overflowing richness of detail. The large guttae are unusual items borrowed from the Doric entablature and, being attached to the entablature as if underneath triglyphs, are intended to make the onlooker forget the absence of pilaster capitals.

One leitmotiv in the design of the Porta Pia lies in the contrasting and interlacing of individual elements resulting in tension and a close interlinking of the wall panels. This applies to such individual forms as firstly the triangular and segmentally arched gable and secondly the arrangement of individual fluted pilasters below and double, unfluted pilasters above; but it applies still more to the design as a whole, as the central section stands out clearly against the lateral wings, the reasons being the building materials (travertine and brick), but also the abundance of ornamental forms and the tall, vertical upwards towering of the centre. The brick masonry, and the merlon-like superstructure on the flanks, possibly allude to the Aure-

H44 SS. Trinità dei Monti

lian city wall. The way in which the central section is so strongly contrasted may therefore all the more clearly show the manner in which this gate penetrates the wall. Like the newly built street, this vertical central part of the gate passes through the transversely located bar shape built of brickwork masonry.

The Porta Pia is a very original monument, and as it is a gate structure it offered the opportunity – more perhaps than would be the case in other architectural tasks – of producing a free abundance of ideas and creating an alienating design. Being a late work by Michelangelo, it clearly displays his later design method, and is thus an important example of Mannerist architecture in Rome. DH

Bibliography: K. Schwager, »Die Porta Pia in Rom«, *Münchner Jahrbuch der Bildenden Kunst*, 1973, p. 38.

H44 SS. Trinità dei Monti
Piazza Trinità dei Monti (plan II 1/E)
begun 1502, c. 1570 to 1587
Giacomo della Porta (?)
Along with the small church of S. Atanasio dei Greci, SS. Trinità dei Monti is one of the few examples of a double-tower façade in Rome. The church and monastery of the Minim friars were founded and supported by the French crown. Charles VIII made available the

funds which enabled the complex to be built from 1502 onwards on the rising ground called the Pincio. The main longitudinal section of the church seems to have been completed in 1519, the year in which Francis of Paula, the founder of the Minim order, was canonized. The monastery buildings were finished in 1550. According to the façade inscription, the two-towered façade must have been largely built by 1570. The main portal, the bell towers and the two flights of stairs were completed by 1587. It has not yet been ascertained who was the architect of the church, and in particular of its double-towered façade. Only Domenico Fontana is mentioned in connection with the stairs, and the sources show no trace of della Porta, to whom the façade has been attributed.

SS. Trinità was planned as a late-Gothic building in the French manner. Glass windows in the apse (not preserved), the still-surviving ribbed vault in the crossing, the peaked arch at the end of the main longitudinal section of the church, and the double-tower façade which may have been planned from the outset, all suggest prototypes from north of the Alps. Today's interior is an early example of a barrel-vaulted hall church with apses (cf. also H26).

The towers are the dominant elements of the façade. The outer bays of the façade project somewhat, forming solid tower substructures framed by pilasters. The central bay, on the other hand, is opened up firstly by a portal – which is framed by an aedicule – and secondly by a thermal window, and thus, being non-supporting intermediate space, contrasts with the substructures of the towers. AS

H45 S. Maria di Loreto

H45 S. Maria di Loreto
Largo del Foro Traiano / Piazza Madonna di Loreto
(plan V 1/B)
1522–52, 1573–83
Antonio da Sangallo the Younger, Giacomo del Duca

This building was erected in two stages. A. da Sangallo the Younger designed the box-like, austere substructure which has an immensely plain architectural order. Some fifty years later, del Duca placed on top of it the octagonal drum and the dome, breaking open the central gable in the process. In this way the only work, apart from St Peter's, came into being in which the severity of Bramante's world and the imaginativeness of Michelangelo's are both present.

A. da Sangallo the Younger was Bramante's draughtsman. Bramante's spirit is seen in the severity of the exterior, to which double pilasters lend solidity, subdividing it according to the principle of the rhythmic bay (cf. H6, H7). That spirit is also found in the interior, where the square shape was bevelled into an octagon, and slender apses were hollowed into the angled sections thus created, with the thickness of the wall becoming visible as a result (cf. H5, H7). The centrally planned building was the ruling discipline of the High Renaissance. Nevertheless, apart from S. Maria di Loreto, only a few such buildings, usually smaller in size, were actually erected in Rome (H4, H7, H10, H12, H20, H40).

Del Duca pursued the rhythmized arrangement of the substructure onwards into the drum which has windows of alternating size, and also into the ribs of the dome. Michelangelo, del Duca's teacher, had already used uniting vertical lines with the same individual shapes (projections, ribs, columns standing out in front) in the exterior of St Peter's (H31). The basic style also looks Michelangelo-like: the drum and dome appear enormous, heavy and onerous by comparison with the substructure. There are also details typical of Michelangelo's style: these are the door frames added by del Duca, and the oculi above (cf. H43). It was unusual and Mannerist to have large windows piercing the dome. Del Duca's design hardly had any successors. Instead, Vignola's more moderate style dominated Mannerist architecture in Rome after Michelangelo's death. SG

2 days: From early to High Renaissance: F4, F5, F6, H22, H1 and F19, (H2), H3, (H12), H14, H23, H24, (H32); -- Michelangelo: H25, (H32), H27, H30, H45, (H40), H42 and A46, H43.
1 day: H4, H7, H31, (H6), H22, H25, (H24 or H32), H27, H30, H43.

Baroque and Rococo

Il Gesù and its period (B1–B25)

The 1560s were a watershed in Roman architecture. Michelangelo died in 1564, at the age of ninety-two, the last great artist of the Roman High Renaissance and its individualistic view of life. Work started on Il Gesù (B1) in 1568, showing an approach to church building that deviated radically from centrally planned architecture, the preferred type for the High Renaissance, laying the foundations for Baroque architecture in terms of type and artistic treatment. The Catholic church took on a new form in 1563 at the conclusion of the Council of Trent, and thus became the most important, indeed the only, source of architectural commissions in Rome. At this point the Catholic church moved from the defensive into the offensive in its confrontation with the Protestant church. Serlio's treatise on architecture (1566) ended a good century of Renaissance treatises (starting with Alberti), all of which showed a remarkable level of theoretical, if not philosophical, abstraction. Nothing comparable was to follow throughout the Baroque period, and the most important by (Borromini) was not published until 1725, and then posthumously. Baroque architecture was more sensual in its direction, less intellectual and theoretical. However, there was one great architect, Vignola, who spanned the 60s watershed. He was the creator of S. Andrea in Via Flaminia (H33) and S. Anna dei Palafrenieri (B5), the first oval rotundas, and he was also responsible for the interior of Il Gesù.

A completely new type was developed in the interior of this church; it may have had some precursors, but it was considerably more powerful (see B1 for detail). Overall form was at least as important for Baroque architecture as establishing a type. Compared with its most important predecessor, Alberti's S. Andrea in Mantua, the side chapels in Il Gesù were much lower and the transepts much less deep, and also the spaces between the side chapels were reduced to double supports. Il Gesù is dominated by the barrel-vaulted uniform space, the pull to the light-filled dome, while more stress was placed on the autonomy of the parts in the Renaissance building. As the wall there was designed as a series of triumphal arch motifs it is also markedly ancient in character. In Il Gesù the rhythm too is faster and more dynamic in its effect because the pilasters are placed so close together. Compactness, the dominance of the overall form rather than individual parts, dynamic features and rhythms in the movement – all these are favourite Baroque design devices. Finally Il Gesù succeeded in something that High-Renaissance buildings had failed to do: in this case the Roman style became generally accepted not only in Italy but in France and Germany as well, and swept away the last Gothic net vaulting there.

After Il Gesù the basilican structure with high nave and lower aisles was almost completely abandoned in favour of a single space with low chapels set at right angles. Exceptions occur when older foundations had to be used (cf. B16) or in the case of the Oratory Chiesa Nuova (B17) the commissioning order was fond of the image of the early-Christian basilica with a rapid series of arcades set close together. The Il Gesù type was then taken up for the great churches of the orders, and though it was never equalled in quality all the buildings that followed it were bigger, and increasingly so: first by the Oratorians in the original church of S. Maria in Vallicella (B17), then by the Theatiners in S. Andrea della Valle (B26) at last by the Jesuits themselves in S. Ignazio (B46). This rigid fixing of type, which completely contradicted the whole (High) Renaissance striving for individual design (then to be rejected again in the High-Baroque period), should be seen as a parallel with the domination of the whole over the individual parts in the overall form.

Indeed a comparable fixing of type can also be seen in palace building. After all, the most important papal palaces, the Quirinal (B15), the Lateran (B21) and the Vatican (B19) were all built or completed in these decades. Also in this respect the institution was obviously dominant and not, as later happened again, the family of the pope who was in office, all of which were to build palaces of their own in the 17th century. In all the palaces only one of the two dominant High-Renaissance façade schemes was adopted, the less articulated one, which appears in its classic form in the Palazzo Farnese (H25), though there it was incomparably more majestic in its proportions (cf. only B2, B14, B15, B19, B21, B22, B23, B24). Here palace building seems much less original than church building, where use was not being made of an earlier building type and in which there was more scope for variation. This imbalance between originality of palace and church building was to persist into the 18th century, while in the (High) Renaissance almost as many palaces had been built as churches, and they included buildings of great individuality and even type-establishing force, above all the (type of the) Palazzo Vidoni-Cafarelli (H22), the Palazzo Massimo (H24) and the Palazzo Farnese (H25). Even the scheme for the main façade of the Palazzo Borghese (B3), the most important palace of the late 16th century, does not follow the standard type but had already been developed in one of the great earlier palaces, the Farnese palace in Caprarola (H38). One original trait that was to be found in palace architecture was that windows were sometimes brought together in groups, i. e. placed rhythmically (B14, B23), which was not to develop into an overall system of articulation until the 18th century. Only one type was also fixed for the building of villas and casinos: all of them were built as façade museums, in which the wall seems to be covered with a carpet of reliefs and busts, in other words was treated as a support for images, for example in the Medici (B4) and Borghese (B35) villas, the germs of which can already be seen in the Casino Pio (H37). The bodies of the buildings themselves also seem to run wild, and are no longer as lucidly formed as those of the villas or even the palace cubes of the High Renaissance. In both series of types. i. e. both in palace and villa building, one aspect that the High Renaissance had especially emphasized as appropriate for the building task was isolated and exaggerated: in palaces the defensive-looking cube, and in villas and casinos an imaginative and fanciful quality. These values were there in embryo in the High Renaissance, but others had always been possible, e. g. lavish magnificence in palace building (cf. the type that goes back to Raphael's house, H22), or splendour in the building of villas (in the Villa Madama, for instance, H16).

This technique of isolating and exaggerating one central, striking quality of High-Renaissance art was considered typical of Mannerism. But in Roman architecture Mannerism is less important as an intermediate period between High Renaissance and Baroque than the clash of very different ways of thinking in the 1560s. For buildings in which, as in many works of northern Italian Mannerism, the Palazzo del Tè in Mantua, for example, a bizarre pleasure taken in lavish inventiveness was on the foreground, were a rare exception in Rome. With the exception of Michelangelo's Porta Pia (H43) and some subsequent works by his pupil del Duca (H45, B8) only one artist's house, the Palazzo Zuccari (B25) can be mentioned. It is true that Mannerism can be found in the second decade of the 16th century, in the Alberini and Maccarani palaces (H14, H19), and then on into the 17th century, for example in the Villa Borghese (B35), but Mannerism always remained a subordinate trend. Before the 1560s the spirit of the High Renaissance was dominant, with very individual and ambitious solutions developed from the particular commission, for example in the long perpetuating school of Bramante, but above all in the great personality of Michelangelo. After the 1560s this changed radically, and the design modes that have already been mentioned were to remain dominant throughout the 17th century. Thus in Rome High Renaissance and Baroque are more impactful in their meeting with each other than Mannerism. The constant characteristic of the façades, especially the church façades of the last decades of the 16th century is not so much Mannerist complexity as their board-like flatness (B6, B10, B11, B17, B29). Churches and palaces seem uncommonly stiff, especially in their exteriors. A tendency to try stepping the façade towards the middle started only hesitantly, at first only in isolated details such as the strongly three-dimensional frame for the portal (B6, B 29, also B1), but later was part of a general tendency towards early- and High-Baroque design. (Maderno then made the decisive step with S. Susanna, B30). Even so, typical Mannerist complexity is not entirely missing from Roman architecture. This can be seen above all in the work of Vignola, for example in the Villa Giulia (H35), but more generally in two elements: architects were very fond of multiple layering (first developed by Michelangelo, H30), and thus vertical strips frequent-ly appeared within a church façade, especially in the centre (cf. A4, B1, B11). Secondly, the coherence of the articulating elements was blurred because they were linked in a chain and not arranged in a loose row. The design of the façade of Il Gesù (B1) was typical, where each time the outermost bay, which is to be thought of as being framed on both sides by a coupled pair of supports, thrust under the adjoining bay, which was placed further inside, so that parts of the support system disappeared (similarly difficult to read: B6). In contrast with this, how simply Maderno placed the articulating elements in S. Susanna (B30)!

The period of Il Gesù is associated above all with the Counter-Reformation. The Council of Trent was more concerned with painting than architecture, and the postulate that art should make Christian values and history available to everyone was certainly implemented much more effectively in the High Baroque period than at the time of Il Gesù. And yet the values of the Counter-Reformation can definitely be identified in late-16th-century architecture, above all in the almost monastic, »reformist« bleakness of the interiors, which was later sacrificed in many cases, especially in Il Gesù (B1) and S. Maria in Valicella (B17) to High-Baroque painting and furnishings. This tendency was not abandoned until the Sistine Chapel, and here we find a horror vacui of the kind that had previously been typical of villa façades in church interiors as well (B20). But above all the move away from the centrally-planned design, the return to dominance by the Latin cross, was justified liturgically, and by Carlo Borromeo even iconographically (cf. B1). Vignola and Maderno also largely turned against central planning in their (relatively simple) treatises. In fact the foundations of the Baroque were laid in the second half of the 16th century with the emergence of new orders and (in the early 17th century) with the canonization of their founders (and mystics). Thus the Barnabite, the Theatine – and most importantly for Rome – the Oratorian and Jesuit orders were founded in the course of the Counter-Reformation. The latter in particular turned against medieval determinism and considered it essential that everyone should contribute to the story of his or her own salvation.

Just as the time of Il Gesù is a time of laying of foundations, it is also a time when types were established. The Il Gesù type has already been addressed. Almost as important in church architecture is the development of the oval space. The High Renaissance had preferred the static circular rotunda, but this was now replaced by a form of rotunda with a greater dynamic potential (H34, B5, B28). In the field of palace building the introduction of rhythmically placed windows was something of a peripheral development;

it was probably more important for the future that Vignola started to use multiple flights of steps even in the late 50s (H36). In fact all three typological developments can be traced back to Vignola. Especially if one also considers his other main works, the Villa Giulia (H35) and the Palazzo Farnese in Caprarola (H38), it is clear that he is generally the central artistic personality of the Il Gesù period.

Sixtus V and Paul V are the outstanding popes at the end of the era. Roughly as many churches were built in their pontificates as there had been in the previous 150 years. Admittedly it is not easy to call many of them to mind. Three, which herald the early-Baroque period, are an exception to this. Architecture under Sixtus V seems somewhat abstruse: the magnificent vista of the Belvedere courtyard was destroyed by building a transept arm (H6); the Colosseum (A25) was to be converted into a wool factory, and the funerary chapels of two popes in S. Maria Maggiore are lacking in a big idea (B20). Only in terms of organization (the completion of Michelangelo's St. Peter's, H31) and in urban development did the period have significant achievements to show. In particular, the way in which Rome was opened up by the building of long axial streets was a major feat under Sixtus V (for detail cf. p. 14–16), and also the first tapping of rich water resources since ancient times, which led to the construction of large fountain systems under both popes (B18, B41), into which water did not just run (as in the Fontana delle Tartarughe, for instance), but poured out in a Baroque surge. Admittedly these streets seem narrow and cramped; it was not until the High-Baroque period that broad and pleasant places in which to linger would appear. In urban development matters too there was a tendency to over-emphasize the whole as against the detail.

The image of the time of Il Gesù is an austere one, with little time for the individual. The two principal achievements were the fixing of types and the creation of (urban) order. This may be seen as an echo of the austere basic attitudes of the Counter-Reformation in the artistic field. A stiff approach to design took the lead over more imaginative varieties. Later there was always an appropriate tension between Baroque Classicism and rich and complex Baroque, in the high phase even with the latter dominating.

Early Baroque from the early 17th century (B26 to B41)

When making a distinction between Early, High and late Baroque this applies mainly to architecture (and not so much to painting and sculpture), and then above all to Roman architecture. The great patrons of early Baroque were the Borgheses and Scipiones, and also Paul V, who was able to immortalize himself on the façade of St Peter's as the man who completed that church. The main works commissioned by the Borgheses show that pioneering works in the early years of the century were built at the same time as others in which a horror vacui or other Mannerist design peculiarities persisted (for example in the Villa Borghese, B35). Three or four works define the step to Roman early Baroque: S. Susanna for façade design (B30), and also St Peter's (B34), S. Salvatore in Lauro (B27) and parts of S. Andrea delle Valle (B26) for interior design, and the Palazzo Barberini (B45) for palace architecture.

Maderno was the most important of the creators of these works. He too was definitely influenced by late-16th-century architecture. thus for instance the preference of his period for the oval rotunda led him to design the few sections of the nave of St Peter's in which he was not bound by Michelangelo's design as a series of oval spaces. He also took up the façade museum type in the Palazzo Mattei (B31). As well as this, the cross-section façade of Il Gesù was the typological model for his main work, the façade of S. Susanna. Nevertheless, at the time of Maderno – in the work of other masters – a first alternative type to that of Il Gesù appeared in Rome, that of the panel façade with both storeys of equal width (B11, B47–B49, also B43). The actual innovative feature of the art of Maderno and his period was not in the development of new types, but in changes in the way in which they were designed in detail – above all in two respects: in their three-dimensional quality and simplicity, and in the use of proportion.

If the façade of S. Susanna is compared with those of earlier years it seems incomparably more sculptural, more compellingly articulated and more compact; the use of two steps is handled much more energetically and at the same time more simply than before (cf. for detail B30). The sculptural filling between the elements became much fuller, the chiaroscuro seems more accentuated. This façade has depth, the stiff, austere, flat style of previous decades seems to have been forgotten.

Something similar can be said about the courtyard of the Palazzo Mattei di Giove (B31). On the façade of S. Susanna the support system (pilasters and columns), which previously appeared in a complicated set of links, also became very simple: each bay acquired two supports as a border, and the bays were juxtaposed loosely and completely. This achievement predestined Maderno for the post of architect of St Peter's, and by building the façade (B34) he completed something that had been started a good century before. In many respects he was tied by Michelangelo's design for the outside of the building, above all in terms of the gigantic attica and the colossal order that had replaced the two-storey design. But its stepped quality makes this façade, which was conceived without the outermost axis, seem similarly simple and energetic to that of S. Susanna. Thus in St Peter's too Maderno continued existing excellence rather than establishing a fundamentally new direction. Nevertheless is again showed that building St Peter's never thrust forward until a telling solution had been found.

Maderno also changed the proportions. Henceforth and in the (High) Baroque it was to be much steeper, even though the façade of St Peter's is actually an exception in this respect. From Maderno's time onwards an element of height was built into most works, which then frequently also became the bearer of the expressive values of the mystical and miraculous. In comparison with the façade of Il Gesù that of S. Susanna seems upright and steep (cf. B30), and the same is true of the dome of S. Andrea della Valle (B26) in comparison with that of St Peter's (H31). And however much the interior design of S. Andrea owes to Il Gesù, it was very clearly different in terms of proportions. Additionally the vertical connecting lines (from the pilasters via the shoulder pieces to the transverse arches) have become very much thicker.

Mascherino's S. Salvatore in Lauro (B27) remains something of a solitaire; it is the most important of the Roman early-Baroque interiors. He knew how to breathe new Baroque life into the old value of gravitas romana, with the sonorous tones of the double column and the heavy transverse arches, rather like Maderno's approach to the art of the façade. It is astounding that this church did not have any successors. Perhaps it was because the greatest church in Christendom was being completed at precisely this time and that its interior and exterior were articulated by pilasters almost without exception (H7, H31, B34). In any case articulation with pilasters dominated until the mid-17th century, until the façade of SS. Vincenzo e Anastasia (B64) was built.

The Palazzo Barberini, Maderno's most important secular building, is the principal work in the field of palace building. It is one of a series of palaces commissioned by the family of the ruling pope, extending through the early- and High-Baroque periods (1605 to 1676; cf. B3, B45, B62, B68, B93). The palace opens up to its surroundings like no other before it in large arcades, and thus seems accessible to the outside world. This is a clear manifestation of the newly awakened Baroque pleasure in prestigious show. At the same time it demonstrates the outstanding role played by principal works of antiquity and the High Renaissance in this new beginning. Just as Il Gesù (B1) would have been inconceivable without the Pantheon (A31), the façade of St Peter's would scarcely be conceivable without Michelangelo (H29 and H31), and the Palazzo Barberini equally little without the rows of arches placed one on top of the other in the Colosseum (A25), of the Damasus courtyard (H11) and also the »three-winged complex« of the Capitol (H27; B45 for detail). The Palazzo Barberini, for which Maderno already shared responsibility with Bernini, was already the prelude to High Baroque.

Many of the High-Baroque church designs owed a great deal to a second event, which happened at almost the same time and was not directly related to architectural history: on 22.5.1622 the most important protagonists of the Counter-Reformation, Francis Xavier, Ignatius Loyala, Teresa and Filippo Neri were canonized. The spiritual position that they represented could be expressed in the High Baroque from then onwards. They had been preceded by Carlo Borromeo in 1610, which very quickly led to the building of three churches (B39, B40, above all B52).

Bernini, Borromini, Cortona and the High-Baroque period (B42–B96)

The Pontificate of Urban VIII (1623–44)

»It is your great good fortune, Cavaliere, to have Matteo Barberini as your Pope, but we have the even greater good fortune that Cavaliere Bernini lives in our Pontificate.« Urban VIII (Barberini) who wrote these lines, awoke a new feeling for life, full earthly joy, for the first time since the Sack of Rome (1527), almost one century later. He saw himself as the successor of Julius II, wrote Latin and Italian poetry, and his court included poets and scholars, first and foremost Galileo. The Counter-Reformation was not forgotten, but was now seen and celebrated as a victorious and magnificent movement. Art was now not just to instruct, but to please as well. But perhaps Urban VIII's greatest achievement was that he discovered the architect Bernini. No one knew like him how to give expression to this new feeling in the 20s, no one made such a mark on the decade as he did – with two works, the Baldacchino (B42) and S. Bibiana (B43). Both share the qualities of the Palazzo Barberini: Bernini also devised a quite new staging device – for the St Peter's tomb the monument that combines architecture and ephemeral structure, and the detached aedicule for the statue and the recently found reliquaries of S. Bibiana. With the Baldacchino Bernini also solved a whole new problem of contextual relationships. He was able to place it in the massive structure of St Peter's as a work that was large enough also to be experienced as architecture but small enough to form a transition to human scale.

In the 30s the great congregational churches, which were always of the same type, started to give way to smaller churches that could be built more rapidly and individually and that largely showed an creative spirit of their own. The new trend extended into the Pontificate of Alexander VII. After the destruction of Bernini's chapel In Propaganda Fide, Cortona's SS. Luca e Martina (B51) and Borromini's S. Carlino (B52) represent this change of trend. But at the same time Martino Longhi brought new and tighter life into the standard type of the cross-section façade. His S. Antonio dei Portoghesi (B50) drew life from a new picturesque quality, with the upper part of the central section acquiring unambiguous overemphasis for the first time – something typical of High Baroque. A quality of height was produced, in this case by the use of prominent sculpture, while the surface of the façade remained quite flat, flatter even than Maderno had made it for S. Susanna (B30) thirty years previously.

Typical of the new line and of both works by Borromini and Cortona are above all the reappearance of centrally organized ground plans, the use of curves for façades and interiors, the striking enhancement of the idea of height (in Borromini's case by detaching the dome, in the case of Cortona by stretching the drum dome), shifting the spiritual centre from the altar to the dome, replacing pilasters with columns, sometimes even prostyle columns (at first usually in the interior), an increase in plasticity and complexity and the imposition of rhythm on the wall structure (while retaining a simple overall impression). Frequently the contextual relation was more strongly emphasized as well. An example of increased complexity is Cortona's tendency (and indeed repeatedly Bernini after him) to combine different elements like the rib (which bears) and the coffer (which makes the ceiling seem lighter) in his dome calottes (B51, B40). And Borromini's building is also the first example of the (typically High and late Baroque) concept of universal architecture, which strives for the infinite and in which the extremes seem to meet, in Borromini's case above all those of an enormous variety of styles. At the same time wonder was clearly expressed for the first time by an architectural design, here in the dome calotte, which seems to hover. Both features were to be found increasingly from this time onwards. »Full Baroque« is a very eloquent term for this general tendency. For half a century Baroque-Classical works, in which all these values are not to be found, or are rather more weakly expressed, form an exception alongside the other works.

The three main masters who were to share all the major contracts between them from this point onwards were all born at about the same time, Cortona in 1596, Bernini in 1598 and Borromini in 1599. The first two were again (as was customary in the High Renaissance) painter – or sculptor-architects. Despite their common thrust the breadth of variation between them was enormous, and the individual profile was as striking as it had last been in the first decades of the cinquecento. Cortona's SS. Luca e Martina has the first curved church façade, with the exterior again as strongly a copy of the interior as it had been in the High Renaissance. He was the first to combine rib and coffer, an example of the uncommonly full, deep wall structure of his interiors. He, a Florentine, adopted many of Michelangelo's ideas, especially from St Peter's, and made them Baroque. Overall the elements seem to be loosely placed, not tightly linked. He was a great innovator, but (at least in the 30s) in many respects as much a decorator as an architect, so that his spatial forms seem less innovative than the individual forms. Borromini loved to make forms flexible, and his relish for the bizarre was much criticized. He knew how to bring together a multiplicity of styles, alongside Gothic above all that of antiquity and the legacy of Michelangelo. The use of stucco, the rounded corners, the soft, imaginative individual forms (frames, for example), which he developed above all in Oratory complex (B53), were to make him a dominant influence in the 18th century. In Rome his influence was more on the design of wall and surface, and in Central Europe on spatial forms. He was much less influential in the 17th century. A second work built in the 30s was even more important than the Oratory complex, S. Carlino, in which all his basic ideas on shaping space and walls can be seen in embryo. Here he was already successful in building a space not just on the basis of a single geometrical shape, but by composing it in a complex fashion from a wide variety of such forms, while at the same time invoking an essentially spiritual, almost monastic impression. Complexity and spirituality (and inventive use of individual forms) were always accompanied by one other value in Borromini's work: he also gave the individual parts enough autonomy to allow them to fit together as a unit but still never to appear subordinate. This is the unique feature in Borromini, and probably contributed to his great influence in the Rococo period, which had an aversion to hierarchies. Bernini's work has a much more thrilling dynamic, genuine, high drama. Bernini was also much more concerned with subordination, with a general design idea. His architecture never seems bizarre, and conversely also not cool. Borromini had largely formulated his architectural legacy in the 30s, Bernini had not yet done that.

In the last years of the Pontificate of Urban VIII, in the 40s, Borromini was nevertheless to receive two more contracts (B56, B57). In the first (for S. Ivo) he again, as in S. Carlino, perfectly balanced main and subsidiary spaces, along with lucid geometry and a spiritual overall impression. But again the feeling of spirituality was unspecific; Borromini did not create a great, clear and simple symbol here either. But in contrast Bernini's Raimundi Chapel (B54) is a mystery of light, much more simple but also much more eloquent. The chapel attracts less attention than it might today if Bernini had not considerably enhanced the expressive devices he used here in the Cornaro Chapel (B60).

The Pontificate of Innocent X (1644–55)

Just as Urban VIII promoted Bernini, Innocent X allowed him to fall out of favour, at least for a time. It is unlikely that this was mainly for artistic reasons, but much more that he blamed their favourite for the Baroque lifestyle of the Barberinis. The paradox is that

Bernini created more important work under Innocent X than Borromini, who was now being favoured. Working for others, Bernini built the first (mystical) »universal work of art« of the Baroque, the Cornaro Chapel (B60), the first Baroque palace, articulated in various sections and towering up proudly, the Palazzo Montecitorio (B72). Then came the Fontana dei Fiumi, an important urban project (B61) and this also led to a change of mind by Innocent X. Conversely, Borromini was so little able to use the great commission of providing a Baroque design for the second most important basilica of Catholic Christendom, S. Giovanni in Laterano (B66), to develop his repertoire further that this work scarcely comes to the mind of the modern visitor of Baroque Rome. New for Borromini here and in the contemporary Palazzo di Propaganda Fide (B65) were nevertheless his increasing delight in mass and monumentality and now his almost wanton pursuit of formal invention. The stucco surface now seems more unctuous and creamy. The problem is that his inclination to the bizarre and the lack of firmness in edges and lines mean that a feeling of monumentality is produced only with difficulty. Innocent X also promoted Algardi, allotting him the corresponding role as sculptor-architect that Bernini had played for Urban VIII. The result was disappointing. The Villa Doria Pamphili is his main work (B59), and with this he never got much further than Mannerist villa architecture, and created one of the few examples of Baroque Classicism in the High Baroque.

Innocent X initiated a truly new dimension in building when he had the Piazza Navona redesigned, which contained his family palace, the Palazzo Pamphili (B62). The church in the centre of the broad side, S. Agnese (B71), was obviously perceived as a reformulation and Baroque correction of St Peter's. Impersonal in style, and built by many architects, it is nevertheless very individual as a Baroque work, and this pointed well beyond Rome: here we see the beginning of the classical two-towered façade with dome and wide concave curve, uniting all contrasts within itself, spreading out and yet towering up, concave and convex, lightly oscillating and yet tense. The Baroque delight in prestigious show now went so far that St Peter's and the Papal Residence were to be moved out of the Vatican into the reigning Pope's private palace (see F5, F6). As the most coherent square design since the Capitol, a typical Baroque square was now created here, which deviated markedly from the stylistic preferences of the High Renaissance with considerably increased dominance for the middle and less balanced proportions (the square follows the shape of the ancient stadium of Nero).

In the 40s Cortona spent most of his time in Florence(1637, 1641–47), but Bernini built the Cornaro Chapel (B60), which was the first building to show the mysticism that started in the middle of the century. Here the High Baroque was much more sensual and mystical than the founding phase of the Counter-Reformation. The same is true of the painting in the congregational churches that now followed. Other than in the Counter-Reformation and early Baroque, efforts were now made to place visitors vividly and directly within the sacred experience, to make them experience this mystically. Thomas Kempis's medieval work on the Imitation of Christ was Bernini's favourite book. For this Bernini chose the device of double vision: just as the saint saw heaven, a (sculpted) observer, the founder, should see the saint and heaven and the visitor then sees the marble observer, the saint and heaven; the intention was to introduce him stage by stage. Bernini's biographer Baldinucci rightly stressed that here the master was uniting all the arts for the first time (to make a »universal work of art«).

In palace architecture as well, for the first time since the High Renaissance, there had been innovations, which at least came close to those in ecclesiastical building: the first great Baroque gallery was created in the Palazzo Colonna (B76), and from the same architect the first large open-air flight of steps with double-curved stairs (albeit for SS. Domenico e Sisto, a church, B48). But above all with Palazzo Montecitorio the first proud Baroque palace arose (B72), which dominated the square like no other before it, degrading it to a real forecourt. But these works were not commissioned by Innocent X, his palace and the Collegio in Piazza Navona seem much more like annexes of the church. Innocent X did not reach the same status as a great Baroque prince and patron as either his predecessor or his successor.

The standard cross-section façade type also became more Baroque, as it had two decades earlier under Martin Longhi. Longhi now gave the façade of SS. Vincenzo e Anastasia (B64), with encapsulated aedicules, that moreover do not completely correspond in both storeys, a high degree of complexity and now also increased depth and plasticity: Longhi introduced the column in massed and sonorous mode and placed two shallow porticoes in front of the wall. For façade art this shift away from the pilaster was completely new, and a step in terms of quality that no architect was to get around in future.

The Pontificate of Alexander VII (1655–67)

Alexander VII was the great completer. Bernini and probably also Cortona had their most productive years under him, the first with eight architectural masterpieces, including the proudest Baroque palace, the Palazzo Chigi-Odeschalchi (B93), the most beautiful centrally-planned buildings (B82, B85, B89), St Peter's Square (B80) and the Ponte Sant'Angelo (B96), and the second also produced highly individual work, especially what is probably the most compact small design for a Baroque square in front of S. Maria della Pace (B79). There were other important projects like

Cortona's design for a Palazzo Chigi and Bernini's proposal for the Spanish Steps, unbuilt (but not without considerable repercussions) and the most important architect of the younger generation, Rainaldi, created his major works. Queen Christina of Sweden, the daughter of Gustavus Adolphus, had converted to Catholicism; her entry into Rome in 1655 was almost a symbol of the new era (cf. B77).

The further increase in dimensions appears first of all in the urban projects. The most beautiful square designs come from this period. These are the colonnaded squares for S. Maria della Pace and St Peter's, above all the latter, which practically embraces the visitor, but also the Piazza del Popolo (B87/B88). These also include the Piazza in Ariccia (B89) and the square in front of S. Maria sopra Minerva (B95). More progress was also made in the design of routes, and a new dynamic was found, a new place for ceremonies. Bernini's Scala Reggia was built (B92) and – on the procession route to St Peter's – the Ponte Sant'Angelo (B96), another example of Bernini's ability to combine various art forms, and at the same time a step towards a light-hearted and scenic approach, which was to persist in the 18th century. Routes were not just laid (as under Sixtus V eighty years previously), but also fully designed and staged. The most magnificent of these designs, the Spanish Steps (B115), was not to be realized until the 18th century, but owed a great deal to a Bernini project for these very steps that emerged under Alexander VII.

The Pope went without his own palace for the sake of all these projects; it would have meant that the Piazza Colonna was designed as a newly unified square. If Cortona's project for this had been built it would have been a very forward-looking structure. For Cortona abandoned the palace cube in favour of the multiply staggered High-Baroque approach, and this influenced Bernini's Palazzo Chigi-Odeschalchi in particular (B93). The Fontana di Trevi (B126) also owed something to this project, because it was also intended to combine a palace façade design (more mobile than that of the Fontana de Trevi) with a gigantic fountain basin, and would have been supplied from the Aqua Virgo spring, which was later used for the Fontana di Trevi.

The Pontificate of Alexander VII was a time of great gestures. Colours became particularly saturated, S. Andrea al Quirinale appears as the epitome of dark Roman-Baroque colour tones (B85). The quintessence of the »universal work of art« was distilled in the Ponte Sant'Angelo, the Colonnades and the late-Baroque painting in church interiors like Il Gesù (B1) or S. Ignazio (B46). The treatment of antiquity became as masterly and original as rarely before. But nothing was more excellent than the ecclesiastical symbols, the all-embracing »arms« (Colonnades) in front of the principal church of Catholic Christendom and – no less intense, but spiritualized – Bernini's

idea of portraying the initiation, the soul's passage into a more holy sphere, by architectural means in the church for the Jesuit novices (B85). To this end porticoes were used to separate two areas from each other, but the boundaries were kept so permeable that human being and soul could manifestly step through them. Now whole church interiors – as had happened to chapels twenty years earlier – became the place where the mystery was completed before the visitor's eyes (B82, B85, B89). This permeability was omnipresent in architecture under Alexander VII, in Bernini's Colonnades, but also for examples in the virtual shells that surround Borromini's dome design for S. Andrea delle Fratte (B74).

S. Andrea al Quirinale and Borromini's main work, S. Carlino (B52), are barely 200 metres away from each other. They provide the clearest demonstration of the difference between Bernini's and Borromini's art. They had both trained under Maderno in St Peter's and the Palazzo Barberini, and Borromini in particular felt the rivalry painfully throughout his lifetime. Bernini used almost only familiar devices, but creates something quite new in total. Classicism and dynamism were probably never so naturally in harmony as in Bernini, especially in S. Andrea, highly complex, universal architecture and yet uncommonly simple in its appearance. Wonder and Ascension were probably never again so convincingly demonstrated architecturally, extroverted – because the saint is bursting out of the Holy of Holies – and introverted – because the novice empathizes with this path taken by the soul. In contrast with Borromini, who conversely reinvented each individual form, Bernini always remained a classicist. Thus Bernini loved to divide façades into three (cf. only B43, B82, B85, B89, B93), and he loved the shallow pilaster. He was never a classicist, even though his legacy was later to develop into Baroque Classicism. Borromini's weakness was that he sometimes built too much for effect, always looking for something unusual, but never finding the compelling simple formula. His strength was that he made all parts autonomous, and gave them the same weight, characteristic as well of his last work,

Pietro da Cortona, Palazzo Chigi

the façade that he built in front of his first work, the interior of S. Carlino (B52). In its consistency it seems typically Roman, impenetrable, like leather, completely innovative in its undulating lines, but by no means as compellingly simple and eloquent as the façade of S. Andrea. Despite all the delight he took in invention, Borromini was in many ways more intent on heeding a recognized architectural canon than Bernini. Borromini would have detested a monumental pilaster standing half in empty space, like the slanting flanking pilaster on the façade of S. Andrea. Bernini chose it because he was concerned about continuity – here in forging a link with the oval body of the building – rather than »correctness«. He liked hard transitions for the sake of their dynamism and eloquence (cf. also B43, B93).

The great feature of High Baroque was polyphony: classical and inventively complex elements, which sometimes seemed bizarre, were combined in a style. This is similar to what had happened under Hadrian with the Pantheon (A31), which Bernini loved, and the Villa Hadriana (A32), which Borromini frequently visited. Bernini was incomparably more influential at first, and as he dominated Roman architecture, he dominated late-Baroque architecture in the rest of Europe. Borromini's influence did not make itself felt until the 18th century, and then not everywhere in Europe. Bernini did not realize his architectural legacy until very late, under Alexander VII, with his three contemporary plans for the three basic forms for the centrally-planned building, the Greek cross and the circular and the oval rotunda (B82, B85, B89). In addition to this there was the quintessential Baroque palace, no longer just cubic, but broken down into several blocks, differentiated at several decorative stages, tripartite in structure and now also fluid (B93). Cortona's project for the Palazzo Chigi in Piazza Colonna and Bernini's project for the Louvre would even have gone further. In the overall picture the inventive churches came first, and the palaces, but also the squares and routes, did not come until much later.

The younger generation, born in the 1630s, followed on. Rainaldi was their most important representative, the architect of S. Maria in Campitelli (B91) and (with others) of S. Agnese (B71) and the twin churches in the Piazza del Popolo (B87/B88). In the first of the three he successfully achieved a most magnificent revision of the traditional Roman cross-section façade, even more splendidly than Longhi had done it just under twenty years before, connecting it with the ancient aedicule façade. The architecture of the interior is similarly universal, the fusion of central planning and nave, of transept, depths (perspective view) and height. A similar dynamism had never previously been achieved in a rectangular composite, a more sonorous sound of pillars. North Italian and Mannerist features were to be found in Rinaldi, the result was always unreservedly High Baroque. This also applies to

S. Agnese, and to the great urban idea of the twin churches. De'Rossi was hardly less original, but less spectacular. His most important palaces (B68, B84) were to have a considerable impact in the 18th century. As in the case of Fontana his principal active period, involving highly complex church and chapel interiors, came in the period after the death of Bernini, in which he developed into one of the few (slight) opponents to Fontana's Baroque Classicism.

Baroque Classicism in the four decades after Bernini (B97–B109)

Borromini and Pope Alexander VII died in 1667, Cortona in 1669, then Bernini in 1680. The Pope had completely exhausted the Vatican funds with his building activities, so money was available only for functional buildings, particularly as holding off the Turkish threat was swallowing enormous sums of money. In the just under forty years we are talking about here only a handful of outstanding works (cf. B94–B107) was produced (along with five chapels). The fact that Bernini survived the two other great architects of the High Baroque by a good decade, combined with the fact that his pupil, Carlo Fontana, overemphasized the more strongly classical features of Bernini's architecture and thus also influenced Carlo Rinaldi to a very great extent, led to a clear overweighting of this tendency and consequently to a breakthrough for Baroque Classicism in the four decades after the death of Bernini.

The situation in the late 17th century was new. The whole repertoire of the cinquecento and High Baroque was in evidence. The idea of universal architecture – influenced by all styles – had long been considered in Rome, in S. Carlino (cf. B52). This repertoire was especially available since special academies of architecture had been founded (in Paris in 1671, in Rome as part of the Accademia di S. Luca, which operated according to the statues of 1599). Fontana was its director nine times in succession. Many more architects had the same teacher all the time, and so stylistic preferences tended to become more uniform. Fontana himself started as a colleague of Rainaldi in designing the twin churches in the Piazza del Popolo, the first with a free-standing columned portico since antiquity (cf. B87/88). S. Biagio (B94) and – after Bernini's death – S. Marcello (B103) followed as independent commissions. Both buildings give an impression of fluency, but on closer analysis it is clear that Fontana was just reproducing Bernini's ideas on a reduced scale: in S. Biagio the creation of several viewpoints for the observer (cf. B85) and the dominance of windows with perspective reveals (cf. B45), in S. Marcello the concave façade, intended to embrace the visitor as if with outstretched arms (cf. B80) and the same kind of window in the centre, and lastly a combination of the

Il Gesù type (B1) with a concave façade familiar in Rome since the Banco di S. Spirito (H23). Fontana assembled the sections on a very simple scheme, which was never sublimely varied, as if they were parts of a construction kit (cf. for detail B103). A comparison with SS. Vincenzo ed Anastasia just under three decades earlier is revealing (B64). Even the tiniest chapels, for instance the Capella Cybó (B105), seem to be similarly orchestrated throughout.

Other artists like Cortona and Rainaldi were also subject to the trend towards Baroque Classicism: dome designs from Cortona's early and late work are very different indeed (B51, B40). Rainaldi's late façade for Gesù e Maria (B99) seems extremely stiff, especially in comparison with the same architect's own earlier masterpiece, S. Maria in Campitelli (B91), or with the last great Baroque aedicule façade, which Rainaldi took as a model, S. Andrea al Quirinale (B85). Even in the years of Fontana's dominance, at least before the turn of the century there was still a slight counter-movement. This includes de'Rossi's late interior design (B100, B106) and – already exotic for a Roman view of art – Gherardi's chapels (B101, B107), which, even though few in number, are a perfect example of an ultra-Baroque counter-movement. But in the early 18th century Fontana's dominance was absolute.

A reawakened interest in large, open façades or axes went hand in hand with the preference for stiffer Baroque classical design approaches in the urban context. The enlargement of the Piazza del Popolo (K1) was one of the first projects of this kind. Fontana also planned to repeat the trapezium-shaped Piazzetta in front of St Peter's beyond the oval Piazza, at the point at which Via della Conciliazione starts today, in other words to pull down the existing Borgo buildings from the square downwards. He was responsible for clearing the Piazza Colonna in front of the Piazza Montecitorio. In comparison with this, High-Baroque architects had tended to create more restricted recreational spaces, each with a clear centre of interest (cf. p. 16).

Perhaps the most important change after the death of Borromini, Cortona and Bernini was that Rome lost its place as the leading architectural city of the West, and was never to get it back again.

Rococo, Barocchetto and the Neo-Classical counter-movement (B110–B140)

In the late 17th century the Turks were defeated outside Vienna and in the Balkans, Louis XIV died in 1715. Once these two main threats had been removed architecture in Rome started to flourish again, in the second decade with two works in which the stylistic supremacy of Fontana was questioned. In the first, S. Agatha in Rome itself, this happened in a more muted way. It was the decoration that was in-novative, not the spatial configuration. Drama gave way to refined taste, forms were developed above all along Borromini's lines, and seem as though they have been melted and softened. This anticipated the development programme for almost all late-Rococo works, even though this church had to wait for ten years before there was any reaction to it. The second work, in the countryside outside Rome, S. Maria del Rosario in Marino (B111), was quite different, a real jewel in its spatial configuration as well, a complete exception, bursting with ideas, lucid and light, probably the most beautiful church in Roman Rococo. The broad stream of new architecture did not start to flow until the third decade, with a multiplicity of talents, above all Raguzzini (B118, B120), Valvassori (B122), de Sanctis (B113, B115), Sardi (B111, B 129), Fuga (B125, B128, B138), Galilei (B124), Gregorini (B134) and Salvi (B126). Unlike even the 17th century, there were not just two or three dominant architects, but conversely none produced more than two or three masterpieces.

In three decades about 25 outstanding works were produced, including large commissions like the Spanish Steps (B115), the Fontana di Trevi (B126), also the Piazza di S. Ignazio (B118) and what is probably Rome's most magnificent palace façade on the Palazzo Doria Pamphili (B122) and the façades of the three great basilicas (principal churches) in the old city of Rome, S. Maria Maggiore (B132), S. Giovanni in Laterano (B124), and S. Croce in Gerusalemme (B134). These works are also very important in urban terms. The square designs that are still most popular today are part of this, and this even though the first urban development design of Roman Rococo, the Ripetta harbour, fell victim to the straightening of the Tiber in the late 19th century (K10). In this design Specchi gave the Tiber what was almost a façade, the undulating movement of the series of steps, as familiar today from the steps on the banks of the northern Italian lakes, had the effect of a cascade, which was very appropriate to the nature of the river. A great deal of attention was paid to contextual relations in general. Frequently church façades, for example, and those for annexe buildings were perceived as an overall composition (B119, B132, also B122), or closeness to nature was a theme (B115, B124). It is probably equally important that Roman Rococo produced numerous small palaces, whose refined, slightly fanciful appearance now make a stronger impression on the image of the city as a whole than buildings of any other period. And yet it is also true that in these three decades Roman architecture no longer set the tone for Europe. In ecclesiastical building in particular scarcely any innovations were created (of the kind that one finds in Austria, Bohemia, Franconia and northern Italy) – the exceptions are S. Maria del Rosario (B111) and S. Croce in Gerusalemme (B134). On the contrary, only surface design changed, in the Rococo period almost always using

Harbour of the Ripetta

motifs developed by Borromini, while works from the Baroque Neo-Classical counter-movement, which started again from 1730 and pushed out Rococo, which had been dominant for two decades, often seemed hollow and echoing. The masterpieces remained isolated phenomena.

The great period coincided with the Pontificates of the Neopolitan Benedict XIII (1724–30), who favoured his fellow-countryman Ragguzzini, and the Florentine Clement XII (1730–40), who withdrew his favours from Ragguzzini and turned to his fellow-countrymen Galilei and Fuga. Under the former the Rococo or Barocchetto tendency reigned almost supreme, and under the latter a form of Baroque Classicism again became widely accepted, in which Fuga and Galilei appeared as successors of Fontana, although this new form of Baroque Classicism was incomparably more complex and varied. A persisting ultra-Baroque tendency can be seen in one work at the most, the porch of S. Maria Maggiore (B132). The years from 1731 to 1733 could be seen as the heyday and turning-point, in which the Palazzi of Doria Pamphili and della Consulta (B122, B125), the Fontana di Trevi (B126) and above all the façade of S. Giovanni in Laterano (B124) were built, the latter as a result of the biggest architectural competition that Rome had seen until then. Galilei won it as a protagonist of the Baroque Neo-Classical counter-movement.

Roman Rococo, sometimes known as Barocchetto, was the dominant force first of all, especially in the 20s. The principal works are those of Ragguzzini and the Spanish Steps, after 1730 the Palazzo Doria Pamphili, also S. Croce (B134 and – slightly atypically – S. Maria Maddalena (B129). In the Barocchetto period in particular secular building once more became as important as ecclesiastical building, and

was even slightly more important if harbours, fountains and steps are included. In particular, a quite independent formula for palaces was devised. In the 18th century it was admittedly mainly building for rented accommodation that followed this pattern. The growing middle class started to assert itself architecturally as well. Typical features were more storeys with lower individual storeys, windows set more closely together, and also arranged in groups (frequently for smaller rooms behind them), linking windows in particular in vertical strips, which were also emphasized by linking sections, replacing the traditional horizontal articulation (by cornices and evenly placed rows of windows), and also the fusion of many articulating elements, for instance the (mezzanine) windows and entablatures (cf. in particular B122). Costs were lowered (as well as by reducing storey heights), by the use of stucco – which had previously happened only in the case of Borromini (cf. B52).

Important above all were the individual forms, not so much the spatial forms. Even structural elements, capitals, for instance, were very frequently reduced (to bands) or dissolved. Borromini's influence is omnipresent in terms of individual forms. The ear motif (at the side of the windows) is to be found almost everywhere, which satisfied 18th-century pleasure in inventing stories, and so is the pagoda gable, the Syrian arch and – inside – rounded corners and stringcourses laid diagonally across the ceiling. Borromini had devised all these forms in an early work, the Oratorio dei Filippini (B53). It is significant that his treatise was not published in his lifetime, but only in 1725. In contrast, the influence of French Rococo, with one exception, the façade of S. Maria Maddalena (B129), remained weak; its most important individual form, rocaille, is rarely found (other example B114). For this reason the term Barocchetto, the diminutive of Baroque (High Baroque) is more apt than Rococo. The surfaces (in ecclesiastical architecture as well) always seem soft, multi-layered, happy to take a very complex approach again (as in Mannerism), the forms vegetable, fused, the colours delicate, like pastels shades. Unlike similar designs in the 16th century the surface now seems elastic, like a living skin, with swellings and parts that »shine through« more strongly. The fusion of the multiply broken angles on the Spanish Steps (B115) is masterly. Ragguzzini also had a very independent role to play here, by thrusting decoration well into the background. With some lines, stripes and elegantly fluent surfaces, he created a quite particular aesthetic of simple elegance, in which layers, lines and panels made decoration, order and ornament superfluous.

There are a very few Barocchetto masterpieces that successfully combine the elegant, smaller forms of the period and the great tradition, the monumental quality of many centuries, not least of the High Baroque. These are the Spanish Steps, in which the majestic should always be comfortable, in keeping with the times, and the Palazzo Doria Pamphili (B122), perhaps also S. Croce (B134). The Barocchetto element was pushed into the background with the accession of Clement XII in 1730, but still had a part to play for at least twenty years, for example in the second façade of the Palazzo Doria Pamphili (B133), in S. Croce (B134) and in the façade of S. Maria Maddalena (B129).

Monumentality was the chief concern of the Baroque Neo-Classical counter-movement, and thus it is hardly surprising that its breakthrough came with the first commission for building the façade for one of the three great basilicas, S. Giovanni in Laterano (B124). Restoring the basilicas then also became one of the principal fields of activity after 1730. Protagonists of this approach were Galilei, Vanvitelli, Salvi and increasingly also Fuga, whose later work is considerably different from his early work (cf. for instance B125 and B128 with B131 and B138). There is clearly a greater French influence than in the Barocchetto strand, there was a tradition of classically monumental tendencies in the land of absolutism. Even in works that tend this way in Rome there are parts that owe more to Barocchetto, for example the upper conclusion of the Lateran façade, reworked in the other two basilica façades (B132, B134), but above all in the Fontana di Trevi (B126): there the façade was structured classically, as it was based on a Roman triumphal arch, conversely the rock and fountain landscape underneath was classical in no respect. The two parts had still been uniform in a (fluid) style in Cortona's fountain-palace project. The Baroque Neo-Classical tendency never once found the happy balance between elegance and grace on the one hand and monumentality on the other. Nevertheless the sprinklings of Barocchetto show that 18th-century Baroque Classicism was much more diverse than it had been earlier, and that the idea of »universal architecture« could now be detected within it. A particularly fine example of the integration of great contrasts is the skeleton construction method that can be seen in the Lateran façade and then in the two other basilica façades as well. The classical feature is that it was borrowed from the High-Renaissance model of the Capitol, but it is typically Baroque that it is taken so far, that a highly picturesque and dramatic contrast between light and dark values was created and then placed at the service of an enormous height development. Even this last phase of Baroque Classicism still felt obliged to the proportions that had been introduced in the early Baroque.

These were not abandoned until the Villa Albani (B139). With S. Maria del Priarato (B140) this is one of the works that are not yet dogmatically Neo-Classical, but in which the Neo-Classical element has clearly detached itself from the Baroque element. Fuga left Rome in 1751, the last great late-Baroque architect. SG

B1 Il Gesù

Piazza del Gesù, Via degli Astalli 16 (plan IV 2/B)
1568–84
Giacomo Barozzi da Vignola, Giacomo della Porta

Il Gesù, being the first large church structure of the Counter-Reformation, established a programme for the development of Baroque architecture. For over two centuries, its architectural type shaped the appearance of countless churches, particularly Jesuit churches, all over Europe. As early as 1549, nine years after their order had been approved by Paul III, the Jesuits planned a prominently located large new building, replacing the small church of S. Maria della Strada which belonged to their order. Designs for it were drawn up by Nanni di Baccio Bigio (1550) and Michelangelo (1554). It was not until 1568 that it was possible, with the financial support of Cardinal Alessandro Farnese, to acquire all the necessary plots of land and to begin building the church, which had now been designed by Vignola.

The Jesuits had secured for themselves a generous promoter in Cardinal Farnese, but he did have some precise ideas regarding the architecture of the new church, in which he also wanted to be buried. Alessandro ensured that Vignola, his court architect, was appointed rather than Giovanni Tristano, the religious order's architect who then supervised the building work. Cardinal Farnese ordered the nave to be given a barrel vault, although the Jesuits initially opposed this, fearing an echo inside the church. Where the design of the façade was concerned, the great interest taken by the patron in the artistic appearance of Il Gesù finally resulted in Vignola's being replaced by the younger della Porta, as the Cardinal preferred della Porta's draft for the façade.

Della Porta took the building work over from Vignola in 1571. It had been completed up to about the level of the main entablature. By 1577, the nave, in which there were some changes as against Vignola's plans, had been given a vault, and the façade had been completed to a new design. The crossing, along with the dome, transept and choir, was – once again to altered plans – built in a second phase of construction lasting from 1577 until the church's consecration in 1584.

B1 Il Gesù

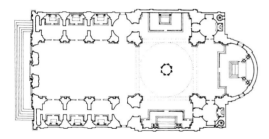

B1 Il Gesù

In spite of the compromises which Cardinal Farnese imposed upon the Jesuits, the ground plan and elevation of the church essentially take account of the practical and theological requirements of this Counter-Reformation order. The ground plan is in the shape of a Latin cross, which the Counter-Reformers (St Charles Borromeo), in distinguishing it from a centrally planned building, praised as being the most appropriate spatial form for churches. The interior consists firstly of a wide but relatively short nave, on each of whose flanks there are three side chapels with altars, and secondly of an adjoining crossing with drum dome, transept and choir.

The barrel-vaulted nave is subdivid-ed by a rhythmic succession of arcades and double pilasters. The pilasters support a broad entablature which surrounds the entire nave and, without projections, continues as far as the crossing. The three arcades on each side open up into chapels. They are kept low so that, between their apex and the entablature, space is left for lattice-work galleries, the »coretti«. The faint lighting of the chapels make the arcades look like dark openings which are of hardly any significance to the spatial effect of the relatively bright nave.

The emphasis is on the spatial unity of the barrel-vaulted nave. As it is not very long, but has a wide nave, the onlooker obtains an unrestricted view of the crossing and the altar as soon as he enters the church. The rapid succession of bays, and the entablature which continues smoothly throughout, both emphasize the movement towards the crossing, the liturgical centre upon which the entire architectural concept is oriented. The crossing is marked by a great abundance of light, is topped by a drum dome, and is expanded by the wide but short arms of the transept and choir, and also by the narrow bay at the end of the nave. All this gives the crossing area something of the character of a Greek cross and thus of a centrally planned area.

The significance of Il Gesù lies in the idea of linking a short nave to a dominating crossing which is full of light and is designed as a centrally planned area. This solves an old fundamental problem, that of combining a longitudinally with a centrally planned building, in a way which is as simple as it is ingenious. Vignola's interpretation of a room church became the most successful architectural type in Roman Catholic Europe, and this was due both to the beauty and, still more, to the functionality of that interpretation.

The spatial impression created today has been entirely altered by the 17C decorations (ceiling frescos by Giovanni Battista Gaulli, transept altars to designs by Andrea Pozzo and Pietro da Cortona). The building by Vignola and della Porta was kept in plain white and grey, thus according with the Counter-Reformation ideal of a church. The capitals and bases of the double pilasters were of grey travertine, while the shafts and the entirely unsubdivided barrel had white stucco plastering. It was only the side chapels that were more richly decorated. The dome area should be thought of as having frescos, and mosaics were planned for the apse.

The façade by della Porta emphasizes some new features in the development of Roman church façades. This can be seen by a comparison with earlier façades, such as S. Spirito in Sassia (H26) and S. Caterina dei Funari (H39), as well as with Vignola's façade design, which has two storeys of equal height, and five axes in three layers. The axes, which are formed into bays, are articulated by alternately small

B1 Il Gesù

and large niches. The main and side portals correspond to the axes, and the middle and side windows of the upper storey relate, in their turn, to the portals. The niches and openings are topped by unadorned wall panels in both storeys. This façade by Vignola has a relaxed structure, and the storeys and articulating elements relate to one another in a well-balanced way. On the other hand, the façade by della Porta, with its five axes and two storeys, shows a marked reduction in the height of the upper storey, and concentrates all the design elements on the central section. It is true that, here too, three wall layers are placed one in front of the other, leading from the outside towards the centre of the façade, but the consistency of the layered structuring is reduced by recesses in the entablature of the lateral central axes. The outer façade axes were left plain, whereas the two central axes are decorated with niches above the portals. Thus the decorative richness increases towards the centre. To conclude matters, the central axis is wider, and the motif of two aedicules placed one inside the other makes this axis into the culmination of the entire façade. The double aedicule, whose segmented and triangular gables extend into the base-course area of the upper storey, is a portal motif intensified so that it attains massive proportions.

Della Porta's façade is at a transitional stage leading to the Baroque, and differs from earlier façades in that it is layered in the manner described and becomes more intense in its articulation as it approaches its centre. Nonetheless, Mannerist principles are discernible in the proportioning and in the unclassical motifs, two examples being firstly the segmented and triangular gables inserted one inside the other, and secondly the fact that the gables of the niches are raised up into the capital zone. This becomes clear from a comparison with the tall façade – which is conceived in a very three-dimensional way, and is consistent down to the details – of S. Susanna (Maderno, B30), the first real Baroque façade. Such a comparison assigns to the façade of Il Gesù the character of a significant transitional work. AS

Bibliography: P. Pecchiai, Il Gesù di Roma, Rome, 1952; J. S. Ackerman, »The Gesù in the light of contemporary church design«, in: R. Wittkower and I.Jaffe, Baroque Art: the Jesuit Contribution, New York, 1972, p. 15; K. Schwager, »La chiesa del Gesù del Vignola«, Bolletino del Centro Internazionale di Studi di Architettura Andrea Palladio, 1977, p. 251.

B2 Palazzo Sciarra-Colonna
Via del Corso (plan IV 2/A)
c. 1560 (?)
Flaminio Ponzio (?)
The wing facing towards the Corso has the main façade of the building. Part of the palazzo was built on the foundations of the ancient Acqua Vergine aqueduct. When the Via del Corso was straightened in the 19C, the result was that the necessary forecourt

disappeared. Part of the façade has so far been attributed to the Bolognese architect Flaminio Ponzio, but may also have been constructed in c. 1560, earlier than the time when he was active. The building was probably completed by Orazio Torriani after 1630 according to the system fixed earlier.

This structure is a typical example of palace architecture following in the wake of the Palazzo Farnese (H25): the division of the storeys is simple, the smooth wall appears to be articulated only by windows, and the edges are reinforced by rusticated strips, which become flatter, and more finely worked, the higher up the building they are. Another feature producing only a subdued effect is the three-dimensional features which are emphasized in the surrounding cornices, in the flat roofings over the windows in the lower storeys, and in the shaped travertine frames of the upper-storey windows. Only in the piano nobile are the cornice and window sills more strongly delineated. The windows above the travertine-clad base course with its openings providing air for the basement storey are supported on scrolled pedestals, and so too are the roofings above the upper windows. The protruding entablature, with its lions' heads, Lesbian and Ionic cyma, and egg-and-dart moulding, has an ancient, classical appearance.

The middle portal, probably the work of Antonio Labacco, is framed in rustic masonry, is intended to impress, and is rich in individual ancient classical shapes (Doric columns with rosette strip and egg-and-dart moulding, and also a Doric frieze).

B3 Palazzo Borghese
Piazza della Fontanella di Borghese 22 (plan IV 1/A)
c. 1560–86, 1st decade of 17C
Giacomo Barozzi da Vignola, Martino Longhi the Elder or Flaminio Ponzio

The nucleus of the Palazzo Borghese, which is oriented on the new Via Trinitatis (on the subject of which cf. B14), was built under Monsignore Tommaso del Giglio shortly after 1560. The palace as a whole is a kind of architectural museum of developments in the late 16C, ranging from Vignola's more ingenious style to the dry Mannerism of the concluding decades.

The façade facing the Via Trinitatis (today's Via Fontanella Borghese) is attributed to Vignola, mainly due to the fine surface articulation which is typical of him, and also because of the observable eclecticism (similar to the earlier Palazzo Farnese in Caprarola, H38): delicate rustic-work ashlars were imitated in stucco on the ground floor and in each of the outside axes of both upper storeys, whereas the seven central axes of the upper storeys have flat frames and the wall here is layered accordingly. Flat surrounding travertine cornices divide the storeys and provide the horizontal articulation. Thus, in the final analysis, various types were employed here: that of the Palazzo Farnese (H25), a type in which the façade block is horizontally subdivided only by cornices and is strengthened at

B3 Palazzo Borghese

the edges by rusticated strips, and that of Raphael's house (cf. on this subject H22), in which the individual storeys are subdivided not only by windows, but also by supports such as columns and which was used in the case of the Palazzo Cicciaporci (H14), for a similarly flat and layered wall structure. Following the hierarchical system, the roofings over the windows in the piano nobile have triangular and segmented gables, the ground floor and upper storey only have flat conclusions, and the two lower storeys each possess in addition a mezzanine with two-dimensionally framed windows. The only three-dimensional feature emphasized is the central portal, which is flanked by columns and has an architrave and the coat of arms of the del Giglio. A balcony on the upper storey corresponds to the portal, and is topped by an aedicule with flat pilasters and a triangular gable.

On the side facing the garden, this building had a loggia on double columns. This design probably derives from a Northern Italian architect, either Longhi or Ponzio, and is an imitation of Northern Italian, or to be more specific Genoese, buildings. Later owners (including, from 1604 onwards, Cardinal Camillo Borghese, the later Pope Paul V) continued this leitmotiv in the extensions which they built along the flanks, with the result that one of the finest inner courtyards in Rome was created. The third storey was later given a Corinthian order of pilasters, and thus accorded with the classical architectural order. The fourth, open wing, built in 1607/08, gave a view of the trapezoidal garden which lay behind it and had fountains in the walls and ancient statues (similar to the Palazzo Mattei di Giove, B31, the former design of the Palazzo Farnese, H25, and many late-16C Genoese city palaces, built into the hills).

The lateral wings of the palace (in the Via Monte d'Oro and Via Borghese) were erected later than Vignola's time and look much plainer. The Palazzo Farnese was now the only architectural type shaping the style, but its masterly proportioning and the conciseness of its subdividing work were not achieved here. The reason for the slight kink in the Via Borghese is that the foundations of a previous building were included in the structure. The scheme of the main portal was also adopted in the side portal leading on to the Piazza Borghese. The square in front of it originally belonged to the palace, and the simpler structure on the square's western side (1624–26) was used by the retinue of Cardinal Scipione Borghese.

Finally, the »keyboard« of the »harpsichord«, as the Romans jokingly refer to the palace on account of its ground plan, was built in 1612 on the narrow rear frontage looking on to the Tiber. Flaminio Ponzio's design for this façade facing the Tiber includes robust rustication at the corners, and a two-storeyed order of pilasters whose arcades lead to a »hanging« garden with a balcony. In 1676, Carlo Rainaldi placed in front of the former garden portal on the ground floor a freestanding Tuscan columnar frontage supporting a narrow, covered balcony. Thus to Ponzio's well-balanced but slightly stiff façade, which remains discernible in the upper storeys, there was added a piece of architecture with all the qualities of the High Baroque: close and dynamic placing of supports, much articulation, preference for curves which are geometrically not clearly defined, deep relief, light and shade. SG

B4 Villa Medici
Viale Trinità dei Monti 1 (plan II 1/D)
begun 1564, from 1576 onwards
Nanni di Baccio Bigio, Annibale Lippi, Bartolomeo Ammanati

In 1564, Cardinal Giovanni Ricci acquired a vigna located on the Pincio. He commissioned Nanni di Baccio Bigio and his son Annibale Lippi to build for him, on this location, a villa with a garden attached. In

B4 Villa Medici

1576, after Ricci's death, the building passed into the possession of Cardinal Ferdinando de' Medici, who ordered it to be completed by Bartolomeo Ammannati.

The façade towards the city presents itself as a massive, wide frontage. It is subdivided with restraint, being divided horizontally into two halves, each of which includes a full storey and a mezzanine. The lower section, with its slight inclination and its corner reinforcements made of bossed travertine ashlars, is clearly discernible as a base course, and, because the building stands on a slope, really only constitutes the basement storey. By contrast with the side towards the city, the façade facing the garden, originally the main entrance, is designed much more elaborately: an open loggia, located on the ground floor of the central structure and marked by a Serliana and rhythmically placed columns, forms the vestibule, which is enclosed on both sides by slightly projecting wings that stand at the corners and have towers above them. The side towards the garden is repletely decorated with sculptures and reliefs that are classical in origin, and is in this respect a characteristic example of horror vacui in Mannerism. In its form, the Villa Medici follows the type of the palazzo suburbano, a hybrid form which is somewhere between a city palace and a villa with a garden and was created by Peruzzi when he designed the Villa Farnesina (H8). This type was imitated in numerous buildings, mostly in the immediate vicinity of the city. The form of the villa, with towers on both sides of the central structure, was in turn adopted again in subsequent villa complexes. DH

B5 S. Anna dei Palafrenieri
Via S. Anna (plan III 1/A)
1565–83 (with later modifications)
Giacomo Barozzi da Vignola

In this building, whose construction was begun in 1565, Vignola created the first oval rotunda in the history of architecture. After Vignola's death, his son continued the building work in accordance with the plans as far as the principal cornice. It was consecrated in 1583. A plan of Rome by Dupérac and Lafréri, and an engraving by Tempestà, (1577/93), show the building as having a simple roof, with the façade subdivided by pilasters (like S. Andrea, H34), but without a gable. It was probably not until 1728-45 that the building was given a vault, the work of Navona, who also modified the façade. Today's design for the sanctuary, and the travertine incrustation (in some parts of the interior and on the façade), both date from the 19C.

The main façade by Vignola had no travertine incrustation, no split gable or flanking columns at the portal, and no campaniletti. These features are absent from the reproductions dating from 1577/93. In its plainness, it was evidently similar to the surviving lateral façade. Like other buildings and plans by Vignola, the structure had two shells (cf. p. 121): it was the right angle that was dominant in the exterior (the tall oval drum was only added in the 18C), and in the

B5 S. Anna dei Palafrenieri

interior it was the oval. Contrary to what occurred in the early 16C, for example in Bramante's works, the shape of the interior did not produce an effect on the exterior. The outer and inner structures were not closely related, and the same applies to the two façades. It is true that they both had five axes and were comparably plain. But the main façade was developed as a main façade in Vignola's plans and was marked by a temple frontage, whereas in the lateral façade it is precisely the centre that is the most weakly developed, a typically Mannerist feature. Thus, as is generally the case with Vignola, the oval building was not understood as being an elongated centrally planned structure with almost identical sides, but was evidently thought of as an oriented building.

The interior goes beyond the first beginnings found in S. Andrea in Via Flaminia (H34), an early work. The oval now shapes the whole structure from the ground plan up into the dome, and now no longer only applies to the dome. The elongation, which in that early work was still fairly restrained given that the ratio of length to breadth was 8:7, now became fully developed. The design of the wall, which is now a curved structure, derives its life from the colonnade. The columns are free-standing in the rich structure of the wall, and continue up into the vault area via the moulding and the wall arches. The wall compartments form separate bodies of their own, and have main and diagonal axes which differ in width. Arcades intersect the compartments on the main axes. This creates not only a rhythmic bay, but also an impression of interlinked triumphal-arch motifs (as had happened in the belvedere courtyard, also in the Vatican, H6). It is doubted whether the columns and their moulding are taken from Vignola's plans, as both features are said to have been unusual in Rome in Vignola's day. However, similar skeleton-like support systems which are detached from the composite wall structure, are found quite frequently in Vignola's work, examples being his inner courtyards (H35) and also the interior of S. Andrea (H34), where the impression of a rhythmic bay was created, although it was not yet in an oval

shape. What is more, the rest of the subdividing work is based on the existence of columns, as they look like links between the rectangular adjoining rooms and the main oval area. Moreover it is natural that Vignola, when developing the oval rotunda, should also have had in mind the ancient oval buildings, chiefly the Colosseum (A25) with its half columns which form bays. This is because it was during those very years that Serlio and Lomazzo, the proponents of the oval shape, were, in order to justify it, beginning to make reference to ancient buildings.

Although Vignola's choir was smaller, it probably formed a Greek cross, and in the main area of the church is also an incipient Greek cross. Rectangular and round sections rebound unabatingly against one another in the arch between the two areas, as they also do in the exterior, in S. Andrea, and very frequently elsewhere in Vignola's work.

S. Anna became the prototype for late-16C oval churches. In the religious buildings he designed, Vignola was always selecting this shape for the most widely varying architectural tasks, ranging from churches for religious fraternities (the Palafrenieri are one example) to memorial buildings such as S. Andrea (H34). Vignola differs from Peruzzi before him in that Vignola seems to have interpreted the oval not only as being an enrichment of his repertoire of shapes, but rather as the only adequate shape for his intentions. This is probably because Vignola understood religious buildings as consisting mainly of a route leading from an entrance, which was the façade, to the altar. The oval is the only logical form of a shell for this route. This is why his works have what is an entirely new feature for centrally planned buildings, namely a main façade and a specially marked-out choir. SG

B6 S. Maria dell'Orto
Via Anicia (plan VII 1/A)
incl. 1554, 1566–85
Guidetto Guidetti, Giacomo Barozzi da Vignola

S. Maria dell'Orto was built for a miracle-working image of the Virgin Mary. Due to lack of documents, the early history of construction between 1495 (the most likely starting date) and 1513 cannot be established with certainty. Probably a centrally planned building had been created above a Greek cross by 1524, it remained uncompleted and, under the supervision of Guidetti the architect, was from 1554 onwards expanded into a pillared basilica with a nave and two aisles. The façade follows a design by Vignola, who though probably only built the ground floor (1566/67). It is likely that Francesco da Volterra, imitating Vignola's plans, completed the upper storey by 1579. The church was consecrated in 1585.

The exceptionally wide brickwork façade with its two storeys is subdivided by flat pilasters into seven axes below and three above. Their rhythmic succession creates a series of wider and narrower wall panels, which are appropriately fitted out with niches and

B6 S. Maria dell'Orto

portals. The storeys are divided by an entablature
which projects only above the portal. Pyramid-shaped
guglios located above this entablature, and also
above the entablature (it has a triangular gable) of the
upper storey, adopt the rhythm of the pilasters. The
main portal, which is topped by an arcade and framed
by a columned aedicule, is the only element of the
façade to be given three-dimensional emphasis. Precursors of Vignola's façade design for Il Gesù (B1) are
discernible in the rhythmizing of the façade and in the
emphasis on the central portal. But the continuous
steps in the façade, leading towards the centre, are
still absent here. Elevations in the terrain have resulted
in the loss of the base course and of the sets of three
stairs in front of the portals, so that today the façade
stands directly on the pavement.

The interior, which is a structure with a nave, two
aisles, side chapels, a transept and a crossing with a
flat dome, contains a decoration (begun 1699) which
is among the first examples in Rome of the ornate and
graceful »Barocchetto« style. The late-Baroque Cappella di S. Giovanni Battista, the work of Valvassori,
also deserves attention (c. 1750). AS

B7 S. Maria in Via
Via del Tritone, Via S. Maria in Via (plan V 1/A)
1570–1600
Giacomo della Porta
This sacred structure attained a certain celebrity when
a miracle occurred in its immediate vicinity in 1256.
A portrait of the Madonna, which had been floating on
the water of an overflowing well and was displayed in
the church, was a centre of attraction for many pilgrims. A new building was planned in 1541, but it is
not known exactly when the construction work began.
According to Baglione, the plans for the structure as
a whole go back to Giacomo della Porta.

The interior is of a plain design, and is a room
church with apse aisles (the Il Gesù type). In terms of
della Porta's œuvre as a whole, the façade is inferior
to that found in the churches of Il Gesù (B1, 1577) and
S. Maria dei Monti (B10, 1580), and is also of somewhat earlier date. But it must still be regarded as a
step in the development that led to the first animated
Baroque façade (S. Susanna, B30). The façade relief

has three axes below and one above, and is gently
accentuated by recessed pilasters; this means that
the centre of the façade, and the corner pillars, project
the furthest, but only in a very restrained way. The fact
that the layering remains subdued brings other details
to the fore all the more strongly: accentuation is given
firstly to those aedicules of the portal and of the upper
window which are moved a little way into the wall and
have a second architectural order behind them, and
secondly to the triangular gable which surmounts the
façade and has a segmentedly arched gable inscribed
within it. Here, the window aedicule serves as a transitional stage, because it employs a rounded-off triangular gable to prepare for the concluding segmented
arch. Thanks to its slightly elongated upper storey, the
façade as a whole possesses a notable upwards urge
which gives it a certain dynamism. PZ

B8 Porta S. Giovanni
Piazza di Porta S. Giovanni (plan IX 1/E)
1573
Giacomo del Duca
The Porta S. Giovanni was one of the city gates in the
Aurelian Wall (A44), created in 1573 under Gregory XIII,
replacing the ancient Porta Asinaria located a little to
the west. It was significant by reason of its location
close to the Lateran basilica, but also provided an
easier link with Frascati, which lay to the south-east
and was the pope's summer residence. The plans for
the design of the Porta are by Giacomo del Duca, a
pupil of Michelangelo, and are among the few examples of imaginative Mannerism in Rome. The side facing the city is as usual very plain, as it consists only of
brick masonry and is given a restrained elaboration
only in its upper area. But the exterior façade facing
away from the city is of greater interest. Its form follows only in a very remote way the architectural type
for ancient triumphal arches which is customarily employed in city gates: the large archway and the attic
zone above it are comparable, but the lateral bays
have become debased into narrow wall panels. This
main frontage is built exclusively of travertine, and its
strongly three-dimensional design relates it to the
frontage of the Porta Pia (H43). The pilasters are articulated by rough bossed ashlars alternating with plane
stone layers projecting at the sides, while in contrast
to this the capital zone remains undecorated and angular. A characteristic feature is the very three-dimensional language of shapes which operates with contrasts and results in strong effects of shade. Customary architectural shapes are varied in an original
way (pilasters, capitals, cornices) and imaginatively
combined. This gate, despite its comparatively modest size, may thus be regarded as an interesting example of Mannerism in the succession of Michelangelo. DH

B9 Palazzo della Sapienza
Corso del Rinascimento 40 (plan IV 1/A)
incl. 1577–1670
incl. Giacomo della Porta, Francesco Borromini

From the late 15C until 1935, the university founded
by Boniface VIII in 1303 was housed in the Palazzo
della Sapienza, a building characteristic of university
architecture. In 1497 Alexander VI ordered a new
building to be erected, and it was continued by Guidetto Guidetti in 1562 and by Pirro Ligorio from 1564
onwards. Della Porta, the architect of della Sapienza
from 1577 onwards, planned today's inner courtyard
with its two-storeyed porticoes and an exedra to the
east. He advanced the construction work a great
deal, but did not finally build the chapel which was to
his design and was a customary feature in university
buildings. On that site, Borromini, who became the
university architect in 1632, built S. Ivo (B56), which
was one of the most spectacular Baroque church
structures. He also designed both the northern section of the palazzo and its eastern outer façade.

The palace frontage facing the Corso Rinascimento makes a very self-contained impression, because
its ground floor has almost no windows and is opened
up only by a portal. A striking feature of the southern
long side is that the rhythmizing of the windows,
which are arranged in pairs, is not entirely consistent.
Here della Porta was following the structure of the
previous building erected under Alexander VI. The
frontage facing the Piazza S. Eustachio (Borromini)
continues the three-storeyed elevation of the palazzo,
but only on the flanks. The central section, with its two
portals and balconies and three window axes, is one
storey lower and concludes in an attic which curves
concavely backwards. It encloses Borromini's dome
and allows an unobscured view of it from the city
square below.

The two-storeyed porticoes of the inner courtyard
are, after the manner of the tabularium motif (cf. A9),
fitted with arcades having the Doric and Ionic orders
(cf. illustration B56). AS

B9 Palazzo della Sapienza

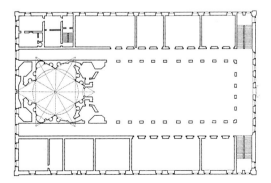

B10 S. Maria dei Monti

B10 S. Maria dei Monti
Via Madonna dei Monti 41 (plan V 1/B)
begun 1580
Giacomo della Porta

When it comes to the development of church façades
in the period of Il Gesù (B1), S. Maria dei Monti is an
important milestone in the work of Giacomo della
Porta.

A miracle-working image of the Madonna was discovered in a haystack in 1579, and is said to have
thereupon caused numerous miraculous cures. Work
on building the church on the site of the haystack was
begun as early as 1580. The architect was the forty-
year-old della Porta, and this church was the first
building he completed. The architectural type which
he wanted for the interior was a room church with
apse aisles (the Il Gesù type), with particular emphasis
being given to the large-scale crossing and its dome.

The façade, too, must be compared with that of Il
Gesù, which della Porta had completed to his own
plans three years previously, in 1577. Some decided
correspondences are firstly the way in which the tripartite central section projects slightly, with the pilasters intersecting at the joints (in Il Gesù they only do
this on the lower storey), and secondly the varying
width – increasing towards the centre – of the bays,
with the central section being marked by niches.

But S. Maria dei Monti is much smaller than Il
Gesù, and this is why double pilasters were not employed. But the energetic radiation proceeding from
the church is not thereby impaired. Rather, the ideas
found in Il Gesù are adopted anew and put into effect
with still greater consistency: the projecting centre is
maintained right up into the gable, which has three

B11 S. Luigi dei Francesi

layers behind it. Della Porta also diminished the over-emphasis placed on the portal area in Il Gesù, and this he did by adapting the size of the portal to that of the upper window and by lending greater value to that window by including an aedicule on columns. By distributing the emphasis in this harmonious way, della Porta took the genesis of the Baroque façade an important step further. PZ

B11 S. Luigi dei Francesi
Piazza S. Luigi dei Francesi (plan IV 1/A)
begun 1580
Domenico Fontana, Giacomo della Porta

S. Luigi is the national church of the French. The tradition of such a church dates back to Charlemagne. Its functions included caring for poor pilgrims (there was always a hospice attached) and holding religious celebrations. The original site was immediately next door to S. Andrea della Valle. The intention in 1518 was to build a new church on today's square. The first architect, Chenevières from Rouen, designed a large, octagonal, centrally planned building, whose construction was interrupted in 1524 due to lack of funds. Work was only continued in 1580, but it was now to an entirely different design. Domenico Fontana and Giacomo della Porta are mentioned as architects in the account books, but a large part of the payment went to Fontana, who may be regarded as the leading architect. A stylistic argument in favour of this theory is the existing façade, which does not bear comparison with della Porta's façades (Il Gesù, B1, S. Maria dei Monti, B10). The abundance of shapes indicates the architect's uncertainty. Fontana was reverting to Michelangelo's plans for the façade of S. Lorenzo in Florence and thus the equally wide storeys, brought together by a triangular gable, but the façade of S. Luigi turned out to be much less energetic. The attempt to suggest two layers is fainthearted and unconvincing. The pilasters intersect with cornices, whose architectural value is therefore questionable as they are not stringently carried through, and the result is that the façade displays an appallingly insipid two-dimensionality. This building, whose interior is also lacking in quality, is famous for its cycle of depictions, by Caravaggio, from the life of St Matthew the Evangelist. PZ

B12 Collegio Romano
Piazza del Collegio Romano (plan IV 2/B)
begun 1582
Giuseppe Valeriano

Work on building a new Jesuit school (Collegio Romano) of grammar and theology was begun in 1582. The executive architect was Giuseppe Valeriano, who was later involved in other Jesuit buildings in Naples and Genoa. The entire complex occupies a plot measuring 13 000 m². The façade had to be correspondingly large, and the architect faced the challenge of giving this enormous area a homogeneous shape.

Two lateral sections flank the central structure, which has a third storey, projects somewhat as it is a risalto extending across an entire flat surface, and presents itself as a separate section of the building. This dividing-up of the various sections was taken into account in the articulation of the wall. The windows with their mezzanines are framed by pilaster strips so that they appear either individually or in groups of two or three, and are placed in a rhythmical relationship with one another. In the lateral sections, the framing surrounds three windows and one window alternately, whereas in the central section this slight pulsation comes to a standstill, as the articulation makes an additive and unconnected impression. The unsubdivided wall area dominates, and is penetrated at the sides by martial portals with aedicules. Only towards the middle are double windows once again framed by pilaster strips. The central axis remains windowless, and the narrow wall panel on the ground floor contains a bizarre niche – an original expedient, a better version of which was adopted on the façade of the Jesuit church of St Michael in Munich.

The façade of the Jesuit college deliberately dispenses with any splendour, and this is why the piano nobile is not specially marked out. The emphasis is on plain severity, and the edifice becomes a sombre teaching building. Although the windows are rhythmically grouped, their rigid uniformity hardly alters the building's prison-like appearance. PZ

B12 Collegio Romano

B13 S. Maria Scala Coeli and S. Paolo alle Tre Fontane

B13 S. Maria Scala Coeli and S. Paolo alle Tre Fontane
Via delle Tre Fontane (plan G2 3/B)
begun 1582, 1599 resp.
Giacomo della Porta

Della Porta built two new churches in the Cistercian complex of the Abbazia alle Tre Fontane (C34). S. Paolo, the later, is built around the three sources related to the execution of St Paul. The name of the older and more important church commemorates that ladder (scala) reaching up to heaven which is said to have appeared to St Bernard during a Mass. Its crypt is regarded as the place of Paul's captivity.

This centrally planned building rises above a ground plan which is in the shape of a Greek cross with bevelled corners. The arms of the cross are kept extremely short. The three conchae, and, on the portal side, a transversely rectangular entrance area framed by an aedicule, are no more than additions to the cross-arms, because they are less wide and the conchae are also less high. Apart from the aedicule, the exterior is subdivided only by upright surrounding frames, behind which the wall filling the remaining space recedes by one layer, as in the case of the conservators' palace by Michelangelo (H30). The simple geometrical shapes, such as the conchae and triangular gables, contrast in an almost brutal way. The rich structure of te building is energetically bound together by the corbelled cornice and the attic.

The basic principle of the interior area is of a similar clarity. This area makes a sober impression in the style of the Counter-Reformation, and is surrounded by a number of tripartite triumphal-arch motifs, each with a large central arch and two small flanking ones. The articulation for this motif is here no longer a flat wall as was the case with Bramante (cf. H6), but is the three-dimensional octagon. The architects who, in their rigid late Mannerism, were laying the foundations for the Baroque found their way by means of simplification and clarification, and also by recollecting the architecture of the High Renaissance. SG

B14 Palazzo Caetani-Ruspoli
Largo Goldoni 55 (plan IV 2/A)
around and after 1583
Nanni di Baccio Bigio (?), Bartolomeo Ammanati

In 1583, Orazio Rucellai, a scion of the Florentine family of bankers, purchased an as yet incomplete urban palace on the Via Trinitatis (today's Via Condotti). This new stretch of road, which led from S. Trinità dei Monti (H44) to the Ripetta port, had once again lent attraction to the city district at the northern edge of the ancient field of Mars.

The main façade faced the new road. By 1583 its construction had probably progressed only as far as the portal, but the rhythmic grouping of the windows in a scheme of 1-2-3-2-1 had thereby already been determined, so that the central axis containing the portal was accentuated. This formation of groups

B14 Palazzo Caetani-Ruspoli

within a series of windows is sometimes found in the late 16C (cf. B23), is frequent in the 18C, and points to Nanni di Baccio Bigio as the architect responsible. The second chief feature of the palazzo is that two equivalent double storeys were formed, separated only by a delicate travertine strip (and this differed from what was more customary in Rome, namely three storeys with a piano nobile). This variation on the type of the Palazzo Farnese (H25, cf. also B19, B21) was felt by contemporaries to be »too plain«.

This building was formerly attributed to Bartolomeo Ammanati, the architect of the Rucellai family, but he probably only continued what had already been begun, creating firstly the courtyard with its multi-storeyed loggia and secondly that celebrated gallery in the piano nobile (on the Corso) which was painted by Jacopo Zucchi in 1586. In 1629 the palazzo passed to the Caetani family who commissioned Martino Longhi the Younger to incorporate a splendid marble staircase, and in 1712 to the Ruspoli family who ordered the extension on the Via del Leoncino to be built.

B15 Palazzo del Quirinale
Piazza Quirinale (plan V 1/A)
begun 1583, 1730
Ottavio Mascherino, Domenico and Giovanni Fontana, Flaminio Ponzio, Ferdinando Fuga

Today the Quirinal palace is the residence of the President of Italy and is not accessible to visitors. The palace, and the design of the square, form what is among the most important examples of the strait-laced late-Mannerist style which predominated in Rome in the late 16C. The hill was dominated in ancient times by the temple of Sol and by Constantine's thermal baths, which were the last imperial thermal baths in Rome. Some remnants of that complex are the very angular statues of the Dioscuri in the middle of the square. Typically late classical, they look cumbersome despite being so animated.

Gregory XIII set about building the monumental summer palace in 1583, incorporating within it some existing garden walls and smaller palazzi by Ippolito d'Este. The starting point here was a loggia structure which had only two storeys, was designed by the architect Ottaviano Mascherino and stood on the slope of the hill. Today this can be discerned from the outside only by its central tower, which stands on its roof and has a belfry.

It was during the pontificate of Sixtus V that Domenico and Giovanni Fontana – by way of a kind of counterpart – built, at the outset of the Via Pia, firstly another two-storeyed section which had seven axes and a central portal and secondly the connecting wing between both parts facing the square. That wing, which looks infinitely long, therefore actually consists of two façades placed side by side. The left-hand façade is long and has seventeen axes, and the façade attached to it on the right is symmetrically organized and has seven axes and a central portal. The

B15 Palazzo del Quirinale

two façades are separated by a rusticated strip such as was used to reinforce the edges in the type of palace deriving from the Palazzo Farnese (H25). The other main features also correspond to this type: they are the smooth wall and the great reduction in the subdividing elements, which run in a horizontal direction throughout and consist only of cornice strips and rows of windows located in the undecorated area. It is only the triangular gables of the windows in the piano nobile that lend three-dimensional life to the monotonous succession. But what is entirely different from the Palazzo Farnese is the proportioning: the classical balance between height and width was abandoned here. It was the first time that such decided overemphasis was given to width in a façade that looked infinitely long, and this is particularly striking because the other features of this architectural type were retained.

Finally, Paul V commissioned Flaminio Ponzio to complete this four-winged complex by adding the long northern connecting wing which, like its southern counterpart, has a portico opening on to the longitudinally rectangular inner courtyard that came into being as a result of the wing's construction. But the central part of the northern wing had a storey added to it, because it contains the two-storeyed consistory hall. In the same way, the wing facing the road was expanded to include 16 axes and contained the official reception room on its new topmost storey. That storey had been built on top of the Fontana section, and was subdivided in the cumbersome overloaded manner of the period of Paul V (cf. B20, which is similar.).

In 1638/39, Gianlorenzo Bernini placed the benediction loggia on top of Maderno's columnar portal on the façade which faces the square, dates from 1615 and has recumbent figures by Maderno (Peter) and Berthelot (Paul). The loggia is framed by fluted pilaster strips with Corinthian capitals and a split gable. The semi-round tower for the artillery standing at the link with the Dataria defensive structure belongs to the same epoch.

The so-called »manica lunga« (long sleeve) along the Via Pia is a low wing with successive additional storeys added to it. It housed the staff, was designed like a garden wall and has a loggia opening on to the gardens of the Quirinal. Fernando replaced it in 1730 by a façade which had eleven axes and which he provided with rustic-work pilaster strips subdividing it in a rhythm of 1-3-3-3-1. He designed its central axis, where the portal was, to project like a risalto. The segmented split gables above the windows of the piano nobile, and the curved gables on the upper storey, are typical of the early 18C.

Bibliography: F. Borsi et al., *Il Palazzo del Quirinale*, Rome, 1974.

B16 S. Giovanni dei Fiorentini
Via Giulia (plan III 2/A)
begun 1518, 1583–1614
incl. Antonio da Sangallo the Younger, Giacomo della Porta, Carlo Maderno

S. Giovanni, the national church of the Florentines, is of great interest for its planning history, and may be regarded as the most magnificent fount of ideas for a centrally planned building ever to have come into being in the cinquecento (apart from St Peter's). Nearly all the significant 16C architects submitted designs for this building, and although they were not put into effect, they are of great importance to architectural history.

Raphael, Baldassare Peruzzi, A. da Sangallo the Younger and Jacopo Sansovino all submitted designs for a competition, and it was Sansovino's draft that was selected by Leo X, the Medici pope. But his design (c. 1518) for a centrally planned building was not put into effect. Instead, building work was begun in 1520 to a design for a longitudinal structure, drawn up by Sangallo. But the choir section of the church extended down into the bed of the Tiber, and this

B16 S. Giovanni dei Fiorentini. Project by Michelangelo

meant that the foundation works swallowed up such amounts of money that the construction work, after several interruptions, came to a complete standstill, probably in 1534. Renewed attempts were made in 1550, probably with Vignola being involved, and in 1559, using designs by Michelangelo. Michelangelo drew up several designs for a centrally planned building, and caused the foundations by the side of the Tiber to be completed in accordance with the final design, of which a model was also built. The work was interrupted again in 1562 due to lack of funds. Only after some wealthy Florentines had committed themselves to making donations did della Porta resume the construction of the church in 1583. He reverted to Sangallo's longitudinal scheme, and by 1593 he had completed the nave of the church using the already existing foundations. Maderno, his successor, completed the choir and transept in 1608-14, and placed a concluding dome on the crossing. Plans for the façade had been available from the start, but it was not until 1733/34 that Alessandro Galilei placed in front of the existing church structure a façade which he had himself designed.

The already existing foundations by Sangallo are the reason why S. Giovanni is not architecturally oriented on Il Gesù (B1), but follows an older spatial form consisting of a pillared basilica with a nave, two aisles, a transept and a domed crossing. As regards the building's overall proportions, della Porta was bound by the guidelines of the cinquecento. Della Porta varied from Sangallo's plans in subdividing the pillared arcades of the nave not by half columns standing in front, but by flat pilasters. What he therefore required was not an entablature with projections above the pilasters, but one which had a straight shape throughout. He therefore dispensed with the strong relief work which would have characterized Sangallo's nave. What della Porta achieved was that the effect of the nave was determined not so much by the projecting pilasters, but rather by the tall arcades themselves. Della Porta's non-Baroque approach found its successors in two buildings by Martino Longhi the Elder (S. Maria in Vallicella, B17, and S. Maria della Consolazione, c. 1600). The domed crossing by Maderno (who lies buried here along with Borromini) is, where the shape of the pillars is concerned, also indebted to High-Renaissance methods, particularly the crossing of St Peter's (H7): the dome is supported not by simple pillars fitted with pilasters, but by massive, broad pillars which are bevelled in the middle and are faced with bent pilasters. The crossing is cut off from the other areas by the projecting pilasters at the edges of the massive structures, and it thus gains spatial independence.

The choir chapel was designed by Borromini, who reworked Cortona's design for the high altar and designed the tombs at the sides. The Falconieri chapel, also to Borromini's plans, is below the choir. AS

B17 S. Maria in Vallicella (Chiesa Nuova)

B17 S. Maria in Vallicella (Chiesa Nuova)
Piazza della Chiesa Nuova (plan IV 1/B)
begun 1575, 1586–1605/06
Matteo da Castello, Martino Longhi, Fausto
Rughesi
Work on the new building which was the church of
the Oratorian order was begun in 1575, the same year
in which the order was approved by Pope Gregory
XIII. Da Castello's design was for an aisleless church
which had side chapels, a transept and a domed
crossing and whose scheme was based on the Jesuit church of Il Gesù (B1), still under construction.
The nave and the side chapels were built to this design until the time when Longhi was engaged as architect. In 1586-88, for reasons which are not yet
clear, Longhi converted the existing structure, which
had a nave but no aisles, into a basilica with a nave
and two aisles, on the model of S. Giovanni dei Fiorentini (B16). The existing decorations in the apse
chapels were abandoned, and those chapels were
provided with passages and linked to form aisles,
with the altars thereby lost being formed into semicircular additions to those aisles. The transept, choir
and crossing were added to the nave from 1588 onwards. The dome (which has no drum) over the crossing was vaulted in 1590, the nave and the transept,
however, were given a vault in 1592/1593.

The fact that the interior has a nave and two aisles
is scarcely significant. The wide nave, the low arcades
and pilasters which subdivide the walls of the nave,
and the retention of the transverse barrels in the former chapels which are now part of the aisles, are all
features clearly reminiscent of the originally planned
aisleless church of the Il Gesù type. The decorations
(frescos by Cortona in the main lon-gitudinal section
and dome, paintings by Rubens in the choir) make a
unifying impression. They are the first set of High-
Baroque redecorations in which the originally rather
sparse character of the Counter-Reformation
churches gave way to exuberant stucco and fresco
adornments. Rughesi, a little-known artist, was the
winner of a competition, announced in 1593, for the
design of a façade. According to the inscription, he
had completed the broad, unaccentuated frontage
by 1605 (but the true date is probably after 1606).
AS

B18 Acqua Felice
Piazza S. Bernardo (plan V 2/A)
1585–87
Domenico Fontana
Rome's water supply was outstandingly good even
in ancient times. Aqueducts conveyed the water from
the mountains into the city. This supply network de-
generated in the Middle Ages, and only in the 16C
did the popes take the initiative and once again ensure an adequate supply of fresh water. Rome is today still supplied by six aqueducts, four of which were
built on the popes' initiative. In classical times, each
aqueduct ended in a splendid fountain structure, a
castellum or a nymphaeum. The castellum of the more
recent aqueducts is called a mostra. As in ancient
times, each aqueduct supplied one district of the
city. The mostra was the end of the water pipe, and
from it the water was distributed to some small fountains.

Every time the water supply was expanded, and
thus safeguarded, this was of vital importance to the

B18 Acqua Felice

tailed inscription in the broad attica. The papal coat of arms shines forth resplendently on the crowning segmented gable. The coat of arms of the Chigi, who were the pope's family, was placed on top of this. The splendid architecture seems not only to provide an effective scenario for the water, which is guarded by four lions carved from Egyptian originals, but also to celebrate the founder. The whole structure is a monumental show wall oriented on the Piazza S. Bernardo (B32). When compared with the façades of S. Susanna (B30) and S. Maria della Vittoria (B44), this fountain maintains its secular character thanks to its visible links with classical antiquity. The achievement, and thus the person, of this work's patron is placed on display in triumphal fashion. AG

B19 Palazzo del Vaticano: front building (on right)

city of Rome. In these urban planning measures which favoured the welfare of the public, those who placed the individual orders for the work were able to gain the best possible reputation for themselves. If they did not want the fact that they were the donors to be forgotten, it was therefore in their interests to give the fountains an adequate architectural form.

In the early 16C, the popes planned to provide a new water supply on the Quirinal hill by restoring the ancient Aqua Alexandrina, but it was not until the time of Sixtus V that the project was put into effect by building the Acqua Felice. In 1585-87, Matteo da Città and Giovanni Fontana, the two assistants of Domenico Fontana who supervised their efforts, carried out the work on the mostra. The massive and somewhat hulking figure of Moses in the central niche was created by Prospero Antichi and Leonardo Sormani. The flanking reliefs depicting Aaron escorting the Israelites to the water and Joshua leading them dry-footed through the Jordan are the work of G. B. della Porta, Flaminea Vacca and Pier Paolo Olivieri. The fountain is also known as the Moses fountain, owing to the colossal statue of Moses.

The revival of the ancient tradition can also be seen from the architectural design of the fountains. This is particularly clear from a comparison with the ancient predecessor of the Acqua Felice in the Piazza Vittorio Emanuele. The so-called Trofei di Mario were an enormous fountain fed by the water of the Aqua Iulia, which also brought water down from the Alban Hills. The façade of this fountain was subdivided by a central niche and two open arches at the sides. The unmistakable similarity between this and an ancient triumphal arch demonstrates the great significance attached to flowing water. Fontana again adopted this architectural type when designing the first concluding castellum to have been built since the Roman imperial period. Three arches are given a monumental setting by the half columns which are placed triumphally in front of them and support the architrave. As was also the case in the Roman triumphal arches, there is a de-

B19 Palazzo del Vaticano: front building
Città del Vaticano (plan III 1/A)
1585–90
Domenico Fontana

Fontana built a new, three-storeyed residential section for Pope Sixtus V. It was a complex which had four wings, stood on a simple, almost square-shaped ground plan, and had an inner courtyard. The rear side of the western wing forms the eastern conclusion of the Damasus courtyard (H11), through which the residential section is entered. Its main façade with ten axes dominates St Peter's Square from above, like a fortress, and there is no portal or balcony opening the palace up towards the outside. The walls on which the palace is built have been concealed ever since Bernini constructed the colonnades (B80).

As an architectural type, the palace is less exciting. The model of the Palazzo Farnese (H25), the most significant High-Renaissance palace, was adopted here by Fontana in a prominent, free-standing position, and was made block-like, with a smooth wall subdivided (horizontally) only by cornices and rows of windows. Fontana later adopted that shape for the Lateran palace (B21). A feature typical of Fontana in the Palazzo del Vaticano is the contrast between the heavy three-dimensional details and the smooth brickwork surface with its chiaroscuro effect.

Sixtus V also created a new urbanist system: by placing the obelisk outside St Peter's, he gave the basilica, for the first time ever, an axis which ran towards the centre of it and which, in turn, he was taking away from the palace's previous main façade, namely the three-storeyed loggia by Bramante (H11). This he did by placing his residential section, and the new courtyard, between that façade and the Via Alessandrina which divided the Borgo. From then on the palace only looked like a secondary aspect of St Peter's Square, from which access to it was now gained. Aside from the work done in the 19C and 20C, Sixtus V completed the Vatican complex of buildings, but also deprived it of much of its imposing character by obstructing the main axes – something which he incidentally also did in the belvedere courtyard (H6). SG

B20 S. Maria Maggiore: Cappella Sistina and Paolina
Piazza S. Maria Maggiore (plan VI 1/B)
1585–90, 1605–15
Domenico Fontana bzw. Flaminio Ponzio

These two centrally planned structures mirror one another and were built on to the northern and southern aisles of the church. Their interior decorations, typical of late-16C chapels, consist of small-sectioned, overabundant marble incrustation, which renders the overall architectural structure unclear. This is the first prominent example in Rome of Mannerist horror vacui in the interior of a building.

The earlier of the two chapels is that to the north, and in 1585–90 Fontana, who had been commissioned by Pope Sixtus V, designed it as a centrally planned building standing above a Greek cross and having a drum dome resting on pendentives. The lateral arms contain the tombs of Pius V and Sixtus V, each of which, in the manner of a triumphal arch, has a central arcade, an attic, and three axes flanked by columns. The wall surface opposite the entrance wall is not accentuated. The liturgical focal point of this Cappella Sistina is in the very middle of this centrally planned building, as it includes the following items: a confessio containing Arnolfo di Cambio's »Adoration of the Magi«; above this a bronze tabernacle borne by angels; and an altar on the rear side of the tabernacle. That focal point is located elsewhere in the Cappella Paolina (1605–15), in which Ponzio was though in other respects largely imitating the Cappella Sistina. The massive altar, which provides a setting for a much-venerated image of the Virgin Mary, stands against the rear wall of the chapel. This position is more appropriate liturgically, and gives the chapel area a clear orientation, to which the shape of this centrally planned area does not though do justice. AS

B21 Palazzo del Laterano
Piazza S. Giovanni in Laterano 6 (plan VIII 2/A)
1586–89
Domenico Fontana

B21 Palazzo del Laterano

B20 S. Maria Maggiore: Cappella Sistina and Paolina

During his pontificate which only lasted five years, Pope Sixtus V ordered a replacement for the old, tumbledown Lateran palace (C15), a building which had become the model for others of its kind in the Middle Ages. This was shortly after he had already added entire wings and edifices to two other papal palaces by building the Quirinal palace (B15) and the Vatican palace (B19). The new Lateran »palace« was never used as the pope's residence, and today it houses the vicariate of Rome.

This new building should be regarded as part of an ensemble which includes the two framing buildings erected at the same time, namely the Scala Santa and the two-storeyed loggia outside the northern entrance of the basilica. As is typical of late Mannerism, the transitions between them are abrupt, hard and not very organic. The ensemble is also evidently aimed at the unusual slanting view obtainable from the Via S. Giovanni in Laterano. This form of design was also always avoided in the High Renaissance, and the result of it was that what had been a taut series of windows was doubled, and thus became endless and monotonous. Fontana was once again following the Palazzo Farnese as an architectural type (H25; cf. also B15, B19): this applies to the formation of blocks, to the rustic work used to reinforce the edges, and to the smooth wall which is (horizontally) subdivided only by cornice strips and rows of windows. But it is precisely from this comparison that it becomes clear that Fontana did not understand what were Michelangelo's two most important interventions in that palazzo, namely the heightening of the wall at the upper conclusion and the introduction of a far-projecting corbelled cornice. Thus the Lateran palace, by comparison with its prototype, looks strangely cut off at the top. SG

B22 Palazzo Albani, today »del Drago«
Via delle Quattro Fontane (plan V 1/A)
1587–90
Domenico Fontana

This palace immediately next door to S. Carlino was probably built in 1587–90. The question of who the architect was has not been fully clarified. Baglione, the 16C author of vitae, attributes the work to Giacomo della Porta, but his contemporary Bellori gives Domenico Fontana as the architect, and this is also confirmed in other sources. The palace was constantly changing hands: it initially belonged to Cardinal Camillo Massimi who was a friend and patron of Poussin's, then to Cardinal Neri, and finally, after 1725, to Cardinal Albani, who erected a large library which was managed by Winckelmann.

The bashfulness of Fontana, who was not a Roman, is noticeable when one takes a look at the decidedly unadorned palace walls. Among the three storeys with their smooth plastering, the piano nobile is accentuated only by a slight superelevation. The palace has an interesting corner facing the crossing where Via Sistina and Via Quattro Fontane meet. That corner is bevelled off, and it develops a certain splendour, thus contrasting with the other walls which are of plain design. In this way, by corresponding with the other three corners of the crossing, it becomes part of a city square. Three different arcades placed one above the other subdivide the wall three-dimensionally and form the real façade. (The fourth storey standing above the corner like a tower, was added in the 17C.) The topmost arcade, with its intrados suggested by foreshortening, is in imitation of the façade of the Palazzo Barberini (B45) and dates from the mid-17C.

As is usual in 16C urban palaces, the cortile is the more splendid feature. But there is a lack of energy in the effect produced by the articulation of its two loggias standing one above the other, which were originally open, but were closed up in the mid-18C. PZ

B22 Palazzo Albani, today »del Drago«

B23 Palazzo Aldobrandini-Chigi

B23 Palazzo Aldobrandini-Chigi
Via del Corso, Piazza Colonna (plan IV 2/A)
begun 1588
Giacomo della Porta

This palace at the corner of Via del Corso and Piazza Colonna has often changed hands. Pietro Aldobrandini, the first member of a certain Florentine family to make a career for himself, acquired the plot of land at the column commemorating Marcus Aurelius. But no building work was done until 1588, the year in which Fabrizio Fossano took over the plot. It is thanks to him that Giacomo della Porta was persuaded to build the palace; innovative work could be expected from the architect of the Il Gesù façade (B1).

Della Porta designed, and probably also built, the oldest part of the palace: the wing on the Via del Corso. The façade's three-storeyed structure (the attic storey was not added until the late 17C) accentuates the tall piano nobile with its integrated mezzanine. At that time the wall remained to a very large extent unsubdivided and was plastered evenly. This places the building still within the Renaissance tradition, particularly that of the Palazzo Farnese (H25). On the other hand, a tremendously new step was also being taken because della Porta was placing the window axes in a rhythmical arrangement: »The windows conglomerate towards the centre in an animated movement, whereas the outer windows, by their isolated location, mark the tranquil point of departure.« (Wölfflin). This anticipated an influential stylistic element of the Baroque (cf. also B14).

70 years later, in contrast to this, the architect Felice della Greca, working on the façade facing the Piazza Colonna, decided to make the axes coolly and almost rigidly symmetrical. But this too probably results from the tradition of hardly rhythmizing anything except the lateral façades (cf. e. g. Palazzo Maffei).

The inner courtyard by della Greca shows a surprising abundance of shapes. An aerily decorated piano nobile almost hovers – only the windows rest on the Doric entablature – above a solid pillared arcature (with a loggia) in the tabularium motif (cf. A9). The approach adopted for the corner is unfortunately unsuccessful. PZ

B24 Palazzo Altemps

B24 Palazzo Altemps
Via S. Appolinare 8 (plan IV 1/A)
c. 1480, c. 1590
unknown, Martino Longhi

This palace owes its creation under Girolamo Riario, the nephew of Pope Sixtus IV, to an appeal issued by the Pope to the effect that the monumental element in the reawakening Eternal City should be intensified. Some typical features – such as the still considerable distance between the windows, and the plain framing work – from the period of the building's construction have been preserved, but its present appearance was perhaps still more strongly shaped by the radical conversion and expansion work which the Altemps commissioned Martino Longhi to carry out in the late 16C.

The three storeys of the main façade, which has seven axes and stands in the Via S. Apollinare, are separated by surrounding cornice ribbons, the lower of which is more elaborate, as it is moulded and has a frieze. The architraves of the windows in the piano nobile are decorated with a curry-comb pattern and delicate egg-and-dart moulding, two elements of a Renaissance repertory of shapes which was oriented on the ancient classical language of shapes. The windows in the other storeys only have flat frames. The surface looks very two-dimensional, quite in the style of the quattrocento, and the entablature also projects only a very little way. The rough rustication of the edges is of a different character and was added in the 16C, being included in the framework of the round-arched central portal with its framing pilasters. This made the palace typologically dependent on the Palazzo Farnese (H25).

The Piazza S. Apollinare is enclosed by two façades of this palace. They display, on their ground floors, features typical of 16C palace architecture and adopted from ancient Roman prototypes: these are the openings for shops, with a mezzanine. The gallery on top of the building, one and a half storeys tall, is another 16C addition, with round-arched openings between the double pilasters, and decorative obelisks.

B25 Palazzo Zuccari
Via Gregoriana 28/Piazza Trinità dei Monti 14
(plan II 1/E)
1590–1603
Federico Zuccari

The Mannerist buildings in Rome usually look stiff, and are in any event not as ornate and imaginative as in Northern Italy. The most prominent exception to this is the Palazzo Zuccari. It is in a district which, in ancient times, contained the villa and gardens of Lucullus, the Roman epicure and military leader. Gregory XIII and Sixtus V developed this district again for the first time since ancient times by building the Via Gregoriana and Via Sistina. Zuccari, who had probably gained a liking for the district when he was painting the decorations in SS. Trinità dei Monti (H44), was able in 1590 to acquire a plot of land in the spandrel between the two streets. This tripartite ensemble suffered from numerous later conversions.

The studio is in the four-storeyed head section of the ensemble. The view on to the Piazza di SS. Trinità dei Monti is today partially blocked by the portico which Juvarra added in 1711 for Casimira, the ex-queen of Poland who was living in the building at that time. The original façade consists of two units which are equal in height, are located one above the other, and each have two storeys and three axes. The central axis is wider, thus forming a rhythmic bay, but also recedes slightly. This creates continuous vertical paths which emphasize the narrow, tall, tower-like impression. The corners are of differing design in the two units: below there are columns placed diagonally in the otherwise plain façade, while in the upper unit the corners are bevelled off and hollowed out. Thereby emptiness and the opposite of load is placed on top of the support. A Mannerist spirit expresses itself

B25 Palazzo Zuccari

in the following features: the formation of vertical
paths on the wall; the way in which structural laws are
called into question; the use of few isolated three-dimensional elements (the columns); and the formation
of two equally strong units one above the other, neither of which can be the main section.

The two-storeyed residential section, which is attached at the rear and was originally only half as tall,
is of less interest. Four pilasters subdivide the five
axes into two wings and a wider central section.

The rearmost section originally only had one storey
and was a garden wall which was itself structured in
three parts. Now its centre is narrower, but at the
same time more prominent, particularly from the design point of view. This, the most famous section, is
also the most freely designed: it is the »bizarre« section. Three ghost masks, which adorn the garden gate
and two »windows«, are each composed of anthro-
morphic and architectural sections merged together,
examples being eyebrows as a gable in the entablature of the gate, and split gables as hats for the masks
at the windows. The masks are depicted with less
tension than in Michelangelo's Porta Pia (H43), the
archetype for this design, and are meant as a joke.
These untamed beings were regarded as suitable for
gardens. A similarly shaped gate – a hell gate – is to
be found in Zuccari's illustration of the *Divine Comedy*.
God created the gate in that poem, and the artist here
worked like a creator. The best-known comparable
example, which is a little older, is the mouth-like gate
in the garden of the Vicino Orsioni in Bomarzo, 50 km
north of Rome.

In the early 19C, this house, which Zuccari intended should be a residence for poor artists after he had
died, actually did become a home for painters of the
German Nazarene school. It finally became the property of H. Hertz, an art lover who made it and her library available for the purpose of founding the German Institute for Italian Art History in Rome. SG

B26 S. Andrea della Valle
Corso Vittorio Emanuele II (plan IV 1/B)
1591–1666
Francesco Grimaldi, Giacomo della Porta, Carlo
Maderno, Carlo Rainaldi, Carlo Fontana

Only a few years after the imposing Jesuit church of
Il Gesù (B1) had been completed, the competing, but
not nearly so popular, Theatine order planned a corresponding new church of considerable size. Grimaldi,
the order's architect, presented some initial plans even
before a benefactor had been found for this ambitious
building project. Cardinal Alfonso Gesualdo agreed in
1588 to finance the construction work and wanted his
architect della Porta to design the building, but all he
achieved was that della Porta revised Grimaldi's plans.
It was in accordance with this design that in 1591, after a small church had been torn down, work was begun on the foundations of the first two bays of the
nave. By 1599, they and their side chapels had been

B26 S. Andrea della Valle

completed and vaulted. At this time the Theatines
were proceeding with the construction work on credit,
as Cardinal Gesualdo's payments were coming to a
standstill. In 1600, Gesualdo ordered designs to be
drawn up for the façade which faced the Via Papalis
and was to be placed out in front of the two bays,
completed by then, of the nave of the church. But
when he died in 1603, he only bequeathed an extremely small sum of money to the highly indebted
Theatine order, and this meant that there could be no
possibility of completing the torso of the church. After
construction work had been interrupted for several
years, a new benefactor, Alessandro Peretti, Cardinal
Montalto, and his architect Maderno resumed it in
1608. Maderno completed the nave, the transept
and the choir to plans which had probably been altered, and he designed the dome and presented
plans for a façade. Rainaldi and Fontana completed
the church façade in 1662–66, with some further
modifications.

The interior of S. Andrea is an aisleless church with
side chapels, a transept, a domed crossing and a
choir, and thus basically follows the scheme of Il Gesù (B1), but the broader proportions of the Jesuit
building have been abandoned in favour of a taller
room. Other differences are: the subdivision of the
room; the proportion to one another of arcade, pilaster and entablature; and the expressive significance
of the chapels to the room as a whole. Thus, wide
and tall arcades alternate with layered pilasters. Not
only the coretti, which in Il Gesù are to be found
above the arcades, but also the double pilasters

which, in that prototype, subdivide the walls of the nave, have disappeared. The relatively self-contained wall of the nave of Il Gesù has thus given way to arcades which do not leave space for much wall surface. The opening and widening of the nave are accentuated, rather than the seclusion of the single space. The entablature, which in the Il Gesù church runs smoothly all the way across, is here projecting above the pilasters. Thus, in the vertical extension, a relationship is created between layered pilasters and wall arches in the vault area, and in this way a vertical movement which has its effect on the entire structure comes into being. The taller spatial effect, already planned for in the spatial proportions, is in this way further enhanced. Finally, the side chapels, contrary to what is the case in Il Gesù, are very bright and, due to the wide arcade openings, contribute considerably to the lighting and spatial effect of the nave of the church. The unity and balance of the area were predominant in Il Gesù, whereas, in S. Andrea, Baroque tendencies are observable in the verticalizing and in the resolution of the wall into openings. This is not the least reason why contemporaries generally regarded S. Andrea della Valle as a corrected version of Il Gesù.

The façade was built from 1661 onwards, is a variation on plans by Maderno, and reflects the spirit of the later Baroque. Rainaldi, whose design was executed by Fontana in a smoothened, classicizing version, made the column the leitmotiv of the façade. Two layers of domed half and three-quarter columns are placed in front of a rear wall layer which is subdivided by pilasters and is visible only in the outer axes of the ground floor. These columns stand in small recesses and are outlined by narrow areas of shade. Four pairs of double columns in each of the storeys form the expressive framework of the façade. The entablature is projecting above each of the pairs, standing on separate plinths, of columns, and it forms in its turn the base for the pair above. The columns at the sides of the portal and of the central window constitute the front layer, and support an appropriately projecting entablature. Even the projections of the gable correspond to the position of the double columns. The consistency seen in the vertical development is probably attributable to Fontana's alterations, but the idea of choosing columns as the leitmotiv of the façade design may be regarded as a trait of Rainaldi.

The dome by Maderno also deserves attention. Its drum is taller in relation to its cupola, and the window areas larger in relation to the wall, than is the case with the dome of St Peter's. Maderno's dome may be reckoned among the finest in Rome. AS

Bibliography: H. Hibbard, »The early history of Sant'Andrea della Valle«, *Art Bulletin*, 41, 1961, p. 289.

B27 S. Salvatore in Lauro
Piazza S. Salvatore in Lauro (plan IV 1/A)
1592–98
Ottavio Mascherino

The church, together with its annexes (but not including the early-Renaissance courtyard, F18), burned down in 1591. It became necessary to rebuild it. The façade dating from 1862 is banal, but the interior is energetic and noteworthy. The dome, which had always been planned for, was not built until 1727–36.

The architectural type is that of Il Gesù (B1): it is a barrel-vaulted homogeneous room, is flanked on each side by three chapels, has a transept which is wider and higher than the chapels but hardly any deeper than them, and the crossing is filled with light. The nave and crossing are intended to look closely linked. The architectural order is entirely different from Il Gesù, where the structure is shaped by pilasters and the entablature which runs evenly and continuously across, whereas here there are full, twin columns – true monuments –, whose moulded entablature continues into weighty arches in the vault. In Rome, the great prototype, namely the exterior of St Peter's (H31), was responsible for the fact that most walls were subdivided by pilasters until the mid-17C (but cf. also B5). Columns, for example those in Palladio's works, were more common in Northern Italy, where Mascherino came from. But Palladio only used half columns, normally not double, not moulded and without arches. Only in the ancient Roman period was Mascherino able to find such expressive weightiness and free-standing full columns or columns standing out in front. Examples are the Diocletian thermal baths (cf. A46, H42), but they too are not double. Michelangelo, in the dome of St Peter's (H31), had been the first to bunch the columns and add arches. Mascherino transferred the pathos of that dome to the church interior, using these means to render it rhythmic throughout and give it the united appearance of a single backdrop. Not until the High Baroque, in S. Maria in Campitelli (B91), is such a forest of columns found again. In High Baroque, the core area seems to breathe in and out, whereas in Mascherino's work it still has exterior limits. SG

B 27 S. Salvatore in Lauro

B28 S. Giacomo degli Incurabili

B28 S. Giacomo degli Incurabili
Via del Corso 499 (plan I 2/D–3/D)
1592–1600
Francesco da Volterra, Carlo Maderno

S. Giacomo degli Incurabili marks a stage in the development of the tradition, founded by Peruzzi and continued by Vignola, of the Roman oval building. The church is part of the complex of the hospice for incurable patients (incurabili). In 1590 Francesco da Volterra was commissioned to design the new building, and Carlo Maderno completed it.

The two-storeyed pilastered façade, which is tied into the street alignment, is a show wall placed out in front and does not render discernible the structure of the church interior. The latter opens up into a large oval domed room which is longitudinally oriented and is set inside a series of square-shaped chapels. The choir and entrance vestibule occupy the short sides of the interior. A Corinthian order of pilasters subdivides the walls and is concluded by a rail-like entablature which redescribes the oval. The long walls of the oval are conceived as monumental interior façades, and are placed in a setting of tripartite triumphal arches enclosed by narrow wall bays. By means of this triumphal, dignified motif, which had previously been a topic for exterior structures, the church interior is ennobled in a new and previously unknown way. The large arcades which are placed at right angles and lead to the choir and vestibule are a secondary motif when compared with the monumental show walls, and mark a sharp break. These arcades do not form a frontal arcade, are slightly set back, make the walls of the oval area appear to be moved forward by one layer, and thus emphasize the shell-like character of those walls. Thus the façade walls, which are monumentalized in the manner of a triumphal arch, are once again emphasized. In adopting Vignola's ideas and combining them with the motif of the triumphal-arch wall, Volterra was, in S. Giacomo degli Incurabili, creating a monumental oval building which attained far-reaching significance in 17C church architecture. EJ

B29 S. Giuseppe dei Falegnami
Via Tulliano (plan V 1/B)
1597–1602
Giovanni Battista Montano

Montano designed, for the fraternity of the joiners (falegnami), a church building which is noteworthy mostly for its Mannerist façade that was completed in 1602. It has three axes, two storeys and is topped by a triangular gable. A columned aedicule marks the portal and characterizes the centre of the façade, while the lateral axes on the ground floor are pilastered bays with rectangular panels. The upper storey, which is not tall, is designed in whimsical contrast to the ground floor: the aedicules are now to be found in the lateral axes. They are flanked on both sides by scrolls, and present themselves as self-contained shapes independent of the remaining articulation. This provides the lateral axes of the façade with a highly individual independence. This effect is intensified by the façade's »empty« centre. Above the entrance aedicule there are two vigorous pilasters which support an entablature projecting above them, but are topped not by an architectural gable, but by a decoratively winding shape. This leap from the architectural to the decorative within an architectural motif gives an impression of something unfinished. The Ionic capitals of

B29 S. Giuseppe dei Falegnami

the upper storey are turned through 90 degrees and display the side rather than the front of a scroll. They should also be thought of as being playful, decorative items. Montano was a member of the joiners' fraternity and the author of *Scielta d. varii tempietti antichi*, Rome 1624, a collection of significance to 17C architecture. He is here using a language of shapes which has no parallels in Roman Mannerism, but is reminiscent of furniture design and resembles the architectural shapes in his book. AS

B30 S. Susanna
Via XX Settembre 14 (plan V 2/A)
1597–1603
Carlo Maderno

This, one of Rome's oldest churches, was built in the 3C on the site of the villa of Pope Caius (282-96), the saint's uncle. In 796 it was replaced by a new building which Sixtus IV, in 1475, ordered to be restored. Cardinal Rusticucci had it radically redesigned from 1593 onwards, initially under the supervision of Domenico Fontana. After Fontana's move to Naples, the construction of the church was in the hands of Carlo Maderno, and it is his first work.

The typology of the façade follows that of Il Gesù (B1), but is, by comparison, more upright, less bull-necked and less uncheerful. It is another cross-section façade (showing that the interior is a basilica), and has two storeys and a linking scroll which is again taller. But the design is entirely new. The chief topic is

B30 S. Susanna

the crescendo which, axis by axis and with a tremendous simplicity, develops towards the centre: pilaster, half column and three-quarter column, each of them assigned to a bay, follow in succession; their contours stand out strongly against the shade of the narrow niche into which Maderno placed them. The best assistance in interpreting the crescendo is the entablature with its threefold graduation. The width of each bay increases towards the centre, with the wall sections being more and more reduced and supplanted by niches containing sculptures, so that the bays are structured more richly and deeply. The greatly increased three-dimensionality signifies a break in style as against the stiff, severe, two-dimensional approach which previously was generally to be found, one example being Il Gesù. At the same time, the bays are not interlinked and hemmed in (except for the subordinated outer bay). Instead they stand freely and relaxedly side by side, and each consists of two supports connected by a section of entablature. This form of design is typical of Maderno's works and is the sign of a magnificent new spirit of simplicity. The centre is additionally emphasized in that the columns come together at the sides of it and are doubled, whereas previously supports were distributed evenly across the façade. In order to prevent the supports from making another doubled impression at the transition between the central and outer bays, the outer bay had to be moved closer to the second bay and lose part of its pilaster.

Maderno adopted the same approach in the design of the façade as Mascherino had in the interior (B27): he based himself on the Il Gesù type, but the three-dimensionality and pathos were immensely intensified. The columns in this façade, and its relief work, are precursors of the High Baroque. They are themselves early Baroque, because the façade was still being interpreted as a plane.

The dynamic movement found in the façade was framed by the upper conclusion which takes the shape of a gable that is as plain as possible. This was why Wölfflin thought that the façade combined »energy and moderation«, and this description might be continued: three-dimensionality and two-dimensionality, dynamism and tranquility, pathos and severity. What is more, by means of the motif – new in church architecture – of the balustrade, Maderno was linking the façade to the adjoining building. This inclusion of satellite buildings within the design was a new feature (with the possible exception of S. Giorgio Maggiore in Venice). It became a central device in the design of Baroque city squares (one example is B79). The year S. Susanna was completed, Maderno became the architect in charge of St Peter's (B34). It had evidently already been sensed that he had overcome the rigid Counter-Reformation and introduced the Baroque.

The interior of the Carolingian basilica was from 1593 onwards converted and then followed the example of Il Gesù in that it had a nave and no aisles, but did have side chapels. The crypt is typical of Carolingian churches (C18, C26). Maderno redesigned it as a Baroque confessio, and it is one of the first examples of that cult of martyrdom which arose in the wake of the Counter-Reformation. The shape selected by Maderno was an oval rotunda with a flattened dome. The rotunda is linked to the outside by a central, stepped, merely visual well, and also by two curving stairwells which can be walked on. Maderno evidently adopted the oval or ellipsoid spatial shape from Vignola's pupil Daniele da Volterra, whose S. Giacomo degli Incurabili he continued (B28). But the type of innovation typical of Maderno is once again seen: for him, the area has two focal points, namely the saint's altar and the slab of the cardinal's tomb. In 1604, for the first time in post-classical literature, the elliptical shape was described by Kepler as being determined by the fact that there are two focal points. Thus, here we find the first occasion on which that shape was so simply and clearly motivated. SG

Bibliography: B. Apolloni Ghetti, *Santa Susanna*, Rome, 1965.

B31 Palazzo Mattei di Giove
Via Caetani 32 (plan IV 2/B)
1598–1617
Carlo Maderno

Beginning in 1598, Maderno built the city palace of Asdrubale Mattei, Duke of Giove, at the corner of Via Caetani (nine axes) and Via dei Funari (eleven axes).

The palace is a simple but compact building following in the type of the Palazzo Farnese (H25): it is block-like, with a smooth wall articulated (horizontally) only by cornice strips and rows of windows. Two more richly decorated features are the windows of the piano nobile, and the projecting corbelled entablature with components of the Mattei's coat of arms. The pride of this three-winged complex is the courtyard with long sides which are closed to form a wall, and short sides which open up into a row of three arches that are lent shape by a tabularium motif (cf. A9). The courtyard, particularly on its long sides, is overabundantly adorned with decorative figures (part of Marchese Mattei's collection of antiques). Thus Maderno adopted the Mannerist architectural type of the façade serving as a »museum«, but what was typical of his art was that he provided this type with a new tautness and a new depth of relief (cf. the similar case of the façade of S. Susanna, B30). This is demonstrated by the example of the short sides: Maderno varied from the tabularium by selecting pilasters as supports between the arcades, because the flatness of the pilasters contrasts better with the three-dimensionality of the busts; he placed the busts diagonally into the openings, so that spatial depth becomes perceptible. United wall as opposed to spatial depth, and flat, hard architectural shapes as opposed to the round shapes of the sculptures: these are the contrasts from which Maderno develops fascinating tensions. SG

B31 Palazzo Mattei di Giove

B32 S. Bernardo alle Terme
Piazza S. Bernardo (plan V 2/A)
c. 1600

In c. 1600, the Cistercian church of S. Bernardo was, by order of Caterina Nobili Sforza, established in the westernmost of the round structures belonging to the buildings surrounding the Diocletian thermal baths (A46). The structure and its vault had survived since ancient times, and all that was required was a radical reworking and redesign of the spatial shell.

In the exterior, the massive ancient cylinder still produces its full effect, and an articulated portal, faintly reminiscent of triumphal arches, was placed in front of it for show. The cylinder is topped by a projecting final cornice, above which there is a polygonal wall superstructure whose sides curve slightly inwards. This superstructure renders the inner vaulting of the building invisible from the outside. It is therefore a surprise to find that the interior is a circular rotunda 22 m in diameter, with a semicircular dome as its vault. As with the Pantheon (A31), whose architectural type this building follows on a small scale, the opening in the apex of the dome is the only source of light for the interior. Originally itself open, it is today closed by a modern structure. The redesign of the lower part of the interior has a single-storeyed articulation, with flat pilasters and statue niches between them. Here, the transverse axis was accentuated and the wall rhythmized by placing altar niches at the sides and by layering the pilasters and placing flat recesses behind

some of them. The dome was articulated by stucco-work coffering, making the building resemble the Pantheon even more. But its dimensions were only about half the size, so that, thanks to the single-storey articulation, success was achieved in modernizing the ancient building while still giving it classical forms.
DH

B33 Villa Aldobrandini, Frascati

Frascati, Piazza Roma (plan G2 4/B)
1601–11
Giacomo della Porta, Carlo Maderno and others

In 1601–11, Pietro Aldobrandini, a nephew of Pope Clement VIII, ordered an existing 16C villa to be converted into what, for Frascati in the 17C, was an exemplary structure (to plans by Giacomo della Porta, and from 1602 onwards by Carlo Maderno). Apart from the residential complex, the villa comprises some extensive gardens, which are subject to a strictly subdividing system of axes. The transverse axis is formed firstly by the residential structure which is conceived as a palazzo, and secondly by three terraces which are directly connected to that structure and are interlinked by staircases and ramps. The lengthwise axis, on the other hand, starts from the Frascati town square, continues in a steeply and axially ascending approach road, crosses the centre of the terraces and palazzo and, behind the palazzo, proceeds up the hill in various waterworks.

That façade of the palazzo which faces the town is rather restrained and derives its particular charm solely from the outline of the broken gable. But the façade towards the garden, on the side where the entrance originally was, has a more playful and intimate central section which projects and contains loggias and cornices. This tendency culminates in the ingenious gardens and fountains which are allusively enriched by programmes of sculptures. The type of villa with the palace structure as the point of departure for extensive gardens clearly traces back to models as the Villa d'Este in Tivoli (H33); on the other hand it paved the way for many 17C villas in Frascati. DH

B33 Villa Aldobrandini, Frascati

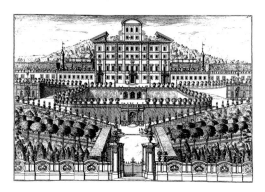

B34 St Peter's: façade

B34 St Peter's: nave and façade

Piazza di S. Pietro (plan III 1/A)
1606–26
Carlo Maderno

When Giacomo della Porta, Michelangelo's successor in the position of the architect of St Peter's (cf. H31), died in 1602, he left the new church of St Peter's largely complete. The exterior was complete except for two sections: the eastern arm of this centrally planned building, and the building's façade which is oriented towards the city (St Peter's is oriented towards the west). A wall temporarily separated this new building from the still existing nave of the Constantine basilica. After being elected in 1605, Pope Paul V pushed ahead with the further building work on St Peter's. He ordered the remains of Old St Peter's to be torn down, but without having a definite plan for the eastern conclusion of the new structure. Various drafts submitted by architects in a competition show that it was initially still an open question whether St Peter's was to be completed as a centrally planned or as a longitudinal building. The only requirement was that the building should have a sacristy, a canons' choir, and a benediction loggia in the façade – Michelangelo had not included these areas in his building. There was probably never any doubt that Maderno, who had been the architect of St Peter's since 1603, was to complete the building. Maderno drew up several plans, which themselves fluctuated between centralizing approaches and designs for a longitudinal section, but all the plans were marked by the endeavour to retain Michelangelo's structure as far as possible.

A wooden model was made of one of the designs, and in 1607 Paul V ruled that its façade was to be built. When the foundation stone for the façade was laid, it had thereby been finally decided that a nave was to be added to Michelangelo's structure. In making this decision, Paul V was ignoring numerous critics of the plan for a nave who were concerned about the unique artistic conception of Michelangelo's centrally planned building, and particularly about the effect produced by the dome.

After some foundations which had already been begun had been torn down again, work on the nave was commenced in 1609 to plans by Maderno, and completed by 1616 (consecrated in 1626). The façade was finished by 1612. In the same year, Paul V ordered that bell towers be built, with the result that the façade was widened by one axis for each bell tower. In 1617, the northern tower was completed up to the height of the façade. The southern campanile was begun in 1618, and after some difficulties with the foundation works it was in 1621 also finished up to the height of the façade. The single-storeyed tower superstructures planned by Maderno were never built. In 1637, Pope Urban VIII commissioned Gianlorenzo Bernini to complete the towers to his own plans. But the foundation of the southern tower proved too weak for Bernini's three-storeyed tower superstructure, so that the torso had to be pulled down again in 1646. This mishap was one of the greatest upsets in Bernini's career.

The appearance of Maderno's façade today is, to its disadvantage, determined by the incomplete bell towers. The wide stumps framed with pilasters lack their superstructures, and thus make the façade appear too wide and settled, as well as disturbing the way in which the subdividing elements are carefully designed to intensify as they approach the central axis. Maderno's original façade (the tower substructures must be thought of as not being there) is a frontage which has seven axes, is subdivided by colossal pilasters and columns, and is concluded by a wide attic. Three layers, consisting of pilasters, half columns and three-quarter columns, are placed one in front of the other, extending from the outer axes towards the middle, and culminate in the temple-frontage motif which is at the centre of the façade and is formed by four three-quarter columns with a triangular gable. A similar intensification is discernible in Maderno's façade of S. Susanna (B30). But today the temple frontage is »sinking« amidst the transverse bare shape of the façade. The colossal architectural order visually combines two storeys – the porch on the ground floor and the benediction loggia on the upper storey.

In designing the façade, Maderno was in several respects reverting to Michelangelo's ideas. Firstly, Michelangelo's use of colossal pilasters and a wide attic in order to subdivide the entire structure is adopted anew. Michelangelo's exterior articulation is copied in Maderno's façade right down to the details of the windows and niches. The temple-frontage motif also adopts one of Michelangelo's plans for the façade of St Peter's. Secondly, Maderno took over the leitmotiv of the façade of the conservators' palace (H30) by employing inserted columns to accentuate the three main entrances and by using colossal columns in combination with this small architectural order. Although Maderno's façade has often been criticized for being too wide, it does successfully resolve the dilemma of how to make a dignified and lavish im-

B35 Villa (Casino) Borghese

pression without conflicting too much with Michelangelo's exterior design, in particular with the dome.

The basilican nave of the church reveals Maderno's restrained and empathetic spirit. The dimensions and articulation of the nave, two aisles, and flanking chapels, are oriented on the western structure by Michelangelo. In his design for the nave, Maderno adopted that succession of pilastered bays and round-arched openings (rhythmic bay) which was already sketched out in the arms of the transept, and thus achieved a formally uninterrupted link between the newly built nave and the existing structure. But Maderno also seems to have been endeavouring to mark the original shape of the centrally planned building and to set his attached structure off against it. The barrel of the nave and its walls are all recessed at the point at which the longitudinal section joins Michelangelo's centrally planned building. Maderno had originally emphasized this borderline still more strongly by lowering the floor and by changing the building materials. The lighting in his nave is also different: six windows in the barrel provide light, while the vault remains closed in the area of Michelangelo's centrally planned building. In the aisles, Maderno resolved the problematical lighting situation by placing a row of domes whose lanterns give sufficient light. The decoration of the nave was converted under Innocent X to designs by Bernini. AS

Bibliography: H. Hibbard, *Maderno*, London, 1971.

B35 Villa (Casino) Borghese
Piazzale del Museo Borghese (plan II 1/D–2/D)
1608–13
Flaminio Ponzio

Cardinal Scipione Borghese, a nephew of Paul V, ordered a palazzo suburbano (cf. B4 for this architectural type) to be built for him from 1608 onwards above the spurs of the Pincio Hill amidst extensive parks. The chief purpose of the palazzo was to house his collection of ancient and contemporary sculptures. The design is by Flaminio Ponzio.

This symmetrically designed building consists of various structures whose independence is particularly noticeable in the roofing. The central area of the many-shaped main façade opens up into a pillared loggia which is surrounded by side wings extending through two storeys. The block, set far back, of the central structure rises above this, and is topped by two tower superstructures which particularly dominate the rear façade. Almost the entire building is covered still in Mannerist style with rich sculptured decorations which are mainly of ancient provenance. Only some of them survive today.

What is characteristic of the architecture of the Casino, in contrast to that of some clearly structured earlier Renaissance villas, is its composition made up of different structures. The forms of all these structures are, thanks to their articulation, recognizably independent, and it is only when they are all taken together that they result in a conglomerate which is harmonized within itself in a complex way and, owing to its contrasts, is rich in tension. The Casino clearly relates to the nearby Villa Medici (B4), not only in the use of the villa as a type – and here, the loggia inserted between two lateral wings is a form which ultimately goes back to such Renaissance villas as the Villa Farnesina (H8) –, but also in the employment of the two characteristic tower superstructures. But by comparison with the Villa Medici (B4), the structure of the Casino, a more recent building, is more energetically articulated throughout. DH

B36 S. Francesca Romana
Piazza S. Francesca Romana (plan V 1/B)
1608–15
Carlo Lombardi

The original church (S. Maria Antiqua) was built by Pope Paul I in the 8C on the site of an ancient double temple from the period of Hadrian. About 100 years later it was replaced by a new building (S. Maria Nuova). The apse, transept and campanile were rebuilt in 1161, and these components still survive today. The apse mosaic probably also dates from that period. The charitable Francesca de Ponziani (known as Romana) was buried in the church in 1440. She was canonized in 1608 and gave the building its new name. The main longitudinal section and the façade were re-built between 1608 and 1615 by Carlo Lombardi (1554–1620) from Arezzo.

B36 S. Francesca Romana

The chief feature of interest is the façade, which consists of two layers one in front of the other. The rear layer is the customary Roman Renaissance façade having three axes in the lower storey and only one axis in the upper, with scrolls linking the two storeys. Large pillared arcades open the ground floor up into a triumphal vestibule. Upon this rear layer, a second layer is placed, embodying another type of façade: a large aedicule motif frames the entire central axis, with two double pilasters standing on high pedestals, and a massive triangular gable. Lombardi had already, in the façade of S. Prisca (C23), employed an aedicule of this type, again with these slender proportions which do not exactly accord with the ideal of gravitas romana. Now he was combining it with a second aedicule in the rear layer. This method is known as »Palladian« because it was in 1576, in S. Giorgio Maggiore in Venice, that Palladio, for the first time ever, placed two façades one behind the other, thus combining them into a composite façade scheme. Lombardi adopted the Palladian style and notably synthesized it with the Roman style. PZ

B37 S. Sebastiano fuori le Mura
Via Appia Antica 136 (plan G2 3/B and plan VIII 2/C)
1609–13
Flaminio Ponzio

This is one of Rome's seven pilgrimage churches. It was built during the rule of Emperor Constantine, in the midst of the most distinguished Christian catacombs in Rome (entrance to the right of the portico). The relics of St Peter and St Paul are said to have been brought here during the troubles which arose under Decius. This is the origin of the church's old name of »Basilica Apostolorum«. Its present name refers to the tomb of St Sebastian. It was built as a basilica (one nave, two aisles), with one peculiarity in that weighty pillared arcades separated the nave and aisles and the aisles were routed around the choir. This is an early example of an ambulatory, and is typical of cemeterial basilicas (cf. p. 69, A54, C13). Roman burial houses (subterranean), residential houses (in the terrain, but above the ground) and the Constantine basilica were excavated in the early 20C.

Scipio Borghese placed the order for the Baroque conversion. Ponzio retained only the nave (and not the aisles), but this is is concealed by the façade structure. Three arcades above very thin double columns open up into a portico on the ground floor. Above this, there is a closed, palatial-looking storey in which the double columns are taken up in the form of pilaster strips. The conclusion is an energetic triangular gable which runs across the whole frontage and has the Borghese coat of arms. The »Chiesa in Palazzo«, the façade that included elements from both church and palace architecture, was invented in this façade (cf. the later B43). Here it is probably something like a reformulation of that interplay between open portico and closed-up wall which is found quite frequently in medieval façades (e.g. C2, C28). Despite the delicacy of the components, the structure is clear and is rich in tension.

The interior space is more rigid and more closely related to the contemporary late-Mannerist style. It is conceived as a row of triumphal-arch motifs. SG

B38 Palazzo Pallavicini-Rospigliosi
Via XXIV Maggio 43 (plan V 1/A–1/B)
1611–16
Flaminio Ponzio, Carlo Maderno (gardens: Giovanni Vasanzio)
The last still-standing remains of the Constantine thermal baths had to be abandoned in favour of the palace and gardens for whose construction Cardinal Scipione Borghese placed the order. The core structure was a three-winged portico made up of three tiers, each consisting of three pillared arcades in front of which double pilasters were placed. Its northern wing led to the terraced garden with the Casino dell'Aurora. It was probably only the middle (eastern) wing that had two additional, not very deep storeys with mezzanines, with the window axes of those storeys corresponding vertically to the arcades. The southern wing today takes the shape of a self-contained cube and is probably the product of an initial, asymmetrical extension. The arcades are closed here, and the windows are placed closer together and more numerous. A splendid Baroque balcony stands on the cube. This nucleus, particularly the cube, determined the vocabulary employed when another wing, which formed a U-shaped courtyard, was added in the south. That wing was built under Cardinal Mazarin, who was in search of a headquarters for the French embassy. It was not until 1704 that the Pallavicini-Rospigliosi family placed the order for yet another wing which was attached to the western side of the previous one. In this way a very asymmetrical, unhomogeneous complex came into being,

From 1611 onwards, Vasanzio designed the early-Baroque gardens and, in their north-eastern section, the Casino dell'Aurora, whose carpet-like, overabundant decorations are an example of Mannerist horror vacui. Guido Reni painted his famous ceiling fresco in the Casino in 1614.

B37 S. Sebastiano fuori le Mura

B38 Palazzo Pallavicini-Rospigliosi

B39 S. Carlo ai Catinari
Piazza B. Cairoli (plan IV 1/B)
1612–50
Rosato Rosati, Giovanni Battista Soria
S. Carlo ai Catinari is one of the three churches in Rome (B40 and B52) to be dedicated to Charles Borromeo, who was canonized in 1610. This church of the Barnabite order was built between 1612 and 1620 to designs by Rosati the architect. The choir, with its apse and the rooms behind it, was only added from 1638 onwards, after Rosati's death. The interior follows the scheme of a Greek cross with an elongated longitudinal axis and a drum dome above its spacious crossing. Chapels are fitted into the angles of the cross-arms (cf. also B107).

It is notable that, in S. Carlo, Rosati does not adopt the architectural type – widespread in Counter-Reformation religious orders – of an aisleless church with chapels (Il Gesù, B1), but seeks to combine it with a centrally planned Renaissance building, specifically a Greek cross. The elongation of the cross in the longitudinal direction clearly orients the interior towards the altar. The liturgically unfavourable spatial shape of a Greek cross, in which all four directions are equally strongly marked, is thus modified in favour of a more strongly emphasized longitudinal axis.
In Il Gesù, a barrel-vaulted space is allocated to the congregation area and the dome is assigned to the liturgical centre, whereas in S. Carlo the domed crossing marks the congregation area. Thus this concept of an architectural synthesis of a centrally planned and a longitudinal building is, in the final analysis, not functional.

The façade by Soria (1635–38) has five axes on both its storeys, and the three central axes project like a risalto and are topped by a triangular gable. AS

B40 SS. Ambrogio e Carlo al Corso
Via del Corso 437 (plan IV 2/A)
1612–84
Onorio and Martino Longhi, Pietro da Cortona and others

On the site of an oratory dedicated to Ambrosius, the national saint of Milano, a new building was erected on the instructions of the fraternity of the Lombards, being their national church. It was also dedicated to Charles Borromeo, who had just recently been canonized. Onorio Longhi began the construction work in 1612, and after his death in 1619 it was continued by his son Martino Longhi the Younger. After an interruption, Pietro da Cortona completed the choir and the drum dome. The façade, to a design by Luigi Omodei, was not built until 1682–84. Oriented on the Corso, it obscures the basilican structure of the church, and instead (following the type of façade found in St Peter's) derives its life from a monumental articulation consisting of a colossal order of columns and a surmounting triangular gable.

The interior is a pillared basilica with a transept and an apse around which – a unique feature for Rome – there runs an ambulatory. The latter probably derives from a special wish expressed by the orderers of the work, and is perhaps to be regarded as an imitation of medieval Lombard models. But as its longitudinal axis does not open towards the main choir, it contributes only slightly to the spatial impression.

The choir with its drum dome provides a backdrop visible from afar, and this is a very good feature in terms of the urban situation. That dome is the last architectural work by Pietro da Cortona. The lower

B40 SS. Ambrogio e Carlo al Corso

B41 Acqua Paola

section of the choir is articulated by unadorned panels and is made up of two energetic cylinders linked by volutes. Above this the drum dome rises triumphally, three-dimensionally articulated by cruciform pilaster pillars and inserted colonnades. Here too, strong three-dimensionality and differentiated wall layering are characteristic of Pietro's late work (cf. B83). DH

B41 Acqua Paola
Via Garibaldi (plan G1 2/C and plan VII 1/A)
1612–90
Flaminio Ponzio

The water supply on the right bank of the Tiber was insufficient until the ancient Aqua Traiana (AD 109) was rebuilt. The new aqueduct supplied the fountains on the Gianicolo and in Trastevere. Paul V Borghese, competing with his predecessor Sixtus V, planned to build a fountain as early as 1605. In 1610–12, the Acqua Paola and another smaller fountain were erected opposite the Ospizio de' Mendicanti at the end of Via Giulia. Giovanni Fontana and Flaminio Ponzio were the technical supervisors. The architecture of the fountain is also attributed to Ponzio. The entire complex was probably not completed before 1690, and the water receptacle was added later by Carlo Fontana.

Although, in using the triumphal-arch motif, the architect is imitating the model of the Acqua Felice (B18), an entirely different concept is dominant in the more recent fountain. The Acqua Felice is a self-contained structure within a city square, whereas the Acqua Paola stands detached in park-like surroundings. In the three central arches, from which the cascades

pour down like a waterfall, there are openings providing a view of the gardens behind them. The arches are flanked by smaller arches set further back. The far-projecting entablature is bent backwards to right angles at the sides, and is supported by three-quarter columns. The view through the arches, and the three-dimensional articulation, cause the show façade to appear like a corporeal structure, a real triumphal arch so to speak, through which the water flows into the city. But the water mainly flows in honour of the owner, because the monumental arch is to a certain degree only the base course for the wide panel of inscriptions and the surmounting segmented gable, in which lavish homage is rendered to Pope Paul V.
AG

B42 St. Peter: Baldacchino
Piazza di S. Pietro (plan III 1/A)
1623–33
Gianlorenzo Bernini
The baldachin above St Peter's tomb is known to be a work by Bernini, but is considerably influenced by Maderno and Borromini. It is the last in a series of ciboria which, from Constantine's time onwards, were used to accentuate the apostle's tomb and the high altar. When Urban VIII, in 1623, entrusted Bernini with the task of building the baldachin, Bernini had to deal with the staircase structure that was built by Carlo Maderno in 1615–17. It was intended to give access to St Peter's tomb which was at a lower level. In this connection, Maderno had also designed a baldachin with twisting columns, and Bernini probably drew lar-

B42 St. Peter: Baldacchino

gely on that baldachin when producing his bronze columns in 1626/27. The design of the superstructure of the baldachin was difficult both statically and artistically, so that Bernini caused two wooden 1:1 models of the superstructure to be built in order to be able to test the effect of the baldachin.

Bernini's baldachin takes into account the way in which the structure of the ciborium had been handed down by tradition from the Constantine period: the four twisting bronze columns relate to eight columns (today they are in the upper parts of the crossing pillars) from Old St Peter's, and it was believed that Constantine took them from the temple in Jerusalem to use them for St Peter's. The four scrolls in the baldachin's superstructure also allude to the original ciborium. A baldachin canopy, held on ribbons by angels, is fitted between the twisting columns, and its substantiality is emphasized by the animated cloths and irregular tufts. Bernini is here using an element of festive decoration to replace the architectural structure expected in ciboria. The architectural ciborium is thus combined with the portable baldachin to form a new dignifying shape. AS

B43 S. Bibiana
Via Giovanni Giolitti 154 (plan VI 2/B)
1624–27
Gianlorenzo Bernini
S. Bibiana opens a new chapter in Roman Baroque art. Not only does Bernini's career as an architect begins here, but this small church also harbours Bernini's first religious sculpture and the earliest fresco cycle by Pietro da Cortona. Today the church is squeezed in among the Stazione Termini complex of buildings; it formerly stood detached on the Esquiline in a distinctly rural area. According to legend, this cultic site dates from the 4C and was built in honour of St Bibiana who was martyred under Julian Apostata. Simplicius built a new church in 468. The core structure of today's complex is the basilica built under Honorius in c. 1220. Not until 1624 did the canons responsible for S. Maria Maggiore once again take notice of that much-dilapidated church. Work on carefully restoring the old church began as part of the Counter-Reformation revival of early-Christian traditions. After a spectacular discovery of relics in August 1624, Urban VIII himself took over the rebuilding work. This was the first prestigious architectural project in which the new pope presented himself to the public in the jubilee year of 1625.

It was required of Bernini that he should, without fail, retain the original design of the church, its »forma vecchia«, and merely ennoble it by building a new façade. He resorted here to the architectural type of the palace-like portico façade with three axes. Maderno had recently built a façade of this type in St Peter's (B34). The characteristic of this façade scheme lies in retaining the same width for the lower and upper storeys, which in this way form a box-like

B43 S. Bibiana

block. The ground floor is designed as a portico which has three axes and is opened up by arcades on all sides. Above it there is a self-contained storey which, in contrast to the Ionic order below, has as its orchestration an architectural order related to the Tuscan. The concluding balustrade, and the flaming vases, lend the façade a distinctly secular character, possibly in deliberate allusion to the ancient palace of Bibiana, which is said to have stood here. The emphatic division into three bays remained from now on a characteristic stylistic principle of Bernini's.

The scheme of the portico façade continued to be a preferred architectural form of the classical tendency within the Roman Baroque until well into the 17C (B47, B49), but was modified in unusual fashion in S. Bibiana. Bernini moved the entire central axis forwards, and designed the upper bay as a large aedicule which seems to thrust its way through the building's upper conclusion. The hard transition between the lateral and central bays is expressive in making the central structure appear to protrude still more distinctly – a principle which Bernini later applied again (B93). Not the least feature is that in this way the aedicule is a dignified motif placed within a setting. It frames a deep box-type niche, and also forms a genuine gallery concluded by a balustrade. The entablature of the lateral bays continues into the niche, so that the aedicule appears to be imposed upon a smaller system. This mutual penetration of a small and large architectural order accords with a design method which Michelangelo first realized in the conservators' palace (H30).

The striking setting given to the aedicule is explained by the particular cultic requirements. The gallery framed by an aedicule served as a platform for the relics, upon which the relics of the head of S. Bibiana were displayed on her holy day. The aedicule was visible from afar as a magnificent framework for the relics gallery. It was the eye-catching feature of the street which had been newly laid out at that time, led towards S. Bibiana and, outside the church, expanded into a small square. Placed in its setting in this way, the façade clearly displays the two major themes: the portico and the aedicule, which here enter into a novel and unusual synthesis. In the 17C, the portico was regarded as a specifically Roman architectural motif which, in ancient times, was a distinguishing feature of heathen temples as well as the early-Christian churches. Combined with the aedicule, which received the relics of the titular saint, the architecture demonstrates not only the ancient origin of the church but also the cult of Bibiana.

The dominant motif of the aedicule was adopted again by Bernini at a central point inside the church. The aedicule frames the high altar and thus becomes the focus of the room. The sumptuous marble housing harbours the statue of S. Bibiana, who is depicted in the »visio beata«. The saint, supported on the whipping post, has accepted her martyrdom in all humbleness, and is now to be received into heaven. An exactly calculated path of light entering from the top left through a specially opened shaft causes the saint to light up brightly in longing expectation of the divine experience.

The basilica (one nave, two aisles) has a flat roof and is subdivided by four pairs of columns which are ancient spoils. The windowless clerestory above the colonnades contains a fresco cycle by Pietro da Cortona (northern wall) and Agostino Ciampelli (southern wall), showing scenes from the life of S. Bibiana. Stimulated by the frieze compositions by Polidoro da Caravaggio and by the reliefs of the Roman imperial period, Cortona created a novel and masterly »all'antica« style, which depicts the early-Christian martyrs as heroes of antiquity. This new style of fresco made Cortona famous at a stroke. From that time on his artistry was a determinant factor on the Roman art scene.

S. Bibiana is a high-quality building which unites the early works of first-ranging artists and thus expresses the far-ranging pretensions, and the clever patronage, of the newly elected pope, under whose pontificate the art of the Roman High Baroque was to develop to the full. The church, being Bernini's first architectural work, points to later buildings by him. In particular, in S. Andrea al Quirinale (B85), Bernini developed the dominant façade motif into a high point of Roman façade art. EJ

B44 S. Maria della Vittoria

B44 S. Maria della Vittoria
Via XX Settembre 17 (plan V 2/A)
1610–12, 1625–27
Carlo Maderno, Giovanni Battista Soria
This building is notable as a piece of town planning,
and also because it houses the Cornaro chapel (B60).
Initially a church of St Paul was planned. After Tilly's
victory – in which a miraculous image of the Virgin
Mary is said to have provided assistance – over Protestant Prague in the battle on the Weißer Berg in
1620, the image was transferred hither and the building was dedicated to the victorious Virgin Mary. The
image was later destroyed by fire.

Maderno was already working on the nave of St
Peter's (B34). In the interior of S. Maria della Vittoria,
he did not go beyond the architectural type of Il Gesù.
Both interiors were also similarly sparse in their decorations at that time; it was only much later (1663–75)
that they became an overall Baroque work of art
made up of painting, sculpture and ornamental
stucco. The façade is more significant. It was Soria's
first work for Scipione Borghese, the nephew of Paul
V (cf. also B49). The model for it was the façade of S.
Susanna (B30), but Soria's façade, despite the comparable location, is taller, almost too narrow, and less
solid, because only pilasters were used, and the forward layering in the centre is less energetic, because
there is no such layering in the upper storey. This
makes the large aedicule of the portal look out of
place, not very well motivated. And the bays no longer
stand so freely side by side, but instead look constricted.

Both façades are related to one another, although
at that time there was also a palace between them (on
what is today the Largo di S. Susanna). They stand in
a very significant ensemble of the later 16C, on one of
the first narrow streets of houses of that period, close
to the Acqua Felice (B18) and S. Bernardo (B32), two
still-recent buildings. When compared with a similar
High-Baroque configuration, namely the Piazza del
Popolo (B87/88), the layout of the buildings here looks
confined in the Mannerist style. The overall arrangement is not yet clear and free. SG

B45 Palazzo Barberini alle Quattro Fontane
Via delle Quattro Fontane 13, Piazza Barberini
(plan V 1/A)
1625–37
Carlo Maderno, Gianlorenzo Bernini
The Palazzo Barberini was built at a time when Urban VIII (Maffeo Barberini) was pope and his nephews
Francesco and Taddeo were gaining great wealth from
nepotism. In 1625, Cardinal Francesco Barberini acquired the Palazzo Sforza with a garden on the Quirinal, not far from the Piazza Barberini. The ground plan
of the old 16C palace had the same proportions as
today's northern wing. That palace was also lower in
height, and the way in which it was divided into rooms
was unacceptable. Contemporaries found it simply
ghastly. Nothing was more natural than to convert the
existing structure and integrate it into a large new
building. The result is one of the most significant palaces of the Roman High Baroque.

These are really two palaces in one, because Taddeo, the building owner, was responsible for the
northern wing, while his brother Cardinal Francesco
began building his own southern wing in 1632. Finally, the central section became the imposing linking
section, with a vestibule, a great hall and a rich façade. Thus the entire palace, when seen from the outside, is a homogeneous structure. But in the interior,
the division of the rooms in the two wings accorded
entirely with the individual pretensions of the two owners. This division into two may have contributed to
what is an unusual shape for Roman city palaces.

The traditional shape for the architecture of a Roman city palace was a self-contained building in the
shape of a rectangular parallelepiped with one or
more inner courtyards. In contrast to this, the Palazzo Barberini is an open structure. The palace has an
H-shaped ground plan, and its central section gives
it two imposing wings, one facing the garden and one
facing the city, with the wing facing the city exhibiting
a particularly gorgeous façade. That splendid abundance of shapes which, in the case of palazzi, had
previously been limited to the cortile – a good example
is the Palazzo Farnese (H25) – was now placed on external display. The flanking wings, which project beyond the central section, mark out a courtyard area,
whose function is similar to that of the French honorary courtyard (cour d'honneur). This architectural

B45 Palazzo Barberini alle Quattro Fontane

type was of course not entirely unknown in Rome, because it was used in the rural villa and the villa suburbana of the Italian Renaissance, an example being the Villa Farnesina (H8), whose wings also extend beyond the central section. But, despite the similarities, the Palazzo Barberini is not a villa suburbana. This contention is supported by its main façade, which is not oriented on the garden, but instead unfurls its splendour in the direction of the city. What is more, the dimensions of the apartments are those of a palazzo, and not those of the smaller rooms of a villa; the fact that there are both summer and winter rooms makes it possible to stay here all the year round. Finally, the building was regarded by contemporaries as a palazzo, and not the least indication of this is its massive size. Thus the architect combined the architectural type of a villa suburbana with that of a palazzo, in this way creating the new, Baroque palazzo. It is not so easy to ascertain who really created this innovation. Initially, Maderno was persuaded to design the new building. When, after four years, he died in 1629, the project had hardly gone beyond the planning stage. Bernini then took over the supervision of the building work, and Borromini also worked under both architects and was probably responsible for parts of the execution. It can though be assumed that Bernini was merely pulling Maderno's plans into effect, while of course also making the odd modification.

The entrance façade mainly derives from Maderno. He was planning a three-storeyed show frontage seven axes wide. Three open loggias placed one above the other were meant to surprise the onlooker's eye. All the relevant plans here are drawn up by Maderno, and only the two upper loggias were closed by windows, thus enabling the great hall in the centre to be enlarged to accommodate the famous ceiling fresco by Cortona. The foreshortened window frames in the upper storey are probably an invention of Bernini's. The loggias are designed to have the tabularium motif (cf. A9), and their columns are located in the ancient superposition. Previously, a maximum of two loggias placed one above the other in the cortile had been customary in city palazzi, and the upper storey was always closed, as for example in the Palazzo Farnese

(H25). The former benediction loggia (torn down in 1616) in the Vatican might have provided the model for Maderno's idea. There is also a close stylistic link with the Damasus courtyard in the Vatican (H11). The Barberini's private palace was evidently intended, in its high artistic pretensions and its perfect synthesis, to surpass the most distinguished sections of the Vatican palace. But the Quirinal palace near to the Palazzo Barberini should also not be forgotten. Its façade facing the inner courtyard is by Mascherino (16C) and consists of two open loggias one above the other. Maderno certainly also intended to excel this design. Another interesting feature here is that the early Roman Baroque architecture is still entirely in the Roman tradition, and is thus strongly oriented on the Renaissance or even on the ancient classical period. But the effect is quite different, and the character is a new one. The façade, formally kept flat, now produces an overall effect of three-dimensionality. The differing but united wall layerings, such as those by Michelangelo, had previously been relief-like and strictly frontal. Now there are large groupings, so that particular points are emphasized and the total uniformity is therefore abandoned. The façade of the Palazzo Barberini is, in its entrance frontage with its seven axes, very intensely accentuated by the order of columns, the entablature and the loggia motif. It is flanked on both left and right by a lower bay which, lacking an architectural order or an entablature, seems to be set back. All this may be described as a risalto which extends across an entire flat surface and makes the seven axes in the centre appear to project,

The low bays of the central section form an adroit transition to the wings, whose plainness makes the façade stand out by contrast. Their function is that of a picture frame, and they contribute to the spatial effect of the façade; they sometimes protect the façade and even conceal it. It is necessary here to visualize the approach route followed by a visitor at that time. There were two alternatives: coming from the Piazza Barberini, the traveller drove either into the Via delle Quattro Fontane, passing some low houses which were for the servants and surrounded the palazzo like a castle wall, until he arrived at an inconspicuous gate on the left through which he made his direct entrance into the »honorary courtyard«. Or else he went through a small gate in the south-eastern corner of the Piazza Barberini, drove up to the long side of the northern wing, went straight towards its main entrance, drove westwards along that wing, and finally turned into the »honorary courtyard«. In short, there were surprises on both approach routes: the façade suddenly appeared, contrasting very strongly with the rest of the architecture, with plainness being intensified into opulence. The articulation of the wings is similar to that of conventional Roman palace architecture, and anyone standing outside the façade of the northern wing might be inclined to assume that this was a traditional Roman palace having the well-known shape of a self-contained rectangular parallelepiped. The effect produced when the visitor enters the open courtyard is thus all the more surprising. A poetic idea has been put into effect at the main entrance of the southern wing, where a bridge in the form of a double arcade crosses the ditch between the piano nobile and ground level. The bridge is designed as a ruin, and the arcade next to the southern wing has »collapsed« from the middle onwards. The gap is spanned by a drawbridge. This double arcade was built in 1678/79, being an early example of ruin architecture. The architect is not known. The idea may have come from Cardinal Francesco himself.

The visitor coming into the central section from the west enters what, for the period, is an unusually spacious vestibule. Its western end has seven bays, but it tapers off by two bays at a time, concluding with only three bays in the east, and it ends in an exedra. The vestibule has massive cross pillars and a groined vault, and resembles a substruction. A vestibule had previously been a barrel-vaulted colonnaded passage (as in the Palazzo Farnese, H25), but here it expands into a large pillared hall. The passage into the garden was not opened until 1670. Before that the exedra had been closed, and there was no link with the garden.

The great hall is in the centre of the piano nobile. The ground plan initially planned by Maderno was square-shaped, but Bernini enlarged the hall by closing the loggias, thus giving them their present volume (15 m wide and high, 25 m long). The only item intended to produce an effect is the famous fresco by Cortona (an allegory of Urban VIII's pontificate, 1633–39).

Maderno's important idea was the oval hall, which adjoins the great hall in the east and can be reached from it. This transversely oval hall is of a classicistic plainness, as if the onlookers' feelings, heated by Cortona's exuberant ceiling fresco, were meant to be cooled again here. Oval-shaped secular architecture was unknown at this period (in religious architecture, cf. H34, B5). The exact function of the oval hall in the Palazzo Barberini is not known: it may have been a room preceding or following the great hall, or else, as there is no fireplace, a garden room for summer use, or perhaps a small gallery of sculptures.

Each wing of the palace is accessible by a separate staircase which is entirely different from the others. On the right, an oval spiral staircase leads to the cardinal's wing. Tuscan double columns support the flight of stairs leading to the open centre. This is a fairly exact copy of the staircase by Vignola in the Palazzo Farnese in Caprarola (H38), but stands above an oval ground plan, which was probably suggested by the oval shape of Mascherino's spiral staircase in the Palazzo del Quirinale. The staircase leading to the left wing of the palace was designed quite differently. The visitor first climbs a long, corridor-like ramp up to the first platform. This section has the standard shape for Roman palazzo staircases in the cinquecento. But then there is a surprising opening towards the centre,

as there is in the oval spiral staircase with its double Tuscan columns. However, the whole structure stands on a square-shaped ground plan. PZ

B46 S. Ignazio

Piazza S. Ignazio (plan IV 2/A)
1626–50, 1685
Orazio Grassi and others

S. Ignazio, the church of the Collegio Romano, is the second large Jesuit building in Rome. In 1626, four years after the canonization of Ignatius de Loyola, a generous donation by Cardinal Ludovico Ludovisi made it possible to erect this new and imposing building in the north-western corner of the school area. Six months after the foundation stone had been laid, a group of architects met to discuss the design. Sketches showing Domenichino's ideas, and a Maderno design drawn by Borromini, indicate that both these artists were involved in the planning at that time. A wooden model was built in 1628 to designs by Grassi, a mathematician who was the architect of the Jesuit order. Grassi's ground plan adopted important ideas from the plans by Maderno and Borromini, but his façade design and the interpretation of the exterior displayed some original thoughts.

Grassi planned an aisleless church which had chapels with apses and, with its transept, domed crossing and choir, followed the ground plan of Il Gesù (B1). In contrast to Il Gesù, however, the small bay at the transition to the transept is abandoned in favour of three larger chapels. The chapels in the nave follow Maderno's design in that they are linked by passageways and marked by free-standing columns located at the entrances and in the passageways. The chapels in the presbytery are compressed into oval shapes. Grassi's model also included a screen façade with five axes on both storeys, and an external articulation which would have presented the church as a uniform, decorative structure that could be looked at from all sides.

B46 S. Ignazio

Alterations made by Antonio Sasso, the building supervisor who worked here from 1633 onwards, ruined this concept. The nave was built by Sasso and completed in 1650, but he made its roof truss too high, thus inevitably altering the façade.

In a second phase of construction ending in 1662, the transept and choir were provided with vaults. Sasso's changes to the plans caused such great difficulties with the design and lighting of the dome that, in 1685, it was decided temporarily to close the dome opening with a canvas painting: this was Pozzo's famous mock dome.

In the interior, the chapels are of greater significance in relation to the nave than is the case with Il Gesù. Grassi gave them pendentive domes as vaults, and linked them with passageways. In this way he created a number of small centrally planned buildings whose model is to be sought in the design of the chapels by Maderno in the nave of St Peter's (B34).

As in Il Gesù the room area of the nave has double pilasters, an entablature continuing straight across, and arcades. But the arcades are wider and taller here, and are accentuated by the full columns which support them. The proportions of the room are also taller than in Il Gesù. The quadratura painting work by Pozzo (later than 1685) in the barrel of the nave seems to continue the real architecture, and makes a decided contribution to the effect produced by that nave.

The façade is based on that of Il Gesù. It has five axes in its lower storey and three in its upper, with scrolls linking the two storeys. It adopts two features found in Il Gesù, namely the layered double pilasters and the large (but in this case simple) aedicule, formed using half columns, above the central portal, but it dispenses with making the elements of design more intense as they approach the centre: all the axes are subdivided by portals and niches. The remaining wall panels are filled with blind windows front, recessed rectangular panels, and festoons. This façade therefore looks unaccentuated and old-fashioned when compared with Il Gesù. AS

B47 S. Caterina da Siena a Magnanapoli
Largo Magnanapoli (plan V 1/B)
1628–40, 1641
Giovanni Battista Soria
This former monastery church on Monte Magnanapoli has an interesting two-storeyed portico façade. The church was begun in 1628 and, after several pauses in the construction work, was both completed and consecrated in 1640. Its façade was built in 1641. There is documentary proof that Soria was the architect of the façade, and he probably also designed the church. He erected a frontage with two storeys and three axes, and concluded it with a triangular gable.

The portico façade is subdivided into two storeys, but there are three storeys concealed behind it: the

vestibule which is accessible via the arcades on the ground floor, the upper storey, and a mezzanine extending from the capitals of the ground-floor pilasters to the external sill of the upper-storey window. The mezzanine gives access to the nuns' choir and to the gallery-like coretti inside the church. Thus the rooms concealed behind the portico façade are not related to the subdivision of the façade, but are designed with a view to the church interior.

In employing the architectural type of a portico façade, Soria is reverting to his masterpiece, the façade of S. Gregorio Magno (B49). But at the same time he is using an architectonic language which is indebted to Mannerism. This can be seen in the triangular gables in the upper storey, which seem too small and are combined with ear-like frames, and also in the window's broken gable, which is combined with a small segmented gable. The two flights of stairs were added in the 19C, in connection with the lowering of the ground level.

The church interior is a barrel-vaulted room with apse aisles but no transept. Coretti for the nuns of the convent are recessed into the entablature, supported by simple pilasters, of the church's nave. AS

B48 SS. Domenico e Sisto
Via Panispera, Largo Angelicum 1 (plan V 1/B)
1569, 1628–63
Domenico Dario de Mezzana, Giacomo della Porta, Nicolò Torriani, Vincenzo della Greca and others
The monastery church of SS. Domenico e Sisto was built over a period of almost 100 years, with eight architects being involved.

The question of attribution is correspondingly complicated. It is likely that de Mezzana designed the ground plan of this room church which has apse aisles and lacks a transept, and that he also built the sections behind today's choir. Della Porta, who was mentioned in the sources in 1579, constructed the the presbytery, part of the nave of the church, and the

B47 S. Caterina da Siena a Magnanapoli

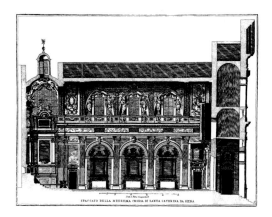

SPACCATO DELLA MEDESIMA CHIESA DI SANTA CATERINA DA SIENA

B48 SS. Domenico e Sisto

bell tower. He was succeeded in 1609 by Torriani, who completed the nave by 1632 after some interruption, and added the façade. The portal and the two-flighted staircase are the work of della Greca (1654–64). A lowering of the terrain in the 19C made it necessary to lengthen the staircase and caused the frontage to produce today's excessively tall effect.

The two-storeyed façade with its three axes (1628 to 1632) is subdivided by flat double pilasters and topped by a triangular gable. Niches and decorative filling motifs fit in between the pairs of pilasters. The façade stays flat and unaccentuated, because the pilasters are not layered, the entablature is not projecting above them, and all the free spaces are visibly designed to express a horror vacui. The architectural type of a screen façade with an equal number of axes in both storeys is typical of Soria's buildings (cf. B39, B47, B49). This is why the design of the façade of this monastery church has been associated with Soria, who worked on SS. Domenico e Sisto in 1637–51. There is a strangely tense relationship between the Mannerist church façade and the High-Baroque staircase, built by della Greca in 1654–57. The staircase, being a two-flighted structure proceeding from a plateau, introduces for the first time an element of villa architecture to Rome, and is regarded as a precursor of the Ripetta harbour and the Spanish Steps (B115). AS

B49 S. Gregorio Magno
Piazza S. Gregorio (plan VIII 1/A)
1629–33
Giovanni Battista Soria

The proud showpiece façade of S. Gregorio Magno on the Caelian Hill is the main work by Soria, who represents in exemplary fashion the classical tendency in Roman Baroque architecture. From the mid-1620s onwards he was the preferred architect of Cardinal Scipione Borghese. The restoration of S. Gregorio, a building of great significance to ecclesiastical history, was begun in the 16C and was continued by C. Baronio. The 11C basilica (modernized in 1725–34) had been built above the birth- and workplace of Gregory the Great, who converted his palace into a Benedictine monastery in c. 580 and, from here, conducted the conversion of England to Christianity. With the façade, Borghese completed the rebuilding work, which was designed on Counter-Reformation principles.

The travertine façade, towering high above a monumental outdoor staircase, is thrust well forwards and forms a united front against the Palatine Hill opposite. In designing it, Soria, like Bernini with S. Bibiana shortly before (B43), was reverting to the architectural type – perhaps suggested by the conservators' palace (H30) – of a palatial portico façade. Ponzio and Vasanzio adopted this type when restoring S. Sebastiano (B37) in 1609, and from that time on the portico façade was the preferred architectural form for the classical tendency in Roman architecture. This show frontage has three axes, is articulated by angular pilasters, and opens up into a three-gate portico on the ground floor. The upper, self-contained storey adopts the articulation of the ground floor, orchestrated by a Composite order and accentuated by rich balustrades and aedicule windows. The entire central axis projects like a risalto, surmounted by a triangular gable containing the Borghese coat of arms. The accentuation of the aedicule frontage is clearly reminiscent of S. Bibiana (B43), but with the block-like character of the façade more strongly emphasized. The central risalto is enclosed by double pilasters with recesses, and is overlaid upon the flanking bays. The principle of ener-

B49 S. Gregorio Magno

getic wall layering – invented in the façade of Il Gesù (B1) and developed further in the façade of S. Susanna (B30) – continues into the individual bays, where sunken framing panels are set in between the pilasters and intensify the vigorous wall relief. The severe, angular pilaster architecture is aimed at giving effect to the hardness and weightiness of the travertine stone. The dignity of ancient Roman architecture is revived in the sober seriousness, lapidary plainness and stony majesty of the façade. This inwardly relates it to the Colosseum (A25) and the Constantine arch (A52), two neighbouring buildings. What is more, the massive eagle above the central portal makes a distinctly ancient impression. Like the dragons above the side gates, the eagle is a heraldic animal of Scipione Borghese, who built himself a proud monument in this façade which greets the Palatine Hill opposite.

This massive show wall, intended to be seen from afar, is not the real church façade which it initially appears to be. That façade is hidden behind the projecting frontage, and is placed at a distance by an atrium. The latter is a two-storeyed pillared courtyard which Soria built above the ground plan of the previous structure. This is the only example of an early-Christian atrium being adopted into a Baroque building. The abbey commandery was housed in the western wing, and this may explain the secular nature of the church façade. The eastern wing opposite still preserves the old church frontage of the Romanesque

basilica. It formerly resembled an ancient temple frontage with Ionic columns placed in pairs. But the temple-like character was lost when the triangular gable was removed.

The church interior was modernized by Francesco Ferrari in 1725–34. Working on the model of S. Ignazio (B46), he designed it as a room church with domed apses and inserted free-standing columns (spoils). Today it shows no remnants of the Romanesque basilica. Two of the oratories (S. Andrea, S. Barbara) assigned to the church derive from donations by Gregory the Great, while the third is dedicated to S. Silvia and dates back to a campaign by Baronio who, around 1600, ordered the chapels to be combined into an integrated group of structures.

The majestic travertine façade of S. Gregorio Magno expressively demonstrates the classical artistic tendency which existed in Rome in the first third of the 17C and accorded with the Counter-Reformation in endeavouring to revive ancient Roman traditions. EJ

B50 S. Antonio dei Portoghesi
Via de' Portoghesi 2 (plan IV 1/A)
1631–36
Martino Longhi the Younger

This Portuguese national church was dedicated to St Antony, the patron saint from Lisbon. The interior by Gaspare Guerra (1629–36) is an insignificant successor to Il Gesù (B1), and the crossing and choir were added later by Carlo Rainaldi (1674–76).

Longhi's façade also follows the Il Gesù type: it is a cross-section façade in which scrolls (here, they are crowned by hermae) link the single-storeyed wings to the two-storeyed centre. The details of the design are new. The ground floor is subdivided by three bays which stand freely side by side, a feature that had been known since Maderno's S. Susanna (B30). The central bay projects by a layer, but it is only from another protruding pair of pilasters and from the frame – again projecting – of the gabled portal that the bay derives its great three-dimensional effect. That steady crescendo approaching the centre which is found in Maderno is here replaced by an exuberant accumulation around the centre. The same structure, right down to the inner pilaster of the wings, is employed in the upper storey. But here the gables extend further and span the central pair of pilasters and the two pilasters in the wings. In all this, the façade represents three values which Longhi was to shape still more incisively in SS. Vincenzo ed Anastasio (cf. B64): the grandiloquent accentuation of the top centre as being the centre of three-dimensionality (here it has the coat of arms of the Portuguese royal dynasty, the Braganza); the generation of much greater depth in relief, with Longhi even shaping the flanks of the façade (by means of the hermae) and thus suggesting depth beyond the front of the façade (cf. here B30); and the greater complexity of the relationships between elements of the architectural order – in this case the

B50 S. Antonio dei Portoghesi

gables – on the one hand and the various bays on the other. All three values characterize the step towards the High Baroque, and the only similar contemporary example of them is the church of SS. Luca e Marina (B51). SG

B51 SS. Luca e Martina
Via Tulliano, Via della Curia (plan V 1/B)
1634–50
Pietro da Cortona

SS. Luca e Martina, the main architectural work by Pietro da Cortona, is regarded as one of the earliest buildings of the Roman High Baroque. This church belonged to the Accademia di S. Luca, which was housed in some adjoining buildings until the route of the Via dei Fori Imperiali was cut in 1931–33. In 1634, Pietro da Cortona, being the chairman of the academy, was permitted to expand the existing lower church and form it into his tomb chapel. It was only when the relics of St Martina were discovered in the course of this work that it was decided, at the instigation of Cardinal Francesco Barberini, completely to rebuild the church to designs by Pietro da Cortona. The building work was largely completed in 1650.

This domed building, visible from afar, stands at the edge of the Forum Romanum above a ground plan which is a slightly elongated Greek cross with its arms ending in apses. The upper conclusion of the two-storeyed façade is a horizontal entablature, so that the massive drum dome contributes to the outward appearance. The chief characteristic of the façade occurs here for the first time in Rome and is the slightly convex forward curvature of its central section which, on both storeys, is inserted between sturdy corner piers with double pilasters in front of them. The entire façade is united by the uniform base course and entablature, but the central section is nevertheless marked out as an independent component by its articulation: the determinant elements on the lower storey are full columns; these had previously only functioned as a frame for the façade sections, but they are now loosely inserted into those sections, thus forming an almost independent colonnade. A recessed layer of wall panels is fitted into the intercolumniations. This impression is intensified by a strip of cornice which unites this rear layer of wall but is overtopped by the columns. The design of the central section is chiastically reversed in the upper storey, with pilasters appearing instead of columns and the angular reinforcements of the central portal zone being replaced by framing columns. This is accompanied by what, overall, is a lighter design for the upper storey: it is of lower proportions, and the Corinthian order is employed instead of the Ionic. This chiastic effect is intensified by shapes – such as a curving frieze, oval framing panels, and the triangular gable – which contrast with those found on the ground floor. The façade is characterized by very intense three-dimensionality and the ingenious mutual embracing of its elements.

B51 SS. Luca e Martina

The interior initially presents itself to the visitor entering it as a centrally planned building with a dominating drum dome; only on closer inspection does it turn out that the transverse arm is subordinate and that the apses are not semicircular. An energetically subdivided storey is the substructure for the dome and vault. The entire interior is firmly united by the base course and entablature, and also by the homogeneous, continuous Ionic order. It is striking that none of the design is coloured: white stucco sculptures in the vault area are the only decoration added to the architectural articulation.

The wall structure is subtly differentiated like the façade, and the very fact that there are several layers may be regarded as a significant new element in wall design. The central dome rests on four massive piers; the bipartite arches of the crossing are each supported by a full column and by a wall pillar articulated by a pilaster, and an intermediate wall panel is also continued in the pendentives of the dome. Such pillars are also found in the transverse arms, while in the side apses there are full columns placed into the wall. The theme of the colonnades, also found in the façade, recurs here, and the rear wall layer, the real outer wall of the apses, does not merely seem inserted between the columns, but now actually forms a layer of its own behind the colonnades. The columns and pillars also accord with this differentiated wall design, in occupying the front layer as pivotal points. This layering of the wall is appropriately mirrored by the articulation of the entablature. The columns of the crossing are here given a linking function which is particularly well expressed because they are free-standing; they also relate to the colonnades of the apses and optically link the whole room together.

A combination of stucco-work coffering and ribs laid above it is found for the first time ever in the vault area of SS. Luca e Martina. These two features formerly belonged to two types of vault which were entirely independent of one another. A two-layered structure is found here too. The sources of light are mainly in the vault area, which is therefore very bright and provides the room with well-balanced lighting.

SS. Luca e Martina occupies a prominent place in Roman architecture. Various elements – the tension-filled juxtaposition of columns and pillars, and the inserted colonnade in general – appear to be inspired by Michelangelo's buildings (H30, H31), whereas Pietro da Cortona, at about the same time as Borromini, created forms of design – one example is the convex or concave curvature of the wall – which were to point the way in Baroque architecture. SS. Luca e Martina must therefore be regarded as an important initial building of the Roman High Baroque. DH

Bibliography: K. Noehles, *La Chiesa dei SS. Luca e Martina*, Rome, 1970.

B52 S. Carlo alle Quattro Fontane, also SS. Trinità di S. Carlo Borromeo
Via delle Quattro Fontane (plan V 1/A)
begun 1634, 1638–41, 1665–67
Francesco Borromini

S. Carlo alle Quattro Fontane (or S. Carlino) changed the architecture of the Roman Baroque. The era of sparse, almost stiff longitudinal buildings ended with this first building (apart from SS. Luca e Martina, B51) to display the complex, inventive and dynamic tendency found in the Roman High and late Baroque. The indigent Trinitarian order possessed only a small plot of land on which the monastery building and the church had to be accommodated. The dormitory, the courtyard, and the refectory (today the sacristy) with its corners rounded out in Borromeo's style, were the first to be built, and were followed from 1638 onwards by the church, which was constructed in two phases: first the interior, completed by 1641, and then the façade, begun only in 1665. Apart from this, there were the old sacristy and a lower church in which the complex spatial shape of the church interior is almost identical to that of the church above, as can be very clearly seen, owing to the sparse orchestration of the design work. The use of stucco (this had previously been uncommon) made the building work cheap (S. Andrea al Quirinale cost five times as much but was the same size) and was appropriate to Borromini's preference for softly moulded shapes.

Two leitmotivs of the overall complex are found in the monastery courtyard: they are the rhythmized colonnade with intercolumniations of differing widths, and the avoidance of corners and thus of abrupt transitions. Borromini selected a sequence of interlinked

Palladian motifs (an old idea, cf. H6) on the ground floor, and a colonnade on the upper storey, but what was entirely new was that he gave both of them convex curves in the corners. The shape of the balusters in the upper-storey balustrade is also new. They were round and slender in the Renaissance (cf. e. g. H4), and the bulge was in the middle and, from Michelangelo's time onwards, was moved downwards to give an impression of weightiness (e. g. H25). Borromini chose a triangular shape, made the bulges point alternately upwards and downwards, and thus invented the Baroque balustrade. Borromini did not give the capitals and architraves their complete classical form, but instead abstracted them. The full architectural order began to be replaced by mere squares and panels.

The complex interior is more easily understood when looked at a stage at a time, starting with the lower section. For the ground plan, Borromini initially considered employing the Latin cross which St Charles Borromeo had propagated for liturgical and also for iconographic reasons, but then Borromini thought of using an oval with a ring of chapels. In this latter case, the chapels with their altars would though have been mere annexes. Borromini probably wanted to avoid this: he cut some of the chapels off altogether (they became side rooms), but emphasized the others: the sweep of the building stretches towards them, and there is an expressively formed movement proceeding towards them (intensified by coffer work which tapers off in perspective). The oval became more complex. The triangle, symbol of the Trinity, is doubled in the ground plan, and – not only in the drawings but also in the building – can still be felt in the architrave sections of the diagonals. What is typical of Borromini's thinking is that geometrical shapes are no longer added one to another, but are combined into a new enriched shape having many elements, so that only fragments of the original shapes are still noticeable. This principle gained acceptance in the 18C.

B52 S. Carlo alle Quattro Fontane

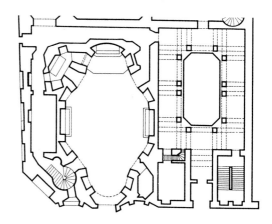

The front elevation of this section is no less complex. It is structured in two layers: the wall and the colonnade placed loosely in front of it. The wall is subdivided in the manner of a rhythmic bay. Compartments having three axes are created. The altar bay, and the convex bay of the diagonals, can be regarded as the centre of each compartment. Thus each of the unaccentuated axes is a part of two compartments each of which has three axes. Thus the compartments appear interlinked. Due to the niches, the wall looks like a deep, three-dimensional mass. In front of the rhythmic bay – a design form of the Roman High Renaissance (e.g. H6, H7) –, and almost unconnected with it, Borromini placed an ancient colonnade (cf. the very similar case of the Piazza d'Oro in the Villa Hadriana, A32). The details of the colonnade are differentiated in masterly fashion, for example by reversing the scrolls and splitting the abacus, but only on the articulating columns. However, the colonnade mainly looks agreeably simple, especially as it is surmounted by the continuous, weighty architrave. The colonnade unites all the parts of the room, and the highly complex play of the interlinked bays becomes mere background music.

The wall and colonnade in the lower section look unconnected (but are harmonious in their interplay), and also the sections themselves look heterogeneous in their relationship with one another. The intermediate zone is unusual, consisting of four arcades and pendentives which provide a link with the oval dome. The arcades were closed by conchae, so that the whole intermediate zone again looks to have many elements and to be almost additive, with the combining effect of the colonnade in the lower section being abandoned here. The form with four arcades and pendentives had been developed for St Peter's (H7), but is unusual here, because such a transitional form is not necessary between an oval lower storey and an oval dome (cf. B5 and A31).

The dome is of a simple oval shape. All the tensions in the lower sections are therefore resolved in it. The light it contains makes it look like a »higher« place of a different nature. It also seems to hover, as the incipient part of it is full of windows and invisible. This design had its aftereffects in the late Baroque (e.g. Weltenburg). The decorations consisting of crosses, hectagons and octagons intersecting like a honeycomb are adopted from the ceiling in S. Costanza (C1), and are again only a more complex background music for the clear shape of the dome, especially as their perspective design also makes the dome look more elevated. The interior is concluded by a lantern made up of concavely curved facets.

The room develops in three zones in which the elements are at the same time independent and united, starting with the more complex and entirely dark zone below, proceeding through an intermediate area in which the cruciform shape takes effect, and going on into the simple, light-containing area at the top. Such

B52 S. Carlo alle Quattro Fontane

a distribution of light and darkness is natural in cultic and church architecture – we need only compare the Pantheon (A31) or S. Andrea al Quirinale (B85). The entirely new feature was that the ancient colonnade was placed in front of the wall which was articulated in High-Renaissance style. In the late Baroque, Fischer von Erlach made this close symbiosis and synthesis of design shapes from different epochs into the basis of his »universal architecture«. It was the many elements used in this method of construction that made it so new. The term »additive« would obscure the essential factor here: what is unique about Borromini's art is that he releases the particular from the grip of the general, so that the one is not subordinated to the other. This is probably why he was so much imitated in the Rococo. The head of the monastery very sensitively wrote the following at that time: »Everything is assembled in such a way that one item supplements the next and the onlooker is stimulated into always letting his gaze wander around on to something new.« The rooms appears to be in a state of constant development, and corners and angles are avoided.

The façade was built from 1665 onwards (it was complete in its decorations too in 1682), but had probably been devised as long before as 1634. At that time, even the most progressive façade of the period, that of SS. Luca e Martina (B51), would have looked traditional next to it. Oval rooms, too, had always been given flat façades (cf. e.g. B28). Even in 1665, Borromini's façade was still the first in which the concave and convex curve were not added to a flat surface as they still were in S. Maria della Pace (B79), but formed the façade on their own. There were no prototypes for this in ancient times. For the first time ever,

The colonnade looks like the skeleton for the wall, which presents itself as a softer mass. Another rhythmic bay was formed. Each individual axis, including the portal axis, was again divided horizontally, with the very tightly packed individual shapes being arranged in one way on the ground floor and in the reverse way in the upper storey. As in the interior, the wall is everywhere three-dimensional in the High-Baroque style and is entirely impenetrable. The individual shapes are very complex. This applies to the statuary shapes which everywhere replace tectonic ones and emphasize the vertical movement proceeding from the praying saint, and also to the small inserted columns which Borromini – contrary to what occurred on the Capitol or on the façade of St Peter's (H30, B34) – no longer interpreted as being intended to link an individual storey to the façade as a whole. Complexity or diversity was here intended to be presented within a uniform basic framework. It is not clear whether the top conclusion with the medallion that pierces the architrave is the work of Borromini. Although this form was to recur in many places in the 18C, Borromini can scarcely be thought capable of it, because Bernini, his worst enemy, had introduced it similarly just before (cf. B85). Borromini probably planned a lower second storey.

This building stands at a short distance from S. Andrea al Quirinale, Bernini's main building (B85). Borromini evidently wanted to lend vibration to the classical Roman façade and to enrich it by adding an ancient colonnade. Placed at a street corner, diagonally and thus not very stable, this building is innovative and striking in that it combines autonomy of the single parts and unity of the whole. In Bernini's building it was the whole which dominated, he always found a more striking, convincing simple idea. SG

Bibliography: L. Steinberg, *Borromini's San Carlo alle Quattro Fontane. A Study in Multiple Form and Architectural Symbolism*, New York and London, 1977.

B52 S. Carlo alle Quattro Fontane

the stone wall became an elastic material. The façade which extends across an entire surface and has two equally wide storeys (for the architectural type, cf. B49) consists, on the ground floor, of a concave curve, a convex curve and a concave curve and, in the upper storey, of three concave curves which, further up, are echoed in the tower and dome. Burckhardt's guide and companion nevertheless mocked the curves and felt reminded of dried apple peelings, while others perceived the new way of moulding the space as being revolutionary in a manner similar to the delicate chiaroscuro of a Rembrandt. This main overall shape is restrained by the colonnades placed loosely in front of the wall and by weighty architraves. The latter are the only parts of the façade of which there is also a transverse view. Thus the organization is again decidedly two-layered, and again has a deeply structured, three-dimensionally moulded wall with a simpler colonnade in front of it.

B53 Oratorio S. Filippo Neri in S. Maria in Vallicella

Piazza della Chiesa Nuova (plan IV 1/B)
1637–59
Francesco Borromini

Filippo Neri founded this oratory in 1561 as a place of discussion, sermon and scenic singing. His close friend Palestrina composed many of his works for the Oratorians. The name »oratorio«, describing a musical genre, originated here. The religious order was recognized by Gregory XIII in 1575. It was a Counter-Reformation order which opened itself up to the world like the other orders, but also wanted to live in early-Christian spontaneity and love. A »Chiesa Nuova« was built (B17), and a little later a section became necessary which adjoined it to the left and housed the monastery and oratory. Paolo Marucelli drew up the overall plans in 1620-27 and, from 1629 onwards, also erected the backbone of the complex: this consisted of the long corridor and the rectangular sacristy. He was replaced in 1637, probably after a competition, by Borromini, who did what no one else did at that time, namely to describe, in his Opus Architectonicum which appeared posthumously in 1725, the process of how he found his artistic form. The façade of the overall complex, the oratory (1637–40), the oval refectory (1641), as well as the two courtyards, the staircase, the library above the oratory (1641/42), and the ingeniously structured clock tower, all derive from Borromini (the final work of execution was done by Camillo Arcucci starting in 1652). All the components were thought of as belonging to a single unit. It is for this reason that rounded-off corners occur in all the rooms and the wall articulation of the façade recurs in the courtyards and oratory. Thus, in addition to S. Carlino (B52), a second early work, very logically formed throughout, came into being. It was somewhat less compact, but no less original and rich in consequences.

The façade extends across the entire surface, has two storeys of equal width (cf. B49 for this façade type), is concavely shaped overall, but is more strongly curved in the middle. This basic shape appears in pure form in the upper storey and is accentuated by the insertion of a central niche. But on the ground floor the central bay is convexly curved; the two adjoining bays pursue an inward but flat course. The trend-setting feature, which at the time was found elsewhere only in SS. Martina e Luca (B51), was not the concave curve itself – such a curve had been known in the High Renaissance (H23) –, but the many elements that became part of the main overall shape. Although the curve here is still subdued and not very sweeping in the High-Baroque sense (cf., later, B58 and B79), it was precisely this feature that caused the façade to have a strong influence on the Rococo of the 18C. Borromini's own explanation of the basic shape was that the five elements of the façade were meant to embrace the onlookers, with the chest in the middle and the upper and lower arms as wings. This indicates a basic difference between Borromini and Bernini. The latter lent shape to the same idea in a way that may have been simpler and less original, but – for example in the colonnades (B80) – was always more readily understandable.

Pilasters subdivide the façade into five bays, the central three of which project by one layer and, thanks to the gable, appear combined. The form of the gable is new, because round and straight shapes were here united for the first time. The gable also very decidedly lends to the façade – which looks like a palace, one reason being the large number of windows – the necessary religious element, and does not unshakably compel the other façade sections to come under its dominion, but – and this is typical of Borromini – allows them their independence. The inner shapes on both storeys are also noteworthy. A whole style – the Borromino style – was born in them, and without it the Rococo would be unthinkable, not only in Rome:

B53 Oratorio S. Filippo Neri in S. Maria in Vallicella

features to be emphasized are the pagoda-shaped, pointed window coverings, the capitals which were deliberately left unarticulated (cf. e. g. B110 for the 18C), and that famous ear shape on the door of the upper storey which is a further development of the transversely placed corbels in Michelangelo's work (e. g. H43) and is found in almost all Barochetto buildings. The inner shapes also display a particular dynamism. They cut far into the wall on the ground floor, while on the upper storey they are placed more loosely, because only one row of windows had to be accommodated. The reason for this is that on the ground floor the two rows of windows are assigned to the main room and the gallery of the oratory, while on the upper storey the gallery of the library is at window level and its main room is at door level.

This refers to the façade's relationship with its surroundings. The oratory behind the façade stands transverse to it, and the portal leads into a corridor to the side of the oratory. Thus the façade only partially corresponds to the interior. The relationship with the neighbouring church façade, which is taller but also much stiffer, is also problematical. Borromini was allowed to use only bricks for the oratory (except in a few structural sections), but employed an immensely precise technique to make the façade look as though it had been baked as a single unit.

Maruschelli had conceived the oratory as a purely rectangular room, but Borromini gave it a new face by providing two inventions which are central to the history of architectural development. He found a very elegant solution to a problem which had been a matter of concern for centuries: the problem of how to orchestrate a corner. He called a corner »the enemy of architecture«, and simply eliminated it by making it round. He designed the room as a skeleton structure by providing horizontal strips which started from the pilasters and were laid diagonally above the ceiling. This enabled the shell of the wall to be opened in some places such as the short sides, and was a first step towards the most permeable spatial creations of the late 17C and early 18C (e. g. B101, B111).

B54 S. Pietro in Montorio: Cappella Raimondi

Borromini's hand is also seen in the refectory and courtyards. The refectory was initially planned as a rectangle, but was finally built in an oval shape in order to obtain some extra space for service purposes and the spiral staircase, and also to facilitate the table discussions which were so important to this religious order, so that there were also some sensitively discerned functional reasons for this shape. Two features of the courtyards, whose arcades were later closed by Carlo Rainaldi, are the rounded-off corners and the use of colossal pilasters. These are unusual for courtyards, but are all the more surprising here because the exterior façade had two pilasters one above the other (see above). The confined courtyards look as if they have been orchestrated almost forcibly. The intention was probably to make the architectural elements of both façade and courtyard equal in size, and thus to emphasize the openness of this religious order. SG

Bibliography: J. Connors, *Borromini and the Roman Oratory. Style and Society*, New York, 1980.

B54 S. Pietro in Montorio: Cappella Raimondi
Piazza S. Pietro in Montorio 2 (plan VII 1/A)
1640–47
Gianlorenzo Bernini
Bernini, in one of his first family chapels, put into effect two new design ideas which became increasingly characteristic of his later work: the integration of all artistic genres into a uniform system of decoration, and the well-directed lighting. Half columns with pilasters behind them divide the oblong room of the Raimondi chapel into two parts: a square section housing the tombs, and a semicircular choir. This division was also adopted in the floor design and the vault decoration. In the design of the wall elevation, however, great importance was attached to uniting the two parts of the room. A uniform base-course and frieze area does not merely combine the choir with the tomb room, but also links the altar structure and tombs to the architecture of the chapel. The sculptures are fitted into the architectural ensemble by employing the same white type of marble for the busts of the deceased, the sarcophagi, the altar relief and the architectural elements.

The tomb chapel is dedicated to St Francis, whose ecstasy is depicted in the altar relief. This relief is set back about 70 cm from the altar architecture, and a narrow window which remains concealed from the onlooker lights it up with a glancing light. The lighting situation thus created makes the figures of the relief look almost like sculptures in the round and highlights the alter area. As in the later Cornaro chapel (B60), the »other-worldly« happenings at the altar are contrasted with this world in the chapels by the tombs with their busts of the deceased.These provide a link between the onlooker and the happenings at the altar. AS

B55 Palazzo Madama
Piazza Madama 11 (plan IV 1/A)
1642
Paolo Marucelli
This palace, today the seat of the senate, was owned by the Medici since 1505 and belonged to Caterina de' Medici, the queen of France. It owes its name to Margherita d'Austria, who was the daughter of Emperor Charles V and the widow of Alessandro de' Medici and had been granted the right of residence and usufruct in it for the rest of her life. The conversion goes back to Duke Ferdinand II and the architect Marucelli.

The façade with its nine axes was completed in 1642, and from then on criticism was directed against its luxuriant ornamentation. The palace, like so many palaces of its period, follows the typology of the Palazzo Farnese (H25), but is mostly of interest for its abundance of decorative shapes. First there is the contrast between the brick masonry and the travertine of the frames, reliefs and double corner rustication;

B55 Palazzo Madama

the central balcony is borne by marble columns. Then there are the window frames: on the ground floor, their abundant scrolls and Ionic pilaster capitals make them look like wood carvings, and the imitation of roof tiling on the flat coverings over the windows makes an almost odd impression. The lions' heads are, rather unusually, employed as keystones, and are explained by the heraldic vocabulary found elsewhere in the façade: lions appear in numerous parts of it, mainly in the piano nobile; Hercules, the symbolic figure of the French royal dynasty, is seen here in the form of a herma pilaster with the hide of the Nemean lion. Scrolls seem to push upwards the segmented gables of the window coverings, and there are also shell shapes with rosettes. And in the upper storey, the French lily is to be found in the split gable of the windows. At the very top, the mezzanine windows move up into the frieze of the classical entablature. SG

B56 S. Ivo della Sapienza

Corso del Rinascimento 40 (plan IV 1/A)
1642–60
Francesco Borromini

The chapel of the former university is among the most original buildings of Roman Baroque architecture, and is regarded as a key work by Borromini. This centrally planned building owes its outstanding position in the history of European architecture not only to the unusual shape of its ground plan, its unusual architectural details and a novel design for the interior, but also to a political and theological programme which the experts are today still engaged on deciphering.

The dimensions of the church, and its site in the eastern part of the Palazzo della Sapienza (B9), were already decided before the foundation stone was laid in 1643. Borromino had, in his plans, to take account of the exedra which had been begun by his predecessor Giacomo della Porta. It forms the eastern conclusion of the inner courtyard, and is at the same time part of the church façade. The church was probably finished as a shell by 1650. But the decoration work continued long into the pontificate of Pope Alexander VII and was only completed in 1660.

The exterior, that is to say the juxtaposition of della Porta's exedra and Borromini's dome, looks irregular when seen from the inner courtyard of the Palazzo della Sapienza. The concave exedra is articulated by five two-storeyed blind arcades with pilasters in front of them (tabularium motif, cf. A9), and is penetrated by windows and doors. In this way the two-storeyed porticoes which surround the courtyard on three sides are continued as blind articulation on the fourth side of the courtyard, and the exedra is assigned not to the church, but to the courtyard as its fourth arcaded wall. There is no church façade in the true sense, and the form and function of the space behind the frontage remain unclear. Borromini's dome structure is a programme contrasting with della Porta's exedra. A convexly curved drum which has a flat dome, a lantern

B56 S. Ivo della Sapienza

and a spiral lantern superstructure stands in opposition to the concave frontage. Simple and layered pilasters alternate rhythmically in subdividing the drum. The volume of the drum presses towards the outside, and is held together by the layered pilasters as if by buttresses. These pilasters continue along the flat dome to the lantern, and find their equivalent in the double columns of the lantern's articulation and in the concluding torches. Above this, a spiral adorned with jewel-like decorations winds its way heavenwards, and ends in a flame, ball and cross. Della Porta's delicate relief-work façade, almost graphic in appearance, is thus confronted by a dome superstructure which is designed to be round-bodied and three-dimensional.

Borromini deviated from della Porta's plans, which were probably known to him, in the design of the interior too. His predecessor intended a centrally planned building above a circular ground plan, whereas Borromini designed a complex figure for the ground plan, marked by spatial sections curving inwards and outwards. Drawings by Borromini show that the figure was developed from the geometrical shape of an equilateral triangle with its apex at the main portal and its base on the side including the altar. Semicircular extensions on the longitudinal sides, and flat-arched insertions at the extremities, make the triangle approximate to a star shape with a hexagonal core area.

From this ground plan, Borromini developed a revolutionary spatial idea. Instead of emphasizing the hexagonal core area as such and giving the star's extremities the character of side rooms, he combined everything into a unified room. The pilastered articulation which surrounds this room has a wide entablature and follows with great exactitude the inwardly and outwardly curving line of the ground plan, thus em-

B56 S. Ivo della Sapienza

bracing all the sections to form them into a unified space with a curving outline (cf. B52). This makes the church interior look uniform and readily surveyable, despite the complexity of the ground plan and the undulation of the wall. Borromini is striving, in the articulation of the wall elevation, to achieve a liberal and unifying effect. The wall is divided into two storeys by niches and stucco profiles, but colossal pilasters, which are an architectural order extending beyond a single storey, link up the wall and subdivide it into rhythmic bays. A curved wall panel, open in both storeys, is on each occasion flanked by two narrower wall sections which are largely closed. Borromini dispensed with any kind of small sectioned wall design, such as stuccoed ornaments or subordinate architectural elements, and decided that the only identifying subdividing motif would be the rhythmized succession of pilasters. This spatial concept aims at unification and also applies to the dome which, without any linking intermediate zone, starts directly from the wide entablature that reproduces the ground plan. In this way the dome assumes the building's complicated basic shape. The delicate transition from the convex and concave dome segments to the strutted circle of the lantern is a masterly artistic and technical achievement of Roman architecture.

The well-thought-out design for the ground plan, interior articulation, and dome shape of S. Ivo desists from the otherwise customary hierarchy of main space and side rooms, and combines all the sections to form a main space (cf. B52). The fact that S. Ivo was nevertheless scarcely imitated later may be due to its complexity and artistic originality, and also to the technical difficulty of the building work. Thus S. Ivo remained an exotic individual phenomenon in the history of Roman architecture.

Borromini's church has been interpreted in the most widely differing ways. It is dedicated to Ivo, the saint of jurists, is the chapel of a university called »Sapienza« (wisdom), and has a corresponding programme. An early overall plan for the building shows a design for the choir having seven columns and the

planned biblical inscription »Wisdom has built her house, she has hewn her seven pillars, and she has spread her table.« (Proverbs, 9, 1–2.) Outlines for this interpretation as a »house of wisdom« are, in the present structure, to be found in the six cherubim which were part of the university coat of arms, in the Holy Ghost dove and in the lamb with the book with seven seals on the exterior of the church. All these features are attributes of wisdom. What is more, the building is related to the popes ruling at the particular times. Contemporaries recognized the bee, the heraldic animal of Urban VIII, in the ground plan of the church. During the pontificate of Alexander VII, professors at the university pointed out that the ground plan imitated »the shape of a flying bee«. Engravings indicate that flying bees were also planned for in the design of the dome. But Alexander VII, more obviously than Urban VIII, ordered parts of his coat of arms, the »three mountains«, to be mounted on the interior and exterior of the church.

The unusual superstructure of the lantern in the exterior structure has not yet been explained and is difficult to decipher. It has been variously interpreted as the Tower of Babel, that is to say as an instance of the hybris of human knowledge, with the Christian cross then rising above it, or as an allusion to Mount Purgatory in Dante's Divine Comedy. The many interpretations strikingly include one in which it is understood as a stylized papal tiara. Borromini himself spoke of the coils of the spiral as being »three crowns« set with »jewels«. This makes the comparison with a tiara plausible. The »house of wisdom« would then be very closely related to the papacy. AS

Bibliography: H. Ost: »Borrominis römische Universitätskirche«, *Zeitschrift für Kunstgeschichte*, 1967, p. 101; J. B. Scott, »S. Ivo alla Sapienza and Borromini's symbolic language«, *Journal of the Society of Architectural Historians*, 1982, p. 294; F. Rangoni, *S. Ivo alla Sapienza e lo »Studium Urbis«*, Rome, 1989.

B57 S. Maria dei Sette Dolori
Via Garibaldi 27 (plan IV 1/B)
1642–65
Francesco Borromini

Soon after Camilla Virginia Savelli Farnese had founded the order of the »Oblates of the Seven Sorrows of the Blessed Virgin«, Borromini was commissioned to build a convent with a church for this order of nuns (1642). He drew up designs but, owing to other commitments, left the execution to Antonio del Grande. An invoice signed by Borromini indicates that the shell of the façade, the vestibule behind it, and the convent church, were all largely completed in 1646. The church interior was stuccoed in 1648/49. The convent building was erected from 1658 to 1665 without any further involvement on Borromini's part.

The façade remained incomplete, and today it is an unplastered brickwork frontage flanked by two semi-elliptical »turrets«. The seven projecting façade axes, which curve concavely backwards at the centre and are subdivided by pilasters and niches, were completed up to half their height. All the windows, the right-hand side portal, and the shape of the central portal, are later, disfiguring additions. It is also unclear whether the right-hand tower-like extension really accords with Borromini's plans. This »tower« is missing from a drawing, by Borromini, of the façade (Albertina 645). Strange to say, this drawing has itself only been completed up to half the height. The drawing also shows that no windows or doors other than those in the central axis and the left-hand »tower« were planned. It was intended that only pilasters and niches should subdivide the façade. The façade of this convent thus looks emphatically self-contained, and differs in this from the façade of the S. Filippo oratory (B53), which is formally comparable except for the windows. Although the inserted niches give the wall surface a more varied appearance, they also demonstrate the thickness and massiveness of the wall. The strict seclusion of the order is thus taken as an artistic theme in the design of the façade.

A vestibule with an approximately square-shaped ground plan is concealed behind the main portal. The vestibule's convexly bending long sides and bevelled corners give the room a curving outline. Researchers have repeatedly pointed out that this basic shape is similar to that of a room in the small thermal baths at the Villa Hadriana in Tivoli (A32). The vestibule allows access to the convent church, which is oriented parallel to the façade. This longitudinally rectangular room has rounded-off corners (typical of rooms by Borromini), one choir chapel and two side chapels, and is subdivided by a rhythmized colonnade of half columns. The spaces between the columns are filled with wall panels with niches let into them. There is a clear distinction between the colonnade and the wall sections. The columns are separated from the filling walls

B57 S. Maria dei Sette Dolori

B58 Palazzo della Congregazione di Propaganda Fide: façade facing Piazza di Spagna

by a kind of opening, and support an entablature which projects further than the walls. Borromini routes the colonnade uninterruptedly through all four sides of the space. The entablature does not break off even at the openings for entrance, choir and side chapels, but bends upwards in the manner of a Syrian arch and forms an arcade. In this way Borromini succeeds in uniting this oblong into a kind of elongated centrally planned space. S. Maria dei Sette Dolori can in this respect be regarded as a simplified variation on the earlier monastery church of S. Carlo alle Quattro Fontane (B52). The space originally had white stucco decorations. The coloured decorations, and the ceiling design, are the result of later alterations. The lighting of the space was also originally different: it is not known when the rectangular windows on the long sides were added. AS

Bibliography: M. Bosi, *S. Maria dei Sette Dolori*, Rome, 1971; P. Portoghesi, *Borromini*, Milan, 1977.

B58 Palazzo della Congregazione di Propaganda Fide: façade facing Piazza di Spagna
Piazza di Spagna (plan V 1/A)
1644
Gianlorenzo Bernini

The architecture of this palace is particularly instructive, because Bernini and Borromini, the two chief architects of the seicento in Rome, played a prominent part in the history of its construction. Their differing architectural styles are clearly revealed in it (on the history of its construction, cf. B65).

In 1644, the Congregation commissioned Bernini to design the façade facing the Piazza di Spagna. Ten years previously, he had built the same client's private chapel (later torn down by Borromini). The façade is very restrained and plain – it is as if it attracted the onlooker's attention more by its exposed location

B59 Villa Doria Pamphili: Casino Bel Respiro

than by its architecture. Its severe elegance may be related to the fact that the client was the Society of Jesus. But Borromini's façade on the south side is an argument opposing this idea. Apart from this, it is still unclear to what extent Bernini may only have been making some corrections to the plans – which cannot be reconstructed – drawn up by Valerio, the father of the Theatine order.

This is an unplastered brickwork shell construction not frequently met with in Rome in such monumentality (Collegio Romano, B12, Cortile del Belvedere, H6). The only subdividing elements are two cornices and pilaster strips. The pilaster strips continue unbroken through all three storeys, as the cornices do not interrupt them but are moulded around them. This gives the façade a strong vertical movement. The central wall panel consists of a widened pilaster strip, which does not merely accentuate the centre, but rather – along with the lateral pilaster strips and the recessed panels which are interspersed by way of interruption – illustrates the thickness of the wall. The wall thus becomes a relief, and the mass of the wall becomes perceptible. The façade as a whole may make a sever and sober impression, but as a brickwork shell construction it is conceived on a grand scale and its execution is successful. PZ

B59 Villa Doria Pamphili: Casino Bel Respiro
Via S. Pancrazio (plan G1 1/C and plan VII 1/A)
1644–48
Alessandro Algardi
This, the second largest park in Rome, is today Rome's finest Baroque garden ensemble, with statues, waterworks, lakes and pastures. It has hardly suffered from 19C expansions and alterations. The casino and gardens were designed by Algardi: in front of the casino there is a garden with beds, and behind it a Giardino Segreto which has stairs leading down to it beside the casino and is enclosed by walls with columns, niches, statues and flaming vases. Diagonally to the right of this, a very regularly planted wood of

stone pines extends transversely to a canal which linked an oval lake (still visible in the ground) to a cascade (c. 1730).

In placing the order for this work, Innocent X and his nephew Camillo Pamphili intended to make Algardi their sculptor-architect (as Urban VIII had previously done with Bernini). Borromini's plans were rejected. Algardi interpreted the façade of the casino as being a bearer of images, which were ancient busts. This also occurred in Mannerism, an example being the Villa Medici (B4, and also B31, B35). Algardi gave the tall block a clearer structure, but it was not dynamic in the High-Baroque style: the two-storeyed lateral façade with its six axes has lateral risalti which each occupy one axis, and the centre recedes; the main frontage with its seven axes, on the other hand, has three storeys facing the garden, and the three central axes project to the extent of a full window axis. Above this there is a gallery-like storey which is also cube-shaped, but smaller. The building has a block-like outline which is foreign to the idea of a villa, but is made to appear less unfriendly by the decorations on the walls, and also by two terraces with statues and vases. What is more, the planned flat wings would have provided the transition to the world of nature. The symmetrical arrangement of the rooms around a central rotunda goes back to Palladio, and all these rooms were used for festivities and the installation of antiques. The dwelling quarters were in the old Casale. The stucco is more splendid than anywhere else in Rome. SG

B60 S. Maria della Vittoria: Cappella Cornaro
Via XX Settembre 17 (plan V 2/A)
1644–52
Gianlorenzo Bernini
It was in the Cornaro chapel that Bernini put into effect, in perfect form, his guiding artistic idea of uniting architecture, sculpture and painting into a *Gesamtkunstwerk*. When seen from the ideal viewpoint in the centre of the crossing, the chapel, which occupies the left arm of the church's transept, presents itself as a room incrusted with coloured marble and restrainedly subdivided by delicate pilasters. Features within this subdivision are the altar architecture, an oval rotunda framed by an aedicule, and the illusionistically expanded balcony niches on the side walls. The altar tabernacle is the setting for Bernini's masterly group, the »Ecstasy of St Theresa«. It receives its own light from a concealed window, and its atmosphere thus contrasts with the rest of the chapel. Opposite the mystic happenings on the altar – an angel is wounding Theresa with the arrow of divine love – Bernini places an audience: six members of the Cornaro family are watching the happenings from balcony loges. Two planes of reality confront one another in this relationship between stage and audience: firstly there is the visionary, supernatural character of the happenings at the altar, and secondly the worldly, observant attitude

of the Cornaro family. Bernini expands this relationship once more: in the chapel vault there is a painted angel's halo accompanying the sudden descent of the Holy Spirit. These supernatural happenings now concern not only Theresa alone, but also the members of the founder family above whose heads the miracle is happening. Architecture, sculpture, painting and light unified in a way that each genre is involved in its own way in realizing the concept of this subject matter. AS

B61 Piazza Navona
Piazza Navona (plan IV 1/A)
incl. 1645–55

The Piazza Navona can be reckoned among the chief Baroque city squares in Italy. This oblong square surrounded by houses, palaces and two churches concludes in a straight row of buildings on its southern short side, and in a semicircular row on its northern. The piazza is accentuated by three fountains, one at each of its two ends and one in the middle.

The unusual ground plan of the piazza derives from the shape of a Roman stadium which was built under Domitian in c. AD 92–96 and was used for athletic games and, for a time, gladiators' fights. Remains of the walls of this stadium were incorporated into the foundations of today's building work in the square, and are still visible in the basements of individual

B60 S. Maria della Vittoria: Cappella Cornaro

B61 Piazza Navona

buildings and on the northern short side of the square, by Piazza Tor Sanguigna. The name »Navona«, a vernacular derivative of »agon« (contest), is itself reminiscent of the square's ancient function. After becoming desolate in the Middle Ages, it was not until the early Renaissance that the piazza again increased in economic significance, to which the work of setting up the market (1477), paving the square (1485), and building the church of S. Giacomo degli Spagnuoli (F2) at its south-eastern edge, all bear witness. Aristocratic families, including the Pamphili, moved here, and as a result the Piazza Navona developed into a residential district for the upper social stratum. In 1574–76, Giacomo della Porta built the fountains on the northern and southern sides of the square as part of an extensive fountain-building programme which affected 18 water supply points in Rome. After 1652, the southern Fontana del Moro, which was decorated with Tritons, was fitted out by Bernini with another basin and adorned with the figure of Moro which gives the fountain its name. The figures on the northern Fontana di Nettuno are 19C.

The square was given its present shape mainly during the pontificate of Innocent X Pamphili (1644 to 1655). Soon after being elected pope, Innocent X ordered extensive construction works and other regulatory measures to be carried out in this city piazza: they consisted of expanding his family palace (Palazzo Pamphili, B62), rebuilding S. Agnese in Agone (B71), and building the Fountain of the Four Rivers.

The Fountain of the Four Rivers is an immense mass of rock which rises from a round basin and is surmounted by an obelisk. Four larger-than-life figures, being personifications of the rivers Ganges (with an oar), Nile (with covered head), Rio della Plata (with silver coins) and Danube (supporting the papal coat of arms), rest on rocky platforms.

There had been a simple fountain structure in the middle of the square since the late 16C. Borromini was one of those who submitted designs for the monumental fountain commissioned by Innocent X., which was given a water supply of its own. If contemporary sources are to be believed, Borromini's project already contained two aspects which are the basis of today's fountain: the notion of placing an ancient obelisk above the fountain, and the idea of connecting the base of the obelisk with the image of the four continents in the shape of the four rivers. But it was not Borromini whom Innocent X, in 1648, commissioned to build the fountain, but Bernini, and sources relate that this was after he had seen a silver model of Bernini's design. Bernini developed the basic ideas in a way which was brilliant from the point of view of both form and subject matter: instead of an architectural base, he selected a massive, weighty piece of rock as the substructure for the obelisk. The rock looks monumental and gives the impression of a great abundance of water. Bernini skilfully obscured the real problem of the fountain, namely the fact that the water pressure was too low. The outlet points for the water are all in the lower areas of the massive rock. There are no gushing water outlets or cascades in the upper parts of the fountain. The irregularity of the water routing, the emergence of the water in a wide, fan-shaped jet, and the interplay of rock and water, all disguise the fact that the water is flowing down from only a slight height. The figured decorations of the fountain are also new: the four river gods are no longer axially arranged base-course figures as they were in cinquecento fountains. Instead, they are depicted in an intense state of movement, and they relate to their spatial surroundings.

In regulating the shape of the square, constructing fountains, enlarging the Palazzo Pamphili and building the church of S. Agnese (B71), Innocent X was pushing ahead with urbanist modifications for which there were probably very specific reasons. The Pamphili pope's plan to move his residence from the Vatican into his family's palace on the Piazza Navona seems to have been the determining factor behind the work of redesigning this city square in imposing fashion. The Piazza Navona was intended to become the forecourt of the papal residence, and as such to convey a vivid impression of the family's fame (consider the numerous Pamphili coats of arms) and of papal world dominion (the allegory of the four rivers). AS

Bibliography: R. Preimesberger, »Obeliscus Pamphilius«, *Münchner Jahrbuch der Bildenden Kunst*, 1974, p. 77.

B62 Palazzo Pamphili
Piazza Navona 14 (plan IV 1/A–1/B)
1646–49
Girolamo Rainaldi, Francesco Borromini

The buildings along the western edge of the Piazza Navona (B61) are the Palazzo Pamphili and the church of S. Agnese in Agone (B71). G. Rainaldi, an architect who had moved to Parma, was recalled to Rome to expand the small Pamphili palace which was set back somewhat from the line of buildings. Within the short space of three years, Rainaldi doubled the size of the

B62 Palazzo Pamphili

palace by incorporating into the structural complex the adjoining palaces, acquired for this purpose, of the Rossi and Cybo families. Some small streets which originally separated the buildings were built over in this process (today they are the main portal and the galery building). A uniform façade to Rainaldi's plans was placed in front of the irregular complex of three buildings. The gallery structure between palace and church follows a design by Borromini.

The lengthy frontage is subdivided by two lateral risalti, each having one axis, and by a central risalto with five axes. The front elevation consists of a tall base-course storey with rusticated slabs, followed by two main storeys, a mezzanine and an attic. The central risalto, and the set-back sections of the façade, each have an accentuated central axis which is emphasized by portals, balconies and the window coverings.

The appearance of the façade in the lateral sections is determined by the horizontal succession of the windows. That succession is broken up in the area of the risalti. Blind arcades and pilastered articulation recur in all the storeys of the risalti and create vertical relationships which form a counterpoise to the horizontally defined lateral sections. A comparison with Borromini's narrow gallery façade, which strives for the effect produced by large individual motifs (Syrian arch) and for greater three-dimensionality in the sub dividing elements, shows that Rainaldi's façade is still rooted in the spirit of Mannerism. AS

B63 Palazzo Falconieri
Via Giulia 1 (plan IV 1/B)
1646–49
Francesco Borromini

Borromini's creative intervention is a lesson in how an everyday 16C building could be turned into an impressive Baroque palace by means of some moderate changes. The city palace of the Odescalchi brothers was a standard 16C building of the Palazzo Farnese type (H25): it was block-like, with three storeys and eight window axes (the portal with its rustic frame was located asymmetrically), and the flat wall was subdivided horizontally, and only by flat cornices which divided the storeys and by rows of windows with flat roofings (the rustication of the upper storeys is 19C). The conclusion was formed by the corbelled entablature with weapon symbols and the Odescalchi's coat of arms.

In 1646, Orazio Falconieri, the new owner, commissioned Borromini to lend the palace a certain greatness. Borromini enlarged the frontage by supplying three additional axes in the north (on the right), added a portal which provided symmetry but was blind (its keystone was the falcon, the heraldic animal of the Falconieri), and built a separate L-shaped section which faced the Tiber and was an extension of the more northerly of the two originally very short wings attached at right angles to the rear of the section. (That L-shaped section was later largely demolished due to the straightening of the Tiber.) The building achieved its greatness thanks to two interventions. The first of these was that Borromini basically retained the old structural scheme (with rather small windows placed at intervals) of the main façade, but by building his extension he gave the frontage new and broad proportions which look majestic, and he also supplied it with a monumental frame consisting, at the sides, of the famous falcon hermae with their energetic appearance (alluding to the owner's name) and, at the top, of a continuous attic with small dormer windows. The second intervention consisted of Borromini's placing a belvedere on the southern wing, facing the Tiber. The belvedere with its three arches competed with that by Giacomo della Porta on the famous Palazzo Farnese next door (H25), and was evidently intended to surpass it in terms of the view across the Tiber. The belvedere differed from della Porta's not only because it was not linked into the main structure below the corbelled entablature, and instead was a free-standing component extending beyond that structure, but also because Borromini did not limit himself to simple arches; but, in using the Palladian motif, selected a much richer form which was once again ennobled by the columns placed in front of the pillars and by the balustrade with Janus-faced busts on top. SG

B63 Palazzo Falconieri

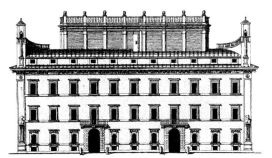

B64 SS. Vincenzo ed Anastasio

B64 SS. Vincenzo ed Anastasio
Piazza di Trevi (plan V 1/A)
1646–50
Martino Longhi the Younger

In 1612, Paul V gave to the Hieronymite order, as a gift, the old parish church of the Quirinal. As that parish church, it preserves in its apse the entrails, removed prior to embalmment, of popes from a period of four centuries. The new building erected in 1614 gave way to another in 1640, because Urban VIII wanted Bernini to redesign the Fontana di Trevi (cf. B126). Cardinal Mazarin, at that time the adviser of Louis XIII, financed the construction of the façade and probably also of the interior which is by Gaspare de' Vecchi and is an insignificant structure imitating Il Gesù (B1, before 1643, choir and decorations by Ferroni, c. 1760). Sedlmayr acknowledged the façade as being the first of the five great High-Baroque façades in Rome.

In the façade, Longhi continued with the ideas he had developed for S. Antonio (B50). The starting point was again the cross-section façade of Il Gesù, with a scroll (here it has hermae) linking the two-storeyed centre to the single-storeyed wings. The wall once again remained traditional, and the façade is to be interpreted from the point of view of its orchestration, which here is the architectural order. It develops freely in front of the wall, and differs from the wall in that it does not remain flat. Similarly free-standing columns are only found in ancient Rome (cf. e.g. A52).

The chief element of the façade is the full column, which was hardly used in exteriors in Rome before Longhi's time, because Michelangelo, in St Peter's which was the most prominent structure for centuries, had preferred the pilaster (H31, B34). The use of the full column is therefore often understood as being a French influence (because of the client!). For Longhi, the full column was decisive: the columns create a vertical strip in the middle, and the width of the façade becomes hardly noticeable. This example soon met with many successors in Rome, an example being S. Maria della Pace (B79). The question of whether columns are being used is less important than how they are used. The central section of each storey is subdivided by three columns which project one in front of the other. But the subdividing work diverges in the two storeys, and subtle shifts arise: above, each pair of columns supports a gable which is clearly assigned to it, whereas, below, one gable is missing and the existing gables do not clearly begin above the columns. Instead, the outer gable is between the two outer columns of each triad, and the inner gable is too narrow to be assigned to the innermost pair of columns. This incongruity is also seen in the relationship with the mouldings of the entablature. Below, the columns seem to have been pushed away underneath the gables which they support, and therefore do not stand so freely as they do above, the expressive aim probably being to leave room for the portal. All this shows a typically High-Baroque preference for dynamism and for the ambivalences which did not disappear until the first peak phase of Baroque Classicism (from c. 1670 onwards). It is instructive to make a comparison with the column placings in S. Marcello (B103). Gables of this size inserted one inside another are – like the accumulation of full columns – a novelty for Rome, 150 years after Michelangelo invented them in the Biblioteca Laurenziana (but cf. B1). They can be found in Longhi's Northern Italian home territory and in his earlier façade of S. Antonio (B50).

With the gables too, it is how they are used that is more important. The gables, too, project further above than below. This fact and the increased three-dimensionality and diversity of shapes result in an upwards movement. They also make the upper conclusion appear mightier, because it is a conclusion not only of a storey, but of the façade as a whole, and is a counterpoise to the greater width , i. e. more quantity, below. The reverse of this is that, below, the design of the stairs is simpler. They are used as a combining element: the lowest step is for the whole façade, and the highest is for the particular triad of columns, while the break line runs diagonally towards the innermost column.

The way in which the façade relates to its surroundings is also new. Only from this time on did it became fashionable in Rome to place church façades on the edge of a street and relate them diagonally to a city square (B52, B87/88). The column at the flank of the façade also continued to be a dynamic element: it is a prelude to the theme of the façade for the visitor approaching from behind. When, 90 years later, the Fontana di Trevi (B126) supplanted the city square, the dynamism and full sonority of the façade were confronted with an almost superior opposite number. Some leading façades of the Roman High Baroque (S. Maria della Pace and in Campitelli, B79, B91) would be unthinkable without Longhi's design, the first in the Roman Baroque to have full columns, gables inserted one inside the other, and references to different visual angles. SG

B65 Palazzo della Congregazione di Propaganda Fide: side façade and Cappella »Re Magi«
Via di Propaganda Fide (plan V 1/A)
1646–66
Francesco Borromini

The lateral façade of the Palazzo facing the Via Propaganda Fide, and the palace chapel of the »Re Magi« which is dedicated to the Three Wise Men, are part of Borromini's architectural legacy.

The Congregation of Propaganda Fide, founded in 1622, was intended for the training of Jesuit missionaries. The palace was given as a gift by a Spanish priest, and in 1634 Bernini enriched it by adding a chapel and the façade facing the Piazza di Spagna (B58). In 1646, after the Congregation had acquired some neighbouring plots of land in order to expand the palace eastwards, Borromini was commissioned to redesign the southern side. While he was planning the façade he demanded that Bernini's chapel be torn down, as it tied him down too much when it came to designing the façade. His request was granted and Borromini probably felt entirely gratified, as he is likely to have felt satisfaction at replacing a work by his rival by a work of his own. The work that came into being stands alone in the history of art as, owing to its extraordinary shape, it found no successors.

The plain wall of the northern façade is continued by Borromini in the southern façade and to some extent serves as a frame for the central section, which is thereby more strongly emphasized by being different. The left half of the central section includes the »Re Magi« chapel, and the portal leads into the vestibule from which the chapel and the cortile are reached; the right half contains bottege (shops) and a staircase. The façade has symmetrical axes and does not indicate what the interior rooms are like (cf. the earlier B53). The façade is shaped by its skeleton architecture, in which colossal pilasters extend through the base-course storey, mezzanine and piano nobile. They look so mighty and supporting that the wall panels between them are merely a visual filling and lose the character of a wall. Michelangelo had created the characteristic prototype in the conservators' palace (H30). The window frames seem squeezed between the pilasters. They are curved concavely here, and convexly at the centre. In this way they enhance the round windows are let into the vault which consists of diagonal ribs running in parallel and is of a kind reminiscent of late-Gothic net vaults.

The further development of the architecture here lies in the consistent avoidance of a readily apparent wall. This avoidance can be sensed in the niches for the portrait busts, and also elsewhere. The wall of those niches has a dark covering, and this makes it it seem to open up into the unlit apse aisles. The room becomes an airy »pillared hall« with a colossal order. The corner reinforcement (consisting, in the Oratorio dei Filippini, of diagonally placed pillars) is dispensed with here, because Borromini consistently pursued the leitmotiv of his chapel architecture: the rhythmic bay is guided once around the rectangular area without any abrupt transitions. The required suppleness was given to the room in the narrow bay found in the corners, which have gentle curves consisting of pilasters with hollows in them. In addition, all architectural elements were combined into a uniform, interwoven net. PZ

B66 S. Giovanni in Laterano: interior
Piazza di Porta S. Giovanni (plan VIII 2/A)
1647–49
Francesco Borromini

This church on the Lateran is the pope's real cathedral and is regarded as the mother and head of all the churches in the world, whereas St Peter's, by contrast, is merely the burial church of St Peter and the palace church of the Vatican. The landed property of the Laterani, an ancient Roman family, fell into the hands of the imperial family in AD 65. In AD 314 it passed to the church, thanks to a donation by Constantine the Great. The basilica, which had a nave and four aisles, but probably no transept, was built shortly thereafter with the aid of generous support from the emperor. It suffered greatly from wars, the weather and earthquakes, but was repeatedly restored, and in consequence the substance of its structure is still preserved today. Domenico Fontana built the northern transept façade (cf. B21) in 1586–90, while Giacomo della Porta was responsible for the thorough rebuilding of the transept itself (1597–1601). A generation later, the walls of the nave of the church were threatening to collapse, and in addition the holy year of 1650 was coming ever closer. These were reasons enough to publicize a plan to rebuild the nave. But in contrast to St Peter's, the aim was that the old basilica should to a very large extent be integrated into the new structure, and this requirement restricted the architect's freedom. Francesco Borromini won the competition. Conversion work was begun in 1647, after a planning phase lasting several months. Thanks to great speed and purposeful organization, success was achieved in completing the final building works on time in October 1649.

In the nave of the church, the old substance of the building consisted of 15 low, arch-supporting

B65 Palazzo della Congregazione di Propaganda Fide: side façade and Cappella »Re Magi«

buoyancy of the façade and even seem to bend beneath the power of the pilasters. The façade is itself curved: at the sides, it protrudes diagonally from the smooth framing wall, and then, guided by the pilasters, proceeds evenly across three axes before curving concavely inwards in the central bay. This unprecedented interplay of the curves is rich in tension and is accentuated by the aedicules of the windows, whose effectiveness exceeds anything previously known. Borromini also remains unorthodox in the details: the capital of the pilasters now only consists of five grooves, and the cornice with its corbels curving backwards and forwards rests directly upon it; the architrave and frieze, which until then had been obligatory, are both absent. Borromini is no longer adhering to the classical principles of architecture (cf. the earlier B53); the free development of his abundance of ideas lends living and energetic movement to the façade.

The building work on the chapel (the porter opens it in the mornings) was preceded by numerous preliminary designs which developed from the plans for the previously erected Oratorio dei Filippini (B53). By this example, Borromini once again shows us how seriously he takes the subject of skeleton architecture. The chapel consists of massive four-cornered pillars (the first architectural order) which support an architrave running all the way round. A colossal order of pilasters placed out in front (the second order) extends through both storeys and supports the moulded entablature upon which the vault rests. But the windows pierce the architrave and frieze of the entablature – once again, classical values are negated. Above this,

B66 S. Giovanni in Laterano: interior

marble columns on each side. These arcades came only a third of the way up the nave wall, and therefore made a small and squat impression. What Borromini had in mind during the planning phase was a liberal and colossal articulation of the wall, but this large-scale idea was incompatible with the old, small-sectioned structure. In his third draft, which was finally put into effect with minor alterations, he made only limited use of the original, time-honoured arrangement of the columns, because he eliminated every third column and designed the nave wall at his own discretion. The main ideas are the colossal pilaster which extends up the entire nave wall, and the associated rhythmic bay. Here, wall panels with niches alternate with a large arcade extending half way up the nave. The narrow bays in the wall are the pillars which really provide the support, and Borromini expressively emphasizes their function, for the colossal pilasters support, at their top, an entablature upon which, finally, the flat ceiling lies. On the other hand, the wall sections consisting of wide bays are – while having arcades below – fitted with windows all the way across above. The window and its frame (an aedicule) extend up to the beginning of the ceiling. According to classical principles, the entablature ought to run continuously along above this point, but it is interrupted, negated and supplanted. The entire wall section seems to be suspended between the pilasters – it is not a supporting element, but fills a space.

At the same time, Borromini prevents the cubically shaped pillar from looking like a massive bar. In his striving simultaneously to penetrate both mass and space, he hollows out the pillar and inserts a niche, a relief panel and an oval panel with an image. The concavely shaped figured niche below has a three-dimensionally shaped counterpart in the aedicule, which curves convexly outwards in black, gloriously contrasting marble. The aedicule seems too wide for the wall panel, and its outward curve lends the colossal pilasters a sinewy strength. This growth in strength culminates on the eastern short side in the entrance

area, where the portal arcade curves outwards and is surmounted by a free-standing aedicule in front of the upper window. The colossal pilasters are slightly bent in this area, as the narrow bays lead diagonally from the nave walls to the eastern wall. In this way Borromini avoids the formation of corners, which his contemporary Martinelli called »these enemies of good architecture«. The spatial continuum thereby created is given a centred effect in the middle of the church's nave. Above the arcade, the window aedicule extends across the entire wall width of the intercolumniation, and corresponds formally to its counterpart above the eastern entrance. The independence of the nave derives mainly from the emphasis placed upon its central longitudinal and transverse axes, which are surrounded by the vividly articulated wall.

There are two aisles on each side of the nave, and their height decreases towards the outside, thus giving the inner aisles a clerestory. The rhythm of the nave, the succession of arches and longitudinally rectangular pillars, is transferred to the aisles.

However, in the inner aisles, Borromini did not limit the rhythm to the wall, but transferred it to the entire area by forming bays by the use of vaults: the narrow bays starting from pillars have a longitudinal barrel vault, and the larger bays that proceed from the nave arcade have a shallow dome. Only the large bays are lit up by a clerestory window, and in this way Borromini transferred the theme of the rhythmic bay from the wall to the space and, what is more, to the light; dark and light bays alternate in sprightly fashion, and the alternating lighting makes the rhythmic succession easy for the eye to comprehend.

A plain colonnade of pillars separates the outer aisles from the inner. Due to their lack of height, arcades could not have been installed without making the springing height of the pillars appear compressed and unattractive. Thus, if the spatial unity was to be elegantly preserved in the inner aisles, a colonnade was the only alternative. By using cherubim heads to smooth over the transitions from the pillars to the entablature, Borromini once again avoided hard corners. PZ

B67 Casino Giustiniani-Massimo
Via Matteo Boiardo 16 (plan VIII 2/A)
conversion 1649
Francesco Borromini

Vincenzio Giustiniani, whose main villa was outside the Porta del Popolo, built himself this Casino as a small country house in his vineyards near the Lateran. In 1637 the estate passed into the possession of his adopted son who, in 1649, decorated the building with ancient reliefs and busts from Vincenzio's famous collection. The traditional attribution of the work to Francesco Borromini has been confirmed by researchers.

Before being converted, the Casino was a plain rectangular structure, subdivided by flat pilaster strips and concluding in a rich entablature which was adorned with the Giustiniani's eagle and tower. In order to obtain a larger area for the new decorations, the loggia in the entrance frontage was walled up (the garden loggia followed in the 19C). Borromini created a convincing synthesis in the decorations which consisted of ancient marble works and imaginative stuccoed adornments. Basing himself on the design principle employed in the courtyard of the Palazzo Mattei di Giove (B31), he developed a clear system of decorations which replaced the intricate articulation which was begun in the Villa Medici (B4). A decorative frieze, in which the Giustiniani eagle alternates with the Pamphili dove (the coat of arms of Maria Pamphili who was married in 1640), runs around the entire building; the ancient sarcophagus reliefs are integrated as window parapets. Busts, and medallions with profiled heads and relief panels – the latter are surrounded by garlands and decorative frames – are set in above the windows. The quality of the work, and the abundance of the decorations, both clearly betray Borromini's hand. Today the Casino is known for the frescos which C. Massimo, the new owner, commissioned from Cornelius and Overbeck (1817–29). EJ

B68 Palazzo Altieri
Piazza del Gesù (plan IV 2/B)
1650–54, 1670–76
Giovanni Antonio de Rossi

The lower section of the large palace between Via and Piazza del Gesù and the Vie del Plebiscito, degli Astalli and S. Stefano on the Piazza del Gesù was built in 1650–54 and included the lateral façade, which was in the Via del Gesù to the left. This section was financed by Cardinal Giambattista Altieri, the brother of the later Pope Clement X (1670–76). After the latter's election, a second and taller section was added to the right. Its entire length extends along Il Gesù, and its main façade faces east and is in the Via degli Astali. It was financed by Cardinal Albertoni, the uncle of Gaspare

B68 Palazzo Altieri

B67 Casino Giustiniani-Massimo

Albertoni, who was the husband of the pope's niece Laura and entered into the inheritance after the Altieri had died out. The palace is the last in a series which had continued since Paul V and in which every High-Baroque pope built an almost new family palace.

The main façade of the old section continued to determine the design. Its articulation follows Sangallo's typology (H25), in which the wall is dominant, is subdivided only by the rows of windows and the horizontal cornices upon which they stand, and is reinforced at the edges by a strip of bosses. The shape of the window coverings (with the heraldic star of the Altieri) looks sparse too and remains unaltered in each row of windows, although the alternation of segmented and triangular gables had been known for over a century. Borromini's palace-type façades (B53, B65) and the façade of the Palazzo Barberini (B45) had already been built, so that this façade is regarded as old-fashioned. It does though have two points of great quality. Firstly, de Rossi, who was still of tender years, was able in 1650 to lend a new rhythm to the old typology by inserting a central risalto with five axes. Bernini later gave this rhythm a splendid form (B72 and especially B93). Not only does this structure harmonize well with that of the façade of Il Gesù (B1), which also has a central section and (lower) wings, but it was also evidently felt to be so convincing that Fuga adopted it again in the building opposite (B138). Secondly, de Rossi recognized in the course of the extension work that the old façade on the Piazza del Gesù was, by reason of its location, the only one suitable as a main façade, that that part of the palace was of human proportions, and that all the other endless façades therefore had to be adapted, that is to say subordinated, to this scheme. Thus he did not succumb to the temp-tation of revising the work from the days of his youth, as this would have been contrary to the requirements of the building site. The main façade today therefore makes the building look much smaller and more easily surveyable than it is. There was no characteristic endless façade as there later was in the 18C (B122). A competing design by Carlo Fontana was rejected probably precisely because it would have preserved the continuity only to a much lesser extent.

Rossi achieved a major breakthrough in this façade. When attaching other building sections, his aim was to preserve the autonomy of the façade while nonetheless creating a continuum. This was why an element of vertical articulation was given only to the last and furthest removed axis of the adjoining section, with its seventeen axes, in the Via del Plebiscito.

One of the great staircases of the Roman Baroque was built by de Rossi between the two inner courtyards around which the building sections are arranged. Once again there is a tendency towards regularization: the asymmetry of the complex was not laid bare. The attraction of asymmetries was not recognized until the 18C (an example is the stairs which are the chief object of interest of the Palazzo Pichini). SG

Bibliography: A. Mezzetti, *Palazzo Altieri*, Rome, 1951; A. Schiavo, *The Altieri Palace*, Rome, n. d. (1965).

B69 Carceri Nuove
Via Giulia 52 (plan IV 1/B)
1652–55
Antonio del Grande

In 1652, Pope Innocent X placed the order for a new prison building which was to replace the old Carceri di Borgo, di Tor di Nona and di Corte Savella. Apart from humanitarian considerations, one major reflection giving rise to the new building was probably that the last residues of the privileges, dating from the Middle Ages, of the Savelli family were to give way to papal judicial enforcement. Whatever the case, the subdivision into solitary cells inside the building was new and trend-setting.

Antonio del Grande, the architect whom Virgilio Spada commissioned on behalf of Pope Innocent X, designed – possibly with the aid of Borromini's advice – a brick building whose main frontage facing the Via Giulia looks uncommonly severe. This four-storeyed façade with its seven axes has a central rusticated portal which tapers towards the top and is reminiscent rather of a castle gate than of a door. The lower storey, which is in the form of a retaining wall and has transversely rectangular barred windows, also has more of the character of a fortress. Like a base course, it is set off from the upper storeys by a strip of cornice.

All the forms in the upper part also make a sparse impression: each storey has seven rectangular windows which are the only subdividing elements; there is a contrast in colour between them and the brick wall, but the window frames are still kept very plain. The functional character of the building was made more clearly visible than was the case centuries later (cf. e. g. K8).

Today this building houses a museum of the history of crime and is the headquarters of the United Nations Institute of Criminology and Social History. SG

B70 S. Girolamo della Carità with Cappella Spada
Via Monserrato 62/A (plan IV 1/B)
1652–60 (or 1654–59)
Domenico Castelli, Virgilio Spada

This church which was redesigned by Castelli after a fire has a double-storeyed façade, a variation on the theme of one aedicule placed inside another. The interior is an aisleless church with chapels and transept. The rich wooden ceiling (probably 1587) was taken over from the previous structure. Two chapels deserve attention: the Antamoro chapel, an early work by Filippo Juvarra (B109, to the left of the choir), and the Spada chapel (1st right-hand lateral chapel), long attributed to Borromini.

Sources which have been discovered suggest that the highly original design of the Spada chapel should be attributed not to Borromini but to Virgilio Spada, the Oratorian priest and architectural dilettante who was his patron. What is unusual for the Roman Baroque is the absence of architectural articulation: the balustrade which otherwise separates chapels from the church aisle is replaced by two angels spreading a cloth. The walls and floor are decorated with marble inlay work reminiscent of carpets and wall coverings. The altarpiece, a small panel of the Virgin Mary, was not given any altar architecture, and it hangs on a hook on the wall, as do the relief medallions of St Francis, St Bonaventura and deceased members of the Spada family. The impression of a private room, which looks more like a living room than a chapel, is conveyed by seating benches decorated with figures of Tommaso and Orazio Spada, and also by the small cupboards which are covered by a cloth and have urns standing on them. The use of coloured marble to depict fabrics or cushions is known from Roman tomb art. The wall design with its ornamental marble inlay work has no Roman prototypes. AS

B71 S. Agnese in Agone
Piazza Navona (plan IV 1/A)
1652–72
Carlo Rainaldi, Francesco Borromini

It was as part of the redesign of the Piazza Navona (B61) that Pope Innocent X Pamphili ordered a splendid palatial burial chapel to be built for him in the immediate vicinity of his family's city palace (B62). Over a period of twenty years (1652–72), a church which may be regarded as a »High Baroque reworking of the centrally planned design for St Peter's« (Wittkower) was built on the site of a small previous structure. Girolamo and Carlo Rainaldi were initially commissioned to build the chapel. But Girolamo withdrew in spring of 1653, and in summer of that year, a year after construction work had begun, Borromini replaced Carlo because the latter's plans had been publicly criticized. At that time the interior had been built up to the level of the pillar niches, and the façade, which was then at Borromini's request taken down again, had been bricked up to a height of several metres. When Innocent X died in 1655, Borromini had himself again built the façade up to the level of the entablature and had completed the shell of the church interior, including the dome. In the years that followed there were disputes with the heirs of Innocent X, resulting in Borromini's withdrawal from the work. By 1672, a team of architects which was appointed in 1657, and of which Carlo Rainaldi was once again a member (Bernini also intervened in the building work in 1666), had completed the façade, the upper tower storeys, the dome lantern and the interior decorations. With its wide façade surmounted by two towers and a dome, the church dominates the city square. The façade curves concavely backwards between the two towers which stand in the straight line of the other buildings in the square. A temple façade, which is backed by pilasters and has three-quarter columns and a triangular gable, emphasizes the main portal of the church and accentuates the central axis of the façade. Smaller secondary portals are set into the curving lateral sections of the façade. The dome rises above an attic, and has a tall drum and parabolically tapering cap and lantern. The towers form an optical counterpoise to this, and have oval cores which become more and more apparent from one storey to the next. The articulation of the columns and pilasters forms a network of delicate relationships within the façade: the tower substructures are fitted with double pilasters, whereas the centre of the façade has double

B71 S. Agnese in Agone

columns which are arranged in approximately the same rhythm and accentuate the central axis. The topmost storeys of the towers are equipped with columns, while the pillars of the dome have pilasters in front of them which are arranged so as to relate to the central aedicule. The curving axes of the façade possess colonnaded articulations, with sections of wall seemingly inserted between them.

Three themes of Baroque façade design have been adopted in S. Agnese: the alternation of concave and convex shapes, the contrast between solid and deformable façade sections, and the contrast between actively supporting and passively filling wall compartments. Thanks to the dominantly convex dome and the broad concave façade, the alternation which is the first of these themes becomes dominant in the façade (and this can also be seen in the university church of S. Ivo, B56, built by Borromini at about the same time). The tower substructures express the idea of placing, inside a frame of solid double pilasters, a convex core which seems to bulge forth under the pressure, and this idea is based on the contrast between solidity and softness. This is also seen in the tensionless insertion of concave façade sections between the solid tower substructures and the temple façade. Some years before, Pietro da Cortona had taken this contrast as a basis for the façade of SS. Luca e Martina (B51), where the distinction between the supporting columns on the one hand, and the secondary wall panels which appear merely to fill up space on the other, is again a matter of artistic concern. The curving façade compartments of S. Agnese are, in accordance with this principle, articulated by blind colonnades and wall panels which occupy the lateral portals and other sections.

Despite its concave shape, the façade relates in various ways to the frontage of St Peter's (B34). The

B71 S. Agnese in Agone

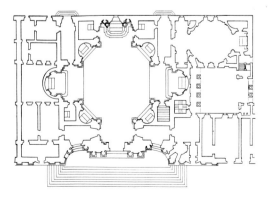

onlooker is reminded of this firstly by the single-sto-reyed structure which is subdivided by columns and ends in an attic, secondly by the temple façade placed out in front, and thirdly by the bell towers which were also planned for St Peter's but never built. Something which Maderno had made impossible by attaching the nave of the church to Michelangelo's centrally planned building was though achieved by the architects of S. Agnese: this was a direct view of the dome, with that dome being artistically included within the façade complex.

The interior of the church is a domed centrally planned space above the ground plan of a Greek cross. It was designed by Girolamo and Carlo Rainaldi and built up to three quarters of the height of the pillars. This determined the arrangement of the interior, and Borromini was left with little scope for putting his ideas of spatial design into practice. The interventions he made seem slight, but are decisive in terms of the spatial effect. Rainaldi originally placed the columns in small niches, but Borromini brought them out into the open by reducing the mass of the pillars. They were now three-quarter columns placed in front of the edges of the pillars of the crossing, and had thus been given a new three-dimensional character. They support a strongly moulded entablature which comes out into the open above the columns. Round arches placed upon a base course rest on the entablature. The eight columns are in this way combined into four arcades. They are dominant motifs which shape the area, and each of them marks the beginning of the four cross-arms. Borromini's alterations also make the massive, bevelled-off pillars look wider than was intended in the Rainaldis' design. They are now nearly of the same width as the cross-arms. The shape of the domed area thus approaches a regular octagon with small arcades (the pillar niches) and large arcades alternately cutting into its sides.

The closeness to St Peter is still more perceptible in the interior than in the exterior. This is noticeable from the bevelling of the crossing pillars, from the resultant broadening of the domed area, and from the niches which have sculptures (here these are reliefs rather than statues) placed in them. But the drum dome, which is as tall again as the church area up to the principal cornice, lends to S. Agnese a tallness unknown in St Peter's. The Baroque reinterpretation of the prototype consists in this tallness, and also in the three-dimensional articulating effect produced by the three-quarter columns, the moulded entablature and the dominant niches.

It must have been clear to contemporaries too that, in S. Agnese, Pope Innocent X was ordering St Peter's to be rebuilt in a reduced-size and a corrected version. After several palaces in the Piazza Navona had been converted into a single Pamphili residence (B62) and the city piazza (B61) had been given a new de-sign, the main part of Innocent X's plan to move the papal residence into the heart of the city lay in building a church serving as a private chapel and burial site. Plans for the construction of a papal tomb in S. Agnese did not go beyond the design stage. Thus it was decided in 1698 to place the tomb of Innocent X above the church portal, where it still is today. AS

Bibliography: G. Elmer, *La Fabbrica di S. Agnese in Navona*, Stockholm, 1970; P. Portoghesi, *Borromini*, Milan, 1977.

B72 Palazzo Montecitorio
Piazza Montecitorio 33 (plan IV 2/A)
begun 1653
Gianlorenzo Bernini

When Bernini was planning the family palace, begun in 1653, of Prince Ludovisi, he had to cope not only with the sloping terrain on the gently descending Montecitorio Hill, but also with other adverse circumstances: the plot of land was extremely wide, and was limited in the south by a curving street of houses.

This palace sets new standards by its dimensions alone. It surpasses other Roman palaces with its 25 window axes, and its height degrades the neighbouring Palazzo Aldobrandini-Chigi (B23). But what is more significant is the architectural idea, which was novel for Rome, and was developed from this situation: the distinguishing of several components in the façade. For this purpose Bernini firstly took the wings, and to a greater extent the corner risalti, out of the frontage of the central section and swung them towards the rear, so that the centre, in an image of provocative pride, seems to be thrusting its way forwards. Secondly, he demonstrated what can be achieved by the pointedly expressive use of an order of pilasters: the few pilasters do not form bays arranged in rows, but instead, being placed on a high base course, are the guiding forms of a colossal order. They mark the edges of the structures and thus lend them shape. Two pilasters combine the seven central axes, while bent pilasters attached at the sides move the centre forwards by one layer; the centre therefore presents itself as a majestically broad middle section, a feature which the superimposed attic again makes

B72 Palazzo Montecitorio

plain. The lengthy wings are subdivided only by cornices and by the vertical equivalent of the longitudinally rectangular windows. The term »risalto«, though lexically correct, is much too weak to describe the lateral conclusions of the façade. Their tall and narrow proportions make them look like solid towers, and this is effectively emphasized by the rustication both of the pilaster base courses and of the external window sills. But the difference between the central block and the corner towers does not mean that the structure is disconnected; the broad façade with its 25 axes can still be sensed, particularly in the magnificent, monotonous rows of windows and in the continuous cornices. This contrast between individual components and the unified façade, and the sparing but purposeful use of the architectural order, are the factors responsible for the peculiar effectiveness of the Palazzo Montecitorio. At the same time, the Roman character remains preserved in the plain shapes of the details and in the austere severity of the wall relief.

In 1694, under Innocent XII, the incomplete building was acquired for the papal court of justice, and Mattia de Rossi, the building supervisor, acted upon Carlo Fontana's suggestion in adapting it to its new function. A set of bells for opening the tribunals was installed above the central section; the attic was also increased in height. The threefold portal, reminiscent of ancient triumphal arches, caters for the throng of visitors and the building's higher claims to impressiveness.

Fontana's plans to build a semicircular forecourt were unfortunately not put into effect (the ground plan is in Fontana's *Discorso sopra l'antico Monte-Citatorio*). The square which was then built in the course of the 18C merely met the requirements of being inexpensive and making good use of what already existed, but at least it opened to view this leading work among Roman Baroque façades. The concluding feature, erected in 1792, was the obelisk, which Augustus had used as the hand of his large sundial. UF

Bibliography: F. Borsi, M. del Piazza et al, *Montecitorio. Richerche di Storia Urbana*, Rome, 1972.

B73 Palazzo di Spagna
Piazza di Spagna (plan II 1/E)
begun 1653
Antonio del Grande (?)

For a long time the Spanish embassy in Rome had its offices in rented rooms in various private palaces. But from 1622 onwards the officials looked for a permanent headquarters of their own, and found it in the Palazzo Monaldeschi in the Piazza della Trinità dei Monti. The piazza and palazzo soon adopted the name »di Spagna«. In 1653 the old palace was replaced by a new building. The question of who the architect was is unresolved. Antonio del Grande is named in the documents, but some structural details argue in favour of Borromini's having been the architect. The palace as a whole accords with one of the two standard types for Rome: it is a self-contained, cubic structure with

a base-course zone, a piano nobile and a mezzanine (cf. H22). The base-course zone also has a mezzanine and therefore makes a very stretched impression. The centre of the façade is accentuated not only by the tripartite rusticated portal, but also by the rhythmic arrangement of the vertical window axes across the entire width of the façade. A fairly long intermediate area sets off the five axes at the centre from the two outer axes on either side (cf. B14, B23).

The vestibule is a hall with a nave and two aisles. The narrow aisles are separated from the nave by a Serliana. The proportioning of the Tuscan order of columns with its epistyle (three fascias) very much points to Borromini as the architect (cf. B52).

The main focus in the inner courtyard is on the eastern side. The two enormous self-contained loggias, which are located one above the other and display the tabularium motif (cf. A9), look somewhat bizarre: two large arcades in the middle are adjoined at the sides by two squeezed-in arcades which look somewhat weak. The lower pilaster capitals are replaced by strange, stunted pilasters; the upper, particularly long pilasters stand on outsized scrolled bases. The staircase is 19C. PZ

B74 S. Andrea delle Fratte
Via Capo le Case, Via S. Andrea (plan V 1/A)
1653–65
Francesco Borromini

From 1605 onwards the Margraves del Buffalo, whose palace is not far from here, promoted the construction of this church. It is part of the very intense building programme carried out under Paul V. Gaspare Guerra's interior is an aisleless space of middling quality, has side chapels and is of the Il Gesù type (B1). It was not until 1653 that Borromini, still following the original plans, added to it the crossing and choir. The façade – the shapes of its ground floor had already been decided by Guerra – was added by Giuseppe Valadier or Pasquale Belli in 1826.

The chief attraction is the exterior of the dome and the tower. As is often the case with Borromini, it by no means corresponds to the interior. Even the more tolerant onlookers – who, like de Brosse, praised other works by this master – spoke of the »bizarre taste« seen in the dome. The latter remained incomplete in two respects: there had been plans for a lantern (again with concave and convex curves) and a stuccoed facing. Thus the »infinito« was unintentional. The dome would have overtopped the tower and thus been more clearly dominant. The rotunda in the interior was, in the exterior, designed by the master in such a way that four identical, curving façades were created. Columns anchored in the walls, and a weighty architrave, lend shape to each façade.

The main overall shape of each façade is in three parts, with each façade having a convex curve at its centre and a concave curve in each of its two wings. A vibrating rhythmic bay was thus created. The cen-

B74   S. Andrea delle Fratte

tral section is, on each side, flanked by a column with an additional rear pilaster, and is made to project beyond the wings by the layering of the wall. The centrepiece's large and ingeniously framed window Is the chief motif of the inner articulation. The concave sections therefore never are to be seen as the centre of a tripartite ensemble, although theoretically they could because of the rotunda form. Things are different again in the corner bastions, whose short wall section facing outwards is again convexly shaped and has two columns. Thus the orchestration is in each case limited to the convex sections. The corner bastions are genetically dependent on the dome of St Peter's (H31) because doubled columns are used. They can therefore – in similar fashion to St Peter's – virtually be completed so that they form an outer circle, the last remnant of a drum. Like this outer circle, an inner circle consisting of the convex middle sections of the four façades is an ensemble which the onlooker should see in his mind's eye. The lantern would have rested on this circle, and that lantern's slender shape would have been visible in the drum. The concave sections would then have been understood as being something different, a mere foil, an exedra which runs behind the convex central sections and combines the fragments of an inner rotunda with those of the outer rotunda. The two rotundas, being the drum and the lantern growing up from underneath, would have been the more strongly accentuated sections. Thus, as is usual for Borromini, the invention would at first have looked bizarre or complex, but would when analysed have been seen to be a logically thought-out assem-

bly of individual shapes which at the same time retain an unusual autonomy. These façades are less similar to Borromini's S. Carlino – in which the wall layering and the orchestration show that the concave and convex curves are equal in value, so that a genuine undulation is created (B52) – than they are to S. Maria della Pace (B79). In one point Borromini was certainly successful: the rotunda and ordinary dome found in the interior became a monument in the exterior. Whether the four wings are intended to be associated with the cross of St Andrew is then a secondary issue.

The structural principle of the tower is different again. I ike the dome of S. Ivo (B56), it is built up of differing sections (or storeys). Underneath there is a classically orchestrated block with a central aedicule which is the rectangular counterpart to the domed drum. Above this stands a classical tholos, whose roundness is strongly emphasized by the weighty balustrade above, which looks like a wheel. The combination of these two storeys is very similar to that of ancient tomb towers, particularly the Conocchia in Capua. As with S. Ivo, the sculptural element increases as the building grows in height, and tectonic sections are replaced by figured ones. Here these are double hermae occupying a piece of architecture which, with its deep and narrow concavely curving architrave, is again very similar to ancient Roman buildings (the Venus temple in Baalbek, adopted in the Villa Adriana, A32). The close juxtaposition of classical shapes (they are almost quotations) and inventions which are all Borromini's own is a peculiarity of his way of thinking. Flaming vases, scrolls, and a thorny crown, surmount the tower, whose design contrasts with that of the dome, because the tower is made up of heterogeneous sections and has a much more slender structure. But both are united by the continuous search for the unusual. SG

B75 Collegio Innocenziano
Piazza Navona, Via del Anima 32 (plan IV 1/A)
1654
Francesco Borromini

After Pope Innocent X had, with difficulty, acquired in 1653 the plot of land north of S. Agnese in the Piazza Navona, he ordered the »construction of a college which was to be used for »young men's religious education«. A year later, the project was put into effect to plans by Borromini. The façade of the Collegio Innocenziano faces the piazza, whereas the entrance is on the rear side of the building (Via dell'Anima).

Borromini attempted to make the frontage into an adequate conclusion standing north of the church façade and corresponding to the gallery and the Palazzo Pamphili south of the church. He managed to do this by first repeating the four-storeyed gallery structure which is the link connecting the palace to the church: the splendid piano nobile rises above a base-course storey and consists of a large window panel framed by a well-proportioned Syrian arch. The three axes are prescribed by this arch motif and continue vertically up to the beginning of the roof. They are framed by pilaster strips which, on the top storey, are linked by scrolls to pilasters. All this is adjoined on the right by an axially symmetrical repetition of the first two bays of the palace façade; the only differences are the aedicule windows in the third storey, and the addition of a fourth storey. The two bays, consisting of a risalto and an outer axis which is set back, give the impression of being only the beginning of an additional palace façade which can be imagined as continuing northwards to any distance desired. This links the palace façade into the heterogeneous palace architecture, and S. Agnese (B71) is vividly seen to be an integrated palace church. PZ

B76 Palazzo Colonna
Piazza SS. Apostoli 66 (plan V 1/B)
1654–65, begun 1730
Antonio del Grande, Niccolò Micchetti

This enormously large palace takes up the area between Via 4 Novembre, Pilotta, Vaccaro and Piazza SS. Apostoli (including the church, F9, B108), and was initiated by Pope Martin V of the Colonna family. But the first section built was the one located in the second courtyard for which Giuliano della Rovere was responsible, who later became Julius II. When he was a cardinal of the church he bought up some plots of land which, after becoming pope, he gave away to Lucrezia della Rovere when she married Marcantonio Colonna. The splendid building sections from the 17C and 18C were built on them.

The core section of the complex was created by del Grande when he built a gallery which ran along the upper storey of the palace, next to the church. Although the arcades of his façade were soon closed in the main courtyard, the gallery remained unaltered. Built in 1654-65, it was not completely furnished until

B75 Collegio Innocenziano

B76 Palazzo Colonna

1703, so that the decorations make less of a magnificent High-Baroque impression than does the architecture. The order was placed by Girolamo, the great-grandson of Marcantonio Colonna who, in the ceiling painting showing the papal troops, was glorified as the victor of Lepanto. The long main hall has two storeys on both sides and is brightly lit by rows of rectangular windows. Two colossal yellow columns form the border between it and the almost square-shaped adjoining rooms which are of equal width. Each of the columns belongs to a recurring pair of supports which otherwise consists of pilasters. These pairs form a succession which is of identical design and colour and runs around the entire hall. Above it there are a richly gilded architrave and corbelled cornice which also run uninterruptedly all the way round. An enfilade which is 76 m long overall and is the most splendid Baroque interior in Rome was thus built a good 25 years before the hall of mirrors in Versailles, and is a genuine early work in its field. The way in which this hall is lit from both sides remained unsurpassed. The hall lives mainly by its inserted columns (colonne). Great architects in Rome had devised such colonne previously, but had not made such magnificent use of them (H30, B34; cf. the later B85). The columns guide the onlooker's gaze from the Dughet hall with its landscape paintings, through the main hall, and across some steps into a second adjoining room, from which the vista continues across a balcony and a bridge (one of four) over the Via della Pilotta into the gardens. In these gardens, built a little later, the visitor immediately meets with a statue of Marcantonio Colonna in a wall

B77 Porta del Popolo

of columns. This great and grandiloquent sequence starting from a room with landscape paintings, continuing through the splendid lighted gallery and proceeding out into the gardens is unique among secular interiors in Rome.

One of the finest endless Rococo façades in Rome was added to the façade side of SS. Apostoli from 1730 onwards. However, the only part of it surviving in the original is the right of two corner pavilions which were linked by a lower section, formerly the riding stable. The system of articulation used in that section was retained in the lower parts of the pavilions. The three windows (reduced to two today) which were placed one above the other and, typically for the 18C, were merged into one vertical band were a characteristic feature, as were the subdividing strips of bosses. The compartment (it has three axes) next to the pavilions was provided with portals, and resembled the still richer compartment in the tower section of the pavilions. The problem of endless length was – and this is quite frequent in the 18C – solved by creating two poles. The individual shapes here are very soft and cheerful in their lines. The softness of the Barocchetto, and Roman monumentality, are here showing the first signs of working in combination – as later occurs in the Palazzo Doria Pamphili (B122). The still-surviving coffee house in this pavilion is a square-shaped room which is rich in elegant Barocchetto decorations and, at the level of the architrave, becomes an octagon with eight arcades. SG

B77 Porta del Popolo
Piazza del Popolo (plan I 2/D)
1561–63, 1655
Nanni di Baccio Bigio, Gianlorenzo Bernini
As part of the urbanist renovations performed under Pius IV, the Porta Flaminia, the northern city gate of the Aurelian Wall (A44), was rebuilt in 1561-63 and named after the neighbouring church of S. Maria del

Popolo (F7). In 1655, on the occasion of Queen Christine of Sweden's entry into the city, Alexander VII commissioned Bernini to redesign the inner façade. The Porta originally only had the central gateway and tower-like corner reinforcements at the flanks. Those reinforcements were replaced in 1879 by the lateral openings, and the articulation of the central section was transferred to the entire structure. The outer façade of the Porta was designed by Nanni di Baccio Bigio. The original form of the structure had a central gateway between two lateral bays and an attic above this, and thus followed the typology of ancient triumphal arches. The wall panels are framed by freestanding columns of the Tuscan order (some of them are ancient spoils).

Bernini supplied the design for the façade facing the city at the same time as he was reworking the interior of S. Maria del Popolo. In his design, he inevitably copied the way in which the outer side of the gate was structured and proportioned, but he replaced the full columns by pairs of flat pilasters and therefore dispensed with the intense moulding of the cornice, and as a result the structure became more uniform. In addition, the fact that the pilasters were placed closer together meant that the portal was given a more energetic double frame instead of the lateral bays. The portal is surmounted and dominated by the gable which rises up above the attic and includes the monumental Chigi coat of arms. DH

B78 S. Nicolà da Tolentino: façade
Salita, Via S. Nicolà da Tolentino (plan V 1/A)
1655–70
after Carlo Rainaldi
In 1620, the barefooted friars, who in 1599 had been recognized as a reform order of the Augustinians, moved their headquarters to the Viminal in the middle of a vineyard on which they built their church of S. Nicolà. The supervising architect was Carlo Buti from Milano, who in 1624 had completed the shell construction to such an extent that it could be used as a church. The dome was added in 1641, but the building work stagnated, and only in 1651 was it resumed by Don Camillo Pamphili, the only nephew of Pope Innocent X. Don Camillo entrusted the construction work to the stonemasons' lodge of S. Agnese in Piazza Navona, and this led to delays and lapses in efficiency on both building sites.

The style of the façade (1665–70) probably derives from plans by Carlo Rainaldi, given that he had particularly good relations with the Pamphili family. A comparison with S. Maria in Campitelli (B91) makes this supposition a certainty. In both cases, the architectural leitmotiv of the façade is the permeability of the layers. The colonnade and the columned aedicule both replace the wall and make the layer behind visible. In this way the column attains a previously unknown significance as an element subdividing, supporting and replacing the wall. In the façade of S.

Nicolà, there is also another phenomenon: the process by which the wall surface is dissolved is displayed step by step. The central bay with its two storeys consists of a wall layer subdivided by pilasters. This bay is particularly accentuated in that it is framed by two orders of columns, which are placed one above the other in front of the wall and are themselves coarsely fragmented because they have only one columnar axis. The accentuated wall panel becomes dissolved in the lateral axes of the façade and passes into the colonnade. The latter makes visible the rearmost façade layer with its niches containing figures. Here, Rainaldi dispenses with an angled pilaster with which to reinforce the outer edges. In consequence, the wall seems to vanish towards the sides. PZ

B79 S. Maria della Pace: façade
Piazza di S. Maria della Pace (plan IV 1/A)
1656/57
Pietro da Cortona

The reason for the fame of this church (F16), built in 1482 on the occasion of the peace with Milano and Naples, is the cloister (H3) by Bramante which dates from just under 20 years later. Alexander VII wished to fulfil a vow by adding a façade to enrich the church. He was seeking peace from the plague and from the threat of Louis XIV.

Cortona created the archetype of the three-dimensional Baroque-style show wall. Its significance can only be measured against the background of what had preceded it. A flat façade had always been enlivened only by means of layering and column positioning (most recently in SS. Vicenzo ed Anastasio, B64), and Cortona had himself done this in SS. Luca o Martina, his first leading work in Rome. He had though already achieved it by bending this surface (B51, cf. also B53), and this can be seen again here in the upper storey, which is very similar to the earlier work. But the primacy of the surface had never been questioned, and its concave and convex curves had never been opposed to one another. The two storeys are designed differently. The upper storey is still in the tradition of the Roman wall façade. Nevertheless the upper storey differs from Il Gesù (B1) in that it looks as powerful and wide as the lower storey, even though the scroll linking the storeys is not absent here. The façade of the upper storey resembles that of SS. Luca e Martina – the façade front is again framed between two massive edge structures and curves forwards, – but is nevertheless more mature: the upper conclusion with its gable is more harmonious, the elements have a masterly firmness as each of them is doubled and enormously intensified by the pairings consisting of a pillar and a column. Every element is clearly marked and is autonomous. The most recent façade in Rome was that of SS. Vincenzo ed Anastasio (B64), and had caused a stir. It was copied here too, for example in the gables inserted one inside another and in the column at the flank of the façade, but it was also im-

proved upon: the gables – there are only two of them – are more prominent, and the flanking column gains in solidity by being combined with a pillar. Thus the upper storey displays tradition in maximum perfection. Anyone who feels that it is not so original when compared with the ground floor is overlooking the fact that the high quality of the façade as a whole lies precisely in the contrast and in the way in which new features are developed out of the tradition.

By dissolving the façade of the ground floor into a vestibule, Cortona was making a radical break with the traditional type of façade. Even ancient vestibules (A31) and vestibules found in Michelangelo's drafts for St Peter's are scarcely comparable, because they do not cover the entire structure but instead ennoble only the centre of it and, what is more, they lack the convex curve which is irreplaceable in the complex as a whole. Here, it was not merely half of a round tempietto that was placed out in front – in ancient times, this shape always aroused the association of a temple of peace -, but the façade was instead formed by the more powerful shape of half of a transverse oval. The strength of Cortona's sculptural sense is shown by a comparison with the vestibule of the slightly later S. Andrea. That vestibule really does consist only of half a tempietto (B85). The relationships between the columns are also much more complex. Rarely indeed does the term »Full Baroque« more appropriately describe the High Baroque. The importance which Cor-

B79 S. Maria della Pace: new design of square

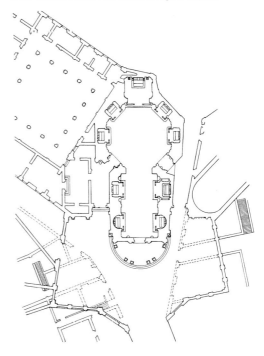

B79 S. Maria della Pace

tona attached to unification and weightiness is seen
from the fact that he selected the strict – doubled –
Doric column for the entire lower storey, but combined
it with an Ionic architrave which was continuous and
was not resolved into metopes and triglyphs. Bernini
adopted this approach for the colonnades (B80). The
centre is left open and becomes the enlarged portal,
so that the vestibule is a new assembly point between
the outside piazza and the church interior.

A concave curve in the upper storey is the response to the convex curve in the vestibule. The
façade itself continues in neighbouring façades on
only one storey, and these are flat sections set well
back. On the other hand, the walls on the upper storey run above a curving ground plan and surround not
only the façade, but the whole nave of the church.
The nave is thereby ennobled, like a pearl in a large
open shell. When seen from close up as is dictated
by the small size of the square, the centre towers up
high, as the adjoining walls – and this is particularly
obvious in the upper storey – start further back. The
increasing concentration which is typical of High-Baroque architecture and proceeds both towards the
centre and upwards has been given a new dynamism,
especially as the crescendo is much longer than usual
and the most complex section of the whole façade,
the section containing the sum of all the possibilities,
is located here.

The individual parts of the façade are themselves
very strongly united. But the full extent of the mutual
relationships only becomes clear when all the buildings in the square are looked at. In a way not customary until the 18C, they were interpreted as being part
of a uniform overall composition: the cornice, the attic
storey, and the order of pilasters in the exedra, are, in
the other buildings in the square, all continued, but are

at the same time somewhat lower. The lines are definitely interrupted, so that hierarchies become visible.
The exedra is part of the articulation of the buildings in
the square, and stands above the broad lower storey
which, across the whole width of the square, is provided with columns, has a scroll above it, and is thus
characterized as being part of the church façade. At
the same time, the exedra, due to the superposition
of the supports, also gives the impression of being
vertically linked to the lateral parts of the church façade. The vertical and horizontal links look equally
strong and perfectly well-balanced. In addition, both
storeys are clearly separated, because the Corinthian
order, which extends across all the sections, belongs
only to the upper storey as does the concave curve,
while the Doric order, and also the convex curve, belong only to the lower. On the other hand, the vertical
relationships are also very intense: double supports in
the upper storey are the response to the double supports below, the window above corresponds to the
central opening in the portico below, and the interruption above, which is continued in the gap between the
two gables, echoes the side openings below (cf. the
contrasting B64). Such unifications are also omnipresent in the third dimension. This is shown firstly by the
walls of the palace exedra which curve so far backwards that the church nave appears in the middle
of the palace building, and secondly by the portico
which, in the exterior, forms a part of the interior. Such
intensity in the spatial permeability of different sections
had not been seen since late-ancient days (e. g. A53,
C10). There is an interplay between two- and three-
dimensional tension, between self-contained and
open structures, between wall and hall, between complicated layering and classical simplicity, between a
gable and a horizontally concluding colonnade. This
complex work required no decoration. There is almost
none. It is all architecture. All that is permitted in order
to prevent any interruption of the architectural shape
is the effect produced by the texture of the stone.

Cortona was meant to design a façade, but what
was created is a leading work of Roman urbanism.
The interplay between the concave and the convex
curve is itself very impressive, one reason being that
the more distant parts are orchestrated more flatly
(only pilasters are used) and without altering them so
much, with the result that the perspective effect is exaggerated, as the effect produced by the structures
approaching us from the depths is intensified. Towards the front, everything becomes more sculptural
and the surface loses in significance. Contrary to what
occurred in the 18C – the Piazza di S. Ignazio (B118) is
one example -, the impression being aimed at was not
one of intimacy, but one of High Baroque large size,
as is clearly indicated by the formation of hierarchies
and central axes. But the large size, and this is typical
of the early and High Baroque, was meant to be confined within one location and stay there, and not be
moved into long axes as happened in the late 16C

and then again from c. 1670 onwards. Here, the confined space is a precondition for the highly charged dynamism. A space and the buildings surrounding it, that is to say an area consisting of building work and an area consisting of air, are closely interwoven here, and the autonomy of the High-Renaissance buildings (e.g. H27) is forgotten. What had been begun by adding secondary buildings (B30) and, in the Piazza Navona (B61), had resulted in a uniformly designed square with a strongly accentuated centre was here completed. Differing sections had not previously been so closely interwoven, and the result is that most sections gain a new value from being part of the whole. It became possible to look at a church nave from more than one vantage point, and this had previously only been the case with centrally planned buildings. The use – not new in itself – of a column in every flank of the façades enhanced this possibility. The square becomes the atrium of the church. Transport considerations (the difficulties arising when coaches were approaching the church) were probably the chief reason for building the square, which was cut deep into the existing urban fabric (see plan). But the square became a genuine teatrum sacrum because – this was another novelty – it was also designed as a theatre: the church was the stage, the square was the auditorium, and the houses were boxes at the theatre.This was the teatrum urbis while, soon later, Bernini's Colonnades (B80) became the teatrum orbis. SG

Bibliography: H. Ost, »Studien zu Pietro da Cortonas Umbau von S. Maria della Pace«, *Römisches Jahrbuch für Kunstgeschichte*, 1971, p. 231.

B80 Piazza di S. Pietro
Piazza di S. Pietro (plan III 1/A)
incl. 1657–67
Gianlorenzo Bernini
In the late Middle Ages, and also after the new church building had been completed, the square outside St Peter's was a sloping area surrounded by irregular building work. The façade group (later, Maderno's façade) of St Peter's stood along the eastern edge of the square, while in the north the square was concluded by the buildings of the Vatican palace and the Leonine wall. On its opposite southern side and on its western edge, St Peter's Square was surrounded by residential houses, so that it had an irregular shape, somewhat wider in the north. Initial efforts to regulate the square and link it in with the urban scene were made by Nicholas V, the pope who, in the mid-15C, also pressed ahead with rebuilding St Peter's church (Rossellino choir, H7). The design for the square at that time was inspired by Alberti and included two ideas which continued to be important for many later planners: building some streets which lay between St Peter's Square and the Tiber and which were meant to lead directly to the church portal and palace portal, and, secondly erecting an obelisk in the middle of the square. Nicholas V's ambitious project was not realized. In 1490, a fountain was built in the northeastern section of the still-irregular square. In 1500, Alexander VI ordered that a street be built which linked Ponte Sant'Angelo to St Peter's Square and was oriented on the portal of the Vatican palace. It corresponds approximately to the buildings on the northern edge of the Via della Conciliazione. The site of the fountain and the orientation of the street both clearly show that, in the early 16C, St Peter's Square functioned as the forecourt not only of the church, but primarily of the Vatican palace.

In 1586, Sixtus V commissioned Domenico Fontana to set up in St Peter's Square the obelisk of the neighbouring Circus Neronis. Today, that still amounts to an astonishing feat of engineering. Sixtus thereby established a fixed point which all later architects had to include in their calculations.

Before Bernini, in 1656, began on his plans for St Peter's Square, three other architects, namely Carlo Maderno, Martino Ferrabosco and Carlo Rainaldi, submitted plans from which the problems posed by a well-regulated square can well be discerned. Maderno and Ferrabosco, like Bernini after them, started by dividing the square into two parts: a smaller forecourt outside the church (Piazza Retta), and a lower section of different design (Piazza Obliqua). The reasons for this division were the Vatican palace which flanked the church to its north, and the portal of that palace. Maderno therefore intended to design the Piazza Retta as a kind of principle courtyard which was to be framed by four storeys of palace architecture in the north and south, and by the façade of St Peter's in the west. Ferrabosco planned to have flat buildings (the northern building was actually erected) flanking the Piazza Retta. Finally, in c. 1646, Carlo Rainaldi submitted a design which adopted Ferrabosco's Piazza Retta and combined it, in the lower half of the square, with a hexagonal area surrounded by porticoes. In this design, Rainaldi came very close to Bernini's later plans, and it is known that Bernini, and also Pope Alexander VII, knew Rainaldi's design and made profitable use of some of its ideas.

B80 Piazza di S. Pietro

The unusually high quality of Bernini's design when it was actually put into effect can be clearly seen against the background of the previous plans, particularly when it is compared with Rainaldi's project for St Peter's Square. The complicated basic shape of the complex – the Piazza Obliqua is an ellipse made up of two segments of a circle and some curving intermediate sections, and the Piazza Retta is a trapezium tapering off towards the east – links the two parts of the square in a self-evident way. It takes into account the fact that the obelisk stands in the middle, and, as far as is possible, respects the historic limits of the area (e. g. the Leonine wall). Although Rainaldi's regular area with buildings surrounding it in a hexagonal shape would have emphasized the great expanse of the complex, it would also have made the church seem remote. Bernini, on the other hand, made the short axis of an ellipse into the square's main axis, and thus brought the optical target, namely the church façade, closer, but without abandoning the impression of expansiveness found in the transverse axes.

Due to its trapeziform ground plan, the Piazza Retta was often regarded as an optical trick by means of which Bernini was trying to correct the fact that Maderno's façade was too wide. There is no doubt that Bernini did know how to relate dimensions and distances to one another from the onlooker's optical point of view. But the ground plan of the Piazza Retta seems to have been at least influenced by Ferrabosco's northern structural section, which itself ran diagonally towards the façade of St Peter's.

Bernini selected, for the conversion of the Piazza Obliqua, a structural form unknown to the architecture of his times: it was a free-standing colonnade consisting of four rows. This architectural form, which Bernini justified to his contemporaries by referring to ancient models, concludes the square towards the outside, but at the same time opens it up: it is possible to walk through the colonnade at any point, and it makes the square accessible from all sides. However, inside the square, the view towards the outside is obscured by a forest of columns. Only at two points in the square, namely the centres of the semicircular colonnades (notice the mark made between the obelisk and the fountain), is it possible to look through to the outside. This is because at those points the columns of the four concentrically arranged colonnades are in an exact straight line. Where motifs are concerned, Bernini is reverting to the temple frontage, which is the chief motif of Maderno's façade: The ends of the colonnades have temple frontages of the same kind. Rainaldi's plans included porticoes with a single storey built above them, whereas Bernini did not in any way use the architecture of the square as a residential area, because he designed a colonnade concluded by a balustrade with figures. The architectural framework of the square thus has no practical function other than that of being a processional route protected from sun and rain. The square is now oriented only on the

church, and the former link with the buildings of the Vatican palace has been abandoned. St Peter's Square thus becomes a church forecourt comparable with medieval atria. Bernini and his contemporaries compared the design of the square with the outstretched arms of St Peter.

The impact of the square, which was originally planned to have a third colonnaded area as its eastern conclusion, is today impaired by the Via della Conciliazione which was built under Mussolini. This wide street anticipates the width of the square, which was formerly entered from narrow alleyways. AS

Bibliography: H. Brauer and R. Wittkower, *Die Zeichnungen des Gianlorenzo Bernini*, Berlin, 1931, p. 64; C. Thoenes, »Studien zur Geschichte des Petersplatzes«, *Zeitschrift für Kunstgeschichte*, 1963, p. 97.

B81 Palazzo Nuñez Torlonia
Via di Bocca di Leone 79 (plan IV 2/A)
1658–60
Giovanni Antonio de Rossi

De Rossi who, in his Palazzo Altieri (B68), had built one of the first High-Baroque palaces to have a graduated structure, was here commissioned by Marquese Nuñez to design a façade on the Via Condotti. Instead of a structure having several blocks or risalti, de Rossi now surprisingly chose to employ a single uniform block and, in other respects too, the principle of dividing the storeys in the manner developed in the Renaissance (cf. H22 and H25). The ground floor with its windows leading into the basement, the piano nobile, the upper storey with its reinforcement, and the corbelled entablature, are all again present here.

B82 S. Tommaso a Villanova, Castel Gandolfo

It is mainly the individual shapes that betray the fact that the palace was built at an advanced stage of the Baroque. They are marked by the simple elegance of their lines and by a restraint which had not been since the Palazzo Farnese (H25), but was trend-setting: the rhetoric and decorum seem repressed. In particular, the window frames and window roofings are, in terms both of three-dimensionality and of decorativeness, scarcely emphasized, except perhaps for the rudimentary capitals of the window frames in the upper storey and the stylized supporting corbels of the ground-floor windows. Even the piano nobile is not emphasized. The Torlonia family acquired the building in 1842.

B82 S. Tommaso a Villanova, Castel Gandolfo
Castel Gandolfo, Corso (plan G2 4/C)
1658–61
Gianlorenzo Bernini

Bernini built a church high above Lake Albano for Thomas of Villanova (1488–1555), who was canonized in 1658. He evidently had to adopt the rectangular foundation walls of a church of St Nicholas and provide stabilizing corner compartments on the side towards the lake. He thus selected a Greek cross as the ground plan and placed the façade on the inland side.

A genuine façade was created, because it was only the walls facing inland that were articulated with sober Tuscan pilasters. This orientation led to a tripartite structure with an energetically projecting centre (similar to B43). It is true that the other two centrally planned buildings which he erected at the same time make a less cool impression, due to their round shapes and the flanking buildings (regarding the three possible types of centrally planned building, all of which Bernini tried out, cf. B85). But the resemblance of this church of St Thomas to the severe early work of Raphael (cf. H10) is only one aspect, the other being that the design of the façade was new for a cross-shaped building.

The interior again looks severe as in the early works of Raphael, of whom Bernini himself stated that he was his greatest model. The proportions are as plain as possible, with the chapels being about twice as wide as they are deep. But the respect shown for the High Renaissance here applied more to St Peter's (H7), whose interior, with its bevelled pillars, was copied, but with taller Baroque proportions in the centre, in which – and this is typical of Bernini – the decorations were concentrated, with coffer work being combined with wall arches. Medallions showing images of the life of St Thomas were hung up in St Peter's when St Thomas was canonized. Bernini wanted to copy this temporary ceremony in a small St Peter's, now surrounded by a ring of angels. The small centrally planned church which becomes a place of mystery, and not the rather severe style, is the main idea here as elsewhere in Bernini's work (cf. B85) SG

B83 S. Maria in Via Lata: façade

B83 S. Maria in Via Lata: façade
Via del Corso 306 (plan IV 2/B)
1658–62
Pietro da Cortona

The interior of this basilica originating from a 15C conversion was redesigned by Cosimo Fancelli in the mid-17C. In 1658–62, the façade, to designs by Pietro da Cortona, was built as a structure which was entirely independent of the interior, is more significant than it, and deserves attention as a late architectural work by Pietro. It towers up in two storeys, and its subdivision consists of two closed lateral wall panels framed by pilasters and of the slightly projecting central section which is accentuated by open colonnades on both storeys and is crowned by a low triangular gable. The colonnades are rhythmized and leave a wider opening in the centre, the upper one of which is marked by a Syrian arch. Both storeys open into porticoes, resulting in a three-dimensional front section with strong contrasts in the lighting. The lower vestibule contains interior colonnades in the narrow sides of which are inserted independent lateral apses, so that markedly different wall layers are discernible.

This façade contrasted with Pietro da Cortona's earlier works (B51, B79) in that the structure had to be fit into the straight line of a street, and he attempted to cope with this different architectural task by employing classical, monumental forms – the colonnades and the Syrian arch – while abandoning any devices, such as convexity, to shape the space. The colonnade is an important element in Cortona's art of wall design and, when compared with that found in SS. Luca e Martina, was given a decisive development here, because it is not merely a separate layer of its own which is placed in front of the wall and contrasts with it, but is free-standing and itself forms the rhythmizing front of the façade. DH

B84 Palazzo d'Aste-Bonaparte
Piazza Venezia (plan V 1/B)
1658–65
Giovanni Antonio de Rossi

From 1815 to 1836, this palace built for the d'Aste brothers was used as a residence by Letitia Ramolino, Napoleon's mother. The Bonaparte eagle commemorates this.

The main façade has three storeys, and the third storey has a mezzanine. This façade with its five axes is markedly narrower than the lateral façade. This makes the building appear compact, well-proportioned and upright. This cubic shape follows the typology of the Palazzo Farnese (H25) in having pilasters reinforcing it at the edges, while the wall is kept neutral and is subdivided only by horizontal cornices and the rows of windows. A new feature is that de Rossi rounded off the edges, and this assists with the continuity in the context of the rest of the street, and also contributes to the compact impression. The balcony extending above the edge underlines this effect.

B85 S. Andrea al Quirinale

Overall, much of the rhetoric otherwise found in 17C palaces is reduced here. The individual shapes are also delicately formed, but are restrained. The window roofings are indebted to Borromini for some features such as the pagoda shape (cf. B53), and to Cortona for others such as the shell (B51). The combination of these motifs was though new. The windows of the mezzanine area are very original in that they are integrated into the entablature and are of alternating sizes. Although playful, they nevertheless emphasize the main axes. All these innovations were to become exemplary for the 18C.

Until that time, however, this building met with no successors, despite its prominent position in the cityscape. But there are also differences between it and 18C buildings: the wall is still dominant, the windows are arranged regularly, stand on the cornice and do not extend to the cornice above, and the subdividing elements (except in the mezzanine) remain independent and unmerged (for further points of comparison, cf. Ameli's façade next door, B133). SG

B85 S. Andrea al Quirinale
Via del Quirinale 29 (plan V 1/A)
1658–70
Gianlorenzo Bernini

The Jesuit novitiate founded in 1566 was housed in the Quirinal palace. On the other side of the road, Bernini, who had been commissioned by Camillo Pamphili, erected a centrally planned building, something very unusual for Jesuit churches. It is one of a series of three centrally planned buildings from the same period, and the two others, in Castel Gandolfo and Ariccia (B82 and B89), were commissioned by the papal family, the Chigi. But the richer decorations in S. Andrea required much more capital and time. The reason why all three buildings are so important is that Bernini's earlier works had, with one exception (B43), been destroyed: this applies to the towers of St Peter's (cf. B34) and to the chapel of Propaganda Fide (B65). Domenico, the master's son, reports that he often saw his father praying in the church, and that, when asked, he said that no other work gave him so much joy in his old age.

The main overall shape of the façade consists of an interplay of flatness, concavity and convexity. This had already been seen in S. Maria della Pace (B79). All three elements are clearly separated from one another in terms of size, energy and substantiality: the small brick walls which form a square were low, delicate, negative in terms of relief, and had hanging scrolls. The convex sections are taller, and some of them were also of brick (this applies to the church rotunda which is also visible), while others were of travertine; these sections, along with the split gable and the lissom, upwards-striving heraldic motif in the centre, are full of energy. The simple, solid, flat element is the largest of the three. Made entirely of travertine, it stands between the restrained concave element and the energetically formed convex one. Bernini loved tripartite structures with a central section, which stands out prominently among the other sections and clearly shows that it has been formed by human hand, (cf. e. g. B82, B93). The flat element is an enormous aedicule. This was not in itself new (for example, it was found shortly before in S. Maria di Monte Carmelo and also, in concise form, in Bernini's work, B43). But Bernini made a gate out of it by adding an arch, and he caused the wall cylinder to look permeable by cutting a window into it. The façade is more of a monumental entrance than a façade in the conventional sense.

The happy link between the interior and the surroundings is therefore a prominent feature. This transversely oval building presents itself towards the outside as a combination of two cylinders of differing heights, with the chapels being grouped in the lower cylinder. Scroll-shaped struts link the two cylinders. The contribution made by the building itself is that of an optical background rather than an independent shape. Many previous oval churches had been given flat façades which appear designed for a church with a rectangular nave, whereas here the structure behind the façade becomes perceptible, and the flat element is only the door between the outside and the inside. This link is provided by two elements: the cornice of the lower cylinder was continued in the portico of the façade, and the roundness of the church itself was, in the overall arrangement of the façade, in turn suggested by placing the outermost pilaster diagonally. This has been criticized as a not very correct lateral conclusion, but it bears witness to Bernini's genius for making both elements, continuity and at the same time diversity, noticeable at this point. The surrounding area is a place framed by concave walls which make the convex structure look more dynamic and reflect the shape of the interior in the exterior, although in the latter the three-dimensionality is less strong. Thus the façade is given an area of its own; in order to enter it, the visitor must turn away from the axis of the street. Walls originally shielded that area off from the street. The visitor arrived in front of the façade by approaching it diagonally through two side entrances, and did not immediately come up against it frontally. Bernini planned a similar method for the colonnades (B80), so that he was probably not responsible for tearing down the wall. In any event, he built only three steps, intended for the portico alone, and the widening of the street made this area lose some of its depth. The link with the urban scene is suggested in the hanging garlands, which are borrowed from Michelangelo's Porta Pia at the end of the street which runs past (H43).

The aedicule framework and the portico were combined in the core façade. The individual components are known from epoch-making works, but what is new is the result. The aedicule which has a surrounding frame as a recessed layer and has smaller columns inserted within it had previously been found in

B85 S. Andrea al Quirinale

the conservators' palace (H30). The portico, which of course also owes something to S. Maria della Pace (B79), was first combined with a rotunda in the Pantheon (A31), the chief work of ancient Roman architecture. But as in the case of Ariccia (B89), Bernini corrected the vestibule of the Pantheon, and now did so in a particularly radical and subtle way because, on the one hand, he monumentalized the triangular gable in front of the rotunda – how much higher indeed does the gable rise up! – and, on the other, he made the vestibule itself less square and rigid, smaller and therefore more flexible and more human in its size (cf. the similar case of B42). At the same time the vestibule is not impenetrable but is permeable, and gives the rotunda a much stronger contributory effect. The façade is meant to be the gate, and the vestibule the prelude, to the interior. This is why, in the vestibule, the façade is brought to the same height as the elements of the interior, in particular the colonnade located there, and it is also why the High-Baroque concentration of the three-dimensional elements at the top centre is so happy, because an upwards movement is created and the main theme of the interior design is thus already suggested. The excellent quality of the façade is due to the inexplicable combination of very great simplicity and very great abundance, of classical style and High Baroque.

The interior consists of a transversely oval rotunda which is the main area and a smaller such rotunda which is the choir. Four chapels, of alternating size, shape (rectangular and oval), and entrance height, are set into the thickness of the wall of the main area. The chapels are kept dark, especially the outer chapels which at the same time adjoin the well-lit choir, thus forming the most energetic foil to it as regards the lighting. The red colour of the substructure also makes a weighty, dark impression. In almost all the points mentioned, the design is indebted to the Pantheon (A31 and then Il Gesù, B1). Thus the visitor is here standing inside a massive Roman building. But its transversely oval design gives it a more dynamic effect than the ancient rotundas. That design is not in itself new, but what is new is that Bernini chose to have an even number of chapels on each side, and thus made the transverse axis end in a pilaster, not in a chapel. This meant that the most important dynamic aspect of the transversely oval design was preserved in all its purity: the onlooker's gaze cannot wander off to the side into a chapel, but instead is guided to the choir by the shortest route. The choir is therefore immediately present.

In the choir, known as the sarcellum, the onlooker witnesses the phenomenon known as a teatrum sacrum, which is though at the same time set off from the surrounding structure. All the means of design were used to achieve this aim. The light enters this area, which stands out amidst the substructure because it is the only area to be lit up. The rays fall upon the saint in his moment of martyrdom, and the image is slightly tilted. This arouses the impression that the angels are on the point of bearing it off heavenwards. The altar looks more spatial than ever before (cf. B52, B60). This scene is separated from the main area by a curtain of columns which is set up in an expressive way, as can be seen from the fact that the columns are rhythmized and that the outermost column is not fully in front of the pilaster behind it. The screen-like sets of columns found in ancient architecture (e.g. A31) now breathe the rhythm and dynamism of the Baroque. The saint, and with him the light, both break through them into the main area. The permeability and the column structure are directly reminiscent of the topic of the façade. The main room becomes a vestibule, an anteroom and auditorium for the holy events. The classical vestibule is indeed transversely oval in shape.

The bright, golden dome rises above the weighty substructure of the main area, and is strongly separated off from it by a heavy, continuous, unmoulded architrave. The dome has no drum, is very flat, and thus makes a light impression. It is built up of individual segments which follow the alternation of wide and narrow chapels, something which is also subtly suggested by the fact that the segments are sometimes peopled by apostles (fishermen such as St Andrew) and sometimes only by putti. These segments look full of air (and do not look folded as in Borromini's work, B56), and seem to hover and to be held only by the ribs (as by the strings of a captive balloon), which do not so much grow tectonically from the bottom upwards, but instead radiate from the top downwards and – this is typical of the High Baroque – are again combined with coffer work. The impression of something airy and full of light is intensified by the large, simple windows, which cut into the base of the vault and cause the light to flow in with an intensity similar to that found in St Peter's, where this design first occurred (H31). This part of the church is of a quite different character from that of the worldly part below, which is built in the massive, classical Roman style. The saint ascending heavenwards appears between the two. All the lines run towards him, and the gable is bursting to free him from earthly anguish. The owners of the Quirinal forbade the building of a drum, in order to prevent the church from obscuring their view. This had a positive effect: a drum would only have been a disturbing factor placed between the sarcellum and the heaven of the dome. The saint was depicted as he was passing into heaven: the ignudi (apostles) are already reacting to him, whereas the angels have not yet perceived him; neither is their circle in the lantern entirely closed as yet. Once again, every detail supports the impression of a holy mystery taking place at this very moment.

Two design ideas make it possible for the onlooker to experience this anew in an intense way. Firstly, the ascension into heaven does not take place in the choir. Instead, the portico gable cuts off the view of the lantern in the choir, and introduces a retarding element. In this way the ascension was compelled to pursue a much longer and more emotionally charged axis running transversely across the whole church and the onlooker's world. Secondly, the emphasis placed upon the gates makes it possible to experience anew the soul's transition. The separation of the substructure from the dome, and the emphasis placed on the portico, can only be explained by this topic of transition. The matter of walking through the gate becomes a guiding idea. The saint's journey is a model, which can be reconstructed just as well in the world of the onlooker, because the gate leading into the church from the outside area is designed in the same way, with light breaking through there too. In a church for novices preparing to enter upon a sanctified monastic life, this is a tremendously expressive image. The way to heaven is similarly uplifting to that from the outside area into the church. On the outside the portico is convex and inviting, while on the inside the colonnade curves backwards as if internalized. Outside, the portico deprives the design of any severity. Inside, the oval shape reverts ingeniously to the shape taken by martyrdom in the late-classical period in which St Andrew lived. Bernini's unsurpassed greatness lies in his making his architecture speak so clearly. On the other hand, he subordinated all the details and, in contrast to Borromini, did not allow the components to retain their autonomy. This makes his buildings appear clearer and more classical, and at the same time more emotive. This is because there are two features which extend beyond the classical models: firstly the permeability which he lent to the rotunda at the decisive locations at the gates for man and man's soul, and secondly the dynamism which he caused to prevail in the structures. What Bernini was building was no longer pure architecture, but was a link between different genres. Formally speaking, the figures and the building work are much more clearly separated than in the case of, for example, Borromini, but in terms of subject matter they are more closely linked, because the building becomes the area housing the sculpture. What is expressive is no longer the decorations, but rather the building itself. In the Cornaro chapel, the altar contained space (B60), whereas here the entire building becomes the space in which the holy event is taking place. The large gate, the anteroom, and the small sanctum from which the chief energy bursts forth – all these are elements of a very trenchant narrative, and they prove that Bernini was a pictorial artist in his architecture too. Bernini differed from Borromini in that Bernini hardly invented a single new individual component, whereas, when it came to the overall view, simplicity and abundance, classical style and dynamism, were, in the works of Bernini, united in a manner not found in any of his contemporaries. And this was entirely new. SG

Bibliography: J. Connors, »Bernini's S. Andrea al Quirinale. Payments and planning«, *Journal of the Society of Architectural Historians*, 1982, p. 15; Ch. L. Frommel, »S. Andrea al Quirinale: Genesi e struttura«, in: *Gian Lorenzo Bernini architetto*, Rome, 1983, p. 211.

B86 Acqua Acetosa
Via Flaminia (plan I 2/A)
1661
Andrea Sacchi

In the mid-16C, a medicinal spring began to bubble forth north of the Ponte Milvio, not far from the bank of the Tiber. Its curative effects attracted numerous patients, so that in 1613 Pope Paul V ordered the construction of a simple fountain for the spring. In 1661, the great popularity of the spring induced Pope Alexander VII to order a more elaborate structure to be built instead of the basin. The inscription on the gable of the fountain praises the initiator of this project, who provided an appropriate architecture marking out this delightful spot with its purifying spring and also planted shady trees to invite the visitor to stay here.

The tradition which relates that Gianlorenzo Bernini designed the new fountain architecture probably does not accord with the facts. It is more likely that Andrea Sacchi carried out the design, and Marcantonio de Rossi the actual building work. Apart from the chapel of S. Caterina da Siena in S. Maria sopra Minerva, the fountain is the only architectural work of which it is certain that Sacchi produced.

A ramp framed by a surrounding wall leads to the fountain which is located below ground level and, on its rear wall, concludes in a curving façade with three axes and a gable. But it is not so much the character of the façade that dominates here, but rather the impression of an ancient, grotto-like nymphaeum. The three round-arched niches form something resembling a detail from an ancient garden room. Sacchi is basically copying ancient triumphal-arch architecture in employing this structure, but the flat subdivision by pilaster strips, and the curving gable, are no more than

reminiscences of rulers' triumphal buildings. A much stronger emphasis was placed on the way in which the framework of the fountain is harmoniously embedded amidst the surrounding nature. AG

B87/88 S. Maria di Montesanto and S. Maria dei Miracoli
Piazza del Popolo (plan I 2/D)
1662–75, 1661–79

In his urbanist redesign of the Piazza del Popolo, Carlo Rainaldi was creating a unique piece of Baroque entrance architecture: the sacred city gate, formed from two churches, of the papal city of Rome. It is an inner gate standing immediately behind the defiant Porta del Popolo (B77). The present-day design of the square goes back to Giuseppe Valadier (cf. K1). The ancient field of Mars in the north of the city was for a long time an irregular area which was not built up. The Porta del Popolo was at its northern end, while in the south three streets lined with houses led into the city in radial formation. They included the ancient Via Lata, today the Via del Corso. When the obelisk was set up under Sixtus V in 1589, this was an initial step towards regulating the terrain. Standing at the point of intersection of the three streets, it is a signpost which marks the centre of the square and is visible from afar. Bernini redesigned the Porta del Popolo (B77) on the occasion of the Queen of Sweden's entry into the city in 1665, thus giving the square a second point of emphasis. A comprehensive effort to restructure the square was not made until 1658, when the Carmelites were planning to build a church at the front of the block of houses between Via del Corso and Via del Babuino and were thus touching upon decisive questions of city planning. Alexander VII now himself intervened in the project by ordering the construction of a second, identical church. The motif of twin churches, S. Maria di Montesanto and S. Maria del Miracoli, was an elegant way of solving that problem of city planning which lay in lending architectural integration to the three radiating streets and in making the

B87/88 S. Maria di Montesanto and S. Maria dei Miracoli

B87/88 S. Maria di Montesanto

square perform its function as a distributor of traffic. The present architectural shape of the churches derives from a lengthy planning progress in which not only Carlo Rainaldi, but also Carlo Fontana and later Bernini, were involved. Large, voluminous domes rest on eight- and twelve-sided drums. Free-standing columned porticoes in the form of classical temple frontages stand in front of the churches; incipient concave curves provide the link. The delicate campanili are 18C additions and concentrate the overall complex still more strongly on the central axis. The massive churches, three-dimensionally designed throughout, are monumental structures which stand at the heads of the streets without blocking their course. The way in which the perspective of the street lines moves into the background can thus be combined with the large-domed buildings to form an impressive backdrop to be viewed. The main topics of this theatre-like view of the square are the dome and the temple frontage, two motifs which are monumentalized in an unusual way. They point towards St Peter's and the Pantheon, and reveal to the onlooker's eye Rome as the papal city and centre of Christendom. The churches do not merely monumentalize the entrance into the city, but they also make it sacred: they are the first harbingers of St Peter's, which is the destination of the pilgrims arriving here from all over the world.

The architectural history of the twin churches of S. Maria di Montesanto and S. Maria del Miracoli is directly related to the rearrangement, for purposes of city planning, of the Piazza del Popolo. When, in 1658, the Carmelites were planning to build a new church, Alexander VII handed over to the Franciscan tertiaries the church of S. Orsola in the block of houses opposite, between Corso and Via de Ripetta, and required them to build an identical structure. The foundation stones of the two churches were laid in 1661 and 1662. By way of an initial step, Rainaldi, assisted by Carlo Fontana, designed two domed churches with cruciform ground plans. But these slender domes above tall drums, and the flat pilastered façades, would scarcely have had the strength really to dominate the square. In 1665, in order to meet the require-

ments of city planning, Rainaldi, with Bernini also possibly participating, made the decisive change of plan and turned the churches into domed structures with circular ground plans. This made it possible considerably to increase the volume of the domes and to achieve that monumentalization of them which was necessary for the backdrop-like view of the square. The plot of land for the Montesanto church extends further back and is narrower than that of its sister church, so that the circular form could only be made into an oval there. During the second phase of construction from 1673 onwards, Bernini put all his skill into optically adapting the different domes to one another.

With its longitudinally oval interior, which is probably Bernini's idea, S. Maria di Montesanto is a direct successor to S. Giacomo degli Incurabili (B28). Here too, a ring of chapels surrounds the main area, and is concluded by a continuous, unmoulded entablature. The triumphal-arch motif of the interior façade walls of S. Giacomo has though been abandoned in favour of a paratactic row of arcades of equal height. The narrow surrounding bays, which in S. Giacomo were self-contained and formed the wall, are here broken up by inserted arches and balconies, and are made to contain space. The large arcades leading to the choir and vestibule are placed above an oval ground plan, and are genuine arcades with arches. They are now no longer being employed to mark an abrupt transition. Instead, every device is used to integrate them into the continuous surrounding ring of chapel arcades. The system of wall articulation thereby achieved is made to flow uniformly, resulting in a self-contained spatial continuum which – in complete contrast to the

B87/88 S. Maria dei Miracoli

curving façade shells of S. Giacomo – emphasizes that the area has the character of a rotunda. The idea of a centrally planned building makes the room circular despite the oval ground plan, and – contrary to what is the case in the twin church – is guided by the principle of homogeneity.

The front elevation system of S. Maria dei Miracoli, whose interior was designed by Rainaldi, is closely related to S. Giacomo degli Incurabili (B28), although the ground plan is not so similar. The rhythmic bays with the three round-arched arcades which are graduated in the vertical direction once again form the triumphal-arch motif on the side walls of the circular main area. The central arcade is additionally framed by a large aedicule. Only the arcades of the entrance and choir can compete with this strongly emphasized motif. They contrast with the sister church and with S. Giacomo in that they are fully developed: the fronts of the arches are richly shaped, and the arcades have their own massive pilasters above which the main entablature is bent to right angles. The emphasis placed upon the arcades of the choir and entrance on the one hand, and upon the aedicules on the other, vividly expresses the mutual penetration of the longitudinal and transverse axes, and thus illustrates the Greek cross. This may mean that Rainaldi was deliberately remembering his first, rejected draft for a church above a Greek cross. Despite the emphasized crossing of the axes, and despite the circular shape, this is an oriented area. All the articulating elements culminate in the choir, where the abundance of architectural details is developed to the full. An entirely new feature, when compared with all the related structures, is the way in which the wall is shaped. It follows the layering principle. The pilasters form the front spatial layer, followed, in the narrow bays, by the wall proper. It is only behind the wall that the straight arcades of the chapels are to be found. These arcades do not follow the circular ground plan. Thus S. Maria dei Miracoli is the richer and more splendid of the twin churches. EJ

B89 S. Maria dell' Assunzione, Ariccia

Ariccia, Piazza Repubblica (plan G2 4/C)
1662–65
Gianlorenzo Bernini

S. Maria dell' Assunzione is of interest as a centrally planned church building, but must also be acknowledged as a brilliant urbanist achievement by Bernini. The family of Alexander VII Chigi, the ruling pope, acquired the little town of Ariccia in 1661. A year later, building work began on the church which was to be constructed opposite the large palace in which the Chigi now lived. Surrounded on three sides by single-storeyed buildings, the church dominates a square which has two fountains and was originally open only towards one side (in the 17C, the Via Appia led to the lower part of Ariccia, and did not run across the church square as it does today).

B89 S. Maria dell' Assunzione, Ariccia

A portico with three arcades and a temple frontage placed flatly in front of it stands outside the cylindrical structure of the church. This rotunda concludes in a hemispherical dome and lantern, and its self-contained, block-like structural effect is emphasized by plain pilaster strips and thermal windows. Both structures, the portico and the church, are of a geometrical clarity, and their restrained articulation makes an un-Baroque impression. It was evident to contemporaries that Bernini, in using this architectural shape, was repeating the ancient Roman Pantheon (A31) in a stylized form. This copying from ancient Rome may be related to Bernini's plans to restore the Pantheon in a purifying way in those same years, but might also derive from a wish expressed by the pope himself.

Drawings show that Bernini's chief problem lay not so much in the design of the rotunda, but more in the effect which the church and square would have in terms of city planning. On the one hand the building was meant to relate to the palace, while on the other it was also necessary to consider the topographical situation of the city behind the palace. Bernini supplemented the rotunda by adding low flanking buildings with porticoes (three axes apiece) on their front sides, and thus formed it into a group of buildings with a uniform, though not self-contained, frontage. Thus, opposite the Chigi palace, there stands an architectural ensemble which is homogeneous within itself. Two bell towers, barely visible from the square, stand to the sides of the sacristy on the rear side of the rotunda and relate to some alleyways in the city.

The design of the interior is as clear as that of the exterior. Eight niches determine the appearance of the area, with the longitudinal axis being cautiously emphasized by placing larger niches at the entrance and altar. In the manner of the tabularium motif (cf. A9), Corinthian pilasters are placed in front of the arcades housing the niches. The circular base of the hemispherical dome stands on the pilasters, and there is no drum. The church is of simple proportions: the height of the cylinder up to the circular base of the dome is the same as that of the dome. The Pantheon may also have determined this feature, as well as the absence of a drum and the plainness of the architectural subdividing work.

Bernini's style here is that of a Baroque Classicist. But the concept for the decorations is High Baroque and, to a certain extent, contrasts with the architecture. The stucco work in the dome area is on the same level of subject matter as the altar fresco depicting the Assumption of the Virgin Mary. Thus the painted holy mysteries in the altar area continue throughout the area of the church. This kind of decorative concept which extends beyond a single area is typical of Bernini. AS

B90 S. Maria del Suffragio
Via Giulia (plan III 2/B)
1662–69
Carlo Rainaldi

The fraternity of »intercession« (suffragio) was founded in 1592. In 1616, this charitable fraternity was awarded the higher status of arch-fraternity (Arciconfraternità). The plan was that the headquarters of the fraternity should be adapted so as to express this increase in significance. Previously, S. Biagio della Pagnotta had been the fraternity's headquarters. But it now moved into the Via Giulia, and work on building a medium-sized church was begun in 1662. Carlo Rainaldi was engaged to design this new building.

However, the design of S. Maria del Suffragio, both inside and outside, turned out to be so plain that it would scarcely be attributed to Rainaldi if the sources did not clearly refer to him. In particular, the column, which is an important component in Rainaldi's architecture, is entirely absent here. The barrel-vaulted interior is a room structure with apse aisles, is of the same type as Il Gesù (B1), and is subdivided by pilasters. Rainaldi initially planned a longitudinally oval building, which would certainly have been more interesting. But the conservative fraternity apparently adhered to traditional architectural shapes. The façade is similarly unremarkable. The overall appearance of the street was the decisive factor: the façade is an almost flat surface, the aim being not to disturb the homogeneity. Only the three central bays – they are subdivided by

B91 S. Maria in Campitelli

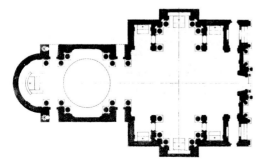

pilasters – are accentuated by the projecting cornice below, the combined gable above, and the three entrances. The outer bays resemble buttresses supporting the sides of the high-rising façade. PZ

B91 S. Maria in Campitelli
Piazza Campitelli (plan IV 2/B)
1662–75
Carlo Rainaldi

The plague church of S. Maria in Campitelli is the chief work by Rainaldi and is among the most significant Roman High-Baroque buildings. An image of the Virgin Mary in the small church of S. Maria in Portico worked miracles in the plague year of 1656, and induced the Roman Senate to vow to place this miracle-working image in a dignified setting. At the insistence of Pope Alexander VII, it was decided to transfer the image from the overpopulated Ripa district to the church of S. Maria in Campitelli on the Piazza Campizucchi. It was probably at that time, in January 1658, that the plans to convert the existing church were abandoned and it was decided to build a new church. Rainaldi was appointed as architect. The pope received the initial architectural plans four months later. These are very likely to have been Rainaldi's design for an oval building, a plan which is known from drawings but, for reasons of cost, was not put into effect. Finally, starting in 1662, the church was built to new plans by Rainaldi, being consecrated in 1675. Its decorations were completed by 1725.

Great interest is commanded not only by today's structure, but also by Rainaldi's plan- it was not put into effect – for an oval building. The surviving drawing (Rome, monastery of S. Maria in Campitelli) shows a longitudinal section running through the façade, the longitudinally oval laymen's room, and the circular presbytery, which are all spatial units following one after another along the main axis of the church. The façade of that project is a two-storeyed vestibule and is clearly an imitation of Cortona's façade for S. Maria in Via Lata (B83).

The laymen's room and the presbytery are interpreted as being two independent spatial units which are combined with one another without abandoning the self-contained character which each of them has. This is related to the design of these two rotundas: a structure consisting of columns or pilasters, an entablature, and a dome, is reminiscent of the design of a round temple, and is filled up with secondary insertions such as chapel entrances and coretti. At the point where the laymen's room and the presbytery come into contact with one another, the only feature that produces any effect is the fact that these two rooms are structured like round temples. This emphasizes their character as two independent centrally planned buildings. The idea of combining two such spatial units into a longitudinal structure was put into effect in another form in the church as it was actually built.

The double-storeyed façade is subdivided into five axes below and three above, and concludes in a triangular gable. The axes of the façade consist of bays made up of pillars which have pilasters on three sides. Three-quarter and full columns stand in front of the pilasters in the three central axes. The axes alternate in containing either portals or windows, or else have full columns placed within them. On both storeys, the central axis of the façade is emphasized by large aedicules consisting of full columns and a triangular or segmented gable, and small aedicules serving as frames for doors or windows are placed within these large aedicules.

The façade essentially follows the classical scheme of a basilican cross-section façade. But the new orchestration of the façade is a notable feature: the most important element is the full column, and the leitmotiv is the aedicule. The effect produced by the façade is determined by its extremely complex three-dimensional structure. The façade is made up of three layers. The rear layer is the wall in front of which the whole of the articulation by means of pilasters and columns unfolds. It is directly visible at the extreme axes of the façade and, as a rear wall, also appears between the columns of the central axes. The layer in front of it consists of six pilastered pillars and the full columns which are inserted into the lateral central axes. The front layer is formed of three-quarter and full columns placed in front of the pilastered pillars. The interplay between the middle and front layers of the façade can be seen from the main entablature and from the concluding triangular gable. These are projecting above the columns of the front layer of the façade, and set back in the sections which belong to the middle layer.

Rainaldi is thus abandoning the design principle which had been customary since the façade of Il Gesù (B1) and which consists in continuously intensifying the three-dimensionality towards the centre of the façade. Rainaldi is to some extent displaying all the layers simultaneously in all the axes. columns, This lends a previously unknown dominance to the system of articulation.

Rainaldi is alluding to famous prototypes in his use of full columns. The full columns inserted into the lateral axes are a motif borrowed from the conservators' palace (H30); the columns placed in front of the pillars suggest ancient design principles (triumphal arches). But the many columns also prepare the visitor for the interior, which is similarly orchestrated.

The ground plan of the interior combines two centralized spatial units. The nave is designed biaxially. Unlike, for example, Il Gesù (B1), it does not have, on each side, three chapels of equal size. Instead, the middle chapel on each side is clearly accentuated, is considerably wider and deeper than the other chapels, and attains the same springing height as the vault of the nave itself. The nave is subdivided only by pilasters, whereas Rainaldi fits out the middle chapels with full columns. This upgrading gives the middle chapels a significant status in the ground-plan system: they attain the character of a transept. This means that the entire space has approximately the shape of a Greek cross.

The adjoining presbytery consists of a domed centrally planned area with low transverse arms and an apse, and has a self-contained character of its own. Eight full columns serve to mark the transitions from the nave to the presbytery and from the latter to the apse. Those columns, along with four more columns in the low transept arms, support the wall arches upon which the dome rests. The crossing is lit by oval windows in the dome and is markedly brighter than the nave.

The transition from the nave to the presbytery is designed by Rainaldi as a constricted area taking the shape of a double arcade which is not concentric. The outer arcade on its high piers follows the course of the barrel vault of the nave, resembles the wall arches of it and, like them, rests on pilasters, while the small arcade borne by full columns is part of the presbytery and finds its equivalent in the transition to the apse. Rainaldi shows by this that the nave ends at this point and that a new and independent spatial unit begins. A more obvious point of change can scarcely be imagined.

The church interior captivates the onlooker by the impressive scenic effect which Rainaldi achieves by subdividing it with full columns. The columns of the choir combine optically with those of the transept-like chapels of the nave to form a backdrop of columns which becomes increasingly narrow, tapering off towards the miracle-working image of the Virgin Mary which is the target of this visual setting. Rainaldi stresses the significance of this part of the church by providing as great as possible an abundance of light in the dome area. Thus, despite the point of change referred to, a visual movement in the direction of the altar is created and ultimately does combine the two very independent spatial units into a longitudinal structure.

Rainaldi's church of the Virgin Mary has no direct predecessors in Rome, but it does follow the model of some prototypes in Northern Italy in which the accentuation of the middle chapels, the use of full columns, and the linking of two centrally planned areas, are all to be found (S. Salvatore in Bologna by Magenta and S. Giuseppe in Milano by Ricchino). Rainaldi's achievement lies in employing lighting and a backdrop effect in order to unite the very complex spatial system. AS

Bibliography: R. Wittkower, »Rainaldi and the Roman Architecture of the full Baroque«, *Art Bulletin*, 1937, p. 242; H. Hager, »Zur Datierung des Ovalprojektes von S. Maria in Campitelli«, *Römisches Jahrbuch für Kunstgeschichte*, 1967/68, p. 297; M. Pedroli Bertoni, *S. Maria in Campitelli*, Rome, 1987.

B92 Scala Regia

Piazza di S. Pietro (plan III 1/A)
1663–66
Gianlorenzo Bernini

The design of staircases was an important architectural topic in the Baroque period, when impressiveness played an important part in the ceremonial. The elaborate Baroque staircases usually took up a good deal of space. This was exactly what was not available in the buildings of the Vatican palace with their many nooks and crannies. When, in 1663, Pope Alexander VII (1655–67) commissioned Bernini to build an impressive stairway for the Scala Regia along the right arm of the colonnades, there was only one narrow room still available for the new stairs. But thanks to an ingenious lighting scheme and a brilliant trick with the perspective, Bernini managed to eliminate this disadvantage altogether. The narrow room meant that there could only be one flight of stairs. The flanking walls unfortunately taper towards one another, and the result is that the stairs seem even deeper than they really are. This situation could only be remedied by making a correction to the true dimensions. Bernini achieved an impression of liberality by using only one design device in the stairs, although the stairs themselves become narrower as a result. The entrance motif of the Serliana is continued up the whole staircase in the colonnades which stand away from the

B92 Scala Regia

walls, and the result is that greater width is suggested than actually exists. This trick also makes it possible not to make the columns approach one another towards the top as much as the lateral walls do. This corrects the visual impression of immense depth. Optical foreshortening is though also achieved by rhythmizing the column positioning and by making a change in the tunnel vaulting. The inserted resting place is accentuated by the light cascading into the room, and the long tunnel-like area is artistically shaped by light and shade. AG

Bibliography: E. Panofsky, »Die Scala Regia und die Kunstanschauung Berninis«, *Jahrbuch der Preußischen Kunstsammlungen*, 1919.

B93 Palazzo Chigi-Odescalchi

Piazza SS. Apostoli 80/81 (plan V 1/B)
begun 1664
Gianlorenzo Bernini

In 1661, the Chigi family purchased from the Colonna, whose palace located diagonally opposite (B76) had just been extended in imposing style, a plot of land with some palace sections standing on it (built by Maderno, 1623; the arcaded courtyard decorated with statues still survives). Like every papal family since Paul V, the Chigi (Flavio Chigi) ordered the construction of a palace which was to point the way forwards: this was the Roman city palace which set the trend for the era of Alexander VII. This is true chiefly of Bernini's new façade with its thirteen axes. The impression it created was destroyed when the Odescalchi acquired the palace in 1745 and commissioned Nicola Salvi and Luigi Vanvitelli, from 1750 onwards, to extend its central section, which had seven axes: the right-hand wing section of Bernini's structure disappeared in the central section, which was now extended by a further eight axes and to which a new wing section with six axes was also attached. A typically 18C endless façade, which now had two portals, came into being. The frontage facing the Corso (by Raffel Ojetti, 1887 to 1889) imitates that of the Palazzo Pitti.

Bernini's work is reproduced in Specchi's engraving. Like the famous Palazzo Farnese (H25), this palace had thirteen axes and three storeys and its edges were reinforced by bosses. It thus represented the highest possible pretensions. Another link between it and that High-Renaissance palace was the shape of the roofing on the ground floor (flat shape) and in the piano nobile (an alternation of segmented and triangular gables). But the structure and orchestration are quite different: Bernini made the central section project, and gave it a colossal order of pilasters in the piano nobile and the upper storey. To this extent, a second tradition was also being followed, namely that of Michelangelo's design of the Capitol (H27, H30). The axes at the ends of the senators' palace are tower-like structures formed into risalti, and this is a method which Bernini had adopted ten years earlier (B72). And all these buildings are articulated by a colossal order

244 Baroque and Rococo

of pilasters (H27, H30, and cf. H23), which in the senators' palace stands on a base course consisting of a rusticated storey. Michelangelo and Palladio, the masters of the cinquecento, did though usually make the colossal order begin on the ground floor, examples being the conservators' palace (H30) and the Palazzo Valmarana in Vicenza. But since then the colossal order had no longer been employed in Rome.

Accordingly, the main section with its seven axes is richly articulated. Here, Bernini was reverting not only to the design of the Capitol, but also to the second standard High-Renaissance type, embodied in what is known as Raphael's house (cf. H22). But since the mid-16C at the latest, the only architectural type which had been copied was that of the Palazzo Farnese: the wall of the block was articulated only by windows and cornices between the storeys. In contrast to this, Bernini now once again selected a very dense, tight articulation which he also placed within the storeys. The relief was simpler and more delicate than in the conservators' palace, and there were no frames or recessed layers. Except for the window frames, Bernini was relying solely on the effect produced by the pilasters. But the reduced number of means employed gave a clear prominence to the particular impression being created. Bernini provided the articulation with a tremendous energy. The pilasters are placed close together in a rapid rhythm, so that the window roofings now fill up the whole width of the intercolumniations. The 18C tendency to allow the wall to be consumed by the windows was thus sketched out for the first time. In Bernini's work, all the elements and their orchestration derive their very tightness and energy from this arrangement. This effect produced by the two main storeys was emphasized by the fact that the ground floor, more clearly than ten years previously (B72), was characterized as being merely a base course. Bernini then gave each storey its very specific character. Here, the mood is determined by the window frames. They are self-contained on the ground or base-course floor, festively and majestically rich in the piano nobile with its columned aedicules, and playful in the upper storey, where the private character comes expressively to the fore: in the small, transversely placed corbels at the upper conclusions of the sides, Bernini was here using a motif which his rival Borromini had gone on to develop into an »ear shape« and which was then to be found everywhere in the more intimate Rococo. Everything has its place in this façade, and everything fits in with the overall context. Examples proving this are firstly the balcony supported by Tuscan columns, and secondly, in the piano nobile, the central window which, with its inserted columns, is an imitation of that in the Palazzo Farnese. In the latter, these parts burst forth from the overall context, whereas here they are logically developed from the rest of the system of articulation.

In Bernini's work, the main section of the building is a block. This palazzo differs from the senators' palace

B93 Palazzo Chigi-Odescalchi

in that it is the centre that projects, not the outermost axis. The projecting centre, and the resultant tripartite structure, had characterized many of Bernini's previous buildings (B43, B82, B89). But after ten years (cf. B72), the relationship between the centre and the wings had become tighter and more strongly regularized, and the centre was more clearly ennobled. What had formerly been a good way of dealing with an individual case now became the norm. Bernini now no longer designed the central section as a risalto, but as a separate block, so that the Roman cube is still kept fully intact and preserved as the basic form of the palace, the only point being that it is very much enriched. This is the very reason why the transitions between the central and wing sections, particularly where the orchestration was concerned, had to be kept as hard and unharmonious as possible. This was why the two sections had to be contrasted with one another, so that the central section projected higher and the corbelled cornice and the balustrade (the plan was that it should be decorated with figures) were reserved only for the central section and the wing sections remained largely undecorated (for example, the windows do not have an aedicule framework). The succession of window roofings in the piano nobile is reversed at the point of transition between the central section and the wing. It was a stroke of genius to build the wing sections in rustic work which was not, as it always had been before, used in order to make the base course appear very weighty, but instead to characterize the wing sections as being different. Thus, from these sections of the building which do not seem to have been designed very much, but still to have been left in their natural state, the central section emerges which splendidly proves itself to be a work of human hand and truly to dominate the wing sections.

Others had copied St Peter's (B71, B82), the Chigi ordered a senators' palace of their own to be built for them, combined with some shapes taken from the Palazzo Farnese. Bernini invented the language of the Baroque princes; it was a matter of the unlimited subordination of the individual to the entirety. This manner of design found successors all over Europe, particularly in the radiant Viennese Baroque, an example being Fischer von Erlach (the most brilliant example is in the Palais Trautson), while in Rome this was more subdued (B126, B138). At the same time, there is hardly another building in which it becomes more clear than Bernini was everywhere basing himself on classical models, preferably those of the High Renaissance, whereas although the individual parts which he was using were basically always known, he was combining them into something completely new. What is new can best be seen by comparing the palace with the Farnese palace. This one appears to be massive whereas the new building is an articulated structure, a skeleton structure, very upright. Not only the horizontal lines are important now but also the vertical ones. And the insula, the block with four equal sides, has been enriched by the *facciata,* the fronting, although the block experience is still maintained. SG

Bibliography: P. Waddy, *Seventeenth-century Roman Palaces*, Cambridge and London, 1990, pp. 291 to 320.

B94 S. Biagio in Campitelli (also: S. Rita da Cascia)
Via Montanara (plan IV 2/B)
1665
Carlo Fontana

The church of S. Biagio originally stood at the foot of the Capitol, immediately to the left of the stairs of S. Maria in Aracoeli (C36). The building was torn down in 1928, and rebuilt on its present site in 1940. The church itself dates back to the year 1653; the architect is unknown. The real interest of the building lies in the façade, that is to say in the cladding of the building. It was added in 1665 by Carlo Fontana, who worked in Bernini's studio for ten years. The façade of S. Biagio is his first known work, and is a two-storeyed frontage. The standard type for a Roman façade has a narrow upper storey, but here the upper storey extends across the entire width of the ground floor. However, the concave lateral bays lead towards the rear, whereas in the centre the front surface is accentuated. The

B94 S. Biagio in Campitelli (also: S. Rita da Cascia)

upper storey is a three-dimensional structure and thus contrasts with the lower, which remains two-dimensional. This makes the façade into a structure rich in tension. The three-dimensional structure leads the onlooker's gaze onwards, inviting him to walk around the building and to encircle it as if it was a sculpture; but it must not be forgotten that on the original site a narrow alley made this impossible.

The idea of a three-dimensionally designed façade in which two different architectural structures supplement one another antagonistically derives, as Wittkower has observed, from plans which Bernini drew up for a tomb. The perspective window frames are also taken from Bernini's repertoire of ideas (cf. B45). The cladding work by Fontana refreshingly enriched this small church by making use of different structures in a manner which was rich in tension. PZ

B95 Elephant carrying an obelisk in front of S. Maria sopra Minerva
Piazza della Minerva (plan IV 2/A–2/B)
1666/67
Gianlorenzo Bernini

An Egyptian obelisk from the 6C BC, the smallest to have been found in Rome, was discovered in 1665 in a former shrine of Isis in the garden of the Dominican monastery, beside the church. Pope Alexander VII took over the guardianship of the obelisk and decided to set up this monolith in the square outside the church. The pontifex was not pleased with some plans drawn up by the Dominicans for the pedestal, and he asked Bernini for some better proposals. After a consultation with the polymath Athanasius Kircher, it was decided in 1666 to build an elephant which symbolizes the bearer of wisdom (the obelisk). The inscription on the pedestal panegyrically relates the elephant to the pope: what a strong mind Alexander VII must have to be able to hold so much wisdom. This ensemble was evidently suggested by a woodcut of the same motif in the Hypnerotomachia Poliphili, an allegorical novel dating from 1499 in which Francesco Colonna praised Christian art as being the perfection of ancient art. The elephant appears as a symbol of God-given wisdom in the novel too. It probably took the greatest artist of those times to form, from the heathen solar symbol of the obelisk and the wild animal, an ensemble which was able to embody a state of inspiration.

Bernini wanted to set up the elephant so that the axis of its body was parallel with the church façade, as it still is today. But the planning documents reveal that the head was intended to be oriented towards the left (the north), so that the monument was meant to be turned through 180 degrees. The chief building of the Dominicans forms the left-hand boundary of the square, and they were meant to be given a good view of the monument. But Bernini entered into an unpleasant dispute with the jealous members of the order, and decided to instruct Ercole Ferrata to sculpt

B95 Elephant carrying an obelisk in front of S. Maria sopra Minerva

the elephant in a mirror image. Thus the Dominicans, up to the present day, have to look at the elephant's creased hindquarters. This is an exemplary instance of the mockery and cynicism which a self-confident artist such as Bernini was able to permit himself.

All in all, the piazza containing the obelisk monument turns out to be a »bel composto« full of delightful tensions. The contrasts were emphasized even within the monument: on the one hand there is the round, soft, living element and on the other the pointed, slender, angular, inanimate element. Bernini did all he could to make the elephant into a bundle of energy. This explains its intense gaze, its strong hump, and the movement in its trunk, ears and drapery. The monument thus contrasts very sharply with the monotonous, flat façade behind it (cf. C37), which was thus upgraded and effectively and cheaply given the Baroque style. On the other hand, the obelisk is integrated into the system of the church façade and is thus subordinated to it. The round window, which was the chief point of emphasis in the old façade, gained from this interplay with the obelisk. It now appears as a disk of light behind the obelisk. How differently indeed were obelisks used under Sixtus V, when they merely pointed the way in long axes. In contrast to this, Bernini created not only a pleasant square which was appropriately filled up by the monument, but also, at low cost, a »new façade«. SG/PZ

B96 Ponte S. Angelo
Lungotevere di Castello/Lungotevere Tor di Nona (plan IV 1/A)
1667–72
Gianlorenzo Bernini

The Ponte S. Angelo, which at the time was called Pons Aelius, was built together with Hadrian's mausoleum (cf. A33) and was interlinked with the masonry of it. The three central arches still date from ancient times. It was given more and more fortifications. Aurelian built walls linking it to the mausoleum, while Alexander VI placed bridge towers out into the river and made the arches narrower. This resulted in flooding. It was only when Urban VIII ordered the bridge towers to be razed in 1628 that there was a turning point in the history of the bridge, and it finally became the most sprightly bridge in Rome. This was because Urban VIII's architect Bernini – forty years later, under Clement IX – proposed that a row of angels be built for the bridge.

The old Bernini was thereby once again initiating the basic tendency of a new epoch, which was the late Baroque (and the Rococo): this was the tendency towards cheerful, scenographic architecture, particularly in staircases and fountains (B115, B126). Paul III had previously, in preparation for Charles V's visit to Rome in 1535, ordered the statues of Peter and Paul to be erected at the head of the bridge, along with eight stucco figures on the bridge itself. Although the stucco figures disappeared, the idea remained. The balustrade supporting a row of figures was also known from the same period: it is found on Michelangelo's

B96 Ponte S. Angelo

Capitol (H30) and in Sansovino's library of St Mark in Venice. Credit is due to Bernini for having lent significance to the statues, and emotionalism to the idea. Both these factors helped that idea to achieve fruition (cf. e.g. B124 and B134). He had already, in the colonnades (B80), abandoned wall architecture, and had conceived the surmounting figures as being more tremendous than a century before. He now further increased both of them. Against the background of sky and water, and also in what, in terms of style and colour, was a very fine contrast with the Castel Sant' Angelo, the angels on the bridge were certain to produce a much more intense effect than their predecessors. The task was also more demanding, because the statues had not only to have a silhouette effect, but also to produce an impression at close range. Bernini therefore called in the cream of the younger sculptors who were trained in his style. They were: Ferrata (angel with cross), Raggi (angel with column), Lucenti (angel with nails), Fancelli (angel with veronica), Giorgetti (angel with sponge), Naldini (angel with dice and robe), Morelli (angel with whip) and Guidi (angel with lance). The angels with the crown of thorns and the inscription are the work of Bernini himself, but they were so well liked that their originals were not installed here (today in S. Andrea delle Fratte, B74). Statues are often found on palace balustrades, but only twice elsewhere on bridges (in Würzburg and Prague).

Where the dynamism of its design is concerned, the bridge is also notable in terms of city planning. Bernini interpreted the angels (particularly the angel with the crown of thorns) as being in a state of transition in which they are just arriving in front of the pilgrim: they are on clouds and their wings are still active. They are signposts of heaven, and are also signposts across the bridge and in the direction of St Peter's: the processional route towards that church led across the Ponte S. Angelo. Thus Bernini was now also allowed to design the last stage of this route (coming after the colonnades, B80, the decoration of the nave of St Peter's, the crossing, B42, and the cathedra). The central theme was transition, set forth in the idea of the procession and the ephemeral elements of heaven and water. The bridge selected was one which linked the congregation (the city) to its prelate (in St Peter's). At that time it was the only bridge, and was thus the Vatican's gate into Rome. SG

Bibliography: H. Evers, *Giovanni Lorenzi Bernini. Die Engelsbrücke in Rom*, Berlin, 1948.

B97 S. Maria Maggiore: apsis
Piazza del Esquilino (plan VI 1/B)
1673
Carlo Rainaldi
When the pilgrim coming from the city approaches this basilica, he first sees the church's rear façade, which for a long time was not designed in a manner appropriate to its significance. The problem lay in

B97 S. Maria Maggiore: apsis

combining the church's structure with its numerous heterogenous additions into one uniform façade.

The first steps towards extending the rear façade were undertaken by Pope Sixtus V from 1586 to 1590 when he added the Cappella Sistina (B20) to the north-eastern side of the basilica. He was followed by Pope Paul V who, in 1611, added the Cappella Paolina (B20) on the opposite side. Due to lack of funds, the magnificent plans for a show façade by Bernini were not put into effect, but they provided the initiative for building the apse. Bernini wanted to conceal the old apse behind a closed wall. But the apse motif would have been taken up again by the massive round shape of a tribuna which was situated immediately in front and was surrounded by a ring of columns. An immense staircase would have optically accentuated the central section still more. The whole complex would have been articulated by graduating the various structures including the chapels.

Compared with this tremendous architectural project, the design actually executed, namely that by Carlo Rainaldi dating from 1673, was an economizing measure. The two dome structures retained their important function as a design element of the façade. The apse was left in its old size and shape. It does not now form a dominant central motif such as had been planned by Bernini, but was inserted as an animated surface between two flanking chapels. The link between the apse and the laterally attached chapels is the rectangular rear wall which follows the shape of the church structure. The attempt was made, by means of a large order of pilasters and a tall attic, to combine the building into an integral whole. But the façade lacks a proper centre. AG

B98 Villa Altieri
Viale Manzoni 47 (plan IX 1/D)
1674
Giovanni Antonio de Rossi
This splendid villa had a terraced garden, a forecourt and lively decorative statues. Today, all these only survive in some engravings. After designing the Palazzo (B68), de Rossi also built here the villa suburbana of the Altieri family.

It was a rectangular, three-storeyed block with eleven window axes which were combined into pairs by fluted pilaster strips. The block was surmounted by a balustrade with busts and a single-storeyed belvedere (three axes) which itself had a balustrade and decorative statues. The façade facing the garden had three large archways on the ground floor. Two flights of stairs led down laterally from that façade to the terraced Baroque garden with its niches, statues and waterworks.

The entrance façade greeted the visitor with two extended semicircular flights of stairs by which he walked directly from the square up to the piano nobile. These flights of stairs surrounded a theatre-like watery scene consisting of a basin, a fountain and statues, all against a rustic-work background which looked like stage scenery and was intended to underline the bucolic mood of the scene. The divided staircase made room, underneath the central section, for an arched opening giving a long-distance view going through the underneath of the entire building and out into the garden behind it.

In addition, de Rossi, in designing the bold curve of the flights of stairs and in providing the opening in the central part of the ground floor, was creating a delightful contrast with the rest of the façade which is dominated by the closed wall and by rectangular shapes which are only slightly three-dimensional and make that façade look tessellated like a carpet. SG

B99 SS. Gesù e Maria
Via del Corso 45/Via di Gesù e Maria (plan I 3/D)
1674–75
Carlo Rainaldi

In 1615, during the rule of Pope Paul V, the order to build the church of SS. Gesù e Maria was placed for the eremitani scalzi of S. Agostino. Carlo Milanesi began the construction work, which however remained incomplete. Cardinal Giorgio Bolognetti commissioned Carlo Rainaldi to complete the façade and redesign the interior. This work was done in 1674/75.

B98 Villa Altieri

B99 SS. Gesù e Maria

The slightly disproportionate façade design, with the large aedicule motif, may derive from Milanesi, as the colossal domed pilasters standing on tall pedestals have a contemporary parallel in the façade of S. Francesco Romana (B36). On the other hand, the design of the two lower lateral sections can certainly be attributed to Rainaldi. They are not linked to the central section by scrolls, although such scrolls were probably originally planned. Instead, they are related to the adjoining house fronts by means of a straight line with a concluding balustrade. Another Rainaldi motif is the corner pillar in the central section which, given the narrowness of the street, is designed to be looked at from an oblique angle.

Rainaldi lent additional shape to the simple, room-type interior by providing apse aisles and a barrel vault. In order to give a more varied appearance to the rigid wall structure between the arch openings, he inserted into each pair of pilasters a three-storeyed architectural structure which was interlinked within itself. Richly articulated balconies open up above the inserted confessional boxes which are framed by Ionic columns and gables. An illusionistic depiction on the balconies shows members of the Bolognetti family apparently taking part in divine service. The third storey is in each case formed by a niche with figures of saints. The articulation of the wall with layers placed in front, the steps and interlacings found in the wall, and the illusionistic openings, all produce a lively wall relief in order to prepare for the choir which was entirely rebuilt by Rainaldi. Convexly curving colonnades which have a richly moulded entablature and stand behind a much-recessed triumphal arch provide the setting for the solemn sacellum. AG

B100 S. Giovanni in Laterano: Cappella Lancellotti

Piazza di Porta S. Giovanni (plan VIII 2/A)

c. 1675

Giovanni Antonio de Rossi

In this chapel built in c. 1675, de Rossi employed the design principle of the double-layered wall. Michelangelo had introduced this principle to Roman architecture in the Sforza chapel (H40), but it was only rarely adopted in Rome. The chapel is built above a circular ground plan with extensions in the entrance and choir areas, and is characterized by the motif of an inserted architectural baldachin. A sail vault with ribs and a lantern rests on four pillars which have pilasters at the sides and a three-quarter column in front. These four supports are placed in front of a wall which is itself subdivided by pilasters (see the entrance and choir walls). The pilasters subdividing the wall are overlapped along half their length in the area of the baldachin pillars, and thus look like recessed layers. They support a wide entablature which runs round the entire chapel and projects above the baldachin pillars.

B100 S. Giovanni in Laterano: Cappella Lancellotti

The pilasters subdividing the wall support two-dimensional blind arcades, and part of the baldachin starts from each of the pillars in front of those pilasters. The lateral pilasters prepare for the cross girders of the arcades, while the ribs of the baldachin begin from the three-quarter columns. The four supports relate exclusively to the sail vault and are linked with it to form an independent architectural motif, namely the baldachin. But at the same time the surrounding entablature also relates the supports to the outer wall.

The baldachin is placed upon a circular ground plan. The pedestals of the pillars, and of the columns placed in front, follow the line of the ground plan and are therefore slightly concave. The course taken by the arcades also retraces the circular ground plan. They curve not only upwards but also laterally outwards, thus describing an arc. This type of arcade, known as »Bogenarkade« in German, was to attain great significance in the South German Baroque (Balthasar Neumann was among those who designed it), and the first consistently produced example of it is found here.

The »Bogenarkade« arcades cut into the dome of the baldachin. Their intradoses, which are decorated with stars and stucco-work shapes, are therefore to be understood as being as a cross-section through the thickness of the vault. Accordingly, the associated pilasters which are placed to the sides of the pillars are the cross-section through the supports. This becomes particularly clear at the transition to the choir, where there is no wall in the rear and the arcade therefore stands alone. The arcades in the area of the side windows are treated less obviously, but no less consistently. One third of the arches is, so to speak, located within the wall, and the window roofings cover the stucco decorations in the intrados, so that only half (of the star, for example) remains visible. The wall and baldachin meet one another, but remain distinguishable. The baldachin is thus displayed as a motif which is independent of the wall surrounding it and has the character of a separate, second shell.

Like Michelangelo in the Sforza chapel a century earlier (H40), de Rossi thus turned two topics into an artistic theme: firstly the independence of the baldachin from the rest of the chapel architecture and, secondly and consequently, a structure consisting of a double-layered wall. The Lancellotti chapel is a Baroque translation of its prototype. The new features, however, lie in the circular ground plan, the »Bogenarkade« motif, the complicated structure of the pillars with the pilasters that form a cross-section, and the refined consistency of the detail.

The Lancellotti chapel is a masterpiece by de Rossi. The mere fact that Bernardo Vittone adopted the chapel in his works is proof of its pathbreaking character. AS

B101 S. Maria in Trastevere: Cappella Avila

Piazza di S. Maria in Trastevere (plan VII 1/A)
1678–85
Antonio Gherardi

In 1678, Gherardi designed for Francesco Avila, who was his patron, a tomb chapel which can be interpreted as an experiment in terms of both lighting techniques and architecture. Two shallow niches and a deeper area are attached by arcades to a square-shaped main area which is marked out by a baldachin motif formed by four diagonally placed columns. The dome-like chapel vault looks contorted, because the circular base of the dome is not strictly horizontal and the rectangular panels are deformed. A stuccoed balustrade placed on the dome leads up to the large apex opening in which four angels are to be seen as if floating in from outside. They carry a small round temple on their shoulders. (This extremely unusual motif appears to be borrowed from dome frescos in which painted angels seem to hold in suspense the real lantern of the dome, as for example in S. Maria in Vallicella.) Oval tabernacles curving concavely in the middle and standing on high pedestals are placed in the niches to the left and right of the entrance and contain the urns of the deceased. They not only fill up the entire height and width of the niches, but even seem too large for it. They thus give an impression of architectural structures which are straining within themselves and threaten to burst the niches apart. The deep choir opposite the entrance contains a foreshortened »colonnade« of pilasters with a sarcophagus in the middle of it. The insertion above the colonnade looks like a theatre balcony. Like the other insertions in the lateral niches, it is too large for the opening available and intensifies the bizarre impression which arises at the sight of the chapel.

Gherardi, who had trained as a painter, here shows himself to be a very ingenious experimenter. The spectacular structure of the architecture is designed to bewilder and to create optical illusions, and seems to have been suggested by stage architecture and ephemeral festive decorations. But imitations of architectural motifs by Borromini are discernible in some points, such as the design of the little balcony (cf. S. Andrea delle Fratte, bell tower, B74). The tendency to fit individual components expressively into their surroundings is also reminiscent of Borromini. What is more, Gherardi's lighting arrangement betrays a knowledge of Borromini's and Bernini's lighting techniques, but is of a variety which goes far beyond these models and must therefore be acknowledged as a unique achievement by Gherardi. Of the five sources of light, only one, the lantern in the apex of the dome, is visible. It surrounds the angels and the tempietto with a flood of light which blurs their outlines. Two further light-wells (one of them is walled up today) lead to the lateral niches, where they yield a weak half-light. The foreshortened »colonnade« is lit from above by a lantern behind the little balcony. Finally, the altarpiece

B101 S. Maria in Trastevere: Cappella Avila

at the end of the line of pilasters is given some additional brightness of its own by a stovepipe-shaped light-well. Examples for each one of these lighting techniques can certainly be found in Rome, but it is their unique combination that makes Gherardi's chapel into a didactic model when it comes to lighting arrangement.

By dispensing with a clear tectonic structure and by slurring and contorting some subdividing elements, Gherardi was going in a direction which was inevitably going to isolate him artistically in an era which inclined towards forms of a classicizing kind. His architecture was therefore hardly imitated in Rome (cf. also the Cappella di S. Cecilia in S. Carlo ai Catinari, B107). AS

B102 S. Francesco a Ripa

Piazza S. Francesco d'Assisi (plan VII 1/A)
1681
Mattia de Rossi

The Benedictine monastery with its church of S. Bagio was founded in the 10C and was fitted out as a hospice for pilgrims. It was much frequented, owing to its favourable location near the port on the Tiber called Porto di Ripa Grande, and Francis of Assisi, its present patron saint, lodged in it in 1210. The Franciscans took over the monastery in 1229, and in 1681 they entrusted Mattia de Rossi, who was Bernini's favourite pupil, with the task of designing a new building. Among the decorations in the church, Bernini's sculpture of St. Ludovica (1671) is definitely worth seeing.

The five axes of the façade indicate the inner spatial structure of the church: in the middle is the nave, flanked by two low aisles which finally extend into two chapels on the outside. The architecture of the façade expressively marks off the basilica (one nave, two aisles) from the attached chapels: the borderline between the basilica and the chapels is indicated by double pilasters and by the fragment, rising above them, of a gable with a segmented arch. The outermost bays are of less significance, but are still part of the interconnected system of the façade, as they are on the same level as the layer of stereobate, are linked to the moulded entablature of the entire façade, and have windows of the same square shape. The fragmented gables with their segmented arches seem to be torn apart and be positively burst asunder by the central façade bay which thrusts itself between the remaining sections like a wedge. This tension is conveyed through the scroll-like wall into the upper storey of the central axis, where it is harmoniously resolved in the well-proportioned, unsplit gable with its segmented arch. The façade is made up of flat areas, but is richly layered and not without tension, while at the same time the frame around it is plain and severe. Thus Bernini's stock of ideas has been translated in a very individual way, but without a great potential for innovation. PZ

B103 S. Marcello: façade
Piazza S. Marcello (plan V 1/A–1/B)
1682/83
Carlo Fontana

Marcellus, the patron of this church, was a pope at the time of Emperor Maxentius, who is said to have consecrated, and thus declared to be a church, a building which stood in the same location as today's place of worship. The 12C Romanesque basilica burned down in 1519, and all that remained was the walls of the western transept. Parts of those walls can still be seen today on both sides of the Baroque façade. Immediately after the fire, a new building was erected. It was designed by Jacopo Sansovino, who also supervised the building work until he left Rome in 1526. After this, construction work was continued under Antonio da Sangallo the Younger, being completed in 1593. The façade was added ninety years later (1682/83). The typology of the conventional interior of the church is that of a room church with side aisles on the model of SS. Annunziata in Florence.

Today's façade faces westwards on to a square whose overall appearance it dominates. Church façades traditionally always occupy a key position in the Baroque design of city squares, and thus this façade

B103 S. Marcello: façade

follows in that tradition. Its architectural shape is an invention. Curving façades became a characteristic stylistic device of the Roman Baroque from no later than the time of Pietro da Cortona onwards. They had previously lived by the contrasting interplay of the concave and convex shapes, whereas Carlo Fontana limits himself in S. Marcello to a façade which is concave throughout. A similar design by Sangallo was previously to be found in the façade of the Palazzo del Banco di S. Spirito (H23). The effect produced by the façade within the framework of the square is that of a body whose outstretched arms embrace the square. The threefold layering of the façade opposes its concave shape. The width of the rearmost layer defines the width of the church interior and forms the basis for the concave main overall shape of the façade. Its outermost bays are subdivided by pilasters, have figured niches, are made up of flat areas, and frame the central panel. Only in the latter does the façade grow up into the top storey and increase its own volume. The layers placed in front of one another are of almost equal width, and give the impression of being crowded into a confined space, as if they were competing for priority. This results in plasticity. The composite column now replaces the pilaster and is entirely separated from the wall behind it. Thus the entire thickness of this layer is visible in front of the layer behind. Only in the upper storey are the double columns reduced to pilasters in order to lend prominence to the entrance area. The façade sections seem to be placed in front of one another like building blocks, and look as though they are individually detachable. There are no transitions created by half or three-quarter columns or by allowing the layers to project slightly. Instead, the layers stand out with an individual life of their own. The entire façade is imbued by a clarity, almost a simplicity, and is free of the complexities which were to be found fifty years earlier (cf. B64); the layerings run cogently through the building from the top downwards, and are themselves so clearly thought out that they might also exist in isolation. They are like chords which, taken together, provide a theme for a symphony, but it is a theme which rests within itself and does not live by the strong agitation of Borromini or the dramatic play of the light and shade found in Rainaldi. To prevent the clarity from turning into rigidity, Fontana gave the architecture a more varied appearance by placing a split, round gable above the portal area. In the middle of the gable there is an empty frame for an image – it was meant to be filled with a relief -, and behind the frame an arched niche is suggested by foreshortening. This frame is very reminiscent of Bernini's foreshortened window frames in the Palazzo Barberini (B45). The stone palm-tree branches which lean against the sides of the upper storey and assume the function of scrolls are a curious decorative element.

Fontana's façade is a reversion to Martino Longhi the Younger's façade of SS. Vicenzo ed Anastasio (B64), but the graduated way in which the columns stand closer together as they approach the centre is here relieved by the more extreme layering, the complexity of the shifts is entirely lost, the upper storey is reduced by the central order of pilasters, and the concave shape gives the façade a character of its own. It was precisely because of its simple, clear structure that the façade was much disputed among Fontana's contemporaries (for an assessment of its quality, see p. 170 above and B113 below). It nevertheless had an umistakable effect upon Juvarra (S. Cristina, Turin) and Johann Dientzenhofer (Neumünster, Würzburg). PZ

B104 S. Maria in Campo Marzio
Piazza in Campo Marzio 45 (plan IV 2/A)
1682–85
Giovanni Antonio de Rossi

S. Maria in Campo Marzio is not de Rossi's most spectacular building, but deserves attention for its gentle re-interpretation of the scheme of the Greek cross. This monastery church has a front side oriented on the Via della Maddalena, and relates to the city planning in this district of Rome. A semicircular apse with an oval target window, the block consisting of the arm of the choir, and the polygonal sheathing of the dome with its lantern, all look effective. They stand above some low functional buildings. The exterior is subdivided in a restrained way which emphasizes the cubic value of the components. To an onlooker standing outside, de Rossi shows the basic shape of the building, namely the Greek cross, and gives away the design of the dome by the lantern which is extended into a transverse oval shape.

The interior, which is to be reached through the main entrance of the monastery and through a portico in front of it, confirms and adds to the impression produced by the exterior. Small chapels are installed in the corners between the barrel-vaulted cross-arms. This means that de Rossi is coming very close to the ground plan and front elevation of the church of S. Carlo ai Catinari (B39), built some 60 years earlier. But S. Maria differs from that church, because the interior of S. Maria has a transversely oval dome and a slightly flattened apse is attached, without a bay in between, to the arm of the choir. The movement in the direction of the altar is moderated, and the transverse axis is cautiously emphasized. The drumless dome – de Rossi had previously planned a sail vault – means that the space is not experienced primarily in an upwards direction. The church derives a restrained nobility not only from the plain articulation of its wall, but also from its spatial proportioning and the abundance of light. AS

B105 S. Maria del Popolo: Cappella Cybo
Piazza del Popolo 12 (plan I 2/D)
1682–86
Carlo Fontana

The tomb chapel of Cardinal Alderano Cybo is a leading work by Bernini's pupil Fontana, and contemporaries regarded it as one of the most important chapels in Rome. Attached to the right aisle like a small church within the church, it is a centrally planned building above the ground plan of a Greek cross, and has a drumless pendentive dome and a barrel-vaulted vestibule. The spatial impression is characterized by double coupled columns which accentuate the main area and at the same time support part of the load of the dome. As a drawing shows, Fontana included in his plans the viewpoint and visual angle which would be adopted by visitors to the chapel: from the en-

B105 S. Maria del Popolo: Cappella Cybo

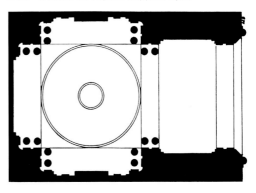

trance, the onlooker cannot judge whether the transverse arms of the chapel extend a long way or are short. The view is so narrow that only the double columns are visible. The altarpiece by Carlo Maratta is not surrounded by altar architecture as is otherwise usual, but hangs in front of a roughly patterned alabaster background. Thus the impression arises that it is hovering in front of a restless, not precisely locatable background. The absence of a deep choir is thus covered up. In the Cappella Cybo, Fontana presents himself as a Baroque Classicist who pays attention to the severity and clarity of the architectural subdividing work and completely eliminates any frolicsome details, particularly stucco decorations. The entire interior was faced with the most widely varying types of marble, covering large areas in some cases. The sumptuousness and aesthetics of this material are thus of great significance in terms of the spatial effect produced. After the chapel had been consecrated, the public, who were accustomed to stucco-work fantasies, paid attention to it mostly because of its splendid varieties of marble, and the fact was praised that »not even a minimum of stucco is to be seen« in the entire area. AS

B106 S. Maria Maddalena: interior
Piazza della Maddalena 53 (plan IV 2/A)
begun 1673, 1690–99, 1735
Carlo Fontana, Giovanni Antonio de Rossi, Felice Pozzoni, Carlo Giulio Quadri
The monastery church of S. Maria Maddalena is an imaginative variation on the Il Gesù (B1) type of church. Five architects, the extent of whose participation in the church in its present shape cannot ultimately be exactly determined, must be named in connection with the building: Fontana, who began the northern transverse arm (1673); de Rossi and his pupil Pozzoni who constructed the choir, the crossing, and parts of the nave (1690–96); Quadri who completed that section (ending in 1698); and Giuseppe Sardi who, in 1735, completed the façade of the church (B129) whose shell had been built by Quadri.

The interior of the building is an aisleless church with apses, a domed crossing, a transept and a choir. However, in contrast to other aisleless churches, the nave is here conceived of as an independent,

B106 S. Maria Maddalena: interior

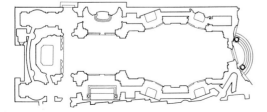

centralizing section the shape of whose ground plan is an extended octagon. The lateral bulge of the area is indicated by the four apse chapels which are not oriented rectangularly on the longitudinal axis of the church, but on two focal points in the middle of the main longitudinal section. The entablature, which is borne by simple pilasters, is also interrupted above the chapels and replaced by segmented gables supported on corbels. This once again underlines the effect of the chapels.

The combination of firstly the centralizing section, namely the crossing, and secondly a nave which has the character of a centrally planned area, is a High-Baroque re-interpretation of the well-known longitudinal architectural scheme of Il Gesù, but does not lose that scheme's essential feature, namely the decided lengthwise orientation. Although the idea of forming a longitudinal building as a combination of two centralizing sections is not in itself new (cf. S. Maria in Campitelli, B91), new devices for putting it into effect have been employed here. AS

B107 S. Carlo ai Catinari: Cappella di S. Cecilia
Piazza B. Cairoli (plan IV 1/B)
1691–1700
Antonio Gherardi
In 1691, the fraternity of Roman musicians commissioned Gherardi to fit out a chapel in honour of St Cecilia, their patron saint. As can be discovered from engravings and old drawings, Gherardi found here a dark area whose only window was obstructed by adjoining buildings. The architectural design of the chapel is therefore in part marked by the matter of solving the lighting problem. The vault of this transversely oblong area is an oval dome at whose apex a large opaion opens up. Through the opening there is a view of a very bright area which is located above and, in contrast to the lower chapel section, is decorated only with plain pilasters and bright stucco-work relief. Gherardi uses this area as a light trap by opening up a large window there and indirectly lighting the chapel by the light coming in from above. At the same time he links this »lantern area« to the chapel decorations in terms of subject matter too (there is a relief of the Saint's assumption into Heaven), so that the entire structure looks like an architectural version of a quadratura painting.

The stucco decorations in the main area are based on the model of Bernini. Gherardi gives the onlooker the impression of suddenly bursting in upon a group of angels going about their activities. These decorations are designed as an instantaneous portrayal. The concert of angels in the altarpiece, with St Cecilia as the singer, is continued in the chapel area. The stucco-work angels are singing and playing instruments. Some of them are presenting martyrdom implements or are drawing curtains open to reveal a view of paintings (which were not though actually painted) in oval frames. An angel is engaged on at-

B107 S. Carlo ai Catinari: Cappella di S. Cecilia

taching an inscription to the entrance arcade. In the decorations, Gherardi is here relying on representations of figures, and in this respect this chapel differs from his earlier Avila chapel (B101). AS

B108 SS. Apostoli
Piazza SS. Apostoli 51 (plan V 1/A–1/B)
incl. 1474–81, 1702–24, 1827
Baccio Pontelli, Carlo Fontana, Giuseppe Valadier
This basilica was founded by Pope Pelagius I in the 6C, and was considerably altered and restored several times in the Middle Ages. Apart from tombs (Andrea Bregno) and frescos (Melozzo da Forli, Vatican Picture Gallery), all that survives of the early-Renaissance alterations is the double-storeyed portico, probably built by Pontelli, outside the façade (1474–81) (F9). This arcaded Renaissance façade had nine axes and was originally open on both storeys. Carlo Rainaldi altered it in 1665 by inserting the windows on the upper storey. Behind this portico, the façade proper is to be seen. It was subdivided by flat pilasters in accordance with Valadier's design.

The appearance of the interior is largely determined by the conversions (1702–24) carried out by Francesco Fontana and his father Carlo. The proportions and design of the side chapels are reminiscent of S. Ignazio (B46). But the church interior has a short nave and no transept (this may be related to the ground plan of the previous buildings), and has a crypt beneath the choir. The idea of characterizing domed side chapels as small centrally planned areas and linking them by pas-

sages flanked with columns was previously seen in S. Ignazio. The wall articulation of the area has a varying succession of arcades and double pilasters, above which the entablature projects: this is the scheme of the Jesuit church. However, the real effect is produced not by the architectural articulation, but by the decorations of the church, in particular the ceiling fresco by Giovanni Battista Gaulli. AS

B109 S. Girolamo della Carità: Cappella Antamoro
Via di Monserrato 62/A, (plan IV 1/B)
1708–10
Filippo Juvarra
This chapel built as the burial place of the Antamoro family is the only work by Filippo Juvarra to have been completed in Rome, where he spent his apprenticeship. Initial designs were produced in 1708, and an inscription gives 1710 as the time of completion.

A simple, rectangular space was prescribed for the chapel dedicated to St Filippo Neri, and Juvarra used various devices in order to enliven that space. Four columns inserted into hollowed-out corners are diagonally oriented, and their bases, as well as the altar, are concave and exactly follow a circular line. The entablature running around above the columns, and wall pilasters is also rounded at the corners. In addition, the flat vault, which has coffer-work diagonal ribs and a

B108 SS. Apostoli

lantern, approximates to an oval dome, so that the overall spatial impression is that of an ellipse. One important element is the background, designed as a large oval window, for the altar figure of the saint (a work by Pierre Legros). The result of this is to make the spatial boundaries unclear, thus providing effective background lighting for the statue. Another feature shaping the spatial impression is the way in which the chapel is entirely decorated with coloured marble, contrasting with the golden adornments and the white stucco-work sculptures in the vault area.

In placing the columns diagonally, Juvarra seems to be adopting the theme of Michelangelo's Sforza chapel (H40), whereas parallels with the work of Bernini are found in the use of figured stucco-work sculpture, and with that of Juvarra's teacher Carlo Fontana in the coloured marble decorations employed in the chapel design. Further features, which also characterized his later work, are the centralizing treatment of the area and the effective lighting arrangement. DH

B110 S. Agata
Via della Lungaretta (plan VII 1/A)
begun 1710
Giacomo Recalcati

The church of the »Madonna de Noantri«, the patron saint of Trastevere, is the focal point of many festivals held in summer. The architecture is suited to festivals, and deviates – though hesitantly – from Carlo Fontana's strictly academic style which had been predominant in Rome for some decades.

The typology of the cross-section façade which has two storeys and a linking scroll still follows that of Il Gesù (B1). But the scheme was given new life, firstly by the re-introduction of some soft, playful elements: the upper-storey pilasters with their unworked capitals, the oval window with angels' wings (both these features are adopted from Borromini, B52, B53), and the multiplicity of gable shapes. The shapes were then tempered, for example in the central axis: the triangular gable above, which in Fontana's works usually concluded the entire façade (cf. e. g. S. Marcello, B103), is now only the central part of a more widely-stretched, split, sweeping gable and, a little lower down, recurs in tempered form as a pagoda-shaped window roofing.

The segmented gable underneath this is split, and in the middle of it there is a very soft shape. Finally, the wall layers became more significant: although Recalcati did create vertical relationships by the superposing of columns (this had been customary previously, cf. e. g. B91), he also achieved it by means of vertical wall layers, and from then on this was the only usual method. What is being done in all of this – as repeatedly occurred in the »Barocchetto« from then on – consists of lending additional, punctual form to traditional types rather than creating a demanding new invention.

B110 S. Agata

The interior also follows the typology of Il Gesù. But a comparison with the slightly older paintings in Il Gesù shows that, in S. Agata, a soft subdivision into strips, neutral areas and small, delicate centres replaces impassioned masses of figures and architectural projections. These are the seeds of a Rococo style which, although created at the same time, were to blossom more richly in other parts of Europe than in Rome. SG

B111 S. Maria del Rosario, Marino
Marino, Piazza Garibaldi (plan G2 4/C)
begun 1712
Giuseppe Sardi

From 1712 onwards, Sardi, who was 32 years old at the time, created, for the religious order founded in 1675 by Princess Colonna, one of the most original church interiors of the early Roman settecento. It is concealed behind long, austere monastery walls which do not suggest the presence of such a gem here. Only the entrance is marked by a lively, two-storeyed framing motif consisting of two aedicules merged together.

The visitor enters the church through a narrower, tripartite longitudinal section above an approximately rectangular ground plan, and the area then widens out into a very splendidly and richly designed rotunda which has eight arches and, opposite the longitudinal section, leads into a shorter choir which is equally narrow and is again rectangular. The centre curves concavely in the longitudinal section, and the columns, which are inserted into softly hollowed-out corners and are used like joints, are the dominant feature.

All this is then much intensified in the main area, which is subdivided by a circle of eight Tuscan columns with eight arches which, in the diagonal axes, are narrower, placed closer together and look as though they are on stilts. The arches in the main axes lead into short chapels, while underneath those in the diagonal axes there are two-storeyed structures as in the façade, but now they project vigorously convexly forwards. Only Borromini had modelled diagonal axes in a similarly energetic way, and that was only on paper (the design for S. Agnese). The very delicate stucco work in the interior is also reminiscent of Borromini, especially the conclusions which literally crown the two-storeyed structures (cf. e. g. B74). These structures show a taste for ornament and for the merging of shapes. This taste is omnipresent and, like the soft hollowings-out which are everywhere to be found, it is one of the central characteristics of the Rococo and the Roman Barocchetto. For example, the abacus of the capitals is very ambivalently conceived, and seems to melt into a ribbon which surrounds the whole church.

But the showpiece of the main room is the flat dome. Lacking a drum, and also lacking the emotionalism and upwards movement of the High Baroque, it looks lightweight and is exuberantly decorative. The impression of lightweightedness derives from the fact that it stands, as if on stilts, on sweeping pedestals between which there are windows and openings de-

B111 S. Maria del Rosario, Marino

signed with differing lines (as also in the apex of the dome). It is possible to look through the windows and, conversely, invisible sources of light are opened up. The design of the flattened dome with intersecting ribbons has been compared with designs by Guarini, the architect from Piedmont who also used intersecting ribbons, although his were more similar to those found in Arab architecture. However, there is hardly an element in which the difference between the High Baroque and the Roman Barocchetto or Rococo is more clearly seen than here: both architects were certainly concerned to achieve dynamism. In Guarini's work, these ribbons were intended to be a supporting structure, while in Sardi's they are to be understood as being mere ornaments. Sardi was concerned with breaking up the self-contained shape – for example, the hemisphere – and making the surface appear to vibrate. It is a genuine Rococo dome and looks intimate and rural.

The significance of this building can scarcely be overestimated. Perhaps only a self-taught person like Sardi, who never came under the influence of the academic, rigid Fontana school, was capable of such a sensational stroke. After almost fifty years of strict and regular building work in Rome, 18C architecture in Rome was born out of nothing in a provincial town, and it was born in a way that was so perfect that there may perhaps, at least in church architecture, be no example like it in Rome. SG

B112 Palazzo del Grillo
Piazza del Grillo 5 (plan V 1/B)
begun 1675, c. 1720
pupil of Giuseppe Sardi

The del Grillo family acquired the plot of land near the Augustus Forum (A20) in 1675. The 13C family tower, one of the few surviving in Rome (cf. C35), was integrated into the new structure. The palace is not very significant as a building, is not uniform, and therefore scarcely fulfils any grand pretensions. One might almost think that it consisted of two palaces, but according to the sources both buildings were erected at the same time. This »disrupted« form derives from the shape of the plot of land, which has a road running through the middle of it. This was why the two halves of the palace were combined by a connecting passage above a tall, undecorated arcade. The storeys of the two halves hardly relate to one another. The piano nobile of the right-hand section is on the first floor whereas, owing to the difference in the level of the building, it is on the third floor in the left-hand section. The piano nobile can only be distinguished by the Rococo decorations, and particularly by the convincingly employed segmented-arched gable whose cornice is pierced by stucco work. These decorations are the reason for the palace's artistic value. Along with the rest of the decorative work in this building, they were probably carried out in c. 1720 by an artist associated with Giuseppe Sardi. The gable design re-

ferred to, with its delicate Rococo stucco-work insertions, greatly enlivens the otherwise rather sterile façade. The aedicules make the palace into one of the
more interesting examples of the Roman Rococo, but
it is only in the palace garden, the so-called »teatrino«,
that the ensemble displays its full splendour (entrance,
with the porter's assistance, can be gained only with
difficulty). In the portal, the artist displayed a cheerful
imaginativeness in the well-balanced combination of
arches and straight lines, and of convex and concave
curves in the stucco-work frame. PZ

B113 SS. Trinità dei Pellegrini
Piazza Trinità dei Pellegrini (plan IV 1/B)
1722–23
Francesco de Sanctis

It was in imitation of Il Gesù (B1) that Martino Longhi
the Elder, in 1587–98, built the banal interior of this
church for a fraternity which was founded by Filippo
Neri and accepted pilgrims in Rome as its members.
The interesting columned architecture in the crossing
was added in 1690, because the structure was in
danger of caving in.

The 18C façade is more original. Its basic shape
is concave and it arouses thoughts of S. Marcello
(B103), but is much more complex. Each of the two
storeys, which are linked by a scroll, of this cross-section façade is concave. But de Sanctis kept the lateral
sections flat, thus differing from Fontana. The curvature, as in the case of SS. Luca e Martina (B51), is
thus fitted in between rectangular corner sections

B113 SS. Trinità dei Pellegrini

and is thereby motivated. The layering, too, is more
subtle in the work of de Sanctis. This is because, following the logic of a convex curve, he set the centre
of the façade back. The resultant pronounced vertical
articulation followed in a good High-Baroque tradition
(B91). This central section now had no architectural
order and was once again flat. It was evidently intended to create a neutral area between two sections
which are being pushed open like the two leaves of a
door, thus releasing the centre, but are prevented from
this by the flat, fixed lateral sections, and therefore
curl up. In this way the entire height of the centre of
the façade was opened up and became an enormous
gate for troops of pilgrims. In the Spanish Steps (B115),
de Sanctis created a synthesis between gracefully di-
vided-up variety and Roman monumentality. It is the
second aspect that is more strongly emphasized in
this church façade, which is of slightly earlier date and
opens up in a large and impassioned way. But the
other aspect is also, in a restrained way, suggested in
the multiple layering, the transitions at the angles, the
small sections, and the detailed shapes such as the
roofings over the niches. SG

B114 Palazzo Centini-Toni
Via Capo le Case 3 (plan V 1/A)
1722–42
Francesco Rosa

The city palace of the Conte Felice Centini, rebuilt
between 1722 and 1742, has the nickname of »Casa dei Pupazzi« (jumping jacks, dolls), alluding to the
stuccoed figures in the window frames in the piano
nobile. These are caryatids growing up out of a blossom, and their extremities are formed into scrolls.

The façade of this four-storeyed palazzetto with five
axes is built on a slope, and its ground floor has not
only two portals and three small additional doors with
transversely oval openings, but also a mezzanine. The
division into storeys, and the outward appearance, of
the large city palaces imitating the Palazzo Farnese
(H25) were both basically retained, despite the limited
space. Thus the façade is horizontally subdivided only
by cornice strips, and is expressively reinforced at the
edges.

The smooth wall is otherwise subdivided only by
the windows which, in the piano nobile, rest upon the
cornice strip. However, the surface here makes a
much richer visual impression than that of the Palazzo Farnese, because the windows have been moved
closer together, and the number of storeys has been
increased and their respective height reduced. Thus
the wall is consumed by window openings, and this
is typical of the 18C, when palaces were increasingly
being designed to suit middle-class standards. The
Barocchetto can everywhere be sensed in the individual shapes too: the window frames (for example,
those of the mezzanine windows in the ground floor)
merge with the cornices, the shapes (scrolls, shells,
shabracks, festoons and blossoms) become rich, and

the C-shaped arch is used several times. An classical-looking language is used in the roofs of the »Pupazzi« windows, with their scroll-shaped split gables with shell decorations and Medusa heads. SG

B115 Spanish Steps
Piazza di Spagna (plan II 1/E)
1723–26
Francesco de Sanctis

The Piazza di Spagna (standing beside the Spanish Embassy, 1647) was part of the urban structure, and streets intersected there since ancient times. In contrast, the surroundings of SS. Trinità dei Monti (H44), one of the two French national churches, were rural, and only in the late 16C were two roads built to make them accessible. It took a century and a half to build a link between these heterogeneous neighbourhoods, and this was after the idea of building some steps had been considered in 1559, and later under Gregory XIII.

It was initially under Urban VIII that the Piazza di Spagna began in the 17C to assume a more definite shape, when the Collegio di Propaganda Fide (B58) and Pietro Bernini's Barcaccia (1626–29) were built there. The water which flows abundantly from the Pincio, and the intersection of the two roads, were, for the first time ever, taken as a theme in the fountain, which almost remains at street level. This theme is seen in the fact that the steps open up routes not only from the Tiber in the west across the Via Condotti to the Pincio, but also – and this had long been planned – from the Piazza del Popolo in the north to S. Maria Maggiore (C7).

From 1660 onwards, the aid provided by the French crown was increased by Mazarin and by a legacy granted by Gueffier in the amount of 10 000 scudi, which by the year 1720, by means of compound interest, rose to 20 000 scudi, the projected cost of con-

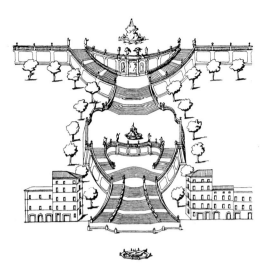

B115 Spanish Steps. Design as actually built

struction. In 1660, Bernini, in submitting his design, laid the basis for all the later plans: he rejected, for the first time, the rectangular staircase designs of the 16C (e. g. H6, H36). They were replaced by curving ramps, resting places, the division of the steps into three parts, and separate flights of steps, and thus differ from the steps on the Capitol (H27) and in S. Maria in Aracoeli (C36). Bernini combined ramps, staircases, the fountains, and an equestrian statue at the centre (here it depicts Louis XIV). But Alexander VII was not pleased with the idea of the site being occupied by the French in this way, and so the project stagnated until the death of Louis XIV. It was not until 1717 that Clement XI announced the decisive competition, which resulted in a dispute between two names: Alessandro Specchi, the architect of the Roman people, and de Sanctis, the architect of the French monks of the Trinità. The dispute was not settled until 1723, when de Sanctis adopted some ideas from Specchi's designs and Innocent XIII acceded to the French request. The structure was completed only three years later. Not until 1786 was the obelisk erected on the instructions of Pius VI. The extent of the contributions made by both master architects is disputed. The structure planned by Bernini continued to determine the design. All that was abandoned was its width (based on the transverse oval and on the introduction of a transverse bar-shaped building above) and the combination of stairs and ramps (the latter, which were intended for state coaches, were regarded as superfluous). In other matters, Specchi followed Bernini almost entirely: as with the Ripetta port previously (cf. p. 170 f.), whose importance for the Spanish Steps is always emphasized, he created the basic shape in accordance with the principle, customary in the 17C, of combining individual sections having clear

B115 Spanish Steps. Design by Bernini

geometrical shapes, particularly segments of circles. This principle is first found in the stairs of SS. Domenico e Sisto (1654–57) (B48). They were a model which strongly influenced the three designs by Specchi, and their upper section also had an effect on Bernini's plans. Of the three sections, de Sanctis built only the upper and lower one according to this principle, and in his plans he found a diction of his own for the main overall shape, the most appropriate expression for his times. He resolved the overall form into many small facettes that were no longer clearly conceivable individual geometrical shapes, but instead a multitude of little bits and pieces.

The most convincing design is that actually built. In de Sanctis' plans, the lower section was still divided into two flights of steps, and did not consist of one compact flight which is enclosed between the two flanking buildings as between two doorposts and is subdivided only by low walls intended for sitting on. De Sanctis sometimes intended that the middle section should be a narrow, steep central staircase, and sometimes that it should be a thin, two-flighted staircase with a wide, empty space between the two flights. In the version actually built, this empty space became the large square in the centre. The planned statues, trees and fountains were, for reasons of cost, not realized. The cascading, flowing quality nevertheless remained the predominant characteristic. The appearance was not – as it had been in Bernini's design – determined by deep changes of direction and sharp curves. De Sanctis himself stated that he wanted to create a place of leisure. This aim was served by such differing elements as the low walls for sitting on, the inclusion of small pedestals after every twelfth step, and the visibility, so important psychologically, of all the sections. The soft outline, free of any sharp angles in the steps as actually built, also fits in with this idea. When it is considered how unsafe, steep and unfortified the hill had previously been, this is the most magnificent of all the changes that could possibly be made to it. Seldom in architecture have function and contemplation been so closely linked. The large number of open squares in the completed project, and also its complexity and the diversity of angles in it, make it different from any other staircase. By employing those cascades of angles, de Sanctis was adopting in his design the rural character of the surroundings on the hill and was thereby inventing a chief characteristic of 18C architecture. He also found in the angles the best means of covering up the great irregularity of the site. This is because the main lines which he found in the already existing buildings and streets obviously do not run in parallels or rectangles. What is more, the transitions at the angles give the impression, highly esteemed in the 18C, that the stairs are part of a larger system in which the church façade above was already following yet another axis extending beyond the city.

Despite the pauses for rest and the angles, the staircase created here was, as a structure, more gran-diose and more independent than any previous staircase. Only here is Roman monumentality, which was the heritage of ancient times and was the most prominent feature of the 16C and 17C, so entirely in harmony with the complexity and gracefulness of the 18C Barocchetto. Almost the only example of any comparable accomplishment is the façade of the Palazzo Doria Pamphili (B122). De Sanctis wanted »what was majestic also to be convenient, wanted what was funtioncal also to be melodious, and wanted those who walked up the steps to sense quite a new spirit of life« (Bruhns). De Sanctis thus lent most spectacular expression to the spirit of the times – they were no longer High Baroque – in which he was living. He also combined the late-16C concept of building narrow routes with the 17C concept of creating places where one could stay at leisure. SG

Bibliography: W. Lotz, »Die Spanische Treppe. Architektur als Mittel der Diplomatie«, *Römisches Jahrbuch für Kunstgeschichte*, 1969, p. 39.

B116 S. Gallicano
Via S. Gallicano (plan VII 1/A)
1724–26
Filippo Raguzzini

In 1724, Pope Benedict XIII founded the hospital for skin and venereal diseases, and also the church, and commissioned his architect Filippo Raguzzini to build them. The design follows the usual scheme which had been developed for the Ospedale di S. Spirito (F8): the men's and women's sections are housed in two long buildings which are separate but at the same time linked – to one another, and also to the world outside – by the centrally located church.

The two-storeyed façade extends in an infinitely long straight line. The vertical proportions, when both storeys are compared with one another, are also extreme, with the tall ground floor contrasting with the very low upper storey. This contrast, rich in tension, was also employed by Raguzzini in S. Maria della Quercia (B120). Another feature common to both works is the style, which largely dispenses with decorations, as soft shapes and surface qualities replace ornaments and adornments: the long straight line is, in both storeys, articulated by pilaster strips with recessed layers, and as a result the surface, particularly when looked at obliquely, looks animated.

The panels between these vertical articulations are occupied alternately by windows and blind oculi which, like the front sides of the pilaster strips, are divided up into geometrical patterns made of rough plaster, so that chromatic nuances are also produced. The entablatures – the upper one is slightly fluted – which conclude the storeys are not complete. The balcony in the upper storey is a useful new invention enabling all the rooms to be catered for without any trouble, and is a pronounced horizontal element.

This church façade stands on a high base course, is taller than the hospital buildings to the extent of an attic storey (with a surmounting feature in the centre), and its central axis also projects energetically from the long straight line. The impression is created that this central section is being pushed forwards into the street by the concavely shaped lateral axes. The outer sections and the central part are subdivided by a stylized Composite order, while the curving linking sections are different because they have facings made of roughcast plastering again. The tall entablatures with their various fascias, the pilasters with their recessed layers whose graduation is continued in the moulding of the entablature, and the architrave with its horizontal lines, are also all features which enrich the interplay of light and dark. Scrolls link the taller central section to the lower side sections and the laterally located vases. Such scrolls had been a feature of 15C and 16C churches, examples being S. Maria del Popolo (F7), S. Agostino (F14) and S. Spirito in Sassia (H26).

The façade creates a different urban impression when looked at from the Vicolo di Mazzamurelli which approaches it at right angles: the areas of shade not only in the central window which is cut deep into the upper storey and pierces the entablature, but also in the tall, gate-like portal, produce an effect which is not merely inviting, but positively magically attractive.

The church interior consists of a domed, centrally planned area above a ground plan in the shape of a Greek cross with rounded-off corners. The various layers in the wall give the impression of many coverings inserted one inside the other.

B117 S. Sisto Vecchio
Via delle Terme di Caracalla (plan VIII 2/B)
1724–30
Filippo Raguzzini

S. Sisto dates from the 5C and is one of the oldest churches in Rome. But Innocent III completely rebuilt it in the early 13C and handed it over to St Dominic and his order. The Romanesque bell tower dates from this epoch. The most recent restoration of the church was undertaken by Raguzzini, the architect of Pope Benedict XIII, in 1724-30. It amounted to a conversion which not only obliterated the presbytery and choir, but also reduced the basilica to a structure with only a nave and no aisles.

The façade today still arouses the impression of a nave and two aisles, and when the lower flanking structures – they are subdivided by pilaster strips, and project like risalti – are added, this even increases to a nave and two aisles at each side. The articulation creates a linear, geometrical impression. This applies to the ribbon shapes which replace the architectural order and cover two storeys, to the cornice strips with their embossed stucco work, and to the flat conclusion of the façade, but also to the portal and its double rectangular frame, with a segmented gable on the outside and the portal proper, with its triangular tym-

B117 S. Sisto Vecchio

panum and its finely worked scrolled corbels on the inside. The round shapes, namely the scrolls, oculi and windows, contrast attractively with the linear ones, and sometimes – this is typical of the Barocchetto – merge with them. For example, the windows merge with the entablatures. The articulating elements, taken all in all, arouse rather the impression of a carpet-like tessellation than that of a classical architectural order. Thus Raguzzini once again took the radical step of replacing a tectonic supporting framework by a delicately designed decorative framework, although the shapes are less sprightly than in other works of his (cf. B116, B118, B120). The tessellation, the panels, and the arrangement in rows, are similarly dominant in the interior of the church. SG

B118 Piazza di S. Ignazio
Piazza di S. Ignazio (plan IV 2/A)
1727/28
Filippo Raguzzini

The façade of S. Ignazio (B46) posed a problem for city planners: how could the small forecourt be designed in such a way that it did not appear to be overwhelmed by the façade? The façade was not merely the last large one to follow the typology of Il Gesù (B1), but also had an enormous and rigid structure. Benedict XIII chose Raguzzini as the architect. Raguzzini had come from Naples to Rome in 1724 as part of Benedict's entourage, and he developed a style of a very characteristic and simple elegance. The design of the piazza is rightly regarded as his masterpiece.

B118 Piazza di S. Ignazio

Raguzzini used new weapons when engaging in this struggle. He simply turned the visual angle around, thus solving all the aesthetic problems by a single stroke of genius: from then on, interest was no longer concentrated upon the church façade, but instead upon the new ensemble of buildings, which better suited the prevailing taste and was better graduated. In that ensemble, Raguzzini lent variety to the formerly rigid shape of the piazza. A few houses in the small piazza were torn down and replaced by an animated but nonetheless regularized and largely symmetrically structured ensemble, in which there was a feeling of permeability and, despite the small dimensions, even of spaciousness. The central section of the ensemble is formed by three buildings whose façade curves concavely backwards from the piazza. They stand between two lateral sections which partly enclose the piazza and are wing structures (each with seven axes), each of them with a corner risalto which consists of a single axis and itself has a slight concave curve. The three concave façades – that in the central building has three axes, while those at the sides have only one axis each – follow the ground plan of three ovals which touch one another, the central oval being larger. The central building tapers sharply towards the rear, so that its overall ground plan resembles an equilateral triangle. The rear axes of the side buildings are parallel; between the buildings there are two streets which meet behind the central building. They are not the only access routes to the piazza, as there are four further routes, two on each side of the wing structures. Benedict XIII described the overall ensemble as a large theatrical assembly (fabbrica teatrale). It provided variety, in contrast to the monotonous church façade. The onlooker's attention was attracted to these more interesting aspects. The gently swaying movement of the surrounding city seems here to have turned to stone. On the other hand, Raguzzini succeeded in ensuring that an onlooker in the diagonally arranged access routes could always only see parts of the large façade and that the whole of it could only be seen from a very short distance away, when its sheer size was at least able to overwhelm the onlooker. Raguzzini was still feeling indebted to High-Baroque designs for city squares, such as those of S. Maria della Pace and S. Andrea al Quirinale (B79 and B85), in that he was designing not so much for the onlooker approaching from a distance as for one who is standing in the middle of the ensemble and feeling a positively physical appeal, with his eyes scarcely able to turn away. Nevertheless, this is the only genuine Rococo square in Rome. The many separate elements of its curving structure relate it to the Spanish Steps (B115), it has no central access route, and it is more unassuming than High-Baroque ensembles. Small and unpretentious items are treated like jewels. Blocks of rented apartments were built here, and they, not the large church façade, were the central feature. Concavity dominates, and the houses almost look like a negative impression of the church façade: their frontages recede in the same way as that of the church projects.

Raguzzini, for the first time, designed blocks of rented apartments to look like palazzi. They all have four storeys, are subdivided in the same way, are unpretentious, and – except for the dainty window roofings in the second upper storey – have no adornments, being decorated only by layers, frames and risalti which are all made of lower-cost plaster in delicate Rococo colours. This explains why they were built in such a short time. It is rare, so early in the 18C, to see layering and delicate ribbon shapes so clearly replacing the classical order and decoration. »Weighty stone balconies gave way to thinner iron ones, with the emotionalism of the High-Baroque yielding to the »discreet charm of the bourgeoisie«. Vertical ribboning, the formation of risalti, and the window arrangement, all ensure a pronouncedly vertically designed overall pattern. The whole structure is of a delicacy inherent only to French interiors of the period. SG

Bibliography: D. Habel, »Piazza di S. Ignazio. Rome in the 17th and 18th centuries«, *Architectura*, 1981, p. 31.

B119 Oratorio SS. Sacramento
Via di S. Maria in Via (plan IV 2/A)
1727–30
Domenico Gregorini

The oratory of the fraternity of the same name was built in 1727-30, with a section attached to the right of it. In 1734 that section was given a counterpart, which can still be seen today, on the left. The right-hand section was demolished when the Via del Tritone was cut through here. It had formerly been the wider section, because beyond the pilastered border there were four more axes to the right, which were subdivided in the same way but were placed closer together.

The structure of the oratory's façade is formed by three convex curves below and a succession of one concave, one convex and one concave curve above.

On top of these, in each storey, an aedicule is placed which runs inwards and is thus visually concave. The aedicule on the ground floor has a split gable which thus opens up the way to the upper part of the façade. This rhythm is found in reverse in S. Carlino (B52), and an example of it on the upper storey is the three concave curves and the convex central motif. Individual important shapes such as the curving upper gable and the main window are also in Borromini's style (cf. B53, B56), while the bundling of the pilasters at the façade edges, and the shape of the swellings, are both more like Cortona's work (cf. B51).

The oratory is visibly independent of the other sections, and in this it differs fundamentally from the works of Borromini. At the same time, the liveliness of its façade only becomes fully evident from the fact that it is enclosed by the flat sections. This façade was not only independent, but was also linked in, resulting in a greater visual unity: the edges of the whole building were provided with pilasters similar to those of the church façade, and the main horizontal lines were continued. SG

B120 S. Maria della Quercia
Piazza della Quercia (plan IV 1/B)
1727–31
Filippo Raguzzini

Raguzzini, who was Benedict XIII's architect, created a gem of the elegant, simple style in this church of the butchers. The façade looks rich and noble, although the means employed are as simple as possible. The basic shape is determined solely by the convex for-ward curvature, which has clear lines and gave the impression of being well mounted within what was formerly a confined square. But the curvature contrasts markedly with its High-Baroque forerunners: the shape looks soft rather than taut and is full of emotion, and the surface is creamy, rather than being firm like leather as it is, for example, in S. Carlino (B52). Raguzzini was building the more elegant Rococo kind of curve. The individual shapes convey a similar mood. The jagged lines contrast delicately with the curvature. In the areas of the entablature, those lines were created by the mouldings. The basic shape was subdivided by rhythmically placed, richly layered pilasters which create three axes and entablatures on two storeys which are equally wide but of decidedly differing heights, as in the case of S. Gallicano (B116). The central pilasters are bent, not because the curvature is so impressive (as is the case in the exterior of St Peter's, H31), but because they were meant to look like filigree work. When the panels with their roughened design are also considered, the façade surface looks spread out like a fan, almost like a backdrop of organ pipes. Clear vertical paths are created, like paths of windows in 18C palace architecture (cf. B122). Raguzzini's radically new and undecorative method of design is seen firstly in the portal which, without any adornment, is cut into the soft mass of stone, secondly in the windows, and thirdly in the complete absence of gables above them. The interplay of layers and panels largely replaces the functions which would be fulfilled by decorations and architectural orders. SG

B119 Oratorio SS. Sacramento

B120 S. Maria della Quercia

B121 S. Filippo Neri

Via Giulia (plan IV 1/B)
1728
Filippo Raguzzini und/oder Giovanni Francesco Fiori

Only one church in Rome is dedicated to Filippo Neri, the reforming saint (1515–95) who was canonized in 1622. (The oratory, B53, named after him is only a meeting room for the Oratorians, the fraternity founded by Filippo Neri in 1575.) Today this small church is in a state of dilapidation. Not until 1728 did Pope Benedict XIII commission Raguzzini, or more probably Fiori, to convert a previous structure. The pope had felt a special association with the saint ever since being miraculously spared the consequences of an earthquake in 1688 as archbishop of Benevento.

The small, two-storeyed façade is linked to an equally tumbledown palazzo, and projects by one layer from the surface of that palazzo, as can be seen from the colossal order made up of flat pilasters and other pilasters with recessed layers. The central axis projects by a further layer, and is like a board containing the portal which is surmounted by a segmented gable. Similar layerings are to be found in the stucco-framed facings to the sides of the portal on the ground floor, and in the windows, again framed with stucco work, of the upper storey. Three-dimensional stuccoed decorations accentuate the upper storey. They consist of narrow shaped frames, festoons, scrolls, fluttering ribbed strips, and the shell-shaped agraffe which clasps the oval half-relief in the central axis. That relief shows the Virgin Mary and the Christ-child appearing to the saint, and relates to Filippo Neri's vision of the Virgin Mary which caused him to recover from a serious illness. The façade is surmounted by a triangular gable displaying the coat of arms of the fraternity of Filippo Neri.

B122 Palazzo Doria Pamphili: façade facing Via del Corso

Via del Corso 303/304 (plan IV 2/B)
1731–34
Gabriele Valvassori

This, the largest city palace in Rome, has a long history. The delicate inner courtyard in Bramante's style (similar to that of S. Ambrogio in Milano) still survives from the 15C core structure, which was originally owned by the cardinals of the Collegio Romano. Julius II handed the palace over to the duke of Urbino (della Rovere), it then fell to the Aldobrandini, and in 1647 it passed by marriage to Camillo Pamphili the Elder, the nephew of Innocent X. Camillo commissioned del Grande to construct the wing near the Collegio Romano (1659–61). The two façades to the north and the west, and the splendid vestibule with its stairs, still survive from that wing. The most recent redesigning work was undertaken by Camillo Pamphili the Younger (cf. also B133): Clement XII (1730–40) preferred Baroque-Classicist designs when he was placing his orders (B123–B126), whereas this privately

commissioned building was erected here in a more animated idiom in 1731-34. Valvassori closed the loggias leading to the Corso and replaced them by the façade and the hall of mirrors. In this way he created the most important palace structure of the 18C.

The façade is 17 axes long. It is subdivided into seven groups by vertical wall strips, and here the layers are more significant than the pilasters. Nine axes in the middle are flanked by two wings which each have four axes and recede in several steps. The outer axis projects by one layer, as does the central axis of the middle section. A rhythm of 1:3:4:1:4:3:1 is created, and it lives by the vertical strips. The portals are located in the three single axes, which were all additionally accentuated by delicate stone carvings. In those axes, the windows were widened, with the columns of the aedicules being inserted instead of being placed out in front at the sides.

The window is the really dominant feature of the façade. It is true that the windows of the Palazzo di Propaganda Fide (B65) were the starting point, but Valvassori went a step further. The aedicule architecture of the windows in the piano nobile is softened, particularly in the gables. The mezzanine windows were included in the frame, which is a double frame, rich in curves and sharply cut, and also continues horizontally at the sides. The windows were placed higher than before, and were moved closer together. They consume the wall, and swell the lines of the building. They form groups, as can clearly be seen on the ground floor, and they are no longer regularly placed as they were in the 17C. The vertically elongated windows matched the balconies, which replaced the cornice that was formerly customary but were designed in a similarly imaginative way, rich in curves.

B122 Palazzo Doria Pamphili: façade facing Via del Corso

The most richly moulded balcony is that at the centre. It is fluid in its middle section, and has a retarding element at the sides.

All these elements are not merely animated in an undulating way, but also merge with one another: the windows are merged into long vertical strips, with those on the ground floor being pushed upwards towards the balconies. The latter themselves merge and are combined into strips, and their supporters are alternately the right way up and upside down (Borromini was the influence here too). The mezzanine windows at the very top merge entirely with the frieze.

The link with the surrounding building work, in this case the church of S. Maria in Via Lata (B83), is excellent and unusual. The concave corner creates a pause and at the same time provides the transition.

Valvassori gave the palace a new orientation – towards the Corso, the most important street in Rome. This concept breathes the spirit of monumentality. This was indeed the only palace in Rome in which, with a reversion to Borromini, Roman monumentality and weightiness were combined with the grace and liveliness of the Rococo, which was neither merely graceful as are most of the Barocchetto works, nor merely monumental. A similarly convincing synthesis was achieved only by de Sanctis in the Spanish Steps (B115). The classical, academic era of Fontana seemed to have been long forgotten. But this façade found no imitators. Instead it was the style of the contemporaneous Lateran façade (B124) that led to Classicism at an early stage in Rome.

The hall of mirrors has the same significance for the 18C as the Galleria Colonna (B76) for the previous century. In the latter structure, it was the brightly coloured marble, the columns and the ceiling fresco that constituted the rich abundance, whereas here it is only the gilded mirror frames that do so, with the decorations are merged with the wall and are a part of it. In the Galleria Colonna, the wall and the barrel vault were separated by a weighty entablature, whereas here the windows encroach upon the wall and barrel, and the transitions become blurred. This more recent hall is marked by an alternation between large windows and mirrors. SG

Bibliography: I. Faldi, *Il Palazzo Pamphily al Collegio Romano*, 1957.

B123 S. Giovanni in Laterano: Cappella Corsini
Piazza di Porta S. Giovanni (plan VIII 2/A)
1732–35
Alessandro Galilei

Clement XII commissioned Galilei, a Florentine architect, to build not only the façade of the Lateran basilica, but also Clement's tomb chapel to the left of the entrance there. They both represent the same change in trends. For the chapel this applies to interior architecture, and for the façade it is true of monumental architecture.

B123 S. Giovanni in Laterano: Cappella Corsini

The ground plan is formed by a Greek cross with short arms. The arms are barrel-vaulted, and the core area is surmounted by a drum dome. The dome and barrels are in coffer work without any wall arches, with the radial floor pattern replying to that of the dome. The dome is exactly hemispherical. The dome and barrel vault are free of any figured decorations. The Corinthian order is not obstructed either, and runs regularly around the area without any moulding.

In all these points, Galilei was abandoning late-Baroque stylistic principles and basing himself on classical models: since the time of Cortona, wall arches were placed above the coffer work (B51), and domes tapered towards the top (cf. B51 and H31). Vaults were always peopled with figures. Galilei was once again seeking the clarity firstly of ancient times, as found in the pure coffer work of the Pantheon (A31), and secondly of the (High) Renaissance. The model for this was the severe shapes of the Cappella Chigi from the High Renaissance (H12) and, as regards the spatial form, even Brunelleschi's early-Renaissance buildings. Galilei did not bevel the cross-arms as had been done in the High Renaissance from St Peter's (H7) onwards. The taller proportions are almost the only Baroque-like features.

The decorations are rightly famous, and make less of a moderated impression: there are the sculptures which are animated in the late-Baroque manner, and the very dainty materials which are in delicate Rococo colours and are more subtle than anywhere else in Rome. But everything is kept strictly within architectural compartments. All in all, it is (Baroque) Classicism that dominates - and this at a time when everywhere in Europe late Baroque was in its heyday. SG

B124 S. Giovanni in Laterano: façade

B124 S. Giovanni in Laterano: façade
Piazza di Porta S. Giovanni (plan VIII 2/A)
1732–36
Alessandro Galilei

When Borromini redesigned the nave of this church for the jubilee year of 1650, the façade was left unaltered. Eighty years later, in 1732, Galilei, the Florentine, won the largest architectural competition of his day (with 23 renowned participants). The jury was made up of members of the Accademia di S. Luca, and they selected a classically severe design. Just when the animated Barocchetto had entirely supplanted Fontana's Baroque Classicism, this design brought about a reversion to a preference for severe monumentality during the papacy of Clement XII Corsini (1730–40).

The two-storeyed façade has five axes and is united and subdivided by a colossal order of pilasters having a continuous unmoulded entablature. This was still more clearly expressed in the original design, in which the central axis was simply wider and was accentuated by inserted columns, but there was no enormous aedicule made up of double half columns and a triangular gable. The aedicule was only added upon the advice of Cardinal Albani, in order to lend the façade a more intensely Roman aspect. The façade as a whole has a double frame, as does the centre. The division into storeys is only visible in a second layer. The subdividing elements are firstly pilastered pillars with a horizontal entablature, and secondly arches. There is almost no wall at all. As there is only subdividig work but no wall, the hollows are almost all that produces an effect, so that Galilei's work differs from that of all the competing architects in that both storeys appear as linked together, and that the impression is shaped by the framework made up of supports and entablature, and not by the wall. The centre is also accentuated by the small architectural order, and in the upper storey this is achieved by the Palladian motif (inserted columns with an arch and a section of entablature on each side). This part of the building is the benediction loggia for the pope, and is

more clearly marked than in any of the competing designs, and also than in St Peter's (B34).

The upper conclusion is much more animated. This applies to the moulded balustrade, but still more to the figures that reach out (the two Johns and the doctores ecclesiae) and to the curved pedestal at the centre with its surmounting figure of Christ.

The façade was formerly thought to be Palladian, because Galilei had spent several years in England, although this was before Inigo Jones built his great Palladian façades. However, there are some much more obvious examples of comparable structures. It is instructive to make a comparison with the conservators' palace by Michelangelo (H30). The comparability was more evident in the original design without the enormous aedicule. The new façade by Galilei, having only five axes, looks markedly taller, especially as the hollows continue vertically all the way up, and no wall in the upper storey lends the building expressive weightiness and a horizontal emphasis. The central sections are more strongly accentuated, especially the middle of the building and the upper conclusion. The dynamism urging forth from the building is part of the design. Reduced to a common denominator, what Michelangelo did was to create a stronger balance, a golden mean, between the palazzo wall and the hollow of a courtyard architecture, between the framework and the panelling, between the small and large architectural orders, and he provided much more subtle layering. The main emphasis was not upon sculptures and vertical movement. The new façade is more impassioned, and this suggests a comparison with the façade of St Peter's (B34), which follows Michelangelo's example less clearly and whose unhappily wide design was evidently intended to be corrected. here. The new façade emphasized the height – the closeness of heaven – and in this it differed from St Peter's. Its appearance is shaped by an army of saints in heaven. Verticality and framework once again gain the ascendancy over wall and material, almost as in the Gothic period. Galilei was evidently seeking to compete with St Peter's: the Lateran basilica as being the true mother church, the mater ecclesiarum.

This façade – in its strong imitation of a leading work of the 16C, the High-Renaissance period – is regarded as exemplary for 18C Baroque Classicism. It is Baroque, and not yet Classicist, because there are changeovers within it: the architectural order below is severe while the conclusion above is animated; the articulation and hollowing create a positively late-Baroque contrast of light and shade; and here, at the edge of the city, architecture confronts nature (this is similar to the slightly earlier Spanish Steps, B115, which also have an animated late-Baroque design). Within the context of the Barocchetto with its animated architecture, this façade nevertheless constituted a turning back, a particular event. When associated with the other buildings in the Lateran, all of which are somehow rigid (B21, B123, even B66), this façade makes the mater ecclesiae look unapproachable and ultimately much more static than St Peter's (H7, H31, B34, B42, B80). SG

B125 Palazzo della Consulta
Piazza del Quirinale 41 (plan V 1/A)
1732–37
Ferdinando Fuga

Fuga was commissioned to carry out the first complete rebuilding of a government building in 18C Rome – and this was his first work! Many purposes had to be fulfilled: the two middle storeys were used by the Curia as court rooms for civil and criminal cases, and they were also a general secretariat, while the ground floor, the upper mezzanine and the roof were for military units. Today the constitutional court is housed in this building.

Fuga, who was from Florence, initially planned a façade with a colossal order, similar in structure to the Palazzo Chigi (B93). The very lively design of the wall was reminiscent of church façades with columns inserted in rectangular niches (following the example of Michelangelo's Biblioteca Laurenziana in Florence). In the design as actually built, the relief work is slightly more restrained, so that the contrast with the severe Quirinal palace and square from the late 16C (B15) becomes weaker.

The façade is of wide proportions, and has two storeys each with 13 axes, three in the centre which projects to the extent of two pilasters superimposed on each other, and five in each wing. The wings, unusually, each have a three-dimensionally accentuated portal of their own. Although there is no large triangular gable above the central section, that section is still the only one to have an order of pilasters (in the upper storey) and bossed edges. Both these features only recur at the outer extremities. The wings are subdivided by frames behind which the wall where the windows are located recedes by one layer. All this is reminiscent of the conservators' palace (H30), as is the balustrade decorated with figures. The complexitiy of layers, different materials in articulation and rich sculptures render the façade very lively. SG

B126 Fontana di Trevi
Piazza di Trevi (plan V 1/A)
1732–40
Nicola Salvi

The Fontana di Trevi places the lavishly flowing waters of Rome in an exemplary Baroque setting, and is today still the embodiment of the vital joy of living. In 1453, Pope Nicholas V ordered the rebuilding of the ancient aqueduct (Aqua Virgo) which M. Agrippa had caused to be erected for his thermal baths. Before it was decided to start upon a new Baroque structure, the Fountana di Trevi was a simple rectangular stone basin about the size of a swimming pool.

In 1640, Pope Urban VIII commissioned Gianlorenzo Bernini to carry out the conversion. Bernini's de-

B125 Palazzo della Consulta

sign not only created a new architectural form, but also linked the fountain into its context in terms of city planning. For this purpose he tore down the old fountain in the Piazza dei Crociferi and moved the conduit to its present ending point. This made it possible to orient the fountain on the Quirinal palace both axially and in terms of the line of sight. But this ambitious project for a new structure was ill-fated. When Pope VIII died in 1644, Bernini had only completed the semicircular basin which was not yet decorated.

The immediate successors of Pope Urban VIII showed little interest in continuing the building work. Not until the time of Pope Clement XI (1700–21) were there any plans to complete the basin which was by then dilapidated, but the column of Marcus Aurelius was not erected as planned. When Pope Clement XII (1730–40) finally tackled the Trevi project again by announcing a competition, its completion was at last in sight. The design was drawn up by Nicola Salvi, a philosopher and poet. Salvi had already made a name for himself as an organizer of magnificent fireworks displays. Salvi and Maini, his sculptor, both died during the work on the fountain which, during the rule of Pope Clement XIII, was completed in 1762 by the sculptors Pietro Bracci, Filippo Valle, Andrea Bergondi and others.

Salvi's plans for the fountain were shaped by the world of the theatrical stage. Although the design as actually built did not entirely accord with his original draft, his basic idea was preserved. A splendid show wall outside the Palazzo Poli rises up behind the semicircular basin of the fountain. A strict palatial façade, and the animated architecture of the fountain, were here merged into a single unit. As the fountain proper is the impressive centrepiece, it is accentuated by colossal half columns standing in front, whereas the setback lateral sections are subdivided by flat pilasters. Salvi adopted this principle of arrangement from Bernini's façade of the Palazzo Chigi-Odeschalchi (B93).

Architecture, sculpture, and water which is the living element, function simultaneously as both decorations and actors on the stage of this theatre. Okea

B126 Fontana di Trevi

nos, the god of rivers and seas, makes a spirited gesture in rushing forwards out of the large central niche. He brings with him the water which gushes forth in a wide flood, pouring out of the triumphal architecture whose articulation copies the ancient Roman honorary arch. An attic forms the upper conclusion. Instead of the three openings of a triumphal arch, niches intended to contain statues are let into the wall. The statues include personifications of superabundance and of curative power. The depictions on the reliefs show Agrippa examining the design of the new water conduit, and a scene from that legend of the founding of the aqueduct which relates that a virgin led the Roman soldiers to the source. This illusionist theatrical performance is emphasized not only by the contrast between the severe architectural order and the exuberantly gushing natural event, but also by the fluid transition from architecture into sculpture. The rocks seem to want to burst the palace architecture apart with an elemental force. AG

B127 SS. Celso e Giuliano
Via Banco S. Spirito (plan IV 1/A)
1733–35
Carlo de Domenicis
Julius II ordered a previous structure from the 6C to be torn down, and Bramante, his architect, only laid new foundations (seen in a drawing dating from 1513). Clement XII (1730–40), the pope who elsewhere helped Baroque Classicism to fruition, placed the or-

der for the new 18C building. Only in S. Celso was a Rococo architect given another chance. Although this was not Raguzzini, it was at least his fellow-worker de Domenicis.

The heritage of Borromini, as found in S. Carlino (B52) and the Oratorio dei Filippini (B53), is omnipresent in the façade: it is seen in the concave-convex overall arrangement, in the oval section which takes up the centre of the upper storey and frames the window, and in the curving upper conclusion of the façade. The new era is mainly seen in the reduced tension of the curves (one reason for this is of course the extreme width) and in the fact that the architect, reverting to Mannerist buildings, once again very abruptly employs the aedicule as a key motif.

The interior, a transverse oval, seems related to that of S. Andrea al Quirinale (B85). But its spirit is different. The oval is subdivided by a large architectural order which copies the oval, and by the small order of the chapels which, curving convexly, is repeated in the balconies. The chapels themselves remain rectangular (despite the typically 18C rounded-off corners), and the shape of the core area does not continue into them. The architectural type employed was thus that of a Greek cross merging with an oval. This type was more popular in the late 16C (cf. B5). The area no longer had the clear, tense geometrical shape found in Bernini, but was instead fashioned in a gently undulating way. Also typically for the 18C, elements merge, such as windows and dome. SG

B128 S. Maria dell'Orazione e della Morte
Via Giulia 262 (plan IV 1/B)
1733–38
Ferdinando Fuga
The fraternity of the same name, which organized paupers' funerals, purchased the plot of land in 1572. The church was soon built, but gave way to Fuga's plans for a new building. Although these date from 1722, construction work was not begun until 1733.

B127 SS. Celso e Giuliano

B128 S. Maria dell'Orazione e della Morte

The façade stands at an angle to the street that leads up to it. The onlooker is therefore struck not only by the flat outer surface façade, but also by the ellipsoidal main structure, especially as the campanicletto is also placed diagonally. There is tension between the severe façade on the one hand, and the lower lateral sections and the curving extension above on the other. The two latter features still breath the spirit of the Rococo. The mixture of hardness and softness, and of severity and playfulness, is the leading theme of the design, is typical of Fuga's early style, and is also seen in the Palazzo della Consulta (B125).

The façade itself is two-storeyed, being united in the upper section by a triangular gable, and on the outside by two stretches of wall, each of them with two pilasters which are in superposition and also have a rear pilaster. The central section is similarly angular and is again two-storeyed. Two aedicules consisting of very flat pilasters (without any rear pilasters) and having a strong segmented gable (the lower gable is split) occupy the projecting slab. On each storey, two columns are inserted into each of the rectangular outside niches between the slab and the stretches of wall. This guiding idea, which Fuga the Florentine had also originally intended for the Palazzo della Consulta, an early work by him, derives from Michelangelo's Biblioteca Laurenziana in Florence, and had, in Rome, already been developed further in SS. Luca e Martina (B51) and S. Maria in Campitelli (B91). The projecting wall had either remained radical, without any architec-

tural order (as in Michelangelo), or had been vigorously orchestrated (by columns in Rainaldi's work). Fuga's approach was a compromise. At the same time, the closely placed row of supports is reminiscent of SS. Vincenzo ed Anastasio (B64). In all this, the building is typical of its period: in the virtuosity with which various impressions and prototypes are combined; in the greater »correctness«, because any subtle shifts between the storeys were abandoned (cf. by contrast B64); and in the reversion to Manneristically unwieldy modes of design (cf. the central slab of A4).

Heterogeneous items clashed strongly with one another even in the façade. The same applies to the interior, for which only a narrow plot of land was available. This is why the area was longitudinally ellipsoidal, with chapels located at the »diagonals«. This interior is also marked by an alternation: between the hard rectangular sections of the aedicules which frame the chapels, soft convex bulges are to be found. Borromino's S. Ivo (B56) was evidently the influence behind this. However, in this 18C building, the changes in direction look typical of the period, as they do not so much shape the space, but instead rather mould and enrich it. All that then remains in the dome is a gentle undulation. On the other hand, the dominant aedicule, and the notching which is found in the segmented gable and leads on to the dome, are both reminiscent of S. Andrea al Quirinale (B85), whose dome is also of related design. Some very heterogeneous prototypes, which are the work of the founding fathers of the High Baroque, are once again merged in masterly fashion. Once again, severe sections clash strongly with playful sections. Examples are the severe aedicules and, above them, the fully decorated oval windows which – typically for the period – negate the outer limits between themselves and the dome. Many items look much more moderated than in the High Baroque, for example the dome with its rhombi, which are close to the plain Zopfstil style (cf. by contrast S. Andrea, B85). SG

Bibliography: H. Hager, *S. Maria dell'orazione e morte*, Rome, 1964.

B129 S. Maria Maddalena: façade
Piazza della Maddalena 53 (plan IV 2/A)
c. 1695, 1735
Carlo Quadri, Giuseppe Sardi (?)

This façade came at the end of a long history of building work (cf. B106). Its shell construction by Quadri was a rather conventional late-17C work. It had three axes on each storey and, like S. Marcello (B103), it consisted of a large concave curve.

The façade is famous for its surface design dating from 1735. Two conventional features about it are firstly its articulation by pilasters (with rear pilasters) and an architrave, and secondly also the other major shapes employed, namely the large niche and the framed aedicule, which are the only energetic three-dimensional shapes. What is notable about the large niche is not so much its similarity to Borromini's work (B53) – that similarity is underlined by the fact that the structure curves in a contrary, convex direction – but rather the way in which shapes merge: the façade differed from 17C works, such as S. Carlino (B52), in that it was no longer built up of easily comprehensible geometrical shapes: individual shapes such as the niche went beyond the limits of the storeys, and the conclusion above was not even in a remote sense a gable, but was reduced to two curves. The main quality of the façade lies in that it seems to be dissolved in ornaments, and also in the use of delicately coloured stucco and the preference for asymmetries and freely flickering cartouches. It was the only façade in Rome to have such cartouches, which meant that it was closer to the Rococo north of the Alps, or to the Rococo of Piedmont, than any other façade in the city. But who is the architect of this late, solitary blossom of the Rococo? Two possible artists are under discussion: Sardi's works display a wide range of styles (e. g. B111 and B136), and he did introduce the C-arch in Marino (B111). On the other hand, an argument in favour of Werle, the great organ builder, is that his contemporaneous main work is in the church. SG

B130 SS. Nome di Maria
Largo del Foro Traiano (plan V 1/B)
1736–41
Antoine Dérizet

When Vienna was rescued from the besieging Turks in 1683, Innocent XI – who had supported Emperor Ferdinand I and King Jan Sobieski – attributed this fact to the assistance of the Virgin Mary. He dedicated a holiday to her memory and her name. A fraternity was also created and it ultimately obtained a church here.

B130 SS. Nome di Maria

B129 S. Maria Maddalena: façade

The interior of this oval rotunda has a ring of chapels in delicate Rococo colours (lilac, pink, bright green, gold, white), and tondi in the Bernini style (with scenes from the life of the Virgin Mary) among palmettes in the Borromini style. Its exterior is evidently based on the older church of S. Maria di Loreto next door (H45). However, the entire architectural history of St Peter's comes between the two. The point is that the substructure of the older church is one of the first centrally planned High-Renaissance buildings, while the later edifice is the last of the centrally planned late-Baroque buildings. In the substructure, the solid cube imitating Bramante has become an octagon with unequal sides, narrow in relation to the drum and dome. The equality of all the sides has turned into an alternation between unaccentuated diagonal sides with pilasters on the one hand and, projecting by a layer, main axes with columns and segmented gables on the other. There is also now no contrast between the substructure and the Michelangelo-like dome. Instead, the articulation of the latter is similar to that of the substructure in its elegance and delicacy. It also rises higher. The difference as against S. Agnese and S. Andrea della Valle (B71 and B26) is minor. It can be seen how strongly the 17C traditions lived on in Rome in the 18C. At the same time, the greater moderation which began in c. 1730 is noticeable.

This third pair of twin churches standing at a prominent location and shaped by the ordering power

of the Roman Baroque is the most heterogeneous
(cf. also B30, B44 and B87/88). The visitor will nonetheless remember it as a symmetrical ensemble on
both sides of the column of Trajan (cf. ill. A29). SG

B131 Palazzo Corsini
Via delle Lungara 10 (plan III 2/B)
begun 1736
Ferdinando Fuga
Cardinal Neri Corsini acquired the old 15C palace in
1736 because of its gardens in which, behind the palace, Fuga and Salvi built two casini and an exedra
consisting of pergolas with plants growing on them.
Vasi included them in his collection of engravings of
the Magnificenze di Roma. On the garden side, Fuga linked the old palace sections to the new ones by
means of a balconied bridge above pillared arcades.
The garden ascended behind the palace into the hills,
as was usual for an Italian garden. Today part of it belongs to the Botanical Garden, and part to the park
of Gianicolo.
   The façade facing the street masks the heterogene-
ity of the sections. However, the three-storeyed structure and the window placings derive from the old
building. Two separately orchestrated upper storeys
stand, in endless length and monotony, above a rusticated storey: the risalti at the sides and centre do
not project strongly enough to create any points of
emphasis, especially as they do not have any gables.
Each storey has only one repetitive window shape
continuing across. The risalti again have frames behind which the wall recedes, and are marked off by
rustic-work pilaster strips. The latter also mark the
three central axes of the central section with its large,
tripartite portal. The palace represents Fuga's change-
over from his animated early style (B125) to the regularized Baroque Classicism of his period.
   This also applies to the large vestibule and to the
stairs which lead to one of Rome's leading picture galleries. Although it is three-flighted in the Baroque manner, all the flights are narrow like tubes and do not
stand openly and freely within the area, and the sections are precisely defined and do not merge dynamically: in short, this is as in the 16C. The only dynamically designed item is the (albeit narrow) path leading
from the portal and going through underneath the
middle flight of stairs and out into the garden. SG

B132 S. Maria Maggiore: vestibule
Piazza S. Maria Maggiore (plan VI 1/B)
1740
Ferdinando Fuga
The imposing church vestibule of S. Maria Maggiore
is integrated into a palace façade in masterly fashion.
Since the 12C this basilica had had a vestibule which
was decorated with mosaics and was rebuilt in 1575
by Martino Longhi, with the decorations being re
tained. This Renaissance vestibule was already dilapidated in the early 18C. It was in 1740, during the rule

B132 S. Maria Maggiore: vestibule

of Pope Benedict XIV, that Ferdinando Fuga was commissioned to rebuild the structure. Fuga succeeded in
taking the existing heterogeneous components, such
as the mosaic-work vestibule and an attached presbytery with a palace façade, and in uniting them into a
harmonious synthesis with the ambitious concept of
a church façade.
   The palace architecture on both sides prescribed a
subdivision into two storeys which formally continues
in the tradition of the Roman Baroque façade. In contrast to such façades, the subdividing architectural order here almost attains the significance of a supporting framework, as all the wall areas are dissolved and
replaced by large openings. Galilei designed the Lateran façade (B124) in accordance with the same principle, but its rigid severity gives it an altogether different
character. The façade of S. Maria Maggiore is dominated by the lively relief of the rich step-like shapes
and by the masterly interlocking of the individual elements which are reminiscent of Borromini's language
of shapes. The centre is emphasized by two aedicules, one above the other, with columns standing in
front. Two further aedicules on the outer axes of the
lower storey are less important and therefore only
have three-quarter columns. By repeating the triangular gable, they dovetail the lower storey to the upper.
In the step-by-step layering, in dissolving the wall, and
in relating the architectural elements to one another in
such masterly fashion, Fuga was again reverting to the
elements of the Roman High Baroque. AG

B133 Palazzo Doria Pamphili: façade facing
Via del Plebiscito
Via del Plebiscito (plan IV 2/B)
1740–43
Paolo Ameli
The section facing the Via del Plebiscito was the last
part of the Palazzo Pamphili to be built, and was

B133 Palazzo Doria Pamphili: façade facing Via del Plebiscito

erected under the supervision of Camillo Pamphili the Younger who acquired the necessary additional plot of land (on the history, cf. B122). The second name of the palace goes back to Giovanni Andrea Doria, who inherited it.

The façade has 21 axes, more than that facing the Corso, but does not achieve that façade's grandezza. Although of the same height as the neighbouring Palazzo d'Aste (B84), the palace has five storeys and not three and a half. They are grouped in pairs by pilasters at the edges and by cornices, and none of them is so accentuated as to form the piano nobile. The absence of a hierarchical formation, and the lower height of the storeys, are two external signs indicating that 18C buildings were more strongly geared to middle-class needs. Another feature is that Ameli did not find any design shapes which were adequate to the size of the façade, and instead adopted shapes from smaller palazzi, arranging them in endless rows.

The individual shapes are standard for the period: the curving iron balconies, the Borromini-style window coverings in the fifth storey (cf. B53), and the irregular, frequently grouped arrangement of the points of emphasis (in the windows, balconies and portals). Another feature not untypical of the 18C is that the storey with the most decoration was moved from the centre to the upper edge. The building differs in all these points from 17C structures, even though some of those, such as the Palazzo d'Aste, anticipated 18C ideas. At the same time the end of the Rococo is also felt in Ameli's façade: subdividing elements that merge with one another are largely absent, and there are no delicate layerings at all. SG

B134 S. Croce in Gerusalemme
Piazza di S. Croce in Gerusalemme (plan IX 1/E)
1741-44
Domenico Gregorini, Pietro Passalacqua
Constantine the Great ordered a church to be installed in the late-classical Sessorian palace. The church was intended to house a relic of the Cross which St Helena

had brought from Jerusalem. It was one of the seven pilgrimage churches in Rome, and in 1144, under Lucius II, it gave way to a columned ba-silica (one nave, two aisles), from whose period the campanile and cloister survive in pure form. Benedict XIV (1740–58) ordered the basilica – a second pilgrimage basilica after S. Maria Maggiore (cf. B132) – to be radically redesigned.

The façade is the last chord struck by the Barocchetto in Rome, and is unusually monumental. A large, convex façade surface is a segment of the transversely oval rotunda behind it, and is articulated and held by a colossal order of pilasters. The central pilasters, united by a monumental segmented gable, form an enormous aedicule above the central portal. The two outer pilasters are placed so far forwards that an impression of concave contrary curves arises. The individual forms within this clear overall architectural order are delicately run together: the wall – particularly the pilasters, panels and entablature – is multi-layered, and the storeys look telescoped into one another, as the portal in the central axis extends upwards, and the windows in the lateral axes downwards. The façade is powerfully united at the top firstly by a moulded entablature with a balustrade and figures that reach out, and secondly, above the gable of the central bay, by a curving pedestal with a cross.

This upper conclusion, and the use of colossal pilasters, show a resemblance to the Lateran façade (B124), which is only slightly earlier, and is also physically nearby. The success of the last-mentioned façade in the cultural life of Rome had evidently aroused some attention. Comparability is also seen firstly in the use of the Palladian motif (inserted columns with an arch and a section of entablature on each side) in a central position, and secondly in the skeleton mode of construction in which the supports and entablatures dominate and there is almost no wall. This similarity also applies to the monumentality and clarity, and it means that the more recent façade is a more animated new version – and also a subdued criticism – of the older one.

B134 S. Croce in Gerusalemme

B134 S. Croce in Gerusalemme

The vestibule was also entirely rebuilt: a transversely oval rotunda which is the core area is surrounded by a lower, dimly lit ambulatory. The border between the two is formed by a ring of double supports which are linked by arches in the main axes and by sections of entablature in the secondary axes. In this way a chain of Palladian motifs is created, and the façade and ambulatory are linked in terms of motifs too. Nowhere else in 18C Rome are there any structures which are similarly open with views right across them, are similarly brightly coloured, and are decorated solely by the delicate layering. Counterparts are to be found only in the best Rococo works of Piedmont and Central Europe, such as those by Vittone and Balthasar Neumann. The flattened dome is isolated as a shell in exemplary fashion, and the arches are sharply cut and curved.

The interior was only redesigned, not rebuilt. The floor and the inserted columns date from the 12C building. Tall pilastered pillars were introduced which alternate with the columns and, linked by arches, develop a strong upwards movement. This interior difers from Borromini's redesign in the Lateran (B66) in that the contrast between old and new and also between light and dark and low and high was taken as a theme, so that a leitmotiv was being adopted from the façade. The consistency with which the motifs were carried through is seen from the fact that the new front section of the building, with its rounded

façade and flattened dome, is ultimately only an answer to the other concha which stands at the far end of the nave and likewise is wide. A contrast, rich in tension, to the width of this apse was created in the newly emphasized narrowness and tallness of the nave. The baldacchino is a gem of Roman Baroque architecture. SG

B135 Oratorio SS. Annunziata
Lungotevere Vaticano (plan III 2/A)
1744–46
Pietro Passalacqua

This late work by Passalacqua is the final upsurge of the Barocchetto in Rome. Passalacqua built the oratory for his own fraternity (S. Spirito in Sassia, cf. F8, H26), which only acquired the plot of land in 1744.

The façade is very similar to that of S. Croce (B134), to which Passalacqua had contributed. A colossal order again subdivides the façade (here, of the oratory) with its three axes, a large aedicule motif marks the centre bay which has an oval window and a smaller aedicule for the portal, and the main lines are again multiplied (here, by recessed layers or by repetition). On the other hand, the very differences reveal the dependence on the other façade: the curvature no longer looks tense, but instead as soft as wax, especially where the wall, where it impacts upon the column, was thrust down upon it like a hat; the com-

B135 Oratorio SS. Annunziata

pact assemblage, which consisted of flat pilasters and in which the curvature found a support, was abandoned by introducing columns; everything looks softer and almost effeminate, every outline of windows and doors is less sharply marked, and the decorations are profuse. The approach employed became like that of a painter. The outer two of the three bays were almost reduced to the status of a double supporting motif, and the windows and doors were moved outwards into two further bays.

The façade of the oratory is supplemented by lateral façade sections for functional rooms (one axis each) and by a recessed storey above. Lateral sections had been included in the façade design in S. Susanna (B30), but only in the 18C were the core façade and the outside façade, as well as some other individual components, actually merged. The decorations are though still more lavish in these outer parts of the façade. Contrary to what happened in S. Croce, success was not achieved in adding a touch of Roman grandezza to the Rococo style.

The interior, with its bevelled corners and wall arches, is indebted to Borromini (B53). SG

B136 S. Pasquale Bylon (SS. Quaranta Martiri)
Via delle Fratte di Trastevere (plan VII 1/A)
1744–47
Giuseppe Sardi

The Spanish barefooted order commissioned Sardi to build this church. Little of the style of his previous church buildings, which are the most animated of the Barocchetto (B111, B129), can be sensed in the façade. They had been ill-received. But although the façade is stiff, it does not follow the Baroque Classicism which was coming into fashion, because it is very definitely designed in two layers – this explains the second gable above -, and the order of pilasters or columns is replaced by mere subdividing strips without proper capitals. What is more, the rounded oval shape plays a prominent part in the centre, and several details, such as the portal, are complexly and ingeniously shaped. S. Maria ad Nives (in the Via del Colosseo) has the same structure, but with slight convex curvature.

The interior within this hard shell – in this respect, Bruhns spoke of the Rococo freezing to death – is much softer, and this is a typical 18C contrast. The main rectangular area with rounded-out corners in the Borromini style is dominant here. Protruding wall sections energetically set it off from the smaller entrance area and from the presbytery. The impression of a graduated backdrop is thus created here, as often in the 18C. This barrel-vaulted single space, whose abundance of light itself makes it look like an independent main area, is subdivided all round by double pilasters and by the dark, extravagantly contoured chapel openings. The shapes and decorations are exquisite. Oculi merge with the architrave, in 18C style. Their round shape was, in a less tall version, adopted

B136 S. Pasquale Bylon (SS. Quaranta Martiri)

in the chapel entrances below, and, in a taller version, also in the lunettes above. The shape recurs in the barrel. The altar coverings, window coverings and architrave are softly modelled, are varied within themselves and nevertheless have recurring shapes. SG

B137 Palazzo Rondanini
Via del Corso 519 (plan I 2/D)
1744–60
Alessandro Dori and/or Gabriele Valvassori

The Rondanini family were looking for a city palace to house their collection of antiques, some items of which were used as three-dimensional decorations as though they were prefabricated structural components. They often had to be cut down to the appropriate dimensions.

The late-16C house which was purchased was the dwelling place of Giuseppe Cesari, the well-known painter referred to as Cavaliere d'Arpino. The characteristics of the types of palace customary at that time are still clearly discernible: this is seen in the division into storeys (cf. H25) and in the use of the ground floor as a storey for shops (with a mezzanine; cf. H22). In contrast to this, the design of the surfaces, the smooth stucco work, the vertical articulation – by means of rusticated strips, which in the 16C were reserved solely for the edges – of the long wall, and the linking together of certain frames and forms, are all typical of the 18C. Everything looks classically moderate, and this differs from the Palazzo Doria-Pamphili by Valvassori (B122).

A portal – which is too large, is dominated by columns, and itself suggests the Classicism which was coming into fashion – leads into the interior which has a nymphaeum. Michelangelo's last sculpture, the Pietà Rondanini (today in the Castello Sforzesco in Milano), stood in an intercolumniation of the vestibule which consists of spoils. As in the case of the Palazzo Mattei di Giove (B31), the antiques themselves were installed only in the inner courtyard, being let into its façades (cf. the previous Casino Pio, H37, and the Medici and Borghese villas, B4, B35). A very decorative arrangement was selected which did not follow any discernible strict system and included the 18C stucco-work decorations, examples being two-dimensionally stuccoed obelisks, vases, decoratively fluttering ribbons and flat profiled frames. SG

B138 Palazzo Cenci-Bolognetti
Piazza del Gesù (plan IV 2/B)
1745
Ferdinando Fuga

The Petroni family, mainly of medical doctors and notaries, was not among the most important families in Rome. But by the mid-18C it was evidently becoming acceptable for such a family to order the construction of a magnificent façade on one of the main processional routes, the Via Papalis. This is the last occasion on which the Baroque desire to design city squares is seen in such splendid fashion. Today this building is the head office of the Democrazia Cristiana.

Two storeys, which have seven axes and are subdivided by a colossal order of pilasters, rise above a rustic-work storey. Above them there are a mezzanine hidden in the frieze, and a balustrade. Moreover, there is a residual section to the left. The centre projects only to the extent of one pilaster (similarly on the ground floor). The centre was also accentuated by using the order of pilasters which is absent from the wings, as well as by the increased width of the bays. Pilasters and rustic-work stone ribboning were also employed as a reinforcement at the edges. However, there are no layerings or panels (cf. the contrasting B125). The portal was also kept severe.

B138 Palazzo Cenci-Bolognetti

B139 Villa Albani

Since the time of Bernini's Palazzo Chigi-Odescalchi (B93), the colossal architectural order had only been used for the Fontana di Trevi (B126), a governmental project. But Fuga missed the sought-after grandezza of Bernini's façade because, in his striving for regularity, he overreached himself and went beyond his prototype. Bernini had created a canon, a law full of tension, while Fuga was only regularizing (for example, the centre projects in a subdued way and the balustrade runs continuously horizontally across). After Galilei's death in 1737, Fuga had become a protagonist of Baroque Classicism, before he himself left Rome in 1751. In any event, the vibrantly rich treatment of the wall in the Palazzo della Consulta (B125) had long been past history. SG

B139 Villa Albani
Via di Villa Albani (plan II 2/D)
1756–62
Carlo Marchionni

Cardinal Albani, the chief promoter of the newly arising love of classical antiquity, planned this villa, the largest in 18C Rome, in order to house his collection of antiques there (today most of them are in Munich). His friend and adviser was Winckelmann who, with his *Geschichte des Altertums* (History of Classical antiquity), founded classical archaeology and modern art history as disciplines in Rome.

The two-storeyed main façade faces the garden. Projecting entablatures and a statued balustrade conclude the storeys, and pilasters (rustic-work below, smooth above) subdivide it into nine axes. The pilasters and entablatures have recessed layers surrounding them like a frame. The wall sections themselves recede by a further layer, and have a smooth Palladian motif below and rustic-work windows above.

The design resembles that of the conservators' palace (H30), and the lower storey of the Palladian Villa Mondragone in Frascati is also imitated. Since the time of the Lateran façade (B124), there had been a

B140 S. Maria del Priorato

revival of High-Renaissance prototypes, and in order to favour them Marchionni repressed the Baroque elements still further: the centre is not emphasized, and there is no step-by-step layering. The proportions are no longer tall. Even the colossal order of columns which was introduced by Michelangelo is abandoned in favour of the multi-storeyed order found in Renaissance palaces (H22). A still more faithful imitation of classical models, and an intensified electicism, are elements of the beginnings of Historicism, which started as Classicism. Only in one area, above the windows of the upper storey, do imaginativeness and the Rococo still take effect.

Classicism in painting was seen to commence in the fresco of Parnassus by Raphael Mengs in the salone. The beginning of romantic ruin architecture, and the love arising for the ancient Greek (and not only the ancient Roman) period, were the spirit of the times and had a strong influence on the otherwise insignificant buildings in the gardens. SG

B140 S. Maria del Priorato
Piazza dei Cavalieri di Malta (plan VII 2/A)
1764–66
Giovanni Battista Piranesi
Cardinal Rezzonico, who was the grand master of the Order of the Knights of Malta and the nephew of Clement XIII, commissioned Piranesi to restore the 16C tomb church belonging to the members of the or-

der. Piranesi, from Venice, had become famous for his brilliant series of engravings of Roman buildings, but was an architect by training. Here he designed firstly the Piazzetta dei Cavalieri di Malta in the style of an ancient Roman street of tombs with stelae, inscriptions, obelisks and cypresses, secondly the view of the dome of St Peter's through a covered walk which almost every visitor to Rome enjoys through the famous keyhole, and thirdly the façade and the interior of the church itself.

The façade, a very severe temple frontage, is articulated by fluted pairs of pilasters and a triangular gable. Between them there is a vertical strip consisting of the portal (which itself has a triangular gable), and above it a transversely rectangular strip motif, in the centre of which there is a round window with a rich intrados (in its structure and decorations, this imitates an ancient ashlar sarcophagus with the medallion of the deceased). The use of ancient decorative shapes in the rest of the façade (such as the meandering strip in the frieze and the grotesque candelabrum to the side of the portal), the severity of the delimitations, and the radiant, marble-like white colour, all make the work early Classicist. But the style, particularly the surface crammed full of decorations, was not imitated later: Piranesi differed from Winckelmann (on whose work in Rome cf. B139) in that he was propagating Etruscan as well as Greek sources, and regarded these forms as a storehouse for the decorator. He collected them in books of selections, and also transferred them to items of decoration dating from his times, such as fireplaces.

The interior is in a Classicist white colour. But Piranesi also gave it a specifically Venetian, still entirely un-Classicist touch by raising the height of the presbytery and inserting apse windows which light up the free-standing altar magically from behind. The medallions above and below the surrounding architrave depict apostles, and this probably refers to how the members of the Maltese order perceived themselves.
SG

1 1/2 days: B43, B30, B44 (with B60), B45, B52, B85, B93, B122, B72 -- B56, B71 with B61, B79, B1, B91 (and one evening each: B115 with B87/88 and B126 with B64).

Or more extensively:
1 day: B1, (B26), B27, B3, B28, B25, B18, B30, B44 with B60, B43 (early Baroque and the early Bernini).
1/2 day: B45, B72, B68, B84, (B86), B93 (High-Baroque palaces).
2 x 1/2 day: B51, (B48), B52, B85, B64, B83 -- B50, B56, B71 (with B61), B79, B53, B96 (High-Baroque churches).
1 day: B115, B118, (B129 with B106), B122, (B103 and B133), B126, B125, (B132), B124, B123 with B100 and B66, B134 (Roccoco and Baroque Classicism).

Classicism and Historicism

The period of Valadier (K1–K8)

It was not until four decades after the Villa Albani (B139) and S. Maria del Priorato (B140), the first secular and ecclesiastical buildings in Rome to start to show Neo-Classical features, that Valadier came on the scene as the great classical architect in Rome. There had been no buildings breaking new ground for thirty years.

His first great work, the design of the Piazza del Popolo (K1), was also the most important. It was the first of the great 19th-century urban development measures (K9, K11), which were probably this century's contribution to the cityscape of Rome (and not just Rome). What was to be designed was the square that had been perceived as the vestibule of the Eternal City even in the Baroque period and for that reason – at that time still rectangular in form – had been laid out strikingly with Bernini's gate façade on the city side (B77) and Rainaldi's twin churches (B87/88). The square design is characteristic of its period not just because of its extent – most of the large squares in European metropolises date from about 1800 – but also because Valadier weakened the clearly directed, dynamic Baroque thrust of movement – from north to south – by emphasizing the transverse axis with the creation of parks and viewing points and went back to an important ancient Roman form, namely that of the imperial forums (cf. in detail K1). In fact for a

Giuseppe Valadier, plan for the conversion of the Piazza del Popolo, c. 1794

Classicist architect nothing could commend itself more than to base a square at the entrance to the capital of the empire on an imperial forum – just as a Baroque architect had given to the entrance roads two »ecclesiastical guards« (Giedion) in the form of the twin churches. Conversely, Vala-dier's design for the square was very modern in many respects, particularly in that it linked buildings and green areas with each other, intended to keep many views (for instance from the Pincio over to the Tiber) definitely clear of buildings (and green), and allowed various levels to work along with each other. With breadth as an urban development option and the powerful link with the ancient Roman forums Valadier had formulated the two leitmotifs for the coming century. The coming century itself was seldom as trail-finding and even »modern« in the way in which it solved problems.

Valadier made a name for himself not just as a precise restorer of antique monuments, for example the Arch of Titus (A26) and the Colosseum (A25), and as the designer of a series of (Neo-Classical) façades for older churches (cf. for instance B74, B108), but also as the creator of almost all the pioneering buildings of the first four decades of the 19th century. Probably the most important new design for a church façade was S. Pantaleo (K2). As well as this he devoted himself to building activities as different as the casino in the public park (K3), the theatre (K6) or the façade of a post office (K4).

However, it is difficult to define Valadier's style and that of the period he dominated. He dominated because in his lifetime almost all the major commissions came to him – with the exception of the Braccio Nuo-

vo of the Vatican Museum (K5), but to some extent he created a similarly formally strong, undecorated stereometric style as his great German contemporary Karl Friedrich Schinkel, probably most clearly in the church façade of S. Pantaleo (K2), which seems very cubic and physical. On the other hand Valadier was not a pure Classicist in terms of his sources of inspiration, just as little as other contemporary Roman architects and just as little as Schinkel. For in Rome the development that was so typical of the 19th century in other places and which can be seen in an almost text-book version in Munich in the three great street axes leading away from the Residence practically did not take place. In Munich the sources of inspiration changed from the ancient Greek classical style (in Briennerstraße with the Königsplatz) via a style like that of the Renaissance that was still indirectly classical (in Ludwigstraße) to those styles in Western architecture in which a relation of this kind was clearly weaker, the Romanesque, Gothic and finally Baroque styles (in Maximilianstraße). One refers to the first phase as Classicism, to the latter as Historicism. In contrast with this, under Valadier in Rome even in the early »Neo-Classical« phase (before the start of the Risorgimento in the 60s) there is recourse to the (mainly northern Italian) cinquecento, in S. Pantaleo, for example (K2) and even after Valadier's death in the Manufattura dei Tabacchi (K8) or to the (Florentine) quattrocento in the design for the necropolis of Campo Verano (K7). Conversely, the entrance gate to the last-mentioned work again seems to make a similarly cubic and solid impression to Valadier's S. Pantaleo half a century before. Striking features of ancient architecture – in Rome that of ancient Rome – were always aspired to, but by no means continuously. Such forms can also be found at a very elementary level in Raffaele Stern's Braccio Nuovo in the Vatican Museum, which with its long barrel vaults and niches seems almost like an ancient Roman audience or palace hall (cf. A27).

Thus two other characteristics are just as specific for Valadier's period as the link with antiquity: the increased eclecticism and – still very hesitantly – the emergence of new building problems for which no new formal language was developed yet that was unique to them. The Palazzo Wedekind is an outstanding example of both these points (K4). It was planned as a post office building, which is at best indicated by the clocks mounted on the top. Otherwise this is a palace façade of the Palazzo Farnese type (H25), but with a portico on the ground floor as in the Palazzo dei Conservatori (H30). That Valadier used heterogeneous set-pieces to a very great extent can be seen not just from the combination of various palace types but also from the fact that he also gave his palace a terrace, as had previously been customary in villa architecture, and as a crown the clocks as a symbol of progress. Other buildings of his period also do not betray their changed function. Thus Valadier

shaped the Casino, which was now intended to serve broad swathes of the population (as a kind of coffee-house) no differently from a villa previously reserved for a patrician family (K3). And Antonio Sarti again built a palace façade in front of his tobacco factory (K8). Nevertheless this building points to the future in two re- spects: at least it is clear that new building problems, in this case a factory, were indeed emerging (and the Cavallerizza in Castro Pretorio and the Villa Pia in Via Portense were among the other building projects under Pius IX); also inner courtyards at least were now designed from a functional point of view to an extent (for detail see K8). Also this building was on the brink of an urban development that was very important for Rome: workers' quarters were to be built above all in the south-east, in the lower reaches of the Tiber, at first in Trastevere, where there had been mills even in ancient times. And also in the south-east these workers' quarters were frequently developed as planned estates, thus first of all here in the context of manufacturing, then later (early 20th century) on the other side of the Tiber in the Quartiere Testaccio (K22) and in Garbatella (M2, M3).

The Risorgimento and Rome as capital (K9–K18)

The creation of the Kingdom of Italy and Rome's promotion as its capital had less effect in terms of individual buildings than in urban development. Rome grew explosively as the new capital of a newly united country. The ensuing flight migration from the countryside meant that workers' estates were needed in large numbers. And the new body of civil servants needed accommodation (rented and owner-occupied housing), like for example the Villa Ludovisi. But the most significant urban development was in the city centre. The first measure was the Via Nazionale – the name itself was a programme. The twenty years after the start of the building works (on the street and the buildings along it) were aimed at creating two street axes and regulating the Tiber, until the monument for Italy's first king, Vittorio Emanuele II, was built, the so-called »typewriter« (K15). It was the climax and the centre (spatially as well) of all these urban projects.

The Via Nazionale (K9) came into being largely because of a new means of transport, the railway. The first station was built in 1864, still under the ecclesiastical state (cf. M31). It was finally connected to the city by the Via Nazionale. At first development tended to be random, and was not funded by the city. Construction of the Via Nazionale relied on a private gift from landed estates. It is equally surprising at first that the road did not start in the station square, but in a neighbouring square, the Piazza Esedra, and led from there towards the Tiber bend and the Capitol (A27). But as the »Esedra« (Exedra) from which the square took its name had been part of the baths of Diocletian (A46), and the square was in the southern part of this complex, the context was a powerful one which was appropriate to the imperial and historicist spirit of the times. And indeed the development of this road from the station to the Tiber bend was concluded by the creation of this square (K16), which, like the Piazza del Popolo (K1) a century before was perceived as a new vestibule for the city. In fact Rome could have looked different as a city, as the first intention was to route the end of the Via Nazionale differently, not in two tight bends down to the Piazza Venezia, but in two wider bends, first of all to the right to the Fontana Trevi (B126) and then left to the Piazza Colonna. After the new route was chosen in 1876, access to the Piazza Colonna (from the station) was created via a less lavish street axis (Via del Tritone/Barberini). The Via Nazionale ran mainly through vineyards, so that there was room for public buildings, and a large number were built, and an even larger number planned. All the major projects of the time before and around 1900 were either planned (K15, K21) or built (K12, K13, K16) on the Via Nazionale, or realized in the Piazza Venezia or the Piazza Colonna (K15, K17, K21, K24); and the development of these two squares, as has been said, was closely linked with the construction of the Via Nazionale. Only one major building went up elsewhere, the Palace of Justice (K18).

The Via Nazionale, coming from the east, met the Via del Corso, the ancient Via Lata, at the Piazza Venezia, which was small at the time. The second great road built in the early days of the kingdom, the Corso Vittorio Emanuele (K11), was the continuation of the Via Nazionale to the west – through the whole of the Tiber bend. But its construction posed quite different problems, as it led through a densely populated area with historical buildings in it. Much was destroyed, and much was integrated into the cityscape somewhat awkwardly, but over all this construction project – within the realms of the possible – was historicist and careful in the positive sense, especially in comparison with contemporary urban development of Paris and Vienna, which intervened in the existing building stock much more radically. The road was perceived not just as a traffic artery, but also always as an opportunity to make the great architectural legacy more easily visible. Thus the Palazzo Massimo alle Colonne (H24) lost the dense building around it, which restricted the view and guaranteed a number of surprising close-ups, but it was visible in its entirety for the first time. Additionally, long sections of the new route ran along old streets, although they had to be considerably widened: for example in the old Via Papalis (from the Ponte Sant'Angelo to the Capitol), which followed the same route from between the Palazzo Farnesina ai Baullari (H21) and Il Gesù (B1), but also at the beginning of the old Via Peregrinorum, the second ceremonial road starting at the Ponte Sant'

Angelo – in the direction of the Palazzo Farnese (H25) and the Theatre of Marcellus (A17) – which was used as the last major road crossing the Corso Vittorio Emanuele (now the Via Banchi Vecchi).

Just as Sixtus V improved the infrastructure with aqueducts as well as major roads, the creation of a new infrastructure in the early days of the kingdom was not restricted to the road network: it also included the regulation of the Tiber, which led to the construction of gigantic embankment walls and the roads beside the river (K10). However, this involved the sacrifice of important features like the Ripetta harbour, the first piece of Rococo urban development in Rome. But overall considerable care was taken during all these operations to protect the old building stock, and some of the proposed measures were abandoned, for example the one which would have involved demolishing Raguzzini's Palazzine in Piazza S. Ignazio (B118). Not more old buildings were destroyed, as they had been when Bernini's Colonnades were built, to which Bramante's and Raphael's most important palace designs had fallen victim. And under Fascism as well people were not afraid to intervene very radically in the urban structure, even though it was precisely the relation to the Eternal City and especial-ly its imperial past that was a central element in the way in which the regime presented itself.

The principal Historicist work in Rome is the Monumento Vittorio Emanuele (K15). Though it is possible to quarrel about its quality, it does demonstrate important tendencies of the early kingdom. Classical antiquity (here again the Roman version) was by no means rarer in Rome at the end of the century than it had been earlier. But now it was not just visual features of ancient Roman buildings that were used, but reference was made to specific major works. The Colosseum (A25) and the Arch of Titus (A26) were combined in the Roman Aquarium (K14), with additional articulation derived from the Roman Insula; the triumphal arch also inspired the façade of the Palazzo Esposizioni (K12), and the Monumento Vittorio Emanuele, with its crowning columned portico and white marble splendour was intended to be a reminder of the age of Caesar and Augustus, the latter's marble city of Rome, and above all the imperial forums. Only under Augustus had there been a comparable (better proportioned) monument, the Ara Pacis (A18).

The main difference in the treatment of the ancient Roman legacy in the early and late years of the century was that the language became louder in the latter period. The massed columns seemed overloaded (K12, K15), and the references to great monuments over-assertive and sometimes – as in the case of the Aquarium (K14) – out of place. At the same time the relation to antiquity became for the first time so emphatic in the Monumento Vittorio Emanuele. Reference now was meant to convey an idea, not only a mood. All this is part of the drama of the national state in the process of constituting itself.

In the early years of the kingdom the relation to antiquity was only one of many possibilities. Reference was very definitely made to Renaissance buildings as well (for example K18 and later K24). But under Neo-Baroque there was an additional stylistic tendency that had not been there in the first half of the century, but which was the dominant one in Germany in the period of rapid industrial expansion after 1870 as well. The protagonist of this approach in Rome was Gaetano Koch. His two major works, the Banco d'Italia (K13) and the Piazza Esedra (K16) are to be seen in the context of the plans for the Via Nazionale. In both works he visibly borrowed from Bernini's Louvre project and the design for the Palazzo Chigi-Odeschalchi (B93): in the staggering of the façades and building blocks by the use of projections, in the concave lines of the central section, in the highlighting of a central block which strikingly thrusts through the transverse palace block. A complex (Neo-)Baroque conclusion to the Via Nazionale also seems more consistent than the ancient Roman drama in the Piazza Venezia, as the very fact of forming axes represents a legacy of the Baroque in Western architecture.

A new formal language for new building needs was not developed in the first years of the kingdom either. The formal language of the palaces seemed perfectly appropriate for buildings intended for prestigious purposes (the majority at this time), for example for a state bank or the creation of a complete display square at the entrance to the city. In the second case recourse to ancient Roman building stock was felicitous indeed. But even the monument for Vittorio Emanuele seems slightly unconvincing to us today because no immediately plausible symbols or building forms were found for the »new« ideas that it was supposed to represent, the freedom and unity of Italy. And then the adoption of features of the Colosseum or from triumphal arches seems entirely random in the case of exhibition buildings or aquaria. In the early years of the kingdom it was not just that buildings were needed for new purposes, but new, pioneering building techniques were developed, again without this leading to any fundamental change in formal language. The most important innovation was the introduction of the steel skeleton construction method. It remained completely invisible in the external structure of the Roman Aquarium (K14), whilst in the interior the innovative features could be seen, in other words again first of all in a hidden place. A whole series of other steel skeleton buildings or constructions date from practically the same time – from the Museo Geologico to the steps of the Ospedale del Celio (though a start had been made with buildings under Pius IX, above all the Ponte dell'Industria). In the Rinascente department store (K17) the steel skeleton affected the appearance of the building as a whole much more clearly, although the formal language was still Historicist. Here a new kind of building, the department store (cf. also K24) also led to a new formal

language. The last-named step was admittedly of importance only for Rome, it had been made long ago elsewhere. In fact the Rinascente department store was one of the buildings built at the turn of the century that increasingly showed dependence on international trends. Here the models were department stores in Paris, and the Palace of Justice (K18) was also modelled on the one in Brussels. If there were discussions in Rome at this time about a »national« style that was particular to Italy (cf. K15, K18), this rather proves that it was something that was missing. The best (and entirely particular) achievements of the first decades of the kingdom were in the urban development field. This was expressed outwardly by the large number of urban development - plans (»piano regolatore«), starting with those of 1873 and 1882.

Looking for a style in the early 20th century (K19–K28)

The principal features of 19th-century architecture are also to be found almost unchanged in the first decades of the 20th century. Reference continued to be made to buildings of an enormous range of styles, ancient Roman (for example M1), and also some from the northern Italian High Renaissance (e. g. K26) or (Roman) Baroque (e. g. K24). The latter, trivialized in terms of its forms, became the basis for the accepted style in residential building in particular, so-called Barocchetto. This reference to historical styles and buildings (increasingly from now on) also intended to make points about the message carried by certain buildings – the Vittorio Emanuele monument, for example. A parliament building was built like a castle in the forms of the »fortified« Sicilian-Norman epoch (K21), the Accademia di Gran Bretagna used forms from British Baroque and the country houses style (K25), the German academy borrowed from the Italian Renaissance villa, because this was seen as the quintessence of older art (K26). Also, nothing changed in terms of the dilemma that scarcely any new or appropriate forms were being (sought and) found for new building problems. This is as true of the parliament as it is of the new synagogue, a building that could just as well be a court-house or a palace of justice in terms of its appearance. The story of the shopping arcade in the galleria off Piazza Colonna is extremely interesting (K24). Here public opinion turned against unduly bold innovations. This led to the erection of one of the greatest Neo-Baroque buildings, modelled on one of the principal Baroque palaces, the Palazzo Barberini (B45), with its great round-arched windows. Innovative formal language made the greatest impact in the newly emerging workers' estates, in the Testaccio quarter (K22), but above all in the Garbatella quarter (M2, M3); these estates also marked the beginning of another new urban development, Rome's expansion beyond the ancient Roman city boundaries – the Aurelian Wall (A44). The Quartiere Garbatella in fact dates mainly from a new era, the very late twenties. Still in these years steel skeleton buildings were made to look like traditional brick buildings (K23). Compared with the Rinascente department store (K17) this was in fact a regression.

Signs of a new era tended to be few and far between. Local styles – or put more generally, contextual relations – shifted further into the centre of interest in the late 19th century; this can be seen, for example, from the fact that the International Art Exhibition of 1911 in Rome produced buildings in a wide variety of local styles, and that above all Lutyens designed parts of his Accademia di Gran Bretagna (K25), which was part of this exhibition (cf. also K23), in the Victorian country house style. But this very building provides proof of continuing eclecticism with its break between main façade and side wings; additionally the architect was British, and so the building was an exceptional case in Rome. The asymmetrical layout of the Villa Massimo (K26) also had implications for the future, in which - with a largely symmetrical design overall – the main building and the studio wings were not arranged parallel with each other, but at a strikingly oblique angle. This assymetry was further emphasized by the fact that the wing of ten studios built next to each other was divided by an avenue between the third and the fourth. But these innovations were hidden away in the park at the back, and the main historical building remained untouched by them.

New tendencies were most clearly present in the (few) buildings that followed Jugendstil and the style of the Vienna Secession or even Futurism itself. Two examples in particular represent the first-mentioned tendency, the Villa Ximenés (K19) and even more strongly the Cinema Teatro Corso (K27). Both appear in their architects' oeuvre as »youthful sins«, as both of them went on to create large and eloquent historicist buildings (K21 or M1). But it is almost more important that precisely the second, more important work largely lost its Jugendstil or Secessionist façade as a reaction to criticism by the Roman public. The most important elements had to be knocked off. And equally very little is still standing of the Casa d'Arte Bragaglia (K28), Rome's first important Futurist building, which heralded a new era, along with other buildings, in the 20s. But in this decade the pendulum had already swung in the opposite direction. Historicist buildings were already the exception, Rationalist buildings and those that were very much in the service of Fascism had become the rule. An independent style of architecture, no longer necessarily committed to historical models had come into being for the first time. SG

K1 Piazza del Popolo

K1 Piazza del Popolo
Piazza del Popolo (plan I 2/D)
1793–1824
Giuseppe Valadier

The Piazza del Popolo was Rome's first Classicist square. Passing through the northern city gate – the ancient Porta Flaminia, renamed Porta del Popolo later on – one arrives at the square that terminates at the Tiber on one side and Pincio Hill on the other. The rectangular yet largely undesigned Piazza was distinguished architecturally during the Baroque period by individual buildings – for example, Bernini's gate facing the city (B77) and Rainaldi's twin churches (B87/88), which separate the Babuino, Corso and Ripetta streets beginning opposite the gate.

Given these circumstances, the idea arose to redesign the square as a welcoming space of the city on one hand, and to plan a park on the heights of the Pincio that would be accessible via a ramp from Piazza del Popolo. Giuseppe Valadier's initial plans date from 1793. Another plan dated 1811 was personally accepted by Napoleon but abandoned in 1813 for reasons of unfeasibility; thereafter, the French architect Louis-Martin Berthault was put in charge. After the withdrawal of the French in 1814, however, Valadier once again took up the work on the project.

He added two masonry exedrae towards the Tiber and Pincio. Traffic was to be guided around the square behind them. He thus countered the targeted movement of the Baroque structures with a new axis. The resulting ground plan of the rectangle embraced by two exedrae reverts to the plan of the old imperial forums (A20, A29). Fountains accentuate the exedrae, whilst the obelisk erected by Sixtus V at the centre of the interior region was placed onto a square podium with water-spitting lions. The corners of the square are enhanced by architectural blocks (S. Maria del Popolo (F7), Dogana, Casa Lovati, Palazzo Torlonia). Existing and new buildings were given a unified façade design with rusticated ashlars and spanning arches. Valadier framed the Porta del Popolo with two cupola structures reflecting Rainaldi's twin churches.

The slope of the Pincio had to be provided with ramps and supporting walls for access to the park. Its design is no longer in line with the Baroque styles as can be found, for example, in Frascati's villas, where the slope was crowned by a building. The access road runs in tight hairpin turns across the slope and is lined with freely growing trees. The middle axis, ascending via four large tiers with triple arcades that become richer towards to top, culminates in a terrace terminated by a wide parapet. In a sense, the terrace literally cuts off the top of the hill. The top arcade step, as a kind of grotto, forms an equivalent terrace on the transverse axis towards the gate and city entrance. The abandonment of Baroque movement axes in favour of several equal directions of view and movement goes hand in hand with the denial of ascribing the square to a specific building. Planning a square on several different levels was path breaking, as well. The contemplation of antiquity – here in the shape of the ground plan – is typically Roman. Valadier created a thoroughly modern work in the Piazza del Popolo with its broad spaces and the combination of architecture and plantings and, at the same time, one of the great Classicist complexes of 19C urban culture. IM

K2 S. Pantaleo: façade

K2 S. Pantaleo: façade
Piazza di S. Pantaleo (plan IV 1/B)
1806
Giuseppe Valadier

The small church of the martyr S. Pantaleo (a personal physician of Emperor Maximian) from the time of Pope Honorius III had been renewed by Giovanni Antonio de Rossi in the 17C with a single aisle. In 1806, at the Duke Giovanni Torlonia's expense, Valadier erected the façade that had remained unfinished.

The narrow building volume from the 17C forced Valadier into the design of a steep, narrow façade. After several designs, he found a flat solution reduced in ornamentation that, in the end, reverts to the façade of the Chiesa delle Zitelle by Andrea Palladio (c. 1580–86) in Venice: the two-story façade crowns a triangular gable with an oculus, and the two storeys are separated by a fresco relief. In the centre, the façade recedes in an arch stretching across both storeys. Within the arch is the small portal framed by Ionic columns and a gable tympanum (a hint at the old origins of the building), and on the second floor there is a large thermal window. Thus, a juxtaposition of elementary forms (circular – triangular) is achieved. Shallow rustication covers the entire wall surface. Different from Palladios' church, which is structured by a fine pilaster order, the S. Pantaleo façade appears block-like – almost a fortification. Above the gable, the volume reappears as an intact though narrow cube.

Rustication and thermal window as well as the form of the façade that is reminiscent of an ancient triumphal arch are very Roman indeed. With it, Valadier proves himself to be the leading Classicist of Rome. In the scarcity of the form, he can be compared to the German Karl Friedrich Schinkel. IM

K3 Casino Valadier
Via del Belvedere al Pincio (plan I 3/D)
1813–17
Giuseppe Valadier

The French influence from the turn of the century echoes through the Casino Valadier. The plans for a public park on the Pincio were personally accepted by Napoleon between 1809 and 1811 in connection with the redesign of the Piazza del Popolo (K1). It was to remain Rome's only larger garden complex from this epoch and was intended to provide a relaxing environment for the inner city population. The type of the private country villa was replaced by a public »coffee house« built by Giuseppe Valadier from 1813–17.

The two-storey structure rises up from a square ground plan and a base joined laterally by terraces resting upon massive columns. A dual-flight stairway at the front leads to the entrance. The first floor is structured by ionic pilasters. The corners of the building are accentuated on both storeys by pilaster and lesene pairs in a way similar to a projection. On the upper floor, three windows enhance the middle axis

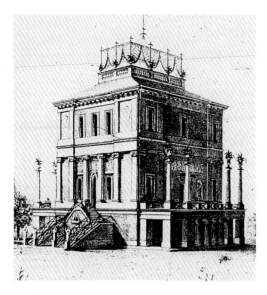

K3 Casino Valadier

of the front façade, whilst the windows on the sides are evenly spread across the entire expanse.

Inside, three square rooms on each side adjoin a central corridor; today, however, they have been refurbished. On the south-west side of the first floor is a large hall divided by two columns. Its décor still matches the design by Valadier: a garland-like frieze in a Classicist form language wraps around the room beneath the ceiling. Blue and silver are the predominant colours of the hall decorated with filigree ornamentation. It remains one of the few preserved interiors by Valadier. IM

K4 Palazzo Wedekind
Piazza Colonna (plan IV 2/A)
1815–38
Giuseppe Valadier, Pietro Camporese
In 1814 the 16C Palazzo del Vicegerente, situated at the west side of the Piazza Colonna, became the headquarters of the General Director of the Vatican post office. In 1815 Giuseppe Valadier submitted plans for a new building that was later realised by Pietro Camporese by 1838. Purchased by the banker Wedekind in 1852, the palace was thereafter named after him, and the interior was completely changed by G. B. Giovenale in 1879.

A distinct building type for post office buildings was not developed; instead, the façade type of the Palazzo Farnese (H25) was copied: the smooth wall is structured horizontally by ledges between the storeys and rows of windows. On the second floor, the windows are placed between columned aediculae (with a widened central window, as on the Palazzo Farnese); the third floor is decorated in a more reserved way.

The mezzanine floors are kept simple. The outside edges of the façade are framed by rustication. As suggested by Valadier, a portico with twelve fluted Ionic columns from an ancient portico excavated from 1812–17 in Veio were placed in front of the façade on the first floor. The portal is flanked by two pairs of columns from the basilica of S. Paolo fuori le Mura, which burnt down in 1823. Above the portico is a terrace, a building style from the villa architecture. Originally, two large clocks, the only signs of progress, decorated the building. Giovenale later replaced them with a single clock. The arbitrary composition of different elements (here, the Palazzo Farnese, the ancient portico, and the villa-style terrace) and the dissolution of once canonical units (here, the storeys) are typical for the 19C. IM

K5 Musei Vaticani: Braccio Nuovo
Città del Vaticano (plan I 1/E and plan III 1/A)
1816–22
Raffaele Stern
To house the antiques that were returned from France in 1816, the papal court architect Raffaele Stern began the construction of a Classicist extension of the Vatican Museums in 1817. After his death, the building was completed by Pasquale Belli in 1822.

The barrel-vaulted hall architecture cuts through the Belvedere yard at a right angle to Bramante's wing buildings. In the centre, above the ground plan of a Greek cross, the tract widens into a central space vaulted by a suspended cupola; it is reminiscent of the Pantheon (A31), not least because of its simple proportions. The north façade facing the Giardino della Pigna rests on a high base and is decorated by a portico consisting of eight Corinthian columns, whereas the adjoining wing wall is framed by projections and is additionally structured by Corinthian columns with an entablature and a roof parapet. The outside staircase

K5 Musei Vaticani: Braccio Nuovo

was added later on. The south façade is decorated only with deep, round niches in the base and a polygonal concha.

Inside, pairs of Corinthian columns (some of an antique origin) and strongly profiled transverse arches distinguish the central space and wings. Rounded arch niches with statues on high bases structure the gallery's walls and suggest an antique massiveness of the wall structure. Antique mosaics are laid into the floors; classical reliefs can be found beneath the entablature. The décor is complemented by busts placed on low columns and on corbels. Openings in the coffered barrel vault provide the lighting. Rectangular niches open up at the height of the bases in the central space; an oculus cuts through the suspended cupola here, as in the Pantheon. The appropriated building elements, quotations from antiquity and the convincingly presented massiveness of the wall structure make the Braccio Nuovo one of the major Classicist works in Rome. IM

K6 Teatro Valle
Piazza Teatro Valle (plan IV 1/B)
1819–21
Giuseppe Valadier
Between 1726 and 1727 the Marchese di Capranica had erected a theatre in the yard of his palace as a wood construction. Following restoration work at the turn of the century, the Roman municipal administration ordered the reconstruction of the heavily damaged theatre in 1819. Giuseppe Valadier received the order, but he was forced by financial restrictions to retain the original building scheme.

The representative façade opens up in seven portals on the rusticated ground floor; a central projection with a large Ionic structure uniting the piano nobile and mezzanine level rises above it. It's framed by wings that have no adornment and are structured only by the alignment of the windows. Behind the façade, the theatre rises into the sky with a triangular gable. Together, the central projection and gable can thus be understood as a sculptural temple façade .

Two triple-flight staircases lead from the side entrances to the stage and to the loges of the horse-

K6 Teatro Valle

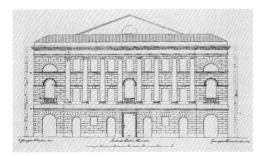

K7 Campo Verano

shoe-shaped, five-story auditorium via lateral foyers and a deambulatory. Though larger than its predecessor and built with masonry walls, the hall's interior design and ceiling are still loyal to the traditional wood construction. Valdier's calculations of the acoustics are new; he wanted to optimise them with a system of windows and doors designed to move the air from the rooms behind the stage towards the audience. What is new aesthetically is the abandonment of the hierarchical structure of the auditorium. Instead, serial motifs – for example, narrow pilasters with volutes – determine the appearance. After the destruction of the Teatro Apollo this is the only preserved example of Valadier's innovative theatre architecture. IM

K7 Campo Verano
Piazzale del Verano (plan IX 3/C)
1855–71
Virginio Vespignani
The Campo Verano, located next to S. Lorenzo fuori lle Mura (C13), was already being used as a funeral site during the late Republican period. The tradition was revived by Napoleon's legislation beginning in 1804: the deceased were no longer to be buried near the churches but in a cemetery surrounded by a wall outside of the inhabited area. The work that had been accomplished since 1809 following a plan by the architects Giuseppe Camporese and Raffaele Stern was terminated upon the return of the papal administration in 1814. Today's complex was realised by Virginio Vespignani only in 1855–71 under Pope Pius IX. During the 80s, it was extended with a charnel and the Hebrew cemetery.

The grounds are surrounded by a wall. The original entrance, a triple-arch portico with seated figures on high bases, is flanked by monumental towers whose forms are reminiscent of a mausoleum. This symbolically charged monument was to separate the city of the living from that of the dead. The latter is kept in the style of the neo-quattrocento: from a square forecourt, an axis runs through two framing corner buildings onto a rectangular square lined by arcades and to the church S. Maria della Misericordia. Outside of this »city«, numerous remarkable family graves were

established in the Historicist style of the end of the
19C along the cemetery lanes that are laid out in an
orthogonal grid. The »Pincetto« on a small, bricked-
up elevation decorated with a chapel is especially
interesting. Until this century, the Verano was Rome's
only cemetery. IM

K8 Manufattura dei Tabacchi

Piazza Mastai (plan VII 1/A)
1860
Antonio Sarti

The tobacco manufacturing plant of Pope Pius IX at
Piazza Mastai, erected in 1860 by Antonio Sarti, was
part of an ambitious urban and social program. Today,
the Viale Trastevere separates it from the surrounding
quarter that had been built at the same time – the
Quartiere Mastai by A. Busiri Vici, with its two- and
three-storey apartment building for workers.

A round plaza decorated with a fountain in its centre is located in front of the factory building. Unlike the
modest social housing, Sarti's three-storey tobacco
manufacturing plant has a detached monumental
façade structured after the Villa Vorlata by Scamozzi.
Above the rusticated base, a large Doric-style structure enhances the seven-axis centre projection. The
half-columns are smooth, and the beams and gable
are kept simple. The staggered five-axis wings form
a projection with three axes at the edges, whereas
the two connecting axes recede towards the central
section.

The reference to Scamozzi's Villa is in line with the
Roman penchant for 16C architecture (Neo-Renais-
sance) during that period. The function of the building
didn't influence the façade; on the contrary, the industrial building was given a palace façade. This discrepancy is characteristic for the end of Classicism and
Historicism.

The rooms of the manufacturing plant are grouped
around several inner courtyards, which are kept simple. The simple walls with their rows of windows
structured according to strictly functional criterion,
lack ornamentation of any kind. For the first time, the
design followed the function in this unrepresentative
part of the building. IM

K8 Manufattura dei Tabacchi

K9 Via Nazionale

(plan V 1/R)
1864–1935

The construction of the Via Nazionale was the beginning of an era of urban planning in Rome following
the unification of Italy. This first measure, however,
was based on a private initiative and proceeded slow-
ly. The new street runs from the Piazza Repubblica
(once Piazza Esedra, K16) to the Piazza Venezia, parallel to one of the city's first axes, the Via Pia from
1560. The course and design are the result of heated
debates and different phases. Large sections of the
area consisting of villas and vineyards – between the
Diocletian thermal baths (A46), Quirinal and Viminal –
had been the property of Monsignore Francesco
Saverio de Merode. Considering the proximity of the
Stazione Termini (M31), the Piazza Esedra took on a
special role for the city. In 1867, de Merode donated
the adjoining grounds, up to the Via delle Quattro Fontane, for a new street. The city accepted the gift; however, it maintained a reserved attitude towards the
new traffic artery. Thus, rather arbitrary connections
with the existing street system resulted for the new
street and its cross roads. It was oriented axially towards the former Diocletian thermal baths (A46), i.e.,
towards Esedra and S. Maria degli Angeli (H42). And
following another donation by de Merode, it ran between the hills of Viminal and Quirinal up to the Via del
Boschetto. The buildings above the intersection with
Via delle Quattro Fontane remained private property
until the unification of Italy.

After Rome was declared the capital in 1870/71,
the first development plan that considered the entire
city was espoused by Alessandro Viviani in 1873. The
plan included the continuation of the street up to today's Via XXIV Maggio; it was to curve through the
Arco della Pilotta to the Fontana di Trevi (B126). From
there it would reach the Pantheon (A31) by way of the
Via del Corso. Contrary to this, today's course – from
the Area di Magnanapoli to the Piazza Venezia where
the street crosses Via del Corso – was decided upon
in 1876. The Area di Magnanapoli was framed by the
Trajan Forum (A29) and Torre delle Milizie (C35), a
medieval weir tower, in a way that the straight course
of the wide street leading directly into the centre had
to be interrupted. Additionally, the steep slope of the
Quirinal Hill had to be overcome. Therefore, the street
was directed in two tight curves through the already
developed historical city area to the Piazza Venezia.

The development of the new street dragged along.
For years several public buildings had been discussed, but, finally, the Palazzo delle Esposizioni
(K12), the Banca d'Italia (K13) and, in 1884, the Teatro
Drammatico Nazionale at the foot of the Quirinal Hill
(destroyed in 1929) were built. The latter offered a Historicist façade at the beginning of the Via Nazionale to
those coming from the centre. Other buildings such as
the Monumento Vittorio Emanuele II (K15) or the Parliament (K21) that had been provisionally planned

along the Via Nazionale were, in the end, built in different locations. Aside from the state's buildings, the course of the street is decorated by more modest buildings in various styles: the American Protestant St. Paul church by the British architect G. E. Street in a northern Italian Neo-Gothic style (1872–92), and the steel construction of the Teatro Eliseo, which was changed several times between 1905 and 1939, are both worth mentioning.

Large sections with parks from the old villas were preserved until the beginning of the 20C. However, there has never been a continuous plan for the Via Nazionale as a boulevard. IM

K10 Lungotevere

Lungotevere Testaccio to dell'acetosa acqua (plan I 1/B–2/C)
1871–85
Raffaele Canevari

Rome's cityscape is largely determined by the Tiber river, which was walled-in during the 19C. Being the main trade and supply route of the city, it had been limited by the numerous, uncoordinated buildings along its banks until 1871. Annual floods through the entire city were the result. From 1871 to 1875 a government commission discussed possible solutions to the problem and decided on Raffaele Canevari's project that proposed the erection of tall protective walls along the river which would cause the harbours and entire districts to disappear. Due to the priority given to technical and economic considerations, a development plan for the river front was never advanced.

High walls were erected on both sides of the river at a distance of c. 100 m; all kinds of buildings were eliminated from the Ponte Margherita to the Testaccio (K22). On the new, high banks, wide streets, the so-called Lungotevere, were built as traffic axes that were soon connected with new bridges and streets – for example, the Corso Vittorio Emanuele II (K11). Beneath them a canal system was designed to run parallel to the river as Rome's sewage disposal system. However, the connection with the historical street network and the housing quarters – approximately 5 m lower – was established for the most part via stairs.

The most striking new building at the Lungotevere inside the Aurelian Wall is Calderini's Palace of Justice from 1887 (K18). Beyond the Aurelian Wall, new administration and housing districts – Prati and Flaminia – were created along the Lungotevere. The redesign of the river and the extension of the city along its banks implied direct competition with the capitals on the Thames and the Seine. IM

K11 Corso Vittorio Emanuele II

(plan IV 1/B–2/B)
1873–1926
The Corso Vittorio Emanuele II is most likely the most important urban change of the 19C. It extended the

Via Nazionale (K9), leading from the Stazione Termini (M31) to the Piazza Venezia, up to the Tiber river. Contrary to the Via Nazionale, however, it was to cut through a densely populated area, the so-called knee of the Tiber, with a width of 20 m and thus opened it up for traffic. The creation of this relatively straight east-west axis and its connection to the north–south axis of the Via del Corso was the core of the urbanisation program from 1873 for the new capital. The cityscape was transformed by the expropriation and demolition of numerous buildings. The interest in a traffic vein was matched equally by the interest in the creation of a representative monument path along which important buildings of Italian and Roman history were to become visible.

The Corso Vittorio Emanuele II was built in three phases.

The first building phase, adjoining the existing Via del Plebiscito, led along the old Via Papalis from the Piazza del Gesù to the Piazza S. Andrea della Valle (1883). Adjacent to the façades of these Baroque churches (B1, B26), the »reconstruction« of the 80 m long façade of the Palazzo Vidoni-Caffarelli (H22) could be seen. New buildings had to fit as well as possible into a unified street image. Later on, the ensemble was disturbed by interventions during the Fascist period: excavations of the Area Sacra di Largo Argentina (A3) and the opening of the Corso Rinascimento tore large gaps into the rows of houses that had already been established.

The second phase (1884) led from S. Andrea della Valle to the Chiesa Nuova (B17). Here, the Palazzo Massimo alle Colonne (H24) on the right side of the street and, on the left, the Cancelleria (F19), »relieved« of its extensions, were preserved. In their immediate vicinity, the Palazzo Farnesina ai Baullari (H21) was isolated through clearing, creating an amorphous square on the opposite side and opening up the view towards the Palazzo Braschi and Valadier's façade of San Pantaleo (K2). Towards the west, the street departs from the old Via Papalis. Numerous buildings

K11 Corso Vittorio Emanuele II

K12 Palazzo delle Esposizioni delle Belle Arti

became its victims – most notable amongst the casualties, parts of the Palazzo Fieschi-Sora (H2).

During the third building phase (until 1888), the old square and the adjoining small buildings opposite the Chiesa Nuova were demolished. The Corso Vittorio Emanuele II now led past the church at an angle and towards the Tiber. Shortly before the end of the street, the Via Paola (named after its builder, Paul III) branches off to the right towards the Castel S. Angelo whereas S. Giovanni dei Fiorentini (B16) emerges on the left. The end point of the new street was decided upon only in 1926. The section leading directly to the Tiber and the new Vittorio Emanuele II bridge which ends in a square 60 m in diameter in the bend of the Tiber dates back to that time.

The Corso Vittorio Emanuele II is one example of »monument protection« in Italy at the end of the 19C: less important buildings were demolished; others, preserved. Aside from the complete »reconstruction«, the façade of a building along the street could be cut off and replaced with a »worthy« façade following the rules of symmetry (e. g. Palazzo Strozzi-Besso). Additionally, only one storey could be changed in order to integrate the façade into the general style of the street (for example, Palazzo Buffalo già Valle). The most important monuments, however, were isolated within the row of façades. IM

K12 Palazzo delle Esposizioni delle Belle Arti
Via Nazionale 194 (plan V 1/A)
1876–84
Pio Piacentini
The appearance of the Via Nazionale (K9) is determined up to this day by the Historicist Palazzo Esposizioni. It was the first public building of the new capital for which a competition was held (1876). The location had not yet been decided upon. Two exhibitions were to be held simultaneously on two storeys. In a second competition in 1877, Pio Piacentini was selected the winner from 74 contestants. The construction started only in 1880, and in 1883 the building was opened with a festive celebration.

The monumental structure was enthroned on a high base next to the early-Christian church S. Vitale and was originally surrounded by a large park. The façade is dominated by a huge triumphal arch, which also determines the height of the building's wings. They are decorated with Corinthian lesenes on the ground floor. The upper floor, with its smooth travertine-clad wall, recedes. The other sides of the building were decorated only with a row of flat blind arcades in order to avoid any competition with the front façade.

A classical vestibule provides the entrance to the interior from whence a wide staircase leads into a broad reception hall with a cupola; on either side of the hall, three large exhibition rooms – similar to side chapels on a church aisle – can be found. Towards the back, the building narrows. Following the middle axis, stairs lead to the upper floor where the spatial structure is repeated around the cupola. Roman Antique style elements are used inside and out – for example, columns or the coffered cupola. The claim of the new empire can already be seen in this first official building. IM

K13 Banco d'Italia
Via Nazionale, Via Mazzarino (plan V 1/B)
1882–92
Gaetano Koch
The main seat of the national bank erected at Via Nazionale (K9) has its origin in a competition to which the architects Gaetano Koch, Pio Piacentini and Fran-

K13 Banco d'Italia

cesco Azzurri were invited in 1882. Azzurri did not
submit a proposal. The management of the bank preferred Koch's functional layout of the rooms. Formally,
however, the bias leaned towards the project by Piacentini, the architect of the Palazzo Esposizione (K12)
across the street. Instead of initiating a collaboration
between both architects, the project by Gaetano Koch
was pursued after 1886. Starting in 1888, the building
was erected behind an original-scale wooden model
of the bank at the Via Nazionale.

The façade with 23 axes occupies a large section
of the Via Nazionale. The building has three storeys:
the rusticated base opened up by round arch windows, and two storeys that differ in their structures
(Ionic on the piano nobile, Corinthian on the third storey) and in the form of the continuous rows of windows. The windows of the piano nobile have round
gables; those on the third floor, triangular gables. The
seven-axis central section is framed by two three-axis
flat projections that appear fortified at the corners
through the use of columns. Thus, the appearance
was loosened up a bit. The centre section and the
projections are composed in like manner with a column order and are distinguished as the only block
within the façade by a common architrave with a
crowning balcony. Koch borrowed his stylistic vocabulary from the Palazzo Chigi-Odescalchi (B93) and from
Bernini's Louvre II façade thus initiating the Neo-Baroque style in Rome. IM

K14 Acquario
Piazza Manfredo Fanti (plan VI 1/B)
1884–87
Ettore Bernich

Modern metal architecture can be seen in a Historicist
form in the Roman Aquarium. In 1882 the municipal
building commission agreed to the building that had
been applied for by the industrialist Pietro Carganico
as an institute for fish breeding at Piazza Manfredo
Fanti. Started by the architect Bernich in 1884, the
Aquarium is one of the semi-public scientific institutions that were purposefully erected in direct conflict
with the clerical orientation of the city. Opened in 1887,
the building's utilisation was changed as early as
1890.

It is located in an archaeological landscape garden.
Two stairways lead to a portico that takes the form
of a monumental triumphal arch. One enters the oval
main tract through its middle niche with its huge
concha. Imperial Roman monuments are referred to
in the portico and main tract: the Constantine Arch
(A52) in the portico, the Colosseum's oval (A25) on
the exterior of the main tract, and the Pantheon (A31)
with the cupola in the Opaeum. The ashlar masonry
covering the metal skeleton on the exterior also points
to the antique Roman tradition with double columns
and rustication. The smooth pockets in the rustication
can be found in the antique Roman insula, as well
(cf. H22).

K15 Monumento Vittorio Emanuele II

The elliptic interior is designed in a different way:
here, a cast-iron column and cross-beam skeleton
supports galleries with traditional theatre loges and
showcases on four storeys. A twelve-cornered pyramid construction is inscribed into the peristyle columns; it is crowned by an elliptic lantern. Bernich enclosed the iron grid of this construction with coloured
glass. Although the latest technology was used, he
hardly developed new forms from it. IM

K15 Monumento Vittorio Emanuele II
Piazza Venezia (plan V 1/B)
1884–1927
Giuseppe Sacconi

Rome initiated an international competition for a monument dedicated to the first Italian king, Vittorio Emanuele II, in September 1878. From 300 proposals for
different types of monuments and origin, that of the
French architect Nenot was chosen. He suggested a
loggia architecture at Piazza Esedra (Piazza Repubblica, cf. K16 for its later design). However, this choice
caused a heated debate about the »national architectural style«. Thus, the preconditions were more precise for the second competition in 1882, and only Italian architects were invited. Above all, the Piazza
Venezia, the terminating point of the Via del Corso,
was declared the future site. Giuseppe Sacconi would
carry home the award in 1884 with a project in a
mixed Roman-Hellenistic style. It was to surpass in
size anything from the past and would outdo the
neighbouring stair complexes of Aracoeli (C36) and
the Capitol (H27).

Preliminary work began in 1885: the quarter at
the foot of the Capitol was demolished, including the
monastery buildings of Aracoeli, the viaduct by Pope
Paul III, churches, streets and numerous apartment
houses. In order to gain space, the hill was cut into.
The weak volcanic tuff base with its caves and galleries necessitated a widening of the monument.

In 1897 Sacconi extended his plans to the entire Piazza Venezia: an altar to the fatherland was to be integrated into the monument; the square should provide an honourable environment. Upon Sacconi's death (1905), however, further buildings needed to be demolished for this purpose: in 1906/07 the Palazzo Torlonia, erected in the early 19C, and an entire block at the old Piazza Venezia were torn down. In 1910/11, the Palazzetto Venezia was moved to the other side of the Palazzo Venezia (see F5). Finally, in 1911 the monumental equestrian statue for Vittorio Emanuele II was erected, and, though unfinished, the monument was inaugurated. The fatherland altar at the foot of the equestrian statue was added in 1921, but the work on the building was finished only in 1925–27.

For Rome, the erection of the Monumento Vittorio Emanuele II may represent the addition of a huge, non-functional structure with pretensions that go beyond the monument itself. On the other hand, a mostly medieval quarter was destroyed and the historical centre completely changed. Also, the cityscape received a new and not always beloved emphasis inasmuch as the monument can be seen from almost any location.

Whereas the Piazza Venezia was a small square prior to this intervention, framed by the Palazzo and Palazzetto Venezia and not oriented towards the Via del Corso, it now had been expanded to such an extent that the Corso approached its centre and the monument at its end. On the side opposite the Palazzo Venezia, the termination is formed by the Palazzo delle Assicurazioni Generali, a new structure erected in lieu of the Palazzo Torlonia following Sacconi's plans; it was conceived as a counterpart to the Palazzo Venezia, providing the square with a seemingly symmetrical layout.

The Neo-Baroque monument, which bears a resemblance to large Baroque palaces (see p. 168), rises to a height of 70 m across (and even 81 m with the superstructures on top) and 200 m wide at the end of Piazza Venezia. A wide, softly ascending staircase leads to a double-level terrace with a semicircular front termination; it forms the foundation for the monument rising behind it: a slightly concave columned walk (portico) terminated on its sides by small temple fronts rests on a wide base. The forms are derived from Hellenistic representational or market buildings that could also be found on Roman forums.

A semicircular podium, accessible via lateral staircases, rises up on the terrace in front of this high portico; its front is decorated with a rich, fully sculpted relief and in the centre with a Roma statue. In the centre of the podium, the bronze equestrian statue of Vittorio Emanuele II is enthroned on a high base, similar to the equestrian statue of Marcus Aurelius on the neighbouring Capitol. The ensemble is completed with an altar table (the fatherland altar) with the grave of the unknown soldier.

The sculptural program is directed towards Rome, the Italian Empire as the fatherland, and towards those who died in its honour. It is completed by the quadrigae – symbols of the unity and freedom of Italy – galloping forward atop the small temples on the sides. The marble in the monument hints on one hand at Emperor Augustus's Rome, who created the only comparable monument, the Ara Pacis (A18); on the other hand, it hints at Greece, which was the first European country to revolt in a modern fight for freedom. The architectural language refers to Hellenistic-Roman forms and, through its exaggerated monumentality, is supposed to express the new Empire. In this case, antique architectural forms were adopted not only in a formal sense but also for their contextual expression, and they were used purposefully. IM

K16 Piazza Esedra
Piazza della Repubblica (plan V 2/A)
1886–1913
Gaetano Koch

A project by the architect Nicola Moraldi dealt with the redesign of the Piazza Esedra (today's Piazza della Repubblica) as far back as 1862: the antique aqueduct of the Aqua Marcia, restored under Pope Pius IX and leading to the church of S. Maria degli Angeli (H42), was to find a magnificent termination in a sculpted fountain. When Italy was unified in 1870/71 and Rome became its capital, the square's importance as an entrance to the city increased due to its vicinity to the Termini station (M31) and its position at the head of Via Nazionale (K9).

After the construction work for the Via Nazionale had begun, Gaetano Koch received the order for the redesign of the square in 1886. The basis for his plans were the semicircular foundations of the huge exedrae of the Diocletian thermal baths (A46). Their large, rounded shapes offered themselves as a backdrop for the new function of the monumental city gate to the same extent as they had been used by various archi-

K16 Piazza Esedra

tects in the past as a representative location for their projects on the monument for King Vittorio Emanuele II (K15).

Between 1886 and 1890 Koch reconstructed the form of the exedrae with two wings on both sides of the Via Nazionale, symmetrically framing the semicircle of the square. Straight wings branching off the square at a right angle lead to the Via S. Susanna and towards the station.

The different tracts, with their Historicist façades and a continuous deep arcade portico, form pavilion-like projections with ornate segmented gables decorated with sculptures at the end points and joints. Additionally, the straight wings were each structured with central projections (similar to Bernini's Louvre II project). The basic construction follows a fundamental Baroque principle of organisation for extremely long buildings; the overall impression of the ensemble can therefore be considered Neo-Baroque. The edges of the pavilions seem to be strengthened by alternating pilasters and columns, and hermae replace the columns on the upper storey. The arcades with the tabularium motif follow the example of the national archives at the Capitol (A9). Above them, a piano nobile – upgraded by an Ionic pilaster order – rises up. The pilasters unite a continuous row of windows with segmented gables and mezzanine. On the short fourth storey, inornate windows alternate with pilasters. The Colosseum was the model for the superposition of the structure (A25).

On the opposite side of the square, the ruins of the Diocletian thermal baths with the façade of S. Maria degli Angeli face this complex; together, they form a magnificent perspective for the Via Nazionale termi-

nating at this site. Moraldi's unfinished four-tiered fountain with its central jet of water in the middle of the square was completed in 1911 with the addition of sculptures by Mario Rutelli at the occasion of the International Exposition in Rome. The choice of a circular form for the square and fountain proved practical over time. On the square, the traffic coming from the station could be smoothly directed into the new axes of modern Rome: the Via Nazionale and the Via S. Susanna. State visitors could reach the most important sites of the capital in a direct way. IM

K17 La Rinascente
Via del Corso/Largo Chigi (plan IV 2/A)
1887
Giulio de Angelis

The La Rinascente department store (formerly Alle Città d'Italia) is located on a property at Via del Corso that had become vacant when old buildings were demolished to make way for the extension of the Via del Tritone. The owners, the Bocconi brothers, held an architectural competition in 1885 that was won by de Angelis. In 1886 his project was approved by the city by virtue of the new function it would bring to Rome, even though it exceeded the permissible height.

The store was erected as a steel skeleton construction above a trapezoid ground plan. Its formal language remains historicising (partly Romanesque, partly Renaissance). Four identically structured façades are resolved into struts and glass between enormous corner pilasters, so that the interior organisation can hardly be guessed. Like a loggia, three large window arches stretch across the rusticated base and the storeys above, united through massive pilasters and heavy entablatures. The upper storeys with their connected window groups are structured by massive pilasters as well.

The interior is divided into four levels; the ceiling heights reduce towards the top. They are supported by two iron peristyle columns arranged around an octagonal glass-covered central court. The décor of the columns becomes simpler towards the top. Aside from the large window surfaces, the glass roof ensures the lighting of the sales rooms that open towards the yard. De Angeli's department store (although the formal language is less progressive) stands in the tradition of Sédille's Magazins du Printemps and Blondel's Belle Jardinière in Paris. In Italy, however, it is a forerunner of the steel skeleton architecture. IM

K18 Palazzo della Giustizia
Piazza Cavour/Lungotevere Prati (plan IV 1/A)
1887–1911
Guglielmo Calderini

With its mixed styles, the Palazzo della Giustizia was a unique object even in the eclectic Rome of the early 20C. This prestigious building of the new capital had already been planned in 1874. In 1880, Guglielmo Calderini received the order as a result of a competition;

K17 La Rinascente

K18 Palazzo della Giustizia

however, given the discussion about the so-called »national style«, he completed the final design only in 1887.

The building is modelled upon the Brussels Palace of Justice by Poelart. The Palazzo rises up with its 30 court halls, huge inner courtyards and staircases above a rectangular ground plan of 165 x 150 m. The façades at the newly created Piazza Cavour and towards the Tiber river display a three-storey central building structured by middle and corner projections, adjoined by two-storey wings that appear to be strengthened at the corners by projections. Following the Mannerist Palazzo Pitti of Florence, the whole building, including the columns, is covered with rustication (except for the upper storey) as were many residences and palaces of justice of the late 19C. The overall impression is determined by an overwhelming décor utilising the formal language of the Renaissance and Baroque as well as oriental stylistic elements.

In the central axis, two yards separate the wings containing meeting rooms and offices that are connected by long hallways and galleries. The large yard behind the Tiber façade owes its debt directly to the Colosseum (A25) with the superposition of the rows of arcades and the use of the Tabularium motif. This typical mixture of styles is repeated in every detail on the inside. IM

K19 Villino Ximenes
Via Cornelio Celso (plan IX 1/B)
1900
Ernesto Basile, Leonardo Paterna Baldizzi, Ettore Ximenes

The Villino of the sculptor Ettore Ximenes in the Nomentano quarter is one of Rome's most important Art Nouveau buildings. It was built in 1900 by the architects Ernesto Basile and Leonardo Paterna Baldizzi according to the sculptor's ideas. It stands isolated within Basile's œuvre of mostly Classicist buildings (Villino Rudini) and the pompous parliament building (K21).

The two-storey building stands as a block in a large garden. A white, archaic, figurative frieze horizontally divides the five-axis reddish tuff façade. As a playful contrast, the round arches of the upper row of windows with their bluish-green ceramic ornaments rest atop the frieze. The central axis is enhanced with a larger rounded arch displaying figurative scenes. The castle-like building is crowned with a richly ornate balustrade with plant motifs; behind it rises a grotesque chimney.

On the L-shaped ground plan, the living spaces on the first floor and the private rooms on the second floor are arranged around a covered statue gallery spanning two-storeys and accessible through a richly decorated vestibule. A third wing completes the U-shaped floor plan at the Via Cornelio Celso. This extension was most likely made by Ximenes himself. Decorated with a horseshoe-gate and female figures, this wing houses a studio and the chapel.

The Villino style used here, a mix between the city villa and bourgeois single-family home, was subject to heated debates around the turn of the century and can mainly be found in the new decentralised residential areas. The statue gallery and rich decoration, however, place this building into the tradition of artist's houses. IM

K20 Sinagoga
Lungotevere dei Cenci (plan IV 2/B)
1901–08
Osvaldo Armanni, Vincenzo Costa

Rome's Jewish population, disadvantaged for centuries, had finally won a new self-consciousness in the united Italy; this is made apparent in the synagogue. In 1880, the city decided on the destruction of the Ghetto between the Teatro di Marcello (A17) and the Tiber in order to reconstruct it in a new form. The grounds were levelled between 1885 and 1887. In 1897 the city sold a tract at Lungotevere Cenci to the Israelite University for the erection of a synagogue. The architects Armanni and Costa, who had won two

K19 Villino Ximenes

competitions, received the building order in 1900. After its opening in 1904 the old cultic buildings, the Cinque Scole, were destroyed in 1908.

The building was erected on two storeys above the ground plan of a Greek cross and was vaulted with a four-part aluminium cupola above a square tambour. The four façades received individual designs: on the western arm, a two-storey columned portico crowned by a triangular gable forms the main entrance. The other façades open up into multiple-storey loggias with decorative Assyrian-Babylonian elements.

A vestibule leads from the portico into the high, cross-shaped prayer hall. Columns and pilasters support the women's gallery on the north, south and west arms. On the east arm, the Torah and reading desk are located in a large aedicula. The orientation of the building – towards the east – is borrowed from the Roman-Christian churches; the building type is derived from the Byzantine cross cupola churches. Like the latter, the Assyrian and Egyptian decorative elements hint at eastern religions. The mixture of all these elements shows that the synagogue is a product of the eclecticism around the turn of the century. IM

K21 Camera dei Deputati
Piazza del Parlamento (plan IV 2/A)
1902–27
Ernesto Basile

Between 1883 and 1897 the competition for the Parliament was held as one of the last big architectural competitions of the young capital. At first, the Area di Magnanapoli at the new Via Nazionale (K9) was the intended site; however, in 1904–27 Basile's Parliament

K20 Sinagoga

K21 Camera dei Deputati

building was realised as an extension to Bernini's Palazzo Montecitorio (B72) at Piazza Montecitorio.

A four-tower complex reaching across three storeys in the connecting sections and erected on a square ground plan adjoins the back of the Baroque palace. At the corners, the towers jut out like projections. The design is oriented towards Sicilian-Norman buildings. Whereas the base zone is rusticated on all sides, the main façade of the extension located towards the back is structured by a pilaster order on the upper floors stretching across multiple storeys. The windows are framed with travertine and decoratively stand out from the red brick walls. Triple windows on the upper floor beneath the entablature of the large order have the effect of a frieze and already express the spirit of the strip windows of the emerging international style. The battlements on the towers are decorated with reliefs. The ornamental structure of the exterior shows Basile's joy in new forms – above all, in Art Nouveau (cf. also K19).

Inside, the rooms are grouped around the parliament hall that extends through all storeys. The rear walls of the balconies are structured by arcades with a large order in the form of the antique tabularium motif (see A9). Above is a gallery. Bernini's Baroque palace shows the same structural form; it is, at the same time, as wide and as high as the parliament hall and appears as the monumental entree to the Parliament. IM

K22 Quartiere Testaccio
Lungotevere Testaccio (plan VII 1/B)
begun 1886, 1903–17
Società Artistica Operaia, Giulio Magni (ICP)

Testaccio, the working-class district at the bank of the Tiber facing the city, was one of the earliest extensions of Italy's new capital. The housing for the workers had been planned here since 1872. Beginning in 1886, the Società Artistica Operaia built the first housing complexes in the quarter reaching to the basilica of S. Paolo fuori le Mura (C2). After a period of degradation, the Istituto Case Popolari (ICP), founded in 1903, received the order to develop the quarter after the first decade of the 20C. Under Giulio Magni's guidance, eleven blocks with 30 houses were realised by 1913, a total of 930 apartments. In 1917, the quarter received a more bourgeois appearance under the direction of the architects Quadrio Pirani and Camillo Pistrucci.

The Società Artistica Operaia had only built small complexes. They consisted of separate houses divided by gardens and yards. Contrary to this, Giulio Magni had to abandon the single-family home type due to the explosion in the population and was forced to move towards multi-storey rental blocks with open inner courtyards. The set-back façades are decorated with simplified Historicist forms. The equally rated first floor replaces the base floor. Enhancing the centre also wouldn't have made much sense in a housing block of this sort. Thus, the classical organisation was abandoned (but the horizontal structure was preserved). Rustication and cantilevered terminal ledges are the few decorative elements that were retained. Next to the apartments, public facilities were built – for example, baths, meeting rooms, washing and ironing houses. The appearance of the Testaccio, determined by economic necessities, is a typical example of Rome's working class districts of that period.
IM

K23 Museo d'Arte Moderna
Viale delle Belle Arti (plan II 1/C)
1908–11
Cesare Bazzani
Today, beside the Accademia die Gran Bretagna (K25) only the Museo d'Arte Moderna reminds us of the 1911 International Art Exposition in Rome. In 1908 six architects were invited to a competition concerning a palace for the fine arts in the Valle Giulia. After the exposition, the palace was to house the National Gallery

K22 Quartiere Testaccio

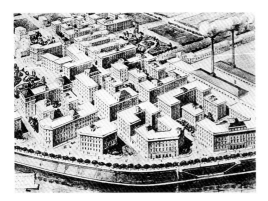

K23 Museo d'Arte Moderna

for Modern Art. The size of the building and the number of rooms were predetermined. In 1909 a commission consisting of architects and sculptors awarded a special prize to Marcello Piacentini; however, Cesare Bazzani received the commission and realised the building in 1910/11.

The building rises up from a high base in a strict symmetrical order above a wide, cruciform ground plan. The façade is staggered: in the centre, a pronaos with Corinthian column pairs projects out, laterally adjoined by wings with prominent corner pavilions. Flat lesenes and a figurative frieze structure the walls of the wings. Beneath the wide entrance staircase, the carriage drive provides direct access to the gallery.

Through a vestibule one enters a central hall on the central axis, adjoined laterally by inner courtyards. It's distinguished only by columns from a deambulatory that continues on into the large, transversely placed exhibition hall. Here, the side wings adjoin, each consisting of a central exhibition room with a loggia architecture opening up towards the outside, with three smaller rooms adjoining on both sides of each exhibition room. The skeleton steel construction, known since the 80s, allowed for all exhibition rooms to be closed off with glass roofs. Semicircular terraces on the side wings lead into a park that was to feature an outdoor sculpture garden. IM

K24 Galleria Colonna
Piazza Colonna (plan IV 2/A)
1909–22
Dario Carbone
Due to Mengoni's contemplation of the continuation of the Via Nazionale (K9), which was under construction and would continue across the Piazza di Trevi and Piazza Colonna to the Pantheon (A31), the area around Piazza Colonna became the centre of attention. Around 1873, Mengoni wanted to provide the square with a completely new look and showcase the monuments along the street. When a different course was decided for the Via Nazionale, a municipal master

plan for the historic centre of Rome was submitted in 1882. Since measures for a new organisation of traffic urgently needed to be initiated, it included, among others, the widening of via del Corso (the antique Via Lata) and the extension of Via del Tritone (as a connection to the station) from the Piazza Claudio to the Corso. This required a wider junction into the Corso. Property seizures and the demolition of the Palazzo Piombino at the narrow eastern side of the square opposite Palazzo Wedekind (K4) on the other side of the Corso created the necessary space for the sophisticated projects pertaining to the redesign of Piazza Colonna.

Thus, a new centre of society and commerce was to be developed for the capital's bourgeoisie. The plan for a large, glass-covered gallery, following Milan's example, tried to meet with this intent. Public competitions with all of Rome's leading architects participating placed the project into the centre of attention but also precluded a quick decision.

The large-scale projects at first referred to the entire area between the Piazza Colonna and Piazza di Trevi on the one hand, and to the Piazza Poli on the other, with the new Via del Tritone as a lateral termination. However, when an appropriate project by Antonio Petrignani was accepted in 1898, the public disapproved of it. They demanded a Historicist architecture because only this would grant a harmonic integration into the existing architecture of Rome. In 1909/10, the decision finally went in favour of a project by Dario Carbone with the added requirement to adapt the building to »the simple lines of the cinquecento«. A temporary wood and steel pavilion by the architects Pio and Marcello Piacentini occupied the site of the planned new structure from 1911–14. The construction of the gallery was begun only in 1916, and it was finished in 1922.

Compared to the first projects, Carboni's structure was much more modest. The gallery takes up only a quarter of the surface than had first been planned. It stretches from Piazza Colonna along the extended Via del Tritone to the corner of Via S. Maria on a rectangular ground plan; it is terminated on the other side by the Via dei Sabini. Within the building, the gallery forms a triangular ray with exits to Piazza Colonna and the corners of the rear façade.

The main façade faced with imitation travertine widens symmetrically at the narrow eastern side of the Piazza Colonna with the column of Marcus Aurelius (A38) in its front. The building has a staggered design. The actual front with the entrance area, whose width is even with the square, is formed by a three-axis central projection with five-axis wings structured according to the scheme of Palazzo Farnese (H25). Further wing tracts with an according structure exceed the alignment of the square to the right and left and recede behind the central tract. Double pilasters strengthen the edges of the separate tracts. The first floor of the main front is designed as a wide columned portico. The entrance to the gallery is enhanced by thick, rusticated columns. On the upper storey of the central projection, the large, rounded arch windows stretching across two storeys and unified through a large-scale Corinthian order bring the nearby Palazzo Barberini (B45) to mind.

A columned portico leads into the hallways of the gallery, which radiate out from it. It reaches up into the upper storey and is covered by a glass roof. The rich ornamentation is structured by pilaster orders placed atop one another. Here, the separate stores and cafés of the young capital's new citizens' centre found their location. IM

K25 Accademia di Gran Bretagna
Via A. Gramsci (plan II 1/C)
1911–13
Edwin Lutyens

At the occasion of the International Art Exposition in 1911, Edwin Lutyens erected the British Pavilion. Following the exposition, it was reconstructed in 1913 at the same site as the seat of the British Academy in a permanent, hardly changed form with an extended back section. Aside from the Museum for Modern and Contemporary Art (K23), it is the only preserved building from the 1911 International Exposition.

On the façade, Lutyens refers to architectural principles typical for the country – similar to many other designers of exposition structures. A broad flight of steps leads to a pronaos in the centre of the façade , representing an almost literal repetition of the upper part of Sir Christopher Wren's St. Paul's Cathedral façade in London from the 17C with the four Corinthian column pairs and the triangular gable. Two corner pavilions terminate the wings on a high base, structured by Corinthian pilasters and aediculae. The rear façade is designed in a similar manner. Both façade tracts are connected through a multiple-wing two-storey building that is erected on an H-shaped ground plan in the rustic country home style of Victorian England and leaves enough space for two transverse inner courtyards. The combination of the »high« – i. e. historicising – and the rural regional style

K25 Accademia di Gran Bretagna

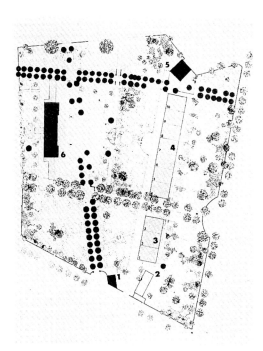

K26 Villa Massimo

is typical for the entire building. The arbitrariness of the architectural references is typical for many architects of the late 19C and early 20C. However, Lutyen's building remains much less theatrical than many other exposition structures, even in its one great reference. IM

K26 Villa Massimo

Largo Villa Massimo 2 (plan IX 2/A)
1911–14
Max Zürcher

The German Academy in the Villa Massimo has its origins in the donation from the Berlin industrial magnate Eduard Arnhold, who in 1910 had bought a tract outside Porta Pia (today: Largo Villa Massimo) from Prince Massimo. In the park, the architect Max Zürcher created a main building and ten adjoining studio buildings between 1911 and 1914. After the expropriation during the wars, the estate came back into German hands in 1956.

The main building and the studio tract running almost parallel are set off by a terrace, a roundel and a fountain. Two avenues with a north–south orientation connect the main and the studio tracts with one of the avenues separating three of the studios from the others.

The two-storey Historicist main building adapts elements from the Tuscany villa. The centre of the strictly symmetrical entrance façade is accentuated by a portal framed with niches and ashlars. It is structured vertically by rusticated columns and horizontally by a continuous double ledge and an inscribed frieze beneath the entablature, alluding to the structural scheme of Villa Giulia (H35). The central axis and corners are accentuated with triple windows in the form of a loggia on the upper storey. Arcades adjoining the façade laterally support a terrace decorated with statues. Inside, three studios and the director's apartment are grouped around a central hall used for festivities and exhibitions.

The decision in favour of a decentralised design of the complex, its modern asymmetry and oblique angles followed contemporary artists' houses in Germany and deliberately abandoned the idea of taking up residence in a historic building (like other academies in Rome, for example, the Villa Medici, B4). IM

K27 Cinema Teatro Corso

Piazza San Lorenzo in Lucina (plan IV 2/A)
1915–17
Marcello Piacentini, Giorgio Venter-Marini

Marcello Piacentini, the architect of the Cinema Teatro (today Cinema Etoile) at Piazza S. Lorenzo in Lucina, dedicated in 1917, had come under the direct influence of the Vienna Secession because of Giorgio Venter-Marini. The façade of the theatre, built in the »style of the Austrian enemy«, had to be changed at Piacentini's own expense given the polemic criticism of the Roman bourgeoisie. The stucco was taken down and replaced with simple reliefs by Alfredo Biagini; the interior decoration was considerably reduced.

Before this change, the façade did without any Classicist structure. The »axes« and storey structures were obscured: the entrance zone consisted of six rectangular portals that left wide white wall compartments open in between. The smooth white architrave was superimposed by a narrow cantilevered glass roof visibly linked to the wall with iron chains. It separated the semicircular windows from the four central portals. Polygonal oriels, so-called bay windows, projected above the outer portals, and, above them, the building receded. The box-like central section of the façade was broken up by four windows that seemed to be hung from a freely floating ledge. A rich stucco decoration with rocaille forms and theatre masks framed the windows. Their plant-like forms enhanced the impression of melting forms and lines.

The rectangular building was cut off at an angle by the façade that had to follow the alignment of the square. In fact, and contrary to any assumptions, there is no symmetrical space behind the façade, but an asymmetrically cut trapezoidal vestibule which mediates into the 1300 seat auditorium. The form of the hall, which widens towards the back, was determined strictly according to the visual axes approaching the stage. The seats along the edge are raised. The ceiling, covered with flowing and dripping stucco forms, terminates the hall in the form of a cupola towards the

K27 Cinema Teatro Corso

top. It is divided horizontally by an undulating balcony overhanging deeply into the hall. The interior lacks any right angles and receives a cave-like character beneath the flatly vaulted ceiling. The functionality, the play of the flowing forms, and the strongly plant-like but more orthogonally disciplined forms on the exterior make the theatre the most important Art Nouveau or Secession building in Rome – despite the conversions and changes. IM

K28 Casa d'Arte Bragaglia with Teatro degli Independenti
Via degli Avignonesi (plan V 1/A)
1921/22
Virgilio Marchi

The Futurist Giulio Bragaglia's Casa d'Arte was Rome's only important Futurist building and most likely was one of the most peculiar structures of the Eternal City. Walls of the so-called Septimius Severus Thermal Baths were discovered during excavations between the foundations of Palazzo Tittoni in Via degli Avignonesi. They inspired Bragaglia to move his »Casa d'Arte« – a meeting place of Italian and international avant-garde artists – from the Via Condotti into the subterranean ruins of the bath. He was able to secure Virgilio Marchi, who designed five exhibition spaces, a small theatre and a so-called »American Bar«, to make the architectural changes. Marchi preserved the antique walls of the thermal bath, and their labyrinth design inspired the artists in charge of the interior decoration: the side walls of a steep and narrow entrance stairway were made more dynamic with highly abstract flames rising from the floor. The ceiling was covered with colourfully painted fabrics and lit by Bergaglia from above. He thus provided the whole space with a dynamic element. A similar proce-

dure was applied to the exhibition spaces. The theatre hall was located in the vaulted pool hall of the ancient bath. The massive column in its centre was preserved and provided the space with a cave-like character. Marchi hung a balcony with a cast-iron volute-decorated railing between the column and the termini of the vault. Thus, he created the space for 200 seats. The balcony was opened in the back, with labyrinthine hallways leading towards the lobby.

The bar area underwent the strongest changes: it received an inner shell made of cement on iron supports, and the floor was covered with asphalt. The cement wall continued around the corners and through all irregularities of the labyrinthine complex. As the material can be freely shaped, the walls were visually structured with folds and spirals. Again, Marchi used the play of light and achieved a synergetic-dynamic effect. The expressive spatial forms were responsible for the architecture's almost futuristic sculptural expression. The Casa d'Arte could, however, be compared with contemporary Expressionist buildings in Germany, such as the restaurant of the Theater Scala in Berlin by Walter Würzbach and Rudolf Belling. For the first time, an international influence thus re-emerged in Rome's architecture. The theatre was closed only a few years later. Today, only the antique ruins and old photographs remain to remind us of the fascinating building. IM

Modernism

The architecture of Rationalism and Fascism (M1 to M29)

Historical forms were a defining element in Rome for a long time. But then in the second half of the twenties important and radical changes set in. In 1928 MIAR, Italy's movement promoting Rationalist architecture (Movimento Italiano per l'Architettura Razionale), founded in Milan in 1926 (as the so-called Gruppo 7), held its first exhibition in Rome. This was about – at least in terms of how the buildings look – the Italian parallel movement to those that were happening mainly in Germany, France and the Netherlands in the 20s as the so-called International Style, developing a genuinely modern formal language, i. e. one that was committed to the industrial age. In Germany its most important exponents worked at the Bauhaus. Hitchcock and Johnson were later to identify three characteristic features – for the exhibition in the New York Museum of Modern Art (1932), which helped make the style to make a breakthrough: liberation from (historical) decoration in favour of pure, smooth, usually white forms, for which the model was the beauty and functional quality of the machine; floating volumes, which took over from rigid, heavy walls (see M33); and asymmetry, which replaced the (inflexible) order of symmetry. MIAR followed this in principle as well. It too forbade historical decoration; floating volumes are to be found in various places in the Rationalist buildings, though it is admittedly rare to find pilotis, the supports used by Le Corbusier to lift buildings off the ground; and asymmetry developed as a specific order, derived from the requirements of a particular building, is a possibility rather than a rule outside Italy as well; there is scarcely an Italian building on which it is demonstrated so compellingly as Moretti's Casa della Gioventù (M18). But Italian Rationalism always had an additional side that was almost always neglected in the International Style, at least in the treatises: an awareness that Modern architecture is also part of a long and exciting line of architectural tradition (the »ricorso arcaico«) and has to use this to find types for new kinds of building.

Between 1926 and 1928 developments took place also outside the MIAR which were fundamental for Rome and its architectural policy in particular. This involves those who commissioned most buildings in the period under discussion here, the Fascist regime. Mussolini made his most important speech on architectural matters on 26 May 1927, with the postulate: let us depopulate the cities. And in fact in the thirties an urban development trend that is typical of the 20th century did start: satellite towns began to be built – in Latium: Sabaudia, Pontinia and – with a different aim – E 42 (M24). But Rome also started to expand into the country, especially towards the sea (Ostia), as had been required by the Duce (M24). The other ma-

jor Fascist projects were also almost all realized outside the ancient Roman Aurelian Wall (A44), outside which there had scarcely been any building before. This goes for the Foro Mussolini (M5) and equally for the University (M9). And as well as this Piccinato in particular developed town planning into planning for the country as a whole (infrastructure, economic centres etc.); this development concluded with the formulation of planning guidelines and instruments in the 1942 act. But above all 1928 was a turning-point for the two central building tasks of the period: the Foro Mussolini (M5) was the first of a series of propaganda buildings; even at this stage we can see Fascism's preference for (mainly Roman) antiquity, and here above all the tradition of the grammar schools and the sporting competition. A copy of an ancient circus was built in the Stadio dei Marmi (M12). Mussolini saw himself as a modern Augustus (cf. M22). Thus not only was the Ara Pacis (A18) revealed, but a series of other ancient monuments, for example the Theatre of Marcellus (A17) and the Colosseum (A25), and a magnificent boulevard, the Via dei Fori Imperiali, was built through the heart of the ancient city. Pioneering developments also took place in social housing – like the Nazis the Italian Fascists also saw the masses as central objects of their (welfare) policy. In 1928 the foundations were laid for social housing in the modern sense, in which the state takes over part of the cost from the owners (cf. M11). In these years the Garbatella district (M2) also saw such projects realized on a hitherto unknown scale. These buildings also show that other architects as well – for example Sabbatini, Capponi and Aschieri (M3, M4, M8, M10) – did not start to build with a specifically Fascist or Rationalist approach, in other words did not subscribe unreservedly to the most recent trends, but almost completely abandoned historical decoration. In the Garbatella district in particular a shift away from the ideal of a garden city that was still built in Barocchetto forms can clearly be seen and that still (as an ideal) was based in the Utopian values of social urban development in England in the late 19th century (cf. also K22), towards a formal language that was already fundamentally undecorated and seemed Modern in its sparseness. And so in 1928 the specifically Modern movement appeared in Rome for the first time, and even the traditionalists moved some way in this direction and the ruling regime had fixed its direction in terms of urban development.

A first period, lasting until about 1936, is marked by a juxtaposition of Rationalism and Traditionalism. Here the Modern tendency – unlike Germany, from which architects emigrated (M20) – was definitely promoted by the regime and conversely frequently saw itself in harmony with the regime and its belief in the future. (M11). The two buildings that most strongly embodied the dynamic, progressive fanaticism of Futurism (M11, M13) were perceived by their architects entirely as expressing the ideals of Fascism. Traditionalist tendencies were rather harder to grasp in stylistic terms than in other countries in the thirties. There certainly were buildings that were linked with the block-like ponderousness of late Secession architecture, and thus followed the mainstream of the thirties in Europe (cf. M9). But most of the more traditional buildings clearly show that profound connection with the Roman and Italian past that is a key theme in all Italian architecture, even in the 20th century. In this world of thinking there is also a completely convincing development of combinations like that of deep cavity, arcade and Travertine (M4) that were later to be among the chief characteristics of the principal Fascist buildings. At this time Piacentini developed the so-called Stile Littorio (cf. M9). This was based – as can be seen from the heavy drama of many of his works (for example M1, M6) – on a programme propagating a return to the grandeur of ancient Rome, published by Piacenti in 1925 under the eloquent title »La Grande Roma«, and committed to the so-called Scuola Romana. Piacenti and del Debbio were protagonists of this school, which devoted itself with particular conviction to that search for a genuine Roman style, »romanità«, that is common to all Roman trends in the 20s. Cohabitation had an even stronger effect on Rationalism, which took on specifically Roman traits at the same time. In the long term Modern architecture, whose central moral thrust was certainly democratic and which thus was denigrated by its opponents as »egalitarian style« (Giunta, 20 May 1934), could not build for the regime without undergoing a profound change. In projects for propaganda buildings in particular there was soon a preponderance of pure forms as opposed to function and content, and this cult of form completely suited Fascist ideology. This is particularly true of the greatest talent, Terragni, for example his Casa del Fascio in Como or the Danteum project in Rome, and it is also true of the marble delights of an architect like Moretti in Rome, who obviously catered for the dominant tastes of the regime (M17). These buildings captivate because of their Rationalist values, above all through unusual spatial continuums and fascinatingly soft and surprising lighting effects. But they are already very smooth, they lack the hardness of Modernism, in the worst case they even take on something of the rhetoric that informs purely Fascist buildings. It is also typical that in important Modern buildings the ratio of closed wall to ribbon windows increasingly shifted to the disadvantage of the openings (M17, M25) – entirely in the spirit of the Fascist preference for stone. Finally, in 1942, even realized buildings by the leading Modernists, Libera, for example, are scarcely distinguishable from the uniform Fascist style (M25). And it was precisely this that Pagano denounced even more bitterly than the results of the relevant competitions. He was the editor of Casabella, the magazine of the Modern movement, and pointed out more clearly than anyone else that this architecture was ultimately based on a morally reprehensible social form. It is only when looking a second time at Libera's Congress Palace (M25) that one can see the same felicitous combination of the elemental forms of architectural history and the leading ideas and techniques of Modernism, as in his post office building for the Aventino district (M15). In fact the best Modern buildings, especially in Rome, were to be functional buildings, in particular the three post offices of 1932–35 (M14, M16), the station in Florence and also some housing. Here the Roman architects set off on a path of their own. Central Roman values were (also) (re-)discovered for Modernism: above all depth of wall, classical Roman gravitas (for instance A31) which is rediscovered in Modern diction (M20, M29, M23 project) and the energy made visible of architecture in which it appears as though an inner energy is forcing its way out and thus forming the external building (M14, M21; cf. H31). It becomes clear that the pure vocabulary of Rationalism, sharply defined, white, and emphasizing form (also because of the polemics of the Scuola Romana) never completely gained a foothold in Rome. Heavy materials that were closer to nature were always included, there was an inclination towards massive walls, towards things that were mixed and expressive, the last above all in the work of Ridolfi. He was the key figure who was to survive the war (artistically as well; M14). And he was also closest to the International Style if not purely in terms of vocabulary, but of the democratic ideal, in that he, unlike the Rationalists, never detached form from function and rejected any hollow drama.

After the conquest of Abyssinia and the subsequent declaration of empire (9 May 1936) a megalomaniac rhetoric dressed up as classicism established itself as the exclusive expressive form. The regime became increasingly aggressive towards rationalist tendencies; the great ancient Roman past became the only model. Even before 1936 prestigious commissions tended to be managed by representatives of the Scuola Romana. Thus Piacenti was responsible for planning the entire university project (1932 to 1935, M9) – and the same is true of the 1942 World Fair, E 42 (M24), after 1936. Similar though they may be in their general layout, especially in their balance of mass and symmetry, and however much the main buildings in each case (in the case of the university by Piacenti himself) have in common, the other buildings are equally different in their appearance. In the university complex these buildings show a wide range of seemingly very Modern solutions, but E 42 has a much more uniform, somewhat stereotypical language that is much more melodramatic and hollow throughout. The transition from diversity (including Modern solutions) to Fascist unity shows in the planning history of this complex: the first draft was still proposing point high-rise buildings with an entirely Modern formal language (in glass and steel), lining on a large highway. The same development within a single project can also be seen in the case of the Palazzo del Littorio. The first competition produced a »stroke of genius« on the subject of «Classicism in Modern diction«, but the second led to a uniform Fascist building (M23). The best work by the opposition – by Ridolfi and Piccinato – was produced by withdrawing to the private sphere in this period (M21, M29). These works in particular are also those that show particularly clearly how much Rome had distanced itself from pure Rationalism – which seemed contaminated by its long liaison with the regime. Here preparations were already being made for organic and Neo-Realistic architecture.

One and a half decades of post-war architecture (M30–M49)

Just one year after the high point of Fascist prestige architecture for E'42, in 1943, Pagano articulated the vision of a »Modern free architecture that would be courageous, spontaneous, uncompromising, master of its own progress, capable of lucid language«. He died not even two years later in a German concentration camp. Post-war Italy's first competition in 1944, was a memorial to 335 victims of Nazism (M30), a work of bleak forcefulness, totally opposed to Fascist rhetoric. It was entirely committed to the ideals of Modernism in the plainness of the pure cuboid forms, the hardness of the material (concrete) and the design, here the raising of the block above ground level, and this is in fact more the harder Modernism of the 50s than the Modernism of the white villas of the 20s. Of course the basic idea of the Roman memorial was later to be taken up by a major work of post-war Modernism, in Ronchamp. The Italian memorial made a completely clean break with Fascist architecture, but architecture immediately after the war almost completely failed to pick up its forms and design.

In Rome the best architects survived, but in northern Italy Terragni and Pagano, who had made Lombardy the centre of Rationalism in the 20s and 30s were dead. Thus Rome had a preponderance in the first one and a half decades after the war. Later this preponderance tended to be reversed – with Rationalist forms again making an impact. It was only then that a building in Rome impinged on developments when Muratori implemented the idea that building types are closely linked with the urban structure in which they stand, in other words that building types are related to their context. For this reason Muratori took the Palazzo Farnese, the most important Roman palace of the High Renaissance (H25), admittedly incorporating a Modern formal language, as his model for the headquarters of Democrazia Cristiana (M44). This building had no effect in Rome, though Aldo Rossi, Giorgio Grassi and also Carlo Aymonino were to allude to it in their architecture in northern Italy.

Neo-Realism, the so-called »Roman School«, the architectural parallel movement to Neo-Realism in film and literature, found the most succinct design ideas for Rome in the period immediately after the war. They were looking for architecture that committed to the people, to rural building forms and to craftsmanship – outdated industrial approaches became a style, and people actually talked about an art of »losers«. The key features are gables, nooks and crannies, angles, earthy materials and delight in patterns. At the same time a Modern legacy was discernible in the standardization of parts, for example, but constantly in individual important forms, for example roof trusses made to stand out from the body of the building. This movement saw its buildings embedded in both the context and the history of Italy. When they related to the past it was not to explicit models, as had been the case a decade earlier – obviously the Fascist example was still frightening. The best possible example of this approach is the INA-Tiburtino complex (M37). Almost all Rome's young architects who were to shape the one and a half decades, in the case of residential complexes even two to three decades, after the war (M38, M55, M40, M67 and Gallaratese as the main complex in northern Italy), worked on this, under the direction of Ridolfi and Quaroni. Only Libera did not take part, continuing to use strongly Rationalist formal stock in one of these residential complexes, the Quartiere Tuscolano; here he succeeded in finding a very convincing solution for individual building combined with increased density (M41), adopting a less »folksy« language. Like Neo-Realism, organic architecture had a concrete relationship with the Modern vocabulary of the 20s, but it rejected the Rationalist approach, though less radically. It wanted to revise it, not to reject it completely. In his manifesto »verso un architettura organica« (1945), Zevi looked toward Frank Lloyd Wright and asked for a Modern architecture that should be directed at man and his psyche as well as function and the precise aesthetics of floating and clear forms. Zevi's postulate, supported by the foundation of a movement (APAO) and a magazine (Metron), remained - largely theoretical; it hardly produced any convincing works. The Neo-Realist key treatise, Ridolfi's *Manuale* of 1946, on the other hand was more committed to practice even as a book and made the crafting of the details in particular a central theme, with craftsmanship and love of small forms above all, frames and handles, unpretentious things. And yet the main masters of the two approaches produced works with clear analogies in their exteriors (M35, M36). But Neo-Realism, with its spare formal language had a much greater potential for the whole range of buildings needed, especially for the simple residential complex. And since 1945 – after a decade of prestigious buildings – simple residential complexes became the most important type for the first time, indeed in the early stages it was the only significant one.

But ultimately it was the strength of the protagonists that made Neo-Realism much stronger in establishing itself than organic architecture. Ridolfi, quite differently from Zevi, knew how to express the frugality and hardness of the times in his various works. He wanted architecture that was rural, craftsmanlike and close to the people. But it never remains mere folklore; Ridolfi became the leading architect of his day by creating great symbols for the values that he wanted to express, enhancing them by contrasts, in a whole range of genres. After the INA Tiburtino complex Ridolfi had to design some high-rise buildings (M40). He recognized that these lose their effect without simple forms. Thus he designed buildings without nooks and crannies, but they were still fragmented and individual, above all because of their striking bevelled roof endings. Additionally he gave these most urban and industrial of dwellings a decidedly rural and crafted quality by making concrete frame and the filling with its craftsmanlike design entirely distinct. In that way Ridolfi established that typically Italian line of »rurally crafted« high-rise buildings that were still making an impact in the Torre Velasca in Milan at the end of the decade – the poetics of poverty. Alongside the INA buildings we have to consider the Palazzini, the small, inner-city type. No more specific anti-urban symbol could be found for this genre than Ridolfi's idea of placing a simple but exquisitely shaped country hut on top of the old Palazzina – the poetics of the countryside (M43). The directness that distinguishes Ridolfi's symbolism is to be found throughout his formal language. An untamed, almost expressive energy is unleashed in his buildings. This can also be seen in all the other Palazzine, whose parts swell and thrust their energy outwards (M35, M42, even M20). In the Palazzina Mancioli I (and II), his last Roman building complex, Ridolfi combined the frugality of the material with the power of his forms, thus demonstrating the sum of his thinking. No other Palazzina seems so chunky – and indeed this is again eternal-Roman, gravitas romana, the poetics of Rome.

Only Moretti found a language that was as clear as Ridolfi's in the first one and a half decades, admittedly one that was quite different, and without political commitment. His Palazzina Girasole (M33) is the best-known building of this type in Rome. The principal emphasis was on beautiful lines, as previously before in the Palazzina Astrea (M32). This rich and fashionable chose the architect who had built most elegantly even under Fascism. Moretti retained the principles of 20s Rationalism most markedly: the dominance of clear and simple bodies, the clear sections, the gleaming whiteness, the quality of being distinct from the surroundings, for example by raising the buildings above them, and also the typically Italian aesthetic exaggeration of this language (as in the work of Terragni) and sometimes also delight taken in asymmetrical design, although this had certainly been more pronounced in the 20s. However, all these principles were now so exaggerated, twisted and over-refined that the works sometimes have a Mannerist quality about them. Nothing is as typical of the opposing attitudes of Ridolfi and Moretti than their way of relating a building's outward appearance and its body to each other. For Ridolfi the façade was never different from the body of the building itself, and this was already the case in the 30s (particularly M14, M35, M42). Moretti on the other hand placed the façade in front of the body of the building, indeed allowed the façade to protrude over it and connected the two only loosely.

But the best project in the first one and a half decades, Ridolfi's proposal for the end section of the Stazione Termini (M31), remained at the planning stage. At the same time the history of this building outlines the most important lines of development beyond the original principal directions in Rome. Thus it is possible to discern a certain continuity even in relationship to Fascist architecture – as in the infancy of its development in the 30s. This is not so much because Ridolfi and Moretti shaped the period between the wars as well as the post-war period, and that the second even realized buildings that came close to Fascism's show buildings in terms of taste (M17). And continuity should also not be seen primarily in the fact that Mussolini himself had demanded that the city be depopulated, and that country-related styles like Neo-Realism dominated after the war: depopulation of the cities was no longer pushed by the regime after 1936, but only by proponents of Modernism like Piccinato and Pagano. The principal source of continuity was the fact that state commissions were being completed in the decade after the war and were very important to the building trade: one was the Stazione Termini as the largest post-war commission, and another the Foreign Ministry (M23), as the ministry that represents Italy in the outside world. The ministry was originally planned as a party headquarters, but it could nevertheless be completed practically unchanged in del Debbio's rigid monumental style after the war. And the ashlar at the top of the station building, emphasizing the smooth, closed wall was close to buildings of the Fascist period. The concourse was equally typical, this time for future development. As the winning project did not contain a concourse in comparable form, Ridolfi's »Expressionist« idea was adopted, but redesigned in a softer, unduly appealing form (cf. similarly M40). Ridolfi strikingly provided a giant open mouth, wide open for all, but the form was smoothed out in execution, less aggressive, curved. Truly expressive buildings were rarely seen in Rome in the 60s, but curves played a central role here, earlier than they had in the international context. Ridolfi left Rome, ruined, say many, by the economic miracle that pulled the carpet from under his poetics of poverty, but possibly also ruined by the violence of his forms.

Architecture around and after 1960 (M50–M74)

Numerous important points change for post-war Roman architecture around 1959/60: the principal protagonists, typology and urban development, and style.

Two architects had shaped the previous period, Moretti and – with an incomparably greater following – Ridolfi. The latter built his last building in Rome in 1959. The three subsequent decades were not to produce buildings with modelled body-structure and block-like values like those of Ridolfi – with one exception: only Portoghesi, himself a great admirer of Ridolfi, occupies a comparable position. Neo-Realism was his direct inheritance, even though he developed in a different direction himself. His very first work, his masterpiece, the 1959 Casa Baldi (M50) drew its life from indigenous material and block-like form. At the same time even this work shows that from this time onwards the relationship with the past was not to exhaust itself in a preference for rural-style craftsmanship, but, if it had a part to play, more deliberately referred to concrete outstanding works and important principles of former periods, Baroque, for example.

Ridolfi made the greatest impression with his INA projects. And these are – with other things – above all an urban development model. Quaroni, himself with Ridolfi the second project director for the INA Tiburtino complex, in his 1959 CEP Project for Mestre, near Venice, set a completely different model against Ridolfi's, which sought to implant staggered or fragmented blocks within the context of an earlier development. Quaroni's project shifted away from the old development and now consisted of uniform buildings with closed large-scale forms. In the 60s these buildings were not very high, rarely more than six floors, and formally they typically tended towards a smooth surface, which emphasized the standardized, prefabricated character of the buildings. Quaroni's fan-shaped complex of uniform buildings for the Quartiere Casalino (M55) in Rome is the principal example of this development phase, and Moretti preceded him with the Olympic Village (M49; closer to the city centre), the first residential complex in the Modern style in Rome, and with the INCIS quarter (M53), in which the exterior space was clearly much better addressed using this formal language. In 1963, during the years in which this new approach was developing, the INA, the institution for which the Neo-Realists had built, was abolished. Towards the end of the decade the new estate types were transformed into gigantic architectural massifs, sometimes even gigantic individual buildings, this time on the urban periphery as well, standing like ships in their surroundings. They included all secondary facilities, were a great deal higher, stood isolated and were still built of prefabricated parts but their surface design seemed more varied and thus more individual. Two architects who worked on the INA Tiburtino project created the key buildings, Aymonino near Milan (Gallaratese) and Fiorentino in Tor Corviale (M67), both with their own »link sections«, both a city in a building. These works still show a predilection for greatness – not just because most of them dated from the period immediately after the war – and were still in the wake of Modernism. At the same time all these developments were strictly linked to the international context, as ultimately they reflect only decisions by the CIAM Congress, which had fixed appropriate estate typologies. Almost at the same time as the further spread of the Tor Corviale type (M64, M68), an estate type developed in reaction that was also placed on the urban periphery – now with a preference for chaotic suburbs just outside the motorway ring – but here the buildings were no longer arranged in a system of large-scale terrace developments. What came into being now were small building units (M65, M66), some with very intricate decoration. They were perceived as small, almost decorative nuclei in these suburban areas. They were Post-Modern above all to the extent that large, melodramatic forms and symbols were avoided and replaced by a playful and ironic treatment of form and symbols. Architects were of the opinion that this language also appealed to ordinary people. In the late 70s and 80s people started to move back into the city, every attempt was made to fit in with existing building stock: in the interiors (M63), by borrowing historical features (M70), most markedly in the years from 1980 to 1985. It was at this time that a left-wing town councillor commissioned a whole series of projects under the direction of Aymonino for carefully context-related interventions in the historical centre, peaking in the plan to rescind the separation of the forums by Mussolini's boulevard and to reconstruct the historic buildings.

Style developed in parallel with urban development. Among the plethora of styles that existed alongside each other from this time onwards two developments stand out clearly, again starting in about 1959. In terms of quantity the strand leading to Post-Modernism is considerably thinner; but it started with the more impressive work, the Casa Baldi (M50), and in Portoghesi (M57, M69, M72) it has the architect who is the only one to have acquired as striking a profile up to the present day as Ridolfi and Moretti in the 50s (the latter in the 60s as well). He started (M50) in a somewhat more modest key, accurately finding only one way, but in each case the right way, of expressing the central requirement: earth-bound material to relate to the (rural) context; a curved wall for the historical reference; and individual tailoring of each spatial area to express the creativity of the residents' private lives. At the end of this development (M72, even M57) the range of these references expanded. A multiplicity of models was drawn in, and the referential structure diversified. This is as evident in the curve as in any element, which now – running concentrically – is multiplied countless times, but no longer freely modelled and thus seeming somewhat stereotyped. Multiplication always ran the risk of inflating the contextual and historical references and thus their random nature (cf. the works mentioned and M65, M70). Sides became reversible, proportions lost their historical order, and a carpet-like surface design replaced tectonics as a fundamental architectural value. Drawing and the way in which it was manipulated dominated everywhere (M65); new techniques were invented (M72); numerous projects were devised that were never intended to be implemented, which can be seen particularly clearly in the leading Post-Modern exhibition, the 1980 Venice Biennale, for which Portoghesi chose the manifesto-like title »Presenza del Passato«. The dramatic slow-down in building activity after 1973, caused by the oil price shock and the first saturation stage in building, was also reflected in this recourse to the project stage. Fewer major works were realized. However, ideas that were later called Post-Modern, especially reference to the past and the rural or urban surroundings and many forms of »double coding« in buildings were found in Rome much earlier than elsewhere, and very convincingly. But even now these Post-Modern ideas have not really taken hold here (or anywhere in Italy) – the most typical Post-Modern building of recent decades in a central position in Rome was actually built by a German (M70)! This is not difficult to explain in terms of a central feature that is specific to Rome: Post-Modernism could not proclaim its principal theme, relation to the past, in a way that was convincing for the public as this relation had always been important for buildings in other Modern styles here, which is hardly surprising in these surroundings.

This is particularly true of the second conspicuous tendency that can be called internationalization in two respects. In 1959 in Otterloo the CIAM, as the great international platform of Modern architecture (in the International Style), condemned the particular route taken by Italy, in which there was scarcely any room for a Modern vocabulary. Conversely, by creating Team X CIAM shifted contextual relations more strongly into the foreground, a feature that has been central to Italian, and particularly Roman architecture in the period immediately after the war. Rome now approached the International Style in diction to the extent that the two most distinguished buildings in the five years after 1959 (M47, M54) were built using the formal language of the International Style of the 50s and 60s – with a steel frame that defines the façade in the manner of Mies van der Rohe or with fair-faced concrete like Le Corbusier. Both buildings were much discussed (outside Italy as well), especially as the theme of the past was integral to their design: in the Rinascente department store in the building itself, in Passarelli's office building (M54) to the extent that the surrounding older buildings are reflected in its glass wall, an approach that was not dis-

covered until a decade later in the USA, but then attracted major architectural prizes there (John Hancock Tower, Boston). However, international tendencies began to make a more general and direct impact on Rome. It became increasingly possible to trace buildings back to international figures like Kahn, Rudolph or Stirling (M62, M54, M61). Again, as under Neo-Realism and organic architecture, as previous independent Roman styles, the development of this approach was accompanied by the appearance of a central architectural »treatise«: in terms of form Benevolo structured his work as architectural history (1960), but in terms of content he was concerned almost exclusively with a (very positively inclined) discussion of various elements of the International Style. Recipes and manifestos were no use any more; a professional approach shaped recent decades. And as the architects' offices thrust in with their more anonymous language in the 70s and 80s (M54, M73), Rome seems to have lost its independent diction – with the exception of Portoghesi. There is no Aldo Rossi with his cool poetics or Carlo Scarpa with his magic of simple things.

The picture seems somewhat blurred by the fact that the two best 60s projects were not realized. Things that are missing make a not inconsiderable

Mario Ridolfi and Wolfgang Frankl, project for the Agip tower, 1968

Giuseppe Samonà, project for the parliament building, 1968

contribution to the character of Rome in the past two decades. This is true for two trends that dominated for a time in the international context. Rome never indulged in High-Tech or even in a significant preponderance of technological values. For example, what a huge difference there is between the Rinascente department store project here and the Centre Pompidou in Paris, even though the latter derived its principal characteristics from the former! And how little technological aspects were emphasized even when it would have been particularly appropriate to do so: Nervi certainly designed the 1960 sports facilities as structurally towering concrete edifices, which helped him to world fame, but the formal language remained classically balanced, with symmetry dominating (M45, M46, M48) and perhaps for that reason the great event remained practically without consequence for Rome; and research facilities – borrowing from Rossi – successfully used the coolest of possible languages (M73). Then again, there is absolutely no sign of Art Brut, the tendency to display raw materials and forms with brutal directness. The residential section in Passarelli's multi-functional building (M54), which came closest to this approach, seems restrained in comparison. Typical though this lack of international stylistic developments in Rome is, the lack of something else is somewhat painful: Ridolfi and Samonà planned work with an expressive quality that is not to be found anywhere else, both in 1968: the AGIP Tower, made up of layers of stellar rings, displaced in relation to each other, and also increasing in size – as if driven by an inner energy – the great »lighthouse«

at the northern entrance to the city would have become »a crystallized image of imminent collapse«. And Samonà's parliament building for the old town would have brought the political drama (and the diction) of the best work of an architect like Le Corbusier to Rome, along with the eloquent symbol of an open hand for a new and more democratic period. The contrast between this concrete cuboids raised into the sky, following the example of the Boston City Hall, with the old building stock would have been enormous. No other Roman architect risked using this language, the most monumental that Modernism ever produced. But would it not also have been the right of a democracy to utter a word of power from a new spirit in the old papal city?

Conversely, the AGIP Tower stands for a character trait that made an impact in Rome in realized buildings as well, at least in the 60s and early 70s. A Roman, southern European quality is inherent in the way in which chaos derived from abundance acquires the status of a principle. Here it is the stars and their exuberant displacement. Only in Rome were so many structures built rampantly on and over other ones, sometimes with jerky breaks of angles (M34, M43, M54, M63). Following the topical trend (and influencing it), Morelli the »Rationalist« became fuller in his formal language (M52, M60) than in his early postwar work. And it is for precisely the same reason that Morandi's style is so well suited to the airport halls (M59). And Portoghesi is still using this kind of effusive formal language today (M72). The coolness of the principal tendency in northern Italy, the so-called Neo-Rationalism, and its preference for parataxis remained a mere episode in Rome, banished into the country (M73). The effusive formal language also characterizes the most recent large-scale projects by Renzo Piano (M75) or by Richard Meier who found here an even more monumental language than elsewhere (M76, M77). SG

M1 Albergo degli Ambasciatori

M1 Albergo degli Ambasciatori
Via Vittorio Veneto (plan II 1/E)
1925/26
Marcello Piacentini, Emil Vogt

IPiacentini built the »Albergo degli Ambasciatori« hotel in Via Vittorio Veneto in 1925 and 1926. It has a strikingly curved façade that reflects the run of the street in the building in an idiosyncratic fashion. The rise in the terrain was camouflaged by a banked base storey. Above this are six floors, but they are so linked as to give the impression of three sections: the two lowest floors with their large areas of window are linked by a large order, the windows of the two floors above them by rusticated pilasters and exploded triangular gables, while the row of windows on the fifth floor seem to be bound into the entablature zone. Loggias topped by statues in front of the rooms in the upper storeys pick up the familiar Roman belvedere type.

Overall and individual forms like column, exploded gables, rustication and loggias topped with statues are quotations from ancient Roman and Baroque architecture. They are used as set pieces, and are placed on the body of the building like reliefs. Viewers should find themselves reminded of an ancient Roman amphitheatre – and not just in the loggia.

Piacentini saw a great deal of work by Ludwig Hoffmann on his trip to Europe, and this was crucial in helping him to get past his Jugendstil period. Piacentini formulated the theoretical basis of his new architecture, which again adopted the values of drama and an almost ancient Roman monumentality, in *La Grande Roma* in 1925. The Albergo is a first step in this direction. But in its formal language it seems retrograde rather than progressive, almost historicist.
IM

M2 Garbatella: garden estate
Via delle Sette Chiese, Circonvallazione Ostiense
(plan G2 3/A)
1920–29
Gustavo Giovannoni, Massimo Piacentini (1st stage);
Innocenzo Sabbatini (2nd stage and hostels); Plinio Marconi (3rd stage)

The site for the workers' estate planned by the Istituto Case Popolari, »ICP for short«, is on a hill near S. Paolo fuori le Mura (C2), which had not been considered in the 1909 urban regulation plan for Rome. It arose from the placing of a large industrial zone along the Via Ostiense south of the old city boundary.

The overall plan devised by Giovannoni and Piacentini provided for a loose distribution of largely two-storey buildings with a garden around Piazza Benedetto Brin. The architects designed multi-storey buildings for the centre and the periphery of the residential area, some with public functions. These represented an architectural target, and were intended to conclude the new urban quarter in relation to the surroundings, that were undeveloped at the time. Behind the concept was the idea of the so-called »garden city«, as already developed in the last quarter of the 19C as a utopian notion of social urban development, particularly in England. The ideal of living in the country as a counterbalance to the unordered and anonymous life of the city was expressed architecturally by using few classical building types and an historicizing formal language. The architecture of farms and village in the Campagna provided a source of inspiration. The architects demonstrated their concern for indigenous culture by adapting this, and distanced themselves from the international eclecticism that predominated at the time. This tendency is also called »barocchetto«, and had already been used by Roman Rococo (cf. p. 172). It remained obligatory for further development of the urban quarter and also shaped the work of many Roman architects in the 20s. The character-

M2 Garbatella: garden estate

istic feature of the design of the individual buildings, which were designed by various architects, is that they link historical motifs and details from the various epochs of Italian architectural history. This gives the exteriors a picturesque feeling intended to symbolize the apparently organic development and change of what has been built over the centuries. The intention was to convey the idea of an old and mature urban core, rather than give the impression of a Modern model estate, something that had simply be redesigned to meet the residents' new requirements. This principle of artificially establishing old traditions by picturesque urban planning also dominated subsequent garden estate expansion, for example Sabatini's projects with his multi-functional buildings in Piazza B. Romano and his hostels in Piazza M. da Carbonara (cf. M3) and the model dwellings in Piazza S. Eurosia planned under the direction of Marconi, and built in 1929 on the occasion of the 22nd Congress of the International Association for Housing and Urban Planning, which was held in Rome. However, there is a sense of reduction and hardening of the formal apparatus in all three concepts, and this contrasts strongly with the overloaded decoration of the original design approach. Then Mario de Renzi used a functionalist formal language for his two buildings in the last-mentioned residential project in Piazza S. Eurosia that has scarcely anything left in common with the essentially folk ideas of the original design. Despite constant expansion and concentration of the building stock, even in its present condition the garden estate still offers a high level of quality. SK

M3 Garbatella: hostels for homeless families
Piazza Michele da Carbonara/Piazza Eugenio Biffi
(plan G2 3/A)
1927–29
Innocenzo Sabbatini

Sabbatini's hostels for homeless families in the northeast of the residential quarter are one of the most interesting expansion developments in the Garbatella garden estate (M2). They were originally intended as temporary accommodation for impoverished families whose rental agreements had been terminated, but they were changed into normal rented accommodation from the very start because of the huge housing shortage at the time. This change of function shows very clearly in the distribution of rooms in the four hostels: a total of 997 living spaces were converted into larger units in the subsequent period. The former collective areas were also gradually restructured as regular housing. The hostels are a striking visual feature within the estate complex with its constantly alternating residential buildings and gardens: multi-storey terrace buildings rise over the ground plan pattern, slightly varied in each case, in tripartite form, and their façades are enlarged to form powerful head buildings. This unconventional ground plan variant was chosen to maintain courtyards between the wings with their

M3 Garbatella: hostels for homeless familes

polygonal bays, which define partly public open spaces because of the changing spatial relations within the hostels. In the same way the inward-curving head buildings at the front were used to transform the street junction into open roundels. Thus the aim of the project as a whole is a clear interplay between the texture of the buildings and the precisely defined exterior space. In order to characterize the individual hostels as separate buildings they were made distinct from each other in their exterior articulation, the choice of architectural details and their colouring. Despite this they have stylistic feature in common that document Sabbatini's personal formal language: the exterior areas are characterized as a homogeneous wall continuum, divided only by the rows of windows and by heavy chord cornices. Another striking feature is the reduction of the design motifs, which concentrate largely on historicizing details, like semi-circular porticoes, triangular gables or base rustication. Typically Modern formal elements, like the frameless windows or glazed staircase cylinders, are placed in contrast with these. Sabbatini translated the folk historicism that predominated in Garbatella in the early 20s, developing the »barocchetto« tendency in its exaggerated interpretation of decoration, into a moderated variant. Certainly reminiscences of the indigenous building tradition can still be discerned, but they are used in isolation as mere formal quotations. The dominant feature of the exterior view is the accumulation of the cubic building volumes that lose their closed, monolithic quality through the stepping of the storeys, thus producing a stereometrically loosened overall ensemble. By choosing terraced buildings Sabbatini was able to do justice even in his larger buildings to the social requirement of garden estates, which was intended to convey a certain rural quality to its urban inhabitants by generous provision of gardens. The stepped floors produced small roof-gardens that could be used privately. He thus took up an important structural principle of Modern architecture that Adolf Loos had applied in his building projects from as early as 1910, and Henri Sauvage had implemented in an exemplary fashion in his famous residential block in Rue des Amiraux in Paris in 1922. This reflects Sabbatini's openness to international architectural trends in the early 20C. SK

M4 Palazzina
Lungotevere Arnaldo da Brescia 9 (plan I 2/D)
1926–29
Giuseppe Capponi

Like Sabbatini's alberghi, this building is in the Quartiere Garbatella (M3), and like these stands between the past and the future. Both draw life from the concave curve as a leitmotif and from rejecting intricate barocchetto decoration. Sabbatini's buildings seem balder, harder and thus more Modern. Capponi's building shows how Modern formal language could seem simply because an architect chose the particular Baroque models in which pure form dominated. He presented a similar project at the 1928 MIAR exhibition (p. 297).

Capponi wanted to break with the past. He abandoned applied decoration. And the deep window hollows are unadorned. This alone was enough to take the building out of the barocchetto context. For the rest is traditional: this starts with the material, Travertine or (at the sides and towards the back) imitation

M4 Palazzina

Travertine. And the body of the building as well, a tripartite block with concave centre and analogous top section, and even the multi-layered surface and the sparseness of the decoration – all this can be found in the work of Fischer von Erlach, and the principle motif even in Bernini's Louvre project. There are no hard transitions and no asymmetry of the kind found in Modern architecture (cf. M50). This took its revenge inside: the rooms no longer have Baroque dimensions; the elegant concave curve meant that each little room lost a little corner. Elegance is the overwhelming quality of the building, and particularly at the heart of the interior, in the ellipsoid staircase, with its four ellipsoid satellite spaces (corridors). Nervi had a similarly beautiful spiral staircase cast in Modern reinforced concrete at the same time in Florence (cf. M46). Capponi's building was more of an end than a new beginning. Modern architecture required more than merely turning away from barocchetto decoration. SG

M5 Foro Italico (formerly Foro Mussolini)
Piazza Lauro de Bosis (plan I 1/A)
1928–60
Enrico del Debbio (1928–33), Luigi Moretti (1936/37)
(cf. also M12, M17)

The 1925 general development plan for Rome anticipated providing a spacious sports centre in the north of the city. This new centre was to be built between the Monte Mario, the Monti della Farnesina and the Tiber; its colossal dimensions were ideal for documenting in an appropriate way the high esteem in which Fascism held sporting activities. Del Debbio was commissioned to produce an overall design in late 1928, after a first introductory project had been devised as early as the previous year. The architect's design had to take account of fundamental aspects like the characteristic landscape structures, links with the city and the national shooting range that was already in existence.

In his first version of 1928 del Debbio fixed a general arrangement that was to remain binding on the later planning variations in its distribution of the important sporting facilities: they were to be arranged in a linear sequence on either side of a large north-south axis, peaking in the gigantic so-called »Stadium of the Cypresses«. Another axis running from the embankment towards the stadium was planned between the large complexes of the two sports academies facing the Tiber. The intersection point of these two axes was extended as a roundel with a massive obelisk in its centre. Two bridges on the edge of the complex linked it with the Flaminio district south of the Tiber. Even this first design by del Debbio symbolized his intended link with classical antiquity, in the choice of building types, like the academy and the Marble Stadium (M12), based on the composition of an ancient gymnasium and modernized to suit the ideological aims of Fascism. Thus both the overall planning and the individual design of the various facilities showed a historical continuity intended to express the abiding quality of »forza italica« by architectural means.

Del Debbio expanded the original concept only two years later, as the shooting range area in the north-eastern part of the Forum had become available for planning. The project now included a total of 200 hectares. The changes in the overall structure associated with this aimed to make the complex more monumental. The addition of a central bridge, the »Ponte Duca d'Aosta«, realized later, made it possible to continue the second main axis to the opposite bank of the Tiber. Entering the sports complex was thus to be celebrated as a massive perspective view, enhanced by moving the obelisk forward from the centre of the roundel to its final position on the northern embankment. Costantino Costantini built this so-called »Mussolini Obelisk« in 1932/33. The whole project had to be adapted to the 1931 land utilization plan in 1932. Work started on the first facilities and buildings in the same year – including sports academies, Marble Stadium, Stadium of the Cypresses – so that the Forum could be officially opened by Mussolini on the tenth anniversary of the »March on Rome«. Del Debbio revised the project again a year later. The most important feature of this planning phase was that the design was expanded to include the original shooting range area. For this del Debbio developed a seemingly almost Baroque symmetrical scheme based on right-angled and radial road systems with several circular open spaces as the central links. The climax was a magnificent street leading from the Tiber to the Monti della Farnesina in the north-west, and culminating in a gigantic 90 metre high statue of Fascism after a sophisticated sequence of different squares.

In 1936 the overall plan was expanded spatially to 410 hectares to accommodate the Olympic Games planned for 1944. Moretti was now responsible for carrying out this gigantic project. He had to include the structures that already existed in the southern part of the Forum. For this reason he was principally interested in the design of the north-eastern section. He replaced del Debbio's original symmetrical street grid for this area with a massive arena for national mass rallies. The gigantic statue of Fascism planned by his predecessor was included in this concept and served as a fixed visual point behind the monumental speakers' platform. Two large theatres were to be built on the northern periphery, joined to the arena by an apparently organic, serpentine system of paths. This would mean that the regime could use the complex for propaganda purposes. Moretti intended to express a similar idea of monumental state architecture when in 1937 he realized the large entrance axis over the Tiber that had originally been planned by del Debbio. He used the mighty Mussolini obelisk as the starting feature of this complex. The adjacent

M5 Foro Italico (formerly Foro Mussolini)

was extended to form a longitudinal square, the »Piazzale dell'Impero« (now Viale del Foro Italico), fringed on either side by a row of polished white marble cuboids. The »heroic deeds« of Fascism were listed in large letters on the front of the stone slabs. This marble avenue led to the roundel whose central fountain with its white marble sphere had been realized in 1933/34 to a design by Mario Paniconi and Giulio Pediconi. Moretti's actual intentions were abandoned in late 1937 in favour of a project whose competitions and submitted entries are part of the most important chapter of Fascist architecture in Italy: the Palazzo del Littorio (M23), the headquarters of the Fascist Party in Rome, was moved from its originally planned site on the Via dell' Impero into the Foro Mussolini. The north-eastern site, a permanent target for large-scale planning since del Debbio's first designs, was thus no longer available for the sports project.

After the Second World War only few changes were made to the existing building stock, including the remodelling of the Stadium of the Cypresses as the Olympic Stadium from 1950 to 1953, but this was changed again in 1990 to provide an expanded building for the Football World Cup (M74). Other particular interventions were made for the 1960 Olympics for the erection of various sporting facilities. In its present form the Foro Italico is an accumulation of various complexes and buildings from various epochs of 20C Italian architecture. Despite the fact that the buildings emerged over a period of 30 years, and almost ten years of planning development with multiple design variants the complex shows a remarkable degree of artistic consistency. It is also one of the urban focal points in the incoherent urban landscape on the northern periphery. In contrast with this, the individual stages of the overall concept, in their enormously increasing extent and the individual sections' and individual complexes' constant tendency to the monumental symbolize the craze for the huge and spectacular with which the Fascist state aimed to glorify itself. SK

M6 Casa Madre dei Mutilati
Lungotevere Castello/Via Triboniano (plan IV 1/A)
1929
Marcello Piacentini
A site on the east bank of the Tiber between the Castel Sant'Angelo and the Palace of Justice was selected for the main building of the National Association of War Invalids. The commission went to Piacentini, who, as spokesman for the so-called »Scuola Romana« tried to bring Neo-Classicism and a rigidly monumental quality into contemporary architecture and rose as the principal organizer of the architecture of the Italian regime from the 30s onwards. The Casa Madre dei Mutilati gave him an early public building project in Rome that unmistakably expressed his personal view of national architecture: in order to make maximum use of the meagre area available, Piacentini designed a triangular building with a central inner courtyard and a main façade facing the Tiber. He chose an intricate, roughly cut tufa as his building material, with a surface that seems to have a patina. The important articulation elements, like the window-frames or the massive concluding entablature, are

M6 Casa Madre dei Mutilati

M7 Musei Vaticani: entrance hall with access ramp

in contrasting Travertine. This gives the impression that the building is already in a ruined state and its apparently old, unclad core is showing through. Thus Piacentini was reacting directly to the dilapidated condition of the Castel Sant'Angelo (A33), whose enormous plasticity he tried to adapt for his dynamically protruding façade, apparently torn open in the middle. Other references to the architecture of Roman antiquity are to be found in the massive round-arched portal with flanking pylons and the tabularium motif with its heavy Doric columns framing the windows in the main storey. Thus the basic tenor of the exterior design is an apparently almost martial classicism, with which Piacentini set the scale for later development of Fascist state architecture in Rome. SK

M7 Musei Vaticani: entrance hall with access ramp
Città del Vaticano (plan I 1/E and plan III 1/A)
1929–32
Giuseppe Momo
The entrance hall is a curiosity in terms of architectural history. Modern architecture, which triumphed in 1932 with its exhibition in the New York Museum of Modern Art, was for a long time condemned by the Curia as distorting and metropolitan, for example as late as 1947 in Metron, Zevi's journal of organic architecture. But the idea of spiral ramps did influence the greatest museum building of a Modern-organic

tendency, Frank Lloyd Wright's New York Guggenheim Museum (1943–59), even though there it was developed much more compellingly in artistic terms: light throughout, no longer in marble and bronze; a dense succession of heavy bands, no longer intolerably light; tapering as it goes down, because the spiral path leads only downwards, into the funnel, passing close to the exhibits, with a compelling dynamic (visitors are taken to the top by lift). In contrast, in the Vatican two ramps placed one above the other lead upwards and downwards; no art is exhibited here. In the New York Museum Wright visually forced visitors to go for a walk through Modern art: this is a special form of the Modern »promenade architecturale«. Vatican architecture served as a model once more, but it no longer pointed the way forward. SG

M8 Casa di Lavoro dei Ciechi di Guerra
Via Parenzo 5–13 (plan II 3/C)
1930/31
Pietro Aschieri

The official programme for the War Blind building included working and administrative areas and also accommodation for 30 people that were to be integrated into the building unit. The available site was a left-over rectangular area bordered to the south by an undulating street. Aschieri now had to arrange a multi-functional building complex in a sensible way on a building plot that was not particularly suitable. The design he devised shows coherent distribution and clear articulation for the individual function areas, and also considers the specific character of the site. The ground plan is based on linking two complex structures that correspond with each in a contrasting fashion: a convex section that curves forward, corresponding directly with the street in its line, and framed by two radially disposed wings. At the rear an oval pavilion is fitted into the concave bay formed by the main volume. This is followed by a small entrance area leading to the three-wing complex with a slightly trapezoid court-

M8 Casa di Lavoro dei Ciechi di Guerra

yard in front of it. Access to this courtyard is emphasized by two staircase cylinders built into the wings. The curve prescribed by the line of the street was taken up by Aschieri as a fundamental design principle and developed in a complex fashion in the design. He also placed the arching elements in stark contrast with the rigorously right-angled spatial sequences. Thus the result is an intricately organized building forming various façade areas which react very sensitively to the urban context. SK

M9 Città Universitaria
Viale delle Scienze (plan IX 2/C)
1930–35
Marcello Piacentini (general plan)

There was stylistic variety in Italian Fascism until 1936. The University complex is the best example of this. It was planned and realized as a prestige object in a very short time. Only three buildings from the first plan (1909–11) had been realized, and these were now included. Piacentini took over direction of the project in 1932, after a competition (1930). He created the overall plan and – as the conclusion of the axis – the main building with hall and rector's building; annexes by Rapisardi in a related style, on the right for the philosophical and on the left for the legal faculty, fuse with it. The other buildings were allotted as a result of individual competitions – to a very varied range of architects: traditionalists like Rapisardi, and Foschini, who designed the other end, the entrance area; architects like Aschieri and Capponi, who were cautiously oriented towards Modernism (cf. M8, M4); prominent protagonists of Modernism like Pagano and Ponti, the editors of Casabella and Domus respectively, or Michelucci, who built the contemporary station in Florence; and young architects like Bini, Minucci, Montuori, Muratori, Fariello. Given the ferocity of the polemics between these groups – Pagano showed the «Table of (traditional) horrors« at the 2nd MIAR exhibition in 1931 – this was a remarkable compromise. Pica then also opened the 1936 Milan Triennale catalogue, a compendium of stylistic diversity until this turning-point year, with the University. The regime had not yet fixed one single preference. Many new buildings were added in the late 50s and the 60s, especially dall'Olio and Lambertucci's pharmacology building (1955–63), architects who were close to Aalto and organic architecture (cf. p. 297).

The overall plan is traditional, structured strictly symmetrically, at a time when architects of the International Style had already started to propagate the idea of asymmetry as an innate, natural order (cf. p. 297). It is also traditional that the axis should lead to the main building and not yet (meaninglessly) into a void. This will change as early as E42/EUR (M24). The individual buildings also seem ossified, even in the monotony of the views on the axis sides, but above all in their size: mobility and a spatial continuum were impossible because of the lack of open spaces. Mies van der Rohe was creating a counter-form, a spatial continuum with a larger number of smaller buildings for the International Style at almost the same time in the IIT university complex in Chicago. Additionally, Piacentini's complex was sealed off to the outside, which was intended to re-enliven the structure of the Fori Imperiali. Otherwise propylaea are placed in front of sacred precincts. Here homage was visibly being paid to progress – and it is precisely in this particular that the Rationalists felt themselves bound to the regime as well (cf. M11). Of the four old faculties, theology is missing completely; philosophy and jurisprudence did not have their own buildings either. (They were accommodated on the sides, in the main building.) The fourth, medicine, and following it, the sciences, were the dominant faculties. They occupied all the other buildings on the axis and the transverse axis. The statue of Athene, goddess of the sciences, was also intended to endorse this sense of a fresh start, here presented in an almost warrior-like fashion, with arms stretched high. Thus there is a strange discrepancy between old form and – in its aspirations – a new spirit. The break can also been seen in formal aspects: behind the ossified Travertine show façades with somewhat hollow dramatic formulae there are quite differently designed, partly bold Modern buildings in simple materials. This is not comparable with the gradations between materials (always visible, conscious) in the Baroque period. The same break ran through the whole complex in just the same way: clinker brick is found – with no recognizable motive – alongside Travertine. Rome built entirely of marble (or Travertine), as under Augustus, was not aspired to until a few years later (M22).

M9 Città Universitaria

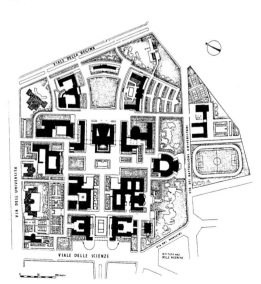

M9 Città Universitaria. Main building by Marcello Piacentini

What is true of the overall plan is also applicable to the main building. Unlike E'42 (M26), it seems sober, without arcades or exedra, right-angled, and not yet imperial either. The portico, the main motif, is closed not by a gable but by a transverse beam, closely related to the Modern flat roof. And yet the building does not seem very Modern. Classical principles are not translated into Modernism, but old forms are simply enriched with a little local Modernism. The Fascist »Stile Littorio« was born in the portico. This is marked by the large, sparse cavities that owed a great deal to de Chirico's Pittura Metafisica (cf. M26), and much even to later works of the Vienna Secession. But for the buildings themselves, few really new, Modern forms were found here.

The transverse axis is occupied by two buildings by distinguished exponents of Modernism. This is scarcely perceptible in the bombastic Travertine section at the front, relating to the ensemble with large openings. Excitingly Modern solutions are found only in the rear section, and this only in Ponti's building for the mathematics department. The building itself was set apart from the high show section by the low middle part, and contains three auditoria, one above the other. The building is cleanly cut; the form alone provides the decoration, here one has a sense of the purist »machine« aesthetic; and the articulation motif, the large window, is a terse device for making the interior complex visible in the exterior. But the Post-Modern variant in the new mathematics building kills the best in horror vacui, in multiple colours and slavish imitation.

The adjacent pair of buildings are also made to look the same in terms of their façades, but this time they are exclusively in brick. Individual features emerge only inside and at the rear. Pagano built the physics building. As an advocate of Modernism he was (politically) closest to Fascism, as he thought above all in urbanistic terms and for this reason was in favour of rigid uniformity. For Pagano the university complex was »worth more than 100 Polemics«. His spatial disposition was unusual: buildings in the form of a small and a large U, with the auditoria at the point of transition, guarantee clear separation of the three areas (advanced physics/theory/mechanics laboratory). In the chemistry building, as in the main building, the planned key motif of a tower was sacrificed to the requirement for a (stereotypical) overall unity. Thus Aschieri's personal style does not come to light until the rear auditorium. But he does place a portico, like that of the main building, though admittedly without spatial content, above his section of the building. There is scarcely any motive for that here.

The most clearly rational building had to wait to be built a little to one side. Capponi was responsible for the pharmacology building with its ribbon windows. Until then Rome had not seen a (glass) building that was so clearly characterized as industrial architecture. But traditional forms live on under the Modern garb, for example the less then powerful concave shape and the structural symmetry (cf. M4). SG

Bibliography: *Architettura*, 1935 (separatum); Regni and Sennato (ed.), *La Città universitaria di Roma*, Rome, 1986.

M10 Palazzina
Piazza Trasimeno 6 (plan II 2/C)
1931
Pietro Aschieri

The palazzina in Piazza Trasimeno is one of a series of urban residential buildings designed by Aschieri in the late 20s and early 30s. The common feature of the individual projects is that the formal repertoire they use is almost identical and was simply varied in its specific composition for the particular building requirements.

For the residential building in Piazza Trasimeno Aschieri had to consider the unusual dimensions of the site, contained by two radial streets and bordering the square with one narrow edge. This unfortunate frontal situation was raised to be the basis of the conception in that the architect designed a triangular building whose narrow façade section opened on the square as an entrance area. Five main storeys and one mansard storey set back from the entrance façade rise above a base storey into which a massive portal is integrated. Two cornices separate the base and the uppermost main storey from the central façade area, so that the outside of the building is divided into three horizontally, which is reminiscent of classical palace articulation. In the same way the dark colouring of the bottom storey and the heavy framing for the square windows indicate a traditional formal language. Then the balconies with their semicircular conclusions intro-

M10 Palazzina

duce a dynamic element that underlines the building's markedly directional tendency. Aschieri created a secular residential type with this palazzina; it has historicist architectural forms and yet its outward appearance is Modern. Despite its somewhat rigid design this structural scheme was a stylistic starting-point for a large number of residential buildings in Rome built by several architects in subsequent years. SK

M11 Casa economica per l'impresa Federici
Viale XXI Aprile 21–29 (plan IX 2/A)
1931–37
Mario de Renzi

On 3 June 1928 a fixed rental price dating from 1917 was lifted. Rents exploded and housing became scarce. Social housing was starting to appear, and led to the uniform urbanization that is still visible today on the periphery of almost all Italian cities, including Rome. In this context de Renzi created the largest block of the inter-war period, containing 442 dwellings and 70 shops. The ground plan is a (slightly curved) H with two long courtyards into which graduated parts of the building thrust. Mario de Renzi, previously director of the exhibition on the Fascist Revolution (Rome, 1932) saw this movement as a treasure trove of progress. Thus in Rome he mediated between Rationalism (a variation on the International Style) and the classical Italian heritage, whose hegemony he promoted in the Tribuna in 1931. He wanted to protect this heritage (abandoning ossification and the excessive quality of late Historicism) against unconsidered acceptance of international tendencies.

M11 Casa economica per l'impresa Federici

His style too remained undecided. The complex with its tremendous leaps in height makes it the largest project realized in the spirit of Futurism. It is above all the high-based, glazed stairwell cylinders that point well into the future. Circulation systems were not emphasized like this until after the Second World War (M67). These sections which made the complex well known, were actually following a famous model: Adolf Loos suggested a similar cylinder for the Chicago Tribune Tower (in the 20C's largest skyscraper competition). It was Loos – whose pronouncement was that ornament was crime – who was the scourge of Historicist decoration like no other and who prepared the way for Functionalism. All other parts of the building were bald in comparison with this, and clumsy in comparison with Rationalist buildings. SG

M12 Stadio dei Marmi
Foro Italico/Viale di Stadio dei Marmi (plan I 1/A)
1932/33
Enrico del Debbio

The name of the stadium derives from the total of 60 marble statues of athletes that top the outer border of the complex; they were a gift from the Italian provinces at the time. The Marble Stadium still offers a clear impression of its original condition, when it was one of the important sports complexes built in the Foro Mussolini (M5) even in the early development stage of the complex as a whole under del Debbio's direction in the early 30s. The site and orientation are determined by a promenade axis that runs from the Tiber through the central passage of the physical fitness academy into the wall-flanked, narrow access to the stadium. A terrace of light, almost marble-white stone encloses the central lawn with outer running track. A large podium edged with steps is to be found on the south-western long side, flanked by two bronze statues of wrestlers. Its low frame and narrowness make the Marble Stadium a balanced and elegant composition, which integrates harmoniously into the surrounding parkland. The choice of traditional materials and the use of classical decorative motifs, i.e. key-pattern friezes and similar, also suggest the formal language of ancient Roman building monuments like the great circuses or amphitheatres. This relation to the artistic values of the national past also shows in the sculptural programme, as famous models from Roman antiquity are reworked in the statues. Thus del Debbio's design shows a kind of Classicism operating with an apparently dramatic architectural language and that is typical for the majority of the buildings in the Foro Italico built under Fascism.
SK

M13 Villini, Ostia Lido
Ostia Lido, Via S. Fiorenzo 2 (type A), Piazzale Magellano 14 (type B), Viale della Vittoria 34 und 43 (type C) (plan G2 1/B)
1932–35
Adalberto Libera

In 1932 the Società Immobiliare Tirrena announced a competition for 15 blocks of flats on the Ostia Lido beach promenade. The participants were Roman architects and engineers who were allowed to submit either a building design or an overall development concept for the site as a whole. Prizes were awarded to the three best overall studies and also to the first three projects for at least two different residential buildings. When the society was commissioned to realize the 15 buildings in 1935 it did not keep strictly to the sequence of prize-winning competition entries. The actual winner of the eventual contract was Libera, who had won first prize for the overall study he had submitted, but was nevertheless permitted to build three different residential types for the project as a whole. The first two variants (types A and B), were intended for the planning area that had originally been

M12 Stadio dei Marmi

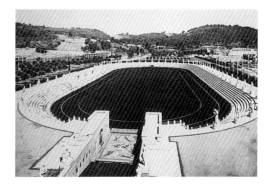

M13 Villini, Ostia Lido

fixed, while type C was realized on a neighbouring site near the Rome–Ostia railway line. Despite the individual character of the three different house types, Libera's building programme is based on uniform design principles that were interpreted differently for each particular building concept.

Type A is a three-storey cuboid building with a basement and an open loggia on the top floor. A total of six flats are accommodated in the three main storeys, and can be reached via a central staircase that protrudes as a semi-cylinder from the closed outline of the block. The rooms are distributed according to a very simple and constant pattern based on maximum exploitation of the building volume. The exterior is dominated by the long side, which faces the sea and has round balconies that thrust far out on the edges of the building.

Although Libera selected a functional design approach that was purifying in the simplicity of its details, the sides that are principally seen are organized on a strict basis of axial symmetry. Type B follows the layout of type A in its basic division. Libera shifted the balconies to the middle of the façade instead of placing them on the flanks of the building. This emphasizes the stereometric basic form of the cube. The narrow sides also have protruding balconies so that the closed body of the building is framed visually by the open railings of the iron balcony balustrades.

Type C is different from the other two to the extent that it is a narrow, vertically rectangular building containing a total of ten flats on five storeys. By using spacious balconies on the narrow sides Libera gave

it a marked sense of orientation that he further reinforced by the outward curve of the roof. Instead of unprofiled windows, which were characterized as sharp-edged incisions in to the mass of the building in the previous types, the square openings on the long sides are sculpturally emphasized by simple framing. The architect also replaced the hard edges of the residential block with a rounded shape.

The basic stylistic quality that the three buildings have in common is that the Neo-Classical formal language is generally abandoned. By using Modern technical processes and structural principles, Libera consciously detached himself from the dictates of the official architecture of the Fascist regime. This may be because the commission did not come from the state, but also because Libera was able to express his rational idea of architecture within the framework of what was then possible. SK

M14 Ufficio Postale
Piazza Bologna (plan IX 2/B)
1932–35
Mario Ridolfi, Wolfgang Frankl

In 1932 a competition was announced for four post offices in four districts, largely at important junctions in the nearer periphery. It was the most successful competition for the Modern movement in Rome under the Fascist regime. It produced three winners: Ridolfi, Libera (M15) and Samonà (M16). The regime was still choosing case by case, a Modernist here and a traditionalist there, though the Modernists tended to win the central competitions for functional buildings – appropriately to their programmatic aims. This applies to the post office buildings just as much as to Florence station (Michelucci). Prestigious buildings of a sporting or cultural nature tended to go to the traditionalists for direction, and to Piacentini in particular (M9, M24). Frankl, Ridolfi's long-term partner, worked on this building for the first time, on the doors and interiors, but they were renovated at a later date, and are no longer authentic today. The building was Ridolfi's first, and the only one of the three post office buildings to deviate substantially from the competition design. The fact that the regime promoted Modernists as well distinguished Italy from Germany, from which Frankl, unemployed because any kind of Modern architecture was anathema, was one among many émigrés.

All three post office buildings are expressive. But Ridolfi's was Expressionist, and the least rationalist of the three. The key for Ridolfi was his trip to Germany in 1930. In terms of Modern tendencies it brought him close to Tessenow and Wachsmann, who were much influenced by the craft movement. When Wachsmann was in Rome he introduced Frankl and Ridolfi to each other. They were not looking for the entirely new aesthetic of floating volumes (like the International Style, cf. M21, M24). Rather they were trying to build on traditional building forms and to stress the basic craft essence of the work. Ridolfi was a member of the Cen-

M14　Ufficio Postale

tral Rationalists' Association, the MIAR (cf. p. 297), but he did not opt either for traditionalism or even definitely for Rationalism, a variety of the International style.

Ridolfi's building is the only large structure in Italy that is rightly labelled Expressionist. A façade placed in front of the building does not fit in with the Expressionist style, which was entirely committed to expressive directness. Here building and façade were already a unity for Ridolfi. The sculptural value of the building was façade enough for him. He was to retain this approach in all his buildings, even in the smaller palazzine after the war (M35, M42); this also distinguished him fundamentally from Moretti, the second post-war protagonist, who had also helped to shape the 30s (M32, M33). This attitude was in the best Roman tradition, following mass building and the most powerful works (A50, H7). Ridolfi was also to cling on to this when he approached Rationalist vocabulary (M20). The large, concave inward curve of the façade was also Expressionist, and the fine roofing over the entrance underlined this by not following it; visually, this created a chasm in front of the glazed »band« door, which sucked visitors inside in visual terms. This was seen as recourse to Mendelsohn and Poelzig, but even Höger's Hamburg buildings seemed more comparable, above all in the handling of material: Ridolfi had Travertine, Rome's most important building stone, laid in thin layers and foot-sized pieces like bricks. This gave the building something of an indigenous quality. It was also sensitive and subtle to keep the rows of windows almost monotonously plain, so that the elegance of the curve could make its full effect. Both, the indigenous quality and the monotony, made it justifiable to speak of »magic Realism«. In contrast, the Roman Rationalists increasingly valued the noble material values of Travertine, and thus created an important link with the tastes of the regime. The key difference between execution and design lay in in-

creased simplicity: three differentiated sections became a single, very impressive one. Rationalist formal language was only sensed remotely: both in the two roofs, which are somewhat long and thin, like discs and (the upper one in particular) seem to float, and in the preference for the elegant curve, which seems a little too smooth for a pure Expressionist work.

Ridolfi demonstrated convincingly that pure, lucid forms did not necessarily need machine aesthetics and floating volumes. He laid the basis for an oeuvre that was expressive and lined with the architecture of the simple, thriving on the corporeal value of the buildings and solid craftsmanship. SG

M15　Ufficio Postale
Via Marmorata (plan VII 2/B)
1933–35
Adalberto Libera, Mario de Renzi

The 1932 competition for the series of new post offices related to the Roman districts of Nomentano (M14), Aventino and Appio (M16). The jury was made up of several architects favouring different styles, and chose, from the large number of entries, works by young Modernists, and these were built from 1933 to 1935 after a revision phase required by the Post Ministry (cf. also M14).

Libera's and de Renzi's project for the Aventino district, which won first prize, could be realized without fundamental revision of the design submitted. As the site available was an open and extensive park, the architects did not have to heed either an urban texture or the requirements of existing axes. The complex they conceived is a symmetrical building with three wings on a high pedestal and open to the street. The spacious forecourt contains a low, longitudinal building that with its glazed upper section and rounded edges forms a startling contrast with the rigid geometry and closed quality of the main volume. The link with the street is a broad flight of steps leading to the raised entrance level with its massive piered colonnade. But the front view of the building is defined above all by the block-like quality and monolithic mass

M15　Ufficio Postale

M16 Ufficio Postale

of the main body: the courtyard façades are articulated only by four rows of square windows, while the front sides of the wings seem almost to have been cut open by large apertures. This unusual dissolution of the wall continuum is intended to lay visual stress on the public staircases, which are in the wings; their ramp structure is emphasized in the exterior view by diagonal latticework. On the side façades, which provide access to the building via small flights of steps, the austere parataxis of rows of windows one above the other is maintained. But the rear façade is almost completely broken up by a network of tiny square windows. The climax of the disposition of the internal space is indubitably the great counter-hall, which is in the central section in front of the main building, with access via a glass membrane. The room is lit from above by transparent glass bricks, and has an open, light breadth that is broken only by two rows of thin metal piers.

The fundamental characteristic of the building is a carefully calculated confrontation of heterogeneous forms and materials: traditional architectural elements and design principles, like the uniform stone cladding, the three-wing building type or the piered colonnade come directly up against typically Modern building techniques like the ostentatious use of different kinds of glass and metal. The two architects did this so that they could do justice both to the state commission and to their own Rationalist requirements. The »spirito nuovo«, the new spirit in Italian architecture that had been called for in the manifestos of the Rationalist un-

ion known as »Gruppo 7« even in the late 20s, required both a Modern, national style and also an enlightened relation to history. By juxtaposing tradition and innovation in their post office building, Libera and de Renzi implemented one of the crucial premises of Rationalist architectural theory in a realized building. SK

M16 Ufficio Postale
Via Taranto 11 (plan IX 1/E)
1933–35
Giuseppe Samonà

The design submitted by Samonà for a competition for a post office in the Appio district had to be revised, just like the majority of the competition entries for the other Roman post office branches (M14, M15). The specific problem lay in maximum exploitation of the development plot that was not only astonishingly small but also had an irregular outline because it was at the junction of several streets. The individual planning phases show that Samonà experimented with the spatial distribution of the various functions and also made a number of changes to the architectural linking points in the exterior design. If one considers the difficulties of this task, the end result can be seen as an entirely convincing solution.

A characteristic feature of the ground plan design is the attempt to use the irregular site for a differentiated separation of functions. The public counter-hall, which follows the prescribed run of the street with its two concentrically organized wing halls, was placed in the triangular area at the front, formed by the combination of two radial streets. This meant that the intermediate area in between could be used for secondary functions. The service and office rooms were accommodated in the rear building, which is based on orthogonal spatial division. Access points and the internal circulation systems like corridors and stairs are placed at the transitions between the two main areas. Thus the spatial disposition relates not only to the requirements of the existing structures, but also to the functional demands. The counter-hall as the key to the interior design is structured by a double row of heavy, granite-clad piers that separate the open public area from the run of counters and divide the outer wall into a regular sequence of glazed intercolumniation. Even though the transparent outer membrane guarantees maximum lighting, an austere, almost cool spatial impression predominates, and this is further enhanced by the fact that the architect chose to reject any form of decoration or surface structuring. The principle of treating the wall as an unarticulated continuum is also maintained for the exterior. While the alternation of column and pier dominates the two important side façades in the lower area, the upper storey is a homogenous, Travertine-clad wall area, running over the edges without profiles or framing, and interrupted only briefly by the two rows of windows. By choosing dark granite cladding for the narrow transitional field between the two main façades, Samonà created contrasts in materials and colour that polarize the front view of the exterior of the building. The concave inward curve of this central wall section is also interesting; it was the architect's reaction to the convex curve of the street corner, intended to form a sight axis. Two tall rectangular windows form the centre of this device: they are arranged one above the other on the central axis, but differently designed in format and internal structure. The basic tenor of the exterior is the attempt to stress the closed quality of the building block by using partially unarticulated wall surfaces. Alongside this, extreme contrasts of material and colour were introduced to counteract monotony in the overall appearance. If one also considers the sophisticated spatial structure, then the building can be judged positively as an artistic piece of architecture. SK

M17 Casa delle Armi (formerly Accademia della Scherma)

Foro Italico/Via dei Gladiatori 4 (plan I 1/B)
1933–36
Luigi Moretti

The Casa delle Armi is one of the most interesting buildings in the Foro Italico (M5). Even before Moretti

M17 Casa delle Armi

M17 Casa delle Armi

was in overall charge of the planning for the Foro Mussolini he designed this building, which is made up of various individual sections. It is sited in the southern section of the sports complex, and consists of two independent buildings that fit together to form an L-shaped ground plan and are linked by an open passage. The narrow, taller wing of the building, which contains the library and a two-storey reading area, ends in an oval space that leads into the open passage like an architectural joint. Adjacent to this is a broad, low block housing the large assembly room. The convincing feature of the interior design is not primarily the austere and sober shaping of the details and articulating elements, but the constant changes in the quality of light. By permanently changing the nature of the lighting, Moretti created unique spatial situations with which the viewer is confronted directly. The dominance of the white, unarticulated walls and the prismatic sharpness with which the different apertures are cut into the wall support this extraordinarily dramatic lighting regime. The exterior is defined by the contrast between the closed wall surfaces and the differently structured window apertures. Despite his recourse to Rationalist formal language, as shown in the free grouping or harmonious balance of the various building volumes, Moretti accommodated the Neo-Classicism of the other buildings with the visible stone of his marble-clad exteriors, and thus created a building that makes a highly controversial statement. However, now that it has been converted into a remand prison, very little can be seen of these original qualities. SK

M18 Casa della Gioventù (GIL)

Largo Ascianghi 5 (plan VII 1/A)
1933–37
Luigi Moretti

The youth building designed by Moretti in the Trastevere district was part of the Fascists' structural programme for educating Italian youth on a basis of clearly delineated ideological state theory. To this end a series of new building types was developed that could be used by the regime's various organizations for their individual purposes. Each building was bound to a type, but the architect was able to make a personal decision about architectural interpretation. When designing the youth building, Moretti was compelled by the scant dimensions of the available site to bring the various functions together in building volumes of several storeys and to group these in the smallest possible space. For this reason he worked with tall building sections that he linked with short, colonnade-like corridors. This produced a complex with staggered heights, which looks very different from different angles. The key element of the exterior design is the remarkable dissolution of the wall continuum in favour of large, rectangular openings contrasting with the stone-clad wall areas. The building seems like a skeleton, reduced to its tectonic structure. The impression often arises that these are just empty casings in which light and shade meet each other abruptly. Moretti created an architecturally convincing design by developing a tension filled composition that is balanced in the distribution of masses from a variety of basic stereometric forms. In its present condition, after radical interventions, a great deal has been lost of the original quality of the building, which used to reflect the guiding principles of Roman Rationalism most impressively. SK

M18 Casa della Gioventù

M19 Ufficio Postale, Ostia Lido

M19 Ufficio Postale, Ostia Lido

Ostia Lido, Piazzale della Posta (plan G2 1/C)
1934
Angiolo Mazzoni

Mazzoni's post office in Ostia Lido is a building that is clearly different in its architectural character from the other post offices built in 30s Rome. Even though Mazzoni had worked in the office of Marcello Piacentini, the leading Neo-Classicist of the so-called »Scuola Romana«, he developed his own personal style, which he implemented in an exemplary fashion in the post office building.

At the centre of the multipartite complex is a circular entrance hall, and behind it is a single-storey building complex that fulfils different functions, joined on like the segment of an outer ring. This portico with its concentrically placed piers and protruding, many-stepped flat roof is an open composition that seems almost filigree; its front thrusts forward in a convex curve into the square in front. A low section with very few windows forms a transition at the side to a tall staircase tower consisting of a vertical rectangular cuboid and a closed cylinder. Three tubes flanking the cylinder correspond with the round piers of the entrance hall.

The principle feature of the post office's ground plan and exterior design is a dynamic component. Whether it is a matter of putting concentric circular sequences together or of the vertical tendency of various round forms, the element of movement is always in the foreground. This reflects Mazzoni's sympathy with the Neo-Futurist tendencies that had established themselves in Italy after the First World War. Even his personal preference for Antonio Sant'Elia can be seen in the design, as that architect's technoid basic elements for a Futurist city are worked into the staircase tower. SK

M20 Palazzina Rea

M20 Palazzina Rea
Viale di Villa Massimo (plan IX 2/B)
1934–36
Mario Ridolfi, Wolfgang Frankl

Ridolfi built his very first town house with Frankl, who had emigrated to Italy because of Nazi pressure in Germany. As usual it has two apartments per storey, but they are both asymmetrical in section: the back left-hand corner is bevelled, and the left-hand apartment takes in only the left balcony axis, and the left-hand and rear façades, whereas the apartment on the right takes up the whole right-hand section up to the staircase in the centre. The building is contemporary with the first competition for the Palazzo del Littorio (M23), at a time in which the regime still accepted Rationalist architecture, though admittedly this did not look the same in Rome as it did in Lombardy.

After Ridolfi's Expressionist post office (M14) a transition to Rationalism came as something of a surprise. Now the main building was raised above ground level, orthogonal and white, all typical of the Rationalist buildings, just like the »floating« strip at the top. Did Ridolfi choose a different formal language because of the other building type (in which the International Style had celebrated its success)? The first impression is deceptive to an extent. Ridolfi did keep behind important principles of the International Style in that he camouflaged the asymmetrical ground plan completely within the (symmetrical) exterior of the building. But it is more important that he went beyond the Interna-

tional Style and found a counterpart to Roman mass building: he used the vocabulary that had been developed for creating »floating volumes« (cf. M30) to show the massive depth of the walls in the corner balconies, thus finding a Modern way of expressing the older Roman style. This corner balcony solution was so powerful that any later corner balcony suspended on the exterior seemed weak. The Roman block was to appear in perfectly mature form in Modern formal language in the Palazzina Mancioli (M42). SG

M21 Palazzina Colombo
Via Valentino (plan I 2/B–3/B)
1936
Mario Ridolfi, Wolfgang Frankl

The second town house embodies a second type within Ridolfi's work with flats occupying a whole storey each. The ground plan is asymmetrical, like an L tending towards a U (with the bit left over opposite the long arm). The staircase is situated in the inner corner of the L and is naturally lit. Around this are grouped three types of room: in the long arm (to the south) are the bedrooms with small balconies; in the short arm (to the west) sitting-rooms with transverse balconies; to the north (in the remaining piece and behind in the long south arm) are the service areas (almost completely without balconies).

The characteristic features of the type are its analytical articulation and the asymmetrical ground plan in contrast with the compact, block-like largely symmet-

M21 Palazzina Colombo

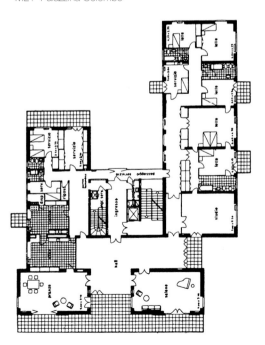

rical »Rea« type for small flats (M20). The freer spatial relationships can also be seen on the outside. One of the main qualities of the building lies in the fact that the exterior structure illustrates the interior space, which was not the case previously (M20). The different nature of the living areas required an asymmetrical structure here. More important are the sleeping and living areas, both allotted to independent sections, and only loosely connected by the balcony. The second main quality of the building is that the volumes are kept »mobile« to a certain extent. The two sitting-rooms are also surrounded by balconies and thus released from the wall pattern, and the balconies are no longer framed by the outer lines of the building. Thus Ridolfi was now able to combine the two principal values of the International Style more strongly with his block-like approach to building. And balconies also convey mood: they are broad in front of the prestigious section, small and intimate in front of each individual bedroom, non-existent in front of the nooks and crannies of the service section. From this point onwards Ridolfi saw »building honestly« also as an accord between interior and exterior. SG

M22 Piazza Augusto Imperatore
Piazza Augusto Imperatore (plan I 2/E)
1936–40
Vittorio Ballio-Morpurgo
Thinking back to the ancient monuments of Imperial Rome was an important component in the ideology of Italian Fascism. Here the historical foundation of the leader cult was equating Mussolini with the emperor Augustus. Against this historical background it is not surprising that new urban design in Rome also concentrated on revealing and presenting Augustan monuments. 1934 saw the start of systematic excavation of the Mausoleum of Augustus by the Tiber, and this was completed in 1937 by the discovery of the missing pieces of the Ara Pacis Augustae (A18), the Altar of Augustan Peace on the western periphery of the tomb precinct. This urban district was declared an archaeological zone, the »Zona Augustea« in the same year; it was to be brought together as a complete building complex by architectural means.

   Ballio-Morpurgo's overall plan suggested extending the excavation area to form a large square, the »Piazza Augusto Imperatore«. This was to be backed by peripheral buildings and would have the mausoleum with the Ara Pacis in front of it as its centre. Large sections of the historic building stock had to be pulled down in order to provide the necessary space. Only the three churches on the fringe of the development area survived and were included in the concept. As no one wanted to lose the important street axes the peripheral development could not be entirely completed, so breaking up into independent building section was the inevitable consequence. To underline the character of these individual buildings even further, the wings acquired different façade designs. These cor-

M23 Palazzo del Littorio (Foreign Ministry)

respond with each other in their rigid formal language, but they are nevertheless articulated as independent building types. The northern edge of the square is bordered by a heavy band of buildings, but the eastern side concludes in a palace-like building. It is only in the treatment of detail that the coherence of these individual buildings is demonstrated architecturally. A colonnade of piers and columns running round the ground floor, the marked parataxis of the window axes and the choice of light-coloured Travertine as a uniform wall cladding guarantee visual coherence and give the complex as a whole a classical but entirely spare appearance. Axial relations are established by the fact that the central façade areas are spatially stressed by column porticoes, with the Mausoleum of Augustus as their architectural focus. Austere formal treatment thus corresponds with precise axiality. The Ara Pacis was also enclosed in a new structure as part of the redesign of the square. Once more a traditional building type from Roman architectural history was chosen. A front-facing podium temple with a massive central ramp was given rhythm by coupled piers and concluded with a massive eaves cornice. Complete glazing of the intercolumniation guarantees a view into the interior from all sides and also underlines the dominance of the tectonic structure. The reduced formal language of this temple-like enclosing structure fits harmoniously into the overall structure of the square.

   The »ricorso arcaico«, Fascist Italy's cult of ancient Rome, was supported by large-scale archaeological excavations and underpinned by the instruments of a new and apparently national architecture. The Piazza Augusto Imperatore is an important example of this. SK

M23 Palazzo del Littorio (Foreign Ministry)
Viale Ministero Affari Estero (plan I 1/A)
1934, 1937, 1938–43, 1956–59
Enrico del Debbio, Arnaldo Foschini, Luisa Morpurgo
This building is remarkable particularly because of its history. 1934 saw the announcement of Fascist Italy's

M23 Palazzo del Littorio. Design by Giuseppe Terragni

biggest building competition, with over 100 projects, and architects including the Modern élite: Libera, Ridolfi, BBPR, Moretti and above all Terragni. The site was to be on the new axial street called the Via dei Fori Imperiali, opposite the basilica of Maxentius (A50), in view of the Colosseum (A 25), at the heart of Ancient Rome. The élite of the Fascist Party were members of the jury, including General Secretary Starace and Secretary Marinelli. The same was true three years later when the second competition was announced, now for a site on the periphery. In the meantime the empire had been declared, after the annexation of Ethiopia. The Moderns no longer stood a chance, all that was wanted now was traditionally charged rhetoric. Del Debbio won. The history of the project reflects a general volte face in the Fascist perception of architecture. Large projects in Modern formal language like Sabaudia or the station in Florence were no longer produced.

Terragni's project for the first phase combined classical and Modern diction: axes were broken, as in the Forum and the Esquiline; building in layers, entirely appropriate to the genius loci (cf. also M34); and engineering achievements of the kind that were also a strong feature of Ancient Roman architecture (here external spiral stairs of the kind used by Nervi for the stadium in Florence in 1929). And Terragni responded to the richly orchestrated, convex forward thrust of the Colosseum with a crowning concave wall, entirely undecorated, narrow and with sharp vertical incisions, massively thick like the walls of the basilica opposite with its gigantic round-arched incisions. Built »pittura metafisica« in old Rome!

The building realized was rapidly redeployed as the Foreign Ministry; it is a rather insignificant cube, completed almost unchanged after 1956 after interruptions during the war. Accessories disappeared – the Torre Littorio, the ramps in front of the entrance, the rear wings. The block remained the same, but the powerfully protruding cornice over the base was cut out, the coffers at the top all opened up as windows (small lights). Del Debbio was not a Fascist architect in the narrow sense, and he used no excessively noisy rhetoric. But what is actually remarkable about the process is that in Italy, unlike Germany, people were not afraid of continuity – at least here in the Foreign Ministry, and soon in the largest post-war competition (M31). Continuity not only led into Fascism, but out of it as well. SG

M24 EUR (Esposizione Universale di Roma), formerly E'42 (Esposizione Universale del 1942)
Piazza Guglielmo Marconi (plan G2 3/B and plan VII 2/C) 1937–42, 1951–60
Giuseppe Pagano, Marcello Piacentini, Luigi Piccinato, Ettore Rossi, Luigi Vietti (first master plan); Marcello Piacentini (definite project); Giorgio Calza Bini (urban conversion project)
Mussolini announced the foundation of the Italian Empire on 9 May 1936. A month later the government in Rome made an official application for the World Fair that takes place every six years. The application was accepted, and the largest international exhibition was fixed for the year 1942, to mark the occasion of the 20th anniversary of Italian Fascism, which come to power in 1922 with the »March on Rome«.

In January 1937 the Duce, following the advice of the General Commissioner of the Exhibition, Vittorio Cini, asked five Italian architects, Pagano, Piacentini, Piccinato, Rossi and Vietti, to draw up a general plan for the exhibition complex. Only four months later the architects submitted a project, and building work started officially on 28 April 1937. Piacentini was commissioned to revise this plan thoroughly in 1938. His alternative project was ready in March, and this formed the basis for the final development plan, which was accepted in 1939 without further reservations. During this phase briefs for the permanent buildings were also announced; this culminated in a major competition in 1941, in which over 100 architects took part. »E'42«, the official abbreviation for the exhibition, was, according to Mussolini's own statement, to be an »Olympics of civilized achievement«. It never took place, because of the war in Europe in the early 40s. Work that had started on the permanent buildings was broken off in 1942, and completely abandoned a year later.

In 1951 work started on completing or restoring the buildings that were incomplete or had fallen in to ruins. In 1955 Calza Bini developed a concept for transforming the exhibition complex into an urban district and integrating this into the city periphery. This project, called »EUR« was realized in subsequent years and concluded in the building of important sports facilities in the new quarter for the 1960 Olympics.

E'42 was not conceived merely as an exhibition, but its permanent buildings were intended to form the core of a future imperial city; a »third Rome« according to Mussolini's own statement, extending from the southern borders of Rome to the sea. The exhibition complex, set on the new monumental axis of the Via Imperiale, which ran from the Foro Mussolini (now Foro Italico, M5) in the north of the city to Ostia Antica (A30), was a record of the petrified vision of a powerful and expansive Rome which was to be a stage for the Fascist regime. Even the first development plan, conceived by the group of architects in 1937, emphasizes this symbolic and propagandistic aspect of the project: the Via Imperiale runs through the whole exhibition area as a dominant symmetrical axis, and determines the position and direction of the other streets and squares. The buildings are distributed on both sides, roughly balanced either as free-standing solitaires or as a linked peripheral development. Alongside their primary function they support the perspective character of the individual street axes, as a visual target or as a kind of architectural setting. This development plan, with its imposing prospects and strict axiality, represents an academic scheme in-

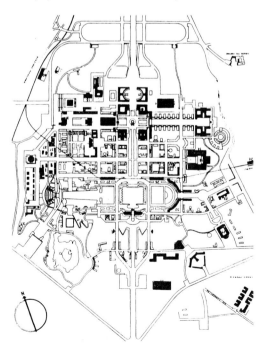

tended as a programme to express the future function of the exhibition complex as the centre of the new Fascist capital. Some of the streets run in curves, apparently organic in nature, to counteract the formal rigidity. In the same way the artificial lake at the centre of the complex is bordered by a natural-looking embankment promenade. In contrast with this, the innovative character of the exhibition is demonstrated by the choice of industrial building materials, the development of new building types and the solution of transport-related problems. The Via Imperiale is a modern high-road, fringed by gigantic point buildings in glass, steel and concrete. Thus the architects' first development plan tried to mediate between academic and Modernist positions.

This strange ambivalence in the concept turned out to be the reason for modifying the first plan fundamentally. In the final version, devised independently by Piacentini, such compromises were no longer accepted and eliminated in favour of a decidedly traditionalist overall solution: the basic disposition is now based on a strictly orthogonal symmetry, reminiscent of the classic Roman »cardo« and »decumanus« in its emphasis of the dominant main and transverse axes. The important main buildings are used much more consistently than in the original version to mark the visual end point of a street. The architectural result is a dialogue between the most important monuments and the emphasis of visual axial relations. Also, the previously even balancing of the architectural masses is regulated more strongly, and replaced by a geometrical grid in places. The sequence of squares is now based on clear theatrical calculation, and the joints are more clearly accentuated by impressive large buildings. The basic tenor of the new design is thus unambiguously concerned with the imposition of strict uniformity on the organizational pattern, schematization and finally a monumental quality for the complex as a whole.

But the greatest difference was in the architectural design of the individual buildings. In the original plan the key was still confrontation between Modern, i.e. Rationalist or Functionalist design principles with the vocabulary of classical architecture, in order to express the combination of old and new in this building, but nothing remained of this in the final version. Despite large-scale competitions involving architects from various camps, the planning process saw the individual building projects brought almost stereotypically into line. This may be because it was necessary to use an architectural language acceptable to the regime if you wanted your project to be successful. Architects were prepared to compromise to an enormous extent, with a result that their projects became so alike that they looked as though they has been designed by one and the same artist: symmetrical ground plans, closed volumes, usually of excessive proportions, stone cladding and the exclusive use of arch, column and pier are the determining characteristics of the built designs (for this cf. M25–27). It was not surprising that Vittorio Cini called the »E'42 style« the ultimate style of the Fascist era. No one wanted to acknowledge officially that this suppressed any individual interpretation and led to barren architectural monotony. Thus the E'42 buildings showed the lack of creative inspiration in Fascist Italian architecture, »Neo-Classical conformism«, as Leonardo Benevolo pointedly put it. SK

M25 Palazzo dei Ricevimenti e dei Congressi
EUR, Piazza J. F. Kennedy (plan G2 3/B and plan VII 2/C)
1937–54
Adalberto Libera

One of the most important competitions for the permanent buildings at the E'42 World Fair in Rome was the Congress Palace for prestigious events. The designs submitted covered a broad spectrum extending from the Rationalist concept by the group around Terragni to the monumental Neo-Classicism of the design by Fariello, Muratori and Quaroni. Libera's original prize-winning project offered a balanced combination of classical architectural forms: the mighty rotunda of the main section, hidden behind the broad bar of the massive portico, was based on a concentric disposition of space. This first design was changed by the architect in favour of an austere solution based on the juxtaposition of cubic volumes. The building was not completed until after the Second World War, but represents one of the high points in the current overall image of the EUR district (M24). As a perspective target in the northern transverse axis it enters into a visual dialogue with the Palazzo della Civiltà del Lavoro (M26).

A longitudinal core building with a broad portico on the main façade contains the key spatial functions for congresses. The central building line is determined by stringent arrangement of a spacious foyer, the large, groin-vaulted hall with several circulation levels and an auditorium at the rear whose main openings lead to the concluding vestibule on the rear façade of the palace. Thus the key feature of the ground plan is a central axis running through the whole building and dividing it into two approximately symmetrical halves. The rooms for their part are subject to a sophisticated

M25 Palazzo dei Ricevimenti e dei Congressi

design approach, which skilfully orchestrates the sequence by constantly changing the height of the rooms. The secondary functions necessary for congresses like offices and service areas are shifted to the longitudinal flanks, so that the consistently executed spatial drama is not vitiated. This meticulously developed planning of the interior corresponds with the harmonious distribution of the cubic masses in the exterior. Here the broad core section functions as an architectural base for the massive central cuboid containing the great hall. The key feature of the front view is the interplay between the heavy, open columned portico and the tall closed cube. Vertical and horizontal as dominant directional tendencies are balanced accordingly. To mitigate the block-like quality of the cuboid is topped by the open segmented arch of the inner groined vaulting. Reduction to historical formal types of architecture, which are excitingly juxtaposed, is the essential feature of the main façade. The rear façade is defined by the open glass membrane of the rear foyer, which formulates a consciously calculated contrast with the rest of the building's stone cladding. Despite the strict treatment of detail and the overall body's almost cold monumentality, the Congress Palace is different from the rest of the World Fair buildings, which tend to be conventional. Precise articulation of the different volumes, juxtaposition of open and closed surfaces and the ostentatious use of modern

M25 Palazzo dei Ricevimenti e dei Congressi

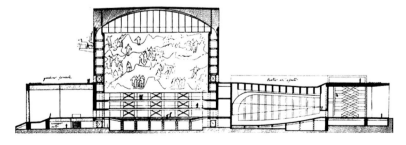

materials like glass and steel develop contrasts that are accepted by the architect and brought together to form a complex whole. SK

M26 Palazzo della Civiltà del Lavoro, formerly Palazzo della Civiltà Italiana

EUR, Piazza della Civiltà del Lavoro (plan G2 3/B and plan VII 2/C)
1937–40
Giovanni Guerrini, Ernesto La Padula, Mario Romano

The competition brief for the main World Fair E'42 building, the Palazzo della Civiltà Italiana, made the very precise requirement that a »classical and monumental feeling« should be the »foundation of architectural inspiration«. A further requirement was the use of local building materials, with restrictions on modern products. With a few exceptions, the designs submitted conformed with these nationalistic ideas. The project by the Guerrini, La Padula and Romano group, which was chosen for realization, stood out because the architects concentrated exclusively on a traditional detail of Roman architecture and the way in which they used it they enhanced it symbolically. After building stopped in 1940 the palace remained incomplete.

The building is a large, almost excessively large cube on a heavy pedestal with access from a broad flight of steps. The closed quality of the cube seems to have been broken almost violently, almost perforated, in that it has a total of 416 arcades on its four sides. This vivid impression is supported by the smooth stone of the remaining wall areas, which are completely undecorated and give the building as a whole a graphic hardness, as though cut with a knife. This produces an apparently empty form, hollowed out by the endless series of arcades, dramatically enhanced by the interplay of light and shade. The arcade motif, reduced to its simple basic form in the exterior design, is a classical element relating to the famous archetypes of Ancient Roman architecture: the arcade was promoted as the dominating design element of the building's exterior in large Roman theatres like the Colosseum (A25) and the Theatre of Marcellus (A17), but reshaped and thus sculpturally revalued by the use of classical column orders to form the so-called tabularium motif (cf. A9). These buildings may form the typological basis that architects wanted to use to express the traditional claim to power made by Fascist state architecture, but they are not a direct architectural model. Something that is more likely to be behind this is a reference to one of the leading tendencies in Italian painting before and after the First World War. The artistic movement called pittura metafisica, represented from about 1911/12 by Giorgio de Chirico, worked with a symbolic revaluation of secular objects that created mysterious and often puzzling pictorial content in their sublime compositional relations. Isolated arcades were a frequently found pictorial element, used as meaningful ciphers and transposed to a metaphorical plane by extreme contrasts of light

M26 Palazzo della Civiltà del Lavoro, formerly Palazzo della Civiltà Italiana

and shade. If one compares these remarkable abbreviations of historical architecture in the images of pittura metafisica with the exterior design of the Palazzo della Civiltà Italiana, the connection is obvious. The architects drew inspiration from a genuinely Italian tendency in Modern painting by making the preferred pictorial object the basis of their design. In this way they did justice to the national requirements of the competition brief and were also able to stake a claim for Modernism by developing contemporary trends. SK

M27 SS. Pietro e Paolo

EUR, Piazzale di SS. Pietro e Paolo (plan G2 3/B and plan VII 2/C)
1937–42
Arnaldo Foschini

The church of SS. Pietro e Paolo in the EUR district is one of the most important examples of Fascist ecclesiastical architecture. It appeared alongside the important exhibition and palace buildings even in the final general development plan for the site, and was raised to the status of being an architectural focal point in the central transverse axis. A powerful ramp, edged with green strips and concluded visually by huge statues of the two apostle princes, leads to the building's raised site. The massive centrally-planned building is set on a Greek cross ground plan. The exterior view is dominated by basic stereometric forms, apparently

M27 SS. Pietro e Paolo

placed additively to form an overall composition: the central block, flanked by the transepts like smaller satellites, is crowned by a drum dome with a lantern on top. The compartments survive as independent primary bodies because the intersections are so precisely articulated by surrounding cornices and as a result of slight variations in the treatment of materials. It is difficult to identify architectural coherence, so the church disintegrates into its component past when viewed from the front and seems remarkably disparate. This may be because the architect drew inspiration from the classical vocabulary of Roman Renaissance and Baroque churches, without possessing an ability to unify in the traditional sense of artistic design. Equally the complete lack of decoration and the undemanding nature of the architectural details mean a conscious rejection of the principles of historical design. Thus a Neo-Classicism is manifest in the conception that tries to convince simply by the sparsely monumental quality of rudimentary geometrical volumes. SK

M28 Palazzina Furmanik
Lungotevere Flaminio 18 (plan I 2/C)
1938–40
Mario de Renzi
De Renzi is a classic case of an 30s architect oscillating between tradition and Modernism: he enjoyed a classical education, and was for a long time commit-

ted to Barocchetto and worked with Aschieri, a principal proponent of the transition from Historicism to Modernism (cf. M8). He did not take part in the 1928 MIAR exhibition, and indeed opposed it in 1931. However, in 1932 (for the Fascist Revolution exhibition) and above all in 1934 (for the post office, M15) he worked with Libera, the leading Rationalist. Nothing was yet to be seen of this in his major social building project (M11). Later as well social building remained de Renzi's principal sphere of work in Orvieto, where his other main Rationalist work of the war years is to be found, and after the war in the Tuscolano quarter (M41). The Palazzina Furmanik was his main work in this genre: broad, with a view of the Tiber and St. Peter's, with two dwellings per floor, and symmetrical in its layout.

The building is considered a main work of Rationalism at a time at which the regime was no longer promoting this direction. The structure, shaped exclusively by the horizontal strip windows and the white bands of wall, is reminiscent of Le Corbusier's Villa Savoye (cf. M33), the principal work of the International Style. And the distribution of rooms with living sections and long balconies at the front and intricately shaped sleeping areas is similar to those in Ridolfi's large palazzina of this period (M21). And yet the building only partially breathes the spirit of Modernism: the sections are fitted together tightly, they do not float. The bands are dominated, as in important prestigious Fascist buildings, by the wall, as the windows are set very far back. This is an elegant building, but it is lacking in asymmetry and dynamics.
SG

M28 Palazzina Furmanik

M29 Villini Accoppiati

M30 Fosse Ardeantine

M29 Villini Accoppiati
Via Nicótera 26 (plan I 2/C–2/D)
1938–43
Luigi Piccinato

A complex was planned in the Vittorie/Trionfale district for the 50th anniversary of Italian independence in 1911, and here the task of building simple rented accommodation was taken more seriously than almost ever before – with moderate success: many parcels remained empty, and a new style was not found for this new building brief. But chance would have it that three decades later Piccinato filled in a gap and decidedly strengthened this modest town-planning genre: but he was not just concerned with planning devices for the town, but for the countryside as well – an idea that Mussolini took up in 1928 when he cried: »Depopulate the cities!« And Piccinato, himself decidedly Modern, was able to implement this strikingly in Sabaudia, about 50 km south of Rome.

After the war Piccinato became a leading figure in the APAO (cf. M36), which promoted individual living. Even here he did not cram eight (artists') apartments per floor into a block, but placed them in the four corners of two blocks with more air and a balcony for each. There are only three apartments in each case in the attic, and communal rooms on the ground floor of the left-hand block. Both blocks retain their freedom of movement entirely in the spirit of the International Style (cf. M30): they are linked only loosely by the central staircase section.

It was not until later that the circulation system was similarly strongly stressed (cf. M67, but also M11). And by using brick he also sounded a rural, almost Neo-Realist note within the orthogonal vocabulary of Modernism – this too had a future in Rome. And ultimately it was also Roman to stress the (wall) depth in the balconies (cf. shortly before even M20). Here the balcony bays become particularly visibly characterized as wall openings, because the street wall had similar proportions. SG

M30 Fosse Ardeantine
Via Ardeantina (plan G2 3/B)
1944–51
Mario Fiorentino, Giuseppe Perugini and others

On 24. April 1944 German troops murdered 335 Roman civilians in a sandstone quarry (fosse) on the Via Ardeantina as a reprisal for an assassination by the Roman resistance – scarcely three months before the liberation of Rome on 4. June 1944. The war had still not ended in northern Italy when the Allies put up the first sums of money and democratic Italy's first competition chose first four and then two from among twelve applying groups – Fiorentino (who had himself been imprisoned as a resistance fighter), Aprile, Calaprina, Cardelli, Coccia (sculptor) and Perugini and Basaldella (sculptors) respectively. The two projects were brought together in the realized work. The jury was made up above all of members of the APAO (including Luigi Piacentini), the Organic Architecture Association, whose journal Metron also published the projects and the built work.

A natural stone wall on the Ardeantine road separates the complex as a whole from its surroundings, like a temenos, the sacred Greek temple precinct. The entrance, designed as a railing made of thorn twigs, is visible from a great distance because of the stone sculpture of two prisoners. Paradoxically this place, where the intention is that victims should be mourned intensively (with borrowings from passion symbolism) is for this reason most strongly trapped in the Fascist past with its inclination to rhetoric, and the figures are scarcely able to detach themselves from this stylistically.

The entrance leads to a square paved with natural stone: here the actual monument appears, raised above a sloping lawn; diagonally opposite to the right is the exit from the old workings (with a path over it). This twists its way across the hilly terrain then back left to the monument. At the corner point in the hills the light breaks dramatically into its darkness through two shafts.

The memorial is plain and consists only of a horizontal, monumental dressed cuboid (25 x 50 m), raised off the ground by eight pilotis (round supports), under which the sarcophaguses were placed in even in three rows in an excavated hollow. The cuboid has a slight concave hollow on its underside, so that it does not seem too oppressive for visitors to the tombs. The design in Rome neither built on the past nor caused any significant effect on the future. And yet weight (gravitas), expressiveness and commitment were specifically Roman values, particularly in the first two post-war decades (more strongly than in northern Italy, for example). At the same time the design was in line with the best inventions of international Modernism. By choosing the simple cuboid, with its allusion to the slab over the tomb, Fiorentino/Perugini first of all chose a form for the monument that emphasized its symbolic value more strongly than a building could have done, but at the same time opted for a silent monument rather than an eloquent one (a sculpture). Silence shaped by human beings was created, at once bedded into and in harmony with surrounding nature. This gave form to basic humanistic values. The rough formal plainness clearly distinguished the structure from the rhetoric of Fascist architecture. Conversely, the future in Rome was to belong to the more intricate Neo-Realism of Ridolfi, the smoother elegance of Moretti and the spatial imagination of Portoghesi. But the cuboid suited the drama of the International Style: only the father of organic architecture, Frank Lloyd Wright, could have made the massive cuboid »float« like this in its surroundings (Falling Water); »floating« masses were also to play a part in the postwar work of one of the main masters of the International Style, Mies van der Rohe. And as early as 1932 Hitchcock and Johnson had identified floating volumes as one of the main characteristics of this style in a book on its fundamentals. But this did not acquire transcendental intensity until the Fosse Ardeantine and the work of Le Corbusier: the raised stone over the tomb, which allows the light to burst in like a halo around it – no symbol coined in the world of Biblical

M31 Stazione Termini

M31 Stazione Termini. Design by Mario Ridolfi

images could be imagined as a stronger symbol of the resurrection. And a monument to war dead has to address resurrection. In Ronchamp Le Corbusier was to replace the cuboid with a monolith and make the image of the rock rolled away from the tomb even more vivid. The first work in democratic Italy combined silence at the sight of the horrors of the past with drama in the hope of a light-filled future. SG

Bibliography: *Metron*, 1947, no. 3 (competition), 1952, p. 2; G. E. Kidder Smith, *Italy Builds*, 1955, p. 174.

M31 Stazione Termini
Piazza dei Cinquecento (plan VI 1/A)
1938–42, 1947–50
Angiolo Mazzoni; Eugenio Montuori, Annibale Vitellozzi

The station of the church-state, built in 1864–71 before the annexation of Rome by the Kingdom of Italy, and redesigned only provisionally in 1911, was to be downgraded as a mere metro station in 1931. But from 1936, when decisions had been taken about the World Fair (M24) and Rome's expansion towards the sea, it was planned by Mazzoni on a new scale. The intimate square in front of it became a Fascist parade ground: the old building was narrower, placed (with the hall end) south of the Servian Wall and with its head near the Baths of Diocletian (A46). The side sections for the terminus station were built by 1942, for departures on the south side and arrivals on the north, also the offices and (not realized) a »Sala Imperiale«. A competition for the head-piece was announced in 1947, and this was built in 1948–50. It was a compromise between the two winning projects (by Montuori, Calini or Vitellozzi, Castellazzi, Fadigati, Pintonello). Today the project by Ridolfi, Quaroni, Fiorentino et. al. is considered superior.

The endless series of blind arcades was intended to give a monumental quality to the side sections, but they turned out to be merely average Fascist values – insignificant when compared with jewels of earlier architecture (A53, B43). When the head section was built the side sections had to be linked, the giant square (shortened only by 50 m in 1947) had to be designed and attention had to be paid to the Servian Wall. Thus a Fascist torso was completed in the most important project of the immediate post-war period (cf. similarly M23). Only Ridolfi addressed the problems this posed.

The completed building is in three parts with hall in front, administrative building and a glazed hall to link it with the tracks, The neutral design of the latter meant that the new building was skilfully distinguished from the side sections. Both groups had proposed a cuboid for the administrative wing. Its form was restrainedly Modern (like the monument to anti-Fascist resistance, M30), and in its execution was like 30s Rationalist buildings, which had Fascist »colouring«: smooth, in house-stone (Travertine), infinitely wide (232 x 28 m) and with extremely narrow ribbon windows (cf. M17, for example). But the building became famous for its entrance hall, which was shifted off the axis to the south because of the ancient Roman wall. The combination of materials – dominating closed stone areas with filigree glass trips – was taken over from the cuboid, though now it had been turned through 90 degrees. The angular, static form was softened and enlivened, as though passengers were to be released into the city with a flourish. Content is plausible as well as form: antithetical principles suggested a turn through 90 degrees. Nevertheless Klotz thought that the canopy expressed the spirit of the kidney table, which could only tolerate the hardness of Modernism with its pure forms when it had been softened down. None of the winning projects, one of which took over the giant arch from Libera's EUR project, contained even a germ of this entrance hall design. A look at the model shows what Klotz meant by his criticism.

The tradition of Rationalism was problematical because it had continued to operate under Fascism. Ridolfi was very sensitive about this, above all with the Neo-Realism of the years to come, but also with this project. One motif is unrestrictedly dominant, the wide-open entrance hall, expressively mobile in outline and in the crossed supports; folded upwards, an open mouth to take in the city; unglazed, a place for true public life, the Res Publica. The past became a genuine concern as well: the jagged line at the top, with no cuboid above it, would have responded to the similarly jagged line of the ancient baths (A46); additionally the entrance hall was shifted (asymmetrically) to the north, towards the old Republican wall (not moved away from it). The wall would have run into the entrance hall, which would have opened up a particularly wide arch to celebrate it. Something new meshed in with the great past! Everything that was built is cheaper: the expressive line is smoothed out – a kidney table; the open roof is down-graded to a small canopy for taxis as they drive up; history is ignored. Ridolfi would have designed the square expressively and addressed the dialogue with the past. He was to make up for this at a later stage. SG

Bibliography: *Metron*, 1947, Nr. 21 (competition); G. Angeleri and U. M. Bianchi, *I cento anni della vecchia Termini*, n. p. (Rome), 1983.

M32 Casa Cooperitiva Astrea

M32 Casa Cooperitiva Astrea
Via Jenner 27–29 (plan G2 2/A)
1947–49
Luigi Moretti

The principal master of the Palazzine realized his first post-war commission with limited means – a Cooperativa was the client. He created a seminal building for the bourgeois type of small apartment »palace«: closed like a block in form, (here) with a flat to the left and right of the central axis on each floor. The middle classes in elegant mood chose the architect who had built the most elegantly under Fascism, the future chief opponent of Neo-Realism.

The façade faces north. Moretti placed the staircases and service rooms on this side. He closed this façade, especially for observers who stand centrally in front of it. The rear he allowed to enjoy its angles and opened it up with windows. This kind of contrast was particularly popular in the early Modernism of the »white« 20s (cf. Villa Stein in Garches, Paris). And as there this basic disposition was not just for functional reasons.

Typical for Moretti's work as a whole was a translation into careful compositions made up of precisely cut, elegant volumes, with carefully calculated handling of light. Thus he bound the balconies in more strongly by treating them like windows, he moved the vertical forms in front of the staircases and devised interesting diagonal sections to capture more light for the kitchens. Moretti raised the main section above the level of the street and designed it – admittedly only with restraint – asymmetrically (cf. also M33), all this a legacy of the 20s. But he clearly turned away from this by merely placing the façade in front of the building (like a shear wall), rather than developing it organically from the inside. With this building Moretti was still wallowing in the clarity of Rationalist forms, but he was soon to start giving his buildings more »Mannerist« disturbing features (cf. M33). SG

M33 Casa del Girasole
Viale Bruno Buozzi 64 (plan I 3/C)
1947–50
Luigi Moretti

In the Casa del Girasole Moretti created the epitome
of the Roman palazzina, the building type that the
newly rich bourgeoisie of Dolce Vita Rome lived in.
The project was under a fortunate star. The client, A.
Fossataro, was a prosperous and art-loving building
contractor and film producer. He wanted to live in the
roof garden flat himself and thus placed almost no
financial restrictions on the planning. The building, in
the middle of the most important palazzina quarter
north of the Villa Borghese, enjoyed the advantages
of extensive development in the surrounding area.

It was Moretti's declared intention, to harmonize the
palazzina, the bourgeois form of the palace, as a type
with Modern individual architectural language. Framp-
ton called the Casa del Girasole the Baroque counterpart to Rationalism in Como, for the building is – in a
Baroque way – almost a temple, but Modern in its language, and that means Rationalist in Italy.

The façade shows Moretti's ambivalent position
between the tradition of Modernism, the International
Style and a preference for mannerisms, with which he
anticipated to principal characteristics of Post-Modernism. Moretti created a »facciata« in the true sense,
a show side, detached both from the ground and the
actual building; it is simply laced in front of it (only
loosely connected), and protrudes beyond it at the
sides. The main section seems to be detached from
the ground, »floating« above the narrower, darkly
earthy lower substructure, and only supported at certain points. This the building had in common with
International Style villas in the 20s, for instance the
Villa Savoye, but it was also linked with classical palace building, in which the piano nobile is also placed
on a plinth in a similar way (H22). Thus Moretti created
an urban counterpart to the Villa Savoye. The clear
horizontal division, the ribbon window, returned, and
so did the smooth, closed, white surface in bands.

M33 Casa del Girasole

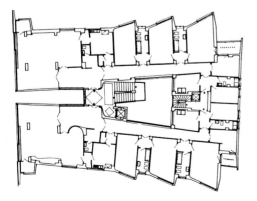

M33 Casa del Girasole

Nevertheless the façade was nothing less than Rationalistic or even International. Even the handling of the
central topoi was characteristic: Moretti cut up the
fixed body vertically and gave it a gable. The masters
of the International Style built closed blocks and flat
roofs. Moretti needed the gable to give his palazzina
the major personal note, its similarity with the temple,
and the cut according to his own words, in order to
establish elevation and provide light for the inner
courtyard, but apparently also to break up the solid
block. The gable was again too flat, to make a decidedly anti-Rationalistic effect – as in Ridolfi's INA buildings (M37). Moretti handled the second, frequently
emphasized characteristic of the large form with similar ambivalence: the façade is asymmetrical in the
base area and the gable. In the leading book on the
International Style Hitchcock and Johnson had called
asymmetry, which took over from (dead) symmetry,
as the second main feature of the style. But Moretti
used it so hesitantly that it looked more as though
he was playing: the lower building was slightly shifted,
the gable was slightly slanting, and symmetry was not
definitely rejected. He did keep the façade in the formal language of the International Style, but by detaching it from the building like a shear wall, he negated
the strong, sculptural corporeality that characterized
building in this style.

The sides give a different impression. Excessive
refinement of materials – an Italian trait that had been
the most striking feature distinguishing Terragni and
his Rationalists from the International Style – is no longer to be found in the rear sections. Moretti concealed

a »Post-Modern« joke here: the topos of anthropo-morphism in art was made banal in the form of a plaster leg in the window reveal of the left-hand flat on the bottom floor. Playful loading with content is also to be seen much more markedly in the upper storeys. Here Moretti had the wall thrust out diagonally outwards three times, to catch the light. This made the building – the name was chosen by Moretti him-self – one that turned towards the sun (gira al sole), and not banally the sunflower house, as the often repeated translation suggests. The bedrooms are behind this wall.

The relationship between the exterior and the interior of a building was rediscovered as a central theme by the International Style. The inner courtyard was already a point of reference for the central section in the façade. The courtyard (and not the light, added façade) in its darkness forms the concealed symmetrical axis (as Moretti called it himself elsewhere), the centre for the disposition of all the interior spaces: in each of the lower three main storeys there are two (almost) symmetrically placed apartments on the left and right with the drawing-room on the façade side, the three widening bedrooms on the side façade and the service rooms towards the back; on the top floor is just a single apartment (attico) with a roof garden and a second unit above it. A ramp in the centre – a microscopic obituary to the Baroque staircase – provides access to the building.

Moretti, like Portoghesi a little later (M50), realized basic principles of Post-Modernism, long before the concept and principles were formulated with a considerably broader response. The Casa del Girasole embodies sensitively, like very few buildings since, »Complexity and Contradiction in Architecture« in the spirit of Venturi. SG

Bibliography: A. Belluzzi and C. Conforti, *Architettura italiana 1944–1984*, Rome, 1985, p. 95.

M34 Villino Alatri
Via Paisello 38 (plan II 2/C)
1948/49
Mario Ridolfi, Mario Fiorentino, Wolfgang Frankl

Ridolfi started his series of private houses in parallel with Moretti (M 32, M33) in terms of time, and with this a second strand of development – usually working with Frankl, while Fiorentino supported him in the development of Neo-Realism (M37). Like Moretti, Ridolfi wanted to give the palazzina type a newly expressive quality. Two years before Ridolfi had promoted good craftsmanlike detail as the key to a new formal language, and the supporters of so-called organic architecture had declared the contextual relation to be the main problem. Ridolfi now added a storey to Morpurgo's 1928 Historicist building, and removed its top balcony, which was similar to that of the Palazzo Falconieri (B63), and filled in the terrace (above the fourth round-arched window on the left) up to the cornice that ran all the way round. In a city that was constantly growing as a result of over-building like no

M34 Villino Alatri

other, he thus created a key building that was innovative in its concrete composition, but old in its concept (cf. H27).

The old building was not continued, but also did not acquire a counterpart. Differently from five years later (M43), floor heights, cornices and the colour of the materials in the new building were scarcely different from those of the old one, but the vocabulary was Rationalistic and Modern like no other building by Ridolfi. The contrast between permeability at the top and closed walls at the bottom could have been more marked, glass and concrete are not very conspicuous here (cf. M54). Conversely Ridolfi took away the best of the Barocchetto building, its staggered arrangement, by cutting it off. From now on the horizontal dominated. The building grew, but seemed lower afterwards. It had not found its own language of contextualism. Only details (breaks in cornices, varied balcony designs) give a hint of Ridolfi's later Neo-Realism. SG

M35 Palazzina Zaccardi
Via de Rossi 12 (plan IX 2/B)
1950/51
Mario Ridolfi, Wolfgang Frankl

Ridolfi created his first post-war palazzina at the same time as Zevi's main work of organic architecture (M36) and his own INA complex (M37), the incunabulum of Neo-Realism. Two loosely linked main blocks each with a staircase provide space for one or two apartments on each floor.

Parataxis dominated, rather than subordination – Wright saw organic architecture as democratic archi-

M35 Palazzina Zaccardi

M36 Palazzina

M36 Palazzina
Via Pisanelli 1 (plan I 2/D)
1950–52
Bruno Zevi

tecture. The main blocks seem just to be loosely combined, in a row. Ridolfi preferred to segregate the blocks – more direct and clear – rather than twist the cube as Zevi did (cf. M36). Their show sides also stand together, turned towards each other through 90 degrees, again built paratactically within themselves with a weak centre and strong sides, more expressive in the diagonal forms, the diagonal walls and the balconies. And so it is not just the building as a whole and the rooms that have individual and expressive forms, but many of the details as well: the irregularly placed windows and the freely modelled lower canopy à la Gaudí. Tafuri criticized this as a »dodecaphony of geometrical distortions«.

But this vocabulary inspired affection, and was adopted. It became the basis for a poetics of poverty. And this could more easily be created by loving attention to detail rather than with invented systems of the kind that Zevi was promoting at the time (cf. M36).

After this came the INAIL palazzina, then the Palazzina Mancioli (M42), with much more block-like ground plans (central planning) and elevations (with corner towers and roof bevelling), and also clearer in the formulation of a personal vocabulary. It was precisely in this point that the Palazzina Zaccardi and the Villino Alatri (M34) were transitional works: before the war Ridolfi's vocabulary was closer to that of the Rationalists (M20, M21). Now it was being carefully revised; it became clearly independent only in the work of subsequent years. SG

Discussion in post-war Rome revolved around Zevi's demand for »architettura organica«, expressed in 1945 in a monograph of the same name and in 1950 in the first Modern architectural history of Italy. Those returning from the USA founded the APAO (Associazione per l'architettura organica) the magazine Metron, while Milan remained Rationalistic with Domus and MSA. Zevi wanted to revise Modernism, Rationalism in Italy: functional building (following Frank Lloyd Wright) was to be understood in a less reduced sense; psyche and well-being of residents was also part of this, He undertook to implement this sensible postulate at 15 Via dei Monti Parioli (1947/48), then in the Via Pisanelli.

Zevi no longer divided the storeys, he piled four complete apartments one on top of the other, villas with many balconies, with a roof garden apartment right at the top. The right angle was eliminated, light and connections became important. In the outer cube Zevi turned the orientation of the rooms through 45 degrees and he placed the stairs in the dark centre. This gave him orthogonally placed corner areas (four independent living areas) with diagonally placed spaces between them. Angling two groups of space against each other led to individual, expressive room sections with a lot of angles, and to wedge-shaped incisions into the cube that were deeper on the broad sides. Thus the rooms were lit from several sides and there was room for terraces on the long sides. Hollow spaces which form a break are the hallmark of this architecture.

Zevi never built another palazzina. On the contrary, Moretti's elegant style (M32, M33) and Ridolfi's block-like style (M42) found favour. In Zevi's case the Modern formal language seemed so distorted that the order of the exterior of the building was lost. SG

M37 Quartiere Tiburtino
Via Tiburtina (plan IX 4/B)
1950–54
Ludovico Quaroni, Mario Ridolfi and others
771 apartments for 4 000 residents were built on 8.8 hectares, buildings with three to five and towers with seven storeys. The commission came from INA, which had been founded by the Legge Fanfani on 28. 2. 1949 to reduce the accommodation crisis by building houses and at the same time to move against unemployment. INA was organized to work in two seven-year periods. Funds were raised and administered by the National Social Security system. The first large INA complex in Rome was built on Via Tiburtina, and was intended to shape style as well. The »Roman school« of Neo-Realism emerged. The architects in charge chose members of APAO (cf. M36) and their own students to work with them. These were Aymonimo and Fiorentino, Chiarini, Lenci, Melograni (all students of Quaroni, with the exception of Fiorentino, who was a student of Ridolfi), and also Menichetti, Gorio, Lanza, Lugli, Rinaldi and Valori. The first named made the greatest impact in the later development of these residential complexes. The programme had a negative effect to the extent that it brought about post-war speculation.

Neo-Realism turned against the Fascist, the Rationalist and an urban formal language. It claimed that

M37 Quartiere Tiburtino

M37 Quartiere Tiburtino

they were inadequate for reconstruction. Ridolfi had already shaped the INA guidelines; he saw a modest style as the right response to the hollow drama of Fascism. The material should be indigenous, to guarantee cheap and rapid building. Rationalism had never clearly detached itself from Fascism in Rome and was considered urban. Ridolfi turned away from this kind of approach in the Palazzina Rea (cf. M20), Quaroni was horrified by cities after spending six years in India. People wanted more than the careful reform of Modern forms that Zevi was aiming for with the APAO.

Quaroni was more interested in the social context, Ridolfi more in the way that things were done. The complex as a whole, the urban development model, the fabric were more important to both of them than the individual buildings. The model that was chosen – and proposed by INA – was not orthogonal and Rationalistic, but full of nooks and crannies, a snake of buildings. It followed Scandinavian models, but did not adopt the passages, so had no homely areas (cf. M38). The complex was arranged in a triangle and designed as a »fortress«, with bulwarks in the form of towers (usually several) at the points. A great deal of heed was paid to the communal areas: the (pedestrian) streets, the shops and the communal building (placed in the centre).

Modernism, Rationalism was also the actual reference point in the design. Some key features were adopted: a striving for condensation, also asymmetry and raising the roof trusses, admittedly in the form of gables, not flat roofs (cf. for all this M33). But the vocabulary of the individual forms was deliberately anti-rational. Gables, balconies, wrought iron railings and outside steps all seemed rural. Local features were the materials, the (Italian) delight in colour and forms like the diamond-shaped railing pattern that Ridolfi used again later (M40) and borrowed from the tobacco halls in the Terni area. Spontaneity and chance were to be expressed, and make their contribution to the well-being of the (mostly poorer!) residents, but in fact they were probably planned. There are certainly also anti-Modern features in the principles. Towers and low buildings were not juxtaposed to form contrasts, as was the Modern way, but here the principle of continuous growth is followed. Also the tower, the quintessentially Modern structure, was subject to the dictates of the gable building method, even though this does seem alienated: with high stilted gables in the front towers (similar to M71) and triple ones in the rear ones, where however the orthogonal forms of Modernism are replaced by extremely complex ones. The towers are intended to be individual pieces, and not duplicated at random arbitrarily as in early drawing board plans by architects like Le Corbusier. Precisely for this reason the complex did not have any successors. It was an experimental laboratory with far too many facets: many motifs were not repeated, gables and nooks and crannies were excessively dominant. Scarcely anything was ordered.

Against this, opposite the centre, Busiri Vici placed a church, built from 1965–71, which followed the best principles of Modernism: the skeleton building method, the flat roof, delight in contrast, unity of material (here concrete, the material of Modernism). SG

Bibliography: *Casabella Continuità*, 1957, no. 215; L. Beretta Anguisola, *I 14 anni del piano INA Casa*, Rome, 1963.

M38 UNRRA Case S. Basilio
S. Basilio (plan G1 3/B)
1950–55
Mario Fiorentino (houses), Serena Boselli (shops)
UNRRA planned smaller complexes than INA (M37), here with war victim funds from UNO and the USA, on 8.5 hectares and for 900 residents. One of the main young architects of the first INA complex was building, again in a Neo-Realistic and rural manner.

He transferred INA virtues to the smaller commission, but diversity and experiment gave way to Fiorentino's calmer language; he was now entirely responsible for the project. This is already true of the detached houses: once more they were rural in concept: with bricks laid in a grid pattern, the changing window size, the little gardens and again with unpretentious lateral stairs. But these motifs were reduced in number and recurred in a more orderly fashion. The complex buildings were replaced by simple, brightly coloured and white-framed gabled houses of the kind found in Scandinavian architecture (here admittedly in the earthier colours of Latium).

The more strongly ordering hand of the single architect also shows in the urban complex, which is once more based on a Scandinavian model: it was a matter of creating homely and private squares. The co-ordinate cross of the two larger streets is intended for the public at large; this was enlarged into a square and slightly displaced at the centre, so that it does not look Modernistically perfect. The shops in the square were conceived in functional Modern terms – the best contrast with the more homely design of the residential complex. The streets lead into a void. This is not so for the paths (which are still passable); one goes of to the left and right of each of the arms of the cross; they are tailored for pedestrians, branch out between the houses and end in quiet squares, surrounded by buildings. But you are not trapped here, a footpath leads back to the centre. SG

M39 Casa Cooperativa »La Tartaruga«
Via Innocenzo X 25 (plan G1 2/C and plan VII 1/A)
1951–54
Ludovico Quaroni, Carlo Aymonino
Two colleagues on the Tiburtino complex (M37), thus protagonists of Neo-Realism, here transferred the stylistic principles of that movement to the palazzina type, the small, middle-class residential block that is complete in itself. At the same time Ridolfi took the same step for high-rise buildings with the INA towers (M40).

The architects chose a U as the basic shape and thus the typically less urban of the classic palazzina models. The staircase occupies the centre of the courtyard, and appears glazed and flanked by two symmetrical apartments in each case, with just one on the ground and attic floors. Even the choice of the basic forms and above all the many slightly distorted angles confirm a preference for the stylistic principles of organic architecture and of Neo-Realism, which were anti-city and close to the people, not elegant and regular. The surface design was also Neo-Realistic and similar to that of Ridolfi: a (concrete) frame was filled with material of a craft origin (brick), thus produc-

M38 UNRRA Case S. Basilio

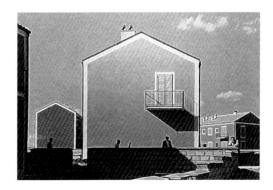

M40 Quartiere Viale Etiopia

ing an agitated, coarse effect. Brutalism, an internationally successful tendency (cf. M54) later tried a corresponding approach with modern materials.

The expressive potential of this surface design was always emphasized, but it had no successors. For the (small) palace was deprived of its own, settled proportions. The architects had created little towers, or highrise buildings like Ridolfi, just lower, and cut off: all the cuboids are set vertically, with no horizontal caesura or fixing. Also the Neo-Realistic language was not that of the middle classes, who preferred the sharply cut, elegant forms that Moretti had al-ready given to the palazzina on a number of occasions (M32, M33). SG

M40 Quartiere Viale Etiopia
Viale Etiopia (plan G1 2/B)
1951–54, 1957–62
Mario Ridolfi, Wolfgang Frankl; Mario Fiorentino
Ridolfi built for INA (for this see M37) a second time, closer to the city centre: eight 9 to 10 storey buildings, each 14 m deep and 23 to 33 m wide. In the wide buildings each floor is quartered in a cruciform shape, and in the narrow ones they are cut into thirds by a T-shaped dividing line. Thus there was room for four or three dwellings per floor, 30 or 40 per building. Portoghesi, protagonist of the development after 1960, called these buildings the best in Italy since the war. In 1957–60 Fiorentino added two pairs of towers (on the right) and two more (in the background (in 1960 to 1962).

Ridolfi's buildings thrive on the combination of Neo-Realistic elements with Modern ones, especially standardization. The rural character of the first INA complex and the highly individual relation to users were weakened, and the new buildings also make an urban effect. This can be seen even in the key forms: roofs were simply bevelled off and not closed with gables, thus combining the Modern flat roof with the old gabled one. This makes the buildings look »round« at the top, and also very physical and solid. The concrete frame, essentially a construction form in terms of function, was given rural craft fillings in the form of majolica, cast iron railings, »bull's-eye« panes and rows of diamond shapes. This gave the overall form a human and manageable quality. Expressive contrasts between light and shade were produced. Filling and frame are clearly distinct, the bevelling of the framing sections adds to this impression and at the same time makes the building look more solid. And the row of balconies on the fifth floor, which provide the over-all form with effective articulation, have their parallel in the rows of shops, which Le Corbusier used to place half way up the building. This storey, in its support element also shows the thickening (which became famous) that was used to make the weight of the building visible; the ancient principle of krasis was greatly exaggerated to this end.

But standardization did not mean any loss of diversity, which was seen as a postulate of being close to users in Neo-Realistic and organic architecture. The buildings differ in width. Two types were developed for each of narrow sides and long sides, and all possible combinations are found. The same details do appear, tiles, for example, but not in the same place. The colours change between yellow and red. The arrangement of the buildings does not follow a grid either; attention was simply paid to the fact that the ensemble should look closed, like a fortress: broader buildings were placed close together on the ends, and entrances and staircases were shifted inside the square.

Fiorentino designed the first towers similarly to those of his teacher, placed them in pairs and diagonally, thus giving rhythm to the run of the street. But the buildings had become more sober, the arrangement more regular, the standardization advanced, most strongly in the rearmost pair of towers (dating from 1962): here only the concrete frame remained a constant. So now diamond bar or windows were in one piece (because the were cast, no longer in brick). Ridolfi's buildings seem to swell, and have a built look about them – like those of Le Corbusier; Fiorentino's buildings make a cooler impression, almost like Mies van der Rohe's metal-frame buildings. The roof pitches became hollow and seem less chunky. In Fiorentino's case standardization became monotonous in large buildings in particular, as can be seen from his later key work in Corviale (M67). Towards the end of the 50s the forms became smoother, Functionalism started to drive out Neo-Realism. Additionally the towers strikingly lost volume, especially the ones that are stepped. SG

M41 Quartiere Tuscolano

Via del Quadraro / Via Cartagine (Tuscolano 2) / Via Selinunte 59 (Tuscolano 3) (plan G2 4/B)
1950–51 (1st stage); 1952–55 (2nd stage, Tuscolano 2); 1953/54(3rd stage, Tuscolano 3)
Mario de Renzi, Saverio Muratori (master plan); Mario de Renzi, Saverio Muratori, Lucio Cambellotti, Giuseppe Perugini, Dante Tassotti, Luigi Vagnetti (individual buildings); Adalberto Libera (Tuscolano 3)

The Tuscolano quarter is the largest housing estate built by the INA Casa housing co-operative in Rome. It was built in three phases, and provided 3150 homes for approx. 18 000 residents on a total area of 35.5 hectares. In the early 50s a start was made on the first section in the south-east of the city, with the extent of the planning area and the distribution of the buildings still relating to the requirements of the 1949 district development plan. For the second phase, de Renzi and Muratori were commissioned to devise a new urban concept that would link up directly with previous development in the south-west. Tuscolano 2 was built from 1952 to 1955, and involved Cambellotti, Perugini, Tassotti and Vagnetti, who were responsible for designing individual sections. An independent component complex was to be built to form a southern conclusion, and Libera was commissioned to plan this. Libera ignored the structures that were already in place and designed an independent small estate, which was realized as Tuscolano 3 in 1953/54.

Although the two last-mentioned residential concepts followed each other directly in terms of time, it is still possible to discern striking differences in spatial arrangement and architectural structure: Tuscolano 2 is based on an approximately orthogonal axis framework with parallel streets and a central main axis, which divides the complex as a whole into two areas of almost exactly the same size. Terraced buildings with five storeys are arranged along the system of roads, and characterized by spatial staggering as independent terraced houses. These were either placed

M41 Quartiere Tuscolano

M41 Quartiere Tuscolano

at angles at the central linking points or displaced diagonally in relation to each other, to avoid monotony in the linear run of the individual rows. Instead of using a rigid disposition the architects chose a diversely articulated organizational pattern, which is intended to convey the impression of a complex that has developed organically. Tower buildings on a cruciform or square ground plan with up to ten storeys were placed as visual focal points at the ends of the street intended to screen the residential area from its surroundings. In contrast with this, Tuscolano 3 consists of a dense texture of building elements of the same shape, cut off from the surroundings by enclosing walls, and accessible from a central garden. The basic module is a sophisticated structural type made up of four L-shaped residential units with their own inner courtyard. The size and interior distribution of these single storey dwellings is based on the spatial needs of a relatively large family, who acquire their own outdoor space in the form of the little inner courtyard. Libera's concept is based on the key thought of making detached houses of minimal size into a continuous fabric of housing, thus creating an architectural balance between private and community building. He thus succeeded, without falling into the conventional view of Modern estate building with its preference for large anonymous complexes, in combining the social requirements of collective living with the right to individual development. This shows Libera's approach to innovative planning theory, as impeccably formulated at the IX. CIAM Congress in Aix-en-Provence in 1953. The idea of raising a precisely articulated residential unit to the parameter of an intact urban organism was taken up again in the late 50s by the international Structuralist movement. SK

M42 Palazzina Mancioli I

Via Vulci / Via Lusitania (plan VIII 2/B)
1953
Mario Ridolfi, Wolfgang Frankl

This palazzina is the second in a row of three with similar themes, between the 1952 INAIL palazzina (96 Viale Marco Polo) and the 1959/60 Palazzina Mancioli II (Via Vulci, next door). The last-named is the Roman legacy of the master before his departure for Terni, which is often explained by the fact that the economic miracle took away the previously fertile ground for Ridolfi's poetry of the »poor«. Later Ridolfi created only the AGIP tower project for Rome (ill. on p. 300). The Palazzina Mancioli I is linked with the 1952 palazzina by the way in which space is distributed on the three main floors: four apartments per storey (with central staircase), two small, symmetrical ones and two large asymmetrical ones. But the attic storey contains only three apartments – corresponding with the division in the 1959/60 palazzina; these are asymmetrical, with bevelled corners.

This series established a type, and fundamental things became standard. All that remained Neo-Realistic were some of the details, the balconies, for instance. But the great step forward was that Ridolfi created a Modern counterpart for the block-like Roman urban palace. Its principle characteristics were: the central plan, which had been traditional for Ridolfi ever since the Palazzina Rea (M20); the solid block formation, out of which even the balconies scarcely broke; and the correspondence between interior and exterior, which can be seen very markedly in the four »towers«. External features are not applied, but are the outer form of the interior spaces. The forces inherent in the building seem to be thrusting outwards. The structure is a solid body, not a mere accumulation of façades. Here the golden mean was found between classical form (H25) and Modern language (e. g. the asymmetrical ground plan and the sparse wall). Ridolfi decided on a classically tripartite structure: with a motor-car workshop down below, a main section and a roof garden (cf. similarly H22). The building also seems well balanced in its horizontal extent, closed at the edges, tripartite in between with dark incisions in the middle and modelled »towers« on the flanks. The roof garden zone seems the most closed and sculptural – like late Le Corbusier at almost exactly the same time (Chandigarh). In these buildings the roof takes up almost as much space as the wall; thus Ridolfi chose the proportions of the roof with a view to the overall façade (and not in terms of the section of which it is a part) – this too had been good practice since the late Baroque (e. g. Vierzehnheiligen). These sections are the key motifs of the building, making it »round« at the top. In the INA high-rise buildings (M40), Ridolfi created an overall roof with the roof bevelling, but each palazzina dwelling – appropriately to its individual character – had its own top section. SG

M43 Villino Astaldi
Via Porpora 22 (plan II 2/C)
1954–56
Mario Ridolfi, Wolfgang Frankl
The Villino Astaldi is situated, like the Villino Alatri (M34) which is five years older, by the Villa Borghese gardens. Once more the architect put an addtional storey on top of an Historicist building.

M43 Villino Astaldi

Ridolfi built a »little hut« in the shape of a Greek cross. Each arm has a plain gable roof for which the brick from the old building was re-used, protruding in each case (except on the side facing away from the park, which is the staircase section). Three arms are brick-built; the one facing the park is all glazed except for the side next to the adjacent arms of the cross.

The building has two characteristic fields of tension, between old and new and between inside and outside. Ridolfi now commits himself more consistently to antithesis in the juxtaposition of old and new. The old building was urban in character, and so Ridolfi – so close to nature – emphasized the rural elements: a roof garden with a country villa was created, set-off by a thick line. The villa seems shallow and modest, but it has a noble core: the Greek cross refers to Palladio's most important villa, the so-called Rotunda, a masterpiece of rural nobility, standing on the top of a hill. Something anti-urban – Ridolfi's guiding theme – here in large format! The relationship between inside and outside was a key theme of Modernism. Once more the modest exterior contains a polished core. The gable as a main motif shifted from the elevation to the ground plan. Four rhombuses were produced as arms, with a domed star in the centre. Stairs and conservatory were separated; a tripartite main space (arm, crossing arm) remained, completely integrated, unlike Palladio's narrow central rotunda. But then each section has its ceiling and thus its own nature (cf. M50). Modest language, big idea – a palace in the form of a hut! SG

M44 Sede della Democrazia Cristiana

M44 Sede della Democrazia Cristiana
EUR, Piazza Luigi Sturzo (plan G2 3/B)
1955–58
Saverio Muratori

The headquarters of the Italian Christian Democratic
Party came into being during the retrospective urban
measures for the E'42 World Fair, with which Giorgio
Calza Bini intended to transform the existing complex into a new suburb from the mid-1950s onwards
(cf. M24). Designs by Adalberto Libera and Saverio
Muratori emerged as victors from a first competition.
A second vote chose Muratori's concept for building,
after previous unsuccessful attempts to combine the
two designs.

The Party headquarters is a longitudinal, closed
building block, developing around a central inner
courtyard. The ground plan is determined by a surrounding spatial arrangement, linked by a corridor
system and enclosing the key functions like auditorium, conference rooms and so on in the core area of
the building. The rigid symmetry of the spatial sequences and the use of traditional access systems
show the conventional nature of this ground plan disposition. The architect used an equally traditional design approach for the exterior: the powerful building,
with storeys of different heights, rises above a base
storey made up of massive concrete piers. The alternation of window axes of different widths, which in its
specific sequence is reminiscent of the traditional design motif of the rhythmic bay, loosens up the austere
articulation of the wall. The first floor is identified as a
piano nobile by its size and the use of heavy segmental arches. This is followed by two intermediate storeys reminiscent of mezzanines, topped by an attic
storey under the eaves. A continuous hipped roof
forms the upper conclusion. Despite the use of Modern principles like the piered foundation and the bands
of windows, Muratori has implemented the theme of
a public show building using the vocabulary of Italian
architectural history. Behind the massive square with
central inner courtyard is concealed the Renaissance
palace type, as represented impeccably in Rome by
the Palazzo Farnese (H25). In the same way the rhyth-

mic quality of the window axes, the hierarchy of the
floors and the detail elements like the segment gable,
the protruding eaves cornice and the hipped roof indicate a historicizing formal language.

Muratori expressed his theoretical and urban studies, which he had pursued since the early 50s, in architectural form in the Democrazia Cristiana headquarters. The starting point of this analysis was the
»tessuto urbano«, the urban fabric, which he exam-
ined using a typological method. His most important
conclusion was to establish a precise interrelationship
between building typology, urban morphology and architectural history. Concise archetypes and fundamental design principles were declared to be constants in
historical development, which the architect could use
as effective and stable instruments in the design process. The Party headquarters reflects this methodo-
logical approach better than almost any other of his
diverse projects. Without falling into the exaggerated
ideas of the earlier Fascist architecture, Muratori distanced himself clearly from the specific procedures of
Modern architecture. Thus he became the intellectual
originator of the tendency in architectural theory that
was founded in the early 60s in Italy by Carlo Aymonino and Aldo Rossi, and is defined by the term »Neo-
Rationalism«. SK

M45 Palazzetto dello Sport
Via Pietro Coubertin (plan I 2/B)
1956–58
Pier Luigi Nervi, Annibale Vitellozzi

Nervi was responsible for the most important sports
facilities for the 1960 Olympics. This round building, a
multi-purpose hall for gymnastics, fencing, volleyball
and basketball etc. seats 5 000 spectators; it is 50 m
in diameter and 14 m high. The services run under the
tiers of seats. Nervi was probably Italy's best-known
architect in the 60s.

Nervi probably owes his fame above all to construction. He called his most important book on architecture Costruire Correttamente. Most of his buildings
were the result of competitions, and he usually (also)
won them on grounds of cost. He used his own con-

M45 Palazzetto dello Sport

M45 Palazzetto dello Sport

struction firm from the late 20s. He had developed the technique of prefabricated reinforced concrete sections for a Turin exhibition hall, as shuttering costs could make up over half the cost in complicated cases. Additionally the building period was reduced – in Turin it could not exceed a winter. Also parts like this could be designed much more freely as they were cast rather than shuttered. In the Palazzetto Nervi used 1620 diamond-shaped cassette sections for the gigantic membrane dome, which was supported by 36 Y-girders, which because of the equality in the angle of inclination prepare visually for the long curve of the shallow dome and carry the thrust with maximum efficiency. The two are linked by triangular pieces that appear to be linked in a jagged continuum by »little gables«. Thus the roof skin, which is drawn down a little deeper than the supporting framework, seems like a tent skin. The thrust is diverted into the ground by a reinforced concrete ring. The filling ring wall of brick and glass is clearly distinct from the supporting framework – as was the case at the same time in the work of the other great reinforced concrete builder of international status, Eero Saarinen (Dulles International Airport and the TWA terminal at John F. Kennedy International Airport).

The aesthetics of Nervi's constructions were praised as exemplary in the 60s. Huxtable said that Nervi had overcome the unnatural separation of construction and form that originated in the late 18C. Nervi liked to quote Sullivan's guideline »form follows function«, and tried to derive new aesthetic charms from each changed prefabricated section. His buildings were considered just as outstanding for our century as engineering structures like the Eiffel Tower or the Crystal Palace had been for the previous one. Here Nervi too was an exponent of the International Style, which was pursuing corresponding aims with

the liberation of the metal frame from its stone cladding in skyscraper building at the same time. But where Mies van der Rohe created a style that could be used for all building projects, Nervi always created buildings for special purposes in the form of megastructures. Raising the spherical cap from the substructure was also in the spirit of the International Style: this created a wreath of light and the dome acquired a floating quality (cf. M30).

But today Nervi's work is seen as locked into tradition, and called Neo-Monumentalism. This does not have to be negative. Nervi really did make use of concrete's ability to be modelled. The Palazzetto in particular seems like a sculpture, a monument. And visitors feel enveloped by the two round shells above and below them. But Nervi, who was from Lombardy, always remains cool. Rigid symmetry, calmed, »classical«, almost monotonously even lines, the circle as the ideal form, are the features that seem traditional in his work. And the toothed wreath of the roof skin outside remained quite inexpressive, compared with the one in the Ridolfi project for the station, where Vitellozzi, the co-architect for the Palazzetto, had already once taken it over and rendered it harmless (M31). SG

Bibliography: A. L. Huxtable, *Pier Luigi Nervi*, New York, 1961; P. Desideri, *Pier Luigi Nervi*, Bologna, 1982.

M46 Stadio Flaminio
Viale Tiziano / Via dello Stadio (plan I 2/B)
1957–59
Pier Luigi Nervi, Antonio Nervi

Nervi had laid the basis for his fame with the stadium in Florence (1929–32) and extended it in the 30s and 40s with works in other cities, always large concrete structures. He had taught in the engineering faculty in Rome since 1945, and built another stadium for the Olympics. This seated 55 000 spectators. The stands are immediately adjacent to the pitch, as there are no running tracks. (In Florence there was one, on one side.) Under the stadium are completely independent sections like swimming-pools.

M46 Stadio Flaminio

The structure surrounding the actual shell remained essentially unchanged from 1929. This is true of the bipartite roof and the way in which it bulges towards the middle, and also of the access points for the stadium from the outside (and a surrounding gallery). In Florence Nervi had devised an additional showpiece in the form of a two-flight spiral staircase for this purpose, which caused a considerable stir. But after the war his style did become more traditional, and his preference for calmer forms more marked.

The shell itself seems unusual – and different from the one in Florence. Not only the prefabricated structure was new: Nervi built up the shell like the hull of a ship, using bearers (like ribs) with tiers on top (like planks). The shape had also changed. Here Nervi had no room for manoeuvre: it had to correspond largely to that of the old 1911 Stadio Nazionale, which had been built to celebrate Italy's 50th anniversary. And so a crescent shape, which would have provided the best visibility, could not be used for the long sides. Nervi tried to achieve a similar effect by making the long sides steeper and the narrow sides shallower. This produces the characteristic form that makes the stadium look as though it is running out at the front and the back. SG

M47 La Rinascente
Piazza Fiume (plan II 2/D)
1957–61
Franco Albini, Franca Helg

When Albini and Helg received this commission in 1957 they were the first representatives of the Lombard school, the second major movement in postwar Italy alongside the Roman school, to build a large building in central Rome. An unprecedented literary argument flared up, involving major theoreticians from Rogers (Milan) via Tafuri to Portoghesi (Rome). Albini himself had decidedly Rationalistic roots, but on the other hand he was a leading representative of contextualism as propagated in northern Italy: alongside Gardella's »old« Venetian apartment (Zattere), Albini's Museo S. Lorenzo (Genoa) was the principal example

M47 La Rinascente

of a 50s building that adapted to the old urban an architectural context. The first, very courageous design (1957–59) and the transition to the built version (1959 to 1961) are to be seen against this background.

Albini combined like no other architect sensitivity to the historical surroundings with Rationalistic elegance and harmonious form. The characteristic feature of the first project was the dark framework of steel T-beams that came together diagonally in the double parking deck, the complete closure of the gaps using windowless Travertine slabs and the external staircase running diagonally across the narrow side. But it was obvious that Albini did not see the Historicist development of the area as the central reference point, but Ridolfi's most important 50s complex, the INA highrise buildings (M40), the principal work of that period in the whole of Rome. Albini recognized the skeleton building method there as a Modern solution, combining functionalism (in the structure) and a high degree of expressiveness, and the short bevelling in the roof area as a form of unity between the Modern flat and the classical gabled roof. Albini certainly did enhance (and close) the surfaces. His building was not intended to look craftsmanlike and rural, but civic. He also allowed the steel frame – following Mies van der Rohe – to protrude characteristically on the outside, and introduced, also following Modern theory, clearly asymmetrical elements. The open parking deck on the roof added a second element to the building's traffic system that was emphasized – the »innards« of the functional structure –, along with the stairs running diagonally over the building. This had a prominent predecessor in the form of the test track on the roof of the Fiat factory in Lingotto; and it was the staircase running diagonally over the building that was the key motif in the Centre Pompidou, the most important post-war building by an Italian architect outside Italy.

Unfortunately the best was lost in the built version, both the asymmetry and the closure of the wall. Huge windows were pierced in this, and their surface was made diffuse by the introduction of vertical bands that concealed supply ducts. The effective force of the simple was no longer being set against the Historicist, decorated buildings in the surrounding area. The built structure is also similar to these in its pink flesh-tints. Also the second striking formula, the kink in the top section of the steel frame, gave way to a heavy steel »entablature« – copied from the cornice of the Palazzo Farnese (H25). Many Modern design ideas remained, including the steel frame protruding on the outside or the fact that the building was raised above the ground. And the building is still appealing amidst its Historicist neighbours because of its greater power and compositional precision. But it is no longer the self-confident »machina« of Modernism, as Albini had called the project in allusion to Le Corbusier's famous saying about the house as a »machine à habiter«. SG

Bibliography: Fiori and Prizzon, *Albini–Helg, Rinascente*, 1982.

M48 Palazzo dello Sport

M48 Palazzo dello Sport
EUR, Piazzale dello Sport (plan G2 3/B)
1958/59
Pier Luigi Nervi, Marcello Piacentini

The Palazzo dello Sport was built in the EUR district (M24) as the last large building conceived by Nervi for the 1960 Olympic Games in Rome. It is surrounded by spacious car-parks and forms the visual focus of the monumental main axis on the southern periphery of the urban complex. As in the case of the Palazzetto dello Sport (M45), which was designed shortly before, this is a circular domes building whose architectural invention lies in the development of a new construction method. The exterior is dominated by the glazed spatial sequence of the staircase, which rises above a massive concrete substructure and conceals the tectonic starting point for the complex vaulting structure. Only the upper segment of the dome is visible from the outside, and as a concrete shell it stands in marked contrast with the circular, transparent curtain wall. The staircase running round the stadium leads to the three spectator tiers with their rows of seats rising in steps. The dominant design element in the high access area are the inclined concrete piers, which thrust out considerably and support the ribs of the massive dome between the concave, inward-curving support structure of the uppermost gallery.

The dome, with 144 braces and a diameter of 100 m, is one of the boldest vaulted constructions of the post-war period. Instead of a homogeneous inner surface Nervi chose folded, pierced dome surfaces between the ribs; all the lighting system is built into these, but yet they give the dome shell an almost fragile character. The convincing feature of this design is not primarily the gigantic dimensions of the interior, but the perfection of the constructional frame, which Nervi raised from being a statical necessity to the plane of aesthetic calculus. SK

M49 Villaggio Olimpico
Viale Tiziano (plan I 2/A)
1958–60
Vittorio Cafiero, Adalberto Libera, Luigi Moretti, Vincenzo Monaco, Amedeo Luccichenti

There had been several sports complexes on the site between the Villa Glori park and the Via Flaminia since the early 19C, like the so-called »Campo Parioli« – a famous horse-racing track – or the National Stadium, which opened in 1911. After a few attempts to systematize the urban pattern from the 30s, a competition for a large traffic axis was announced in 1950, intended to link the urban periphery with the city centre via the Ponte Flaminio. The first legitimate building units on the then derelict site were realized east of the Viale Tiziano on the basis of the prize-winning design by Claudio Longo. A new partial regulation plan was devised for the 1960 Olympics, and this provided for the erection of important sporting and service complexes in this area. As well as the Stadio Flaminio (M46) and the Palazzetto dello Sport (M45), a generous development area was scheduled for the Olympic Villa, and the Housing Department for State Employees, known as »INCIS« for short, was commissioned to build this. After the games the whole complex was to be converted into a new urban quarter for 6500 residents. Five architects were commissioned to design this large-scale residential project, and together they devised an overall concept with a sophisticated distribution of the various residential buildings. The fundamental characteristic of this design is a loose arrangement of the component projects. They relate to the existing road system and are surrounded by extensive parkland. Of the 35 hectares of the site as a whole, 16 hectares were taken up by green areas and only 7 by residential buildings. To guarantee the continuity of the parkland, all the buildings were mounted on polygonal concrete supports, so-called pilotis. The architects chose four different building types that could be varied in several ways, rather than a uniform building structure: block and terraced buildings alternate with square building blocks and cruciform struc-

M49 Villaggio Olimpico

tures, largely connected by a grid system. Despite the typological differences the building programme can be seen to be architecturally coherent in that the individual buildings are unified by a general structural scheme and a characteristic exterior design: as well as a maximum height of five storeys and the fact that the buildings were raised on pilotis, only concrete was used for the construction, clad on its outer surfaces with ochre-coloured brickwork. The storeys are articulated by white-painted bands of windows that differ only in rhythm and in their dimensions.

The Olympic Village is the first manifestation of Modern residential building in Rome after the Second World War. With its low density (150 residents per hectare), the fact that it is broken up by green areas and its impeccable solution of transport problems it is a direct implementation of the urban maxims demanded by the »Charter of Athens« as early as 1933. As a »city in a park« the Olympic Village embodies key guidelines of Modern urban development. But its negative consequences can be seen just as clearly in this complex: the building structure is an accumulation of individual, isolated buildings that are only vaguely connected with each other, and are unable to develop as a closed fabric with a clearly defined exterior space. Failure to heed these factors that help to constitute urban development is thus responsible for the lack of fundamental urban qualities in the Olympic Village. SK

M50 Casa Baldi
Via Labaro / Via Sirmione 19 (plan G1 2/A)
1959–62
Paolo Portoghesi

With his Casa Baldi, Portoghesi summed up 20C Roman architecture's struggle with the building heritage more succinctly than ever before, anticipating the positive developments of Post-Modernism almost a decade before that movement began. Only 28 at the time, he had limited means at his disposal, but complete freedom as far as the design was concerned. The exterior structure is simple, but formally rich. The building consists of a main storey, of a basement storey (on the same ground plan and only at the front) and of a much narrower upper storey. The tufa walls are concave, and gaps for the windows, always set back, are created between the concave sections. Portoghesi addressed his surroundings for everything: the took the material, the tufa, something that Ridolfi had already used, from the Campagna. In fact Portoghesi thought that Ridolfi's INA towers (M40; scarcely five years older) were the best work in post-war Italy. For him using tufa meant humility, craft, religion. He took the curves of the building from the landscape with the Tiber bends; they also refer to Borromini, in other words the architectural legacy and context. Borromini was Portoghesi's preferred Baroque architect. He said that he built not to solve problems, but constantly to create new ones. In the three central build-

M50 Casa Baldi

ing forms the Casa Baldi is reminiscent above all of S. Andrea delle Fratte (B76); the comparison is revealing: Borromini offered concave and convex curves, complex, but regular, with columns as joints and dominant diagonals. Portoghesi also used curves for his walls, but above all they were freely modelled (no longer following geometrically defined forms) and asymmetrical. These last two elements work more freely and more dynamically than under Borromini, and were in the spirit of classical Modernism (cf. p. 297) and unthinkable in the Baroque. Portoghesi also did not want to abandon the articulating column – according to him the »external and internal rhyme« of a building –, nor the decorative entablature. Again he found an equivalent in Modern formal language: he alluded to an entablature in the lines and drew the concave sections forward like a prostatic column, admittedly again without symmetrical balance. He tamed the movement, which was far in excess of the usual, by making the main storey higher than the base storey, in other words heavy, and at the same time emphasized the horizontal strikingly – and all this was once more in harmony with the great models in Rome (H25). The upper storey is again reminiscent of Baroque balconies and also of the roof gardens favoured by the International Style. The slab running between the storeys looks particularly Modern – the counterpart to an entablature in earlier architecture. For here the new building method is clearly demonstrated: the modern material (concrete) was strikingly juxtaposed with that venerable building material tufa. But it is clear above all that this slab was cast in one piece; so it can protrude both more and less like a plank cut with a fretsaw. The transitions to the wall are hard – all inconceivable in the Baroque, and yet elements that give the building the necessary hardness and austerity – a long way from the kidney table and unduly soft curves (cf. for instance M31 and M52). Despite its small size the building seems solid and also closed, as the wall sections are separated, but also broad, low and thus strikingly robust (cf. in contrast M57). The openings hardly separate more than columns.

While the concave curves close the exterior (because the openings almost disappear), the convex curves in the interior almost create suction into the light and opening niches. The room also seems open because two isolated room dividers – as in the International Style in the twenties – replaced the walls (exception: the bedrooms). Portoghesi also designed the ceiling with local brickwork that was different in various parts of the room, so that each area had a character of its own despite the openness of the continuum (M43). The main axis leads diagonally from the eating area, the most important »room«, to the large window facing the Tiber.

Charles Jencks, the spokesman for Post-Modern architecture, saw this building as the first »completely convincing« work in the style. Principles of Modernism and of older periods were fused without constraint to form a cosy, refined and modest whole. Portoghesi asked in an essay on Gaudi: »Why should someone who caresses his wife not caress his house as well?« He is the most lyrical of Italy's author-architects, and the only one to write substantially about past periods. SG

M51 Palazzina Arbia
Via Arbia 21 (plan II 3/B)
1960/61
Carlo Aymonino, Maurizio Aymonino, Alessandro de Rossi, Baldo de Rossi (Studio AYDE)
Carlo Aymonino, who had worked on the INA complex (M37) ten years before, planned a palazzina with a central oval staircase section and three apartments per storey; Aymonino was working for the AYDE studio, founded in 1960. Two of the apartments are placed symmetrically, one at the front and one at the

M51 Palazzina Arbia

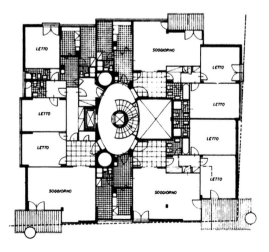

rear, and each run through to the kink that runs vertically to the top of the building on both sides. On the right of the kink is the third apartment, with a large side balcony in the attic storey. The building owes its precision to the fact that Studio AYDE took direct responsibility for it.

A key feature of the building is that various clearly defined bodies seem to penetrate each other strikingly. Thus the part with the two apartments thrusts out over the part with one apartment, and likewise the staircase oval protrudes into the roof garden, where the form was duplicated. Thus the surface seems to be set in motion by forces inherent in the building. Interpenetration of various units and realities represents a constant in Aymonino's work: Thus the familiar Gallaratese complex (1967–73) intertwines with the teeming surrounding development, or Modern projects fitted into historic central Rome, promoted by Aymonino in the left-wing city council in 1980–85. Overall the building makes a very Roman impression. Aymonino translated the tradition of massively solid buildings (cf. for example H31, B93) into Modern formal language as compellingly as only Ridolfi before him (M14). Here the dynamics of the surface are based – in a very Modern way – not on the decoration, but on the body-language of the building. The earthy quality, in the ochre-coloured brick, for example (in contrast with the cool, sharp forms of Lombard Neo-Rationalism), is also typically Roman, but had hitherto only been formulated in a specifically Modern way by Aymonino's teacher Ridolfi (M14). Gravitas romana and abundance too in this building! SG

M52 Palazzina Maurizio
Via Romei 35 (plan G1 1/B)
1962–65
Luigi Moretti
After the Casa del Girasole (M33), Moretti's best palazzine were built outside Rome, and above all La Saracena in S. Marinella (1952–54). In Rome Moretti was starting to produce convincing exteriors with curved buildings in urban development terms as well (cf. M53). The Palazzina Maurizio is fundamentally just a cuboid with a central staircase and two (symmetrically proportioned) dwellings per floor, completely right-angled in its ground plan. It is best seen from below, from the road; there is a hill behind it. The key motif is the swirling balconies on the three front façades.

They are what it is all about; each of the four sets of balconies has a different form, and their curves run against each other. The design was criticized as a piece of formal virtuosity. In fact Moretti fails to meet his self-imposed target of conveying a »feeling of violent expansion, forcing its way outside from within«. This kind of feeling is not produced by the qualities that this building and Moretti's style have in abundance – elegant cut, whiteness, smooth materials. And it was also the case here, as always in Moretti's

M52 Palazzina Maurizio

palazzine (M32, M33), that the façade, here the vi-
brant flood of balconies, is completely detached from
the structure behind it. This building is the perfect embodiment of what Venturi postulated as the model for
Post-Modernism, the »decorated shed«, a plain barn
as a building block, lavishly hung with decoration. But
the criticism was misplaced. The curve was increasingly being rediscovered a counter-form to the cube
of the International Style, by Moretti (La Saracena),
by Portoghesi (M50), even in Chicago (Marina Towers). And why should elegant forms not be suitable
for a villa district, distinct in colour and form from the
rougher wall behind them and set against a sky with
white fluffy clouds of various shapes. SG

M53 Quartiere INCIS
Decima, Via C. Sabatini (plan G2 2/B)
1962–66
Luigi Moretti (master plan); Luigi Moretti, Vittorio Cafiero,
Ignazio Guidi, Adalberto Libera (individual buildings)
Shortly after building the Olympic Village (M49) in the
north-west of the city, which had been changed into
a residential quarter, following the original planning
intention, the Housing Office for State Employees,
known as »INCIS«, was planning a new housing estate for state employees on the southern periphery.
Shifting important ministries and public institutions to
the new EUR district (M24) made a nearby residential
quarter for the public employees a necessity. A 22
hectare planning area north of EUR was sought out to
this end, which could be linked up with the large traffic
axes between Rome and Ostia. Moretti was commissioned to devise an urban concept, and he brought
in three other architects, Cafiero, Guidi and Libera, to
design the individual buildings. This created a planning
group that had already been in charge of building the
Olympic village, though here they had slightly different
roles. Thus the urban development criteria and archi-

tectural design methods are comparable for the two
projects: within the overall structure of the two residential projects the buildings are loosely distributed,
and relate in their siting and orientation to the road
system, and again green areas are stressed as a combining fabric. In the same way different building types
were used, in this case terraced buildings and rectangular or cruciform building blocks, to counteract the
formal rigidity of the architectural grid. Even the fundamental structural principles, like the use of pilotis to
support the four- or five-storey buildings and the brick
cladding are identical. The Olympic Village was typified by an astonishingly low building density on the
basic area, but in the new residential quarter, because
of the limited extent of the planning area and a simul-
taneous increase in the number of residents (approx.
7500), the architectural masses had to be more
closely concentrated. This made the estate complex
tighter; it no longer threatened to disintegrate into its
component pieces, as in the Olympic Village, but
formed a more closely-woven architectural fabric.
The outdoor space is also more clearly defined by
the introduction of rectangular gardens protected from
the surrounding area between the mainly curved terraced buildings. Given that an orthogonal axial frame
was fixed by the line of the two dominant roads, a
large junction is formed in the centre of the estate,
and this is at least vaguely defined as a square by the
buildings on the periphery, with their concave inward
curves.

Although the concept for the residential complex in
the Decima district followed the same Modern building
maxims as the Olympic Village, its urban qualities are
more strikingly demonstrated. The denser building

M53 Quartiere INCIS

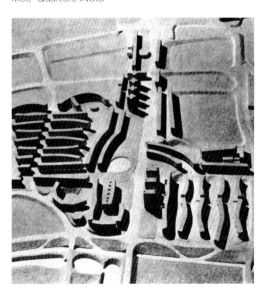

stock and the more precise interplay between building texture and the exterior space represent fundamental, city-creating factors of the kind that are necessary of a uniform organism is to be maintained. Even though the organization of the residential area is far removed from the traditional structure of a historic town fabric, its positive effects and social efficiency still have to be recognized. Without falling into picturesque town planning, the architects used the instruments of Modern town planning to provide an architecturally convincing example of post-war residential building. If one compares the present condition of the two residential complexes their different degrees of preservation are hardly surprising. SK

M54 Palazzo per uffici ed abitazioni
Via Campania (plan II 2/D)
1963–65
Vincenzo, Fausto and Lucio Passarelli and others
Here the Passarelli brothers, working with Cercato, Costantini, Falorni, Tonca (design) and Giangreco, Giordano (statics), designed a multi-purpose building with an underground car-park, shops on the ground floor, offices on the next three floors and flats above them. After the La Rinascente department store no 60s Roman building excited so much media interest, abroad as well.

The Architectural Review wrote: »Rudolph stands on Mies«, and conjectured that each brother planned a separate section. The block-like office building was raised above ground level on quadruple fair-faced concrete piers – absolutely in the spirit of the International Style (M30, M33). Mies van der Rohe, as a master in this field, had established the curtain wall, but with a metal framework drawn outwards, not skin-thin and with a mirror effect. But reflections, especially of older buildings (in this case the Aurelian Wall, A44), were particularly important to the Passarellis, and were to create a stir in the USA as well, for instance in the John Hancock Tower in Boston. This also reinforced the contrast with the »brutal« fair-faced concrete above, which was designed in an entirely higgledy-piggledly, almost anarchic fashion. The quadruple piers thrust right through to here, where the second great Modern tradition comes into play, Le Corbusier and his disciple Rudolph. The office block seems subdued, but the private building is explosive, dissolved, starkly asymmetrical and at an oblique angle to it, an illustration of leisure.

Here a new style had been established for the world, anti-Modern despite its Modern models, as the Modern value of unity was negated. Post-Modern authors (like Jencks) praised the breaks as an expression of functional diversity. But in Rome there was already a long tradition of divergent layers of architecture one built over the other (M34, M43). SG

M54 Palazzo per uffici ed abitazioni

M55 Quartiere Casilino
Viale della Primavera (plan G1 3/C and plan IX 4/D)
1964/65, 1970 ff.
Ludovico Quaroni with Gabriella Esposito, Roberto Maestro, Luciano Rubino
Statute no. 167 of 1962 allowed large local authorities to set aside districts for social housing in their development plans. A plan of this kind was passed in Rome in 1964, the so-called PEEP. The Quartiere Casalino, a residential complex for 12,330 residents on 50 hectares is one of the first generation of PEEP projects.

Ideas were realized in this project that Quaroni had developed for Mestre CEP project in 1959, with which he had taken a step away from the INA philosophy. He later had the following to say about his and Ridolfi's INA project (M37): »We were looking for the city but got stuck in the village.« Intricate, village-like development near the city had been replaced by Quaroni from 1959 by simple, geometrical sections set on the periphery, where they occupied large sites. This was intended to confront the dilemma that Italy had great architects with a feel for urban development questions, but the authorities had no planning powers, so that good individual work sank in the chaos of the suburbs. On this occasion an overall concept that was made clearly visible was followed. This and the restrained design both show that Rome was increasingly following the tendencies of the International Style from the 60s as well. (cf. also M47).

All three projects are examples of this kind of uniform planning: the first has large curved buildings, distantly related to the INCIS quarter (M53), also the second, in which Op Art ideas were implemented (with strict rows of black and white cubes). The project that was built was the third (from 1970 to the mid-1980s), as it seemed that this, unlike the others, could be built by a several construction companies. And yet in this complex as in no other a basic idea was consistently carried out: the overall form is established by 29 buildings, arranged in a fan shape, again forming four smaller groups, each with its own focus that is slightly different from the others. The buildings grow towards the outside; thus the ones that are closer to the focal point rise from two to seven, the outer ones to fourteen storeys at the far end. Low communal buildings were intended to stand at the focal point, and to catch the eye from the Viale de la Primavera. The idea was so convincing that it was much imitated, as in Italy's best-known complex, Gallaratese, by Carlo Aymonino and Aldo Rossi.

The execution was poor. The responsible authority did not allow Quaroni to supervise the project as a whole. At first the authority had itself laid down that all the buildings should be clad in brick, but later they paid as little attention to this as to Quaroni's requirement that their should be no protruding balconies or interruptions of the rising lines (by building on top of roofs, for example). The complex, conceived in austere unity, became a confused accumulation of mediocre individual buildings, in which today the most striking ideas are special touches (like the exterior spiral staircases, for example). The school that now stands at the focal point is a two-storey building, too high (and also too wide). Even more unfortunate was the

lowering of the Viale Primavera: the complex lost its central and focal point.

Finally, when the idea had been ruined, an image of what it might have been worth was created right at the front: this group is made up of geometrical and block-like buildings that follow the law of the constantly rising roof-line and are built in brick. The length of the sections decreases towards the back, so that the perspective effect seems further enhanced.
SG

M56 Sede ENPDEP
Via Giovanni Battista Morgagni (plan IX 1/B)
1964–76
Luigi Moretti and others

Italy's Public Service Pension Fund (ENPDEP) commissioned a new building among a number of Historicist structures. It was to keep to the scale of its predecessor. Moretti employed Silvano Zorzi as a well-known structural engineer.

Three storeys were placed below street level – enough space for the service areas (car-park, copying and counter rooms). The upper storeys were suspended on four gigantic pylons, linked by concrete floors and – at the top – the rafter system, which is visible at the sides. Moretti chose an egg-shape for the pylons, the characteristic motif, a feature they share with the piers in Cologne cathedral, the tallest Gothic structure. The rest was built as a light-weight structure, with cardboard interior walls. This was where Moretti placed the offices, in the light. The entrance section is an independent feature between the two blocks.

As he was to do once more later (M60), Moretti transferred the structure of one of his palazzine to an office building here, not as obviously as later, but including the whole complex. The model was Moretti's most famous palazzina, the Casa del Girasole (M33): with a four-storey main block, articulated above all by ribbon windows, and raised above ground level by a trapezium-shaped entrance floor; with a gable, though here, in the office building it had to be conceived less

M55 Quartiere Casilino

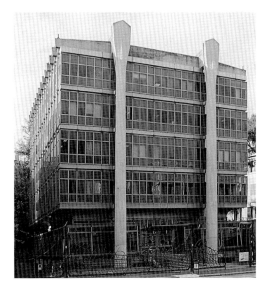

M56 Sede ENPDEP

freely, i. e. it is symmetrical and more strongly functional, a »rafter« in the support system; and with the
vertical section, which again forms a frame for a staircase (here the sophisticated external fire escape), but
now shifted to the rear. It is clear how much Moretti
thought in the aesthetic lines of his formal language
from the fact that he gave functional elements a beautiful outline when he left them visible, as is the case
here. SG

M57 Casa Papanice
Via Marchi 1 (plan IX 2/A)
1966–70
Paolo Portoghesi

The Casa Baldi was followed by two rural Case (Casa Andreis in Scandiglia and Casa Bevilacqua in Fon-
tania). The wall sections became smaller and more
fragmented; the closed impression disappeared. Concentric circles became increasingly dominant. But the
materials remained earthy, and the Casa was thus integrated with its surroundings. The Casa Papanice
took Portoghesi into the city. The development plan
talked of a villino, a palazzina. At first the project suggested one unit occupying the full height, finally three
apartments, each occupying a full floor.

Portoghesi named two basic ideas: he said that
each room (more precisely: functional area), for example eating, relaxing, or the fireplace, had its own quality. He felt that they should be anchored in a centre,
here between the poles formed by entrances and light
sources (openings and balconies). The centres grow
in concentric circles, intersect at the edges and fuse
with each other at this point. They are indicated in the
interior by circular discs growing down like satellites.

Conversely, Portoghesi uses only room dividers (except for the bedrooms), not walls. Thus he preserved
a Modern spatial continuum (cf. also M50), but gave
each area its own set of values. In the exterior the
overall form developed by the fusing circles is illustrated in the wall sections. The second idea (always
central for Portoghesi), was that the building should
fit in with its surroundings. At first he wanted to give
it a mirror surface, so that it would »cancel itself out«.
But when it was built he opted for long strips of dark
green, brown, blue and orange majolica. Here he was
intending to be selective: this was not a response to
the »bad« (largely Historicist) buildings in the surrounding area, but to nature – cedars, tree-trunks, sky and
light –, which he wanted to represent with his strips,
an almost impressionistic technique.

Portoghesi was not commissioned to design a second palazzina, despite his elegant forms. In fact such
buildings require prone forms, as this is the only way
in which they can look solid despite their small size.
But in the Casa Papanice the concave pieces are
long, like piles supporting the earth. They were criticized as »organ-pipes«. The horizontal lines of the
storeys are missing; none of the Baroque models to
which Portoghesi was referring could have coped
without their controlling force (cf. similarly M37). Additionally many parts do not follow the outline of the
building – corners and balconies – and distort it.

Small, lavish town houses can tolerate caprice and
elegant materials. But when the form is very lively, the
material has to provide a counterweight. Caprice and
an all too elaborate intellectual system are also out
of the question. Casa Baldi had lost its spontaneity.
SG

M57 Casa Papanice

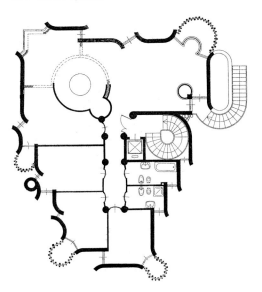

M58 Aula delle Udienze Pontificie

M59 Alitalia, Fiumicino

M58 Aula delle Udienze Pontificie
Città del Vaticano, Via di S.Uffizio (plan III 1/A)
1966–71
Pier Luigi Nervi

Nervi had to take a large number of fundamental planning factors into consideration when designing the audience hall for the Pope in the Vatican: apart from the extremely irregular development site on the southern flank of St. Peter's, it was the enormous dimensions – the hall had to accommodate 14 000 visitors –, the design of the internal area for the Pope and the demands for the best possible lighting and acoustics that presented the architect with a task that was very difficult to solve.

By using a trapezoid ground plan Nervi could respond to the existing axis system and also give the building a marked feeling of orientation. Access to the large assembly hall is through a low vestibule placed in front of the main volume on the east side. As in his two sports palaces (M45, M48), Nervi concentrated on developing a complicated vault structure derived statically from a new kind of construction system. A segmental barrel vault placed transversely to the main orientation arches over the enormous hall, setting an extraordinary dynamic accent with its sequence of 42 arches. This movement is focused towards the audience area, which is opposite the vestibule and visually underlined by two powerful, inclined piers.

This creates a backdrop with an enormous perspective effect, which is perfectly suited to staging the Pope's various activities. The ceiling lighting integrated into the triangular vault areas supports the movement of the barrel vault and with maximum illumination makes the ceiling structure seem like an enormous cascade of light.

In the audience hall Nervi's typical reinterpretation of reinforced concrete leads to an astonishingly direct and symbolic implementation of the functional requirements. SK

M59 Alitalia, Fiumicino
Fiumicino (plan G2 1/B)
1961–65, 1967–70
Riccardo Morandi

Morandi was involved in the building of the first terminal at Fiumicino airport in 1957–60; its dimensions were almost doubled in the late 80s. The two aircraft hangar complexes south of this are more important architecturally.

The first hangars to be built are made up of three units; they are rectangular, symmetrical and placed longitudinally to each other. Almost three quarters of the roof are suspended, floating freely, and rising slightly outwards on girders 35 metres high with concrete-clad steel hawsers stretched over them. These three quarters together with the outside wall, the actual hall (200 x 85 m), are not hampered by support elements, and thus available to aircraft. The supports sit on the wall that divides off the remaining quarter, a concrete cage for the service areas, forming an anchorage for the overall weight. Two shallow sections, again rectangular and placed longitudinally to each other, occupy the space between the two units.

The second hangar (166 x 153 m) has a steeply rising outline, so that there is space for two Boeing 747s with their high tails. Two corridors for the cockpits thrust inside into the shallower office section, that seems to be a distinct cuboid from the outside. In this way the sections were linked spatially. The bracing is tent-like, indeed asymmetrical in design, and is suspended only from three pylons at the front, so that there is space for large gates, and from a row of seven pylons at the back.

Morandi is a Roman who otherwise built hardly anything in Rome, and he rejected the calm, classical forms preferred by Nervi, who was from Lombardy. The structural qualities of concrete are dominant again, and not (as with Le Corbusier), its sculptural ones. But Morandi did select an expressive and daring form, gigantic bracing, Roman abundance. SG

M60 Palazzo per uffici
Piazzale Flaminio (plan I 2/D)
1972–74
Luigi Moretti, C. Zacutti

Moretti's last building in Rome was an office block. This type of building had made him better-known abroad than most post-war Italian architects. The Piazza del Popolo, the city's northern »vestibule«, had often acquired twin designs, domed in the Baroque period (B87/88), temples in Classicism, now Modern cubes – a great urban-development idea.

A terrace, two cubes with several storeys and two cloud-like roof sculptures rise over a ground floor. Moretti wrote as early as 1950 (in Spazio) that a conglomerate was an appropriate form for rich societies with a complex structure of interests. He designed the building in this spirit, taking a lead from Passarelli's multi-functional building of 1965 (M54). Once more the forms of the International Style were adopted, but its basic values were negated (cf. M54 for detail): the building does not seem robust, as the outer skin of the curtain wall is again made of glass and seems »thin«, and also because the white, vertical pilaster strips seem fragile, making the block bases appear unstable. The building seems to have been dissected, thus smashing the unity that was so important for the International Style, as a strongly protruding ribbon runs through it horizontally and the rounded sections stand out strongly, elegant in form and softening the cube, with hints of Moretti's Palazzine Saracena and Maurizio (M52). These rounded sections, the most highly aestheticized parts of the building, contain the supply equipment, its most functional part, so that the unity of form and function is also negated. Unlike Passarolli, Moretti did not use breaks to express different functions. But as far as appearance is concerned its is fair to say: »The Saracena stands on Mies«. SG

M60 Palazzo per uffici

M61 Casa d'abitazioni
Via Camilluccia 341 (plan G1 1/B)
1967–70
STASS

G. Ciucci, M. d'Allessandro, M. Manieri Elia and M. Morandi made their mark in Rome in the 60s as Studio STASS with three buildings: a school (Spinaceto, Via Renzini), a palazzina (M62) and here a block of flats, all on the outskirts, and all using the same formal language based on the International Style.

The overriding form of the building is an L-shape, with the staircase in the corner. Both arms are raised on pilotis in the manner of the International Style (cf. M33). The arms are at different levels in the hilly terrain, the higher one to the south above the sloping roof of the communal rooms. But the corridors that give access to the individual apartments are all on the same level, downstairs in the higher section and upstairs in the lower. The large round windows, which are the principal feature here and in the other two buildings, were borrowed from the vocabulary of architects like Kahn (Dacca) or Stirling (Runcorn New Town), identify the tiny rooms, which are scarcely wider than a single window, 13 per arm. The row of windows was given rhythm by the fact that they alternately face the courtyard, then outside, in pairs. The rooms were placed on the corridors as if on a rail, and the corridors thrust into the staircase are like a hose. This striking principle is montage in the style of Archigram, one of the most prominent 60s groups. Otherwise the values of the International Style were pushed as far as possible and thus reversed (in a Post-Modern fashion): the function, the infrastructure in this case, was given so much space that there was none left to live in: two flights of steps were placed in the large stairwell, which meant that they were both cramped and narrow. Unity of material was lost as well: the ultra-Modern, like aluminium, for instance, was juxtaposed with old-fashioned brick. SG

M62 Palazzina
Via S. Maria Sapienza (plan G1 2/B–3/B)
1968–70
STASS

The Palazzina with its large apartments demonstrated the legacy of Louis Kahn like no other building by STASS (cf. M61 for this group). The typical feature of Kahn's work – and this can be seen very clearly in the parliament building in Dacca – are components that are highly geometrical in themselves and already articulated, which return multiply as modules and grow into a complex, expressive, almost atmospheric whole.

Here the articulated basic module consists of two framing cylinders, and in the centre a cuboid with two rows of large round openings, and set back in between a block with one thin cuboid like a pilaster strip and one wide one. Two of these basic modules are set at right angles to each other. A third forms the remainder of the building, though this one is divided into two equal individual section between the rows of round windows. These are again set at right angles to the framing cylinders, then turn at an angle of 135 degrees and run towards each other. The courtyard and the entrance with the porter's lodge, which screens off the entrance like a diagonally cut baston (as frequently happens in Post-Modern US high-rise architecture, as in its founder Pennzoil Building, for example), are set between the two, at the point where the module is cut.

From about 1970 it is possible to detect an inclination to the formal, the first sign of Post-Modernism. Here the cleverly devised overall structure is already subject to it, but so are all the details: for example the triangular run of the stairs in the staircase cylinder or the grid of squares that was applied to the individual balconies without regard for their height. At the same time forms were no longer clearly ascribed to a particular building tasks, and in this case a residential building acquired a fortress-like tower. SG

M63 Filiale del Banco di Roma: interior
Via del Corso (plan V 1/A–1/B)
1970–85
Ludovico Quaroni, E. Calanca

This branch is diagonally opposite the headquarters of the bank, immediately adjacent to S. Marcello (B103). Previously there had been a gallery here, placed at right angles to the Corso, passing through the 18C building. This had to be preserved. Halfway down this on the left-hand side – on the site of the present counter hall – were two cinemas, separated by a reinforced concrete wall set at right angles to the gallery. The wall was an irritation inside a bank, but the cinema rooms were too low for a single space.

The solution was simple: Quaroni kept the gallery as an axis, as an extended rectangle, and created additionally – shifted slightly in the direction of the former cinemas – a circular main space, which can be recognized in some sections of the wall, fused with the rectangle and bulging out twice more at the level of the

M63 Filiale del Banco di Roma: interior

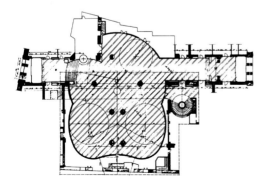

former cinemas. The supporting dividing wall of the cinemas and the northern gallery wall were replaced by supports. All that remained on the first floor was the room above the former cinemas. Two circular breaks were made in the ceiling above the bulges at the back of the room. A third circle is placed in the centre above the two openings, the floor of the first storey. The lines on the floor and ceiling run diagonally, at an angle of 45 degrees.

It is typical of the 70s (and of the onset of Post-Modernism) that compositions became more and more formal, as here, for example, with the superimposition of different geometrical systems (cf. also M62). One feature was unreservedly Post-Modern: remains of the house of St. Marcellus had to be preserved: a glass structure was built over them, which made them lool like a museum exhibit. The symbolic plane was often over-used in Post-Modernism: here the bankers, whom Jesus expelled from the temple, are showing the house of one of the early popes in a bank building. SG

M64 Quartiere Vigne Nuove
Via delle Vigne Nuove/Via G. Conti/Via A. De Curtis (plan G1 2/B–3/B)
1971–79
Lucio Passarelli (project director)

The Vigne Nuove residential area, with the Corviale (M67) and Laurentino estates, is one of Rome's great late 60s urban development projects, which aimed to upgrade and systematize the urban periphery. Large estates with high resident density were intended to be created on the basis of a new organizational pattern for residential building with integrated collective areas. In 1971 the commission for the new residential quarter in the north of the city was given to the IACP planning office, which drew up a mass distribution plan. The institute passed this on to a group of architects under the direction of Passarelli for revision, but they in fact modified the original plan considerably. In 1972 this design variant was accepted by the city authorities, work began in the following year, and was completed with the exception of a few secondary facilities in 1979. A total of 524 residential units were built for 3330 residents on an area of 8 hectares. In contrast with the conventional, urban zoning plans this meant an extremely high density of 416 residents per hectare. This very high concentration was intended on the one hand to reduce the major housing shortage and on the other to provide an urban core for the district, which was very fragmented at the time.

The architectural unity needed for the new centre was intended to be guaranteed by exclusive use of a precisely defined building type, which could be varied only in detail. Simple linear building suggested itself for this purpose, being versatile in its extent. Also its configurational flexibility, with individual linear building on the triangular building site guaranteed a sensible distribution of mass. Seven- or eight-storey residential rows on a piered base with ribbon windows throughout and grey fair-faced concrete outer cladding were assembled in an angled building line running north-south. The link in the south-west between sections A and B is designed as a spatial caesura with obviously broken outlines at the ends of the buildings, so that the continuous linear building seems to be violently torn apart at this point. This reflects the unsuitable proportions of the planning area, which did not permit an ideal layout for the gigantic complex. The group of architects opted for a multiply articulated linear structure for the individual rows, accompanied by an external path system, rather than a stereotypical accumulation of longitudinal buildings. Thus the purpose of this complex building structure lies in creating an individual organization pattern intended to convey a different overall impression within the sequence of differently disposed compartments. The internal circulation system is just as sophisticated as the exterior street network with its multitude of steps and ramps. A characteristic internal feature is a strict distinction between horizontal distribution with so-called »interior passages« and vertical access via gigantic staircase cylinders placed in front of the long façades. Low, interlinked buildings were spread all over the site as a somewhat indifferent fabric; they contain the secondary service sections.

The concept for this residential complex is based on theoretical ideas that were summed up as early as the 50s under the collective idea of »Brutalism«, which continued to influence residential building in Europe until the late 70s. SK

M64 Quartiere Vigne Nuove

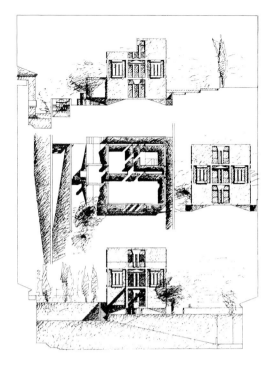

M65 Casa Rosato

M65 Casa Rosato
Casalotti, Via della Cellulosa (plan G1 1/B)
1972
Studio GRAU (Gruppo Romano d'Architetti Urbanisti)
Various teams from GRAU, usually with Martini, built several buildings in the Corona of Rome from 1966 to 1975 (Fratocchie, 3 Via Divino Amore; S. Angelo Romano, Morolungo, Casa Eletti; Vitinia, Via Fosso Fontanile, Casa Mastrojanni). The group called itself »urbanistic« as they wanted to place a special building in the untidy suburb on each occasion.

The overall shape of this building is narrow, cubic, and with three steps. The lowest step forms a portico. The building is articulated by windows and inlaid patterns. GRAU based the overall form on the Villa Pamphili (B59), though the wings were trimmed. The link seems to be less deeply felt than Portoghesi's inspiration by Borromini (cf. M50), and is much more playful: the old building was not taken as the starting-point for a new interpretation. On the contrary, it simply provided a body for the building, which was then covered with a decoration system that does not relate to it in any particular. To that extent we are again dealing with a »decorated shed« here (for this cf. M52). The decoration is viewed essentially as drawing, and covers the wall like a carpet. Thus the temple façade (with gable and pilaster strips) became one with many fields, and the windows became intercolumnia. Moreover, the historical system of classical orders was lost: the metope beside it, formerly just part of a frieze, was now the same size, and the gable could also be placed on the side façade or in the middle of the façade. The aim of bringing art to the people (to the suburbs), the historical link, which can also be quite random, and the dominance of drawing and decorative games rather than deep walls and tectonics are Post-Modern features. GRAU's particular affinity with the early Renaissance can be seen in the field-work of this building, which is like that of Alberti's S. Maria Novella. SG

M66 Casa Cooperativa Aleph, Ciampino
Ciampino (plan G2 4/C)
1972–77
F. Cellini, F. Marchioni
These two semi-detached houses were built for the Aleph Co-operative (with modest funding). – Portoghesi had encouraged Cellini as a Roman hopeful, publicized him and invited him to the 1985 Biennale (Accademia bridge project). These buildings were his first major work in Rome.

This building with a gable roof has a broad façade that is built up in two layers and almost seems to be divided into fields. Its relation to the architectural heritage is obvious – and typically Post-Modern. Characteristic features are the round piers, which are let into the wall and are too massive for it, and a high temple façade (four raised round piers with a small triangular gable bordered by incisions) and a more shallow temple façade supported by all the piers taking up the full width. The model was Michelangelo's Biblioteca Laurenziana (for the inlet round piers) and Palladio's church façade system (for the combination of two temple façades). The structure became Mannerist and Post-Modern because everything is in an unusual context: the intercolumnia in the high temple façade are narrower in the middle, not on the outside (as the dividing wall between the two halves of the building is placed here). And it is also not a state building, as the instrumentation suggest – the drama of earlier epochs, even of the International Style, now

M66 Casa Cooperativa Aleph, Ciampino

becomes available for use in any way. Equally the gable, as in an Upper Bavarian farmhouse, was able to be shifted from the narrow side to the broad side, and thus lost all proportion (cf. M71). The elements are strewn over the façade as if over a carpet, thus seeming remarkably unstable, given their mass. SG

M67 Quartiere Corviale
Via Poggio Verde / Via Casetta Mattei / Via Portuense (plan G2 2/B)
1972–82 and later
Mario Fiorentino and others
This complex came into being on the basis of statute no. 167 and PEEP (cf. M55). The project was directed by one of the young principals involved in the INA complex (M37); groups attached to F. Gorio, M. Valori, P. Lugli, G. Sterbini and – on the construction side – R. Morandi assisted. The 1972–74 project was on 60 hectares and provided accommodation for a total of 8500 residents. Building started in 1975. The main building was completed by 1982, the other residential section and the communal buildings were not complete at the time of writing.

Only one of the residential complexes created as much of a stir as this one, and that was the one that started a few years earlier near Milan, by Carlo Aymonino, the other young principal involved in the INA complex. There the new complex was opened up to the teeming development in the surrounding area. In contrast with this, the main building in Corviale was intended to work as a protective wall, as a bulwark of the open country to the west against the wild expansion of the city from the east; this is how the situation was defined in the development plan. The complex follows a hill that rises slightly to the north in several parallel strips, various chains of buildings, including the main one.

The idea of a residential complex that is a complete town in itself, is an old one, and was first realized in full by Le Corbusier in the Unité d'habitation in Marseilles (1947–52), from which the central articu-

M67 Quartiere Corviale

lating topos, adapted for a gigantic residential block, originated: as in Marseilles, the main building in Corviale also has a storey half way up that is specially treated (cf. also M40). In Marseilles it contained a street of shops, in Corviale the communal rooms and the paths as well. Coloured lines and symbols show the way. The line rises with the terrain. To enhance the impression of unity the height differences were built into the blocks, not into the vertical incisions. There are four floors of dwellings above the line, and four below, right at the bottom is one with garages and one with canteens. The vertical articulation is by four staircases, made into mega-columns with corrugated perspex. Thus the individual sections seem mobile in relation to each other, a legacy of Modernism. But the sections seem Post-Modern and »mannered«: the linking seems excessive in relation to the dubious material used for the »columns«. Emphasizing the circulation system by colours and stressing the staircases and corridors is also typical of the 70s, in which the functional thinking of the International Style was pushed too far (cf. M47, M61, also Olympic Village in Munich).

Parallel chains of buildings occupy an area 200 m wide in all: west and east of the main building and linked to this by pedestrian bridges are four low buildings (kindergardens, shops, bar), or, on the ridge of the hill itself, gardens and communal facilities (from church to arena). This corresponds with the »roof garden« in Le Corbusier's buildings, which was used for communication purposes, and has simply been shifted to ground level here, beside the main building. A commercial estate – adjacent to the east – forms a link with the city, and so particularly does a second residential building set at an angle of 45 degrees to the main building. SG

M68 Quartiere Tor Sapienza

Viale de Chirico/Viale Morandi (plan G1 3/C)
1970 ff., 1973–79, 1981–85
Alberto Gatti and others, Carlo Chiarini and others

Today the complex consists of three sections: the first, for 4650 people, is made up of small units, unusual for the time (cf. M55, M67), but capable of reproduction if needed. It is south-east of the ring road. The second, which was built in 1974–79, is the main complex, situated within the ring-road. Both are by A. Gatti, P. Carci, A. Ferri, S. Rossi and E. Sebasti. The large block by C. Chiarini, L. Cremona and I. Melanesi

M68 Quartiere Tor Sapienza

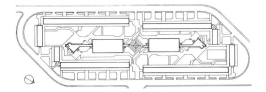

(north-east of the ring road) was built as a third unit in 1981–85.

Le Corbusier's Unité d'habitation was again the model for the main section for 2700 residents (cf. for all these M67): again the »roof garden« (with shop, metro station, playground) was shifted to ground level (the courtyard in this case). The building was articulated horizontally half way up, because a second, deeper type of dwelling protrudes. Once more fair-faced concrete was used, here enlivened with colour. And again the sections seem to move in relation to each other, as the complex breaks down into four L-shaped sections framing the courtyard, again consisting of two individual blocks. But Le Corbusier did not use standardized parts, and in the 70s the circulation systems were more heavily emphasized (cf. M67).

In Chiarini's large block a heterogeneous interior (terraced houses at the bottom, flats occupying full floors above, then duplexes on the 6th floor) is hidden behind a strictly uniform exterior with rows of plain square windows as the only articulating motif. A structure of Lombard coolness (cf. M73), Post-Modern in its paratactic structure, was placed alongside the core complex in its Roman abundance. Only the earth-coloured brick and the rear with its pleasingly lively forms seem Roman. SG

M69 Banco Monte dei Paschi di Siena

Via Cola di Rienzo 1 (plan I 2/D)
1975–78
Paolo Portoghesi

A year before Hollein's famous design for the counter-hall in the Viennese Tourist Office, Portoghesi moved Post-Modernism into the interior. He built in – in a bank counter-hall (!) – (in the back corner) a cosy private grotto. His own view of the two key pieces: the three mushroom columns made up of discs were intended to be reminiscent of piled-up coins, the annual rings on a tree and Michelangelo's idea of the multiple gable (cf. H43); the first idea is banal, the last very learned; loading things with banal and with learned content represents two basic ways of handling meaning in Post-Modernism. The curved counter in the middle is intended to separate the concave private space from the convex public one. Besides, he said, the mixture of two languages, the »double coding« postulated by Post-Modernism, should also be expressed in the materials: plastic, aluminium and carpets are Modern, lead and coloured glass are old.

The chief features of (the exterior and) the interior are the free-flowing large form, which harmonizes with the two key features, and decorative forms that are used intensively in places; these too are fluid, and seem to melt (in the door handles, for instance). It was principally the interior that was designed in the Jugendstil, in the early days of Modernism; even Frank Lloyd Wright, the father of Modernism, de-

M69 Banco Monte dei Paschi di Siena

signed the fixtures and fittings himself; in Jugendstil itself vegetable motifs were crucial – here in the mushroom trees, which shape the space and the light. But Portoghesi offered the vegetable forms in the artificial atmosphere of neon and plastic, cold green and shiny white. Neon became socially acceptable under Post-Modernism: Venturi published a book with the challenging title *Learning from Las Vegas* in 1973! But there is scarcely a trace of the Pop Art that this promoted in Portoghesi's building (he comes closest in the banister, using forms like a drain house and lametta). In Portoghesi's work neon seems cool and sterile, or serene, almost like high art. The materials make an ambivalent impression as well: in the Viennese tourist office Hollein opted unreservedly for precious materials that stimulate dreams, but in Portoghesi's work everything seems more sober, which is appropriate to the character of a banking hall, but it partly seems cheaper as well. However successful the overall form seems, Portoghesi was not able to make up his mind between a cooler form of Las Vegas and Jugendstil. It was not until 1985, in the Galleria Apollodoro, Piazza Mignanelli, that Portoghesi developed a sumptuous language for an interior design. SG

M70 Ambasciata Tedesca alla Santa Sede
Via Villa Sacchetti 4 / Via Tre Orologi 3 (plan II 1/C)
1966–84
Alexander Frh. v. Branca with K. Blum, G.Teebken
The architect who designed the Neue Pinakothek in Munich won the competition for West German architects in 1966/67 for the design of the German Embassy to the Holy Sede.

The building was in an area characterized by Historicist villas. The architect's aim was to »create, in the middle of 19C Rome ... with a view to the ... thousand-year-old link between Pope and empire ... a built structure that would reflect all this.« Paying heed to the architectural and historical context – this was the postulate with which Post-Modernism had confronted the architecture of the International Style. Also, von Branca wanted to conceal the building partially in the rising terrain, thus opening up large terraces. And so practically all one sees of the building (except turrets) are balustrades as a light-coloured horizontal element. Under Post-Modernism building types, here the castle and the orangery of a Baroque garden, can be used and combined at will.

The building is almost invisible from outside. The principal articulating element of the entrance wall is a window with – atectonically in a typically Post-Modern way – continuous pilaster strips. Otherwise it provides only a small peephole with a view of a tower that functions as a chimney. The view from Via Crillo is equally restricted. At the back a porter drives away visitors from the adjacent street. It seems paradoxical that an embassy should hide itself away in a little castle behind walls, when »Opus Dei« established itself next door in a Historicist castle that can be seen from a considerable distance. The – typically Post-Modern – irony of playing with the architectural heritage is also completely missing, and so is any sense of Castel del Monte, of greatness. This is a building for an unkissed Sleeping Beauty. SG

M71 Case IacP, Mazzano
Mazzano (plan G1 1/A)
1979–85
Paolo Portoghesi
In the 80s Portoghesi realized several projects in the country, all near Caprarola and with similarly restricted budgets (here commissioned by IacP): in Mazzano, in Anguillara and in Trevignano. They also share a more moderate tone and clear central themes, in short: the virtues of the Casa Baldi (M50).

The façade consists of five structures, staggered with the rise in the terrain. The highest two seem to

M70 Ambasciata Tedesca alla Santa Sede

M/1 Case IacP, Mazzano

have been fused together like a castle's top wing. Each of the buildings is the same in terms of its major forms: three storeys, with five window axes, with the central one accentuated by a high, outsize dormer window. This main motif is prepared for by transversely placed, vertical concrete walls running through all the storeys: vertical counterparts to the cornices on which the windows sit directly, following the Roman tradition. All of this gives a sense of the (simple) language of our century. How much more strongly than in excessively elegant forms are to we see the effect of the best inventions of High-Renaissance and Baroque palace forms: a risalto gives stability to the sides of the block as a whole (cf. for example H2); the vertical large form is reminiscent of the aedicule, and the five individual components thrust vividly upwards through the whole block (B93). The dormer window became a light balcony, approached by the dynamic staircase. In its permeability to the rear this section has the best qualities of Modernism, which were unknown to the Baroque, in the same way as the block as a whole with its asymmetrical assimilation of the landscape (cf. M30, M33). Such sovereign play was made with what had been inherited that no concrete model had to be adopted. The last Roman aedicule façade makes us curious about the cheerful nooks and crannies of the labyrinth of steps behind. SG

M72 Centro Islamico con Moschea

Viale della Moschea/Via Anna Magnani (plan II 1/A)
1975–93
Paolo Portoghesi, Vittorio Gigliotti, Sami Mousawi
This is the largest mosque outside the Islamic world. Portoghesi included a Muslim, an Iraqi (as well as his partner of long standing), in order to combine the two worlds in this way.

Portoghesi wanted to sum up two great traditions of world architecture, in his words he wanted to use everything: the Pantheon (A31), S. Ivo and Propaganda Fide (B56, B58); Kairouan, Cordoba and the cathedral of Monreale; also the Spanish Steps (B115), Poelzig's Salzburg Festspielhaus, Taut's Haus der Freundschaft and Libera's Congress Palace (M25).

He failed in this in terms of the façade, but in the interior he redeemed his ambition magnificently and simply.

The façade seems resoundingly hollow. The key form of the interior, the budding pier bundle, was dragged into the light here, endlessly duplicated, demystified. Also the large concave form is lacking in tension and out of place for a mosque in Rome because of the model for St. Peter's Square (B80). Also, the exterior of a mosque is usually a closed block, as a contrast with the open, paradisal interior. In fact the other three sides of the exterior were designed as closed block. Only the mihrab, the prayer niche, emerged from them. Another striking feature is the horizontal section, alluding to central topoi of the interior: the antithesis of the lower part of the building and the dome area and the bundling of light-paths. The forest of shallow domes looks fairy-like from a distance. The sawn-up brick technology is local-Roman (A37, B74).

Inside the square of the plain enclosing walls a circle of vegetable-shaped pier bundles dissolved into filigree supports the shallow dome with its forest of braces. Portoghesi rightly chose light as the central element (going back to the 24th Koran-Sure, the Sure of Light): Allah, shimmering indirectly, light in the crystal – all this can be sensed directly. And one can also see, as the Sure puts it, the light of God (from above) meeting the light of man; the latter is admitted through the horizontal cut, which is banked upwards and channels the light appropriately. On can also understand the milky light from the apertures in the prayer wall, which face Mecca. As well as its luminous power, Portoghesi recognized the dematerializing power of light. The atectonic language of Post-Modernism was very appropriate for this. And so he put the two Islamic architectural traditions that were closest to Europe one on top of the other: the pierced Moorish arch is placed on top of the Roman-Byzantine-Ottoman shallow domes, and the two are also differentiated in terms of colour. For him this

M72 Centro Islamico con Moschea

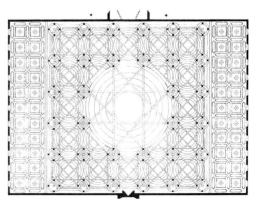

M72 Centro Islamico con Moschea

was squaring the circle, a combination of block and dome, of the earthly and the divine. The concentric circles, which he previously used almost schematically (in Salerno, for instance), he here conceived convincingly as the Koran's circles of heaven. And the vegetable forms that Post-Modernism borrowed from Jugendstil – here swelling, like lianas, dominant – fit in well with Islamic structures, as (only) Islam consistently rejects representations of human beings in favour of plant motifs. The soaring piers look almost as though they are in bud. Post-Modern authors (including Portoghesi) have overinterpreted them as praying hands. Portoghesi succeeded as a non-Muslim in using the resources of an ironic, undramatic style, Post-Modernism, to create a profoundly devout feeling within an alien religion. SG

M73 ENEA: test centre
Anguillara Sabazia, Strada Provinciale Anguillarese 301 (plan G1 1/A)
1979–85
Gregotti Associati
This building was commissioned by Italy's (test) organization for alternative energy (ENEA). Roman architecture had remained largely immune to Neo-Rationalist tendencies. Here, on the periphery, the Lombard architect who had followed these tendencies most strongly, was now building. He had become famous by building the University of Calabria in Cosenza (1973–85), a complex 3.2 km long, in which individual cubes with unequal numbers of floors (for the individual faculties) appear in rows on a narrow, dead straight set of paths. The complex seems like a bridge over the hills, with the tall cubes reaching down into the valleys. Gregotti's basic approach to the ENEA building was comparable.

The exterior, which is made up of 80 cm modules, draws energy from an even alternation between wall and window opening (each a 2 x 2 module, 160 x 160 cm large). The windows are set flush with the inside of the wall, so that their thickness of 70 cm, which contains the supply lines, was visible. The multifunctional quality of the building cannot be read from the exterior. Neo-Rationalist architects are chiefly concerned to achieve one thing – absolute repose – formally the building is very much like Rossi's cemetery in Modena. This was the Lombard response to Post-Modern (sometimes also Roman) formal excesses. For Gregotti a building had to look as though it had been standing from time immemorial.

As in Cosenza the way into the interior is via bridges that thrust into the building like rails; in fact the whole building has an open air or light rail running through it. Inside the laboratories and towers are grouped around a similarly super-cooled design, a square inner courtyard that is divided into two by the instrument bridge. SG

M74 Nuovo Stadio Olimpico
Piazzale di Foro Italico, Foro Italico (plan I 1/A)
1987–90
Annibale Vitellozzi, Maurizio Clerici, P. Teresi, Antonio Michetti (1st extension project); consortium of firms under the direction of COGEFAR (definite project)

M73 ENEA: test centre

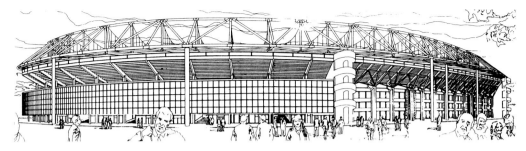

M74 Nuovo Stadio Olimpico

The old Stade Olimpico, the successor to the Fascist Stadium of the Cypresses built in 1950–53 by Carlo Roccatelli and Annibale Vitellozzi, was to be extended and modernized for the 1990 Football World Cup. To preserve an architectural link with the other sports facilities in the Foro Italico (M5), the Travertine-clad outer façade of the stands, which faced the Tiber, had to be included in the new design. After a long-winded debate preceding the competition announcement a planning group consisting of architects Vitellozzi, Clerici, Teresi and Michetti submitted a first extension project in April 1987. The main idea behind this project was to raise the old stands in order to meet the required capacity of at least 80 000 covered seats. The new, heavily protruding tiers were to be covered by a transparent suspended roof construction whose complicated support structure of steel hawsers woven like a net was carried by concrete piers. The enormous dimensions of these supporting piers, which would have severely disturbed the overall image of the Foro Italico, unleashed great controversy and a resultant revision phase with many corrections to the original project. After several legal interventions the group of entrepreneurs under the direction of COGEFAR that had already been nominated by the authorities was commissioned to produce a revised realization project. This design was available in May 1988 and was accepted by those responsible for the decision. The partial inclusion of the old exterior façades and the use of a transparent roof membrane as covering were retained as fundamental design principles from the original project.

In the revised version the secondary functions necessary for the extended event, like visitors' halls, offices and lounges were placed under the newly added rows of seats in the front third of the spectators' stands. This meant both the best possible arrangements for movement within the sports venue and also avoided making the building any higher. The originally planned support structure for the roofing, which had caused a dispute at the time of the first extension project with its external framework of piers, was abandoned in favour of a circular bracing system: an outer ring of triangular bars supported by slender steel girders, forms the upper conclusion of the spectators' area. Strong metal tubes were suspended on this stabilizing ring, running radially to the centre of the stadium and ending in an internal steel ring. Its diameter corresponds approximately to the radius of the outer running track, so that the playing area is open at the top. A concentric sequence of 12 steel hawsers is stretched over this net-like support structure, and they provide the actual support for the light roof. A transparent fabric membrane made of Teflon, reinforced with glass fibres, is hung loosely over the support structure, giving the impression of a thin, tent like roof. Despite its enormous span the suspension structure seems almost weightless, only vaguely setting a boundary to the open breadth of the internal space and scarcely showing on the exterior. Nevertheless the new stadium, because of its huge dimensions and technoid character seems like a foreign body in the overall ensemble of the Foro Italico. SK

M75 Parco della Musica (Auditorio)
Viale Pietro de Coubertin (plan I 2/B)
1994–2000
Renzo Piano

In an area easily accessible for a large number of people, between Palazzetto dello Sport (M45) and Stadio Flaminio (M46), Renzo Piano created a complex of three enclosed concert halls – grouped in a fanlike formation around the fulcrum of a central piazza – and in the centre an open amphitheatre. Thus he gave Rome the long awaited for centre – the »park« – for mainly musical events.

The three halls (Sala Santa Cecilia in the East, Sala Sinopoli to the South and Sala Petrassi in the West) tower high above the open *cavea*, dug into the earth, in the centre. The complex is open to the north, as is the *cavea*, and here is the long and low entrance tract. Thus, when seen as a whole, the open *cavea* is topped by a second *cavea* consisting of the three concert halls. The entrance tract closing the open flank is reminiscent of the stage building in ancient theatres, although much lower. Piano conceived the overall ensemble as embedded into the landscape, like ancient ruins: interwoven open areas and buildings, in a hilly landscape. By chance, during the work on the foundations, walls of an ancient villa of the 6th century BC were found – and integrated.

M75 Parco della Musica (Auditorio)

The three halls, though towering above the *cavea*, are partly below ground. All four theatres are joined at the base by a lobby, thus forming an ensemble of one open and three closed »theatrels«: for winter and summer, closed rooms and open air, inside and outside. Although the halls tower high above the *cavea*, they are both low lying and substantial. In this way they are similar to the nearby Palazzetto dello Sport, in contrast to it, however, irregular and freeform, rather than engineered and regularly constructed. The lead coloured roofs, consisting of several jointed canopies resembling the shell of a beetle, or maybe a musical instrument such as a violin, invoke images of Baroque Rome with ist lead-covered domes.

Piano created three auditoria instead of one – in the interest of better acoustics –, the smallest being the most flexible (mobile floors, ceilings and walls) which allows for adaptation to the size of the orchestra and its style of music. On the other hand, in the largest, the Sala Santa Cecilia, Piano pays homage to Scharoun's Philharmonic Hall in Berlin, his favourite concert house. As in Berlin, the interior appears to be highly fragmented (simulations in the planning phase ensured optimal acoustics) with a central orchestral stage as the focus. Modern architecture in the tradition of the old – how appropriate for Rome!

In the overall design, Piano indeed created a true »Park of Music« or a great ancient *agora* – one of the beloved themes of Piano and perhaps of any Mediterranean architect. This concept was re-invented for modern architecture by Le Corbusier whose influence can be felt in the mighty, sculptural forms of the halls (as in his residential block in Marseilles or his chapel in Ronchamp). But what a contrast between this »park« and the »modern engine« Piano had built for Paris 30 years earlier with the Centre Beaubourg; what a diverse scope of expression from one architect! The ultimate inspiration for the Parco della Musica, however, is Roman: ancient times and the famous »gravitas romana«. Piano has created a congenial framework for modern »events«. SG

M76 Chiesa 2000 (Dio Padre Misericordioso)
Via Francesco Tovaglieri / Largo Serafino Cevasco (plan G1 4/C)
1998–2003
Richard Meier

For the jubilee, the holy year 2000, the Vatican commissioned a church on the outskirts of Rome, in the suburb of Tor Tre Teste, which can be reached on the Via Tor Tre Teste, departing from the Via Prenestina to the south some 2 km inside the Gran Raccordo Annulare. Renowned architects were invited to submit their designs, with Tadao Ando, Frank O. Gehry and Santiago Cavalatra presenting designs typical (for them) in their monastic simplicity, sculptural dynamics and opening-wings design, and as well Günter Behnisch and Peter Eisenman. It seems as if the Vatican wanted to compete with the great Mosque built some years before, also on the outskirts of Rome (M 72).

Meier created a barque – the Catholic church as a ship, an old metaphor, for instance, present in Rome in Giotto's Navicella in Old St. Peter. Meier's church is a barque surrounded by tower blocks, with three sails of white stone, round and »full of wind«, like a succession of three shells. »Behind« these sails is a high white wall, enclosing the church hall, long, plain and precise and complementing the round forms on the other side, like the mast for the sails. »Behind« this mast, similarly white but more substantial, is the campanile. Overall a dynamic, light, concisely organized

M76 Chiesa 2000 (Dio Padre Misericordioso)

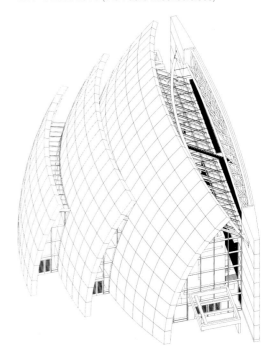

M76 Chiesa 2000 (Dio Padre Misericordioso)

M77 Museo dell'Ara Pacis

and graceful building – just like Meier's version of the »white« villas of early Modernism in the 1920s, for instance Le Corbusier's Villa Savoye.

Like in a similar building by Meier, the Stadthaus in Ulm, the interior is characterized by opening up towards the sky, again with a tilted ceiling in glass (in Ulm framing the high tower of the cathedral). Indeed, the interior is full of light, with its openings, light articulations and slim forms, it is almost like the white modern counterpart to late-gothic chapels (which are so rare in Rome). The interior is divided into a larger main hall – between the plain wall and the inner shell – and a smaller chapel, placed between the inner and the outer shell. In front of one of the openings is the cross, above a simple altar, to the west. Indeed, this little church faces west (towards Rome) – one of the very rare examples besides St. Peter's, where the apostle's tomb justifies this orientation. SG

M77 Museo dell'Ara Pacis
Lungotevere in Augusta (plan IV 1/A = A18)
2000–2006
Richard Meier

Having already worked on the Jubilee Church on the outskirts of Rome, Meier was commissioned for a museum at one of the focal points of Rome, or more precisely: he was commissioned to design a framework to the Ara Pacis, this »altar« of the grandeur of late republican (ancient) Rome (A18).

Mussolini already had given such a framework, he did so, however, by creating a (fascist) square. Meier incorporated the box of glass sheltering the Ara Pacis from the elements, into an enclosed construction, a cube, a real »museum« – although this museum continues to contain little more than the altar. The altar is still partially visible through the glass sides of the structure. Some important features of the altar itself are reflected in the new architecture such as the socle, the long low walls and lines, the rectangle, the horizontal cubic form and the large rectangular openings in the walls. Meier thus makes multiple references

to the Ara Pacis and its architectural characteristics. Meier's love of the white colour helps, but nevertheless the altar is now hidden in the museum. This outstanding example of the heroic period in Roman history, of simple beauty, is no longer really in the public sphere. Meier's building may be light and very simple, but compared to the altar it appears complicated and of exaggerated dimensions. Therefore it is not surprising that Romans continue to criticise it, and delayed the work on it. This building is considered not to respect Roman beauty, the Baroque churches on the other side of the square »disappear«. On the other hand, I have never seen so many visitors around the altar before. SG

1 day: Via large-scale complexes of Fascism (M5, M17, M12, M23, approach possibly via M29) and of the 1960 Olympic Games (M45, M46, M49) to three important pallazzine of the post-war period (M33, M34, M43) and to a major work of Post-Modernism (M72).

1 day: Rationalism, Fascism and liberation from it in the post-war period: M31, M9, M14, M11, M20, (interesting detours to M57, K26, K19), M37, M75, M76.

Selected bibliography

General and topography

Bruhns, L., *Die Kunst der Stadt Rom. Ihre Geschichte von den frühesten Anfängen bis in die Zeit der Romantik*, Vienna and Munich, 1972.

Giedion, S., *Space, Time and Architecture*, Cambridge, Mass., 1941.

Matthiae, G., *Le Chiese di Roma*, 3 vol., Bologna, 1962/63.

Parsi, P., *Chiese romane*, 6 vol., Rome, 1968–70.

Zeppegno, L., and R. Mattonelli, *Le chiese di Roma*, Rome, 1975.

Individual epochs

Roman antiquity

Andreae, B., *Römische Kunst*, Freiburg, Basle and Vienna, 1978.

Bianchi Bandinelli, R., *Die römische Kunst – von den Anfängen bis zum Ende der Antike*, Munich, 1975 (special edition from *Universum der Kunst*).

Crema, L., *L'architettura romana*, Turin, 1959.

M. Grant, *Art in the Roman Empire*, London and New York, 1995.

Kähler, H., *Der römische Tempel – Raum und Landschaft*, Frankfurt a. M., 1982.

Kähler, H., *Rom und seine Welt – Bilder zur Geschichte und Kultur*, Munich, 1960.

Kraus, Th., *Das römische Weltreich*, Frankfurt a. M., Berlin and Vienna, 1984.

Mielsch, H., *Die römische Villa – Architektur und Lebensform*, Munich, 1987.

Ward-Perkins, J. B., *Rom*, Stuttgart, 1986.

Coarelli, F., *Rom. Ein archäologischer Führer*, Freiburg, Basle and Vienna, 1989.

Christian Middle Ages

Brenk, B., *Spätantike und frühes Christentum*, Berlin, 1977.

Huelsen, Ch., *Le chiese di Roma nel medioevo*, Florence, 1927.

Krautheimer, R., *Early-Christian and Byzantine architecture*, Harmondsworth, 1979.

Krautheimer, R., *Rome. Profile of a City. 312–1308*, Princeton, 1980.

Krautheimer, R., et al., *Corpus basilicarum christianarum Romae*, 5 vol., Vatican City, 1937–80.

Stützer, H., *Frühchristliche Kunst in Rom*, Cologne, 1991.

Wulff, O., *Altchristliche und byzantinische Kunst*, 2 vol., Berlin, 1914.

Early and High Renaissance

Ackerman, J. S., *The Architecture of Michelangelo*, Harmondsworth, 1961, new edition 1986.

Frommel, Ch. L., *Der römische Palastbau der Hochrenaissance*, Tübingen, 1973.

Golzio, V., *Palazzi Romani – dalla Rinascita al Neoclassicismo*, Bologna, 1971.

Heydenreich, L. H., *Architecture in Italy. 1400–1500*, New Haven, 1995.

Kauffmann, G., *Die Kunst des 16. Jahrhunderts*, Frankfurt/M., Berlin and Vienna, 1984.

Lotz, W., *Architecture in Italy. 1500–1600*, New Haven, 1995.

Portoghesi, P., *Architettura del Rinascimento a Roma*, 2nd edn., Milan, 1979.

Baroque

Blunt, A., *Borromini*, Cambridge and London, 1979.

Blunt, A. *Guide to Baroque Rome*, London, 1982.

Borsi, F., *Bernini architetto*, Milan, 1980.

Brinckmann, A. E., *Die Baukunst des 17. und 18. Jahrhunderts in den romanischen Ländern*, Berlin, 1915.

Elling, Ch., *Rome. The biography of its architecture from Bernini to Thorvaldsen*, Tübingen, 1975.

Golzio, V., *Palazzi Romani – dalla Rinascita al Neoclassicismo*, Bologna, 1971.

Hibbard, H., *Carlo Maderno and Roman Architecture 1580–1630*, London, 1971.

Hubala, E., *Renaissance und Barock*, Frankfurt a. M., 1968.

Hubala, E., *Die Kunst des 17. Jahrhunderts*, Frankfurt a. M., Berlin and Vienna, 1984.

Kauffmann, G., *Die Kunst des 16. Jahrhunderts*, Frankfurt a. M., Berlin and Vienna, 1984.

Keller, H., *Die Kunst des 18. Jahrhunderts*, Frankfurt a. M., Berlin and Vienna, 1984.

Krautheimer, R., *The Rome of Alexander VII. 1655 to 1667*, Princeton, 1985.

Lotz, W., *Architecture in Italy. 1500–1600*, New Haven, 1995.

Mallory, N., *Roman Rococo Architecture from Clement XI to Benedict XIV (1700–1758)*, New York and London, 1977.

Onofrio, C. d', *Roma nel seicento*, Florence, 1969.

Portoghesi, P., *Francesco Borromini*, Milan, 1977.

Portoghesi, P., *Roma barocca*, Rome and Bari, 1992.

Riegl, A., *Die Entstehung der Barockkunst in Rom*, Vienna, 1908.

Varriano, J., *Italian Baroque and Rococo Architecture*, New York and Oxford, 1986.

Vasi, M., *Roma del Settecento. Itinerario istruttivo di Roma*, Rome, 1970 (new edition of the work by G. Matthiae).

Wittkower, R., *Art and Architecture in Italy. 1600 to 1750*, Harmondsworth, 1980.

Classicism and Historicism

Accasto, G., V. Fraticelli and R. Nicolini, *L'architettura di Roma capitale.1870–1970*, Rome, 1971.

Borsi, F., *L'architettura dell'unità d'Italia*, Florence, 1966.

Golzio, V., *Palazzi Romani – dalla Rinascita al Neoclassicismo*, Bologna, 1971.

Modernism

Accasto, G., V. Fraticelli and R. Nicolini, *L'architettura di Roma capitale. 1870–1970*, Rome, 1971.

Borsi,F., *L'architettura dell'unità d'Italia*, Florence, 1966

Ciucci, G., and F. Dal Co, *Atlante dell'architettura italiana del Novecento*, Milan, 1991.

Galardi, A., *Neue italienische Architektur*, Stuttgart, 1967.

Gregotti, V., *New Directions in Italian Architecture*, London, 1968.

Muratore, G., et al., *Italia – gli ultimi trent'anni*, Bologna, 1988.

Nestler, P., *Neues Bauen in Italien*, Munich, 1954.

Pfammatter, U., *Moderne und Macht – »Razionalismo«: Italienische Architekten 1927–1942*, Braunschweig, 1990.

Portoghesi, P., et al., »Presenza di Ridolfi«, special edn. no. 1 of *Controspazio*, 1974.

Francesco Moschini, *Paolo Portoghesi. Progetti e disegni, 1949–1979*, Florence, 1979.

Portoghesi, P., *I nuovi architetti italiani*, Rome and Bari, 1985.

Rossi, P. O., *Roma – Guida all'architettura moderna*, Rome and Bari, 1991.

Santuccio, S., *Luigi Moretti*, Bologna, 1986.

Seta, C. de, *Architetti italiani nel Novecento*, Rome and Bari, 1982.

Tafuri, M., *History of Italian Architecture 1944–1985*, Cambridge and London, 1989.

Taylor, R., *The word in stone – The role of architecture in the National Socialist ideology*, Berkeley, 1974.

Glossary

Technical terms are best explained in terms of concrete examples. For this reason references are provided, where helpful, to actual buildings in Rome that appear in this guide.

Aedicule (Lat. little house): a pair of *columns* or *pilasters* connected by an entablature and gable, usually to frame a statue (ancient period), an altar (early Christian, medieval), window, door or niche, cf. A25.

Amphitheatre: Roman venue for combat and competitions, usually with an elliptical arena and rising tiers for spectators on all sides, cf. 25.

Apse: semicircular, rectangular or polygonal section, regularly ceremonial in ancient buildings or Christian churches (cf. also *concha*), cf. A11.

Aqueduct: ancient Roman device in which water is carried in a channel supported on arches, following the natural slope, from the source to the place of use, cf. A22.

Arcade: arches cut into a wall and supported on piers or columns, cf. A8.

Architrave: horizontal main beam above a bay of columns, called epistyle in the ancient world, cf. A9.

Atrium: cf. *peristyle courtyard*.

Attica: low wall as upper conclusion for *triumphal arches* or above the main cornice of a building, concealing the roof, cf. A50, H31.

Baldacchino: 1. ceremonial canopy, e. g. above ecclesiastical or secular thrones, altars, portable canopy for the holy of holies; 2. protective of ceremonial roof over statues and pulpits; 3. in architecture (esp. Gothic) the statically important parts of a (nave) bay or a chapel (four supports and the vault resting on them), to the extent that they appear separate from the rest of the building, cf. B100.

Barrel vault: cf. *vaults*.

Basilica: 1. originally king's hall (basileus = king); then 2. Roman market or court hall with several aisles, cf. A11; later 3. type of Christian church with the nave higher than the aisles and lit by a clerestory, cf. p. 67.

Baths: public or private bathing facilities with the following rooms: **apodyterium** (changing room), **frigidarium** (cold-water bath), **calidarium** (room with hot air and heated pool), **laconium** or **sudatorium** (steam bath), cf. A43.

Bay: section, for example a section of space in an axially arranged sequence, or vault section divided off by transverse arches and supports from the adjacent vault or spatial sections, also a section between two columns.

Bottega floor: cf. *floors*.

Cavea: area for spectators in the ancient theatre, usually slightly more than a semicircle, cf. A17.

Cella: windowless main space in an ancient temple, in which the image of the god stood, cf. A34.

Clerestory: section of the nave rising above the side aisles of a *basilica*, generally with windows, cf. A11, C7.

Coemeterial basilica: early-Christian church over a tomb area, usually a martyr's tomb, cf. A54 and C13.

Column order: cf. *order*.

Concha: semicircular niche or apse with domed conclusion, e.g. to conclude an aisle or transept, cf. H31.

Cosmati work: marble encrustations by a group of 12th- to 14th-C artists in and around Rome and Naples, cf. C26.

Cross-section façade: façade that shows the outline of the structure (the aisles) of the interior, cf. F7, H26.

Crypt: (semi-)underground room, usually under the choir of a church as a tomb and place in which to store relics. Important forms are the **circular crypt**, a semicircular corridor with a tomb chamber at the apex, the **gallery crypt**, a space consisting of one or more intersecting galleries and the **hall crypt**, a room with three aisles of equal height, supported by columns or piers.

Cryptoporticus: underground corridor with various functions, often covered with barrel or groined vaults, e.g. as access to a crypt or storage cellar, cf. A21.

Dome: cf. *vaults*.

Drum: cf. *vaults*.

Ear motif: an ornamental form in Mannerism and Baroque, cf. H43, B53.

Enfilade: sequence of rooms with doors on a single axis, making it possible to see through all the rooms (mainly in Baroque architecture), cf. B76.

Entablature: cf. *order*.

Epistyle: cf. *architrave*.

Exedra: round, more rarely rectangular niche or room form, usually more spacious than an *apse*, though often equated with this – and like it an extension of the main space, cf. A27, A29.

Fascia: (two or three) slightly protruding ribbon-like strips, articulating the Ionic and Corinthian *architrave*.

Floors or storeys: From ground level come a **base floor** (sometimes bottega floor, with shops), then the **main floors**, with the first floor possibly emphasized as the *piano nobile*, cf. H22, the other upper floors and the **mezzanine floor**, which is a low intermediate floor (usually just below the roof, or between the other floors), cf. A30, M24.

Fluting: longitudinal grooves on the shaft of columns, pilasters or piers, cf. H12.

Groined vault: cf. *vaults*.

Horrea: storage hall, cf. A30.

Hypocaust: warm-air heating built into the floor, above all in ancient Rome, cf. A43.

Hypogeum: tomb in the form of a room or vault.

Impost: additional slab over the capital or arcade, typical of the Christian Middle Ages, or the area between support and arch or vault, cf. C10.

Intercolumnia: space between two columns or pilasters, cf. A9.

Metope: usually square relief slab under the gutter of a Doric temple; alternates with the triglyph in a **triglyph-metope frieze**.

Mezzanine: cf. *floors*.

Mosaic: Pictorial work made up of small pieces of stone or glass on walls, ceilings and floors.

Nymphaeum: ancient fountain-temple, a place dedicated to the nymphs; it can be designed as a grotto with spring or fountain-house, or also as a lavishly articulated structure, cf. A27, A53.

Opaion: round opening for light at the apex of a *dome*.

Opus caementitium: ancient Roman cast masonry, cf. A8, A54.

Opus incertum: ancient Roman form of polygonal masonry, cf. A8.

Opus quadratum: ancient Roman from of ashlar masonry, cf. A2.

Opus reticulatum: ancient-Roman masonry patterned like netting with joints running diagonally.

Order: articulation of a wall or building by pilaster or (half-)columns and the linking entablature; in ancient architecture there was a prescribed order of certain column, capital and entablature forms (especially the Doric, Ionic, Corinthian and Composite orders), cf. A9, A25.

Palazzo suburbano: palace near the city.

Palladian window: type of window, cf. *Serliana*.

Pendentive: cf. *vaults*.

Peripteral temple: rectangular temple with columns on all sides; in the **pseudo-peripteral** temple the columns are linked to the cella wall on three sides as mere half-columns, cf. A7, A34.

Peristyle: Greek, usually rectangular courtyard form, framed on three or all sides by rows of columns with sections of buildings behind them; usually called an atrium in ancient Roman residential architecture and Christian church building, cf. A30.

Piano nobile: cf. *floors*.

Piered arcade: square piers supporting masonry arches, cf. A9, C37.

Pilaster: Rectangular equivalent of a half-column projecting only slightly from the building; regularly conforms to a column *order*, cf. H12.

Pilaster strip: vertical wall strip, protruding only slightly, but without a pilaster's base and capital.

Pilotis: supports, usually cylindrical that raise a structure above the ground, usually by one floor, with no base, capital or fluting, unlike a column, cf. M30, M33.

Podium temple: Roman temple form with high base, usually with access from a flight of steps occupying the whole length of a building, cf. A7.

Portico: open porch supported by columns or piers, cf. A13, A31.

Presbytery: old term for choir, reserved for altar and clergy.

Projection (Ital. risalto): protruding section of wall extending over all storeys of the building, but unlike the pavilion, not creating the idea of an independent section; called centre, side or corner projection according to its position, cf. F19, H2.

Prostatic columns: columns standing in front of a wall and attached to it only by an entablature protruding from it, cf. A41.

Prostyle temple: temple consisting of a columned portico and a simple cella without any order of columns or pilasters, cf. A1.

Pseudo-peripteros: cf. *peripteros*.

Rhythmic travée (also rhythmic bay): assembly of several *bays* of unequal width, used especially by Bramante, cf. F19, H6.

Ribbed vault: cf. *vaults*.

Risalto: cf. *projection*.

Rotunda: cylindrical building with dome, cf. A31.

Serliana: Architectural device named after the Italian architect and art theoretician Sebastiano Serlio (1475 to 1554) taken up by Palladio in particular and thus also known as the Palladio motif. It consists of a tripartite opening with narrower side openings closed by a horizontal entablature, and a wider, taller arch as the central component, therefore related to the *triumphal arch* and to the rhythmic *travée*, cf. B73.

Spoils: building material reused from older buildings, practised especially in the ancient and early-Christian periods, cf. A52, C18.

Squinch: cf. *vaults*.

Storey: cf. *floors*.

Stylobate: upper part of the stepped substructure of a temple, on which the columns stand, cf. A34.

Superposition: columns or pilasters placed vertically above one another on several floors, cf. A25.

Syrian arch: tripartite motif similar to the *Serliana*, but with a continuous entablature rising to a circular arch in the middle, cf. A32.

Tabularium motif: piered arcade with column order placed in front, cf. A9.

Tholos: round temple with one row of columns, cf. C6.

Titular church: early-Christian church, emerging from a house church (private house used for services and carrying its owner's name), cf. C6.

Travée (cf. bay), otherwise also a complete unit made up of a vault field in the nave and the aisle on the same axis, with their supports, cf. A25.

Triclinium: dining-room in ancient Roman or medieval house, palace or monastery, cf. A27, C15.

Triumphal arch: 1. single- or multi-gated arch in honour of people or historic events, cf. A26, A52; 2. arch dividing the nave from the crossing or choir in churches, cf. C2.

Tumulus: burial mound, cf. A12, A15.

Tunnel vault: cf. vaults.

Twin columns: two columns connected by a common entablature, cf. B27.

Ustrinum: square site for incineration in ancient Rome, cf. A33.

Vaults: **barrel** or **tunnel vaults** consist of a semicircular cylinder that can also be flattened or pointed, in which case the side cells can protrude into the barrels, cf. F13; the **groined vault** consists of two barrels meeting at right angles, with intersection points known as groins, cf. A9; the **ribbed vault** has ribs instead of groins, with thin masonry between them. The **dome** forms a vault for square, polygonal or round spaces, in the form of a hemisphere according to Renaissance ideals. The transition from the angled space to the (hemispherical) upper conclusion is achieved by means of pendentives (spherical triangles, cf. H7) or squinches (arcade-like halved hollow cones). Also a cylindrical masonry drum with windows can be placed on the crossing arches and pendentives, thus regularly from St. Peters to the late Baroque (drum, cf. A53, H31). There are also double-shelled domes, cf. H 31. For a hemispherical dome cf. A31, an umbrella dome is articulated by several cells from the apex, so that the form is reminiscent of an umbrella, cf. F19; domes are usually topped by a lantern.

Vestibule: entrance section that becomes an independent part of the building, in ancient Roman houses or palaces and in medieval ecclesiastical architecture, cf. A32, C8.

Roman emperors (selection)

Augustus	27BC to AD 14
Tiberius	14–37
Caligula	37–41
Claudius	41–54
Nero	54–68
Vespasian	69–79
Titus	79–81
Domitian	81–96
Nerva	96–98
Trajan	98–117
Hadrian	117–138
Antoninus Pius	138–161
Marcus Aurelius	161–180
Commodus	180–192
Pertinax	193
Didius Julianus	193
Septimius Severus among others together with Caracalla (198–211) and Geta (209–211)	193–211
Caracalla	211–217
Macrinus	217/218
Elagabalus	218–222
Alexander Severus	222–235
Maximin	235–238
Gordian I und II	238
Balbinus	238
Gordian III	238–244
Philip	244–249
Decius	249–251
Trebonianus Gallus	251–253
Aemilian	253
Valerian	253–259
Gallienus	259–268
Claudius (II) Gothicus	268–270
Quintillus	270
Aurelian	270–275
Tacitus	275/276
Florian	276
Probus	276–282
Carus	282/283
Carinus	283–285
Diocletian	284–305
Galerius among others together with Maxentius (306–312), Constantine I, the Great (since 306) and Maximinus Daja (310–313)	305–311
Constantine I, the Great	313–337

Popes

Silvester I, St	314–335
Mark, St	336
Julius I, St	337–352
Liberius	352–366
Damasus I, St	366–384
Siricius, St	384–399
Anastasius I, hl	399–402
Innocent I, St	402–417
Zosimus, St	417–419
Boniface I, St	418–422
Celestine I, St	422–432
Sixtus III, St	432–440
Leo I, St	440–461
Hilary, St	461–468
Simplicius, St	468–483
Felix II (III), St	483–492
Gelasius I, St	492–496
Anastasius II	496–498
Symmachus, St	498–514
Hormisdas, St	514–523
John I, St	523–526
Felix III (IV), St	526–530
Boniface II	530–532
Dioscurus	530
John II	533–535
Agapetus I, St	535–536
Silverius, St	536–537
Vigilius	537–555
Pelagius I	556–561
John III	561–574
Benedict I	575–579
Pelagius II	579–590
Gregory I, St	590–604
Sabinianus	604–606
Boniface III	607
Boniface IV, St	608–615
Deusdedit (Adeodatus I), St	615–618
Boniface V	619–625
Honorius I	625–638
Severinus	640
John IV	640–642
Theodore I	642–649
Martin I, St	649–653
Eugen I, St	654–657
Vitalian, St	657–672
Adeodatus II	672–676
Donus	676–678
Agatho, St	678–681
Leo II, St	682–683
Benedict II, St	684–685
John V	685–686
Conon	686–687
Sergius I, St	687–701
John VI	701–705
John VII	705–707
Sisinnius	708
Constantine I	708–715
Gregory II, St	715–731
Gregory III, St	731–741
Zacharias, St	741–752
Stephen II (III)	752–757
Paul I, St	757–767
Stephan III (IV)	768–772
Adrian I	772–795
Leo III, St	795–816
Stephen IV (V)	816–817
Paschal I, St	817–824
Eugenius II	824–827
Valentine	827
Gregory IV	827–844
Sergius II	844–847
Leo IV, St	847–855
Benedict III	855–858
Nicholas I	858–867
Adrian II	867–872
John VIII	872–882
Marinus I (Martin II)	882–884
Adrian III, St	884–885
Stephen V (VI)	885–891
Formosus	891–896
Boniface VI	896
Stephen VI (VII)	896–897
Romanus	897
Theodore II	897
John IX	898–900
Benedict IV	900–903
Leo V	903
Christopher	903–904
Sergius III	904–911
Anastasius III	911–913
Lando	913–914
John X	914–928
Leo VI	928
Stephen VII (VIII)	928–931
John XI	931–935/36
Leo VII	936–939
Stephen VIII (IX)	939–942
Marinus II (Martin III)	942–946
Agapetus II	946–955
John XII	955–964
Leo VIII	963–965
Benedict V	964
John XIII	965–972
Benedict VI	973–974
Boniface VII	974, 984–985
Benedict VII	974–983
John XIV	983–984
John XV	985–996
Gregory V	996–999
Silvester II	999–1003
John XVII	1003
John XVIII	1003/04–1009
Sergius IV	1009–1012
Benedict VIII	1012–1024
John XIX	1024–1032
Benedict IX	1032–1045
Silvester III	1045–1046
Gregory VI	1045–1046
Clement II	1046–1047
Damasus II	1048
Leo IX, St	1049–1054
Victor II	1055–1057
Stephen IX (X)	1057–1058
Benedict X	1058–1059
Nicholas II	1059–1061
Alexander II	1061–1073
Gregory VII, St	1073–1085
Victor III, BM	1086–1087
Urban II, BM	1088–1099
Paschalis II	1099–1118
Gelasius II	1118–1119
Calixtus II	1119–1124
Honorius II	1124–1130
Innocent II	1130–1143

Anacletus II	1130–1138	Urban VII	1590
Celestine II	1143–1144	Gregory XIV	1590–1591
Lucius II	1144–1145	Innocent IX	1591
Eugen III, BM	1145–1153	Clement VIII	1592–1605
Anastasius IV	1153–1154	Leo XI	1605
Adrian IV	1154–1159	Paul V	1605–1621
Alexander III	1159–1181	Gregory XV	1621–1623
Lucius III	1181–1185	Urban VIII	1623–1644
Urban III	1185–1187	Innocent X	1644–1655
Gregory VIII	1187	Alexander VII	1655–1667
Clement III	1187–1191	Clement IX	1667–1669
Celestine III	1191–1198	Clement X	1670–1676
Innocent III	1198–1216	Innocent XI, BM	1676–1689
Honorius III	1216–1227	Alexander VIII	1689–1691
Gregory IX	1227–1241	Innocent XII	1691–1700
Celestine IV	1241	Clement XI	1700–1721
Innocent IV	1243–1254	Innocent XIII	1721–1724
Alexander IV	1254 1261	Benedict XIII	1724–1730
Urban IV	1261–1264	Clement XII	1730–1740
Klemens IV	1265–1268	Benedict XIV	1740–1758
Gregory X, BM	1271–1276	Clement XIII	1758–1769
Innocent V, BM	1276	Clement XIV	1769–1774
Adrian V	1276	Pius VI	1775–1799
John XXI	1276–1277	Pius VII	1800–1823
Nicholas III	1277–1280	Leo XII	1823–1829
Martin IV	1281–1285	Pius VIII	1829–1830
Honorius IV	1285–1287	Gregory XVI	1831–1846
Nicholas IV	1288–1292	Pius IX	1846–1878
Celestine V, St	1294	Leo XIII	1878–1903
Boniface VIII	1294–1303	Pius X, St	1903–1914
Benedict XI, BM	1303–1304	Benedict XV	1914–1922
Clement V	1305–1314	Pius XI	1922–1939
John XXII	1316–1334	Pius XII	1939–1958
Benedict XII	1334–1342	John XXIII	1958–1963
Clement VI	1342–1352	Paul VI	1963–1978
Innocent VI	1352–1362	John Paul I	1978
Urban V, BM	1362–1370	John Paul II	1978–2005
Gregory XI	1370–1378	Benedict XVI	2005–
Urban VI	1378–1389		
(Clement VII)	1394		
Boniface IX	1389–1404		
(Benedict XIII)	1394–1417		
Innocent VII	1404–1406		
Gregory XII	1406–1415		
Alexander V	1409–1410		
John XXIII	1410–1415		
Martin V	1417–1431		
Eugen IV	1431–1447		
Nicholas V	1447–1455		
Calixtus III	1455–1458		
Pius II	1458–1464		
Paul II	1464–1471		
Sixtus IV	1471–1484		
Innocent VIII	1484–1492		
Alexander VI	1492–1503		
Pius III	1503		
Julius II	1503–1513		
Leo X	1513–1521		
Adrian VI	1522–1523		
Clement VII	1523–1534		
Paul III	1534–1549		
Julius III	1550–1555		
Marcellus II	1555		
Paul IV	1555–1559		
Pius IV	1559–1565		
Pius V, St	1566–1572		
Gregory XIII	1572–1585		
Sixtus V	1585–1590		

Index of buildings

Numbers refer to pages, combinations of letters and numbers to buildings as listed in the book.

Index of artists

Numbers refer to pages, combinations of letters and numbers to buildings as listed in the book.

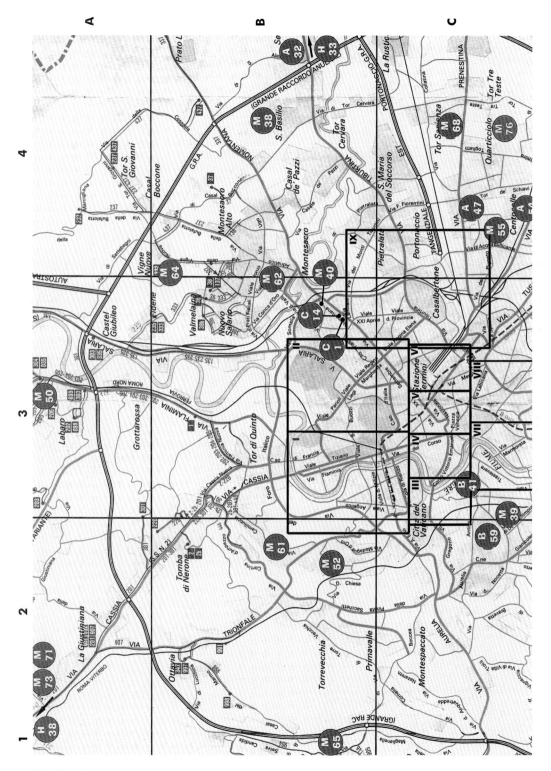

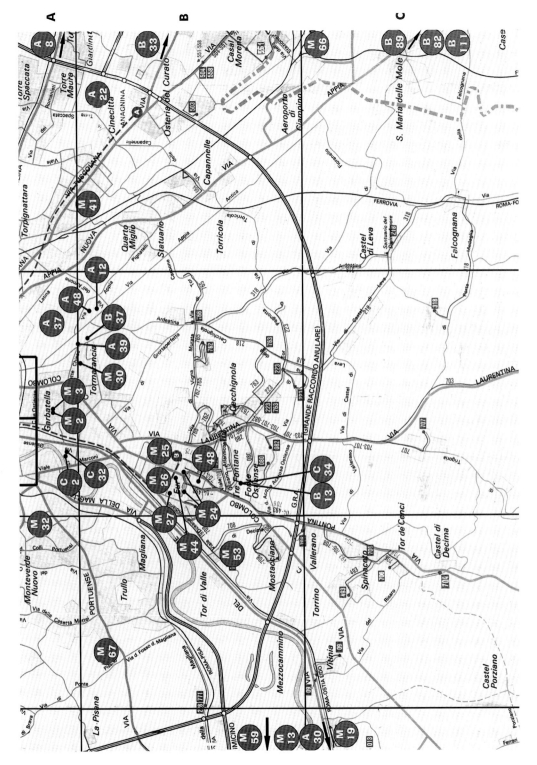

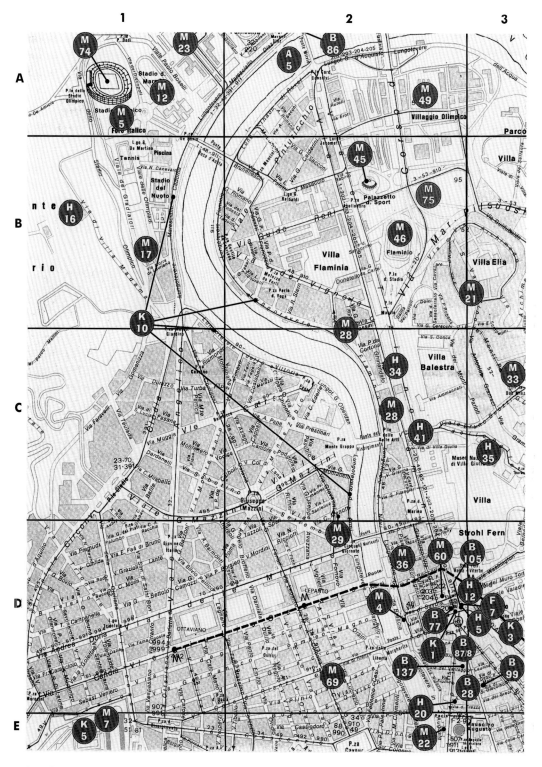

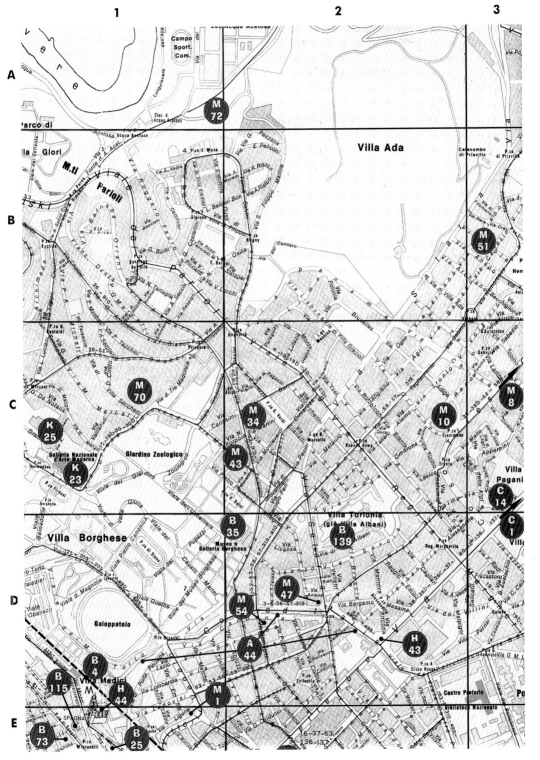

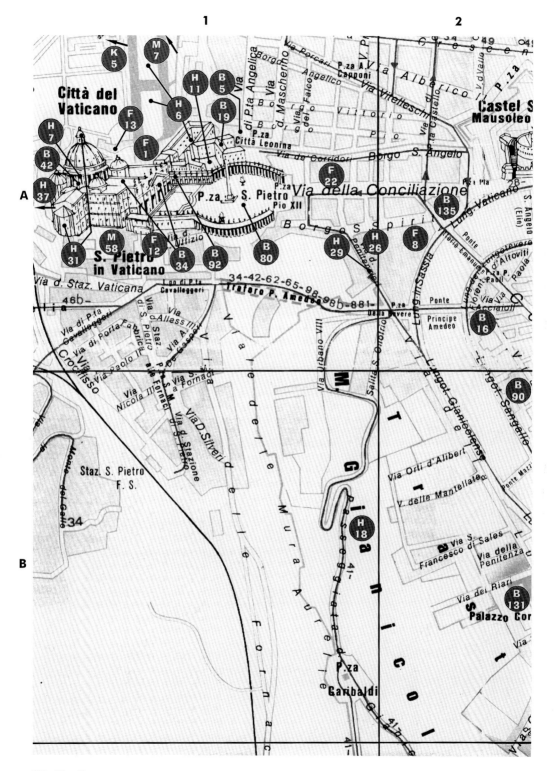

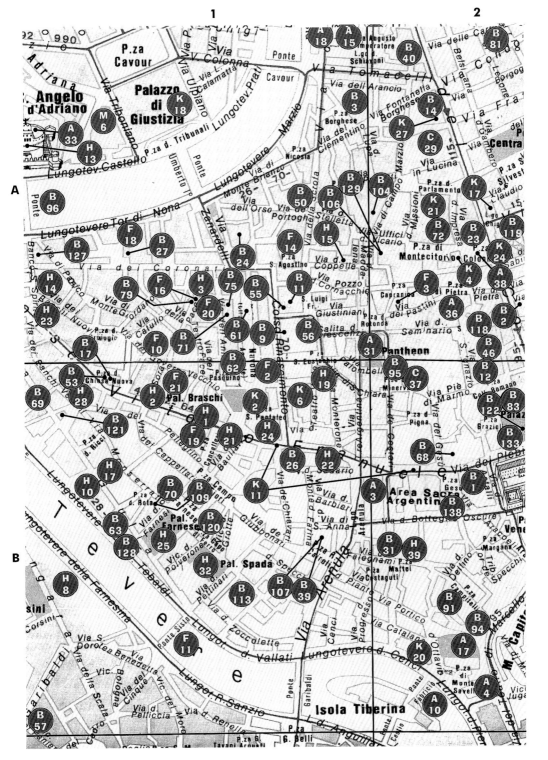

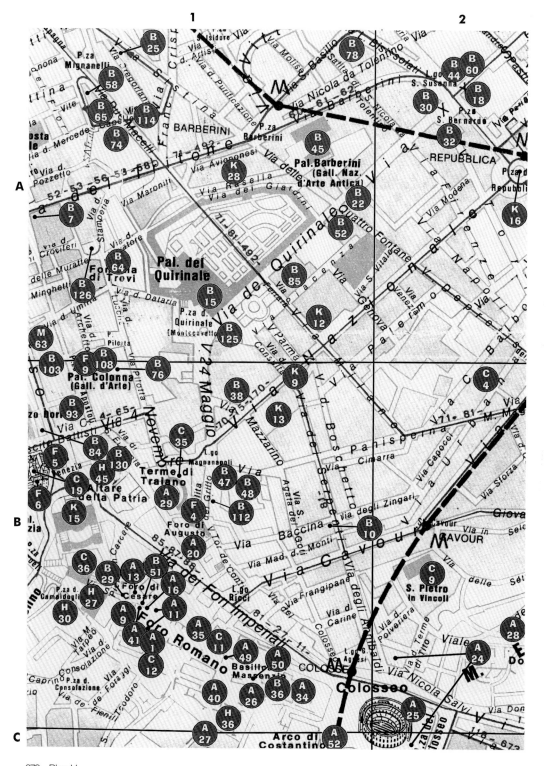

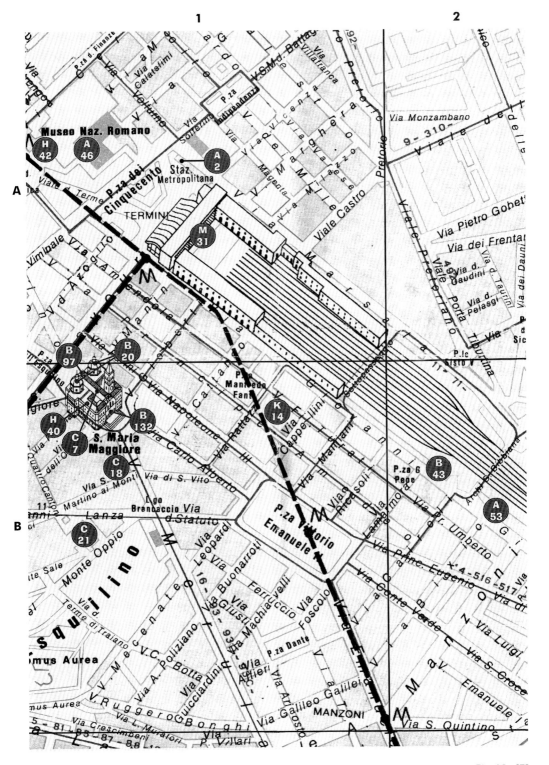

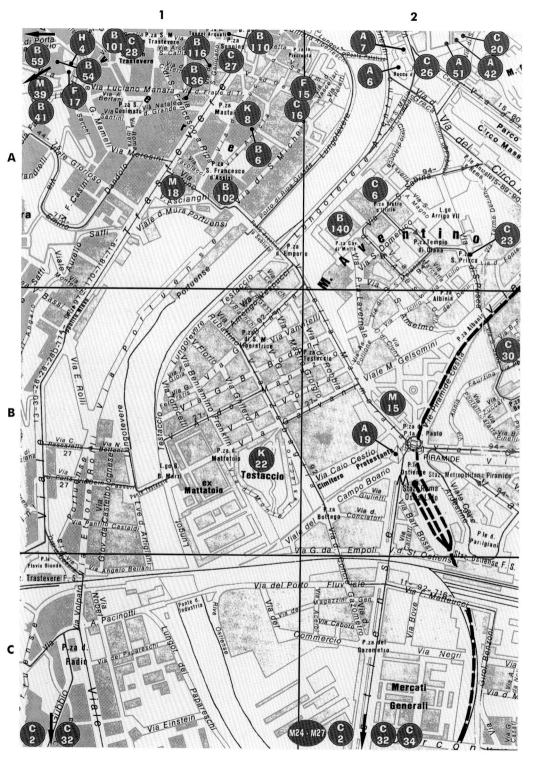

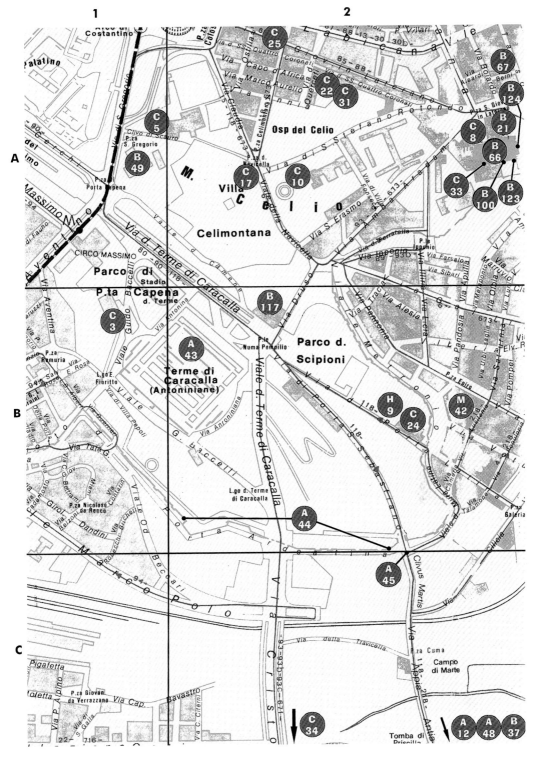

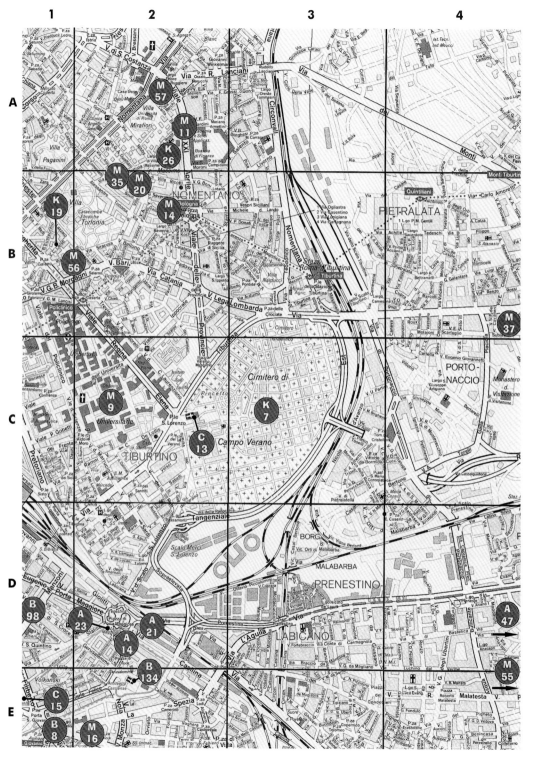

About the tour proposals

The tour proposals (pp. 66, 97, 161, 276 and 355) are arranged by period – like the whole of the guide. Outside the city the reader will have to work by theme because the distances involved are so great.

Here are some suggestions, each for a day's walk:
– ancient tombs, a martyr's church and a war memorial (a good half day), and also key High Baroque and Rococo works (half a day): A12, (A37), A39, A48, (B37), M30, -- B82, B89, B111;
– monumental complexes, villas and gardens of antiquity and their impact on the Modern age: A8, A32, H33, (B33);
– principal works of Mannerism and – as a counterpart in our century – Post-Modernism: H38, M50, M71, (M74);
– the ancient Roman city of Ostia and the Fascist-Imperialist EUR: A30, M24–M27, M44, M48, M53.

It is also worth pursuing central points of the development from early and High Renaissance to High Baroque in cross-section on a single day in the Vatican: F1, F13, H6, H11, (B5), H7, H31, B34; B42, B80, B92. The same is true of the Piazza del Popolo, but here half a day is enough: F7, H5, H12, M65, M74, B87/88, M60.

The walks do not take account of works of Classicism and Historicism whose significance is above all in urban development terms (for example K1, K9–K11, K15–K17), which the visitor is involved with anyway, and the following works, also important, which can be included in one or other of the walks, even though this will involve additional time: A33, A53, C1, C13, C14, C18, C25, H8, H16, H34, H35, B31, B49, B57, B91, B101, B107, B113, B120, B128, M15, M16, M18, M40, M42, M47, M54 and the Quartieri.

Photo credits

Where no credit is listed, photgraphs are by the team of authors, namely by Stefan Grundmann, Steffen Krämer, Philipp Zitzlsperger and Anke Scherner, as well as by Michaela Grundmann and Imke Spannuth.

Accasto, G., V. Fraticelli and R. Nicolini, *L'architettura di Roma capitale. 1870–1970*, 1971 K21, K22, K27, M1

Andreae, B. *Römische Kunst*, 1978 A11

Architektur der Welt: Barock, 1964 B9, B52,1,

Architettura del Settecento a Roma, 1991 277

Blunt, A., *Guide de la Rome baroque*, 1992 B6, B38, B45, B63, B93, B98

Borsi, *Bernini architetto*, 1980 B54, B60, B77, B82, B85,1

Brantl, K., *Glanzvolles Rom*, 1967 B96

Breuning, H.-J. M31,1, M40

Brinckmann, A. E., *Die Baukunst des 17. und 18. Jahrhunderts*, 1915 B105

Bruhns, L., *Die Kunst der Stadt Rom*, 1972 C9, C10, C13, C14, C12, C18, C29, C34, C37, F15, H25,1 H25,2, H26, B20, B21, B30, B46, B123

Ciucci, G., and F. Dal Co, *Atlante dell'architettura italiana del Novecento*, 1991 300, 303, M9,2, M29, M30, M31,2, M37,2, M38, M41,2, M67

Ciucci, G.,and V. Fraticelli (ed.), *Roma capitale 1870–1911. Architettura e urbanistica*, 1984 K11

Dal Maso, L. B., *Das Rom der Cäsaren*, 1974 A22

Debenedetti, E. (ed.), *Casino Valadier. Segno e architettura*, 1985 K3

Enciclopedia dell'Arte Antica 10

Falda, G. B., and A. Specchi, *Palazzi di Roma nel '600*, o. J. B6, B63

Gallavotti Cavalliero, D., *Palazzi di Roma dal XIV al XX Secolo*, 1989 F3, H14, H21, H22, B19, B22

Gregotti Associati: 1973–1988, 1990 M73

Heemskerck 99, H7,1

Henze, A., *Rom und Latium. Kunstdenkmäler und Museen*, 1981 C25

Heydenreich, L. H., *Architecture in Italy. 1400–1500* F2, F5,1, F5,2, F17

Hibbard, H., *Bernini*, 1978 B85,2

Kauffmann, G., *Die Kunst des 16. Jahrhunderts*, 1984 H29

Keller, H., *Die Kunst des 18. Jahrhunderts*, 1984 B140

Kraus, Th., *Das römische Weltreich*, 1984 A47

Krautheimer, R., *Early-Christian and Byzantine architecture*, 1979 C19, C26,2

Krautheimer, R., *Roma. Profilo di una città. 312–1308*, Rome, 1981 72

Letarouilly H36

Lieven Cruyl B126

Lombardi, F., *Roma. Palazzi, palazzetti, case. Progetto per un inventario. 1200–1870*, 1991 17, 18

Lotz, W., *Architecture in Italy. 1500 to 1600*, 1995 H4, H5, H7,2, H7,3, H8, H12, H16, H24, H34, H38, B1, B3, B5

Murray, P., *The Architecture of the Italian Renaissance*, 1963 H10

P. L. Nervi. Neue Strukturen, 1963 M46

Norberg-Schulz, *Barock*, 1985 B26, B45, B71,2, B80, B106

Piranesi B18

Pisani, M., *Paolo Portoghesi*, 1992 M50, M69, M71, M72,1, M72,2

Poliano, S., *Guida all'architettura italiana del Novecento*, 1991 M11, M43, M66

Portoghesi, P., *Francesco Borromini*, 1990 B57

Portoghesi, P., *L'ecletticismo a Roma 1870–1920*, 1968 K17

Portoghesi, P., *Roma barocca*, 1992 B68, B72, B89, B107, B128, B135

Redig de Campos, D., *I Palazzi Vaticani*, 1967 K5

Rossi, de B39, B46

Rossi, P. O., *Roma. Guida all'architettura moderna, 1909–1991*, 1991 M2, M21, M23,1, M37,1, M41,1, M51, M53, M55, M63, M68

Rotondi, S., *Il Teatro Valle*, 1992 K6

Santuccio, S., *Luigi Moretti*, 1990 M17,1, M17,2, M18, M32, M33,1, M52

Salamanca H31

Schulte-Mattler A5, A18, A42, A52, C20, C26,1, C28, C31, H33, H44, B17, B42, B59

Schumacher, Th., *Giuseppe Terragni, Surface and Symbol*, 1991 M23,2

Seidler, Harry H35, M7, M25

Spagnesi, G., *S. Pantaleo*, 1967 K2

Specchi B33, B35, B45, B93, B98

Stützer H. A., *Das antike Rom*, 1979 A9,2, A15, A32,2, A42, A49

Varriano, J., *Italian Baroque and Rococo Architecture*, 1986 168, B27, B47, B50, B52,1, B52,2, B52,3, B56,1 B64, B92, B103, B111, B118, B138, B139

Vasi B4, B38, B76

Ward-Perkins, J., *Rom*, 1986 A24, A37

Willich H34

Wittkower, R., *Art and Architecture in Italy. 1600 to 1750*, 1980 B37, B83

Zantuccio M18, M17,1, M 17,2, M32, M33, M52